A Note from the Publisher

The Educational Book Division of Prentice-Hall, Inc. is committed to the publication of outstanding textbooks. One important measure of a book's excellence is how well it communicates with its readers. To assure a highly readable book, the content for this text was selected, organized, and written at a level appropriate for the intended audience. The Dale-Chall readability formula was used to control readability level. An inviting and meaningful design was created to enhance the book's visual appeal as well as to facilitate the reading process. In addition, a consistent organization was used throughout so that all units, chapters, and sections will meet the reader's expectations. The authors, editors, and designers are confident that the students for whom this book is intended will read it, comprehend it, and learn from it.

The following paragraphs describe additional features that should prove useful to both students and teachers. A page reference is given to provide an example of each feature.

Clear Rules and Examples: Easy-to-read rules for *all* major concepts are presented in colored print throughout the text (page 176). These combined with numerous examples showing the many different ways in which each rule can be applied (page 176) provide the core of the learning experience.

Numerous Exercises and Applications: *Every* subsection has at least one exercise (page 21), allowing a direct and immediate evaluation of skills learned. *Every* section has at least one Application (page 25), which puts the various skills learned to some immediate use, generally through written expression.

Helpful Charts and Checklists: Colorful charts are found *throughout* the text, highlighting the elements involved in understanding basic concepts (page 274) and presenting step-by-step approaches to the mastery of various skills (page 396). Also in chart form are a number of checklists (page 593) that can be used to check mastery of skills.

Composition Steps and Models: Composition skills are taught not through rules alone but through a thorough analysis of the elements involved in *every* form examined (pages 545–564) and through the use of clear and easy-t[illegible] writing and revising steps, again given for *every* fo[illegible]rous student and professional [illegible]*ut* to increase further the reader[illegible]n each form.

Three Easy-to-Us[illegible]ntents (pages 5–16) lists *all* top[illegible]th page references. The Key of [illegible] lists *all* major concepts. The Index (pages 693–702) offers a comprehensive, thoroughly cross-referenced guide to *all* points in the text, with rules and definitions printed in bold.

Prentice-Hall

Grammar and Composition

Level 2

Annotated Teacher's Edition

Prepared by Gary Forlini

Pelham High School, Pelham, New York

PRENTICE-HALL, INC., Englewood Cliffs, New Jersey

ISBN 0-13-696773-6

10 9 8 7 6 5 4 3 2 1

Prentice-Hall International, Inc., London
Prentice-Hall of Australia Pty. Ltd., Sydney
Prentice-Hall Canada Inc., Toronto
Prentice-Hall of India Private Ltd., New Delhi
Prentice-Hall of Japan, Inc., Tokyo
Prentice-Hall of Southeast Asia Pte. Ltd., Singapore
Whitehall Books Limited, Wellington, New Zealand

Contents

Scope and Sequence

LEVEL ONE (Grade 7)	LEVEL TWO (Grade 8)	LEVEL THREE (Grade 9)

UNIT I Grammar

LEVEL ONE (Grade 7)	LEVEL TWO (Grade 8)	LEVEL THREE (Grade 9)
1 Nouns	**1** Nouns and Pronouns	**1** Nouns and Pronouns
2 Pronouns	**2** Verbs	**2** Verbs
3 Verbs	**3** Adjectives	**3** Adjectives and Adverbs
4 Adjectives	**4** Adverbs	**4** Prepositions, Conjunctions, and Interjections
5 Adverbs	**5** Prepositions, Conjunctions, and Interjections	**5** Reviewing Parts of Speech
6 Prepositions	**6** Reviewing Parts of Speech	**6** Basic Parts of a Sentence
7 Conjunctions and Interjections	**7** Recognizing Parts of a Sentence	**7** Prepositional Phrases and Appositives
8 Reviewing Parts of Speech	**8** Expanding Sentences with Phrases	**8** Verbals and Verbal Phrases
9 Recognizing Parts of a Sentence	**9** Expanding Sentences with Clauses	**9** Clauses
10 Expanding Sentences with Phrases	**10** Correcting Sentence Errors	**10** Sentence Faults
11 Expanding Sentences with Clauses		
12 Correcting Sentence Errors		

UNIT II Usage

LEVEL ONE (Grade 7)	LEVEL TWO (Grade 8)	LEVEL THREE (Grade 9)
13 Using Verbs	**11** Using Verbs	**11** Verb Usage
14 Using Pronouns	**12** Using Pronouns	**12** Pronoun Usage
15 Making Words Agree	**13** Making Words Agree	**13** Agreement
16 Using Adjectives and Adverbs	**14** Using Adjectives and Adverbs	**14** Adjective and Adverb Usage
17 Recognizing Special Problems in Usage	**15** Recognizing Special Problems in Usage	**15** Special Problems in Usage

LEVEL FOUR (Grade 10)	LEVEL FIVE (Grade 11)	LEVEL SIX (Grade 12)
1 Nouns, Pronouns, and Verbs **2** Adjectives and Adverbs **3** Prepositions, Conjunctions, and Interjections **4** Analyzing Parts of Speech **5** Basic Parts of a Sentence **6** Phrases **7** Clauses **8** Sentence Faults	**1** The Parts of Speech **2** Analyzing Parts of Speech **3** Basic Sentence Parts and Patterns **4** Phrases and Clauses **5** Avoiding Sentence Faults	**1** The Parts of Speech **2** Basic Sentence Parts and Patterns **3** Phrases and Clauses **4** Correcting Sentence Faults
9 Verb Usage **10** Pronoun Usage **11** Agreement **12** Adjective and Adverb Usage **13** Special Problems in Usage	**6** Verb Usage **7** Pronoun Usage **8** Agreement **9** Adjective and Adverb Usage **10** Miscellaneous Usage Problems **11** Levels of Language	**5** Verb Usage **6** Pronoun Usage **7** Agreement **8** Adjective and Adverb Usage **9** Miscellaneous Usage Problems **10** Levels of Language

LEVEL ONE (Grade 7)	LEVEL TWO (Grade 8)	LEVEL THREE (Grade 9)

UNIT III **Mechanics**

LEVEL ONE (Grade 7)	LEVEL TWO (Grade 8)	LEVEL THREE (Grade 9)
18 Using Capitals	**16** Using Capitals	**16** Capitalization and Abbreviation
19 Using Abbreviations	**17** Using Abbreviations	**17** Punctuation
20 Using Punctuation Marks	**18** Using Punctuation Marks	

UNIT IV **Vocabulary and Spelling**

LEVEL ONE (Grade 7)	LEVEL TWO (Grade 8)	LEVEL THREE (Grade 9)
21 Building Your Vocabulary	**19** Building Your Vocabulary	**18** Vocabulary Building
22 Improving Your Spelling	**20** Improving Your Spelling	**19** Spelling Improvement

UNIT V **Study Skills**

LEVEL ONE (Grade 7)	LEVEL TWO (Grade 8)	LEVEL THREE (Grade 9)
23 Developing Your Study Skills	**21** Improving Your Study Habits	**20** Basic Study Skills
24 Developing Your Reading Skills	**22** Improving Your Reading Skills	**21** Reading Skills
25 Developing Your Library and Dictionary Skills	**23** Improving Your Library and Reference Skills	**22** Library and Reference Skills

UNIT VI **Composition**

LEVEL ONE (Grade 7)	LEVEL TWO (Grade 8)	LEVEL THREE (Grade 9)
26 Improving Your Sentences	**24** Improving Your Choice of Words	**23** Sentence Style
27 Finding the Right Words	**25** Writing Better Sentences	**24** The Use of Words
28 Looking at Paragraphs	**26** Looking at Paragraphs	**25** The Basic Paragraph
29 Writing Paragraphs	**27** Writing Paragraphs	**26** Kinds of Paragraphs
30 Writing Different Kinds of Paragraphs	**28** Writing Different Kinds of Paragraphs	**27** The Essay
31 Writing Essays	**29** Writing Essays	**28** The Library Paper
32 Writing Reports	**30** Writing Reports	**29** Letters
33 Writing Stories	**31** Writing Stories	**30** Essay Examinations
34 Writing Letters	**32** Writing Letters	

LEVEL FOUR (Grade 10)	LEVEL FIVE (Grade 11)	LEVEL SIX (Grade 12)
14 Capitalization and Abbreviation **15** Punctuation	**12** Capitalization and Abbreviation **13** Punctuation	**11** Capitalization and Abbreviation **12** Punctuation
16 Vocabulary Building **17** Spelling Improvement	**14** Vocabulary Building **15** Spelling Improvement	**13** Vocabulary Building **14** Spelling Improvement
18 Basic Study Skills **19** Reading and Test-Taking Skills **20** Library and Reference Skills	**16** Basic Study Skills **17** Test-Taking Skills **18** Library and Reference Skills	**15** Basic Study Skills **16** Test-Taking Skills **17** Library and Reference Skills
21 The Right Words and Tone **22** Sentence Variety and Logic **23** Paragraphs **24** Kinds of Paragraphs **25** Essays **26** Kinds of Essays **27** Library Papers **28** Letters **29** Essay Examinations	**19** Sentence Length and Structure **20** The Use of Words **21** Clear Thinking in Writing **22** Effective Paragraphs **23** Kinds of Paragraphs **24** Essays **25** Library Papers **26** Papers About Literature **27** Letters and Précis **28** Essay Examinations	**18** Word Choices **19** Sentence Style **20** Logical Thinking in Writing **21** Effective Paragraphs **22** Paragraphs with Different Purposes **23** Essays **24** Research and Writing **25** Papers Analyzing Literature **26** Letters and Applications **27** Précis and Essay Examinations

Introduction to the Student's Text

The goal of *Prentice-Hall Grammar and Composition* is one shared by teachers across the country: to help students deal more effectively with the English language. To achieve this goal, the authors and editors began by asking teachers what they wanted in such a series. The answers were not always uniform, but several points were clear. First, a good series must be comprehensive, with enough content, examples, and exercises to meet most, if not all, of the daily classroom needs. Second, a good series must be organized clearly and simply and contain enough learning aids to make it possible for students to become comfortable with the books quickly, both as texts and as reference tools. Third, a good series must present not just a series of exercises but a complete and thorough exercise program, giving students a chance to test their mastery of all skills in a variety of contexts. Finally, a good series must contain excellent coverage of composition, providing material that encourages students to expand their writing skills, not only through rules and analysis but also by following useful steps, studying numerous models, and experimenting with new ideas.

In preparing this series, the authors and editors have focused on these four points, producing a series that is (1) sufficiently comprehensive to meet your daily needs, (2) organized and presented in a fashion that will make each book readily accessible to students as a text and as a reference tool, (3) filled with exercises that offer students a number of different ways to test and use the skills they are gaining, and (4) viable as the basis for the thorough coverage of composition skills. The following paragraphs will give you details about how these features have been implemented.

Content: A Comprehensive Package, Clearly Developed from Level to Level. The Scope and Sequence chart beginning on page T-4 offers a general guide to the coverage in each level. Basic topics are presented in a clear and interesting fashion in the lower levels and then are retaught at each higher level along with new details, giving older students a chance to review previously studied topics while gaining additional information about the way in which the English language works.

To get a clearer idea of what is covered in each unit of your text, you can check the Table of Contents. There, the titles of all subsections are given to allow you and the students quickly to find the topics you wish to cover. A glance through the text itself will show you the wealth of examples and exercises included. Notice no topics are introduced without an accompanying exercise. Notice also the valuable material contained in the study skills unit, material that can help your students succeed not only in their English course but in other courses as well.

Organization: A Clear and Logical Format, Enhanced by Numerous Learning and Reference Aids. By choosing a simple, consistent format for each chapter, each section, and each subsection, the authors and editors have been able to present a series that will be immediately accessible both as a text and as a handbook. Whether the book is being used in class or is being consulted as a reference tool, a student's understanding will be enhanced not only by the consistency and simplicity of the format, but also by the fact that (1) all rules appear in bold, colored type, (2) all examples and models are clearly labeled, and (3) numerous charts are used to offer visual keys to important concepts. In addition, special care has been taken to provide enough examples to clarify the variations that may occur in applying each rule.

Recognizing that not all students use the same techniques for finding information in a text, the series provides three reference aids: the Table of Contents at the front of the book, the Key of Major Concepts at the back of the book, and the fully cross-referenced Index that precedes the Key.

Exercises: A Special Program with Different Levels of Skills Evaluation and Application. The series presents three types of exercises which, when taken together, give the students a chance to practice, combine, and apply skills in endless ways. First, each *subsection* ends with at least one set of basic exercises, giving students immediate feedback, allowing you to conclude a day's lesson at any point, and assuring that no concept is overlooked. Second, each *section* ends with one or more Applications, giving students a chance to begin combining the skills they have learned in a very practical way, generally through writing. Finally, the grammar, usage, and mechanics units end with sets of Review Exercises that give students a chance to monitor their skill development and restudy material they are having difficulty with.

Composition: A Complete Program That Motivates Students to Succeed. In teaching composition, rules and analysis alone are not enough; likewise, special skill building techniques can do only part of the job. Instead of relying on any of these in isolation, *Prentice-Hall Grammar and Composition* presents a solid approach for teaching writing, including a recognition of the importance of both audience and purpose. For each type of writing assignment, students are also given a number of practical steps to follow, numerous fully labeled models, and charts and checklists that highlight the most important concepts. A special section on preparing papers, which includes steps for putting a written work into final form follows immediately after the composition unit.

The series authors and editors believe that these four features—comprehensiveness, clarity of organization, a full exercise program, and an emphasis on writing as a vehicle of clear communication—will make *Prentice-Hall Grammar and Composition* especially valuable to both you and your students.

Introduction to the Annotated Teacher's Edition

Each Annotated Teacher's Edition has been designed to offer not only general strategies for course planning and evaluation but also specific section-by-section suggestions that can be used on a daily basis. The following paragraphs offer details about these particular features.

Strategies for Using the Text. The flexibility of the series is seen in its many possible applications both as a text and as a reference work. Beginning on page T-11, you will find suggestions for using the series in a variety of settings.

Time-Allocation Chart. On page T-16, you will find a chart giving suggested time allocations for each section of the course. Whatever sections you choose to teach, in whatever order you choose to teach them, the chart should prove helpful in gauging time, for a week, a semester, or a year.

Evaluation Procedures. The section on page T-21 starts with a description of the complete test program available with the series, moves on to specific suggestions for developing your own pretests and post-tests using text material, and then offers ideas for charting progress and developing additional exercises based on text material. The final part of the section is devoted to a discussion of various methods that can be used to evaluate student writing.

Bibliography. On page T-29, you will find a bibliography of general reference works that may prove useful in teaching a course in grammar and composition.

Teaching Suggestions. The bulk of the teacher's guide portion of the Annotated Teacher's Edition is devoted to a section-by-section coverage of the text. Here you will find objectives to help you plan your coverage of individual sections, suggestions for adapting each section for more and less advanced students, and specific ideas for additional exercises or activities. The objectives, which are correlated on a one-to-one basis with each subsection, should prove especially useful in planning which areas to emphasize and which exercises to assign to meet the particular needs of your own students.

Additional Answers to Text Exercises. Although most of the answers to text exercises are found directly on the text pages, a few, particularly for the diagraming exercises, are found here.

Strategies for Using the Text

Before starting a course, you will certainly want to consider how best to utilize the text to fit the needs of your students and the curriculum. For example, you may choose to teach the complete grammar and composition course in the order presented or you may choose to emphasize certain aspects of the text: grammar, composition, composition as it relates to literature, grammar as it relates to the improvement of basic skills, or grammar as it relates to the correction of errors in composition. Options and possible strategies for using the text in any of these different settings are given in the following paragraphs.

As a Text for Teaching Grammar and Composition. The units in the text are presented in the traditional order of rhetoric handbooks with grammar taking the preeminent position. Although this order works well, other orders can easily be followed. You may, for example, find it more useful to begin the year with study skills (especially the first two chapters), perhaps combining the unit with vocabulary. If you do choose to begin with grammar, you may want to start with the final chapter on sentence errors, then move into a quick coverage of the parts of speech followed by a more leisurely progression through the chapters on sentence parts.

Still another popular and easily managed strategy is one that merges the work on grammar and usage. The usage chapters on verbs, adjectives, and adverbs can be covered with parts of speech, while the chapters on pronouns and agreement can be taught with the study of sentence parts. Certain sections of the mechanics unit can also be taught with grammar and usage, particularly those dealing with end marks, commas, colons, and semicolons.

Following any of these strategies, you still face two basic choices on the teaching of composition. You may decide to leave all of the composition unit for later in the year, when you can give it your complete attention, or you may want to enliven the study of grammar, usage, and mechanics by interspersing groups of chapters on composition throughout the year.

Regardless of the order in which you choose to teach the course, you will probably find that pretests given early in the year will be very helpful in deciding which sections need the most emphasis. Ideas for pretests can be found in the following section. Once you have basic information about a new group of students, the time chart beginning on page T-16 will help you draft your general plan for the year.

The following chart shows just three of the many possibilities for course organization.

<table>
<tr><th colspan="3">THREE BASIC COURSES IN GRAMMAR AND COMPOSITION</th></tr>
<tr>
<td>Grammar (Ch. 1–10)
Usage (Ch. 11–15)
Mechanics (Ch. 16–18)
Vocabulary and Spelling (Ch. 19–20)
Study Skills (Ch. 21–23)
Composition (Ch. 24–32)</td>
<td>Study Skills (Ch. 21–23)
Vocabulary (Ch. 19)
Grammar (Ch. 1–10)
Composition: Sentences (Ch. 24–25)
Usage (Ch. 11–15)
Composition: Paragraphs (Ch. 26–28)
Mechanics and Spelling (Ch. 16–18, 20)
Composition: Longer Works (Ch. 29–32)</td>
<td>Grammar: Parts of Speech (Ch. 1–6)
Usage: Verbs, Adjectives, and Adverbs (Ch. 11, 14)
Grammar: Sentence Parts (Ch. 7–10)
Usage: Pronouns and Agreement (Ch. 12–13)
Composition (Ch. 24–32)
Mechanics (Ch. 16–18)
Vocabulary, Spelling, and Special Usage Problems (Ch. 19–20, 15)
Study Skills (Ch. 21–23)</td>
</tr>
</table>

As a Text for Teaching Grammar. If your curriculum calls for greater emphasis on grammar, you can use either the first few units of the text in the given order or rearrange them in one of the ways suggested previously. Again the pretest section and the time chart should prove useful in initial planning.

<table>
<tr><th colspan="3">THREE BASIC COURSES EMPHASIZING GRAMMAR</th></tr>
<tr>
<td>Grammar (Ch. 1–10)
Usage (Ch. 11–15)
Mechanics (Ch. 16–18)
Vocabulary and Spelling (Ch. 19–20)
Study Skills (Ch. 21–23)
Composition as Time Allows (Ch. 24–32)</td>
<td>Study Skills (Ch. 21–23)
Vocabulary (Ch. 19)
Grammar (Ch. 1–10)
Usage (Ch. 11–15)
Mechanics and Spelling (Ch. 16–18, 20)
Composition as Time Allows (Ch. 24–32)</td>
<td>Grammar: Parts of Speech (Ch. 1–6)
Usage: Verbs, Adjectives, and Adverbs (Ch. 11, 14)
Grammar: Sentence Parts (Ch. 7–10)
Usage: Pronouns and Agreement (Ch. 12–13)
Mechanics (Ch. 16–18)
Vocabulary, Spelling, and Special Usage Problems (Ch. 19–20, 15)
Study Skills (Ch. 21–23)
Composition as Time Allows (Ch. 24–32)</td>
</tr>
</table>

Because of the written nature of most of the Applications found at the end of every section in the text, your students will have a chance to do some work in composition even if time does not permit much attention to the final unit of the text.

Although the exercise program within the first few units is extensive, in teaching a course devoted mainly to the study of grammar, usage, and mechanics you may find that the practical section-by-section suggestions for additional activities in the later portion of this guide are particularly valuable.

As a Text for Teaching Composition. As already noted, the comprehensive unit on composition has been designed to present a thorough coverage of writing skills with emphasis not merely on rules, analysis, and special techniques, but also on the way these can be combined with a more thorough understanding of the purposes involved and the steps and methods that can be used to achieve success.

For a course that emphasizes composition, text material can be used in the given order, or it can be rearranged or divided in several other ways. Although the two chapters on sentences make a logical starting place, you may, instead, wish to start with paragraphs. One especially useful way of organizing the study of composition is around major assignments, either derived from the Applications at the end of each section or developed to fit your own classes' needs. This system works particularly well if you begin with paragraphs. The following chart shows two of the many plans that might be followed in using the text for a course that emphasizes composition.

TWO BASIC COURSES EMPHASIZING COMPOSITION

Sentences (Ch. 24–25)	Paragraphs—Major Assignment (Ch. 26–27)
Paragraphs (Ch. 26–27)	Kinds of Paragraphs—Major Assignment (Ch. 28)
Kinds of Paragraphs (Ch. 28)	Essays—Major Assignment (Ch. 29)
Essays (Ch. 29)	Sentences—Major Assignment in Paragraph or Essay Form (Ch. 24–25)
Reports (Ch. 30)	Reports—Major Assignment (Ch. 30)
Stories (Ch. 31)	Stories—Major Assignment (Ch. 31)
Letters (Ch. 32)	Other Units as Time Allows (Ch. 1–23)
Other Units as Time Allows (Ch. 1-23)	

Again, the materials in the evaluation section that follows can help you pretest your students to determine which areas need the most attention and how ambitious you may want to be with any group. The following section also offers ideas for evaluating written work—ideas that can help you find enough time to carry out ambitious plans.

The other units in the text will undoubtedly prove of value as you discover mechanical problems in written work. You may want to use the correction symbols in the section on preparing papers that follows the composition unit or work out your own system with the students. From time to time, you may also want to check papers with particular questions in mind. Perhaps most or all of the students could benefit from an extended lesson on a particular section of one of the earlier units. The chapter on sentence errors is especially likely to fall into this category.

Most students will also benefit from coverage of outlining and library skills; both are presented in the unit on study skills.

As a Text to Use in Conjunction with a Literature Text. If you are using the text in a course that combines the study of literature and the study of grammar and composition, you may want to place special emphasis on the composition unit. Students can learn about literature through an analysis of what good writing should be. They can also express their opinions about literature through writing. The following chart shows some of the ways in which the studies of literature and composition can complement each other.

STUDYING LITERATURE THROUGH COMPOSITION

Analysis of Good Writing	Writing About Literature
Sentences (Ch. 24–25)	Persuasive Paragraphs (Ch. 28)
Paragraphs (Ch. 26–28)	Essays (Ch. 29)
Essays (Ch. 29)	Reports (Ch. 30)
Stories (Ch. 31)	

The composition chapters on sentences should prove especially useful in helping students recognize the importance of the way in which authors use words. As the composition chapters increase the students' awareness of literary value, the study of literary models combined with those models already found in the text should expand the students' own ideas of what they can begin to aspire to.

Paragraphs, essays, and stories can be studied, not so much in terms of wording, but in terms of logical communication. Although students will not always find topic sentences, thesis statements, or dialogue in literary models, they will certainly find transitions, persuasive organizations, and a general flow of ideas that can again help them in their own writing.

Persuasive paragraphs, essays, and reports can in turn be used by students to express their own opinions about the works they are studying. In an ambitious combination of the two disciplines, reports and book reports can offer a student the chance, even at this level, to begin analyzing literature on a higher, more critical level.

As a Source Book for Teaching Basic Skills. If your students have had little training in the basic skills needed to achieve success in English classes or in school in general, you will probably want to choose only a few of the topics in the text and give extra attention to each. Perhaps the best place to start is with a thorough pretesting of present skills, following the suggestions in the next section.

Once you have solid data on your students' needs, you can follow any one of a number of plans. The unit on study skills is an excellent starting place for a course of this sort. You may wish to follow this with the material on vocabulary and spelling, again to give students help with skills that can improve their ability to deal with all subject matter. You will probably want to teach most of grammar, dropping occasional topics listed in the objectives and following many of the adaptation suggestions found in the section-by-section portion of the guide that begins on page T-30. In general, you are likely to find that the first few subsections of each section contain the most basic material. This same principle carries, in a general way, throughout the units on usage and mechanics.

The time you wish to devote to composition in such a course will vary. Perhaps the most useful approach is an in-depth coverage of the first two chapters on paragraphs. This coverage, like that of the other chapters and units, can be adapted and expanded by following the section-by-section suggestions that begin on page T-30.

ONE POSSIBLE COURSE EMPHASIZING BASIC SKILLS

Study Skills (Ch. 21–23)	Most of Mechanics (Ch. 16–18)
Vocabulary and Spelling (Ch. 19–20)	The Basic Paragraph (Ch. 26–27)
Most of Grammar (Ch. 1–10)	Some Work on Sentences (Ch. 24–25)
Most of Usage (Ch. 11–15)	Letters (Ch. 32)

As a Handbook for Correcting Errors in Composition. If most of your students are above grade level and can already handle the basic aspects of the composition process with relative ease, you will find that this text fits the reference needs of such students admirably.

If you plan to use the text primarily as a reference tool, you may want to conduct a short workshop session on the use of a handbook sometime early in the course. Students can be asked to brainstorm for ideas about the ways in which they might find a handbook useful—both in correcting mistakes and in developing ideas for compositions. With such a list in hand, they can then be asked to use one of the three reference aids in the text to find the areas they would consult, listing page numbers for each problem or source of ideas.

The following chart lists some of the areas that might be explored in such a session.

POSSIBILITIES FOR A WORKSHOP SESSION ON THE USE OF A HANDBOOK

For Correcting Mistakes	For Getting Ideas
1. What mistakes have students made on past compositions?	1. How can vocabulary be of help in composition?
2. What are their biggest problem areas in grammar, usage, punctuation, and spelling?	2. What should students be trying to achieve with their sentences? Their paragraphs? Their longer works?
3. What are some of the technical problems that may arise in putting their work into final form?	3. How important are audience and purpose?

Time-Allocation Chart

UNIT I

Grammar

Estimated Class Sessions

Chapter 1: Nouns and Pronouns

1.1 Nouns	1–1½
1.2 Pronouns	1–1½
1.3 Four Special Kinds of Pronouns	1½–2

Chapter 2: Verbs

2.1 Action Verbs	1–1½
2.2 Linking Verbs	1–1½
2.3 Helping Verbs	1–1½

Chapter 3: Adjectives

3.1 Adjectives as Modifiers	1–1½
3.2 Pronouns Used as Adjectives	1–1½

Chapter 4: Adverbs

4.1 Adverbs as Modifiers	1–1½
4.2 Adverbs Used in Sentences	1–1½

Chapter 5: Prepositions, Conjunctions, and Interjections

5.1 Prepositions	1–1½
5.2 Conjunctions	1–1½
5.3 Interjections	½–1

Chapter 6: Reviewing Parts of Speech

6.1 Determining Parts of Speech	1–1½

Chapter 7: Recognizing Parts of a Sentence

7.1 The Basic Sentence	1–1½
7.2 Complete Subjects and Predicates	1–1½
7.3 Compound Subjects and Verbs	1–1½
7.4 Special Problems with Subjects	1–1½
7.5 Direct Objects	1½–2
7.6 Indirect Objects	1½–2
7.7 Subject Complements	1½–2
7.8 The Four Functions of Sentences	½–1
7.9 Diagraming Basic Sentence Parts	2–2½

Chapter 8: Expanding Sentences with Phrases

8.1 Prepositional Phrases	1–1½
8.2 Appositives in Phrases	1–1½
8.3 Participles in Phrases	2–2½
8.4 Gerunds in Phrases	2–2½
8.5 Infinitives in Phrases	2–2½
8.6 Diagraming Prepositional Phrases and Appositives	2–2½

Chapter 9: Expanding Sentences with Clauses

9.1 Adjective Clauses	2½–3
9.2 Adverb Clauses	2½–3
9.3 Classifying Sentences by Structure	1–1½
9.4 Diagraming Clauses	2–2½

Chapter 10: Correcting Sentence Errors

10.1 Avoiding Fragments	1½–2
10.2 Avoiding Run-ons	1½–2
10.3 Avoiding Misplaced Modifiers	1½–2

UNIT **II**

Usage

Estimated Class Sessions

Chapter 11: Using Verbs

11.1 The Principal Parts of Verbs	1–1½
11.2 The Six Tenses of Verbs	1–1½
11.3 The Progressive Forms of Verbs	1–1½
11.4 Active and Passive Voice	1–1½
11.5 Glossary of Troublesome Verbs	1–1½

Chapter 12: Using Pronouns

12.1 Cases of Personal Pronouns	1½–2
12.2 Cases of *Who* and *Whom*	1½–2

Chapter 13: Making Words Agree

13.1 Agreement Between Subjects and Verbs	1½–2
13.2 Special Problems with Subject-Verb Agreement	1½–2
13.3 Agreement Between Pronouns and Antecedents	1½–2

Chapter 14: Using Adjectives and Adverbs

14.1	Regular Adjectives and Adverbs	½–1
14.2	Irregular Adjectives and Adverbs	½–1
14.3	Using Comparative and Superlative Degrees	½–1
14.4	Making Logical Comparisons	1–1½
14.5	Glossary of Troublesome Adjectives and Adverbs	½–1

Chapter 15: Recognizing Special Problems in Usage

15.1	Double Negatives	1–1½
15.2	Twenty Common Usage Problems	2–2½

UNIT **III**

Mechanics

Estimated Class Sessions

Chapter 16: Using Capitals

16.1	Capitals for First Words	½–1
16.2	Capitals for Proper Nouns	½–1
16.3	Capitals for Proper Adjectives	½–1
16.4	Capitals for Titles of People	½–1
16.5	Capitals for Titles of Things	½–1
16.6	Capitals in Letters	½–1

Chapter 17: Using Abbreviations

17.1	Abbreviations of Titles of People	½–1
17.2	Abbreviations for Time and Historical Dates	½–1
17.3	Geographical Abbreviations	½–1
17.4	Abbreviations of Measurements	½–1

Chapter 18: Using Punctuation Marks

18.1	End Marks	1–1½
18.2	Commas That Separate Basic Elements	2½–3
18.3	Commas That Set Off Added Elements	2½–3
18.4	The Semicolon	1–1½
18.5	The Colon	½–1
18.6	Quotation Marks with Direct Quotations	1½–2
18.7	Underlining and Other Uses of Quotation Marks	1–1½
18.8	The Hyphen	1–1½
18.9	The Apostrophe	1½–2

UNIT **IV**

Vocabulary and Spelling

	Estimated Class Sessions
Chapter 19: Building Your Vocabulary	
19.1 Ways to Enlarge Your Vocabulary	2–2½
19.2 Using Context	1½–2
19.3 Using Structure	3–3½
19.4 Exploring Word Origins	1½–2
Chapter 20: Improving Your Spelling	
20.1 Solving Your Spelling Problems	2–2½
20.2 Following Spelling Rules	2–2½

UNIT **V**

Study Skills

	Estimated Class Sessions
Chapter 21: Improving Your Study Habits	
21.1 Establishing Good Study Habits	1–1½
21.2 Developing Your Listening Skills	½–1
21.3 Developing Your Note-Taking Skills	1–1½
21.4 Developing Your Speaking Skills	½–1
Chapter 22: Improving Your Reading Skills	
22.1 Developing Your Reading Rate	1–1½
22.2 Reading Textbooks	½–1
Chapter 23: Improving Your Library and Reference Skills	
23.1 Using the Library	2½–3
23.2 Finding Reference Books in the Library	2–2½
23.3 Using the Dictionary	1–1½

UNIT **VI**

Composition

	Estimated Class Sessions
Chapter 24: Improving Your Choice of Words	
24.1 Choosing Precise Words	2–2½
24.2 Avoiding Worn-out and Inappropriate Words	2–2½

Chapter 25: Writing Better Sentences

25.1 Expanding Short Sentences	1–1½
25.2 Simplifying Long, Confusing Sentences	1–1½
25.3 Using a Variety of Sentences	2–2½

Chapter 26: Looking at Paragraphs

26.1 Recognizing Topic Sentences	1–1½
26.2 Recognizing Supporting Information	1–1½
26.3 Recognizing Unity	1–1½
26.4 Recognizing Coherence	1½–2

Chapter 27: Writing Paragraphs

27.1 Thinking Out Your Ideas and Writing a Topic Sentence	1–1½
27.2 Developing Support for a Topic Sentence	1–1½
27.3 Writing the Paragraph	1–1½
27.4 Revising and Rewriting a Paragraph	1½–2

Chapter 28: Writing Different Kinds of Paragraphs

28.1 Writing Paragraphs That Explain	1½–2
28.2 Writing Paragraphs That Persuade	2–2½
28.3 Writing Paragraphs That Describe	2–2½

Chapter 29: Writing Essays

29.1 Looking at Essays	2–2½
29.2 Thinking Out Your Ideas and Writing a Thesis Statement	1–1½
29.3 Developing Support for a Thesis Statement	1½–2
29.4 Writing and Revising an Essay	1½–2

Chapter 30: Writing Reports

30.1 Understanding and Preparing Reports	3½–4
30.2 Writing Book Reports	2–2½

Chapter 31: Writing Stories

31.1 Writing a Character Sketch	2–2½
31.2 Writing a Short Short Story	2–2½

Chapter 32: Writing Letters

32.1 Looking at Friendly Letters, Social Notes, and Business Letters	1–1½
32.2 Writing Different Kinds of Letters	2–2½

Evaluation Procedures

Almost the only things that are certain about the evaluation procedures used in teaching a course in grammar and composition are (1) that they will probably be multifaceted and (2) that they will probably take up a considerable amount of a teacher's time. The following suggestions cover most of the different facets—general pretesting and post-testing, drill work, and the variety of special techniques that can be used in grading compositions. Many of the latter suggestions are specifically directed at reducing the work a teacher of composition can expect to face. Throughout, the focus is on using evaluation procedures to communicate with the students and help them achieve greater success.

Using the Accompanying Test Package. The *Prentice-Hall Grammar and Composition Test Program,* available separately, offers a complete pretest and a complete post-test for each unit in each text, as well as a mastery test for each chapter. Because the various sections involved are clearly marked along the left-hand side of each test, you can use any of the tests to cover any or all of the sections contained in a larger division. If, for example, students are taking a chapter test on verb usage, but you have decided to omit the section on active and passive voice, you can simply instruct the students to omit those labeled portions of the test.

Although the focus in the test package is mainly on objective questions, the tests covering the composition unit combine questions that call for objective identification with other questions that call for writing samples. Possible scoring systems are given for each of the samples, although you can, of course, change the weighting of parts or substitute a more holistic evaluation.

The following charts show some of the possible uses of the various components in the test package. First, they can be used in the most traditional sense of pretest and post-test evaluation.

FOR OVERALL EVALUATION

Unit Pretests	Chapter Tests	Unit Post-Tests
Administer all or most of the pretests at the beginning of the year to identify strengths and weaknesses; then use the section numbers on the tests to plan lessons.	Administer the chapter tests at the end of each chapter in the traditional manner.	Administer all or most of the post-tests at the end of the year, or in groups at the end of each semester, to gauge overall progress during the period by comparison with pretest scores.

The tests can also serve for planning and testing each unit.

FOR UNIT-BY-UNIT PLANNING AND EVALUATION

Unit Pretests	Chapter Tests	Unit Post-Tests
Administer the pretests unit by unit as students approach each new area; encourage students to recognize their own strengths and weaknesses.	Use the chapter tests as the first stage in a recycling system that allows students to note problem areas that need extra attention.	Use the post-tests as the second stage in the recycling system, either by chapter, following the section numbers on the tests, or by unit.

Among the other uses of the tests are previewing, skills evaluation, and student self-testing.

FOR PREVIEWING, SKILLS EVALUATION, OR SELF-TESTING

Unit Pretests	Chapter Tests	Unit Post-Tests
Following the section numbers on the tests, use portions of the pretests before each chapter or section as a preview of a week's lesson.	Use the chapter tests (or the post-tests) as part of an open-book evaluation of students' ability to use the book as a reference tool.	Use the post-tests (or the chapter tests) as a vehicle that allows students to monitor their own progress in mastering basic skills.

Any of the suggestions in the charts can also, of course, be used with tests you construct yourself. The following ideas can help you construct such tests using the material in the text.

Developing Your Own Pretests and Post-Tests. The wealth of exercise material contained in the text makes it possible to pull selected material for special testing purposes without destroying the later value of the exercises themselves.

The following chart lists possibilities for constructing pretests directly from the material in the text.

CONSTRUCTING PRETESTS USING TEXT MATERIAL

1. Pull two or three exercise items from each set of exercises in the section, chapter, or unit you wish to pretest, keying them for later reference.
2. Use or adapt the Applications at the end of each section. Their cumulative nature makes them readily useful in a general pretesting of section objectives. Again, key them for later reference.
3. Use or adapt the Review Exercises at the end of the grammar, usage, and mechanics units, keying them in a more general way to the chapters covered.

Pretests can also be created by using the objectives in the section-by-section portion of this guide. The objectives can be used either to construct a series of individual questions for each objective or as a guide to decide on one or more major tasks the students might attempt in order to show the extent of their mastery of an overall concept. The following chart lists some of the major tasks that might be considered for each of the units in the text.

SAMPLE PRETESTS BASED ON OBJECTIVES FOR EACH SECTION

1. **Grammar:** Students can be given a series of sentences and asked first to label parts of speech, second to label sentence parts, and finally to label the sentences themselves by structure and by function. In addition, you would probably want to include a list of terms to be used in carrying out each part of this four-part assignment.
2. **Usage:** Students can be given one or more passages that contain the various errors in usage detailed in the objectives. After being told the number of errors contained in each passage, they can then be asked to locate and correct each error. Important in this kind of test is the immediate provision of corrections after students have completed the test, possibly through the use of a second sheet of error-free passages that students can study at length after completing the test.
3. **Mechanics:** Again, passages containing the major errors covered in the objectives can be distributed, with an emphasis on those that cause confusion in communication. Students should again be given the number of errors in each passage and corrected passages to study immediately after the test.
4. **Vocabulary and Spelling:** To test general strategies for developing vocabulary, you might give students a sample paragraph, asking them to identify the words they do not know, make guesses about the words telling why they made those guesses, tell how they would check the words' meanings, and how they would go about learning the words for future use. A general spelling test might ask students to choose among ten pairs of correct and incorrect spellings used in context, tell why they picked each word, and then tell how they would go about memorizing any words they have missed. As with the suggested usage and mechanics tests, correct answers should be supplied to the students immediately after they have completed the test.
5. **Study Skills:** To test the students' current knowledge of the study skills taught in this text, you might ask a series of short questions: (1) What study habits should a student try to master? (2) What should a student listen for in class? (3) What methods can be used to take notes and outline ideas for a paper? (4) What features in a textbook can be used in studying and reviewing? (5) How does one find a book in the library? (6) What reference books are especially useful in carrying out school assignments? (7) What can be found in a dictionary other than the meanings of words?
6. **Composition:** Your choices in designing a pretest in composition are perhaps the broadest. You can measure objective knowledge,

identification skills, or writing skills. The best single method is probably to ask for a paper of three to five paragraphs. It can then be analyzed in terms of all the different elements involved. A knowledge of the skills involved in writing reports, stories, and letters can be evaluated following a process similar to that suggested for study skills.

Post-tests for sections, chapters, and units can be constructed in similar fashion, using the text material directly or working with the guide objectives. If you are particularly interested in measuring overall attainment across a period of time, you will probably find it useful to use the same technique in constructing both the pretests and the post-tests. The following chart lists methods that might be used, including those that parallel the methods for constructing pretests.

METHODS FOR DEVELOPING POST-TESTS

1. As suggested for the pretests, pull items from the exercises in each section, use or adapt Applications, or use or adapt Review Exercises.
2. Again, as suggested for the pretests, use the guide objectives to develop individual questions for each objective or more general questions covering broader skills.
3. Use students' corrected homework papers to identify special problem areas, discuss these areas in class, and concentrate on them in preparing tests.

Whatever methods you use to evaluate student progress, you may find it useful to chart results at various stages and share these results with students.

Charting Student Progress. One of the major reasons for pretesting is so that you will be able to measure student progress, especially in those areas where the greatest problems seem to lie. Although grades can certainly be marked in grade-books, a more visual charting of scores can be more dramatic, particularly when it is shared with students at each testing stage. You may even want to ask students to construct their own charts, beginning with the results of their pretests, then moving on to other post-test stages.

To be most valuable, such charts should show individual scores for discrete portions of the work. This will give students a chance to identify those areas that are in particular need of improvement. The following chart shows three sets of scores on the usage unit: the lowest set on the unit pretest, a better set on the chapter tests, and a greatly improved set on the final unit post-test. Since one score in each set is needed for each chapter, the unit tests have been scored not in an overall fashion but chapter by chapter.

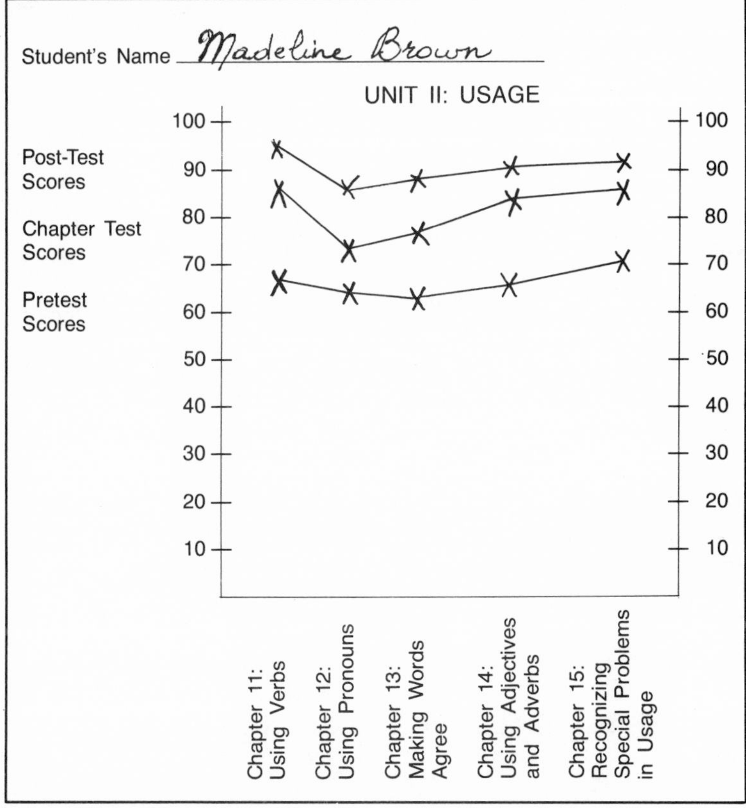

Such charts are probably most useful when teaching grammar, usage, and mechanics. With care, however, they can also be used to measure the more mechanical aspects of skills in other units.

Developing Additional Drill Material. Although you will generally find more than enough exercise material to cover the needs of most classes, individual students or groups of students may from time to time need extra work in some areas.

IDEAS FOR ADDITIONAL DRILL WORK

1. Use the additional activities in the section-by-section portion of the guide, along with the ideas for adapting the sections to fit the needs of different ability groups.
2. Adapt exercise sets from other areas of the book to follow the specific instructions for the exercises you are covering.
3. Have the students themselves construct new exercises, while gaining a new perspective from which to view the task at hand. After you have examined the exercises for accuracy, they can be exchanged repeatedly among the students.

As in charting student progress, you will most likely find that these ideas work best for the units presented at the beginning of the book. The last unit, composition, demands its own evaluation procedures.

Using Special Strategies for Evaluating Composition Skills. A number of different evaluation techniques can be used for grading compositions, some of which take considerable time, others of which can drastically reduce the time you spend without greatly changing the overall benefit to the student. Many experts, however, suggest that you consider using a mixture of techniques, cutting down the time you need to grade most papers while giving a thorough analysis to others.

The most traditional method of grading composition work is the most time-consuming. Each error is marked for correction and an attempt is made to cover all aspects of good writing, from ideas to spelling. The result is generally a single grade covering the entire piece of writing, combined in most cases with comments that will encourage students while directing them to specific areas that can be improved.

A variation of this approach divides the general analysis into specific criteria, which can then be graded individually. The following two charts show ways in which this system can be implemented. The chart on the left gives letter grades for nine equal criteria. The chart on the right gives number grades for seven weighted criteria.

COMPOSITION EVALUATION FORM

Student's Name *Sandy Giullo*

1. Word choices	B
2. Sentence style	B-
3. Clarity of main idea and purpose	A
4. Development of ideas	A-
5. Unity	A
6. Coherence	B
7. Ideas presented	A
8. Grammar and usage	C-
9. Mechanics and spelling	B
Composite Grade	B

COMPOSITION EVALUATION FORM

Student's Name *Greg Campbell*

Criterion	Score	Possible
1. Word choices and sentence style	8	(10)
2. Clarity of main idea and purpose	9	(10)
3. Development of ideas	8	(10)
4. Unity and coherence	8	(10)
5. Spelling	10	(10)
6. Grammar, usage, and mechanics	18	(20)
7. Ideas presented	26	(30)
Composite Grade	87	(100)

The criteria used and any weighting given will depend, of course, on what you are trying to measure in each assignment. The charts, if used, should also be seen as simply one more way to communicate clearly with students. They cannot replace the notes of encouragement and individual directives that may still be included on the papers along with requests for corrections.

Another increasingly popular method of grading composition papers is the holistic method. It has two basic purposes and a number of variations. The first purpose is to save time, thus making it possible to assign more papers, giving students more chances to practice their skills. The second purpose is to keep the focus on the quality of the entire paper and not on individual, miscellaneous faults. The basic method calls for the rapid reading and ranking of a group of papers on a scale of one to five (or one to four, or one to three, depending on the variation). The papers are then rapidly read and ranked by a second teacher and the scores are compared, with perhaps a third teacher acting as mediator on papers where the two sets of scores differ greatly.

The following chart shows an adaptation of the holistic method that you can use alone.

SUGGESTIONS FOR USING A CLASSROOM ADAPTATION OF THE HOLISTIC METHOD

1. Cover the students' names to guard against expectations.
2. Spend no more than a minute reading each page of a group of papers, getting a general feel for the quality of each work.
3. After reading each paper, place it in one of four piles which range from excellent to good to fair to not good. If necessary, include a fifth pile for papers that are for some reason impossible to grade—perhaps because a student has produced a good or promising paper that does not quite fit the assignment.
4. Briefly consider the possibility of reranking some of the papers. (If you are in doubt, you will generally find it best to stick with your first opinion.)
5. Add grades and comments.

The peer-grading method has also gained favor among some teachers in recent years. Like holistic grading, it saves time and makes it possible for the students to complete more assignments. In addition, it widens the audience for which each student is writing, while giving students further models of what the members of their own peer group can accomplish. Unless it is carefully managed, however, it can cause certain problems, including the reinforcement of errors. The following suggestions may make the system more manageable in your own classroom.

SUGGESTIONS FOR USING PEER GRADING

1. Before students are asked to evaluate each other's papers, discuss what specific things they should look for and how they should go about checking and marking these things.

2. Emphasize the importance of noting the good things and offering criticism in a constructive way.
3. From time to time, consider the possibility of having more than one student evaluate each paper.
4. Also from time to time, review sets of papers and conduct a general classroom review of the criteria to be used (not specifying any particular papers).

Perhaps the most ambitious system, not so much in terms of a teacher's workload, but in terms of true student progress, is one that relies on increasing self-evaluation. The revision checklists in the text can be part of such a system, along with any or all of the suggestions in the following chart.

SUGGESTIONS FOR DEVELOPING A SYSTEM OF SELF-EVALUATION

1. As in peer grading, discuss with students the specific qualities they should look for in a written work.
2. Have students begin their self-evaluation simply by conducting two revisions, with the second revision taking place at least a day after the first.
3. In each revision, ask students to mark their original work as a teacher might with internal corrections and margin comments.
4. After they have completed the final revision, ask students to list what they believe are the strengths and weaknesses of the work. These notes should be placed in a notebook along with ideas for future works.
5. Analyze the groups of revised works from time to time to see what progress the students are making. If possible, hold individual conferences.

Few if any of the methods discussed here can be used as the sole method of evaluation in the typical classroom. However, a judicious mixture may save time while giving students greater opportunities to develop their skills.

Bibliography

Armstrong, William B. *Study Tips.* Woodbury, N.Y.: Barron's Educational Series, 1975.

Baker, Sheridan. *The Practical Stylist,* 3rd ed. New York: Crowell, 1973.

D'Angelo, Frank J. *Process and Thought in Composition,* 2nd ed. Cambridge, Mass.: Winthrop Publishers, 1980.

DeSola, Ralph. *Abbreviations Dictionary.* New York: Meredith Press, 1967.

Follett, Wilson. *Modern American Usage.* New York: Hill and Wang, 1966.

Froe, Otis D. and Froe, Otyce B. *Easy Way to Better Grades.* New York: Arco Publishing Co., 1976.

Gilbert, Doris Wilcox. *Breaking the Word Barrier.* Englewood Cliffs, N.J.: Prentice-Hall, 1972.

Gorrell, Robert and Laird, Charlton. *Modern English Handbook,* 4th ed. Englewood Cliffs, N.J.: Prentice-Hall, 1967.

Hill, Robert H. *Dictionary of Difficult Words.* New York: John Day, 1971.

Kilner, Bernard G. *Learn How to Study.* Chicago: Science Research Associates, 1975.

Koch, Carl and Brazil, James M. *Strategies for Teaching the Composition Process.* Urbana, Ill.: National Council of Teachers of English, 1978.

Leggett, Glenn, Mead, David C., and Charvat, William. *Essentials of Grammar and Composition.* Englewood Cliffs, N.J.: Prentice-Hall, 1978.

Macrorie, Ken. *Telling Writing.* New York: Hayden Book Co., 1970.

Marshak, David. *HM Study Skills Program, Part I and II.* Reston, Va.: National Assoc. of Secondary School Principals, 1979.

Memering, Dean and O'Hare, Frank. *The Writer's Work.* Englewood Cliffs, N.J.: Prentice-Hall, 1980.

Myers, L. M. *Guide to American English,* 4th ed. Englewood Cliffs, N.J.: Prentice-Hall, 1968.

Quaintance, William. *Learning to Learn.* Portland, Me.: J. Weston Walsh Publishers, 1976.

Smelt, Elsie. *Speak, Spell and Read English,* 2nd ed. Hawthorn, Victoria, Australia: Longman, 1976.

Spargo, Edward. *The New Student.* Providence, R.I.: Jamestown Publishers, 1977.

Struck, William. *Study Skills for Success in School and College.* Danbury, Conn.: Grolier Educational Corp., 1978.

Two Hundred Tips to Students on How to Study. Danville, Ill.: Interstate Printers and Publishers, 1979.

West, William W. *Developing Writing Skills,* 3rd ed. Englewood Cliffs, N.J.: Prentice-Hall, 1980.

Teaching Suggestions

UNIT I

Grammar

This unit will help students explore and analyze both the eight parts of speech and the structure of sentences. The objectives of each section are detailed in the following pages. In the text itself, each objective is covered by a short subsection of explanatory text, followed by one or more sets of exercises. This arrangement will give the students a chance to test their understanding immediately. The Applications at the end of each section and the Review Exercises at the end of the unit can then be used to help students test, combine, and apply the skills they are learning.

Chapters 1–6 examine the parts of speech in a logical sequence: Nouns, pronouns, and verbs are covered first, followed by modifiers, prepositions, conjunctions, and interjections. The students in most classes will already be familiar with much of this material. They will then have a chance to review earlier work while concentrating on the more technical aspects of recognition and identification.

Chapters 7–10 examine the basic parts of sentences, the way in which sentences can be expanded through the use of phrases and clauses, and the ways in which sentence errors can be corrected. Chapters 7, 8, and 9 end with sections on diagraming. Although the diagraming sections are optional, most students are likely to enjoy this activity. You may also find that diagraming helps many students see more clearly the relationships among the various sentence parts.

The pretest for Unit I, available in the *Prentice-Hall Grammar and Composition Test Program,* can be used to help determine students' need for instruction in the skills presented in the unit. Chapter tests and a unit post-test are also available in the test program.

CHAPTER 1 Nouns and Pronouns (pp. 20–36)

Section 1.1 discusses nouns, Section 1.2 deals with personal pronouns, and Section 1.3 considers demonstrative, relative, interrogative, and indefinite pronouns.

Sections 1.1 and 1.2 can be completed by most classes in one class session each. Section 1.3, however, may take two class sessions for the average class to complete.

■ 1.1 Nouns (pp. 20–25)

Objectives: After completing this section, students should be able to

- Identify nouns as the names of people, places, or things.
- Recognize collective nouns.
- Recognize compound nouns.
- Distinguish between common and proper nouns.

Adapting for Different Abilities. Most students will have no difficulty completing the exercises in this section. For less advanced students, however, you may wish to preview the Application. Before they fill in the blanks, these students can discuss the kind of noun that will fit in each blank.

Advanced students might enjoy playing "Categories." Have the students draw a grid similar to the following model. The object in filling in this grid and others that the students make for themselves is to find nouns that fit each of the categories and begin with each of the letters at the left. Remind students who construct their own grids to choose some categories that require common nouns and some that demand proper nouns.

	Rivers	Vegetables	Cars	Landmarks	Toys
T					
I					
M					
E					
S					

Set a ten-minute time limit for the completion of each grid and have students compare their answers when they are finished. Score 5 for each unique answer, 3 for each shared answer, and 0 for each blank.

Suggestions for Additional Activities. You might want to have each student bring a short newspaper clipping to class. Students can underline all the nouns in each clipping, list them on a piece of paper, and classify them as in Exercise A. If you wish, students can then describe each noun as common or proper and note any nouns that are collective or compound.

■ 1.2 Pronouns (pp. 25–30)

Objectives: After completing this section, students should be able to

- Recognize the relationship between pronouns and their antecedents.
- Identify personal pronouns.

Adapting for Different Abilities. If you feel that less advanced students will have difficulty with Exercise B, you might work with them on the first two or three items. Advanced students might be asked to identify the person and number of each personal pronoun that they use in the Application.

Suggestions for Additional Activities. Ask each student to relate a personal anecdote or to describe a recent experience on paper. Have the students exchange papers and identify the personal pronouns in each story by person and number.

■ 1.3 Four Special Kinds of Pronouns (pp. 30–36)

Objectives: After completing this section, students should be able to

- Recognize demonstrative pronouns.
- Recognize relative pronouns.
- Recognize interrogative pronouns.
- Recognize indefinite pronouns.

Adapting for Different Abilities. Less advanced students might feel more confident working in pairs to complete the Application. In all exercises advanced students can supply antecedents for the pronouns they select. If a pronoun has no antecedent, as in some of the sentences in Exercises C and D, students can write *none.*

Advanced students can also prepare five or ten additional sentences using the Application sentences as models. Students can then exchange papers and complete each other's sentences.

Suggestions for Additional Activities. You might direct students to write an original sentence for each of the four types of pronouns discussed in this section. Students can then exchange papers and underline and label each pronoun.

CHAPTER 2 Verbs (pp. 37–48)

Each section of this chapter considers a different kind of verb: Section 2.1 looks at action verbs, Section 2.2 deals with linking verbs, and Section 2.3 discusses helping verbs. Understanding each type of verb is essential to students' work with sentence structure and will also help students to resolve a number of usge problems.

Average classes should be able to complete each section in one day. Some classes may require additional time or additional drill.

■ 2.1 Action Verbs (pp. 37–41)

Objectives: After completing this section, students should be able to

- Recognize that action verbs represent both visible and mental action.
- Recognize transitive action verbs.
- Recognize intransitive action verbs.

Adapting for Different Abilities. The material presented in this section as well as the accompanying exercises should be manageable for most students. Less advanced students might be asked to write only one sentence for each verb in the Application. You could then review their sentences individually, helping students to distinguish between transitive and intransitive verbs.

Advanced students can write a pair of sentences—one transitive and one intransitive—for each of the following verbs:

1. break 2. climb 3. run 4. throw 5. wash

Suggestions for Additional Activities. If students need further practice in distinguishing between transitive and intransitive verbs, have them work with the visible-action verbs in the chart at the beginning of the section, writing a sentence for each verb and then labeling each verb *transitive* or *intransitive.*

■ 2.2 Linking Verbs (pp. 41–45)

Objectives: After completing this section, students should be able to

- Recognize forms of *be* as linking verbs.
- Identify other linking verbs.
- Distinguish between action verbs and linking verbs.

Adapting for Different Abilities. Remind less advanced students to apply the "*am, is, are,*" test to each sentence in Exercise C before deciding on their answers. Also, you could use the Application as an in-class group activity with these students.

Suggestions for Additional Activities. Students can rewrite the first five sentences in Exercise C, keeping the subject the same but using each linking verb as an action verb and vice versa. Also, you might ask students in turn to read any one of the sentences they wrote for the Application and have their classmates identify the type of verb in each sentence.

■ 2.3 Helping Verbs (pp. 45–48)

Objectives: After completing this section, students should be able to

- Recognize helping verbs.
- Locate helping verbs in sentences.

Adapting for Different Abilities. Few students will require additional help with the material in this section. However, in order to make the Application more challenging for advanced students, you might have them phrase two or more of their sentences as questions so that one of the helping verbs will appear before the subject.

Suggestions for Additional Activities. Students may enjoy comparing their answers to Exercise A. Call on students in turn to read the helping verbs they supplied and ask if anyone chose different helping verbs. Record variations on the board and discuss with the class the different shades of meaning the helping verbs contribute to each sentence. In Sentence 6, for example, *will perform, may perform,* and *should perform* result in quite different meanings. Where no variation occurs, as is likely to happen in Sentence 9, for example, students can discuss why only one choice seems appropriate.

CHAPTER 3 Adjectives (pp. 49–60)

This chapter discusses a number of different types of adjectives. Section 3.1 considers descriptive adjectives, articles, nouns used as adjectives, proper adjectives, and compound adjectives. Section 3.2 deals with the various types of pronouns used as adjectives.

In some classes you may wish to spread Section 3.1 over two class sessions, breaking after Exercise B. Given students' earlier experience with pronouns, you should be able to complete Section 3.2 in one class session.

■ 3.1 Adjectives as Modifiers (pp. 49–56)

Objectives: After completing this section, students should be able to

- Recognize adjectives as modifiers of nouns and pronouns.

- Distinguish between definite and indefinite articles.
- Identify nouns used as adjectives.
- Recognize proper adjectives.
- Recognize compound adjectives.

Adapting for Different Abilities. Less advanced students might work in pairs to complete the Application. Advanced students might be instructed to supply at least one modifier for each noun in the Application.

Suggestions for Additional Activities. Students can exchange the papers they wrote for the Application and list each adjective and the word it modifies.

You might also have each student bring to class a short descriptive paragraph from a magazine or newspaper. Students can copy their paragraphs, substituting a blank space for each descriptive adjective. They can then exchange papers and fill in the blanks with appropriate adjectives. If you wish to extend the activity, ask students to list on the board the adjectives from the original paragraph and indicate any that are nouns used as adjectives, proper adjectives, or compound adjectives.

■ 3.2 Pronouns Used as Adjectives (pp. 56–60)

Objectives: After completing this section, students should be able to

- Identify possessive adjectives.
- Recognize demonstrative adjectives.
- Recognize interrogative adjectives.
- Recognize indefinite adjectives.

Adapting for Different Abilities. Most students will be able to move fairly rapidly through this section. Less advanced students, however, may need additional help in learning to distinguish between pronominal and adjectival uses. Remind these students that when demonstrative, interrogative, and indefinite pronouns are used as adjectives, the noun modified follows immediately. If a noun or pronoun does not follow immediately, the word is used as a pronoun.

Suggestions for Additional Activities. Have students look for sentences in their reading assignments that illustrate each of the four kinds of pronouns used as adjectives. Less advanced students might work in pairs while average and advanced students work independently.

CHAPTER 4 Adverbs (pp. 61–67)

Chapter 4 consists of two short sections. Section 4.1 discusses the three types of words that adverbs modify, while Section 4.2

helps students find adverbs in sentences and distinguish them from adjectives. Since both sections are fairly short and straightforward, most classes will be able to complete them in one class session each.

■ 4.1 Adverbs as Modifiers (pp. 61–64)

Objectives: After completing this section, students should be able to

- Recognize adverbs that modify verbs.
- Recognize adverbs that modify adjectives.
- Recognize adverbs that modify other adverbs.

Adapting for Different Abilities. Most students will have no difficulty with the material in this section. However, the Application can easily be modified to suit the abilities of your students. Average and above average students can simply complete the activity according to the instructions in the text. Less advanced students might be given the following list of adverbs, each of which can be used one or more times in the Application sentences:

1. carefully	6. rather
2. harshly	7. silently
3. late	8. very
4. never	9. here
5. not	10. soon

Suggestions for Additional Activities. Students can compare their answers to the Application, rate the most popular choices, and discuss why certain words seem to be most obvious.

■ 4.2 Adverbs Used in Sentences (pp. 65–67)

Objectives: After completing this section, students should be able to

- Locate adverbs in sentences.
- Distinguish between adjectives and adverbs.

Adapting for Different Abilities. If less advanced students seem to have difficulty with Exercise B, ask them to identify the word that each underlined word modifies and then determine the part of speech of the modified word. Remind students that adjectives modify nouns or pronouns, while adverbs modify verbs, adjectives, or other adverbs.

Suggestions for Additional Activities. Refer students to Exercise A in Section 2.1 (p. 38), and ask them to add at least one adverb to each sentence. If you wish, students can then compare choices and note the different positions in which adverbs can be placed.

CHAPTER 5 Prepositions, Conjunctions, and Interjections (pp. 68–78)

Each section in this chapter considers one of the remaining parts of speech: Section 5.1 discusses prepositions, Section 5.2 looks at conjunctions, and Section 5.3 deals with interjections. You can probably cover Sections 5.1 and 5.2 in one class session each. Section 5.3 can be covered even more rapidly or assigned for independent work.

■ 5.1 Prepositions (pp. 68–72)

Objectives: After completing this section, students should be able to

- Recognize one-word and compound prepositions.
- Identify prepositional phrases.
- Distinguish between prepositions and adverbs in sentences.

Adapting for Different Abilities. Although the material in this section should not be difficult for most classes, you may wish to work through the pairs of sentences in Exercise C orally with less advanced students. You might also ask these students to identify the object of each preposition.

Suggestions for Additional Activities. If you feel that students need more practice in identifying prepositions and prepositional phrases, have them find those that appear in the sentences of Exercise A in Section 3.1 (pp. 50–51). Ask students to write each prepositional phrase they find, and underline each preposition.

■ 5.2 Conjunctions (pp. 73–77)

Objectives: After completing this section, students should be able to

- Recognize coordinating conjunctions.
- Recognize correlative conjunctions.
- Recognize subordinating conjunctions.

Adapting for Different Abilities. Students should have no difficulty identifying the conjunctions in the exercises. However, you may wish to allow less advanced students to skip the second Application. Advanced students might be asked to identify the kinds of conjunctions used in both Applications.

Suggestions for Additional Activities. Students can exchange the sentences they have written for the second Application. They can then circle the conjunction in each sentence and underline the words or groups of words each conjunction joins. Students can also be asked to write at the end of each sentence the kind of conjunction they circled.

■ 5.3 Interjections (pp. 77–78)

Objective: After completing this section, students should be able to

- Recognize interjections.

Adapting for Different Abilities. Most students should be able to complete this section easily and without additional practice. You may want to let less advanced students choose any five of the words in the Application for their sentences.

Suggestions for Additional Activities. To introduce the point that interjections should be used infrequently in formal writing, you may want to have students search for interjections in their reading assignments and then discuss the results.

CHAPTER 6 Reviewing Parts of Speech (pp. 79–83)

This chapter expands and reinforces the concept that a word's part of speech is determined by its use in a sentence. Students who have covered the earlier chapters will have already seen the use of nouns and pronouns as adjectives, the use of a single word as an adverb or an adjective, and the use of a single word as a preposition or an adverb. This chapter extends the idea by showing other words that can be used as many different parts of speech. One class session may be sufficient to cover this material.

■ 6.1 Determining Parts of Speech (pp. 79–83)

Objective: After completing this section, students should be able to

- Identify a word's part of speech from its use in a sentence.

Adapting for Different Abilities. With less advanced students, you might analyze step-by-step the parts of speech of three other words in the example sentence on page 82: *team* (noun), *finished* (verb), and *early* (adverb). After the students have identified the parts of speech, using the questions in the charts, they can be asked to use *team* as a verb, *finish* as a noun, and *early* as an adjective. Advanced students might return to Exercise A and write original sentences using the underlined words in Sentences 4–7 as different parts of speech. If necessary, suggest that students use the dictionary to find the meanings of these words when they are used as different parts of speech.

Suggestions for Additional Activities. Students can read the sentences they wrote for the Application, while classmates identify the part of speech of the key word in each sentence. Instead of stopping after eliciting just two parts of speech for each, ask if any student has another sentence with the key word used as a different part of speech.

Students can also be asked to think of other words that can be used as different parts of speech and to use each of them in sentences illustrating as many parts of speech as possible. The following group of sentences might serve as an example:

1. Sit right here. (adverb)
2. It's important to right the boat quickly. (verb)
3. Make a right turn here. (adjective)
4. Do you consider voting a right or a privilege? (noun)

CHAPTER 7 Recognizing Parts of a Sentence (pp. 84–125)

This chapter will provide students with an understanding of basic sentence elements; the ideas presented here will then be enlarged upon in subsequent chapters. Section 7.1 deals with the need for a subject and a verb in a sentence. Section 7.2 discusses complete subjects and predicates. The material in the first two sections is further developed in Section 7.3, which covers compound subjects and verbs, and Section 7.4, which covers special problems with subjects. Sections 7.5 and 7.6 present direct and indirect objects, and Section 7.7 deals with subject complements. Section 7.8 considers the classification of sentences by function, and Section 7.9 introduces sentence diagraming as a tool for viewing relationships between sentence elements.

Although the time you devote to this chapter will vary depending on a class's ability and background, you will probably need at least two weeks to cover all of the material in an average class.

■ 7.1 The Basic Sentence (pp. 84–89)

Objectives: After completing this section, students should be able to

- Recognize a sentence as a group of words containing a subject and a verb.
- Distinguish between complete thoughts and incomplete thoughts.

Adapting for Different Abilities. The material in this section should be accessible to most students. However, if less advanced students seem to be having difficulty, you may want to do Exercise B with them as a group activity. Ask these students what kinds of words are missing in each item and help them restructure the fragments into complete sentences.

Suggestions for Additional Activities. Students can return to the sentences they wrote for Exercise B, and underline the subjects once and the verbs twice.

■ 7.2 Complete Subjects and Predicates

(pp. 89–91)

Objective: After completing this section, students should be able to

- Recognize complete subjects and complete predicates in sentences.

Adapting for Different Abilities. Less advanced students might complete the Application in pairs. Advanced students might write twenty sentences for the Application rather than ten. To do this, they can be asked to expand each subject and verb separately instead of using the words in the pairs given in the text.

Suggestions for Additional Activities. If students need further practice with this material, you might refer them to Exercise B in Section 1.1 (p. 22). Instruct students to follow the directions for Exercise A in Section 7.2. If you wish, students can also be asked to expand the subject and verb in each sentence into a sentence that is different from the original.

■ 7.3 Compound Subjects and Verbs

(pp. 91–95)

Objectives: After completing this section, students should be able to

- Recognize compound subjects in sentences.
- Recognize compound verbs in sentences.

Adapting for Different Abilities. Less advanced students might profit from a brief study or review of conjunctions (Section 5.2) before undertaking the second Application.

Suggestions for Additional Activities. If you wish to give students further practice in working with compound subjects and verbs, you might refer them to Exercise A in Section 7.1 (p. 86). Ask the students to make the subjects compound in half the sentences and the verbs compound in the other half. If students have not yet studied subject-verb agreement, you may want to do this as an oral activity.

■ 7.4 Special Problems with Subjects

(pp. 95–101)

Objectives: After completing this section, students should be able to

- Recognize subjects in sentences that give orders or directions.
- Find the subject in questions.
- Find the subject in sentences beginning with *there* or *here.*
- Find the subject in inverted sentences.

Adapting for Different Abilities. To make the Application more accessible to less advanced students, you might supply sentences that correspond to the instructions in the text. Students can then underline the subjects once and the verbs twice.

Advanced students can bring to class particularly effective inverted-order sentences from their reading to share with the class. Volunteers can then identify the subjects in these sentences.

Suggestions for Additional Activities. As a special challenge, you might ask students to rewrite some of the sentences in the first Application in Section 7.3 (p. 94) as follows. Warn students that a number of words may need to be changed slightly.

Sentence 1: Invert word order.
Sentence 2: Write as a question.
Sentence 7: Write as an order.
Sentence 8: Write as a question.
Sentence 10: Write as a question.

■ 7.5 Direct Objects (pp. 101–107)

Objectives: After completing this section, students should be able to

- Recognize direct objects in sentences.
- Recognize compound direct objects in sentences.
- Distinguish between direct objects, adverbs, and objects of prepositions.
- Locate direct objects in questions.

Adapting for Different Abilities. If less advanced students have difficulty with Exercise D, you might remind them to rewrite the questions in normal word order. These students might also work in pairs or in small groups to complete the Application.

You might instruct advanced students to write the sentences in the Application in any order they choose, as long as they use all the patterns. Students might then exchange papers and identify direct object, adverbs, and prepositional phrases according to the instructions in Exercise C.

Suggestions for Additional Activities. To reinforce recognition of direct objects, you might have students write answers to the first five questions in Exercise D. They can then underline the direct object in each of the new sentences.

■ 7.6 Indirect Objects (pp. 107–110)

Objectives: After completing this section, students should be able to

- Recognize indirect objects in sentences.
- Recognize compound indirect objects in sentences.
- Distinguish between indirect objects and objects of prepositions.

Adapting for Different Abilities. You might work with less advanced students on the first five sentences of Exercise A. Remind these students that the indirect object always comes before the direct object. Also, suggest that they can test a word to see whether or not it is an indirect object by moving it to the end of the sentence and making it the object of the preposition *to* or *for.* Help students apply this test to the first five sentences and then have them complete the exercise on their own.

You may wish to reserve the Application for advanced students. The sentences they write can then be distributed in random order and analyzed by other students.

Suggestions for Additional Activities. In studying direct and indirect objects, students might also be asked to practice sentence-combining techniques. Ask students to combine sets of sentences such as the following into a single sentence each. Then have students identify the direct and indirect objects in the resulting sentences.

1. The judges awarded Jack a blue ribbon.
   The judges awarded me a blue ribbon, too.
   (The judges awarded Jack and me blue ribbons.)
2. They gave us refreshments.
   They also provided entertainment.
   (They gave us refreshments and provided entertainment.)
3. We brought our hostess some flowers.
   We brought our host some flowers, too.
   We also brought them a box of candy.
   (We brought our hostess and host some flowers and a box of candy.)

■ 7.7 Subject Complements (pp. 110–115)

Objectives: After completing this section, students should be able to

- Recognize predicate nouns and pronouns in sentences.
- Recognize predicate adjectives in sentences.
- Recognize compound subject complements in sentences.

Adapting for Different Abilities. Less advanced students might work in pairs to write the sentences in the Application. Advanced students might be permitted to mix and match the subjects and predicates in the Application and to compare their sentences to see the many variations possible.

Suggestions for Additional Activities. If students need further practice with subject complements, have them identify the type of subject complement in each sentence of Exercise A in Section 2.2 (p. 42).

■ 7.8 The Four Functions of Sentences

(pp. 115–117)

Objective: After completing this section, students should be able to

- Identify sentences as declarative, interrogative, imperative, or exclamatory.

Adapting for Different Abilities. You might suggest that advanced students rewrite the sentences in Exercise A, changing each to another function. For example, Sentence 1 could be changed to a declarative sentence: *It is wise to visit the dentist twice a year.* Other students might carry out the same activity orally.

Suggestions for Additional Activities. Call on students in turn to read aloud in random order the sentences they wrote for the Application while other students identify each sentence by function.

■ 7.9 Diagraming Basic Sentence Parts

(pp. 117–125)

Objectives: After completing this section, students should be able to

- Diagram sentences with subjects and verbs.
- Diagram sentences with adjectives, adverbs, and conjunctions.
- Diagram sentences with compound subjects and verbs.
- Diagram orders, sentences beginning with *there* or *here,* and interjections.
- Diagram sentences with complements.

Adapting for Different Abilities. Average and less advanced students might be given skeleton diagrams to use in completing any or all of the exercises and the Application.

If you decide not to teach diagraming to these students, you can use the exercises for additional drill. Students can write the sentences and label subjects, verbs, modifiers, and complements.

Suggestions for Additional Activities. Many of the exercise sets found earlier in the chapter can be adapted to provide extra practice in diagraming. All prepositional phrases, appositives, and subordinate clauses must be removed, and the sentences should be checked carefully for other words that might give the students difficulty.

CHAPTER 8 Expanding Sentences with Phrases (pp. 126–147)

In this chapter students will build on their knowledge of the basic parts of a sentence by working with sentences that contain different kinds of phrases. In Sections 8.1 and 8.2, students will explore the functions of prepositional phrases and appositive phrases. In the next three sections, they will learn about verbal phrases. Section 8.3 defines the participle and explains how participles can be used in phrases. Section 8.4 defines the gerund and demonstrates how gerunds can be expanded into phrases. Section 8.5 explains the uses of infinitives and discusses infinitive phrases. In Section 8.6 students will learn to incorporate prepositional and appositive phrases into basic sentence diagrams such as those they worked with in Chapter 7.

With most classes you will probably spend one class session each on Sections 8.1 and 8.2. Since Section 8.3 introduces verbals and helps students distinguish between participles and verbs, it may require two days. You might also want to spend about two days on each of the other three sections in the chapter.

■ 8.1 Prepositional Phrases (pp. 126–131)

Objectives: After completing this section, students should be able to

- Identify prepositional phrases used as adjectives.
- Identify prepositional phrases used as adverbs.

Adapting for Different Abilities. With less advanced students, you might want to study or review the material on prepositions in Section 5.1 before beginning this section. Advanced students can complete Exercises A and B a second time, replacing as many phrases as possible with one-word modifiers. For example, the third sentence in Exercise A can be rewritten in the following way: *Mary is the nurses' supervisor.*

Suggestions for Additional Activities. Exercises A and B in Section 5.1 (pp. 70–71) may be used as needed to give students additional practice in identifying prepositional phrases used as adjectives and adverbs. The sentences students wrote for the Application in Section 5.1 (p. 72) can also be used in this way. Since the emphasis in the two exercises is on adverbial phrases, you may want to instruct students to add a few adjective phrases of their own to the sentences.

■ 8.2 Appositives in Phrases (pp. 131–133)

Objective: After completing this section, students should be able to

- Identify appositives and appositive phrases in sentences.

Adapting for Different Abilities. Once again, less advanced students might benefit from working in pairs to complete the Application. You can have advanced students make at least three of the appositives rename direct objects. These students might also be encouraged to expand the appositives with additional modifiers.

Suggestions for Additional Activities. Ask each student to bring to class at least one example of an appositive from a newspaper or magazine article. Then ask students to identify the appositives in each other's selections. For further practice students can work again with the sentences in the Application in Section 1.1 (p. 25). Ask students to identify the sentences that already have appositives (Sentences 1 and 3). Then instruct them to complete the sentences so that each of the ten sentences contains an appositive. Students can then exchange papers to identify the appositives in each other's sentences.

■ 8.3 Participles in Phrases (pp. 133–138)

Objectives: After completing this section, students should be able to

- Identify present and past participles.
- Distinguish between verbs and participles.
- Recognize participial phrases.

Adapting for Different Abilities. It might help less advanced students working on Exercise B if you ask them to write the whole verb phrase for each sentence in which part of a verb phrase is underlined. Remind these students that the helping verbs are what turn these participles into verb phrases. If the underlined word stands by itself and modifies a noun or pronoun, it is a participle.

Advanced students might be asked to use each word they have labeled a participle in Exercise B as a verb and each word they have labeled a verb as a participle.

Suggestions for Additional Activities. You might ask students to copy from their outside reading or from a textbook five sentences containing participles or participial phrases. Students can then exchange papers in class and identify the participles and participial phrases.

■ 8.4 Gerunds in Phrases (pp. 138–140)

Objectives: After completing this section, students should be able to

- Identify gerunds used in sentences.
- Identify gerund phrases in sentences.

Adapting for Different Abilities. Less advanced students should have no great difficulty in identifying the gerunds in Exercise A. However, you may want to give them extra practice in determining each gerund's use in the sentence. Have these students begin by identifying the subject and verb of each sentence, covering only the first clause in Sentence 4. Then students should identify any complements and any prepositional phrases, ignoring the infinitive phrase in Sentence 8. At this point they should readily be able to identify the use of each gerund.

You might give advanced students some leeway in doing the Application. Tell them that they must use two gerunds as objects of prepositions, two as subjects, and one as a direct object. They can then use the gerund phrases given in the Application in any order they wish.

Suggestions for Additional Activities. Students can be asked to rewrite the sentences in Exercise A so that each contains a compound gerund. For example, the first sentence could become *Walking and jogging are excellent exercise.* Alternatively, you might use those same sentences and instruct the students to expand each gerund into a gerund phrase (*Walking at least a mile a day is excellent exercise.*).

■ 8.5 Infinitives in Phrases (pp. 140–144)

Objectives: After completing this section, students should be able to

- Identify infinitives used in sentences.
- Identify infinitive phrases in sentences.

Adapting for Different Abilities. You might give less advanced students some preliminary practice in distinguishing between the use of the word *to* as a preposition and its use at the beginning of an infinitive. Ask these students to identify the prepositional phrase in each of the following pairs of sentences. After they have told why they chose each phrase, you can introduce the idea of infinitives.

1. This is the best road to take.
   This is the best road to Claytonville.
2. I have a letter to mail.
   I wrote a letter to Sandy.
3. Chris came to school late.
   Chris came to visit.

4. I made a promise to Lee.
   I made a promise to call back.

As they complete the exercises, advanced students might be asked to give the function of each infinitive used as a noun and to identify the use of other infinitives as adverbial or adjectival.

Suggestions for Additional Activities. Students can be asked to use the following five infinitive phrases in sentences of their own. Students can then identify the functions of the infinitive phrases in each other's work either by reading sentences aloud to one another or by exchanging papers.

1. to be well liked
2. to play the role of Juliet
3. to miss the train
4. to overcome his fear of heights
5. to finish painting the house by the end of the week

■ 8.6 Diagraming Prepositional Phrases and Appositives (pp. 144–147)

Objectives: After completing this section, students should be able to

- Diagram sentences with prepositional phrases.
- Diagram sentences with appositives and appositive phrases.

Adapting for Different Abilities. With less advanced students and with average students, you may want to review Exercise A orally before they begin diagraming. Be sure the students can identify both the prepositional phrases and the words they modify. Less advanced students and average students might also be given skeleton diagrams to use in completing the exercises and the Application. If you decide not to teach diagraming to these students, the exercises may be used for additional drill material. Advanced students might enjoy diagraming some of the sentences they have written for the Applications in Sections 8.1 and 8.2.

Suggestions for Additional Activities. If students need more practice in diagraming sentences, they might be asked to diagram selected sentences taken from the exercises in Sections 8.1 and 8.2.

CHAPTER 9 Expanding Sentences with Clauses (pp. 148–166)

Each of the first two sections in this chapter introduces a different kind of subordinate clause: Section 9.1 discusses adjective clauses, Section 9.2 deals with adverb clauses. Section 9.3 then explores the classification of sentences by structure, based on the number and kind of clauses a sentence contains. Section 9.4

completes the instruction in diagraming and helps students see more clearly the relationships among the clauses they have been working with.

You will probably need to allow from eight to ten days for the completion of the chapter. Advanced students might proceed somewhat more quickly, but average and less advanced students will need at least eight days to assimilate the material.

■ 9.1 Adjective Clauses (pp. 150–153)

Objectives: After completing this section, students should be able to

- Identify adjective clauses in sentences.
- Use adjective clauses to combine sentences.

Adapting for Different Abilities. Although the section should not prove particularly troublesome for most students, less advanced students might benefit from looking more closely at the words that introduce adjective clauses. Ask students to list the words that introduce each adjective clause in Exercise A. Have each new word recorded on the board as it is given. Leave the list on the board so that students can refer to it when completing Exercise B and the Application.

Suggestions for Additional Activities. To provide additional pairs of sentences for sentence-combining activities, you can have each student find at least five sentences with adjective clauses by looking through magazine articles or books. The students can then construct a pair of sentences from each sentence they find and exchange papers. Finally, they can compare each other's answers with the original sentences.

■ 9.2 Adverb Clauses (pp. 153–157)

Objectives: After completing this section, students should be able to

- Identify adverb clauses in sentences.
- Recognize elliptical adverb clauses in sentences.

Adapting for Different Abilities. You may want to allow less advanced students to refer to the chart of subordinating conjunctions on page 154 when they work on the Application.

Advanced students might enjoy comparing the sentences they write for the Application. They should note the variations in emphasis resulting both from their choices of subordinating conjunctions and from their decisions as to which sentences to subordinate.

Suggestions for Additional Activities. If students need more practice in working with adverb clauses, you can give them copies of the following sentences:

1. We try to cooperate more than they.
2. Alice always tries to remain as fair as she can.
3. Many in the audience fidgeted while they waited for the curtain to rise.
4. Bruno can be vicious when he is angry.
5. Our phone rings as often as theirs.

Ask the students to copy each adverbial clause and to complete in parentheses any elliptical clauses.

■ 9.3 Classifying Sentences by Structure (pp. 157–163)

Objectives: After completing this section, students should be able to

- Identify simple sentences.
- Identify compound sentences.
- Identify complex sentences.
- Identify compound-complex sentences.

Adapting for Different Abilities. If less advanced students proceed in a step-by-step manner through the many exercises in the section, they should have a good understanding of the types of sentence structures by the time they are asked to distinguish among them in the first Application. Before these students begin the second Application, you may want to review and discuss in class their work on the first Application. You might also consider working with these students to help them complete the second Application, or you might decide to exempt some students from it altogether.

Suggestions for Additional Activities. To give the class additional practice in identifying sentence structure, you can have students read aloud in random order the sentences they wrote for the second Application, or you can present some of the best ones on a ditto master.

■ 9.4 Diagraming Clauses (pp. 164–166)

Objectives: After completing this section, students should be able to

- Diagram compound sentences.
- Diagram sentences containing subordinate clauses.

Adapting for Different Abilities. As in previous diagraming sections, you might want to provide skeleton diagrams for less advanced students and average students to use in completing the exercises and the Application. If you decide not to teach diagraming to these students, you might want to use the exercise material to provide extra drill work on clauses. Advanced students might be given the challenge of diagraming some of the compound-complex sentences in Exercise G of Section 9.3 (p. 162).

Suggestions for Additional Activities. If you wish to provide further practice in diagraming compound and complex sentences, you might ask the students to diagram selected sentences from Exercises C and E of Section 9.3 (pp. 159–161).

CHAPTER 10 Correcting Sentence Errors (pp. 167–184)

This chapter concludes students' formal work with sentence parts and asks them to apply their knowledge of grammar in correcting a number of common writing problems. Sections 10.1 and 10.2 deal with the common structural errors of fragments and run-ons. Section 10.3 shows students how to identify and correct misplaced modifiers.

Although some advanced students may be able to move along more rapidly, most classes will benefit from spending up to two days on each section, for a total of up to six days for the chapter.

■ 10.1 Avoiding Fragments (pp. 167–174)

Objectives: After completing this section, students should be able to

- Recognize sentence fragments.
- Recognize and correct phrase fragments.
- Recognize and correct clause fragments.

Adapting for Different Abilities. You may wish to work closely with less advanced students in analyzing the sentences in Exercise A. Students can compare the fragments they find with those in the chart on page 168 and try to determine what is missing in each.

Advanced students can draw one chart showing types of phrase fragments and one showing the types of clause fragments. They can then supply original examples to illustrate each type of fragment.

Suggestions for Additional Activities. If students need more practice in correcting fragments, you can have them write complete sentences using the fragments in Exercise A.

■ 10.2 Avoiding Run-ons (pp. 174–179)

Objectives: After completing this section, students should be able to

- Recognize run-on sentences.
- Use appropriate punctuation and/or coordination to correct run-on sentences.

Adapting for Different Abilities. This section should be accessible to all students. They should be able to move through the presentation comfortably and complete the exercises and the Application with no difficulty.

Advanced students can look for lengthy sentences in their outside reading, copy them down, and bring them to class. The sentences can then be analyzed to show how ideas in long sentences can be correctly coordinated or subordinated.

Suggestions for Additional Activities. If you find that some students need more practice in correcting run-on sentences, you might have them correct the run-on sentences in Exercise A.

■ 10.3 Avoiding Misplaced Modifiers (pp. 180–184)

Objectives: After completing this section, students should be able to

- Recognize misplaced modifiers.
- Correct misplaced modifiers by moving them closer to the words they modify.

Adapting for Different Abilities. If you feel that less advanced students need extra help in correcting misplaced modifiers, you can guide them through the required revisions of the first five sentences in Exercise B. You may also want to work with these students in carrying out the revisions called for in the Application.

Suggestions for Additional Activities. To provide additional reinforcement, you might ask students to return to Exercise A and correct the misplaced modifiers.

■ Review Exercises (pp. 184–190)

These exercises, based on Chapters 1–10, can be used as homework, as classwork, or as assessment material, depending on students' needs and abilities. The number of exercises you use and the time you devote to them is a matter of individual preference.

UNIT II

Usage

This unit deals with the principal parts, tenses, and voices of verbs; the case forms of pronouns; agreement of subjects and verbs and of pronouns and antecedents; the degrees of adjectives and adverbs; and such usage pitfalls as double negatives. Since so much of this material requires an understanding of grammar and syntax, you may wish to deal with these chapters after you have taught Unit I. Alternatively, you may choose to teach the chapters in Unit II along with the chapters in Unit I that offer the necessary background information.

Students learn most nonstandard usage by hearing and speaking nonstandard forms, not by reading them. As a result, oral practice can help many students master the standard English forms. For this reason the teaching suggestions that follow frequently recommend oral drill. You should feel free, however, to use this method at any point in the unit. As often as possible, have students read aloud and repeat completed exercise sentences using standard forms so they become accustomed to hearing the forms used by educated speakers and writers.

The pretest for Unit II, available in the *Prentice-Hall Grammar and Composition Test Program,* can be used to help determine students' need for instruction in the skills presented in the unit. Chapter tests and a unit post-test are also available in the test program.

CHAPTER 11 Using Verbs (pp. 192–223)

Chapter 11 shows how verbs express time and voice. It also demonstrates the correct use of verbs. Students must have the appropriate grammar background in order to understand the content of this chapter. Study or review of Section 2.3 on helping verbs will help students understand Section 11.1 on the principal parts of verbs. Before moving on to verb conjugation in Sections 11.2 and 11.3, students should be familiar with first-, second-, and third-person forms of personal pronouns discussed in Section 1.2. Study or review of Sections 2.1 and 2.2 on action and linking verbs will help students gain a better understanding of Section 11.4 on active and passive voice. Students should also understand subjects and predicates in sentences, as covered in Chapter 7, before learning about the passive voice. Section 11.5, which summarizes some of the major problems that students encounter in verb usage, also depends to some extent on students' knowledge of the basic parts of sentences.

With most classes you may want to allow five or six days to complete this chapter. You will probably want to spend at least half a day on the first part of Section 11.1 (regular verbs) and at least half a day—possibly a whole day—on the second part (irregular verbs). Be sure students have mastered the principal parts of verbs before you move on to Section 11.2. Most classes will be able to cover the four remaining sections in one day each.

■ 11.1 The Principal Parts of Verbs (pp. 192–201)

Objectives: After completing this section, students should be able to

- Recognize and use the principal parts of regular verbs correctly.
- Recognize and use the principal parts of irregular verbs correctly.

Adapting for Different Abilities. While drill work may prove especially helpful with less advanced students, all students can benefit from it. To help students memorize principal parts, draw a chart on the board with the following headings: *Present, Present*

Participle, Past, and *Past Participle.* Fill in one of the principal parts with a verb form and have the students supply the other parts. You might have less advanced students copy the chart into their notebooks.

Students can also benefit from oral practice with principal parts used in sentences. Have students take turns reading aloud the completed sentences in Exercises D through F. If a student makes an incorrect choice, he or she can be asked to reread the sentence, supplying the correct principal part. Less advanced students can again be asked to copy the principal parts of verbs that they use incorrectly, this time giving a sentence that shows the correct use of each part.

Suggestions for Additional Activities. A "principal parts bee," conducted in the same manner as a spelling bee, can be an enjoyable and useful form of practice. Have students form two teams at opposite sides of the classroom. For the most part, choose irregular verbs from the charts on pages 196–198; occasionally, select a regular verb. Call out the verb and a principal part for contestants to identify.

Question: *lose,* past participle
Answer: have lost

Move rapidly through the words, increasing the pace as the bee progresses. If many of the students remain standing after a reasonable period of time, you may wish to make the bee more difficult by asking students to spell the principal part, too.

■ 11.2 The Six Tenses of Verbs (pp. 201–206)

Objectives: After completing this section, students should be able to

- Identify the basic forms of the six tenses of verbs.
- Conjugate the basic forms of verbs.

Adapting for Different Abilities. To reinforce the material on verb tense with less advanced students, you can write the following chart and its first two columns on the board. In class discussion have students supply the information that is in parentheses. Point out that the second column shows how tense is used to tell different times or to indicate when something takes place.

Six Tenses	Tells When . . .	Helping Verb	Principal Part
Present	it happens	(________)	(present)
Past	it happened	(________)	(past)
Future	it will happen	(will)	(present)
Present Perfect	it has happened	(has)	(past participle)
Past Perfect	it had happened	(had)	(past participle)
Future Perfect	it will have happened	(will have)	(past participle)

After completing the third and fourth columns, students can extend the chart by supplying various verbs as examples.

Before less advanced students conjugate basic verb forms, you will probably want to have them study or review the singular and plural forms of personal pronouns. To conduct a quick review, you can write the following chart on the board and have students supply the answers shown here in parentheses:

Definition	Person	Singular	Plural
Person speaking	First	(I)	(we)
Person spoken to	Second	(you)	(you)
Person, place, or thing spoken about	Third	(he/she/it)	(they)

After students have completed the chart, they can be asked to conjugate one regular and one irregular verb in Exercise B. Students might then exchange papers with those who chose different verbs in order to correct each other's conjugations.

Advanced students can be introduced to the idea of short conjugations—conjugations, such as the one in the chart at the beginning of the section, using only a single pronoun. These students can then be asked to write a short conjugation for each of the verbs in Exercise A.

Suggestions for Additional Activities. The sentences students write in Application 2 can be used to provide further practice in identifying and forming tenses. Have students choose one of the six sentences they have written for each word and copy all of the chosen sentences on a separate sheet of paper. They can then exchange papers and identify the tense of the verb in each sentence that they receive. Finally, they can rewrite each sentence using a different verb in the same tense.

■ 11.3 The Progressive Forms of Verbs

(pp. 206–210)

Objectives: After completing this section, students should be able to

- Identify the progressive forms of the six tenses of verbs.
- Conjugate the progressive forms of verbs.

Adapting for Different Abilities. Less advanced students may benefit from beginning this section with a review of the conjugation of the verb *be* on pages 204 and 205. First, drill students on the basic forms of *be.* Then, explain that the progressive forms of all verbs are made by using the appropriate form of *be* plus the present participle of the main verb. The form of *be* shows the tense, and the present participle makes it progressive.

To reinforce the material on progressive verb forms for less advanced students, you can write the following chart and its first two columns on the board. In class discussion have students supply the information shown in parentheses. You can also point out that progressive verb forms show continuing action, while most basic forms show completed action.

Six Tenses	Tells When . . .	Helping Verb	Principal Part
Present	it is happening	(is)	(present participle)
Past	it was happening	(was)	(present participle)
Future	it will be happening	(will be)	(present participle)
Present Perfect	it has been happening	(has been)	(present participle)
Past Perfect	it had been happening	(had been)	(present participle)
Future Perfect	it will have been happening	(will have been)	(present participle)

After completing the columns, students can extend the chart by supplying various verbs as examples.

As suggested for Section 11.2, advanced students can write short conjugations, using a single pronoun, this time giving the progressive forms for ten of the verbs in Exercise A.

Suggestions for Additional Activities. If students need more drill work with progressive forms, you might conduct a "tense bee," following the general rules for the "principal parts bee" on page T-53. Depending on students' abilities, you might include basic as well as progressive verb forms in the bee. This time, call out the verb first, then a subject, tense, and form.

Question: *draw,* she—future progressive
Answer: she will be drawing

■ 11.4 Active and Passive Voice (pp. 210–215)

Objectives: After completing this section, students should be able to

- Distinguish between the active and the passive voice.
- Conjugate verbs in the passive voice.
- Use active and passive voices appropriately.

Adapting for Different Abilities. With less advanced students, you may want to begin by discussing subjects and direct objects. You can do this by writing the following sentence on the board:

John painted the boat.

Ask students to come to the board to complete the following steps:

1. Underline the verb.
2. Circle the subject.
3. Draw a box around the direct object.

Students can then be asked to try to rewrite the sentence, making the direct object into the subject. The results can lead into a discussion of active and passive voice.

With less advanced students, you may also wish to limit the work to the first objective: distinguishing between the active and the passive voice. If so, students need complete only Exercise A. You might then emphasize the greater value of the active voice in most sentences and have students answer Exercise C orally.

Average and advanced students can be asked to select a paragraph or two from their outside reading and to analyze the verbs in the paragraphs for use of active and passive voice.

Suggestions for Additional Activities. If students need further practice with this material, you might have them work again with Exercise A. Ask them to rewrite sentences, changing active voice to passive voice and vice versa. When students have finished, ask them to identify the subject in each of the original sentences and then in their rewritten sentences.

■ 11.5 Glossary of Troublesome Verbs

(pp. 215–223)

Objective: After completing this section, students should be able to

- Use a number of problem verbs correctly.

Adapting for Different Abilities. With a less advanced group, you will probably find it helpful to stop after each group of five verbs and have students complete the corresponding exercises. Since oral reinforcement is useful, you can call on students in turn to read each exercise sentence aloud with the correct answer. If students make errors, they can correct the mistakes by reading the complete sentences aloud, using the correct forms.

Suggestions for Additional Activities. You can use the sentences students write for the Application to review the entire chapter. Have each student read aloud one of his or her sentences. You can then ask the class to identify the verb in the sentence, its tense and form, and its voice.

CHAPTER 12 Using Pronouns (pp. 224–235)

This chapter builds on Chapters 7 through 9, which discuss basic sentence parts, phrases, and clauses. Students can not choose appropriate case forms of personal pronouns in Section 12.1 or interrogative and relative pronouns in Section 12.2 without knowing sentence structure and syntax. You therefore might want to study or review the relevant grammar chapters before teaching this chapter.

Most classes will be able to complete this chapter in three days, with the time divided equally between sections. However, some less advanced groups may require one or two additional days.

■ 12.1 Cases of Personal Pronouns (pp. 224–231)

Objectives: After completing this section, students should be able to

- Identify the case of personal pronouns.
- Use pronouns in the nominative case correctly.
- Use pronouns in the objective case correctly.
- Use pronouns in the possessive case correctly.

Adapting for Different Abilities. With a less advanced group, you may find it helpful to delay Exercise A until students have completed the other exercises. Less advanced students might also benefit from working in pairs to complete the two Applications.

Average and advanced students can rewrite the sentences in Exercise A, using other personal pronouns in place of those that are underlined. These students might also write additional sentences using the pronouns listed in the second Application but changing the sentence part called for wherever possible.

Suggestions for Additional Activities. If students require further practice in identifying case, you might have them write sentences with the pronouns described in the following list:

1. Nominative case as subject of verb
2. Nominative case as predicate pronoun
3. Objective case as direct object
4. Objective case as object of a preposition
5. Possessive case to show ownership

■ 12.2 Cases of Who and Whom (pp. 231–235)

Objective: After completing this section, students should be able to

- Use *who* and *whom* correctly in sentences.

Adapting for Different Abilities. Less advanced students might work in pairs to complete both of the exercises and the Application.

Advanced students can write questions and complex sentences using both *who* and *whom.* They can then exchange sentences and identify the functions of the pronouns in each other's sentences.

Suggestions for Additional Activities. If students need further practice with this material, you can duplicate the following sentences from Section 1.3, omitting the interrogative and relative pronouns:

Exercise B: Sentences 1, 3, 5, 8, 9
Exercise C: Sentences 2, 6, 7, 9, 10

Students can then supply the correct form of *who* or *whom* for each sentence.

CHAPTER 13 Making Words Agree (pp. 236–256)

Sections 13.1 and 13.2 deal with subjects and verbs: Section 13.1 discusses agreement between subjects and verbs, and Section 13.2 considers special problems with subject-verb agreement. Section 13.3 covers agreement between pronouns and antecedents.

You may wish to spend two days on Section 13.1 to be sure that students clearly understand the basic principles involved. One or two days each will probably be enough for the other two sections.

■ 13.1 Agreement Between Subjects and Verbs (pp. 236–245)

Objectives: After studying this section, students should be able to

- Recognize the number of nouns and pronouns.
- Recognize the number of verbs.
- Make verbs agree with singular and plural subjects.
- Make verbs agree with compound subjects.

Adapting for Different Abilities. In Exercise A you may wish to ask less advanced students to give the number of the nouns and personal pronouns only. The indefinite pronouns in the list may pose problems at this time; they will be treated separately in Section 13.2. In covering Exercises C through E, you can provide oral reinforcement for less advanced students as well as average students by having them read the completed sentences aloud. Advanced students, on the other hand, should find most of the work in the section relatively easy and should need little reinforcement.

Suggestions for Additional Activities. After they have completed the exercises, students may benefit from writing original present-tense sentences using most of the words listed in Exercise A as subjects.

■ 13.2 Special Problems with Subject-Verb Agreement (pp. 245–250)

Objectives: After completing this section, students should be able to

- Make subjects and verbs agree in sentences with unusual word order.
- Make subjects and verbs agree in sentences that have indefinite pronouns as subjects.

Adapting for Different Abilities. You might suggest that less advanced students and average students working with inverted sentences (such as those in Exercise A) mentally rewrite the sentences in normal word order to check agreement. To give less advanced students more work with indefinite pronouns, you can have them rewrite in the present tense Sentences 1, 4, 8, and 10 of Exercise D in Section 1.3 (pp. 35–36).

Suggestings for Additional Activities. If students need more practice with the concepts in this section, you can have them work again with the sentences in the second Application. Students can rewrite the sentences, making the following changes:

Sentence 1: Change *he* to *everyone.*
Sentence 2: Change *three old cherry trees* to *an old cherry tree.*
Sentence 3: Change *film* to *articles.*
Sentence 4: Change *flies* to *not one noodle.*
Sentence 5: Change *basket* to *vases.*
Sentence 6: Change *highwayman* to *highwaymen.*
Sentence 7: Change *A few* to *Each.*
Sentence 8: Change *sweater* to *sweaters.*
Sentence 9: Change *relatives* to *band.*
Sentence 10: Change *All* to *Each.*

As students work on this activity, remind them that many of the original sentences are incorrect. Their job now, however, is to come up with ten sentences that are correct.

■ 13.3 Agreement Between Pronouns and Antecedents (pp. 250–256)

Objectives: After completing this section, students should be able to

- Make personal pronouns agree with their antecedents in person and number.
- Make personal pronouns agree with indefinite pronouns.

Adapting for Different Abilities. Before beginning this section, less advanced students may require a brief study or review of pronouns in Sections 1.2 and 1.3. As these students study the present section, you can provide oral reinforcement by having them read aloud the completed sentences in Exercise A and the corrected sentences in Exercise B.

Average and advanced students can work at the board, writing their answers to Exercises A and B. After writing each sentence, they can show that the pronouns and their antecedents do agree by first drawing a circle around each pronoun and then drawing an arrow from the pronoun to its antecedent. Finally, they can list the person and number of the connected words.

Suggestions for Additional Activities. To give students extra practice with indefinite pronoun antecedents, you can ask the class to work again with Exercise C, making the changes given in the following list. Students should note that they do not have to choose one of the pronouns in parentheses. Instead, they should choose a pronoun that will make the sentence correct.

Sentence 1: Change *parakeets* to *girls.*
Sentence 2: Change *Not one* to *Some.*
Sentence 3: Change *each of the girls* to *everyone in the class.*
Sentence 4: Change *Several* to *Many.*
Sentence 5: Change *each* to *one.*
Sentence 6: Change *students* to *boys.*
Sentence 7: Change *all of the actors* to *everyone in the cast.*
Sentence 8: Change *Few* to *All.*
Sentence 9: Change *Some* to *One.*
Sentence 10: Change *all* to *one.*

CHAPTER 14 Using Adjectives and Adverbs (pp. 257–272)

Sections 14.1 through 14.4 deal with the correct use of modifiers. Section 14.1 on regular adjectives and adverbs discusses the usual ways of forming the comparative and superlative degrees of modifiers. Section 14.2 on irregular adjectives and adverbs lists the most common irregular modifiers and lists their comparative and superlative degrees. Sections 14.3 and 14.4 give information that will help students use the degrees of adverbs and adjectives correctly. Section 14.5 lists common problems that students encounter with modifiers and gives solutions for each problem.

The straightforward, step-by-step presentation in the text should enable students to complete this chapter in five days or fewer.

■ 14.1 Regular Adjectives and Adverbs (pp. 258–261)

Objectives: After completing this section, students should be able to

- Use *-er* and *-est* or *more* and *most* to form the comparative and superlative degrees of most one- and two-syllable modifiers.
- Use *more* and *most* to form the comparative and superlative degrees of all modifiers with more than two syllables.

Adapting for Different Abilities. Less advanced students may require a brief review of the material on adjectives in Chapter 3 and on adverbs in Chapter 4 before beginning this section. To reinforce the material on degrees in the present section, you can place the first two columns of the following chart on the board and have less advanced students supply the information shown in parentheses. These students can then supply several different examples of regular adjectives and adverbs and their degrees as shown at the right.

Degree	Formed by Adding ...	Examples
Positive	(________)	sad, sadly
Comparative	(-er) or (more)	sadder, more sadly
Superlative	(-est) or (most)	saddest, most sadly

Suggestions for Additional Activities. To give students additional practice with this material, you can refer them to Exercise B in Section 7.9 (p. 119). Students can identify at least one adjective or adverb in each sentence and then write its comparative and superlative degrees. Note that the sentences contain a few words such as *very* that can not readily be compared. Depending on the ability of your students, you may or may not want to discuss these words.

■ 14.2 Irregular Adjectives and Adverbs (pp. 261–263)

Objective: After completing this section, students should be able to

- Recognize the positive, comparative, and superlative degrees of the most common irregular modifiers.

Adapting for Different Abilities. Both less advanced students and average students are likely to benefit from oral drill on irregular adjectives and adverbs; such practice can help them commit these forms to memory. First, you can drill students on the words alone; then, students can read their answers to the exercises aloud, correcting any mistakes.

Average and advanced students can choose one sentence from each pair of sentences they have written for the Application, copy the chosen sentences on a separate sheet of paper, and exchange papers with partners. The students can then identify the degree in each sentence and then write a compatible sentence for each, using the positive degree.

Suggestions for Additional Activities. If students need further practice, they can reuse the modifiers in Exercise A. Instruct students to divide their papers into three columns with the headings *Positive, Comparative,* and *Superlative.* Students can then write the underlined modifier from each sentence in the appropriate column and fill in the other two degrees.

■ 14.3 Using Comparative and Superlative Degrees (pp. 264–266)

Objective: After completing this section, students should be able to

- Use the comparative and superlative degrees of modifiers correctly.

Adapting for Different Abilities. You may want to ask less advanced students to write only ten sentences for the Application. One way of doing this would be to instruct them to use the comparative degree of the first five words and the superlative degree of the second five words.

Suggestions for Additional Activities. To give students additional practice in identifying and correcting poor comparisons and double comparison, you can use the following phrases. Ask students to explain why each phrase is wrong and then to give a correct version.

1. most hottest afternoon
2. better photograph in the group
3. more sicker
4. best of the two
5. least worst
6. more better
7. the oldest of the two
8. most worst program
9. less farther
10. most saddest

■ 14.4 Making Logical Comparisons (pp. 266–269)

Objectives: After completing this section, students should be able to

- Construct balanced comparisons.
- Use *other* and *else* correctly in comparisons.

Adapting for Different Abilities. With less advanced students, you may wish to review the first few sentences of Exercise A as a class. Students can write the sentences on the board, circle the modifiers, and then underline the words that are being compared. Once the words are underlined, students should easily be able to identify the words that must be added to form a balanced comparison.

Suggestions for Additional Activities. As an additional activity, you can give students the following modifiers to use in sentences that show comparisons:

1. scarier
2. less tasty
3. weaker
4. more friendly
5. more difficult

■ 14.5 Glossary of Troublesome Adjectives and Adverbs (pp. 269–272)

Objective: After completing this section, students should be able to

- Avoid a number of common errors in adjective and adverb usage.

Adapting for Different Abilities. Less advanced students might carry out the following steps in reviewing the first few sentences in Exercise A:

1. Identify the troublesome modifier in each sentence.
2. Identify the word that it modifies.
3. Supply the corrected word, if one is needed.
4. Read the corrected sentence aloud.

Suggestions for Additional Activities. For additional practice you can have students write original sentences using each of the following words correctly:

1. bad	3. good	5. fewer	7. just
2. badly	4. well	6. less	8. only

CHAPTER 15 Recognizing Special Problems in Usage (pp. 273–283)

Section 15.1 deals with the correct use of negatives in sentences. Section 15.2 presents twenty pitfalls in usage, ranging from frequently confused words to unacceptable nonstandard usage.

With most classes you should not need more than a day to cover Section 15.1; considerably more time, however, will generally be needed to cover Section 15.2. With all but the most advanced groups, you will probably want to budget two or more days for the second section, allowing time to discuss the many different problems and solutions presented.

■ 15.1 Double Negatives (pp. 273–275)

Objective: After completing this section, students should be able to

- Recognize and correct double negatives.

Adapting for Different Abilities. Oral reinforcement can be of great benefit to less advanced students. You can have them read aloud both of their corrected versions of the sentences in Exercise A, correcting any continued mistakes as they read. Advanced students can be asked to write compound or complex sentences containing a single negative in each clause.

Suggestions for Additional Activities. To provide further practice, you can have students exchange and correct the papers they write for the Application. The students can then rewrite Sentences 2, 5, 7, and 8, keeping the same meaning but finding a different way to make each statement negative. Again, students can check each other's work.

■ 15.2 Twenty Common Usage Problems (pp. 275–283)

Objective: After completing this section, students should be able to

- Recognize and avoid making a number of common usage errors.

Adapting for Different Abilities. With a less advanced group, you might want to stop after reviewing each set of five items and have the students complete and discuss the corresponding exercise. You might also encourage students to refer to the glossary when they explain their answers.

Suggestions for Additional Activities. Students can be asked to write original sentences using each of the following word pairs correctly:

1. among/between
2. beside/besides
3. in/into
4. like/as
5. than/then

■ Review Exercises (pp. 283–290)

These exercises, which follow the order of the chapters in the unit, can be used as additional classwork, as homework, or as testing material. How you use them will depend on a class's ability and on your own scheduling needs.

UNIT III

Mechanics

This unit presents detailed explanations of capitalization, abbreviation, and punctuation. Although some of the material may be a review for many of your students, you may still want to plan to spend enough time on this unit to cover all the rules and exercises. Most students can benefit greatly from a review of basic points combined, as in the present unit, with new concepts and ideas. The broader view they will gain should help them see mechanics as a means of communicating more clearly.

The material on capitalization and abbreviation in Chapters 16 and 17 does not depend greatly on students' knowledge of grammar or sentence structure. Thus, you may teach the chapters at any time during the year. You can also choose to present sections of the chapters whenever students' compositions demonstrate a need for instruction in these areas.

Comprehension of the material on punctuation in Chapter 18, in contrast, does depend to a large extent on students' understanding of grammar and sentence structure. Therefore, if you wish to teach punctuation in conjunction with composition, you will first need to make sure that students understand the related concepts covered in Unit I. You can do this by skimming the section you wish to cover, noting any terms that the students may have difficulty with, and then studying or reviewing in class the appropriate material in Unit I.

The pretest for Unit III, available in the *Prentice-Hall Grammar and Composition Test Program,* can be used to help determine students' need for instruction in the many different skills presented in the unit. Chapter tests and a unit post-test are also available in the test program.

CHAPTER 16 Using Capitals (pp. 292–312)

Chapter 16 consists of a number of short sections that move from the most basic uses of capitals to more specialized uses of capitals. Section 16.1 covers the use of capitals for the first words in sentences and full quotations. Section 16.2 covers the capitalization of proper nouns, and Section 16.3 covers the use of capitals with proper adjectives. Section 16.4 presents rules for capitalizing a variety of social, professional, and family titles, and Section 16.5 presents the more specialized uses of capitals in the titles of various works of art. The final section, Section 16.6, discusses capitalization in the salutations and closings of letters.

Average and advanced students may be able to study much of the material and do most of the accompanying exercises as homework. Less advanced students are likely to benefit from spending more time in class working through the text and the exercises. Advanced students will undoubtedly be able to master all of the material in about three days; less advanced students may need to spend a day on each section.

■ 16.1 Capitals for First Words (pp. 292–296)

Objectives: After completing this section, students should be able to

- Capitalize the first word in a sentence correctly.
- Use capitals correctly in quotations.
- Capitalize the word *I* whenever it appears in a sentence.

Adapting for Different Abilities. With less advanced students, you may want to work through the first few sentences of the Application in class. These students might also write sentences of their own illustrating the various rules before doing the Application. Average and advanced students, on the other hand, can be asked to supply more than one sentence for each pattern given in the Application.

Suggestions for Additional Activities. To provide extra practice for those who need it, you can select some of the best sentences written for the Application and put them on a ditto master without capital letters.

■ 16.2 Capitals for Proper Nouns (pp. 296–303)

Objectives: After completing this section, students should be able to

- Capitalize the names of people correctly.
- Recognize and capitalize correctly proper nouns that name geographical places.
- Recognize and capitalize correctly a number of other proper nouns including those that name specific events and specific groups.

Adapting for Different Abilities. Less advanced students can be asked to supply additional examples for each of the charts in the section. If students need further practice in capitalizing proper nouns, you might reuse Exercise E in Section 1.1 (pp. 24–25). You might also read aloud sets of items such as the following and ask students to write on their papers the proper noun in each set of words, using correct capitalization, of course:

1. ocean   body of water   Isthmus of Panama
2. Sears Tower   skyscraper   building

Less advanced students and average students can work in pairs or small groups to complete the Application. You may want to give each group a sample brochure to examine. You may also want to encourage these students to use encyclopedias and other reference materials to find specific information to include in their descriptions.

Suggestions for Additional Activities. Students can be asked to find sentences containing proper nouns in magazine and newspaper articles. They can then copy the sentences, leaving out the capitals. In class students can exchange papers with classmates and capitalize the sentences correctly.

■ 16.3 Capitals for Proper Adjectives (pp. 304–305)

Objective: After completing this section, students should be able to

- Capitalize proper adjectives correctly.

Adapting for Different Abilities. For less advanced students who need additional practice, you may wish to provide a ditto of Exercise D in Section 3.1 (pp. 54–55). Omit the capitals and have students capitalize correctly.

Advanced students might be asked to search for and list examples of words that contain proper adjectives that are no longer regularly capitalized. They might start with the following three examples: *dutch oven, french fries,* and *russian dressing.* You can have the students share the additional examples they find in printed materials, and you can encourage them to speculate on why the adjectives in the examples have lost their once-required capitals.

Suggestions for Additional Activities. Students might compile extensive lists of proper adjectives and the nouns they modify, using their own lives as reference points. The proper adjectives might include nationalities, geographical references, and particular months associated with the students' families and daily lives. Students might also include brand names of items found in their homes and in local stores.

■ 16.4 Capitals for Titles of People (pp. 305–309)

Objectives: After completing this section, students should be able to

- Capitalize social and professional titles correctly.
- Capitalize family titles correctly.

Adapting for Different Abilities. Less advanced students may need to discuss the meanings of the terms *possessive noun* and *possessive pronoun* before they can make decisions about the appropriate use of capitals in family titles. Advanced students might be asked to add at least one additional title to each category in the chart on page 306.

Suggestions for Additional Activities. Students can be assigned to read different sections of a newspaper and bring in one or two paragraphs of a story that uses any of the titles covered in this section. Students can then share their clippings and discuss the uses of capitalization.

■ 16.5 Capitals for Titles of Things (pp. 309–312)

Objectives: After completing this section, students should be able to

- Capitalize the titles of works of art correctly.
- Capitalize the titles of school courses when appropriate.

Adapting for Different Abilities. If you find that less advanced or average students need more practice, you might write on the board or on a ditto master Sentences 3, 4, 5, and 6 of Exercise A in Section 18.7 (pp. 367–368) and Sentences 1, 4, 6, 7, 8, and 9 of Exercise B in Section 18.7 (pp. 369–370). Include underlining or quotation marks, but omit the capital letters in the titles.

Suggestions for Additional Activities. Each student can be asked to list the title of his or her favorite work in each of the five categories presented on page 310. Students can then rewrite their lists without capitals and exchange them with their classmates for additional practice.

Since some students may already have thought about what courses they wish to take in high school, you might also ask them to capitalize correctly the names of courses they hope to take.

■ 16.6 Capitals in Letters (p. 312)

Objective: After completing this section, students should be able to

- Capitalize letter salutations and closings correctly.

Adapting for Different Abilities. Before any of your students attempt the Application, you may want to have them refer to the discussion of proper letter form in Section 32.1 (pp. 672–681). After they have mastered the various parts of letters, you may wish to have less advanced students write only the heading, salutation, closing, and signature instead of an entire letter. Average students and advanced students, on the other hand, can exchange the invitations they write and write responses accepting or rejecting them.

Suggestions for Additional Activities. As an additional activity, students can write letters to government officials or local newspapers expressing their opinions about an issue of interest to the students.

CHAPTER 17 Using Abbreviations (pp. 313–326)

Chapter 17 covers abbreviations in four short sections. Section 17.1 covers the titles of people; Section 17.2 covers time and historical dates; Section 17.3 covers geographical abbreviations; and Section 17.4 covers measurements.

A number of the abbreviations in the chapter may already be familiar to your students. However, students may not realize that many of these abbreviations are not acceptable in formal writing. To help students build their awareness, each rule in the chapter includes information on when it is appropriate to use each abbreviation.

Most students should be able to handle at least two sections a day; most classes will thus need only two days to master the entire chapter.

■ 17.1 Abbreviations of Titles of People (pp. 313–318)

Objectives: After completing this section, students should be able to

- Abbreviate social titles correctly.
- Use abbreviations correctly for governmental, military, and professional titles before names and for social and professional titles after names.

Adapting for Different Abilities. Less advanced students may require additional discussion of when to spell out and when to abbreviate titles in formal writing. You might put the following sentences on the board and discuss whether or not titles may be abbreviated in each case. Students can then write the abbreviations for all but the third sentence.

1. Mister Robinson was chosen to be our representative.
2. I wrote a letter to Representative Shirley Chisholm.
3. Did you know that Sergeant Lopez was promoted?
4. Rosemary Martino, Doctor of Philosophy, spoke to us about the responsibilities of a senator.
5. Doctor Fields sent the bill to James Bentley, Junior.

Advanced students might be asked to collect examples of appropriately abbreviated titles from newspapers and magazines.

Suggestions for Additional Activities. As a group project, students might be asked to make a chart of state or local government officials, using abbreviations for all titles. Students interested in the military might enjoy preparing a complete list of ranks and their abbreviations for a particular branch of the service.

■ 17.2 Abbreviations for Time and Historical Dates (pp. 318–321)

Objectives: After completing this section, students should be able to

- Use abbreviations correctly to express time before and after noon.
- Use abbreviations correctly to express historical dates before and after the birth of Christ.

Adapting for Different Abilities. Since the entire section deals with only four abbreviations, all students should be able to master the material easily. With less advanced students, you may want to indicate a preference for one of the two choices given for abbreviating time before and after noon. With other students you can simply stress the need for consistency.

Suggestions for Additional Activities. Students can use abbreviations for time in writing a weekly study schedule as suggested in Section 21.1. You might also ask each student to research and list five historical events that happened before the birth of Christ and five that happened after the birth of Christ.

■ 17.3 Geographical Abbreviations

(pp. 321–324)

Objective: After completing this section, students should be able to

- Use geographical abbreviations correctly and appropriately.

Adapting for Different Abilities. You might permit less advanced students to refer to the charts in the text when completing Exercise A and the Application. Average and advanced students might take part in a spelling bee that tests their ability to give the correct abbreviations for geographical terms.

Suggestions for Additional Activities. Students might enjoy compiling a class list of places of birth, using abbreviations. Students might also make address books listing friends and relatives to gain further practice in abbreviating geographical terms.

■ 17.4 Abbreviations of Measurements

(pp. 324–326)

Objectives: After completing this section, students should be able to

- Abbreviate traditional measurements correctly.
- Abbreviate metric measurements correctly.

Adapting for Different Abilities. With less advanced students, you may need to stress that they should use periods with abbreviations of traditional measurements but *not* with abbreviations of metric measurements. The fact that a single abbreviation can be used for both singular and plural may also need extra attention with these students.

Suggestions for Additional Activities. Students can be organized into groups and given a variety of items to weigh and measure. Students can then record the weights and measurements of the items using the correct abbreviations. If students do this activity in class, you will need a supply of scales and rulers.

CHAPTER 18 Using Punctuation Marks (pp. 327–383)

Chapter 18 is much longer than the other two chapters in this unit. It consists of nine sections, which present an in-depth study of all of the most common punctuation marks, beginning with end marks and commas.

As mentioned on page T–65, the correct use of punctuation marks, such as end marks, semicolons, colons, and especially commas, depends on a basic understanding of both grammar and sentence structure. Therefore, you will want to make sure that students understand the related concepts covered in Unit I before they study each of the sections in this chapter. Once students have the necessary background, the material in this chapter can be used to reinforce as well as add to your students' understanding of both grammar and sentence structure. It will also help students realize that punctuation is a key element in making written matter clearer and easier to understand.

With most classes you will need a little over two weeks to complete the chapter. Section 18.1 on end marks will probably require only one class session for many of your students. Sections 18.2 and 18.3 on commas are more complicated. You will probably want to incorporate a review of grammar and sentence structure into the study of these sections. As a result, you may want to spend as many as five or six days working on the two sections. One or two days should be enough time for students to master the material presented in both Section 18.4 on the semicolon and Section 18.5 on the colon. Section 18.6 on quotation marks with direct quotations may also take two days since it involves the placement of other punctuation marks as well as quotation marks. Section 18.7 on underlining and other uses of quotation marks, Section 18.8 on the hyphen, and Section 18.9 on the apostrophe can probably be covered in one day each, although you may want to add drill time during the study of apostrophes.

■ 18.1 End Marks (pp. 328–333)

Objectives: After completing this section, students should be able to

- Use periods correctly at the end of declarative and imperative sentences, indirect questions, and most abbreviations.
- Recognize the need for question marks with direct questions, incomplete questions, and statements intended as questions.
- Recognize the need for exclamation marks with exclamatory sentences, forceful imperative sentences, and some interjections.

Adapting for Different Abilities. Most students will have little, if any, difficulty with this section. With less advanced students, however, you may wish to incorporate into this section a study or review of sentence fragments and run-on sentences as presented in Sections 10.1 and 10.2. You may also wish to have these students study or review the material on sentence functions in Section 7.8.

Advanced students might be asked to make the sentences they write for the Application as difficult as possible. You can then place their sentences, omitting end marks, on the board or duplicate them to challenge other students in the class.

Suggestions for Additional Activities. For further practice in using end marks, you can use or reuse Exercise A in Section 7.8 (pp. 116–117) and the Application in Section 7.8 (p. 117).

■ 18.2 Commas That Separate Basic Elements (pp. 333–339)

Objectives: After completing this section, students should be able to

- Use commas correctly to separate the parts of compound sentences.
- Use commas correctly to separate items in a series.
- Use commas correctly to separate adjectives of equal rank.

Adapting for Different Abilities. With less advanced students, you may wish to study or review Section 9.3, just before the students are asked to complete Exercise A. As they do Exercise C, you might also remind these students to apply both of the methods discussed in the text in determining whether or not to use a comma to separate adjectives.

Average and advanced students may find that the most difficult part of this section is deciding whether or not to use commas to separate adjectives. You might ask them to look through newspapers, textbooks, or other reading material to find five examples of adjectives separated by commas and five without commas. They can then bring their examples to class and share them with their classmates. You might also choose sentences these students have written for the Application and write them on the board, omitting the commas. Then you can call on other students to add the necessary punctuation.

Suggestions for Additional Activities. Students can construct additional compound sentences joined by coordinating conjunctions and separated by commas, using selected items from Exercises A and B of Section 10.2 (pp. 175 and 178–179).

■ 18.3 Commas That Set Off Added Elements (pp. 339–349)

Objectives: After completing this section, students should be able to

- Use commas correctly to set off introductory words, phrases, and clauses in sentences.
- Use commas correctly to set off parenthetical expressions.
- Use commas correctly to set off nonessential expressions.
- Use commas as needed to set off dates and geographical names.
- Use commas correctly in other situations.

Adapting for Different Abilities. With less advanced students, you will probably want to spend considerable time with the chart of essential and nonessential expressions on page 343. You can discuss with students why the expression in each example is or is not essential and encourage students to try reading each example without the italicized expression. You may also want to suggest that students try reading each sentence in Exercise C without the underlined material to determine whether it is essential or nonessential. Advanced students might enjoy collecting examples of sentences in which commas are especially important in making the meaning and relationships clear.

Suggestions for Additional Activities. Students can be asked to exchange the papers they write for the Application and to check each other's work. Caution them to make sure that each student has followed the instructions and that commas are used correctly. Students can also review some of their own recent compositions to see if they have used commas correctly.

■ 18.4 The Semicolon (pp. 349–354)

Objectives: After completing this section, students should be able to

- Use semicolons correctly to join independent clauses.
- Use semicolons in sentences where additional commas would cause confusion.

Adapting for Different Abilities. With less advanced students, you might wish to study or review compound sentences (in Section 9.3) just before beginning this section. With these students you might also decide to turn the Application into a class activity. Advanced students might be asked to find in their reading additional examples of each type of sentence specified in the Application.

Suggestions for Additional Activities. Students can rewrite Sentences 2 to 5 in Exercise C, Section 9.3, using semicolons instead of conjunctions. In addition, students might benefit from writing sentences of their own to illustrate each of the rules in this section.

■ 18.5 The Colon (pp. 354–357)

Objectives: After completing this section, students should be able to

- Use colons correctly as introductory devices.
- Use colons correctly in special writing situations.

Adapting for Different Abilities. With less advanced students, you may wish to omit the first part of this section entirely and have them study only the subsection on special uses of the colon.

In this case omit the Application. Instead, ask students to give five examples of the use of the colon in special situations.

Average and advanced students might be asked to write one additional sentence for each of the items in the Application; the sentences should be written in random order and all colons should be omitted. Students can then change papers and punctuate each other's sentences.

Suggestions for Additional Activities. Students can get additional practice in using colons as well as in restructuring sentences by rewriting the sentences in Exercise B of Section 18.2 (pp. 336–337) so that each sentence consists of an independent clause followed by a list of items and punctuated with a colon.

■ 18.6 Quotation Marks with Direct Quotations (pp. 357–365)

Objectives: After completing this section, students should be able to

- Distinguish between direct and indirect quotations.
- Place quotation marks correctly in direct quotations accompanied by introductory, concluding, or interrupting expressions.
- Use commas and end marks correctly with direct quotations.
- Use quotation marks appropriately in dialogue.

Adapting for Different Abilities. You may find that the Application is too challenging for less advanced students. If so, you might ask these students to tape-record actual dialogues and then to transcribe them, adding appropriate introductory, concluding, and interrupting expressions. Average and advanced students might be asked to rewrite each indirect quotation in Exercise A as a direct quotation and vice versa.

Suggestions for Additional Activities. To give students additional practice in writing dialogue, you can choose a short passage from a play in a literature anthology or use the following scene adapted from Dickens' *A Christmas Carol* in which Scrooge's nephew invites him to Christmas dinner. Have students rewrite the selection as dialogue. They should include introductory, concluding, and interrupting expressions to identify the speakers, and they may incorporate stage directions if they wish. Less advanced students might work on this activity in pairs or small groups.

> *Nephew.* Don't be angry, uncle. Come! Dine with us tomorrow.
> *Scrooge.* I'll see you hanged first.
> *Nephew.* But why, uncle? Why?
> *Scrooge.* Why did you get married?
> *Nephew.* Because I fell in love.
> *Scrooge (contemptuously).* Because you fell in love! Good afternoon!

Nephew. Nay, uncle, but you never came to see me before that happened. Why give it as a reason for not coming now?

Scrooge. Good afternoon!

Nephew. I want nothing from you; I ask nothing of you; why cannot we be friends?

Scrooge. Good afternoon!

Nephew. I am sorry, with all my heart, to find you so resolute. We have never had any quarrel, to which I have been a party. But I have made the trial in homage to Christmas, and I'll keep my Christmas humor to the last. So, a merry Christmas, uncle!

Scrooge. Good afternoon!

Nephew. And a happy New Year!

Scrooge. Good afternoon!

— Adapted from Charles Dickens

■ 18.7 Underlining and Other Uses of Quotation Marks (pp. 365–370)

Objectives: After completing this section, students should be able to

- Use underlining appropriately with certain titles, names, and words.
- Use quotation marks correctly with titles.

Adapting for Different Abilities. Less advanced students might benefit from supplying their own examples for each of the categories of titles presented in this section. With average and advanced students, you might choose some of the best sentences written for the Application and place them on the board without underlining or quotations for students to write correctly.

Suggestions for Additional Activities. Students might be asked to write a paragraph including their favorite titles from at least three of the categories mentioned in the section.

■ 18.8 The Hyphen (pp. 370–376)

Objectives: After completing this section, students should be able to

- Use hyphens correctly with numbers, word parts, and compound words.
- Divide words correctly at the ends of lines, using hyphens.

Adapting for Different Abilities. With less advanced students, you might discuss each item in Exercise B as well as the reasons why it can or can not be divided. Stress the idea that in dividing a word at the end of a line, students must think about how the word is pronounced. Any division that makes it harder for the reader to recognize the word should be avoided. Advanced students might be asked to find in newspapers examples of words that have been incorrectly divided (a common phenomenon because of narrow columns and computer typesetting).

Suggestions for Additional Activities. To give students further practice with hyphens, have them follow the instructions for Exercise B with the following items:

1. alone
2. self-explanatory
3. haunted
4. ivory
5. erase
6. lectured
7. oval
8. seventy-seven
9. elect
10. all-encompassing

■ 18.9 The Apostrophe (pp. 376–383)

Objectives: After completing this section, students should be able to

- Place apostrophes correctly at the end of possessive nouns.
- Use apostrophes correctly with pronouns.
- Determine where to place apostrophes in contractions.
- Use apostrophes to write the plurals of numbers, symbols, letters, and words used to name themselves.

Adapting for Different Abilities. Less advanced students may need extra practice in deciding where an apostrophe belongs in singular and plural nouns. They might enjoy taking turns making up sentences that use the possessive case of their classmates' names. Students can use first names to practice singular possessives and surnames to practice plural possessives.

Average and advanced students can exchange the dialogues they write for the Application. They can then rewrite each other's dialogue to eliminate as many of the apostrophes as possible.

Suggestions for Additional Activities. For an additional activity, students can write a sentence for each word in each of the following pairs:

1. who's/whose
2. it's/its
3. you're/your
4. they're/their
5. there's/theirs

■ Review Exercises (pp. 384–388)

This material can be used to assess your students' grasp of the material covered in Chapters 16–18. The time you allot for this review will depend on students' abilities and on their need for review and reinforcement. The exercises can be assigned as classwork, as homework, or as testing material.

UNIT IV

Vocabulary and Spelling

Although mastering the content of this unit is critical to success in everyday life as well as in school, the concepts covered are not directly related to those in any other units and may, therefore, be taught at any time during the year. You might, in fact, find it helpful to present Sections 19.1 and 20.1 quite early in the year so that students can set up vocabulary notebooks and personal spelling lists and add to them at regular times throughout the year. In addition, you may wish to set aside a short time each week for students to share additions to their lists of vocabulary and spelling words. This device will ensure that students are using these tools and will also provide an opportunity for their classmates to consider possible additions to their own lists.

The other sections in the unit may also be worth covering early. The vocabulary lessons presented in Sections 19.2 through 19.4 and the spelling rules presented in Section 20.2 can help the students carry out their other course work in English as well as in other areas.

The pretest for Unit IV, which is available in the *Prentice-Hall Grammar and Composition Test Program,* can be used to help determine students' need for instruction in the many different skills presented in the unit. Chapter tests and a unit post-test are also available in the test program.

CHAPTER 19 Building Your Vocabulary (pp. 390–413)

Chapter 19 begins with a general strategy for building vocabulary and then looks more closely at specific aspects of vocabulary building. Section 19.1 gives students a number of concrete suggestions that they can use to learn new words. Section 19.2 explains how to use context clues and provides a variety of selections for practicing this skill. Section 19.3 presents structural analysis as a way to expand one's vocabulary, and Section 19.4 demonstrates how to approach words from the standpoint of etymology, or word origin.

In planning for this chapter, you should probably allow eight or nine days. Most classes will need two days for Section 19.1. These days can profitably be spent having students set up vocabulary notebooks, having them practice the other study devices, and having them work with partners to review new words. Section 19.2 on using context will take most classes a day and a half, one half day for each selection. Section 19.3 on using structure may take three or four days, while Section 19.4 on exploring word origins may be covered in a day or two.

■ 19.1 Ways to Enlarge Your Vocabulary (pp. 390–395)

Objectives: After completing this section, students should be able to

- Set up and make use of a vocabulary notebook.
- Make flash cards or tapes to study and review new vocabulary words.

Adapting for Different Abilities. You might need to help less advanced students set up their vocabulary notebooks and prepare their flash cards and tapes. Average and advanced students can set up their notebooks and flash cards independently and practice alone with a tape recorder or with partners.

Suggestions for Additional Activities. Students can be asked to find in a magazine or newspaper five unfamiliar words to add to their vocabulary notebooks or sets of flash cards. You may want to emphasize the importance of looking up the meanings of these new words in a dictionary.

■ 19.2 Using Context (pp. 395–401)

Objectives: After completing this section, students should be able to

- Determine from context the meanings of words they encounter in daily reading.
- Determine from context the meanings of words they encounter in science books.
- Determine from context the meanings of words they encounter in social studies books.

Adapting for Different Abilities. To ensure that less advanced students are actually using context clues and are not just guessing at the answers, you may want to go over the exercises with them in small groups and have students pinpoint the context clues they have used to arrive at meanings. Advanced students might be asked to bring in paragraphs with particularly good context clues that they encounter in their outside readings—newspapers, novels, and so forth. You might ditto the best of these for use by the whole class.

Suggestions for Additional Activities. A colleague in science, health, or social studies might help you select passages from students' textbooks that contain difficult or unfamiliar terms surrounded by particularly good context clues. Ask students to identify unfamiliar terms and to supply short definitions from the context. Words can then be checked in a dictionary and added to vocabulary notebooks.

■ 19.3 Using Structure (pp. 402–407)

Objectives: After completing this section, students should be able to

- Add prefixes to roots and define the resulting words.
- Use roots to define words.
- Use suffixes to change the parts of speech of words.

Adapting for Different Abilities. You might encourage less advanced students to use the charts of prefixes, roots, and suffixes on pages 403–406 as they complete the exercises. Average and advanced students might use a dictionary to find two additional words that use each prefix in the chart on page 403. They can then quiz each other on the meanings of the new words.

Suggestions for Additional Activities. Students can exchange the papers they write for the Application and write short definitions for the key words in each other's sentences. Students can also make a master list of all the words they construct in the Application, grouping them by root.

■ 19.4 Exploring Word Origins (pp. 407–413)

Objectives: After completing this section, students should be able to

- Recognize words that have been borrowed from other languages.
- Recognize some of the ways in which words may acquire new meanings.
- Recognize some of the ways in which new words are coined.

Adapting for Different Abilities. You will probably want to make sure that less advanced students are able to find etymologies in a dictionary before assigning the exercises. With these students you might also divide the class into six groups and assign each group a different exercise. You can then allow class time for each group to share its work with the rest of the class. Advanced students can compare their answers to Exercise C and compile a master list of possibilities.

Suggestions for Additional Activities. Students can be asked to keep a running list of words that have been taken into English exactly as they exist in another language: *en route, pasta, sheik, tortilla, sauerkraut,* and so forth.

CHAPTER 20 Improving Your Spelling (pp. 414–434)

The first of the two sections in this chapter, Section 20.1, suggests general techniques for identifying and solving spelling problems. It also provides practice in working with one hundred common spelling demons. Section 20.2 identifies basic spelling rules and gives the students a chance to practice applying them.

Most classes will be able to complete this chapter in four or five days. However, you might want to provide additional drill time for less advanced students.

■ 20.1 Solving Your Spelling Problems (pp. 414–422)

Objectives: After completing this section, students should be able to

- Set up and use a personal spelling list.
- Use a systematic method to learn the spelling of words they have problems with.
- Develop memory aids to help remember the spelling of difficult words.
- Use a list of spelling demons to discover additional words that they should learn to spell.

Adapting for Different Abilities. You may have to work closely with less advanced students to help them set up their personal spelling lists. You can then check their notebooks at regular intervals to see that students are keeping the lists up to date.

Advanced students can practice their spelling skills by proofreading each other's written work. Misspelled words should be corrected and added to students' personal spelling lists.

Suggestions for Additional Activities. Students may enjoy a spelling bee based on the list of spelling demons. Students who miss words can add them to their spelling lists.

■ 20.2 Following Spelling Rules (pp. 423–434)

Objectives: After completing this section, students should be able to

- Write the plural forms of most words correctly.
- Add prefixes correctly.
- Add most suffixes correctly.
- Spell *ie* and *ei* words correctly.
- Spell words that end in *-cede, -ceed,* and *-sede* correctly.

Adapting for Different Abilities. You might permit less advanced students to refer to the charts as they complete the exercises. Average or advanced students can make lists of words to add to those contained in the charts.

Suggestions for Additional Activities. The prefixed and suffixed words in Section 19.3 can be used or reused to test students' abilities to add these word parts correctly. You may also want to conduct a spelling bee focusing on individual sets of rules or on all of the rules in the section. You can call out directions such as the following:

1. Spell the plural of *thief.*
2. Add the suffix *-y* to *fun.*
3. Spell *intercede.*

Words for the bee can be taken from section charts and exercises.

UNIT V

Study Skills

This unit covers skills that are useful both in English class and in other subject areas. Since it does not build directly on any other chapters of the text, it can be taught at any time. You may, for example, choose to teach Chapter 21 on study habits early in the year; students can then begin to establish good listening and note-taking skills from the start. Similarly, you may decide to cover Chapter 22 on reading skills and Chapter 23 on library and reference skills at a point in the curriculum when it will be most helpful to your students.

The pretest for Unit V, available in the *Prentice-Hall Grammar and Composition Test Program,* can be used to help determine students' need for instruction in the skills presented in the unit. Chapter tests and a unit post-test are also available in the test program.

CHAPTER 21 Improving Your Study Habits (pp. 436–459)

The first section of the chapter, Section 21.1, deals with general study methods: setting goals, scheduling study time, recording assignments, and creating a distraction-free study area. More specific learning skills are covered in Sections 21.2 through 21.4. In these sections students will find suggestions for improving their listening, note-taking, and speaking skills.

You will probably find that students can cover these sections fairly quickly. Most classes will need only three to four days to complete the entire chapter.

■ 21.1 Establishing Good Study Habits (pp. 436–444)

Objectives: After completing this section, students should be able to

- Set up goals for improving their study habits.
- Schedule their study time.
- Record homework assignments accurately.
- Create a distraction-free study area.

Adapting for Different Abilities. You can use this section to help less advanced students think about how to improve their study habits. To point out examples of study improvement goals, you can review Exercise A with the class. Then, in a class discussion, you can have students draw up lists of both short- and long-range goals that could apply to most of the students in the class. Finally, students can develop their own lists of goals and write them in their notebooks. As you proceed through the section, you can check to see that students are working toward the goals they have set and that they are adding new goals as well.

Average and advanced students can try different methods of recording assignments and report on which work best for them. These students may also want to develop symbols that will show at a glance which assignments are most time-consuming or most important.

Suggestions for Additional Activities. After students have planned their own weekly study schedules (as described in Exercise D), you can have them compare their results. You might group together students who share many of the same school activities, such as sports practice or play rehearsal, so students can see how others juggle the same time commitments. You might also suggest that students revise their schedules each month or whenever outside activities change.

■ 21.2 Developing Your Listening Skills

(pp. 444–448)

Objectives: After completing this section, students should be able to

- Listen carefully for main ideas and major details.
- Restate a set of directions given orally.

Adapting for Different Abilities. The following test can give less advanced students more practice in listening to directions. Make up simple directions from your school to each of the following locations:

1. The public library
2. The closest movie theater
3. The nearest hospital
4. The post office
5. A popular shopping area or store

Read each set of directions aloud to your students *without* telling them where the directions lead. By listening closely, students should be able to figure out the identity of each place.

Suggestions for Additional Activities. To give all students more practice in listening for main ideas, you can borrow from the library a recording of well-known speeches. Play short selections for the class, telling them to jot down the main ideas and major details as they listen. Afterwards, have students discuss their notes to compare what each considered to be the main ideas of the speeches. Ask students to supply the speech details that support their answers.

21.3 Developing Your Note-Taking Skills
(pp. 449–455)

Objectives: After completing this section, students should be able to

- Create a modified outline.
- Create a formal outline.
- Write a summary of the main ideas in a lecture or short reading assignment.

Adapting for Different Abilities. To give less advanced students practice in learning how to group items in categories, you can list the following items in mixed order on the board, using no indentations. Have students discuss how the items can be grouped and then prepare a modified outline covering all of the items.

- Dogs
  - Dachshunds
  - Cocker spaniels
  - Irish setters
  - Poodles
- Fish
  - Goldfish
  - Guppies
- Cats
  - Siamese
  - Persians
  - Tabbies
- Birds
  - Canaries
  - Parakeets

Average and advanced students might use the same items as the basis for a formal outline, adding more detailed subcategories covering such items as color and size. Average and advanced students might also prepare formal outlines from selections in texts used for other classes.

Suggestions for Additional Activities. Students can be asked to practice writing summaries of articles or of classroom notes. Students can then work in pairs to compare their summaries, checking for clarity and content.

21.4 Developing Your Speaking Skills
(pp. 455–459)

Objectives: After completing this section, students should be able to

- Demonstrate improved participation in classroom discussions.
- Prepare and give a demonstration speech, using a short outline.

Adapting for Different Abilities. Less advanced students can be encouraged to set goals for increasing their class participation over a series of weeks. For example, a student can plan to speak at least once in class during the first week, twice during the second week, and so on.

Suggestions for Additional Activities. One good way of evaluating students' speeches is to have members of the class act as critics. Remind students that a critic analyzes and judges a performance and can make both positive and negative comments. Students can work with a ranking sheet such as the one shown below. Evaluations should be made on a scale of 1 to 5—1 for poor, 3 for average, and 5 for excellent.

1 2 3 4 5 (1) Speaker included all necessary information.
1 2 3 4 5 (2) Speaker's use of notes on index cards did not create a major distraction.
1 2 3 4 5 (3) Speaker spoke naturally and comfortably.
1 2 3 4 5 (4) Speaker's ideas were organized and logical.
1 2 3 4 5 (5) Speaker maintained good eye contact.

CHAPTER 22 Improving Your Reading Skills (pp. 460–471)

This chapter is designed to help students improve both their general reading and textbook reading skills. Section 22.1 on reading rate discusses various reading styles and speeds. Section 22.2 on reading textbooks explains how textbooks can become more effective learning tools for students when used correctly.

You will probably need at least a half day of class time for each section in the chapter, although practice of outside assignments may continue for several weeks.

■ 22.1 Developing Your Reading Rate (pp. 460–466)

Objectives: After completing this section, students should be able to

- Recognize when to use three different reading styles: phrase reading, skimming, and scanning.
- Calculate and chart their own phrase reading rates.
- Use different methods to increase their phrase reading rates.

Adapting for Different Abilities. With less advanced students, you may want to conduct individual reading conferences. You can use this time both to help students select the best methods for improving their reading rates and to keep track of each student's progress as shown by phrase reading rate charts.

With average and advanced students, you might wish to assign outside readings for drill work at home. These students can also be asked to bring in charts periodically so you can monitor their progress.

Suggestions for Additional Activities. Students can practice the three kinds of reading styles by carrying out assignments such as the following:

1. Skim the final chapter of your science book to get a general idea of what it covers. In a few sentences, explain what you learned by skimming.
2. Scan your history book to find the date on which a major war began. Then scan to find out which countries were involved in the war. Write your answers in one sentence.
3. Phrase read a short story to find out what happens in the end. Summarize the story in a few sentences.

■ 22.2 Reading Textbooks (pp. 466–471)

Objectives: After completing this section, students should be able to

- Make profitable use of a number of special sections found in most textbooks.
- Make profitable use of the reading aids found within the chapters of most textbooks.

Adapting for Different Abilities. With less advanced students, you may want to review textbook terminology. List the following terms on the board and ask students to define and describe each:

1. Table of contents
2. Preface
3. Index
4. Glossary
5. Appendix
6. Bibliography
7. Titles
8. Headings
9. Subheadings
10. Captions

Then have the students use their own textbooks to locate examples of each of the features.

Suggestions for Additional Activities. Students can be asked to evaluate textbook features in several different books on the same subject. Students can work in groups of three or four to prepare the evaluations and can present them in charts or in several paragraphs.

CHAPTER 23 Improving Your Library and Reference Skills (pp. 472–514)

Knowing how to use research and reference tools can be of great benefit to every student. This chapter discusses some of the valuable learning resources found in both school and public libraries and explains how to use them. Section 23.1 explains how works of fiction, nonfiction, and biography are listed in the card catalog and arranged on the library shelves. Section 23.2 focuses on the use of reference books. Section 23.3 gives detailed explanations of how students can benefit from the many special features of a dictionary.

As with the other chapters in this unit, you may teach this chapter at any time during the year. However, since your school librarian can probably help by demonstrating how to use the school library, you may wish to plan ahead to ensure free use of the library. Students can probably cover this chapter in five to six days.

■ 23.1 Using the Library (pp. 472–486)

Objectives: After completing this section, students should be able to

- Locate information about books in a library card catalog, using the word-by-word alphabetizing method.
- Locate fiction, nonfiction, biographies, and special materials in the library.

Adapting for Different Abilities. If you are working with less advanced students, you may want to have the librarian conduct a very basic and detailed session on using the library. It can include a lengthy demonstration of how to use the card catalog, followed by a tour of the fiction, nonfiction, biography, and reference shelf sections. During or after the session, students can be asked to draw a map of the library that shows the following:

1. Card catalog
2. Study tables
3. Librarian's desk
4. Fiction shelves
5. Nonfiction shelves, divided into the ten Dewey Decimal sections
6. Other special shelves, such as biography or reference

Average and advanced students are likely to benefit from a similar but less basic tour. At the end they can draw the same map, adding specific titles for each of the twelve or more shelf areas described in the last three items of the list.

Suggestions for Additional Activities. To give students more practice with the Dewey Decimal categories, you can list topics such as the following on the board:

1. Musical theater
2. Baseball
3. Sailing
4. Dance
5. U.S. political parties
6. American authors

Pairs of students working together on a topic can then examine library books on their topic and note the Dewey Decimal category in which their topic belongs. Finally, they can answer the following questions:

1. In which main class does the topic belong?
2. What is the number of this class?
3. What are some of the other topics covered by books in this main class?

■ 23.2 Finding Reference Books in the Library (pp. 486–500)

Objectives: After completing this section, students should be able to

- Find, select, and use general reference books.
- Find, select, and use specialized reference books.
- Use magazines and journals to find current information.

Adapting for Different Abilities. A step-by-step explanation showing less advanced students exactly how to use *The Readers' Guide* may be helpful. You can then ask them to pick a subject, to find an article on that subject, and to write a step-by-step explanation of how they found the article, using *The Readers' Guide.* Their explanations should include a copy of *The Readers' Guide* entry used and a translation of the entry. Average and advanced students can follow the same assignment but might omit some of the procedural details and instead read the article that they find and write a summary of it.

Suggestions for Additional Activities. As a homework assignment, students can use almanacs to write five to ten trivia questions and their answers (for example, "Who is the governor of Arkansas?"). You can then use these questions to set up a game. Organize the class into two teams and give the first member of each team an almanac. Using the students' trivia questions, ask one question of the first member of both teams. Both must find the answer quickly in the almanac—the first to raise his or her hand with the answer receives one point for the team. The book is then passed on to each of the next team members for the next question. At the end of the game, the team with the most points wins.

■ 23.3 Using the Dictionary (pp. 500–514)

Objectives: After completing this section, students should be able to

- Choose a dictionary that suits their own needs.
- Use a dictionary to check spelling quickly and easily.
- Find words in a dictionary, using the letter-by-letter alphabetizing method.
- Understand and make use of the different parts of dictionary entries.

Adapting for Different Abilities. Less advanced students may need additional practice in letter-by-letter alphabetizing. If so, you can give them the following list before assigning Exercise C. Point out that the words in this list are arranged in word-by-word order, as in a card catalog, and direct students to place the words in letter-by-letter order. Students can check their answers in a dictionary when finished.

1. New Bedford
2. New Brunswick
3. New England
4. New Year's Eve
5. newborn
6. newcomer
7. newfangled
8. news
9. news conference
10. newscast

You may also want to work closely with less advanced students as they cover the material on the parts of main entries. With these students, you can use the excerpt shown in Exercise E as the basis for a classroom exercise. Have the students read through each entry, looking for and identifying the following parts in each one:

1. Entry word
2. Preferred spelling
3. Syllabification
4. Pronunciation
5. Part-of-speech labels
6. Etymology
7. Definition(s)
8. Usage labels
9. Field labels
10. Idioms
11. Derived words
12. Synonyms

Students should recognize that not all entries will contain all of the parts.

Advanced students might use a dictionary both to define the following words and to research their etymologies. Students should give the language or languages from which each word derives and cite and define the words given in the etymology that help explain the basis for the word's present-day meaning. In carrying out this activity, students will also have a chance to become familiar with the list of abbreviations generally found in the front of a dictionary.

1. Mayday
2. discotheque
3. nostalgia
4. temerity
5. winnow

Suggestions for Additional Activities. Since dictionaries differ, you may want to have students examine copies of different student dictionaries, looking for variations. You may also want to spend additional time examining the pronunciation key found in the dictionary students are most likely to use. Have students read aloud the words given in the key as one student draws on the board the letters or symbols the words are used to illustrate. Then review the letters and symbols by having students give representative words for them.

UNIT VI

Composition

The nine chapters of this unit progress logically from smaller to larger units of writing. In Chapter 24 students practice choosing precise words and lively phrases to improve sentences; in the following chapter, they continue working with sentences—expanding, condensing, and varying the types of sentences they write. Chapter 26 begins a sequence of three chapters about paragraphs. Students first examine paragraphs and learn to recognize topic sentences, supporting information, and unity and coherence. In Chapter 27 students learn to plan, write, and revise paragraphs; in Chapter 28 they learn to recognize the characteristics of expository, persuasive, and descriptive paragraphs and to include these characteristics in their own writing. In Chapters 29 through 31, students deal with longer written forms, examining and writing essays, reports, and stories. The final chapter, Chapter 32, presents ideas for writing both social and business letters.

You may wish to teach some parts of this unit in conjunction with other material in your language arts curriculum. For example, you might begin Chapters 24 and 25, which discuss various aspects of writing sentences, immediately after students study grammar. In this way students can continue to develop their sentence structure skills. Similarly, you may choose to present Chapters 26, 27, and 28 on paragraphs early in the year, before giving students other writing assignments. You might present the sections on writing essays, reports, stories, and letters whenever you feel they are most appropriate.

The pretest for Unit VI, which is available in the *Prentice-Hall Grammar and Composition Test Program,* can be used to help determine students' need for instruction in the skills presented in the unit. Chapter tests and a unit post-test are also available in the test program.

CHAPTER 24 Improving Your Choice of Words (pp. 516–527)

The first of the two sections in this chapter, Section 24.1, is designed to help students choose appropriate, specific words for sentences they write. The second section, Section 24.2, will help students avoid using clichés and slang in their writing. Although you may want to assign some parts of the chapter as independent work, you will probably want to spend considerable class time on other parts, most notably on connotations. Whatever you choose to emphasize, most classes will be able to complete the chapter in about four days.

■ 24.1 Choosing Precise Words (pp. 516–524)

Objectives: After completing this section, students should be able to

- Replace linking verbs and verbs in the passive voice with action verbs in the active voice.
- Use specific, vivid words to enliven sentences.
- Choose words with appropriate connotations for a particular context.

Adapting for Different Abilities. The discussion of verbs at the beginning of the section assumes a working knowledge of the material taught in Sections 2.1, 2.2, and 11.4. With less advanced students, you may want not only to assure previous coverage of the topics but also to carry out a review just before beginning this section. To review action verbs and active voice, these students might do Exercise C in Section 2.2 (pp. 44–45) and Exercise A in Section 11.4 (pp. 211–212). In addition, you might work with these students on the revisions required in Exercise A of the present section. Point out that each sentence already contains a word that can become the main verb and remind students that they may have to change more than just the verb. You might also work with less advanced students on the first few sentences of Exercise B to be certain they understand the process. Average and advanced students can compare their answers to Exercises D and E and discuss the connotations of each specific word as well as the different senses the connotations give to the sentences.

Suggestions for Additional Activities. Students might be asked to collect examples of vivid words they encounter in their reading. The words might then be compiled into lists or into a card file grouped by categories. An entry might be set up in the following way: Ways of Walking—tiptoe, ramble, hobble, meander. Once the lists are compiled, they can serve as resources when students revise their own writing.

■ 24.2 Avoiding Worn-out and Inappropriate Words (pp. 524–527)

Objectives: After completing this section, students should be able to

- Recognize and avoid clichés.
- Use precise language in place of slang expressions.

Adapting for Different Abilities. You may wish to work with less advanced students in class as they revise the sentences in Exercise C. You might also discuss in class the clichés and slang expressions less advanced students plan to use when they write the passages called for in the Application. If you do so, you can then change the second part of the instructions to omit the exchange of papers. In carrying out the Application or as an extra activity, advanced students might enjoy consulting a dictionary of slang to find examples of outdated slang expressions with which to confuse their classmates.

Suggestions for Additional Activities. Students might enjoy compiling a class dictionary of clichés and slang. You can have them work in committees using the sentences they wrote for Exercise A and the Application. Ask students to select the most frequently recurring clichés and slang expressions and give two or three precise revisions for each. They can then enter their results in a notebook or other file to be placed in a central location and used in revising their own writing. The entries might look something like this:

Cliché/Slang	Precise Writing
1. bite off more than one can chew	undertake too large a task overextend oneself
2. blow one's mind	be totally surprised by be overwhelmed by
3. chew one's ear off	chatter endlessly babble constantly talk to no purpose

CHAPTER 25 Writing Better Sentences (pp. 528–544)

Before students begin this chapter, you will want to be sure that they understand the material on phrases and clauses presented in Chapters 8 and 9. In Section 25.1 students will be asked to use prepositional phrases, verbal phrases, and clauses to expand and combine sentences. Section 25.2 demands a knowledge of compound and complex sentences; so too does Section 25.3, which stresses the need for variety in sentence structure.

You will probably need to allow one or two days for each section, a total of four to six days for the entire chapter. With less advanced students, you may need to allow even more time to work closely with the students on the many important concepts covered in the chapter.

■ 25.1 Expanding Short Sentences (pp. 528–534)

Objectives: After completing this section, students should be able to

- Add details to expand short sentences.
- Combine short, choppy sentences in a variety of ways.

Adapting for Different Abilities. With less advanced students, you will probably want to spend some time discussing in detail the sentence-combining possibilities in the chart on pages 531 and 532. You might also want to work with these students to revise the first few groups of sentences in Exercise C and then permit them to work in pairs to combine the remaining groups of sentences.

Advanced students might be instructed to use each of the sentence-combining techniques from the chart at least once in revising the sentences in Exercise C. They can then compare their answers to see which seem smoothest.

Suggestions for Additional Activities. All students are likely to benefit from comparing their revisions of the Application passage and from discussing which possibilities are smoothest and most interesting. However, the most beneficial revision activity you can provide will generally be one in which students revise a composition they have written themselves. If you work with this material before students have done enough writing to provide their own samples, you might provide them with unattributed student writing from a previous year and ask them to revise it for smoothness and detail.

■ 25.2 Simplifying Long, Confusing Sentences (pp. 534–538)

Objectives: After completing this section, students should be able to

- Separate rambling compound sentences into shorter sentences.
- Separate complicated complex sentences into shorter sentences.

Adapting for Different Abilities. Less advanced students will probably need help in revising the sentences in the exercises and the Application. You may thus want to work with them as a group on the revisions. In working with Exercise B, you might have the students identify the most important ideas in each sentence. You can then help them structure these ideas into main clauses while placing the relevant supporting information in subordinate clauses. You might also try having these students do thumbnail modified outlines of the information in the sentences.

Average students may benefit from working in pairs to revise the exercise sentences. Advanced students, on the other hand, will probably find it relatively easy to complete the exercises independently.

Suggestions for Additional Activities. As suggested for Section 25.1, group comparison of the revisions students write for the exercises can be beneficial to most students. Additional revision work with sentences found in the students' own work or with unattributed sentences taken from past students' papers can also be of great value.

■ 25.3 Using a Variety of Sentences (pp. 539–544)

Objectives: After completing this section, students should be able to

- Use a variety of sentence openers in their written work.
- Use a variety of sentence structures in their written work.

Adapting for Different Abilities. Supplying additional examples for the chart on pages 539 and 540 can help less advanced students become more familiar with the varied sentence openers they can use in their own writing. Some of these students may also require supervision in completing the exercises, at least at the beginning of each.

Average and advanced students might be asked to identify the type of openers they use in Exercises B and C. Advanced students might also be asked to select a passage from their literature text or from a book they are reading outside of class. They can then make a list of the various types of sentence openers mentioned in the chart on pages 539 and 540 that are used in the passage. In addition they can label each sentence in the passage *simple, compound, complex,* or *compound-complex.*

Suggestions for Additional Activities. After students have completed the revision called for in the second part of the Application, you might want to discuss the need for proofreading as well as for revising. Instruct them to check their work for problems in both mechanics and spelling (referring them to Chapters 16–18 and 20, if necessary). Then ask them to make any corrections.

CHAPTER 26 Looking at Paragraphs (pp. 545–564)

The four sections of this chapter move logically from Section 26.1 on topic sentences and Section 26.2 on supporting information to Sections 26.3 and 26.4 on unity and coherence. The entire chapter provides a firm foundation for the actual writing of paragraphs, which students will undertake in Chapters 27 and 28.

Since many of the exercises involve only identification, you can probably cover the chapter in four or five days. If you choose to have students complete the Applications in class rather than as homework, you may need to allow slightly more time.

■ 26.1 Recognizing Topic Sentences (pp. 545–548)

Objective: After completing this section, students should be able to

- Identify topic sentences in paragraphs.

Adapting for Different Abilities. The material in this section should be accessible to all students. You may want to go over the sample paragraphs with less advanced students to be sure they understand why each italicized sentence is a topic sentence.

Suggestions for Additional Activities. To provide an additional identification exercise, you might ask students to bring to class one of their textbooks from another class. A social studies or science text might be the best choice. They can then choose a chapter or part of a chapter and locate the topic sentence in each paragraph. If a paragraph lacks a topic sentence, students can supply one, as suggested in the Application.

■ 26.2 Recognizing Supporting Information (pp. 548–553)

Objectives: After completing this section, students should be able to

- Recognize examples, details, and facts used as supporting information in a paragraph.
- Recognize reasons and incidents used as supporting information in a paragraph.

Adapting for Different Abilities. With less advanced students, you may want to omit the labeling requirement in Exercise A and have students concentrate instead on the need for adequate, specific support. Average and advanced students may enjoy thinking up paragraph topics and then listing kinds of support, including combinations of different kinds, that could be used for each.

Suggestions for Additional Activities. After students complete the Application, they can be asked to compare the details about your school that they have listed. They might also develop subgroups of details and think of a topic sentence that each subgroup could be used to support. The following are possible subgroups students might consider:

1. Exterior details
2. Setting
3. Courses
4. Athletics
5. Extracurricular activities
6. Student attitudes

■ 26.3 Recognizing Unity (pp. 553–556)

Objective: After completing this section, students should be able to

- Recognize unified paragraphs.

Adapting for Different Abilities. Few students are likely to have any great difficulty in identifying the unrelated supporting ideas in Exercise A and the Application. However, you may wish to have less advanced students complete at least one of the items in Exercise A orally as a class exercise before they begin work on their own.

Suggestions for Additional Activities. If students carried out the grouping activity described in the suggestions for additional activities for Section 26.2, they can now check the list of details under each of the subgroup headings to ensure that each detail truly supports the topic sentence they have written.

■ 26.4 Recognizing Coherence (pp. 556–564)

Objectives: After completing this section, students should be able to

- Recognize a number of logical orders that can be used to give a paragraph coherence.
- Recognize and choose appropriate transitions to connect ideas.

Adapting for Different Abilities. You may wish to allow less advanced students to refer to the chart of transitions as they work on the two Applications. Advanced students might choose one of the items in the first Application and organize it in two different ways, using different transitions for each order chosen.

Suggestions for Additional Activities. For additional practice, students might work with the sample paragraph on page 552. Ask the students to identify the order used in the paragraph and to locate the transitions used to make this order clear.

CHAPTER 27 Writing Paragraphs (pp. 565–595)

This chapter provides students with a step-by-step guide for planning, writing, and revising a paragraph. The material builds on what students have learned about sentences in Chapters 24 and 25 and about paragraphs in Chapter 26. It also provides a foundation for writing essays and reports as discussed in Chapters 29 and 30.

Sections 27.1, 27.2, and 27.3 can probably be covered in one class session each. If you plan to have students revise their work in class, you should allow somewhat more time for Section 27.4.

■ 27.1 Thinking Out Your Ideas and Writing a Topic Sentence (pp. 565–572)

Objectives: After completing this section, students should be able to

- Find and narrow an idea into a good paragraph topic.
- Decide on an audience, main idea, and purpose in order to focus a paragraph topic.
- Write a topic sentence for a paragraph.

Adapting for Different Abilities. You can help less advanced students develop topics narrow enough to be written about in one paragraph by having them present their paragraph topics from Exercises A and B in class. The class can discuss whether or not the topics are suitable for a paragraph. You can then ask for suggestions to focus those topics that are still too general.

With average and advanced students, it may be helpful to bring a variety of paragraphs to class to demonstrate clearly the need for deciding on audience, main idea, and purpose when writing a paragraph. The paragraphs you bring can be read aloud and discussed in class. You may wish to present paragraphs of the following types:

1. A persuasive paragraph from an editorial written for a general audience
2. A descriptive paragraph from a book for young children
3. An explanatory paragraph from a scientific journal written for professionals
4. An explanatory paragraph from a textbook your students might use

Suggestions for Additional Activities. After students complete the Application, you may find it useful to have students of similar ability work together in small groups so that they can review and discuss each other's work. As students work together, remind them to offer only constructive criticism of each other's work.

■ 27.2 Developing Support for a Topic Sentence (pp. 572–578)

Objectives: After completing this section, students should be able to

- Gather supporting information for a topic sentence.
- Check supporting information for unity and organize it in a logical order to achieve coherence.

Adapting for Different Abilities. Less advanced students, in particular, might benefit from a study or review of the material on modified outlines in Section 21.3 before working on Exercise C and the Application. You might ask advanced students to complete the third item in the Application twice, using a different logical order each time. Remind students that a change in the logical order might necessitate changes in the topic sentence and in the supporting information.

Suggestions for Additional Activities. Students might enjoy an activity based on paragraphs found in magazines. Select at least one paragraph with a clear topic sentence covering a subject with which the students are likely to be familiar. Write the topic sentence on the board and ask the class to brainstorm for supporting information. Then read the full paragraph.

■ 27.3 Writing the Paragraph (pp. 578–581)

Objective: After completing this section, students should be able to

- Write the first draft of a paragraph.

Adapting for Different Abilities. You might want to work with less advanced students to develop the first draft of a paragraph before students write first drafts using their own topics. You can use the work done by one of the students for the Application in Section 27.2, or you can develop another topic of your own choosing.

Suggestions for Additional Activities. Students can be asked to exchange papers and review each other's first drafts. Students can check to see that the topic, focus for a particular audience and purpose, topic sentence, and support are appropriate. They can then check for unity, logical order, and transitions.

■ 27.4 Revising and Rewriting a Paragraph (pp. 581–595)

Objectives: After completing this section, students should be able to

- Recognize and correct topic sentences that are too narrow or too general.
- Recognize and correct supporting information that provides too little support or that contains generalizations and weak opinions.
- Recognize and correct paragraphs that lack unity and coherence.
- Use a checklist to locate problems in paragraphs.

Adapting for Different Abilities. You may want to help less advanced students make the revisions called for in Exercises B and D by discussing in detail the reasons for making the revisions.

Suggestions for Additional Activities. Students may benefit from conducting a class revision of one or more unattributed paragraphs written by students in previous years. As a variation of the basic activity, you might divide the class into eight groups, give each group one of the points in the checklist to consider, and then conduct a revision based on the findings of each group.

CHAPTER 28 Writing Different Kinds of Paragraphs (pp. 596–609)

Each section in this chapter explores a different kind of writing: expository, persuasive, and descriptive. (Narrative writing is treated separately in Chapter 31.) Within each section students will consider both the special features of and the language appropriate to each of the different kinds of writing. They will also have a chance to plan and write one or more paragraphs of each type.

You will probably need to allow approximately two days for each section—one of which can be spent examining the special features of one of the three different kinds of paragraphs and the other planning and writing paragraphs of that type. Section 28.1 is likely to take the least amount of time.

■ 28.1 Writing Paragraphs That Explain

(pp. 596–600)

Objectives: After completing this section, students should be able to

- Develop a topic sentence and support appropriate for a paragraph that explains.
- Use informative language in a paragraph that explains.

Adapting for Different Abilities. You may want to work closely with small groups of less advanced students as they complete Exercise B. Then, in place of Exercise C, these students might simply list supporting information they could use to develop one of the topic sentences in Exercise B. Finally, for the Application, they can write that paragraph rather than develop a new one. Average and advanced students can exchange their finished paragraphs from both Exercise C and the Application and suggest revisions, checking especially for clarity and logical order.

Suggestions for Additional Activities. Students can be asked to look in books and magazines for examples of paragraphs with a clear expository purpose and then to try to identify the topic sentence, the audience, the order used, and specific examples of informative language in each.

■ 28.2 Writing Paragraphs That Persuade

(pp. 600–604)

Objectives: After completing this section, students should be able to

- Develop a topic sentence and support appropriate for a paragraph that persuades.
- Use reasonable language in a paragraph that persuades.

Adapting for Different Abilities. If the recommendations for Section 28.1 worked well with less advanced students, you may want to follow the same procedure here. Work with these students on Exercise B, have them plan in detail for Exercise C, and allow them to use the same topic in place of a new one when they do the Application.

Advanced students might read to each other the paragraphs they write for the Application, omitting the topic sentences. The listener can then try to write a topic sentence that expresses both the topic and the writer's opinion.

Suggestions for Additional Activities. You might want to suggest that students bring to class an editorial from a local newspaper or from the school paper. Students can analyze the editorial, noting in writing as many of the following points as you assign:

1. The writer's purpose
2. The topic sentence of one of the paragraphs
3. The pieces of support used
4. An evaluation of the organization
5. Examples of reasonable or, if such is the case, offensive language used

■ 28.3 Writing Paragraphs That Describe

(pp. 604–609)

Objectives: After completing this section, students should be able to

- Develop a topic sentence that offers a dominant impression and use support appropriate for a paragraph that describes.
- Use a number of different kinds of descriptive language in a paragraph that describes.

Adapting for Different Abilities. Less advanced students might benefit from studying or reviewing Section 24.1, particularly the material on vivid language and connotations. These students could also base their paragraphs for the present section on one of the sentences in Exercise C of Section 24.1. Using that sentence as a topic sentence for a descriptive paragraph, students can make up vivid descriptive details, decide on the arrangement of the details, and then write the paragraph.

Average and advanced students can bring to class a descriptive paragraph from their outside reading and discuss any vivid modifiers or figures of speech used by the writer. The various examples of descriptive language can then be compared and evaluated.

Suggestions for Additional Activities. To emphasize the creation of mood in a descriptive paragraph, you might suggest the following. Have students choose a specific place and write a paragraph describing how it would look on a bright sunny day from the point of view of someone who has just received some good news. They can then write a second paragraph describing the same place on a dismal dreary day from the point of view of someone who has just suffered a disappointment. If students need help deciding on a place, you might suggest the following:

1. The street on which a student lives

2. The school playground
3. An imaginary place
4. A bus, train, or plane
5. A room in a student's home
6. A classroom
7. A beach or lakefront

CHAPTER 29 Writing Essays (pp. 610–634)

Chapter 29 gives students a chance to use paragraph writing skills to create a longer, more detailed composition—an essay. Section 29.1 describes the parts and the organization of an essay. Section 29.2 provides step-by-step guidelines for developing a thesis statement for an essay. Section 29.3 takes students through the planning steps for the body of the essay. Section 29.4 offers concrete suggestions for writing and revising an essay.

You will probably need at least six class sessions to cover the chapter adequately. With less advanced students, who are likely to require substantial guidance during the planning stage, you may need somewhat more time.

■ 29.1 Looking at Essays (pp. 610–618)

Objectives: After completing this section, students should be able to

- Recognize the parts of an essay.
- Recognize how the parts of an essay work together.

Adapting for Different Abilities. You might ask less advanced students to take notes on the explanatory material in this section; they can then refer to these notes as they answer the questions in Exercise B and the Application. You might also have them prepare a modified outline of the annotated model essay. This activity may help them see more clearly the relationship between the ideas in the essay and the way in which the essay is developed.

Suggestions for Additional Activities. To provide students with further practice in analyzing essays, ask them to bring in essays that appear in weekly news magazines. They can then use as many of the Application questions as possible in analyzing the essays they bring in.

■ 29.2 Thinking Out Your Ideas and Writing a Thesis Statement (pp. 618–624)

Objectives: After completing this section, students should be able to

- Find and narrow an idea into a suitable essay topic.
- Decide on an audience, main point, and purpose.
- Write a thesis statement.

Adapting for Different Abilities. For many less advanced students, finding and narrowing a topic can be a difficult task. As the text suggests, these students can brainstorm to find topics. One student can then write the suggested topics on the board. After you have explained ways of narrowing down a topic, with the help of the chart on page 619, you can use one of the suggested topics to demonstrate the narrowing down process. Students should then be able to complete Exercise A. You might also use the same topic for demonstration purposes when students move on to the chart on page 621, thus helping your students with the task presented in Exercise B. With your guidance, less advanced students should then be able to complete Exercise C and the Application. Average and advanced students can help each other by playing in turn the role of audience for a student who is trying to establish a main point.

Suggestions for Additional Activities. Students may be able to see the importance of purpose more clearly if they are asked to rewrite the thesis statements they have prepared for the Application to show another purpose entirely.

■ 29.3 Developing Support for a Thesis Statement (pp. 624–629)

Objectives: After completing this section, students should be able to

- Gather supporting information to develop a thesis statement.
- Organize supporting ideas for an essay.

Adapting for Different Abilities. A study or review of the material in Sections 26.2 and 26.4 on supporting information and coherence may be helpful for all students but vital for the less advanced. Before beginning Exercise A, these students can benefit greatly from thinking about the different kinds of support they can use, as discussed in Section 26.2. Before completing Exercise B, they can benefit equally from a discussion of the logical orders presented in Section 26.4.

Suggestions for Additional Activities. After students have completed the Application, you may want to try to schedule time for individual conferences during which you can discuss the modified outlines they have prepared. Improvements discussed at this point can help students greatly when they begin to write.

■ 29.4 Writing and Revising an Essay (pp. 629–634)

Objectives: After completing this section, students should be able to

- Plan an effective introduction, conclusion, and title for an essay.

- Write the first draft of an essay.
- Revise an essay and make a final copy.

Adapting for Different Abilities. Before less advanced students begin to write, you may want them to study or review the material on transitions in Section 26.4. You can then have a chart drawn on the board, showing the five orders discussed in Section 26.4 with appropriate transitions listed under each. As students revise their essays, they can refer to the chart when they need help in making logical transitions from paragraph to paragraph.

Suggestions for Additional Activities. After students have completed the Application, you may want to ask them to share essay assignments they have prepared for another class. Have them exchange and revise the assignments as they did for the Application.

CHAPTER 30 Writing Reports (p. 635–655)

The two sections in Chapter 30 cover two very different kinds of reports. Section 30.1 is devoted to writing general reports based on research. Because the students are taught to prepare a true piece of research work with footnotes and bibliography, you may wish to omit or modify this section when working with less advanced students. Section 30.2 covers book reports, offering simple steps that should help all students to prepare better reports on the books they read.

Before beginning this chapter, you may want to make sure that students know how to find material in a library. If they do not, you may want to begin with a study or review of the material in Sections 23.1 and 23.2. Whether students are locating information for a general report or finding a book to write a book report on, they must be able to find their way around a library with relative ease.

The time you allot for this chapter will depend to a large extent on other scheduling constraints and on students' abilities. You might, for instance, want to spend two class sessions on each section to get students started and then check with students over a more extended period of time as they progress through the planning and writing steps. When working with book reports, you might also want to reserve part of each class once or twice a week for students to give oral book reports or to share their written ones.

■ 30.1 Understanding and Preparing Reports (pp. 635–648)

Objectives: After completing this section, students should be able to

- Recognize the special features and general structure of a report based on research.
- Carry out a number of steps to plan, write, and revise a report.

Adapting for Different Abilities. To make this section accessible to less advanced students, you will almost definitely want to begin with a study or review of Sections 23.1 and 23.2. Ideally, this review should be conducted in the library so that students can use the card catalog, locate books on the shelves, and handle various kinds of reference books. Less advanced students will probably also benefit from your step-by-step guidance throughout the section.

Average and advanced students can be encouraged to set up a calendar for themselves as they begin their research and the actual writing of their papers. You can give the students an end date and help them allocate time for all the steps along the way—a certain amount of time for doing the research, organizing their information, writing an outline, writing the first draft, preparing the bibliography, and completing the revision and final copy.

Suggestions for Additional Activities. After you have reviewed the students' reports, you can suggest that students create a classroom reference shelf. Have them make up subject, author, and title cards for each of the reports. These cards can then be filed. (A shoebox can act as a classroom card catalog.) Location symbols can be based on the Dewey Decimal System, presented in Section 23.1. When each report has been marked with a call number, students can arrange the entire collection on a shelf in the classroom.

■ 30.2 Writing Book Reports (pp. 648–655)

Objectives: After completing this section, students should be able to

- Recognize the basic features of a book report.
- Plan, write, and revise a book report.

Adapting for Different Abilities. With less advanced students, you may want to use a book with which all of the students are familiar to give step-by-step demonstrations of all of the points covered in the section.

Average and advanced students might enjoy bringing to class book reviews from newspapers or magazines. They can evaluate these reports by using questions similar to those in Exercise A. The reports and evaluations can then be shared with the class and discussed.

Suggestions for Additional Activities. As suggested earlier, you may want to make some provision for students to share their book reports with the rest of the class. The reports may be given orally on designated days and/or collected into a binder or scrapbook. If the reports are placed in a class binder, students can later be encouraged to check the binder when looking for a good book to read.

CHAPTER 31 Writing Stories (pp. 656–671)

Because the elements of narrative writing are somewhat more complex than those of other forms, this genre receives an entire chapter. If students have studied Section 30.2, they will already have encountered the elements of character, plot, and setting in their consideration of book reports. In this chapter, they will explore the development of these elements in original writing. Section 31.1 is devoted to the character sketch, while Section 31.2 brings all the narrative elements into play in developing a short short story.

You will probably need to allow at least two days for each section. If students wish to continue writing, you may want to spend even more time.

■ 31.1 Writing a Character Sketch (pp. 656–663)

Objectives: After completing this section, students should be able to

- Recognize the basic features of a good character sketch.
- Choose an appropriate subject for a character sketch.
- Develop and organize a character sketch.
- Write and revise a character sketch.

Adapting for Different Abilities. With less advanced students, you might want to provide an opportunity to develop a group character sketch. Select a picture of an interesting face from a magazine or have students choose their favorite picture from a book of photographs such as *The Family of Man.* Work together to develop a group character sketch, trying to elicit contributions from all members of the group.

Advanced students might develop two character sketches—both of the same person but written to focus on contrasting aspects of the person.

Suggestions for Additional Activities. As you begin work on this section, students may enjoy listing their own favorite characters from literature or movies, making a class tally of favorites, and discussing why the most popular characters are memorable. Each student can then write a few sentences giving his or her dominant impression of one of these popular characters.

■ 31.2 Writing a Short Short Story (pp. 663–671)

Objectives: After completing this section, students should be able to

- Recognize the basic features of a short short story.
- Carry out a number of steps to plan a short short story.
- Use dialogue to show character and to develop plot.
- Write and revise a short short story.

Adapting for Different Abilities. To increase the confidence of less advanced students in their own ability to write a story, you may want to divide these students into groups for oral storytelling. They can then take turns relating an experience, real or imaginary. Students who are listening can jot down the following:

1. Characters
2. Setting
3. Central conflict
4. Point of view
5. Suggestions for use of dialogue

Each student can then use these notes to develop and organize the story he or she related to the group.

Average and advanced sudents can collaborate on a story either before or after they write their own stories. Working in groups, they can brainstorm for ideas about characters, settings, and conflicts. After they decide on a point of view, they can work together to develop the story.

Suggestions for Additional Activities. You may want to suggest that students bring to class professionally written short short stories to be read to their classmates. Follow the reading with a discussion, using the questions in Exercise A.

CHAPTER 32 Writing Letters (pp. 672–688)

Section 32.1 discusses the form of letters and envelopes, while Section 32.2 emphasizes content. Each section deals with both social and business letters. If you prefer, you may work back and forth from one section to the other, discussing both form and content for each type of correspondence at the same time.

Most classes will be able to complete Section 32.1 in one class period. Section 32.2 may take two or three days to complete, particularly if you have students write the letters in class rather than at home.

■ 32.1 Looking at Friendly Letters, Social Notes, and Business Letters (pp. 672–681)

Objectives: After completing this section, students should be able to

- Set up friendly letters and social notes and prepare them for mailing.
- Set up business letters and prepare them for mailing.

Adapting for Different Abilities. Since friendly letters are conventionally introduced in language arts programs in the lower grades, you may want to emphasize the formal elements of business letters at this time, especially for average and advanced students.

Suggestions for Additional Activities. Students can be asked to exchange the work they prepare for the exercises and to check each other's work for form, use of abbreviations, capitalization, and so forth.

■ 32.2 Writing Different Kinds of Letters

(pp. 682–688)

Objectives: After completing this section, students should be able to

- Write friendly letters and social notes.
- Write business letters.

Adapting for Different Abilities. All students should be able to complete this section successfully. With less advanced students, you can propose a situation and have all the students brainstorm to write an appropriate letter. For example, they can pretend that a classmate was absent and missed an interesting field trip. They can then collaborate on a letter describing the day's events. With average and advanced students, you might want to suggest a similar situation but have each student write his or her own letter.

Suggestions for Additional Activities. Once again, students can review each other's work for form, content, and mechanics. Encourage students to suggest constructive improvements in word choice and sentence structure.

Additional Answers to Text Exercises

Unit I Grammar

Section 7.9 Diagraming Basic Sentence Parts

Exercise A (p. 118)

1. 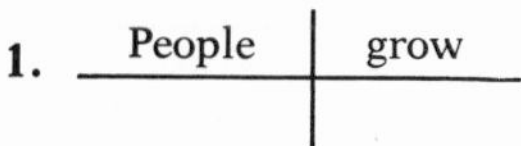

2. Max | spoke

3. Mrs. Rodriguez | has changed

4. Oklahoma State Park | has opened

5. They | have been notified

Exercise B (p. 119)

1.
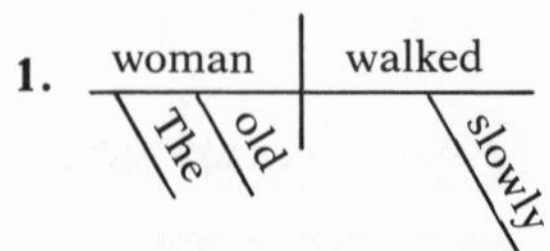

2.
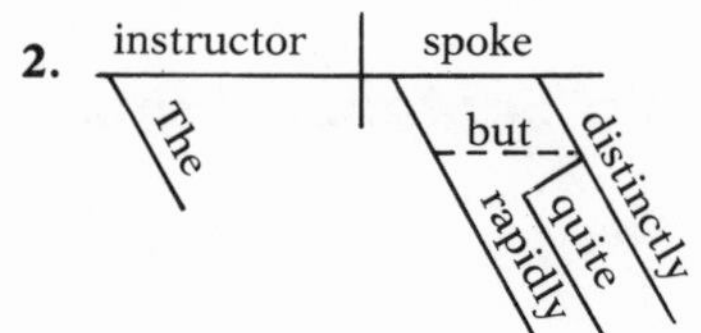

3.
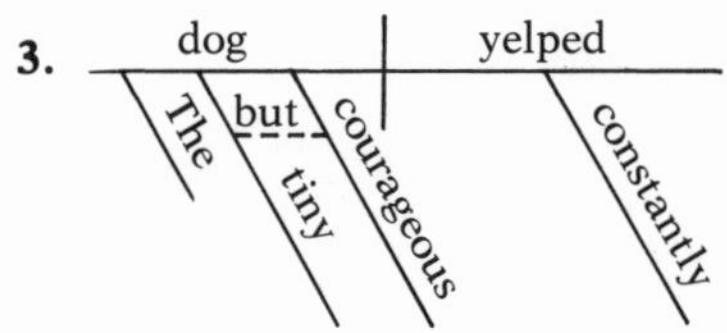

4.
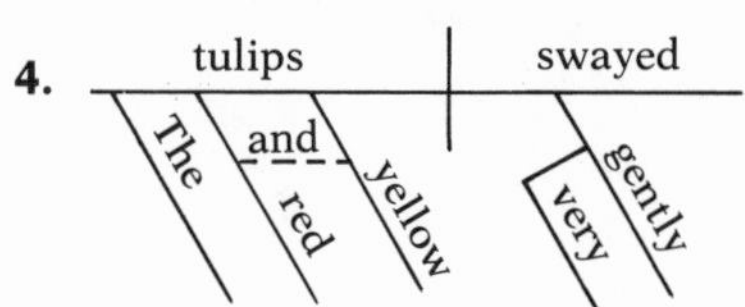

5.
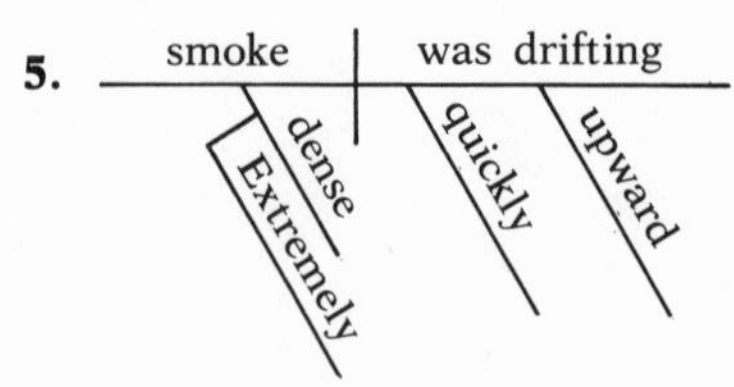

Exercise C (p. 121)

1.
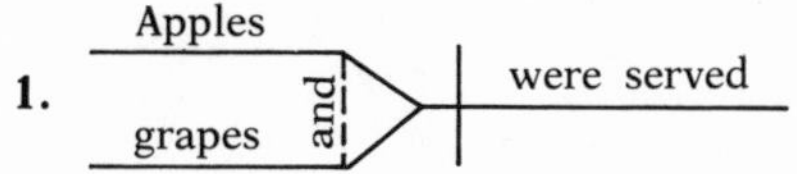

2.
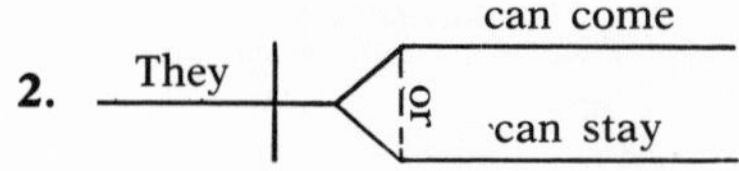

3.
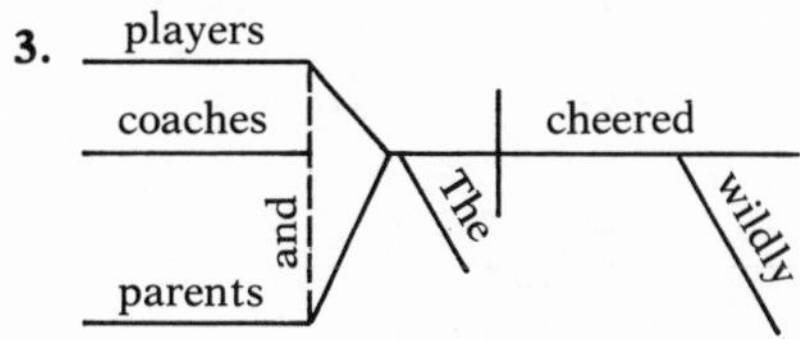

4.
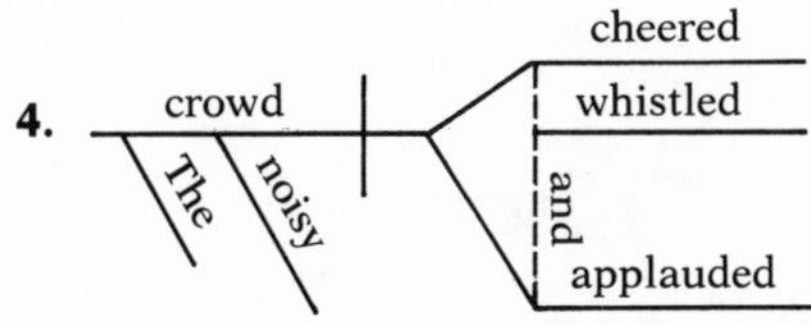

5.
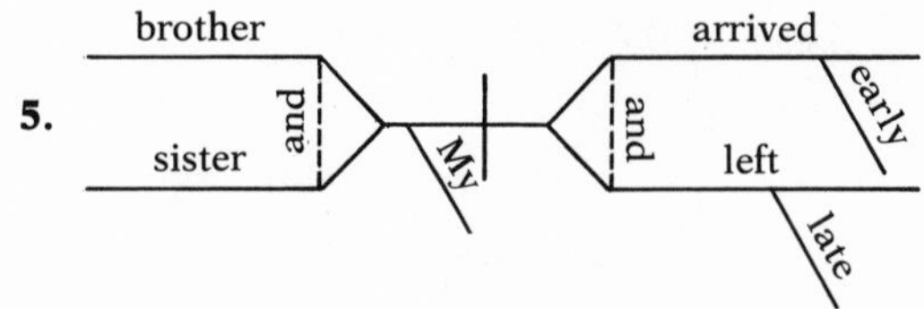

Exercise D (pp. 122–123)

1.
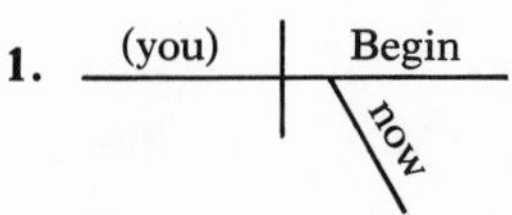

2. 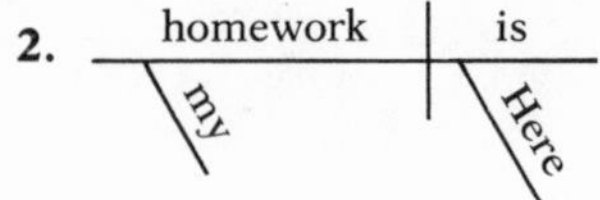

3. 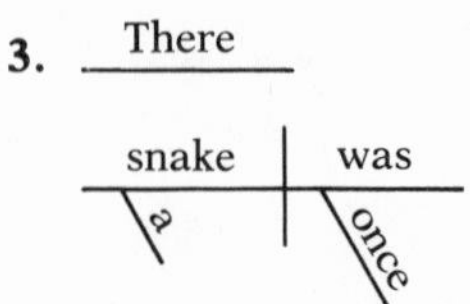

4. 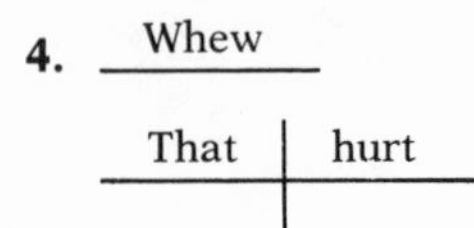

5. Gee

(you) | Watch

out

Exercise E (p. 125)

1. 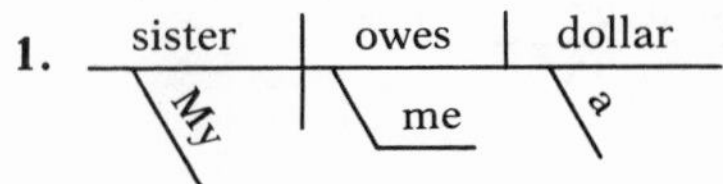

2. 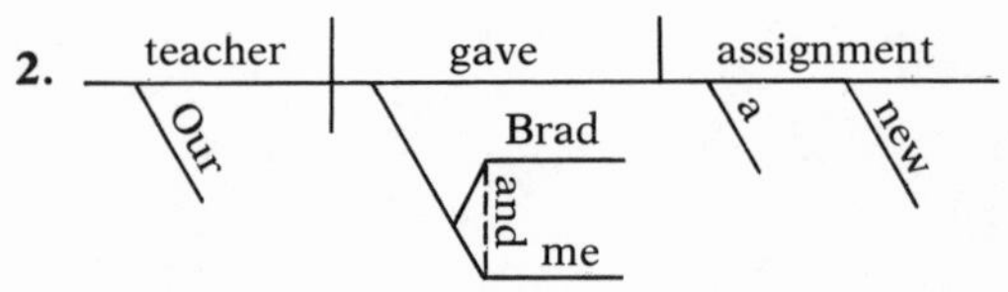

3. 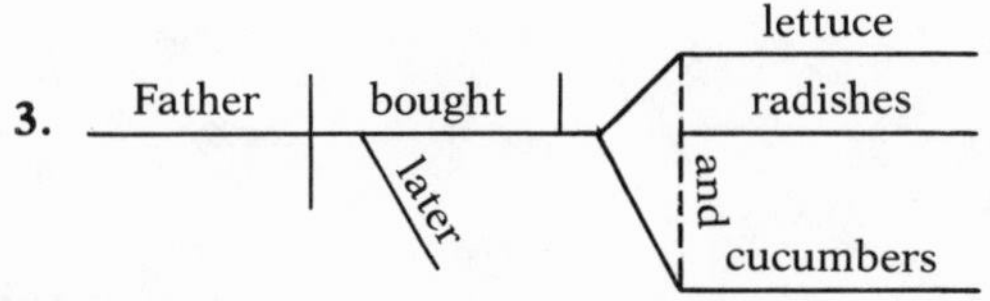

4.

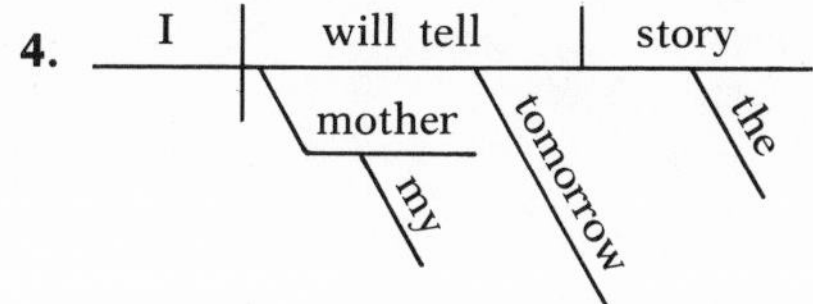

5.

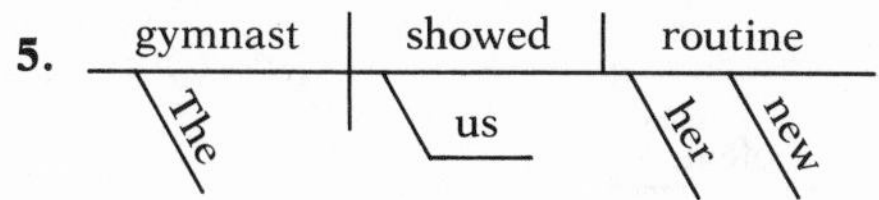

Exercise F (p. 125)

1.

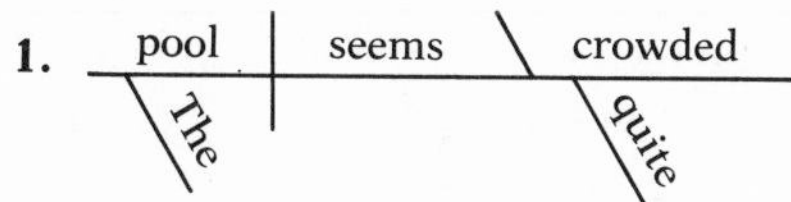

2.

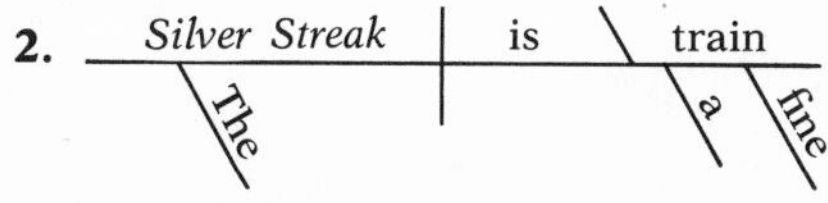

3.

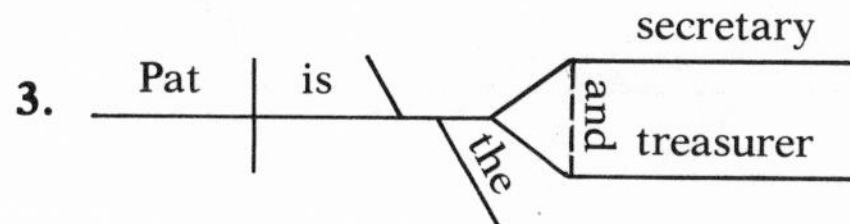

4.

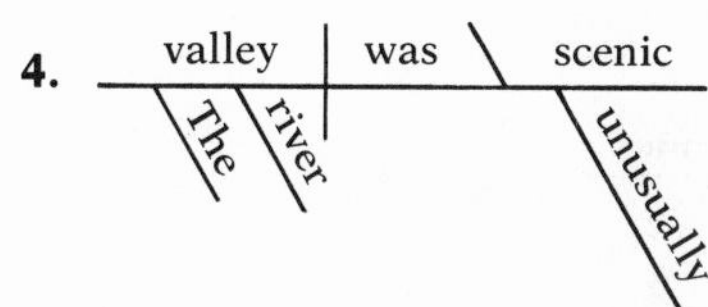

5.

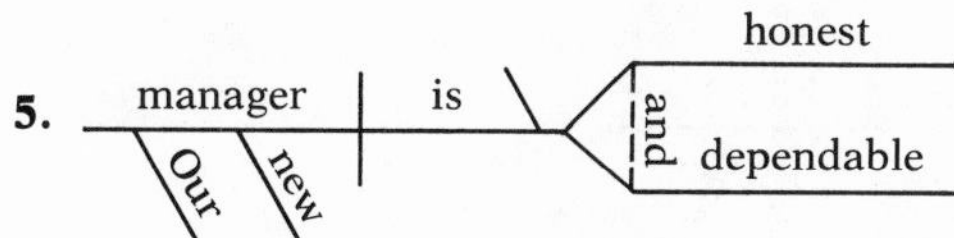

Application (p. 125)

1.
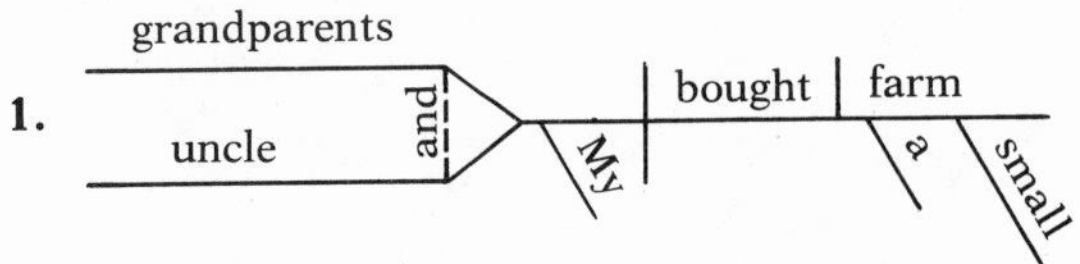

2.
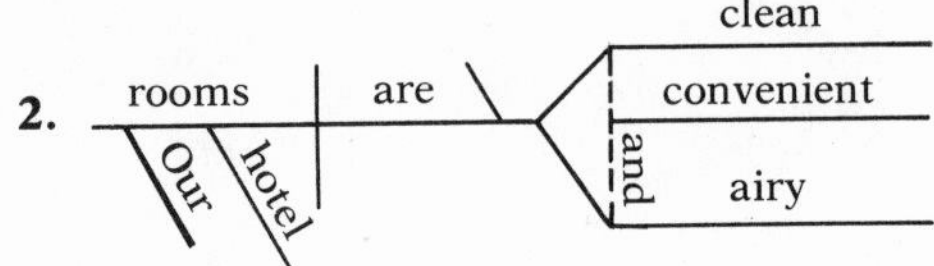

3.
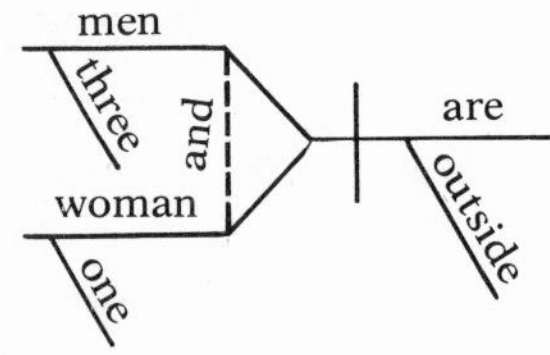

4.
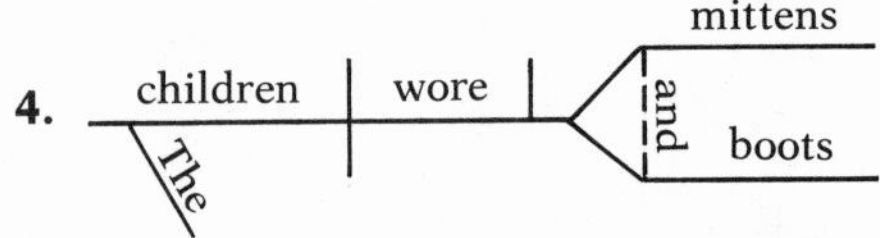

5.
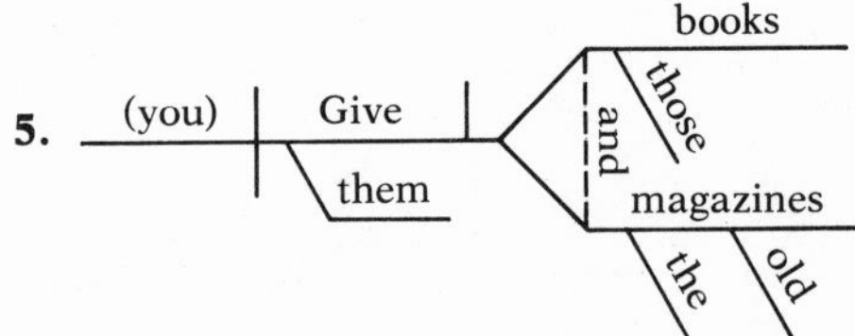

6.
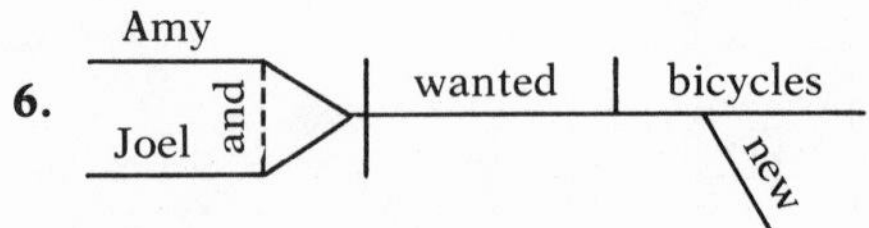

7.

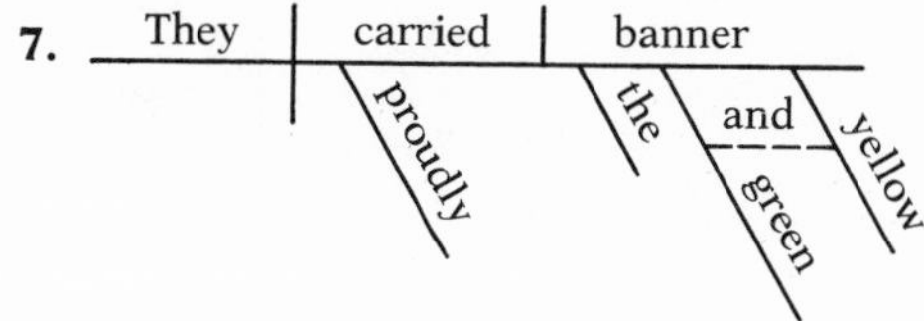

8.

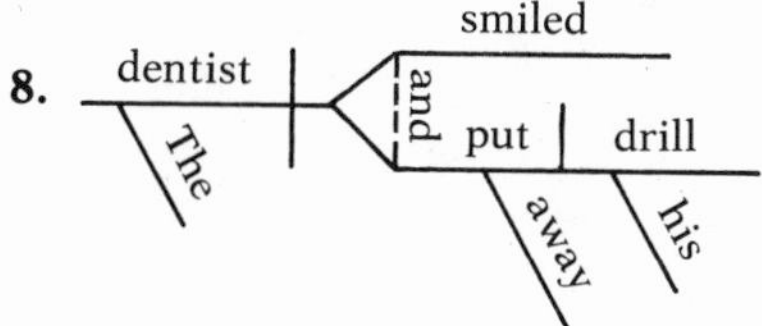

9.

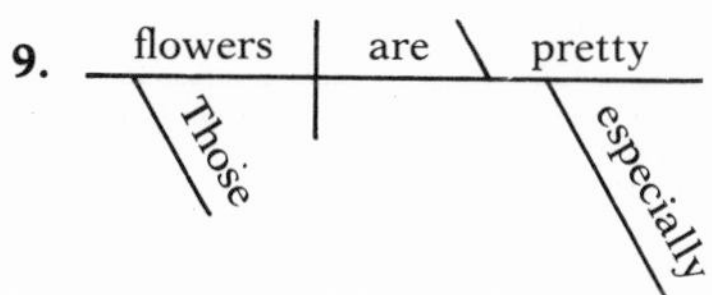

10.

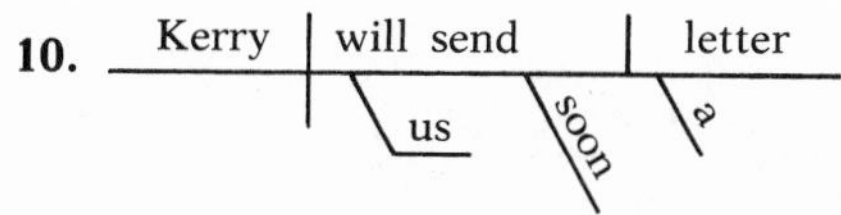

Section 8.6 Diagraming Prepositional Phrases and Appositives

Exercise A (p. 145)

1.

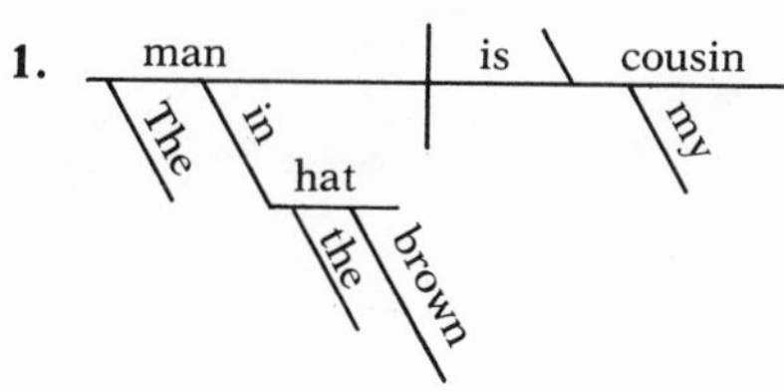

2.

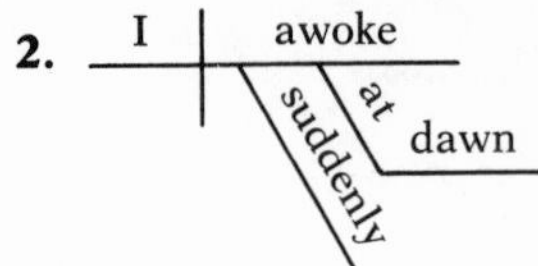

I
awoke
suddenly
at
dawn

3.

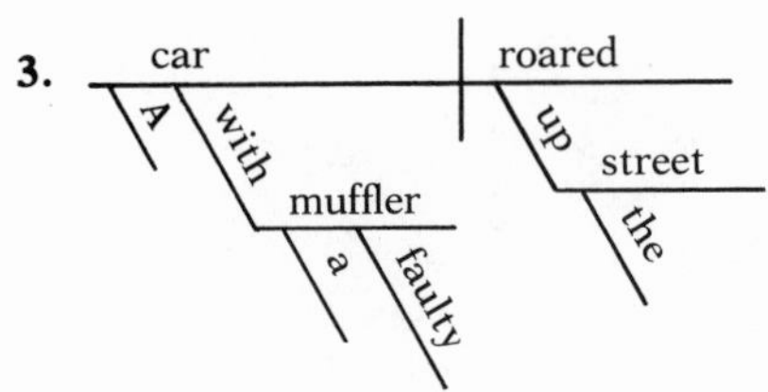

car
roared
A
with
muffler
a
faulty
up
street
the

4.

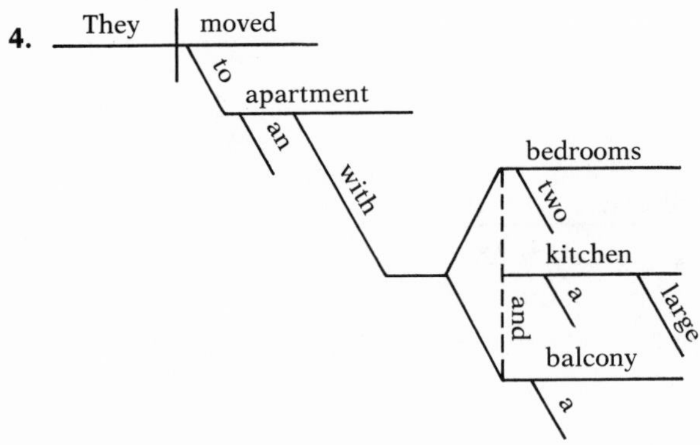

They
moved
to
apartment
an
with
bedrooms
two
kitchen
a
large
and
balcony
a

5.

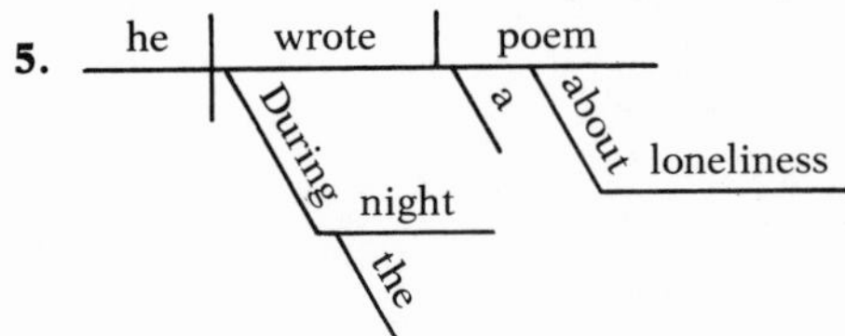

he
wrote
poem
a
about
loneliness
During
night
the

Exercise B (p. 146)

1\.

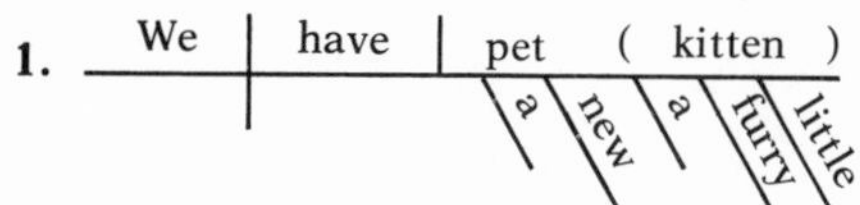

2\.

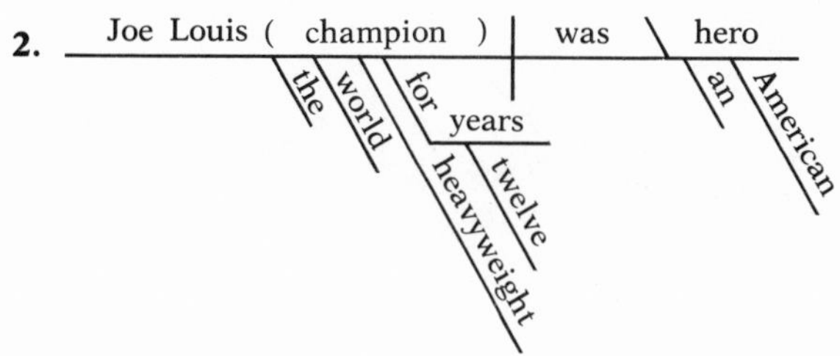

3\.

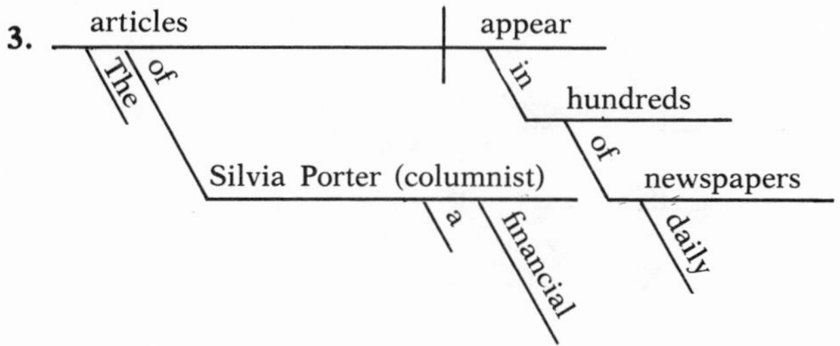

4\.

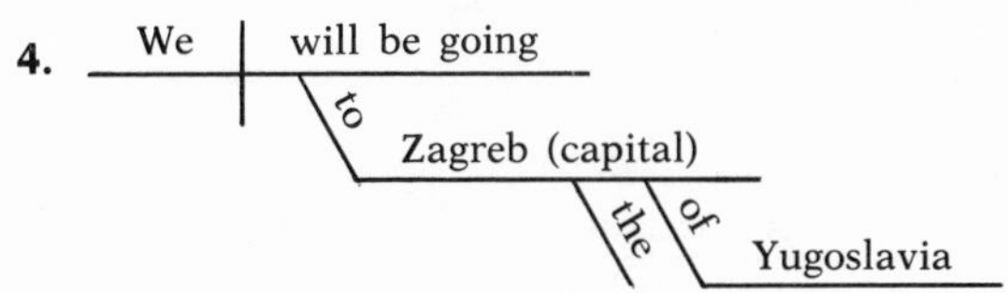

5\.

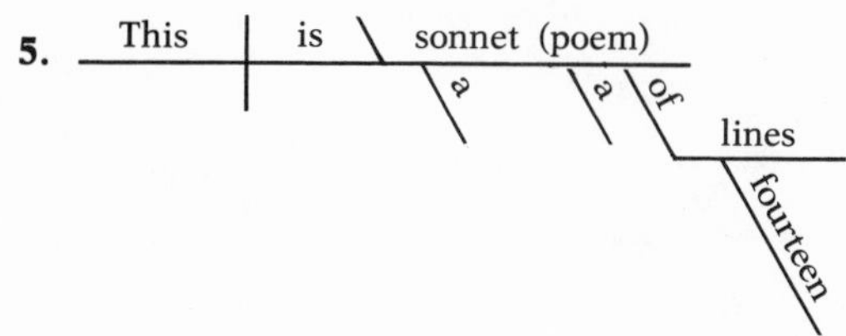

Application (pp. 146–147)

1. 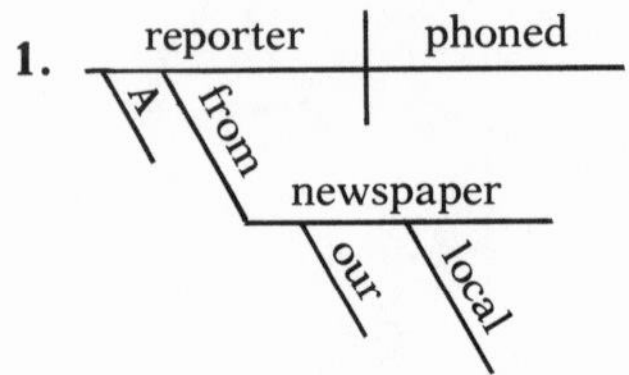

2. 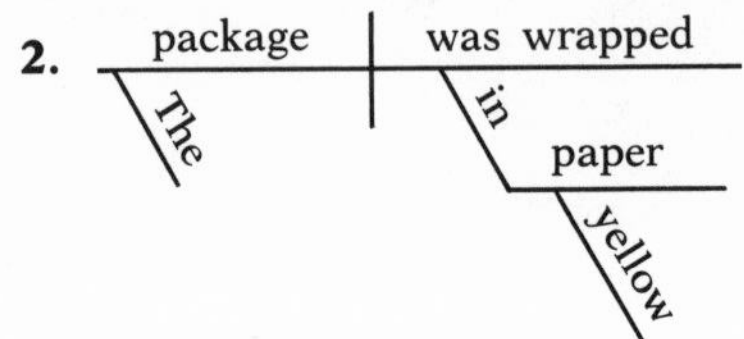

3. 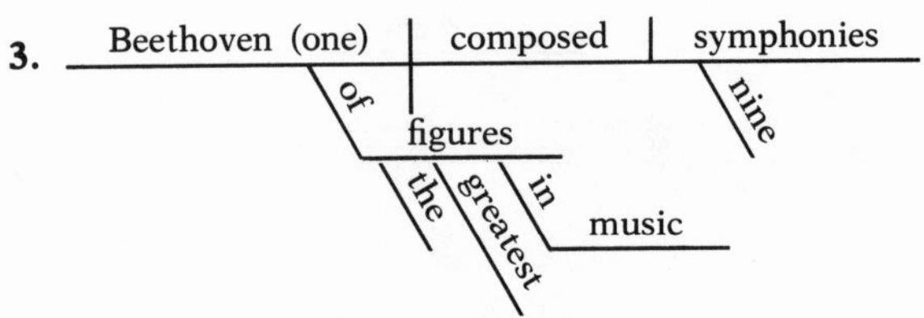

4. 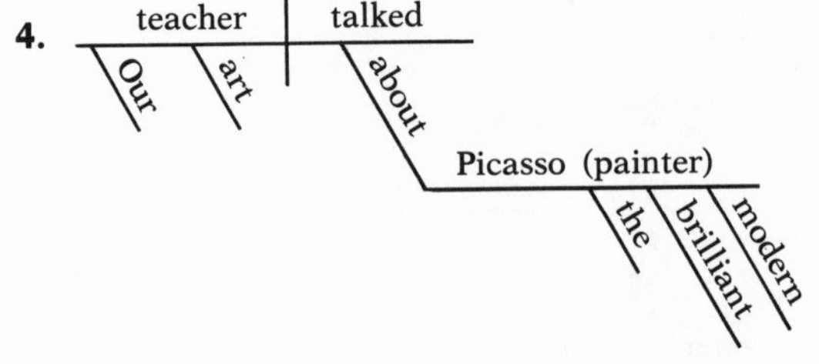

5. 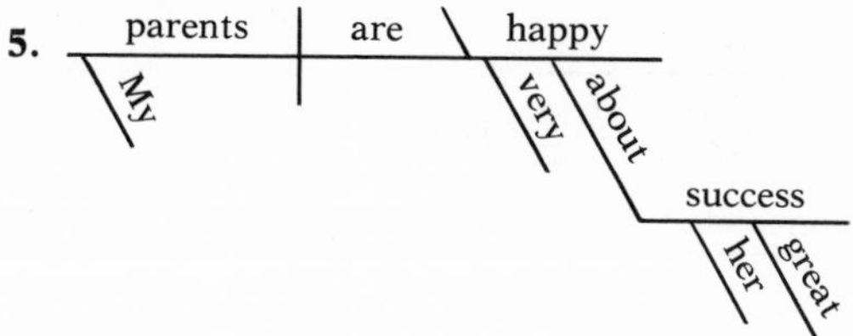
parents
are
happy
My
very
about
success
her
great

6. 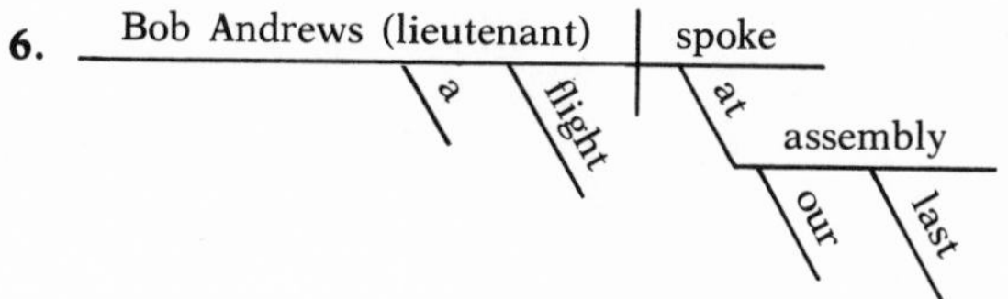
Bob Andrews (lieutenant)
spoke
a
flight
at
assembly
our
last

7. 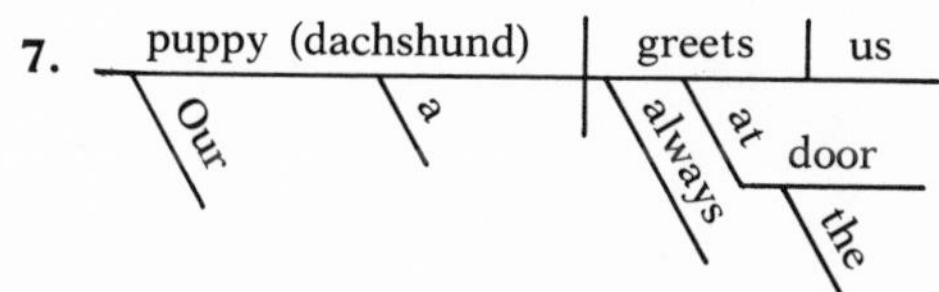
puppy (dachshund)
greets
us
Our
a
always
at
door
the

8. 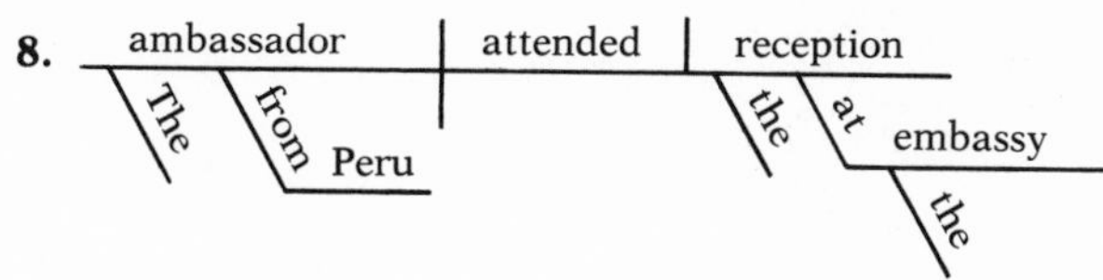
ambassador
attended
reception
The
from
Peru
the
at
embassy
the

9. 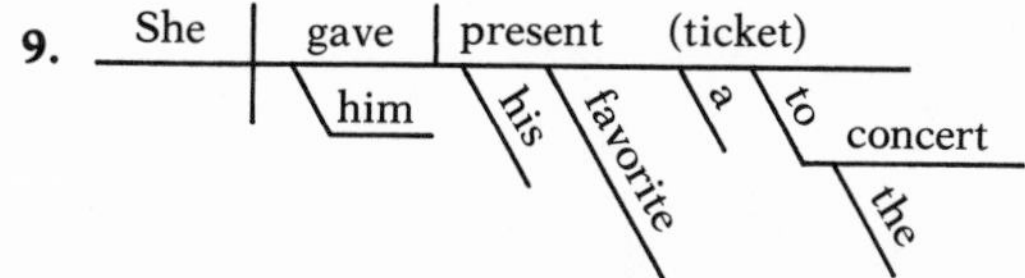
She
gave
present (ticket)
him
his
favorite
a
to
concert
the

10.

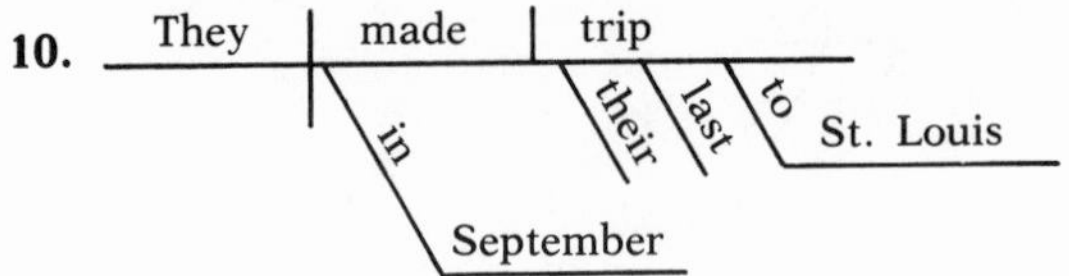

Section 9.4 Diagraming Clauses

Exercise A (p. 164)

1.

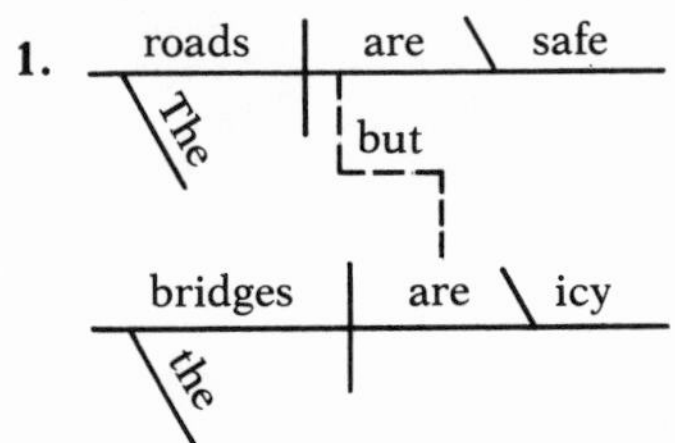

2.

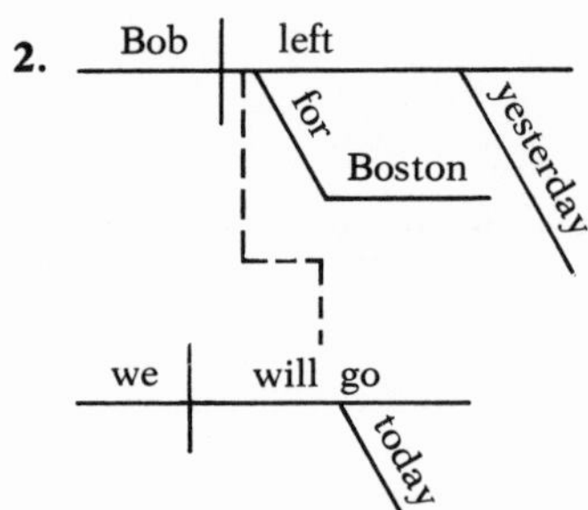

3.

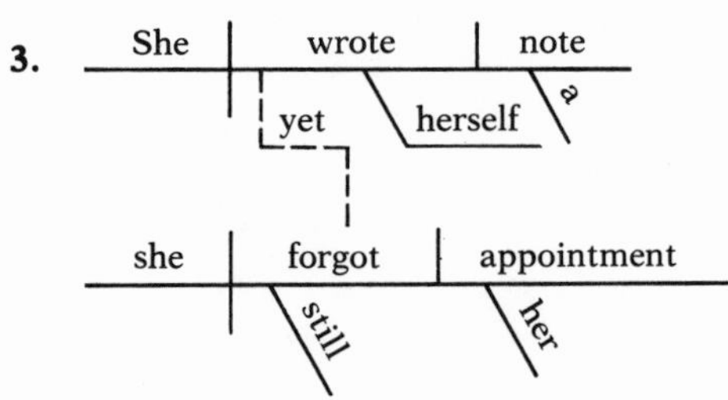

4. 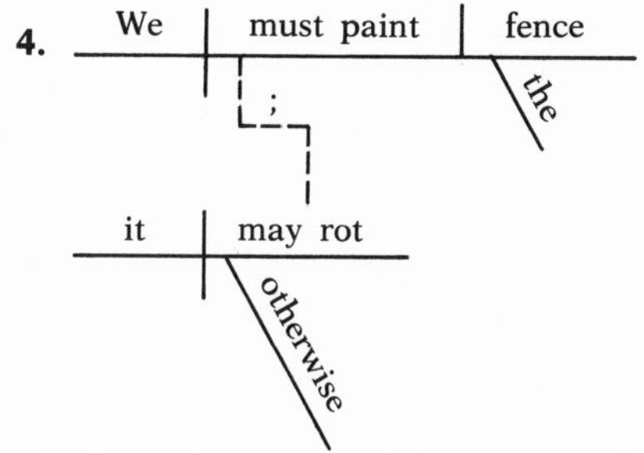

5. 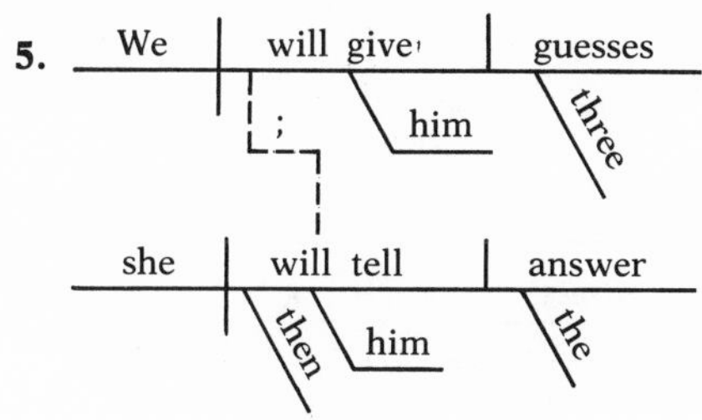

Exercise B (p. 166)

1. 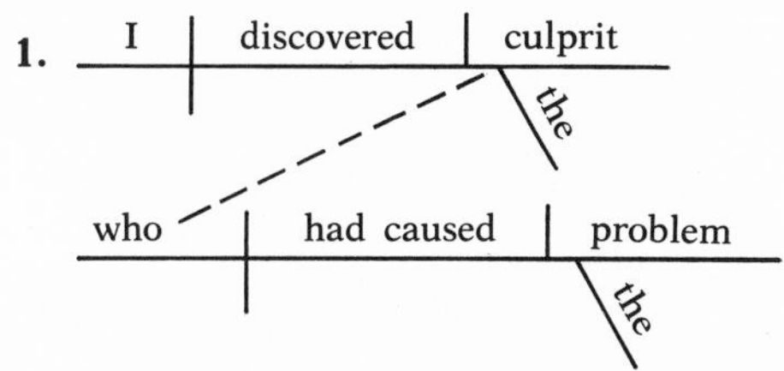

2. 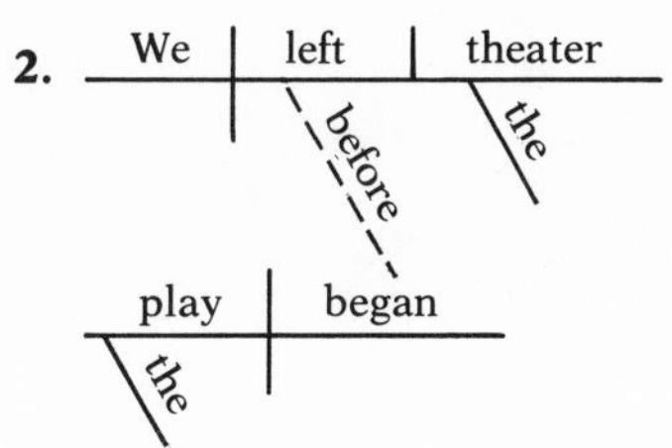

3.

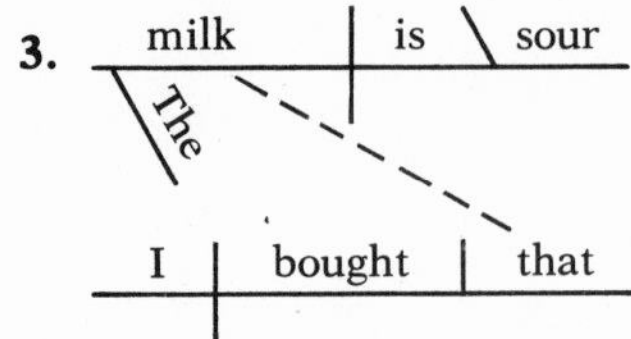

4.

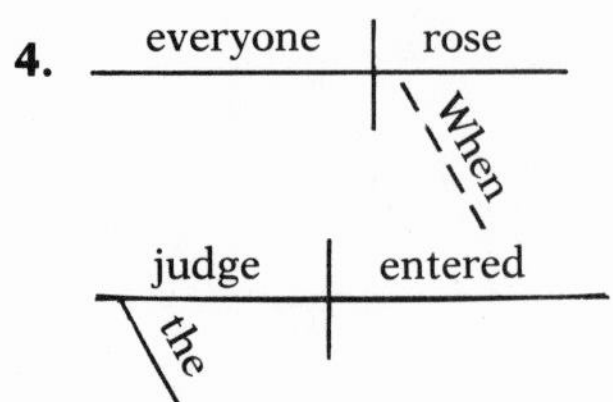

5.

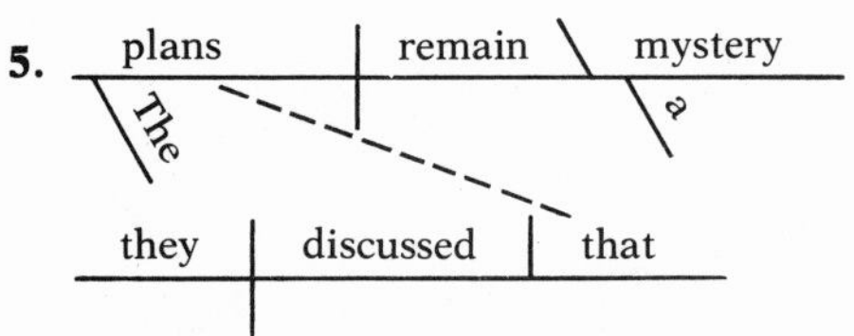

Application (p. 166)

1.

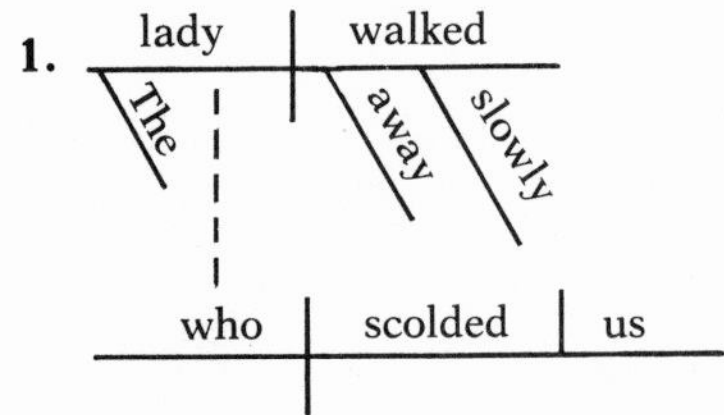

2.

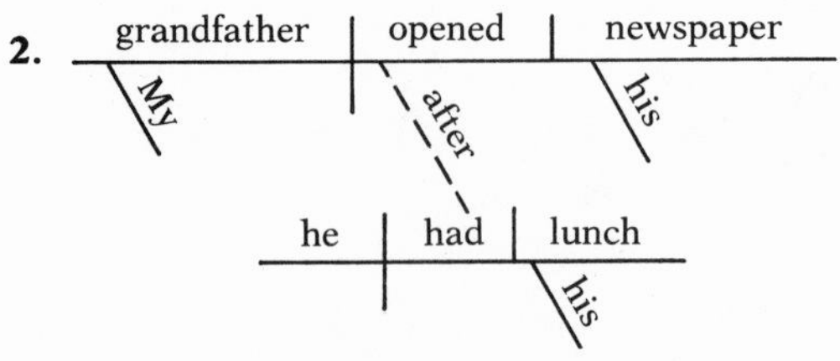

3.

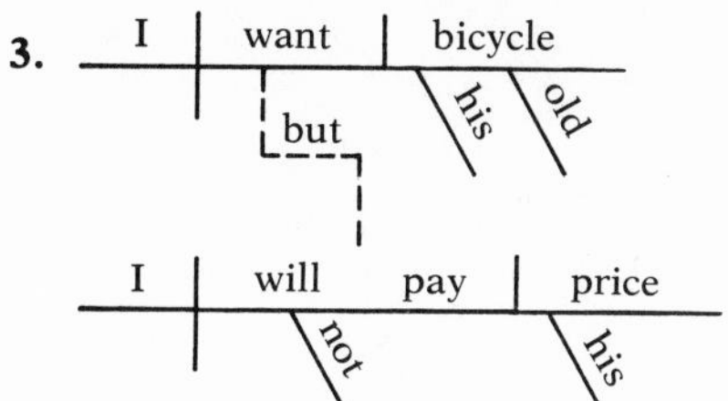

I
want
bicycle
his
old
but
I
will
pay
price
not
his

4.

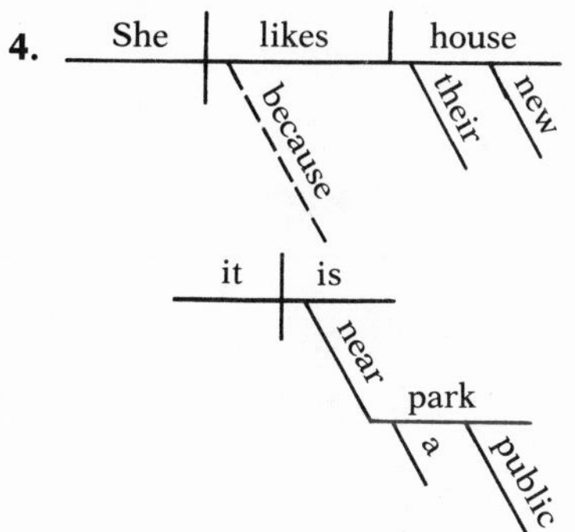

She
likes
house
their
new
because
it
is
near
park
a
public

5.

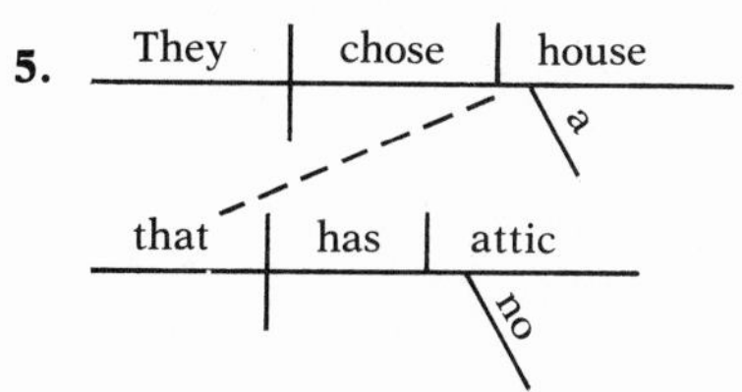

They
chose
house
a
that
has
attic
no

6.

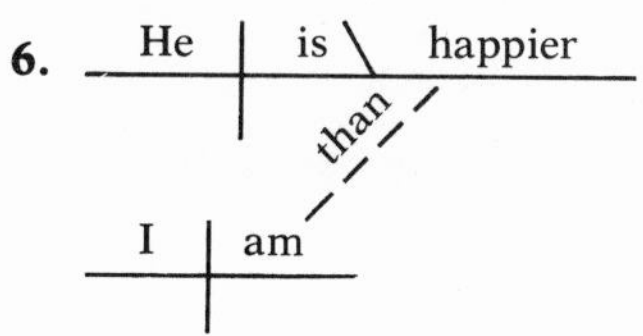

He
is
happier
than
I
am

7.

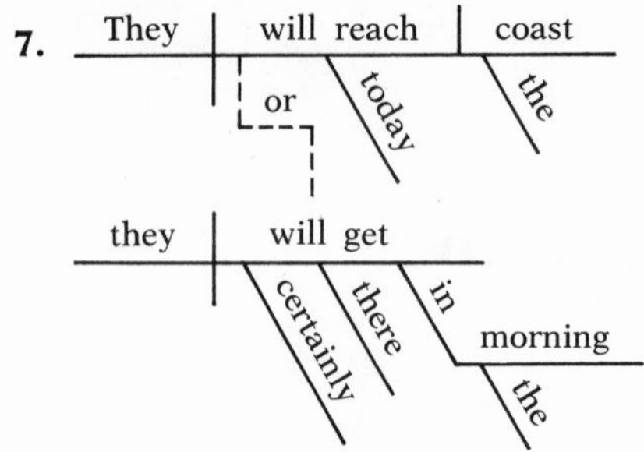

8.

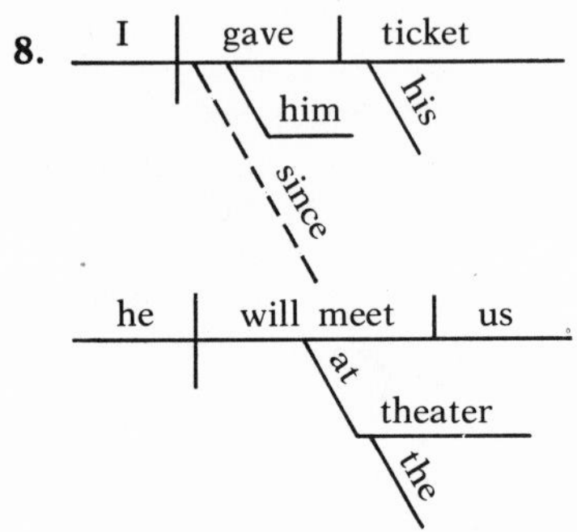

9.

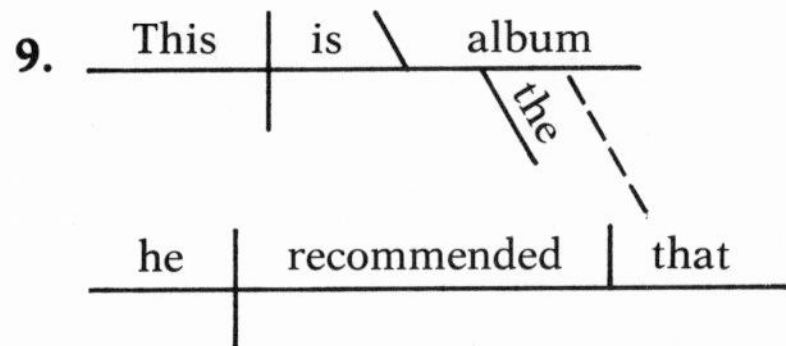

10. We | have been expecting | letter

a

but

none | has arrived

Unit 11 Usage

Section 11.4 Active and Passive Voice

Application (pp. 214–215)

(1) After years of preparation and many delays, the United States launched the first space shuttle in 1981. (2) The shuttle had been designed by NASA engineers to make a number of voyages into outer space. (3) The spacecraft *Columbia* made the very first voyage on April 12, 1981. (4) Astronauts John Young and Robert Crippen manned the spaceship. (5) These men had been carefully trained for many years by NASA to participate in the space shuttle program. (6) The *Columbia* was lifted into space from Cape Canaveral by several rockets that could be reused by the space program. (7) The Navy later recovered these rockets from the Atlantic Ocean. (8) The spacecraft with its human cargo orbited the earth for two days. (9) Astronauts Young and Crippen finally guided it back to the earth and landed it on the ground at Bakersfield, California. (10) Millions of Americans heralded the successful flight as this country's return to outer space.

Unit III Mechanics

Section 16.6 Capitals in Letters

Application (p. 312)

1416 Miller Avenue
Ann Arbor, Michigan 48103
November 19, 1982

Dear Jessica,

We are having a Thanksgiving party at our house this coming Wednesday night from 5:00 to 10:00. There will be ten of our friends, lots of pizza and soda, and stereo at top volume! Do say that you can come, and please bring your latest albums.

Mom and Dad are going to chaperone, so I'm sure your mother will let you come. We all hope to see you here on Wednesday.

Your good friend,
Sandy

Section 18.6 Quotation Marks with Direct Quotations

Exercise D (pp. 364–365)

(1) "This is quite a large crowd," Andrea whispered to her friends.

(2) "You're right," answered Paul. (3) "I understand that this speaker is a famous expert on the Old West."

(4) Bill, who was sitting on Andrea's left, joined the conversation by asking, "Why do you think that topic is so popular?"

(5) "It may have something to do with the programs on television," Andrea suggested.

Unit IV Vocabulary and Spelling

Section 19.4 Exploring Word Origins

Exercise E (p. 412)

1. equipment worn by divers for breathing under water, an acronym for *s*elf-*c*ontained *u*nderwater *b*reathing *a*pparatus
2. unreasoning devotion to one's country, after a soldier of Napoleon named Chauvin
3. a poisonous alkaloid in tobacco, after a French ambassador named Nicot who first introduced tobacco into France
4. a distant, starlike celestial object, an acronym for *quas*i and stell*ar*
5. a system to speed mail deliveries, an acronym for *Z*oning *I*mprovement *P*lan
6. an acronym for *N*ational *A*eronautics and *S*pace *A*dministration
7. to destroy bacteria in milk by heating, after a French scientist named Pasteur who developed the process
8. a type of engine, after a German inventor named Diesel
9. an acronym for *O*rganization of *P*etroleum *E*xporting *C*ountries
10. a sweater that opens down the front, after the seventh Earl of Cardigan

Unit V Study Skills

Section 21.2 Developing Your Listening Skills

Exercise A (pp. 445–446)

Paragraph 1:
1. The importance of water conservation during a drought
2. (a) reservoirs low and dry spring forecast
   (b) need for cooperation from companies and individuals
   (c) specific methods of saving water
3. Failure to conserve water now may mean rationing next summer.

Paragraph 2:
1. Dehydration in winter
2. (a) loss of body fluids caused by cold, dry air
   (b) need for three to four quarts of water daily
   (c) use of melted rather than raw snow
3. Body fluids must be replaced in winter as well as in summer.

Section 21.3 Developing Your Note-Taking Skills

Exercise B (pp. 453–454)

I. Epidemics during Middle Ages
   A. Contributing factors
      1. Poverty
      2. Poor sanitation
      3. Migration
   B. Kinds of diseases
      1. Typhus
      2. Cholera
      3. Influenza
      4. Black plague

II. Extent of black plague
   A. Killed ¼ of Europe's population between 1347–1351
   B. Affected almost every family

III. Resulting panic
    A. People desperate
    B. Doctors helpless
    C. Worthless remedies
        1. Sitting between two fires
        2. Rubbing perfume on walls
        3. Letting spiders spin webs
        4. Drinking red wine in which steel had been cooled
        5. Placing bread on a victim's mouth
IV. Cause and cure
    A. Cause identified in 1894
        1. Bacillus
        2. Carried by fleas
    B. Cure discovered in 1940

PRENTICE-HALL

Grammar and Composition

Level 2

SERIES CONSULTANTS

Level 1

Ellen G. Manhire
English Consultant Coordinator
Fresno, California

Level 2

Elizabeth A. Nace
Supervisor, Language Arts
Akron, Ohio

Level 3

Jerry Reynolds
Supervisor, Language Arts
Rochester, Minnesota

Level 4

Marlene Corbett
Chairperson, Department of English
Charlotte, North Carolina

Level 5

Gilbert Hunt
Chairperson, Department of English
Manchester, Connecticut

Level 6

Margherite LaPota
Curriculum Specialist
Tulsa, Oklahoma

CRITIC READERS FOR LEVEL 2

James E. Coomber
Concordia College
Moorhead, Minnesota

Patricia Edwards
Jordan School District
Sandy, Utah

Elaine Holden
James Mastricola Middle School
Merrimack, New Hampshire

Ruth Hudson
Carnage Middle School
Raleigh, North Carolina

Howard D. Peet
North Dakota State University
Fargo, North Dakota

Irwin P. Riddle
Webber Junior High School
Saginaw, Michigan

Maria Salinas
Camden City Schools
Camden, New Jersey

Barbara Sirotin
Arlington Heights Public Schools
Arlington Heights, Illinois

Mary Smith
Gillespie Junior High School
Philadelphia, Pennsylvania

Harry E. Southey
Memorial Boulevard School
Bristol, Connecticut

Kay Stalcup
Carmel Junior High School
Carmel, Indiana

Prentice-Hall

Grammar and Composition

Level 2

SERIES AUTHORS

Mary Beth Bauer, Language Arts Consultant, Houston, Texas

Lawrence Biener, Chairperson, Department of English, Locust Valley, New York

Linda Capo, Writer and English Teacher, Ithaca, New York

Gary Forlini, Writer and English Teacher, Pelham, New York

Karen L. Moore, English and Speech Teacher, Saratoga, California

Darla Shaw, Reading Coordinator, Ridgefield, Connecticut

Zenobia Verner, Professor of Curriculum and Instruction, Houston, Texas

PRENTICE-HALL, INC., Englewood Cliffs, New Jersey

SERIES TITLES

Prentice-Hall Grammar and Composition: Level 1

Prentice-Hall Grammar and Composition: Level 2

Prentice-Hall Grammar and Composition: Level 3

Prentice-Hall Grammar and Composition: Level 4

Prentice-Hall Grammar and Composition: Level 5

Prentice-Hall Grammar and Composition: Level 6

SUPPLEMENTARY MATERIALS

Annotated Teacher's Editions—Levels 1–6

Test Program—Levels 1–6

Acknowledgments: page 703

ISBN 0-13-696765-5

10 9 8 7 6 5 4 3 2 1

Prentice-Hall International, Inc., London
Prentice-Hall of Australia Pty. Ltd., Sydney
Prentice-Hall Canada Inc., Toronto
Prentice-Hall of India Private Ltd., New Delhi
Prentice-Hall of Japan, Inc., Tokyo
Prentice-Hall of Southeast Asia Pte. Ltd., Singapore
Whitehall Books Limited, Wellington, New Zealand

Contents

Vocabulary and Spelling 389

Study Skills 435

Preface

This book has a single purpose—to help you deal more effectively with the English language. The content, organization, and special features have all been designed to help you reach this goal.

Content

Unit One, Grammar, covers parts of speech and the parts of sentences, while giving you a number of useful methods for correcting basic sentence errors. Unit Two, Usage, zeroes in on problems that may arise in using verbs, pronouns, adjectives, and adverbs and includes a special section listing twenty common usage problems along with their solutions. Unit Three, Mechanics, helps you decide when to capitalize, when to abbreviate, and when to use commas, quotation marks, and other forms of punctuation. Unit Four, Vocabulary and Spelling, provides strategies for building your knowledge of words and improving your spelling. Unit Five, Study Skills, offers numerous ideas for getting more out of the time you spend studying, listening, reading, and using the library. Unit Six, Composition, begins with ideas for making your sentences clearer and more interesting, moves on to steps for writing paragraphs, and ends with steps and other useful methods for writing essays, reports, stories, and letters.

Organization

While your class may study any or all of the sections in the book in depth, you will find that the book has an equally important use as a reference work, not only in your English classes but also on any other occasions when you want to write or speak with particular effectiveness.

As a Textbook. All the units are divided into chapters, each of which is divided into sections. The sections themselves are then divided into subsections. A glance at the Table of Contents, which begins on page 5, and a brief survey of a few of the text chapters should show you how this works.

The sections are short and can usually be covered in a day or two. Before beginning each section, you will find it useful to preview the subsections. Which areas do you consider yourself strong in? Which areas are you weak in? As you work through the subsections, you will find one or more exercises at the end of each subsection. You can use these to preview or test your understanding of the topics covered. At the end of each section, you will find an Application that asks you to put all the skills you have reviewed or learned in the section to work in a practical exercise. This will give you a chance to check your overall understanding and ability to use the material in the section.

As a Reference Tool. In and out of school, you are likely to find situations in which knowing correct punctuation, correct spelling, and standard usage is important. If you have questions on these matters, there are three places you can go in this book to find the answers.

You can check the Table of Contents at the front of the book, you can check the Key of Major Concepts at the back of the book, or you can use the Index. Note that the Index uses bold numbers to show you where to find rules and definitions.

Special Features

In addition to becoming familiar with the overall organization of the text, you may find it useful to explore some of the special features.

Clear Rules. All major rules and definitions are printed in color and written in easy-to-understand language. The bold numbers in the index indicate pages where rules and definitions can be found.

Numerous Examples. For most rules you will find a number of examples, each pointing out a different aspect of the rule. Whether you are studying a section or using it for quick reference, make sure you check all of the examples to be certain you understand all aspects of the rule.

Exercises for Each Subsection. Each subsection has one or more exercises. This will make it possible for you to tell which concepts you have mastered completely and which concepts you will need to review more thoroughly.

Applications for All Sections. The practical Application at the end of each section lets you put to work what you have been learning, generally in some writing exercise. At the same time, you will be checking your mastery of the ideas in the section.

Charts Covering Important Concepts. Throughout the book you will find important concepts highlighted in charts. This will make it possible for you to identify these concepts quickly and check your understanding and knowledge of essential ideas.

Charts Offering Useful Steps. Charts are also used to illustrate step-by-step processes: for using context clues in reading, for writing summaries, for developing different materials in compositions, and for numerous other topics.

Checklists. One of the most important uses of charts is for revision checklists. What should you do when you have finished writing the first draft of a paragraph or essay? The checklists in the composition unit give some valuable suggestions.

Numerous Composition Models. One of the best ways to improve your own writing skill is to examine the work of professional writers and of other students. Throughout the composition unit, you will find models by other writers with important elements clearly labeled.

A Special Unit on Study Skills. The study skills unit can help you review and develop a number of skills that will be immediately useful in a number of situations. The discussion of textbook reading aids in Section 22.2 may be especially helpful.

A Special Section on Preparing Papers. This section, found at the end of the book, can be immensely useful any time you need to prepare a written work that you want to be well received.

Three Reference Aids. The Table of Contents, the Index, and the Key of Major Concepts at the back of the book all can help you zero in on the rules and examples you need when you are using the book for quick reference.

UNIT I

Grammar

Chapter 1

Nouns and Pronouns

Have you ever watched anyone build a stone wall? Choosing each stone for its size and shape, a person must build the wall one stone at a time. Building a sentence is a little like building a stone wall.

Words, like stones, must be chosen carefully, one at a time, and fitted together to make a sentence. The more you know about words, the easier it will be for you to do this. One good way to begin learning about words is to look at the eight kinds of words in English.

The eight kinds of words in English are known as the *parts of speech*. The eight parts of speech are *nouns, pronouns, verbs, adjectives, adverbs, prepositions, conjunctions,* and *interjections.* In this chapter you will learn about the first two kinds, nouns and pronouns.

1.1 Nouns

Nouns are naming words. Nouns help people identify what they are talking or thinking about. *Grandfather, ice cream, loyalty,* and *Ohio* are all nouns.

A **noun** is the name of a person, place, or thing.

People, Places, and Things

Study the list of nouns in the following chart. You may be surprised to find that some of these words are nouns.

People	
farmer	Mrs. Wilson
Bostonians	pilot
Places	
Chicago	waiting room
theater	Madison Square Garden
Things	
Living and Nonliving Things That You Can See	
flowers	ballpoint pen
goldfish	skyscraper
elephant	poem
Ideas and Things That You Can Not Usually See	
success	revolution
happiness	fairness
anger	health

EXERCISE A: Classifying Nouns. All the words in the following list are nouns. Make three columns on your paper and label them as shown. Then place each word in the correct column.

EXAMPLE: People Places Things
carrot

1. teacher *people*
2. grizzly bear *things*
3. sadness *things*
4. city *things*
5. basketball *things*
6. uprising *things*
7. Frank *people*
8. ranch *places*
9. heroism *things*
10. newspaper *things*
11. Maine *places*
12. fable *things*
13. flower *things*
14. justice *things*
15. countryside *places*
16. Mary Stuart *people*
17. vegetables *things*
18. silliness *things*
19. Atlantic Ocean *places*
20. truth *things*

Collective Nouns

Certain nouns name groups of people or things. For example, a *jury* is a group of people; a *herd* is a group of animals. These nouns are called *collective nouns.*

A **collective noun** is a noun that names a group of individual people or things.

Following are some examples of collective nouns.

COLLECTIVE NOUNS		
team	committee	group
class	crowd	audience

EXERCISE B: Recognizing Collective Nouns. On your paper list the twenty nouns from the following sentences. Circle the five that are collective nouns.
Collective nouns are shaded.

EXAMPLE: Marie shocked the audience with her final words.

Marie (audience) words

1. A panel of scientists debated the probability of life on other planets.
2. An outlandish sketch of an imaginary Martian amused the audience.
3. The performance of the team improved tremendously after the speech given by the coach.
4. General Pickett led his brigade in a daring charge at Gettysburg.
5. William Shakespeare wrote his plays for one particular company of actors.

Compound Nouns

You have probably used the words *soft* and *drink* separately many times. When both words are used together, however, they form a single noun that has a special meaning, as in "She drank a *soft drink.*"

A **compound noun** is a noun made up of two or more words.

Compound nouns are usually written in one of three ways.

TYPES OF COMPOUND NOUNS		
Separate Words	**Hyphenated Words**	**Combined Words**
high school	cure-all	congresswoman
chief justice	cha-cha	framework
Empire State Building	mother-in-law	classroom

Check a dictionary for the spelling of unfamiliar compound nouns. If a word is not listed in the dictionary, spell it as separate words.

EXERCISE C: Recognizing Compound Nouns. The following paragraph contains ten compound nouns. Copy the paragraph onto your paper and underline each compound noun.

EXAMPLE: There is no way their high school can beat ours this year.

(1) Yesterday in homeroom, Bob and I discussed sports in our junior high school. (2) We both agreed that our victory in volleyball was the highlight of the year. (3) Bob said he couldn't wait to go to high school, where we will be able to play basketball, water polo, and baseball. (4) I myself would like to be a linebacker playing football.

Common and Proper Nouns

All nouns can be divided into two large groups: *common nouns* and *proper nouns*.

A **common noun** names any one of a class of people, places, or things.

A **proper noun** names a specific person, place, or thing.

Common nouns are not capitalized. Proper nouns are always capitalized.

Common Nouns	Proper Nouns
author	Washington Irving
village	Tarrytown
story	"Rikki-tikki-tavi"

EXERCISE D: Identifying Common and Proper Nouns. Copy each of the following nouns onto your paper. Place a *C* after each common noun and a *P* after each proper noun. Then write a proper noun that gives an example of each common noun. Finally, write a common noun that gives an example of a class to which each proper noun belongs.
Illustrations will vary; samples given.

EXAMPLE: Mars

Mars P planet

1. writer *C—Kurt Vonnegut*
2. Chicago *P—city*
3. Zeus *P—god*
4. river *C—Amazon*
5. street *C—High Street*
6. Louisa May Alcott
7. Jamaica *P—country*
8. horse *C—Secretariat*
9. automobile *C—Ford*
10. Blondie *P—singing group*
11. state *C—Maine*
12. singer *C—Elvis*
13. Rockies *P—mountains*
14. relative *C—Aunt Jo*
15. team *C—Dodgers*
16. Washington *P—state*
17. book *C—Quo Vadis*
18. ocean *C—Atlantic*
19. May *P—month*
20. actress *C—Mary Tyler Moore*

6. P—writer

EXERCISE E: Distinguishing Between Common and Proper Nouns. Each of the following items contains three nouns, one of which is a proper noun that has not been capitalized. On your paper write each proper noun correctly with capitals.

EXAMPLE: lion leo kitten

Leo

1. car convertible oldsmobile *Oldsmobile*
2. state district dade county *Dade County*
3. lake erie ocean river *Lake Erie*
4. magazine bible pamphlet *Bible*
5. nation ghana country *Ghana*
6. singer songwriter john lennon *John Lennon*
7. aunt sally relative woman *Aunt Sally*
8. character tom sawyer boy *Tom Sawyer*
9. cartoon movie bambi *Bambi*
10. poet writer emily dickinson *Emily Dickinson*

APPLICATION: Using Nouns in Sentences. Copy each of the following sentences onto your paper. Fill in each blank with an appropriate noun. *Answers will vary; samples given.*

EXAMPLE: The day I like least is ______.

The day I like least is Wednesday.

1. __*Ms. Beadle*__, our principal, visited our class.
2. My father would like to buy a __*camera*__.
3. I just spoke to __*Aunt Sue*__, my favorite relative.
4. The activity I enjoy most is __*chorus*__.
5. I particularly like __*Loretta Lynn*__'s singing style.
6. __*Boston*__ is a city I would like to live in.
7. Is __*Mark Twain*__ your favorite writer?
8. The capital of our state is __*Austin*__.
9. __*Spanish*__ is the next thing I want to learn.
10. For breakfast I often eat __*oatmeal*__.

Pronouns 1.2

Pronouns are words that take the place of nouns. They are generally used when it would not make sense to repeat a noun over and over again. Imagine, for example, that you are writing about Aunt Jenny. If you were using only nouns, you might write the following sentence.

WITH NOUNS: Aunt Jenny was late because *Aunt Jenny* missed *Aunt Jenny's* train.

To avoid using Aunt Jenny's name too often, you would substitute pronouns.

WITH PRONOUNS: Aunt Jenny was late because *she* missed *her* train.

> A **pronoun** is a word that takes the place of a noun or of a group of words acting as a noun.

Sometimes a pronoun takes the place of a noun in the same sentence.

EXAMPLE: My father opened *his* present first.

A pronoun can also take the place of a noun used in an earlier sentence.

EXAMPLE: My father opened his present first. *He* felt *he* couldn't wait any longer.

Finally, a pronoun may take the place of a whole group of words.

EXAMPLE: Trying to make the team is hard work. *It* takes hours of practice every day.

Antecedents of Pronouns

A pronoun is closely related to the noun it replaces. The noun that the pronoun takes the place of has a special name. It is called the *antecedent.*

> An **antecedent** is the noun (or group of words acting as a noun) for which a pronoun stands.

The Latin prefix *ante* means "before," and most antecedents do come *before* the pronouns that take their place. In the preceding examples, *father* and *trying to make the team* are the antecedents of their pronouns.

EXAMPLES: My *father* opened *his* present first. *He* felt *he* couldn't wait any longer.

(Antec: father; Pron: his, He, he)

Trying to make the team is hard work. *It* takes hours of practice every day.

(Antec: Trying to make the team; Pron: It)

Once in a while an antecedent will come after the pronoun.

EXAMPLE: Since *she* is known as a fine soprano, *Lucy* was offered a part in the concert.

(Pron: she; Antec: Lucy)

Finally, a pronoun will sometimes have no definite antecedent at all.

EXAMPLES: *Who* will represent the class?

Everything was lost in the flood.

In these examples the pronouns *who* and *everything* do not stand for any specific person or thing.

EXERCISE A: Recognizing Antecedents. In each of the following sentences, a pronoun is underlined. Find the antecedent for each pronoun and write it on your paper. *Antecedents are shaded.*

EXAMPLE: Somehow Jeff managed to lose his tuba.

Jeff

1. There is a zoo in Arkansas that trains and houses a remarkable group of animals.
2. Visitors at the zoo can see such marvels as Bert Backquack and his all-duck band.
3. The zoo also includes among its residents a roller-skating parrot.

4. The trainers there believe that most animals behave intelligently if they are treated with respect.
5. Davy Crockett's tales made him a legend in his own time.
6. Davy went to Congress claiming that he had wrestled grizzly bears as a child.
7. Fashionable people found themselves competing for Davy's attention at parties.
8. As children, the Brontës created their own private world.
9. To avoid the prejudice against women who wrote, Charlotte and Emily Brontë took pen names.
10. Charlotte called herself "Currer Bell," and her sister became "Ellis Bell."

Personal Pronouns

The pronouns used most often are called *personal pronouns*.

Personal pronouns refer to (1) the person speaking, (2) the person spoken to, or (3) the person, place, or thing spoken about.

Depending on whom or what a personal pronoun refers to, it is called a first-person, second-person, or third-person pronoun. The following chart lists these pronouns in both their singular and plural forms.

PERSONAL PRONOUNS		
	Singular	**Plural**
First Person	I, me, my, mine	we, us, our, ours
Second Person	you, your, yours	you, your, yours
Third Person	he, him, his she, her, hers it, its	they, them, their, theirs

First-person pronouns, such as *I, my, we,* and *our,* are used by the person or people actually speaking to refer to himself, herself, or themselves.

EXAMPLE: *I* waited for *my* package to arrive.

Second-person pronouns, such as *you* and *your,* have the same form whether they are singular or plural. They are used when a person is speaking directly to another person or to other people.

EXAMPLE: Sheila, *you* left *your* photos on the table.

Third-person pronouns have more forms than do the other types of personal pronouns. Note that there are separate masculine pronouns *(he, him, his)* and feminine pronouns *(she, her, hers)* for people and neuter pronouns *(it, its)* for things. Third-person pronouns are used to refer to someone or something that may not even be present.

EXAMPLE: I haven't seen my grandfather in a year. *He* will arrive from Florida tomorrow.

EXERCISE B: Identifying Personal Pronouns and Their Antecedents. Each of the following sentences contains two personal pronouns. On your paper write each personal pronoun and its antecedent.

Personal pronouns are underlined; antecedents are shaded.

EXAMPLE: Jim, you forgot your hat.

you Jim your Jim

1. Mom, you forgot to call your sister.
2. "I tried to repair my stereo," said Carlos.
3. Since Maggie moved, she has called her friends once a week.
4. Now, boys, you have to clean up your own mess.
5. James tried to reach the doctor, but she was not in her office.
6. My brothers quit the team when they found that their grades were suffering.

7. Marge, yesterday you promised to lend your album to Judy.
8. The book is not as exciting as its jacket suggests, but it has one suspenseful chapter.
9. The McCurdys said that they would volunteer some of their time.
10. Uncle Dan gave his favorite watch to his oldest nephew.

APPLICATION: Using Personal Pronouns in Sentences. Copy each of the following sentences onto your paper. Fill in each blank with an appropriate personal pronoun. *Answers will vary; samples given.*

EXAMPLE: Linus can figure it out if ________ tries.

Linus can figure it out if he tries.

1. ___He___ made another omelet for Keith.
2. ___She___ will make the final decision.
3. They dented ___our___ new station wagon.
4. Betsy finally reached ___them___ by phone.
5. ___They___ carefully prepared for the trip.
6. Unfortunately, ___we___ had broken the window.
7. ___These___ poems are easy to memorize.
8. My sister designs ___her___ own jewelry.
9. ___She___ painted the entire room yesterday.
10. Please give ___me___ five minutes.

1.3 Four Special Kinds of Pronouns

Four other kinds of pronouns play an important part in our language: *demonstrative, relative, interrogative,* and *indefinite pronouns.*

Demonstrative Pronouns

Demonstrative pronouns are pointers.

A **demonstrative pronoun** points out a specific person, place, or thing.

There are four demonstrative pronouns, two singular and two plural.

DEMONSTRATIVE PRONOUNS	
Singular	**Plural**
this that	these those

A demonstrative pronoun can come before or after its antecedent.

BEFORE: *This* is the book I chose.

Those are my new friends.

AFTER: Of all my stamps, *these* are the most valuable.

We stopped in Bad Neustadt and Salz. *These* are the towns where our ancestors lived.

EXERCISE A: Recognizing Demonstrative Pronouns. Each of the following items contains a demonstrative pronoun. On your paper write each demonstrative pronoun.

EXAMPLE: That is not the record I would have chosen.

That

1. Those are the most expensive dresses in the store.
2. Of all the Beatles' records, these are their best.
3. Until recently a knowledge of Latin and Greek was considered essential to a liberal education. These are no longer even taught in many schools.
4. These are the three most popular exhibits.
5. Of all his ideas, those are the strangest.
6. This is the artist I want you to meet.
7. You may help by peeling the carrots. That is your first chore.
8. He raises bromeliads. These are a kind of exotic plant.
9. That seems to be their busiest time of the year.
10. This was all she said before leaving: "I'll be back."

Relative Pronouns

Relative pronouns are connecting words.

A **relative pronoun** begins a subordinate clause and connects it to another idea in the same sentence.

There are five relative pronouns.

RELATIVE PRONOUNS				
that	which	who	whom	whose

The following chart gives examples of relative pronouns connecting subordinate clauses to independent clauses. (See Section 9.1 for more information about relative pronouns and clauses.)

Independent Clauses	Subordinate Clauses
Here is the book	that Betsy lost.
Dino bought our old house,	which needs many repairs.
She is a singer	who has an unusual range.
Is this the man	whom you saw earlier today?
She is the one	whose house has a fire alarm.

EXERCISE B: Recognizing Relative Pronouns. Each of the following sentences contains a relative pronoun. On your paper write each relative pronoun.

EXAMPLE: The person who left has just volunteered.

who

1. A leader whom our nation will never forget is Abraham Lincoln.

2. She chose a hat that matched her gown.
3. I will spend the summer vacation with my cousin who lives in Kingston.
4. The pipe that had leaked for a month finally burst.
5. The woman who was chosen scientist of the year works as a biochemist.
6. We joined the club whose introductory offer was the best.
7. The experimental car, which runs on batteries, does not pollute the air.
8. The pupil who gets the scholarship must excel in mathematics.
9. The dancer whom we admired most performed two solos.
10. Can you find a button that matches the others?

Interrogative Pronouns

Some relative pronouns can also be used as *interrogative pronouns*.

An **interrogative pronoun** is used to begin a question.

All together there are five interrogative pronouns.

INTERROGATIVE PRONOUNS				
what	which	who	whom	whose

Interrogative pronouns often do not have antecedents. In the following examples, only two of the interrogative pronouns have antecedents.

EXAMPLES: *What* did she win at the bazaar?

Here are two choices. *Which* do you want?

Who is the owner of that cassette recorder?

Whom did they want to speak to?

Mine is finished. *Whose* is not?

EXERCISE C: Recognizing Interrogative Pronouns. Each of the following items contains an interrogative pronoun. On your paper write each interrogative pronoun.

EXAMPLE: Which of the colors goes best with this sweater?
Which

1. Which of Ernest Hemingway's novels takes place during the Spanish Civil War?
2. One President of the United States served as Chief Justice of the Supreme Court after he left office. Who was this President?
3. What are the main differences between the rules for professional football and the rules for college football?
4. Which is your favorite Joni Mitchell song?
5. A special symbol is hidden in this painting. What is the symbol?
6. Whom did Tom Sawyer and Becky Thatcher see when they were lost in the cave?
7. Who pitched the only perfect game in World Series history?
8. What did Dorothy do to escape from the Wicked Witch of the West?
9. Who was the first woman to be elected to the United States Congress?
10. For whom did Lewis Carroll write *Alice in Wonderland*?

Indefinite Pronouns

You should learn to recognize one other kind of pronoun—the *indefinite pronoun*.

Indefinite pronouns refer to people, places, or things, often without specifying which ones.

In the following chart, notice that a few indefinite pronouns can be either singular or plural, depending upon their use.

INDEFINITE PRONOUNS			
Singular		**Plural**	**Singular or Plural**
another	much	both	all
anybody	neither	few	any
anyone	nobody	many	more
anything	no one	others	most
each	nothing	several	none
either	one		some
everybody	other		
everyone	somebody		
everything	someone		
little	something		

Like interrogative pronouns, indefinite pronouns do not always have antecedents.

WITHOUT ANTECEDENTS: *Anyone* can volunteer to serve hot dogs at the game.

Many cheered when the President arrived.

WITH ANTECEDENTS: *All* of the students volunteered to sell hot dogs at the game.

The guests gathered eagerly. *Many* cheered when he arrived.

EXERCISE D: Recognizing Indefinite Pronouns. Each of the following sentences contains at least one indefinite pronoun. On your paper write the indefinite pronoun or pronouns from each sentence.

EXAMPLE: Nobody went to see that movie.

Nobody

1. Everyone applauded the winner of the marathon.
2. The coach asked all of the girls to prepare thoroughly for the match.
3. Most of the students are interested in computers, but few know how they actually work.
4. Few of my classmates knew anything about Susan B. Anthony.
5. The auditorium was so dark that we could see nothing.
6. Did someone remember to turn on the lights?
7. Somebody has taken one of the dictionaries.
8. Neither wanted to go, but it was important for both to attend.
9. Little is known about the people who built Stonehenge.
10. No one knew why some of the pages had been torn from his diary.

APPLICATION: Writing Sentences with Pronouns. Copy each of the following sentences onto your paper, filling in the blank with the kind of pronoun indicated in parentheses. *Answers will vary; samples given.*

1. What 2. that 3. Many 4. these 5. Both

EXAMPLE: Where is the person __(relative)__ borrowed my book?

Where is the person who borrowed my book?

6. Who 7. that 8. some 9. this 10. Which

1. __(Interrogative)__ did you expect to find in the cellar?
2. This is the house __(relative)__ I want to purchase.
3. __(Indefinite)__ in the room applauded the decision.
4. Are __(demonstrative)__ the winners of the tournament?
5. __(Indefinite)__ of the girls received a reward.
6. __(Interrogative)__ is going to the party?
7. This is the book __(relative)__ you should read.
8. Would you like __(indefinite)__ of the pie?
9. I don't like __(demonstrative)__ .
10. __(Interrogative)__ of the poems is yours?

Chapter 2

Verbs

The *verb* is a necessary part of every sentence. It helps tell whether an event is taking place in the present, past, or future. Verbs do more, however, than just tell time. Some verbs express action. Other verbs provide a link between two parts of a sentence. Still others simply point out that something exists.

This chapter will describe the two main kinds of verbs—*action verbs* and *linking verbs*—and will show you how these verbs can be used with another kind of verb—*helping verbs.*

Action Verbs 2.1

The following are verbs that are used all the time: *see, plan, run, eat, shout, tell,* and *sit.* All these verbs have one thing in common. They all express *action.*

An **action verb** tells what action a person or thing is performing.

EXAMPLES: My father *waited* at the station for the train.

The swans *float* gracefully on the water.

In each of these examples, the verb describes the action that is taking place. The verb *waited* tells what *father* did. The verb *float* tells what *swans* do. In these sentences the performers of the action *(father, swans)* are the *subjects* of the verbs. (See Chapter 7 for more information about subjects.)

Visible and Mental Action

It is useful to be able to recognize the different kinds of action that action verbs can express. Some actions are *visible*. You can see, for example, a group of swans flying or swimming. You can also see swans floating, even though little movement is going on. You can also see someone waiting.

Some other actions can be seen only with difficulty, if at all. These are usually *mental* actions. Compare the two kinds of action in the following chart.

Visible Action		Mental Action	
walk	spin	wonder	remember
stand	sing	think	dream
put	slide	believe	consider
open	chase	worry	decide

EXERCISE A: Recognizing Action Verbs. On your paper write the action verb from each sentence. After each verb write *visible* or *mental* to identify the kind of action the verb shows. Note that half are visible and half are mental.

EXAMPLE: People once believed in goblins.

believed mental

1. The *Concorde* flies quickly across the Atlantic. *visible*
2. For many weeks Columbus and his crew worried about reaching land. *mental*
3. Juan dreamed of his family in Cuba. *mental*
4. The quarterback threw a long pass. *visible*
5. The receiver barely caught the ball. *visible*
6. Elizabeth Kenny developed a treatment for polio.
7. She considered warmth and exercise to be the best therapy. *mental*
8. He remembers many events from World War II.
9. Weeds suddenly sprouted all over our front lawn.
10. She believed in justice and freedom for all.

6. visible 8. mental 9. visible 10. mental

■ Transitive Verbs

Some action verbs are *transitive.*

An action verb is **transitive** if the receiver of the action is named in the sentence.

The receiver of the action is called the *object* of the verb.

EXAMPLES: Sandy *opened* the window with great difficulty.

The truck suddenly *hit* the pedestrian.

In the first example, *window* receives the action of the verb *opened. Opened* is transitive because the sentence has an object *(window)* that tells *what* Sandy opened. In the second example, *hit* is transitive because the sentence includes a word that tells *whom* the truck hit. This word is *pedestrian.* (See Section 7.5 for more information about objects of transitive verbs.)

EXERCISE B: Recognizing Transitive Action Verbs. Copy the following sentences onto your paper. Underline the transitive action verb in each sentence and draw an arrow from the verb to its object. *Verbs are underlined; objects are shaded.*

EXAMPLE: Andy hit a home run on her first try.

1. Lightning struck the new building.
2. Later in the day, Beth prepared the entire report.
3. Congress bought its first two navy vessels on October 13, 1775.
4. The train reached the station two hours late.
5. According to legend, Lincoln wrote the Gettysburg Address while on his way to Pennsylvania.
6. Tom chopped enough wood to last through January.
7. In the morning the flood waters reached the top of the barrier.
8. Jan put the groceries away.
9. Louise uses a kerosene heater in her room.

10. My parents planted various flowers near the entrance to our house.

Intransitive Verbs

An action verb can also be *intransitive*.

An action verb is **intransitive** if no receiver of the action is named in the sentence.

A sentence with an intransitive verb will not have an object.

EXAMPLES: My sister *smiled*.

The bus *raced* through the traffic light.

EXERCISE C: Recognizing Intransitive Action Verbs. On your paper write the intransitive action verb in each sentence. Be prepared to explain why the verb is intransitive.

EXAMPLE: He runs faster in the morning.

runs

1. Her ring fell between the planks of the boardwalk.
2. My brother laughed for an hour at the joke.
3. The explorers traveled along the banks of the river.
4. We talked for hours after dinner.
5. Fort Pierre grew slowly from a small trading post near Bad River in Missouri.
6. The spider hovered near the top of the lamp.
7. I awoke before dawn.
8. Pieces of glass tinkled to the floor after the accident.
9. Her magnificent voice soared across the auditorium.
10. The tiny poodle stepped daintily around the patches of mud.

APPLICATION: Writing Sentences with Action Verbs. The following ten verbs can be used as either transitive verbs or intransitive verbs. Use each of the ten verbs in *two* sentences of your own, once as a transitive verb and once as an intransitive verb. Label your sentences *transitive* or *intransitive* and underline the verbs.

Answers will vary; samples given for first one.

EXAMPLE: read

He read the novel in a week. transitive

After lunch, he read until dinner. intransitive

1. Frogs eat insects. trans / We usually eat in the dining room. intrans

1. eat	3. grow	5. visit	7. finish	9. shout
2. jump	4. write	6. swim	8. play	10. drop

Linking Verbs 2.2

A few widely used verbs do not show action. These are *linking verbs.*

A **linking verb** connects a noun or pronoun at or near the beginning of a sentence with a word at or near the end.

Study the words before and after the linking verbs in the following examples. Note that the words after the linking verbs identify or describe the words that come before the verbs.

EXAMPLES: Rita *is* a dentist.

The winners *were* Tony and I.

He *looks* old.

The linking verbs *is, were,* and *looks* act almost as equal signs between the words they link.

Forms of *Be*

The verb *be* is the most commonly used linking verb in English. You should learn all of its many forms.

THE FORMS OF *BE*		
am	can be	have been
are	could be	has been
is	may be	had been
was	might be	could have been
were	must be	may have been
am being	shall be	might have been
are being	should be	must have been
is being	will be	shall have been
was being	would be	should have been
were being		will have been
		would have been

EXERCISE A: Recognizing Forms of *Be* as Linking Verbs. Copy each of the following sentences onto your paper. Underline the form of *be* in each. Then draw a double-headed arrow connecting the words that are linked by the verb. *Verbs are underlined; linked words are shaded.*

EXAMPLE: Edgar Allan Poe was a writer of great imagination.

1. Ringo Starr was the drummer for the Beatles.
2. The National League has been victorious in most recent All-Star games.
3. Edgar Allan Poe was for a short time a cadet at West Point.
4. The writer of supernatural tales might have been a strange general.
5. Marie Curie was the winner of two Nobel Prizes.
6. Your first choice should be the new Rod Stewart album.
7. Halley's Comet will be visible from parts of the United States in 1986.
8. Americans were fearful and excited about its last visit in 1910.
9. Ethel Barrymore was part of a famous theatrical family.
10. This family of actors had been successful on the stage before working in movies.

Other Linking Verbs

In addition to the verb *be,* a number of other verbs can be used as linking verbs.

OTHER LINKING VERBS					
appear	feel	look	seem	sound	taste
become	grow	remain	smell	stay	turn

These verbs often set up the same relationship between words as the linking verb *be* does. The words after the verbs identify or describe the words that come before the verbs.

EXAMPLE: Rita *became* a dentist.

Everything *smells* damp and musty.

He *looks* very old.

EXERCISE B: Identifying Other Linking Verbs. Copy each of the following sentences onto your paper. Underline the linking verb in each. Then draw a double-headed arrow connecting the words that are linked by the verb. *Verbs are underlined; linked words are shaded.*

EXAMPLE: The chili tastes delicious.

1. The plant grew sturdy in the hothouse.
2. Gold coins seem a better investment.
3. Although far apart the sisters remained good friends.
4. The new chorus sounds even better than the old.
5. Sometimes Alex feels weak and tired.
6. That plant turns brown in the fall.
7. The roast goose looks sensational.
8. At the moment he appears very unhappy.
9. Both sponges smell sour.
10. The noises from the empty house sound strange.

Action Verb or Linking Verb?

Most of the twelve verbs in the chart on page 43 can be used as either linking verbs or action verbs.

LINKING: Richard *felt* sad.

ACTION: The doctor *felt* my pulse.

LINKING: The cake *tasted* too sweet.

ACTION: The chef *tasted* the stew.

To see whether a verb is a linking verb or an action verb, substitute *am, is,* or *are* for the verb. If the sentence still makes sense and if the new verb links a word before it to a word after it, then the original verb is a linking verb.

Linking	Action
The teacher *looked* angry.	The teacher *looked* for chalk.
(The teacher *is* angry?)	(The teacher *is* for chalk?)
Yes, it's a linking verb	No, it's an action verb

EXERCISE C: Distinguishing Between Action Verbs and Linking Verbs. On your paper write the verb from each sentence. After each action verb write *AV* and after each linking verb write *LV*.

EXAMPLE: Lucy smells a rat.

smells AV

1. My aunt in Iowa grows wheat and corn.
2. Just home from the hospital, my sister looked pale.
3. The ghost supposedly appears every night at twelve.
4. The guests stayed at the cottages near the lake.
5. For some reason he remains angry and depressed.
6. The apple and peach pies look absolutely delicious.

7. Lucinda remained at the convention for a full week. *AV*
8. Suddenly the valley became dark and misty. *LV*
9. The butter turned rancid. *LV*
10. Felix seems happy and rested. *LV*

APPLICATION: Writing Sentences with Action and Linking Verbs. Use each of the following verbs in two sentences of your own. Use the verb as a linking verb in the first sentence and as an action verb in the second sentence. *Answers will vary; samples given for first one.*

1. That cake smells delicious. Ferdinand smells the flowers.

EXAMPLE: sound

Jenny sounds too happy this morning.

The bell sounded over the loudspeakers.

1. smell
2. feel
3. appear
4. grow
5. taste

Helping Verbs 2.3

A verb is sometimes just a single word. At other times, however, one verb may be made up of two, three, or four words. This kind of verb is called a *verb phrase.*

Helping verbs are added before another verb to make a **verb phrase.**

In the following examples, the *helping verbs* are italicized. Notice how they help to change the meaning of *opened,* the key part of the verb.

EXAMPLES: opened

has opened

will have opened

could have been opened

Recognizing Helping Verbs

Forms of the verb *be* are often used as helping verbs. You may want to review the forms of *be* in the chart on page 42. In the following chart, the forms of *be* used as helping verbs are italicized.

SOME FORMS OF *BE* USED AS HELPING VERBS	
Helping Verbs	**Verbs**
is	opening
was being	trained
should be	written
had been	sent
might have been	played

Some other verbs can also be used as helping verbs.

OTHER HELPING VERBS			
do	have	shall	can
does	has	should	could
did	had	will	may
		would	might
			must

Many different verb phrases can be formed using one or more of these helping verbs. The following chart shows just a few.

VERB PHRASES	
Helping Verbs	**Verbs**
does	find
had	gone
should	see
will have	talked
might have	told

EXERCISE A: Supplying Helping Verbs. Each of the following sentences contains one or more blanks. Write the sentences on your paper and fill in each blank with an appropriate helping verb. *Answers will vary; samples given.*

EXAMPLE: Ian ________ ________ ________ told not to ask that question.

Ian should have been told not to ask that question.

1. Jose __has__ decided to go away to college.
2. She __had__ __been__ waiting at the station for more than two hours.
3. __Have__ you chosen a topic for your report?
4. She __is__ going to St. Louis on business tomorrow.
5. In another half-hour, she __will__ __have__ __been__ sleeping for twelve hours.
6. My brother __might__ perform the leading role in the show next week.
7. __Can__ you explain why you are late?
8. When __should__ the winners __be__ notified?
9. This __has__ been an almost unbelievable day.
10. He __has__ __been__ telling all sorts of stories about you.

Finding Helping Verbs in Sentences

Sometimes the words making up a verb phrase are separated by other words, such as *not, slowly,* and *carefully*. In certain types of questions, the parts of the verb phrase are usually separated. In the following examples, the parts of each verb phrase are italicized.

WORDS TOGETHER: She *could have been reached* by phone earlier.

WORDS SEPARATED: She *could* certainly *have been reached* by phone earlier.

This *has* not *happened* before.

Did you ever *expect* to win?

EXERCISE B: Locating Helping Verbs. On your paper write the complete verb phrase from each of the following sentences. Include all parts of the helping verb, but do *not* include any words that separate the parts of the verb phrase.

EXAMPLE: Patty did not leave until after four.

did leave

1. Uncle Bob should have reached Boston by now.
2. Have you ever wanted to ski at Mount Washington?
3. She had carefully arranged her plans a week in advance.
4. Sailboats are often seen on the lake in summer.
5. She probably would have given you her phone number later.
6. Traders would often exchange tools, weapons, and utensils for pelts of fur.
7. That book has been on the best-seller list for ten weeks.
8. Do you know the name of the first state?
9. You should not even have attempted that difficult somersault.
10. Those plants have not been watered in more than a week.

APPLICATION: Writing Sentences with Helping Verbs. Use each of the following verb phrases in a complete sentence. Underline all parts of the verb phrase in each sentence. If you wish you can put the word *not* or some other word between parts of the verb phrase.

Answers will vary; samples given for first two. 1. The new shop will open next week.

EXAMPLE: have been

My favorite books have always been about horses.

2. Could the butler have been behind the screen?

1. will open
2. could have been
3. has been told
4. can be reached
5. have been talking
6. must be tried
7. will leave
8. has decided
9. are hoping
10. may be taken

Chapter 3

Adjectives

Have you ever tried to describe an animal that you saw at a zoo or in a photograph? You may have used words such as *huge, heavy, gray, rough,* and many others. With these words you painted a picture of a specific animal—an elephant—so that other people could see the animal in their minds. The words you used are called *adjectives.*

There are many kinds of adjectives. This chapter will cover some of the most common of them.

Adjectives as Modifiers 3.1

Adjectives are used with two other parts of speech.

An **adjective** is used to describe a noun or a pronoun.

In the following examples, the adjectives are italicized.

EXAMPLES: *sleek* jets

clear violet eyes

tall, majestic oaks

Adjectives with Nouns and Pronouns

To *modify* means to "change slightly." Adjectives are modifiers because they slightly change the meaning of nouns and pronouns. Adjectives modify meaning by adding information that answers one of four questions: *What kind? Which one? How many? How much?* In the following chart, notice how adjectives answer these questions.

What Kind?	
brick house	*white* sheets
Which One?	
that man	*each* answer
How Many?	
one daffodil	*several* roses
How Much?	
no time	*enough* raisins

An adjective usually comes before the noun it modifies, as all the adjectives in the chart do. Sometimes, however, adjectives come after the nouns they modify.

EXAMPLE: The light, *white* and *shining,* fascinated her.

Adjectives that modify pronouns usually come after linking verbs. Sometimes, however, adjectives come before pronouns.

EXAMPLE: She was *tall* and *beautiful.*

Tall and *beautiful,* she walked into the ball.

EXERCISE A: Recognizing Adjectives and the Words They Modify. Copy each of the following sentences onto your paper. Draw an arrow pointing from each underlined adjective to the noun or pronoun it modifies.
Modified words are shaded.

EXAMPLE: His sharp, witty remark was hardly appropriate.

1. The many rings of Saturn glowed in the blurry photograph.
2. The tired old man stumbled down the road.
3. Several books have been written about the last days of Roman power.
4. Willie Mays leaped for the high fly ball and made a brilliant catch.
5. Her third attempt was good, but in her fourth and final try, she broke a ten-year-old record.
6. The house, dreary and uninviting, had not been lived in for seventeen years.
7. Irving Berlin wrote many wonderful songs.
8. The feathery fins of the angel fish drifted in the clear blue water.
9. The marble statue was pale and dramatic against the dark velvet curtains.
10. The crusty little turtle crawled across the deserted parking lot.

Articles

Three commonly used adjectives are called *articles*—*the, a,* and *an.* These three words are adjectives because they come before nouns and answer the question *Which one?* Because of the way it modifies nouns, *the* is called the *definite* article.

The, the **definite article,** refers to a specific person, place, or thing.

EXAMPLES: *the* President *the* auditorium *the* green hat

The other two articles, *a* and *an,* are not as specific as *the* is.

A and *an,* the **indefinite articles,** refer to any one of a class of people, places, or things.

EXAMPLES: *a* president *an* auditorium *a* green hat

A is used before consonant sounds. *An* is used before vowel sounds. Notice that you choose between *a* and *an* based on *sound.* The letter *h,* a consonant, may sound like either a consonant or a vowel. *O* and *u* are vowels, but they may sometimes sound like consonants.

USING *A* AND *AN*	
Consonant Sounds	**Vowel Sounds**
a *c*andy cane	an *e*gg
a *h*ome run (*h* sound)	an *h*onor (no *h* sound)
a *o*ne-way road (*w* sound)	an *o*men (*o* sound)
a *u*niform (*y* sound)	an *u*nhappy child (*u* sound)

EXERCISE B: Distinguishing Between Definite and Indefinite Articles. On your paper write the article that will correctly complete each of the following sentences. The word in parentheses tells you which kind of article.

EXAMPLE: What __(indefinite)__ unusual subject!

What an unusual subject!

1. Did you see __(definite)__ mayor yet? *the*
2. She bought __(indefinite)__ new dress and __(indefinite)__ umbrella. *a/an*
3. Our history teacher mentioned __(definite)__ Battle of Harlem. *the*
4. __(Indefinite)__ old man and __(indefinite)__ young woman slowly approached. *An/a*
5. She was given __(indefinite)__ once-in-a-lifetime opportunity. *a*
6. __(Definite)__ road we must take to __(definite)__ bridge is blocked. *The/the*
7. He was eager to make friends because he was __(indefinite)__ only child. *an*
8. Read __(indefinite)__ book on World War II and then write __(indefinite)__ report. *a/a*
9. Where did you put __(definite)__ combination to __(definite)__ safe? *the/the*
10. Some say __(indefinite)__ apple a day keeps __(definite)__ doctor away. *an/the*

Nouns Used as Adjectives

Nouns are sometimes used as adjectives. When a noun is used as an adjective, it comes before another noun and answers the question *What kind?* or *Which one?*

Nouns	Used as Adjectives
dinner	*dinner* party (*What kind* of party?)
morning	*morning* classes (*Which* classes?)

EXERCISE C: Identifying Nouns Used as Adjectives. Each of the following sentences contains one noun used as an adjective. Write the modifying noun on your paper, and next to it write the noun it modifies.

Nouns used as adjectives are underlined; modified nouns are shaded.

EXAMPLE: Fifteen baby buggies were blocking the path.

baby buggies

1. They brought a long grocery list to the market.
2. Did you attend the evening performance?
3. Guitar music soothes me.
4. Have the street lights been repaired yet?
5. The local bus will take you right to the train station.

Proper Adjectives

Some *proper adjectives* are simply proper nouns used as adjectives. Others are adjectives made from proper nouns.

A **proper adjective** is (1) a proper noun used as an adjective or (2) an adjective formed from a proper noun.

When a proper noun is used as an adjective, its form does not change.

Proper Nouns	Used as Proper Adjectives
Arizona	*Arizona* desert (*What kind* of desert?)
Tuesday	*Tuesday* morning (*Which* morning?)
Churchill	*Churchill* memorial (*Which* memorial?)

When an adjective is formed from a proper noun, the noun form changes.

Proper Nouns	Proper Adjectives Formed from Proper Nouns
Elizabeth	*Elizabethan* literature (*What kind* of literature?)
Boston	*Bostonian* architecture (*What kind* of architecture?)

All proper adjectives, as you can see from both charts, are capitalized.

EXERCISE D: Recognizing Proper Adjectives. Find the proper adjective in each sentence and write it on your paper. Next to it write the noun it modifies.

Proper adjectives are underlined; modified nouns are shaded.

EXAMPLE: Some Victorian antiques are rather ugly.

Victorian antiques

1. My brother is studying Jacksonian democracy in his class.
2. Indian jewelry made of silver is very popular.
3. The weather department predicts a February blizzard.
4. My uncle has four rolls of silver Washington quarters.
5. Reporters watch the first Presidential primaries very carefully.
6. The Thanksgiving dinner was bountiful .
7. A *Newsweek* editor called several hours ago.

8. The January meeting of our club was canceled because of the ice storm.
9. When do you study American history in your school?
10. A Shakespearean comedy is fun to watch.

Compound Adjectives

Just as there are compound nouns, there are also *compound adjectives.*

A **compound adjective** is made up of more than one word.

Most compound adjectives are written as hyphenated words. Sometimes, however, they are written as combined words. If you are uncertain about which way to write a compound adjective, consult a dictionary for the correct spelling.

COMPOUND ADJECTIVES	
Hyphenated	**Combined**
one-sided opinion	*newborn* calf
so-called expert	*heartbreaking* news
worn-out clothing	*nearsighted* professor

EXERCISE E: Recognizing Compound Adjectives. Find the compound adjective in each sentence and write it on your paper. Next to the adjective, write the noun it modifies. *Compound adjectives are underlined; modified nouns are shaded.*

EXAMPLE: Do you think that story is old-fashioned?
old-fashioned story

1. Joanne was an unusually sweet, bright-eyed baby.
2. The Parents Council planned a schoolwide festival.
3. Joe Louis was a popular heavyweight champion.
4. My mother sees well, but my father is farsighted.

5. The hit-and-run driver was later captured by the police.
6. An offside penalty cost our team five yards.
7. A four-inch steel latch protects the office safe.
8. She tells funny stories about her absent-minded friend.
9. That region of New Hampshire has several mountains with snow-covered peaks.
10. Achilles drove his spear into Hector's bloodstained armor.

APPLICATION: Writing Sentences with Adjectives. Rewrite each of the following sentences by adding one or more adjectives. Use at least one noun as an adjective, one proper adjective, and one compound adjective.

Answers will vary; samples given for first two.

EXAMPLE: One night it rained.

One dark Christmas night it rained.

1. We bought a secondhand encyclopedia from the book dealer.

1. We bought an encyclopedia from the dealer.
2. The teacher returned the papers.
3. The truck driver ran out of fuel on the highway.
4. The attic contained cartons, a trunk, and a chair.
5. The intruder could not see and bumped into the furniture.
6. We watched a cartoon and a movie.
7. The locomotive chugged into the station.
8. A man and a woman knocked on our door.
9. The church has walls, a window, and a spire.
10. The sports car careened around the corner and grazed the wall.

2. The English teacher returned the latest papers.

3.2 Pronouns Used as Adjectives

Pronouns, like nouns, can sometimes be used as adjectives.

A pronoun is used as an adjective if it modifies a noun.

Four kinds of pronouns are sometimes used as adjectives. They are *personal, demonstrative, interrogative,* and *indefinite pronouns.*

Possessive Adjectives

The following personal pronouns are often called *possessive adjectives: my, your, his, her, its, our,* and *their.* Because they have antecedents, they are considered to be pronouns. They are also adjectives because they answer the question *Which one?*

EXAMPLE: Anna is doing *her* homework.

This example shows that *her* is an adjective modifying the noun *homework. Her* is also a pronoun because it has an antecedent, *Anna.*

EXERCISE A: Identifying Possessive Adjectives. In each of the following sentences, a possessive adjective is underlined. On your paper make three columns as shown in the example. Write the underlined word in the first column. Then find the noun it modifies and its antecedent and put them in the second and third columns. *Modified words are underlined; antecedents are shaded.*

EXAMPLE: Lincoln gave his life for his country.

Possessive Adjective	Noun Modified	Antecedent
his	life	Lincoln

1. Dori finished her chores and then worked on her report.
2. Leaving his office, Mr. Cruz took a cab to the station.
3. Mary Louise will exhibit some of her watercolors in the village library.
4. My friends were late and could not keep their appointment.
5. Grabbing their lunches, the twins raced from the house.

Demonstrative Adjectives

The four demonstrative pronouns—*this, that, these,* and *those*—can be used as *demonstrative adjectives.*

PRONOUN: I saw *this.*

ADJECTIVE: I'll buy *this* watch.

PRONOUN: I want *those.*

ADJECTIVE: Buy *those* peanuts.

EXERCISE B: Recognizing Demonstrative Adjectives. Find the word *this, that, these,* or *those* in each of the following sentences and copy the word onto your paper. If it is used as a pronoun, write *pronoun* after it. If it is used as an adjective, write the noun it modifies.

EXAMPLE: That is her decision.

That pronoun

1. This room is always light and airy. *room*
2. After thinking it over, he took those. *pron*
3. Have you read that article yet? *article*
4. These photos are among the best I've seen. *photos*
5. I just can't believe that. *pron*

Interrogative Adjectives

Three interrogative pronouns—*which, what,* and *whose*—can be used as *interrogative adjectives.*

PRONOUN: *What* did he want?

ADJECTIVE: *What* name did he give?

PRONOUN: *Whose* is that?

ADJECTIVE: *Whose* umbrella is that?

EXERCISE C: Recognizing Interrogative Adjectives. Find the word *which, what,* or *whose* in each of the following sentences and copy the word onto your paper. If it is used as a pronoun, write *pronoun* after it. If it is used as an adjective, write the noun it modifies after it.

EXAMPLE: What are you going to do?

What pronoun

1. Which route did he decide to take? *route*
2. What can be done now to stop them? *pron*
3. At whose house shall we have the party? *house*
4. What movie do you want to see this weekend? *movie*
5. Which of the routes is the fastest to your house? *pron*

Indefinite Adjectives

A number of indefinite pronouns can also be used as *indefinite adjectives.*

Some indefinite adjectives can be used only with singular nouns, some only with plural nouns, and some with either singular or plural nouns.

INDEFINITE ADJECTIVES			
Used with Singular Nouns	**Used with Plural Nouns**	**Used with Singular or Plural Nouns**	
another	both	all	most
each	few	any	other
either	many	more	some
neither	several		

The following examples show the words in the chart used first as pronouns and then as adjectives.

PRONOUN: I bought one of *each.*

ADJECTIVE: *Each* album costs six dollars.

PRONOUN: *Both* of them called.

ADJECTIVE: *Both* girls called.

PRONOUN: I don't want *any*.

ADJECTIVES: I don't want *any* help.

I don't want *any* string beans.

EXERCISE D: Recognizing Indefinite Adjectives. Find the indefinite pronoun or adjective in each of the following sentences and copy the word onto your paper. If it is used as a pronoun, write *pronoun* after it. If it is used as an adjective, write the noun it modifies after it.

EXAMPLE: Both children adored playing in the mud.

Both children

1. people

1. Several people phoned the police after the accident.
2. Both appeared at the hotel for the contest. *pron*
3. More apples in the bushel have spoiled. *apples*
4. Few winners claimed their prizes. *winners*
5. Neither of the choices was acceptable. *pron*

APPLICATION: Writing Sentences with Pronouns Used as Adjectives. Write ten sentences of your own. In each sentence use one of the following words to modify a noun. Then draw an arrow pointing from each adjective to the word it modifies.

Answers will vary; samples given for first two.

EXAMPLE: that

Bobby will never get that role in the play.

1. this
2. whose
3. both
4. her
5. which
6. those
7. either
8. our
9. their
10. these

1. This drawing might win first prize.

2. Whose idea was it?

Chapter 4

Adverbs

Like adjectives, *adverbs* modify words in sentences. Consider this sentence: *In the afternoon Judy worked.*

Judy could have worked in many ways: *hard, slowly, happily, cautiously, willingly,* or *unwillingly.* Each of these words tells something about how Judy worked. All of these words are adverbs.

The first section in this chapter will explain which parts of speech adverbs can modify. The second section will give you additional practice recognizing adverbs in sentences.

Adverbs as Modifiers 4.1

Adjectives, as explained in Section 3.1, modify nouns or pronouns. *Adverbs* modify three different parts of speech.

An **adverb** modifies a verb, an adjective, or another adverb.

To recognize adverbs, you need to know how they modify each of these three parts of speech.

Adverbs Modifying Verbs

An adverb modifying a verb will answer one of four questions about the verb: *Where? When? In what manner?* or *To what extent?*

ADVERBS MODIFYING VERBS	
Where?	
drove *down*	stay *nearby*
is *here*	jump *away*
When?	
report *later*	come *tomorrow*
will leave *soon*	appeared *suddenly*
In What Manner?	
cautiously approached	walk *quietly*
smiled *happily*	tell *unwillingly*
To What Extent?	
nearly won	had *almost* left
hardly counted	*scarcely* escaped

EXERCISE A: Recognizing Adverbs That Modify Verbs. Make four columns on your paper and label them as shown in the following example. Then find the adverb in each sentence and write it in the appropriate column.

EXAMPLE: The dog slept quietly by the stove.

Where?	When?	In What Manner?	To What Extent?
		quietly	

1. The bus traveled rapidly into the night. *In what manner?*
2. Does he fully understand what is expected?
3. She immediately described the accident to a police officer. *When?*
4. The guests arrived late but found nobody at home.
5. Silently, the detective climbed the stairs to the attic. *In what manner?*
6. Bud has almost finished his model. *To what extent?*
7. Do you expect to move away from Albuquerque?
8. He is always creating problems. *When?*
9. The shopping center has nearly been completed.
10. My sister quickly cleaned the cage. *In what manner?*

2. To what extent? 4. When? 7. Where? 9. To what extent?

Adverbs Modifying Adjectives

When an adverb modifies an adjective, it answers the question *To what extent?*

ADVERBS MODIFYING ADJECTIVES	
sometimes happy	*not* sad
almost right	*unusually* rich

EXERCISE B: Recognizing Adverbs That Modify Adjectives. On your paper write the adverb from each sentence. After each adverb write the adjective it modifies.
Adverbs are underlined; adjectives are shaded.

EXAMPLE: The frog was very happy when the princess kissed him.

very happy

1. We examined an almost new tape recorder.
2. He was somewhat unwilling to answer our questions.
3. Sue was very glad to accept his invitation.
4. These baked potatoes are especially good.
5. He made the whipped cream too sweet.
6. An often noisy crowd waited outside the courtroom.
7. An unusually tall actress is needed for that role.
8. The patient looked decidedly ill.
9. That teacher is remarkably knowledgeable in her field.
10. This trip will be rather dangerous.

Adverbs Modifying Other Adverbs

When adverbs modify other adverbs, they again answer the question *To what extent?*

ADVERBS MODIFYING ADVERBS	
traveled *less slowly*	move *very cautiously*
lost *too easily*	lived *almost happily*

EXERCISE C: Recognizing Adverbs That Modify Other Adverbs. In each of the following sentences, find an adverb that modifies another adverb by answering the question *To what extent?* Write this adverb on your paper and after it write the adverb it modifies.
Modifying adverbs are underlined; modified adverbs are shaded.

EXAMPLE: The movers arrived too early in the day.

too early

1. She worked too slowly to finish in time.
2. After his unfortunate experience, he climbed trees rather cautiously.
3. The train should pull into the station quite soon.
4. After living for years in Japan, the child had almost totally forgotten how to speak English.
5. The vase was almost completely uncracked.
6. Do you think you can talk less rapidly?
7. My best friend has moved far away.
8. Although he lost, the knight fought very bravely.
9. He has been told that he speaks Spanish extremely well.
10. She was only slightly tired after the long race.

APPLICATION: Using Adverbs. Each of the following sentences contains one or more blanks. Copy each sentence onto your paper, and fill in the blanks with adverbs of your choice. *Answers will vary; samples given.*

EXAMPLE: Jeremy__________ yells __________ loudly.

Jeremy never yells too loudly.

1. Lisa *rarely* stays up *late* on Fridays.
2. Follow my instructions *very* *carefully*.
3. Your answers were *remarkably* complete.
4. *Silently*, the tiger stalked the antelope.
5. Mimi spoke *very* *slowly*.
6. Todd skated *quickly* across the pond.
7. I hope they will be *very* *honest*.
8. *Rapidly*, he gave us the message.
9. The dance is *now* over.
10. She was *seldom* *very* happy in Tokyo.

Adverbs Used in Sentences 4.2

Adverbs can be located in almost any part of a sentence.

Finding Adverbs in Sentences

Learning where to look for adverbs will help you to identify them. The following chart shows some of the positions in which adverbs can appear. The arrows point from the adverbs, to the words that they modify.

LOCATION OF ADVERBS IN SENTENCES	
Location	**Example**
At the Beginning of a Sentence	*Quickly,* they gathered the firewood.
At the End of a Sentence	They gathered the firewood *quickly.*
Before a Verb	He *cautiously* approached the dog.
After a Verb	She walked *slowly* from the room.
Between Parts of a Verb	They had *quickly* gathered the firewood.
Before an Adjective	He was *rather* glad about the results.
Before Another Adverb	She walked *rather* slowly from the room.

EXERCISE A: Locating Adverbs in Sentences. Each of the following sentences contains one or two adverbs. Copy the sentences onto your paper and underline the adverbs. Then draw arrows from the adverbs to the words they modify. *Adverbs are underlined; modified words are shaded.*

EXAMPLE: The poet happily inserted the perfect word.

1. She tearfully told us about the accident.
2. Suddenly the train whistle sounded, and the train slowly left the station.
3. Bobby has almost finished his piano practice.
4. He has never asked for help.
5. My mother moved the couch slowly to the left.
6. The lifeguard does not think that the swimming pool will be opened soon.
7. Cautiously, the police approached the building.
8. The wall was brightly painted in yellow and white.
9. He spun too quickly and lost his balance.
10. In 1860 Senator William M. Gwin and several others pushed vigorously for a pony-express route.

Adverb or Adjective?

Some words can be either adverbs or adjectives, depending on the words they modify. An adverb always modifies a verb, an adjective, or another adverb. An adjective modifies a noun or pronoun.

ADVERB MODIFYING VERB: He drove too *fast.*

ADJECTIVE MODIFYING NOUN: He is a *fast* driver.

ADVERB MODIFYING ADJECTIVE: She is *much* happier now.

ADJECTIVE MODIFYING NOUN: I ate too *much* food.

Although many adverbs end in *-ly,* not all words ending in *-ly* are adverbs. As the following chart shows, some are adjectives. These adjectives are formed by adding *-ly* to nouns.

Nouns	Adjectives with *-ly* Endings
a beautiful *home*	a *homely* animal
an *elder* in the church	an *elderly* man
his true *love*	*lovely* flowers

EXERCISE B: Distinguishing Between Adverbs and Adjectives. On your paper indicate whether the underlined word in each of the following sentences is an adverb or an adjective.

EXAMPLE: The poster was <u>finally</u> finished.

adverb

1. My grandfather was a <u>kindly</u> man who always helped his grandchildren. *adj*
2. Aunt Millie drives <u>regularly</u> to Los Angeles to shop. *adv*
3. I always work <u>hard</u> on my class reports. *adv*
4. Mother had a <u>hard</u> time reaching the doctor. *adj*
5. The senator <u>bitterly</u> criticized his opponents. *adv*
6. My science teacher is an unusually <u>friendly</u> person. *adj*
7. Does the <u>early</u> bird catch the worm? *adj*
8. I jog <u>daily</u>. *adv*
9. Taking a coffee break is a <u>daily</u> practice in our company. *adj*
10. Has the engine been running <u>smoothly</u>? *adv*

APPLICATION: Writing Sentences with Adverbs. Write twenty sentences of your own using the adverbs in the following list. After writing each sentence, draw an arrow pointing from the adverb to the word or words that the adverb modifies.

Answers will vary; samples given for first two.

EXAMPLE: not

She has not given us her answer yet.

1. beautifully
2. slowly
3. regularly
4. amazingly
5. never
6. soon
7. sleepily
8. almost
9. happily
10. smoothly
11. seldom
12. very
13. away
14. now
15. quickly
16. yesterday
17. loudly
18. completely
19. always
20. usually

1. The dancer soared beautifully into the darkness. *2. We drove slowly on the wet road.*

Chapter 5

Prepositions, Conjunctions, and Interjections

The three parts of speech discussed in this chapter all play special roles in sentences. *Prepositions* relate nouns or pronouns to other words in a sentence. *Conjunctions* connect parts of sentences. *Interjections* add sudden emotion or feeling to sentences. To understand fully how sentences work, you must be able to recognize these three parts of speech.

5.1 Prepositions

Prepositions are words such as *against, among, at, beyond, during, of,* and *on.* They make it possible to show relationships between certain words used separately in sentences.

A **preposition** relates the noun or pronoun following it to another word in the sentence.

■ Words Used as Prepositions

There are several dozen words in the English language that can act as prepositions in sentences. The following chart lists fifty of the most commonly used prepositions.

FREQUENTLY USED PREPOSITIONS				
about	behind	during	off	to
above	below	except	on	toward
across	beneath	for	onto	under
after	beside	from	opposite	underneath
against	besides	in	out	until
along	between	inside	outside	up
among	beyond	into	over	upon
around	but	like	past	with
at	by	near	since	within
before	down	of	through	without

Prepositions consisting of two or three words are called *compound prepositions.* Some of them are listed in the following chart.

COMPOUND PREPOSITIONS		
according to	by means of	instead of
ahead of	in addition to	in view of
apart from	in back of	next to
aside from	in front of	on account of
as of	in place of	on top of
because of	in spite of	out of

The choice of preposition affects the way the other words in a sentence relate to each other. In the following example, read the sentence using each preposition. Notice how each preposition changes the relationship between *stopped* and *school.*

EXAMPLE:

The bus stopped { at / near / opposite / in back of / next to } the school.

EXERCISE A: Recognizing Prepositions. Find the preposition in each of the following sentences and write it on your paper. Then rewrite the sentence using a different preposition. *New prepositions will vary; samples given.*

EXAMPLE: They left the house at dawn.

at They left the house before dawn.

1. The florist left a box outside the house. *in*
2. After breakfast I walk the dogs. *Before*
3. The baby crawled under the table. *around*
4. He warned us of the danger. *about*
5. The taxi drove in front of the delivery truck.
6. There is a round window near the entrance.
7. She hid her bicycle in back of the fence. *under*
8. What are those flowers growing on the hillside?
9. Put these papers on top of my desk. *on*
10. Three deer loped through the woods. *out of*

5. behind 6. above 8. near

Prepositional Phrases

A preposition must always be followed by a noun or pronoun. The group of words beginning with the preposition and ending with the noun or pronoun is called a *prepositional phrase.* The noun or pronoun that follows the preposition is called the *object of the preposition.*

PREPOSITIONAL PHRASES	
Prepositions	**Objects of Prepositions**
in	the *house*
with	*us*
in front of	the old dilapidated *barn*

Most prepositional phrases are made up of just two or three words. However, as the last example in the chart shows, phrases with compound prepositions or with adjectives modifying the object can be longer. (See Section 8.1 for more information about prepositional phrases.)

EXERCISE B: Identifying Prepositional Phrases. On your paper write the prepositional phrase appearing in each of the following sentences.

EXAMPLE: She opened the gate in the fence.

in the fence

1. She waited all morning near the store.
2. In the morning Mom and Dad prepare breakfast and pack our lunches.
3. They reached the campsite by means of a steep, rocky path.
4. Uncle Steve brought a present for me.
5. According to Mr. Wilson, the math test has been postponed.
6. After much excitement we reached the airport five minutes early.
7. I stored my gear inside my best friend's locker.
8. In front of my house stands a weathered blue spruce.
9. When is she coming home from school?
10. Edith planted flowers in front of the shrubs.

Preposition or Adverb?

Some words can be either prepositions or adverbs, depending on how they are used in a sentence. To be a preposition, a word must be part of a prepositional phrase. If a word modifies a verb and has no object, it is an adverb.

PREPOSITION: The jet flew *over* the house. (Obj: house)

ADVERB: The entire family came *over*.

PREPOSITION: They walked *along* the waterfront. (Obj: waterfront)

ADVERB: Won't you come *along?*

EXERCISE C: Distinguishing Between Prepositions and Adverbs. In each of the following pairs of sentences, one sentence contains a word used as a preposition and the other contains the same word used as an adverb. Find which words appear in both sentences. If the word acts as a preposition, write the prepositional phrase on your paper. If the word acts as an adverb, write *adverb.*

Prepositional phrases are shaded; adverbs are underlined.

EXAMPLE: We found the keys in the car.
They came in and dinner began.

in the car adverb

1. The rabbit would not come near.
   The rose bush is near the white fence.
2. You will find the house if you continue past the traffic light.
   The old man would often walk past in the evening.
3. Turn the lights on before it gets dark.
   The shopping center is two blocks farther on the right.
4. Several vultures soared around gracefully.
   Go completely around the traffic circle.
5. He and his baggage were thrown out the door.
   We all went out to celebrate our parents' anniversary.

APPLICATION: Writing Sentences with Prepositional Phrases. Each of the following sentences has one or two blanks. Copy the sentences onto your paper, inserting a prepositional phrase in each blank.

Answers will vary; samples given.

EXAMPLE: Marie is happiest __________.

Marie is happiest in Colorado.

1. *On pleasant days* we like to walk to school.
2. The room *on the south side* is usually very warm.
3. They decided to drive *into the country*.
4. *After dinner* she went *to the roller rink*.
5. *After the countdown* the space shuttle roared *into the cloudless sky*.
6. *After the game* we decided to stop *at Jim's house*.
7. The messenger *from Dad's office* rang the bell twice.
8. *During the blizzard* the police stopped all traffic *on all lanes*.
9. The doctor asked me to step *onto the scale*.
10. A person *in trouble* can always get help *from someone*.

Conjunctions 5.2

Conjunctions work like cement between bricks. Words such as *and, but, as,* and *when* connect individual words or groups of words. They are the cement of sentences.

A **conjunction** connects words or groups of words.

Conjunctions fall into three groups. There are *coordinating conjunctions, correlative conjunctions,* and *subordinating conjunctions.*

Coordinating Conjunctions

Coordinating conjunctions connect words of a similar kind, for example, two or more verbs. They can also connect larger groups of words, such as prepositional phrases, or even entire sentences.

COORDINATING CONJUNCTIONS			
and	for	or	yet
but	nor	so	

In the following examples, the coordinating conjunctions are circled. The words they connect are italicized.

CONNECTING NOUNS: My *cousin* (and) his *wife* arrived yesterday for a visit.

CONNECTING ADJECTIVES: He had a choice of a *tan, red,* (or) *blue* shirt.

CONNECTING VERBS: The St. Bernard *chewed* (and) *swallowed* its food ravenously.

CONNECTING PREPOSITIONAL PHRASES: Put the package *on the doorstep* (or) *in the garage.*

CONNECTING TWO SENTENCES: *Alison wanted to go shopping,* (but) *she decided to do her homework first.*

EXERCISE A: Recognizing Coordinating Conjunctions. Copy the following sentences onto your paper and circle the coordinating conjunction in each. Then underline the words or groups of words connected by the conjunction. *Conjunctions are shaded.*

EXAMPLE: We nibbled on cheese (and) crackers.

1. We bought a small yet comfortable car.
2. The experiments are conducted in the morning and in the evening.
3. The actor was handsome but untalented.
4. I must catch the train at noon, for I have a doctor's appointment in the city.
5. The eagle soared, swooped, and landed on its nest.

■ Correlative Conjunctions

Correlative conjunctions connect the same kinds of words or groups of words as do coordinating conjunctions. Correlative conjunctions are different, however, because they come in pairs.

CORRELATIVE CONJUNCTIONS		
both . . . and	neither . . . nor	whether . . . or
either . . . or	not only . . . but also	

CONNECTING NOUNS: He opened (both) his *present* (and) her *present.*

CONNECTING PRONOUNS: (Either) *you* (or) *I* will be the lead runner.

CONNECTING VERBS: The sick python would (neither) *eat* (nor) *drink.*

CONNECTING PREPOSITIONAL PHRASES: He will keep the appointment; whether *at one* or *at two,* he couldn't say.

CONNECTING TWO SENTENCES: Not only *is Lila a talented artist,* but *she is* also *a fine writer.*

EXERCISE B: Recognizing Correlative Conjunctions. Copy the following sentences onto your paper and circle the correlative conjunction in each. Then underline the two words or the two groups of words connected by the conjunction. *Conjunctions are shaded.*

EXAMPLE: I can ask neither my father nor my mother for permission.

1. I don't care whether Marla or Lisa represents us.
2. She trains for the marathon both in the morning and in the afternoon.
3. Not only was he a fine athlete, but he was also a fine student.
4. Neither Michael nor she could explain the strange noises.
5. Grandfather was either reading or napping.

Subordinating Conjunctions

To *subordinate* means to "place below another in rank." *Subordinating conjunctions* connect two ideas by making one idea dependent on the other.

FREQUENTLY USED SUBORDINATE CONJUNCTIONS			
after	as though	since	until
although	because	so that	when
as	before	than	whenever
as if	even though	though	where
as long as	if	till	wherever
as soon as	in order that	unless	while

The subordinating conjunction always comes before the dependent idea. The subordinating conjunction connects the dependent idea to the main idea.

EXAMPLES: *I did the planting* (after) *he prepared the soil.* [Main Idea: I did the planting; Dependent Idea: he prepared the soil]

(When) *he phoned this morning, he was unable to reach the senator.* [Dependent Idea: he phoned this morning; Main Idea: he was unable to reach the senator]

The examples show that the main idea can come at the beginning or at the end of the sentence. Notice the important difference in punctuating the two examples. When the dependent idea comes first, it must be separated from the main idea with a comma. (See Section 9.2 for more information about subordinating conjunctions.)

EXERCISE C: Recognizing Subordinating Conjunctions. Copy the following sentences onto your paper and circle the subordinating conjunction in each. Then underline the dependent idea following the conjunction and label it *Dependent.* *Conjunctions are shaded.*

EXAMPLE: (If) he asks my permission, I will grant it. [Dependent: he asks my permission]

1. Since they want to join our club, I will be happy to nominate them.
2. They all went fishing while their father went to the museum.
3. The stamps will be available whenever you wish to pick them up.
4. As if she didn't have enough trouble, she has lost her wallet.
5. As long as I can remember, we have spent part of the summer in Vermont.
6. She went home as soon as she heard the news.
7. I sometimes eat more than I should.
8. He lost his way because he forgot to take a map.
9. I can do it if you help me.
10. You look as though you need a rest.

APPLICATION 1: Writing Sentences Using Conjunctions. On your paper fill in the blanks with words that will complete each sentence. Use as many words as necessary to complete each thought, but keep each conjunction in the position shown.

Answers will vary; samples given.

EXAMPLE: ________ as though ________.

She acted as though she didn't really want to go.

1. Both *Cheryl* and *I jumped up*.
2. If *you can do the work*, *go ahead*.
3. *I hope you can* because *I can't*.
4. Although *the twins are here*, *their brother is not*.
5. Not only does she *ski*, but she also *climbs mountains*.
6. *Felix raised his hand*, but *you didn't see him*.
7. When *we arrived*, *the party seemed to be over*.
8. Either *Jane* or *Diane will bring crackers*.
9. *I was surprised* even though *I knew the story*.
10. While *you were fixing the car*, *we found the map*.

APPLICATION 2: Writing Original Sentences with Conjunctions. Write sentences of your own using each of the following conjunctions.

Answers will vary; samples given for first two.

EXAMPLE: both . . . and

Both Irving and Poe wrote short stories.

1. You don't have to come unless you want to.

1. unless
2. or
3. when
4. neither . . . nor
5. although
6. even though
7. but
8. wherever
9. as if
10. whether . . . or

2. Grace or Mel can give you directions.

Interjections 5.3

The last of the eight parts of speech—the *interjection*—is the part that is used the least. Its only use is to express feelings or emotions.

An **interjection** expresses feeling or emotion and functions independently of a sentence.

An interjection has no grammatical relationship to any other word in a sentence. It is, therefore, set off from the rest of the sentence with a comma or an exclamation mark.

Note the different feelings or emotions interjections can express.

JOY: *Wow!* I can't believe I won.

SURPRISE: *Oh,* I didn't expect to hear from you.

PAIN: *Ouch!* That hurts.

IMPATIENCE: *Tsk!* How long do they expect to wait?

HESITATION: I, *uh,* think you should leave.

EXERCISE A: Recognizing Interjections. Rewrite each of the following sentences using an appropriate interjection in place of the feeling shown in parentheses.

Answers will vary; samples given.

EXAMPLE: (Anger) I wanted to watch the football game.

Darn! I wanted to watch the football game.

1. (Surprise) I never expected this. *Oh!*
2. (Impatience) We have to catch the train. *Hey!*
3. (Dislike) I don't like that hat at all. *Yuk!*
4. (Pain) I caught my finger in the door. *Ow!*
5. (Joy) We're all thrilled you came. *Wow!*

APPLICATION: Using Interjections in Sentences. Use the following interjections with commas or exclamation marks in sentences of your own.

Answers will vary; samples given for first two.

EXAMPLE: uh

My excuse is, uh, not what you might expect.

1. Ouch! I just stubbed my toe.

1. ouch
2. gee
3. oh
4. goodness
5. whew
6. wow
7. darn
8. ah
9. ugh
10. hey

2. Gee, I wish you could come.

Chapter 6

Reviewing Parts of Speech

The preceding chapters have introduced each of the eight parts of speech. Being able to identify the part of speech of each word in a sentence is an important skill. With this skill you will be able to study how sentences are put together. You will also be able to discuss ways of improving your writing.

Determining Parts of Speech 6.1

Studying the English language would be easier if it were possible to say, "This word is always a noun," "This word is always an adverb," and so on. Language, however, is flexible. To identify what part of speech a word is, you must look beyond the word's spelling and pronunciation. You must consider how the word is used in each particular sentence.

How a word is used in a sentence determines its part of speech.

Although it is sometimes possible to guess a word's part of speech just by looking at it, it is important to examine how the word is actually used. Only then can you be sure.

Some words can be used as several different parts of speech. In the four sentences that follow, you can see how the word *past* is used as a different part of speech in each sentence.

AS A NOUN: The *past* is often a guide for the future.

AS AN ADJECTIVE: His *past* actions trouble us.

AS AN ADVERB: A hummingbird just darted *past.*

AS A PREPOSITION: She drove *past* our house.

Identifying Parts of Speech in Sentences

The following charts can help you identify the eight parts of speech in almost any sentence. The middle column—"Questions to Ask Yourself"—should be particularly helpful to you in determining parts of speech.

Nouns and Pronouns. A noun names a person, place, or thing. A pronoun stands for a noun.

Part of Speech	Questions to Ask Yourself	Examples
Noun	Does the word name a person, place, or thing?	*Sue* received a *present* from her *aunt.*
Pronoun	Does the word stand for a noun?	*Each* gets *one* of *them.*

Verbs. A verb generally shows an action or a condition.

Part of Speech	Questions to Ask Yourself	Examples
Verb	Does the word tell what someone or something did?	She *bought* a cake.
	Does the word link a noun or pronoun before it with a noun or adjective that follows?	She *is* the captain. He *seems* sick.

Adjectives. An adjective modifies a noun or pronoun.

Part of Speech	Questions to Ask Yourself	Examples
Adjective	Does the word tell what kind, which one, how many, or how much?	*Several large, heavy* packages arrived.

Adverbs. An adverb modifies a verb, an adjective, or another adverb.

Part of Speech	Questions to Ask Yourself	Examples
Adverb	Does the word tell where, when, in what manner, or to what extent?	Go *there!* You can go *later*. She works *very quickly*. They are *nearly* ready.

Prepositions, Conjunctions, and Interjections. A preposition relates the noun or pronoun following it to another word. A conjunction connects words or groups of words. An interjection expresses feeling or emotion.

Part of Speech	Questions to Ask Yourself	Examples
Preposition	Is the word part of a phrase that ends in a noun or pronoun?	*In* the morning he often jogs. Sit *behind* them.
Conjunction	Does the word connect other words in the sentence?	Bill *and* Mary arrived. He will *either* go *or* stay behind. This is *as* it should be.
Interjection	Does the word express feeling or emotion?	*Gee!* I'm happy to see you.

Using these questions as a guide, you should be able to identify correctly what part of speech a particular word is. Consider the italicized words in the following sentence.

EXAMPLE: The team finished *practice* early since *everyone* arrived on time.

You might begin by wondering whether *practice* is a noun or a verb, since it can be used as either. Does the word name a person, place, or thing, or does it tell what the team did? *Practice,* in this sentence, names something. Therefore, it is a noun.

At first glance *everyone* may seem to be a noun, but does it actually name a person? No. Does it stand for a noun? Yes, it stands for the names of the team members. Therefore, *everyone* has to be a pronoun.

Now try to analyze *team, finished,* and *early* in the same sentence. The more you rely on the questions in the charts, the easier this analysis should be.

EXERCISE A: Identifying Nouns, Pronouns, Verbs, and Adjectives. On your paper identify the underlined word in each sentence as a *noun, pronoun, verb,* or *adjective.*

EXAMPLE: They drink iced tea in July. verb

1. The trip lasted for two weeks. *verb*
2. I think the wooden desk can be refinished. *adj*
3. This rhinoceros seems quite ferocious. *noun*
4. The window frame was green. *adj*
5. *verb* The tourist season reaches its peak in January.
6. These stains can not be removed easily. *noun*
7. *adj* An interested parent can help a student greatly.
8. Will they agree on a choice? *pron*
9. His idea deserves more discussion. *noun*
10. It will be an unhappy day when she leaves. *adj*

EXERCISE B: Identifying Adjectives, Adverbs, Prepositions, and Conjunctions. On your paper identify the underlined word in each sentence as an *adjective, adverb, preposition,* or *conjunction.*

EXAMPLE: Before she arrives, we will have left. conjunction

1. She hasn't said a word since dinner. *prep*
2. She hasn't said a word since they arrived this morning. *conj*
3. He arrived last week and has been here ever since. *adv*
4. They were afraid they would be left behind. *adv*
5. You will find an old broom behind the cellar door. *prep*
6. He staggered about after bumping his head. *adv*
7. She strolled about the botanical gardens. *prep*
8. The garden apartment has an outside entrance. *adj*
9. The tool shed is just outside the door. *prep*
10. Would you like to walk outside? *adv*

APPLICATION: Using Words as Different Parts of Speech. Each of the following words can be used as at least two different parts of speech. Write two sentences for each word, using the word as a different part of speech each time. *Answers will vary; samples given for first one.*

EXAMPLE: question

Her question was very strange.

Do you always question the results?

1. stop
2. past
3. opposite
4. after
5. jump
6. dry
7. mail
8. in
9. hope
10. lemon

1. Does the Number 5 bus stop here? New Haven is the last stop for this train.

Chapter 7

Recognizing Parts of a Sentence

The eight parts of speech are the building blocks of language. By assembling the parts of speech in various patterns, you can express your ideas and communicate them to others. Patterns of words that communicate ideas are called *sentences.*

This chapter will begin by describing the basic patterns of words that form sentences. Each section will build on the one before it to show you how longer, more complicated sentences are put together.

7.1 The Basic Sentence

There are many kinds of sentences. Some are short, and others are long. Some seem very complicated. But all sentences, in order to be sentences, must have certain ingredients. This section will describe those essential parts—the parts that every sentence must have.

The Two Basic Elements of a Sentence

All sentences, regardless of length or difficulty, must contain two basic elements.

A sentence must contain a **subject** and a **verb.**

Both of these ingredients are necessary in order to have a sentence. If either one is missing, what remains is not a sentence.

The Subject. Every sentence must have a *subject.* Most subjects are nouns or pronouns found near the beginning of a sentence.

> The **subject** of a sentence is the word or group of words that answers the question *Who?* or *What?* before the verb.

In the following examples, the subjects have been underlined and the verbs have been labeled.

EXAMPLES: <u>Father</u> bought (V) a present for us.

Our new <u>car</u> was (V) in the garage.

<u>She</u> tried (V) to be good to them.

The noun *father* is the subject in the first example. It tells us *who* bought a present. The noun *car* in the second example tells *what* was in the garage. *Car,* therefore, is the subject of the sentence. In the third example, the pronoun *she* tells *who* tried to be good. *She* is the subject.

Not all subjects are this easy to find. Some are more than one word. Some may not appear at the beginning of the sentence. But the subject will always answer *Who?* or *What?* before a verb. (See Section 7.4 for more information about finding subjects in sentences.)

The Verb. As one of the two essential parts of a sentence, a *verb* simply tells something about a subject.

> The **verb** in a sentence tells what the subject does, what is done to the subject, or what the condition of the subject is.

In the following examples, the verbs have been underlined twice and the subjects have been labeled.

EXAMPLES: Bobby gave an unforgettable speech. (S above Bobby)

Their prize poodle was stolen. (S above poodle)

She has been blue all day. (S above She)

Gave is the verb in the first example. It tells what the subject, *Bobby,* did. In the second example, *was stolen* tells what was done to the subject *poodle. Has been* in the third example is a linking verb. It tells something about the condition of the subject by linking *she* to the word *blue.*

EXERCISE A: Recognizing Subjects and Verbs. Copy each of the following sentences onto your paper. Underline each subject once and each verb twice.

EXAMPLE: One Greek hero spent ten years trying to reach home.

1. The ferry crosses the river twice a day.
2. Our teacher has been more than fair with us.
3. My sister bakes delicious vanilla cookies.
4. The old bridge creaks occasionally under a heavy load.
5. The book describes the causes of the Great Depression.
6. Maybe the old road will be opened in the spring.
7. His handwriting is unreadable.
8. They have told us only half the story.
9. The old rocker was repaired just last week.
10. Without question Cicely Tyson is a brilliant actress.

The Need to Express a Complete Thought

In addition to having a subject and a verb, a sentence must express a *complete thought.* Difficulty in deciding whether a group of words is a sentence often comes down to difficulty in recognizing a complete thought.

A group of words with a subject and verb expresses a **complete thought** if it can stand by itself and still make sense.

Making sure that your words express complete thoughts is especially important when you write.

Incomplete thoughts will leave readers with questions in their minds. Consider the group of words in the following example.

INCOMPLETE THOUGHT: The girl in the green bathing suit.

"What about the girl in the green bathing suit?" a reader may ask. "What did she do?" Standing by itself, this group of words obviously makes no sense. An important element is missing—the verb. Using *girl* as a subject, you can turn this incomplete thought into a sentence by adding any number of different verbs.

COMPLETE THOUGHTS
The girl (S) in the green bathing suit swims (V) beautifully.
The girl (S) in the green bathing suit left (V).
The girl (S) in the green bathing suit is lying (V) by the pool.

Notice that each of the examples in the chart has all of the ingredients necessary for a sentence: Each has a *subject* and a *verb* and each expresses a *complete thought.* Each sentence makes sense by itself.

Sometimes an incomplete thought may be a group of words with no word in it that can be used as a subject. Consider the following example.

INCOMPLETE THOUGHT: Near the stream by the roadside.

This incomplete thought is merely two prepositional phrases. *Both* a subject and a verb are needed.

COMPLETE: Wild irises are growing near the stream by the roadside.

In grammar incomplete thoughts are often called *fragments*. See Section 10.1 for more information about fragments and about how to avoid them in your writing.

EXERCISE B: Correcting Incomplete Thoughts. None of the following groups of words expresses a complete thought. On your paper correct each one by adding whatever words are needed to make a sentence.

Answers will vary; samples given for first two.

EXAMPLE: Three angry ducks in search of corn.

Three angry ducks in search of corn waddled by.

1. The apple peeler is on top of the shelf in the kitchen.

1. On top of the shelf in the kitchen.
2. In the garage near the old newspapers.
3. The clerk behind the counter.
4. A police officer at the top of the hill.
5. Because of all the wrong answers.

2. You must look in the garage near the old newspapers.

APPLICATION: Recognizing Sentences. Only ten of the following twenty items are sentences. The rest are incomplete thoughts. If a group of words is a sentence, write *sentence* on your paper. If a group of words expresses an incomplete thought, add whatever words are needed to make a sentence. Then underline the subject once and the verb twice in each new sentence.

New sentences will vary; samples given.

EXAMPLE: The suitcases from the plane.

The suitcases from the plane were unloaded.

1. She asked me about the next edition of the newspaper. *sentence*
2. The room in the back of the house *is used for storage.*
3. In the desert, tall cactuses *baked in the sun.*
4. We understood her reasons. *sentence*
5. From the observation deck at the rim of the canyon *we could see many hiking groups.*
6. The teacher on the third floor near the window. *often sits*

7. Walter opened the package quickly. sentence
8. He returns there every summer. sentence
9. ~~Under~~ the chair near the window. The dog is under
10. His typewriter has an automatic carriage return.
11. The lawnmower with the green handle. is broken.
12. Her television flickers often. sentence
13. Everyone in the room waited. sentence
14. Because of the low temperature and the icy winds.
15. ~~Near~~ the river by the yellow bench. We ate near
16. This is the second flat tire in less than a week. sentence
17. According to the information on their identification cards. these persons come from another galaxy.
18. The white telephone in the bedroom does not work. sentence
19. The kitchen is small and dark. sentence
20. During the storm, the tree on the north side of the house. toppled onto the garage.

10. sentence 14. we stayed home.

Complete Subjects and Predicates 7.2

Every sentence is built around its two essential elements, the subject and verb. Like the trunk of a tree from which smaller branches grow, the subject and the verb together support the many details that a sentence may contain in expressing a complete thought.

DIFFERENT SENTENCES BUILT AROUND THE SAME SUBJECT AND VERB	
People	swim.
Many people	swim daily.
Many people in our town	swim daily at the pool in the community center.

Notice the lines that divide the sentences. The words to the left of the lines include the subject *people* and any other words that add details to it. In each sentence the words to the left of the line make up the *complete subject.* (The word *people* is often called, in contrast, the *simple subject.*)

> The **complete subject** of a sentence consists of the subject and any words related to it.

As you can see in the preceding examples, a complete subject may be just one word—the subject itself—or it may be several words.

In the preceding examples, the words to the right of the lines include the verb *swim* and any words that add details to it. This part of the sentence is called the *complete predicate.* (The verb itself, a word such as *swim* or a phrase such as *has swum,* is often called the *simple predicate.*)

> The **complete predicate** of a sentence consists of the verb and any words related to it.

As you can see in the examples, a complete predicate may be just one word—a verb—or it may be several words.

EXERCISE A: Recognizing Complete Subjects and Predicates. Copy each of the following sentences onto your paper. Underline the subject once and the verb twice. Then draw a vertical line between the complete subject and the complete predicate, as shown in the example.

EXAMPLE: The man in gray | paced in front of the statue.

1. A sudden storm | swept across the prairie.
2. Two old cargo ships | collided in the harbor.
3. Bruce | described his nervousness about the history test.
4. The lilac bushes in our front yard | burst into flower overnight.
5. Rosalyn | sews all her own clothing.

6. A rather strange event | occurred off the Atlantic coast.
7. Small white spots | appeared on the leaves of our plants.
8. He | described the accident in detail.
9. The local museum | sits on an acre of land near the river.
10. Many new telephones | have pushbuttons instead of dials.

APPLICATION: Developing Complete Subjects and Predicates. The first word in each of the following items is a noun or pronoun that can be used as a subject. The second word is a verb. Develop each item into a complete subject and predicate by adding details to the subject and verb. Write the new sentences on your paper. *Answers will vary; samples given for first two.*

EXAMPLE: tree fell

The tree in our back yard fell during a storm last night.

1. The Missouri River flows into the Mississippi.

1. river flows
2. comedians tried
3. everyone is
4. result was
5. storm lasted
6. train arrived
7. cat jumped
8. audience was
9. answer is
10. kites soared

2. The two comedians tried their best to make us laugh.

Compound Subjects and Verbs 7.3

Many sentences have a single subject and a single verb. Some sentences, however, have more than one subject. Others have more than one verb.

■ Compound Subjects

A sentence with more than one subject is said to have a *compound subject.*

A **compound subject** is two or more subjects that have the same verb and are joined by a conjunction such as *and* or *or*.

The parts of the compound subjects in the following examples are underlined once. Each verb is underlined twice.

EXAMPLES: Ted and Louise are brother and sister.

My sister or she will represent our club.

Apples, peaches, and grapes are sold at that roadside market.

EXERCISE A: Recognizing Compound Subjects. Each of the following sentences contains a compound subject. Copy the sentences onto your paper and underline the subjects that make up each compound subject.

EXAMPLE: Red, white, and blue are popular colors for flags.

1. Skaters and cyclists crowd the park each weekend.
2. After the dance Joan and I stopped for a milkshake.
3. All day wind and rain lashed the tiny island.
4. The coach, the team, and the cheerleaders boarded the bus for the game.
5. Both gorillas and orangutans are in danger of extinction.
6. Along the road daisies, buttercups, lilies, and dandelions grew in profusion.
7. Either the principal or the superintendent will introduce the speakers.
8. Adjectives and adverbs are modifiers.
9. Utah, Colorado, New Mexico, and Arizona touch borders at the same point.
10. San Marino and Liechtenstein are two of the smallest nations on earth.

■ Compound Verbs

A sentence with two or more verbs is said to have a *compound verb.*

A **compound verb** is two or more verbs that have the same subject and are joined by a conjunction such as *and* or *or.*

EXAMPLES: He smiles often and frowns occasionally.

The plan will succeed or fail within a year.

She produces, directs, and often acts in her own productions.

Sometimes a sentence will have both a compound subject and a compound verb.

EXAMPLE: Jane and Sharon both sing and dance.

EXERCISE B: Recognizing Compound Verbs. Each of the following sentences contains a compound verb. Copy the sentences onto your paper, and underline the verbs that make up each compound verb.

EXAMPLE: Carol looked around and then laughed uproariously.

1. Our kite dipped suddenly and wrapped itself around a tree.
2. The workers first dug a hole and then carefully lowered the new shrub into it.
3. The dog turned around three times, settled into its bed, and yawned.
4. The coin slipped from my hand, rolled along the pavement, and dropped into a sewer drain.
5. My parents sold the station wagon and bought a new compact car.
6. I either left my door keys at home or lost them at school.
7. The conductor bowed to the audience, turned to the orchestra, and began to lead them in Beethoven's Fifth Symphony.
8. The snake recoiled and then struck.
9. Jan finished her homework, prepared for bed, and settled down to her favorite TV show.
10. We gathered the ears of corn and put them in bushel baskets.

APPLICATION 1: Recognizing Compound Subjects and Verbs. Each of the following sentences contains a compound subject, a compound verb, or both. On your paper write the compound subjects and the compound verbs. Then label each compound subject and compound verb as in the example.

Compound verbs are underlined twice.

EXAMPLE: He and she are good friends.

He, she compound subject

1. Our old magazines and newspapers are stored in the attic.
2. She opened the door and rushed out of the lobby.
3. My mother and father either walk or drive to the station.
4. The top spun for a minute, teetered, and finally fell on its side.
5. Trains, buses, and taxis are three popular means of transportation in urban areas.
6. Neither Cal nor Peter liked Oliver's poem.
7. She washes and scrubs her face four times a day.
8. "Bonny Barbara Allan" and "Lord Randal" are two of the most popular English ballads.
9. Michelle and she read French well and often translate whole passages into English.
10. A tall man, three girls, and a little boy appeared at our door and asked for a "Mr. Malinowski."

APPLICATION 2: Developing Sentences with Compound Subjects and Verbs. The following items contain compound subjects and verbs. Expand these subjects and verbs into fully developed sentences by adding conjunctions, descriptive words, and other details. Write your complete sentences on your paper.

Answers will vary; samples given for first two.

EXAMPLE: cats, dogs are

Large cats and small dogs are sometimes good friends.

1. That active toddler sometimes reaches up to the table and grabs the silverware.

1. toddler reaches, grabs
2. food was spoiled, could be eaten

2. After the power outage, the food was spoiled and could not be eaten.

3. Barbara, Lisa will agree
4. brother drove, walked
5. singer, musicians will record
6. uncle, aunt visited, stayed
7. Walt Whitman, Edgar Allan Poe have been
8. daffodils, irises were given, were put
9. snow, sleet fell, disrupted
10. friend learned, did

Special Problems with Subjects 7.4

In the first three sections of this chapter, each subject that you were asked to find appeared somewhere early in the sentence, with the verb following immediately or soon after. This pattern, a subject followed by a verb, is the pattern most often used in English sentences. Thus, it is called *normal word order*. As long as the subject comes before the verb, it does not matter whether the subject and verb appear at the beginning, middle, or end of the sentence—the sentence is in normal word order.

NORMAL WORD ORDER: The car (S) raced (V) toward the bridge.

Yesterday morning after breakfast, Uncle George (S) left (V) on a flight for home.

Trapped by the bad weather, cold and hungry, she (S) waited (V).

In several kinds of sentences, however, the subject and verb do not follow normal word order. In some sentences the subject may seem to be missing entirely. In others the subject may follow the verb or come between the parts of a verb phrase. This section will give you practice in recognizing sentences that do not follow normal word order. It will also help you find the subjects in these sentences.

Subjects in Orders and Directions

Some sentences give orders or directions. In most of these sentences, the subject does not appear before the verb.

In sentences that give orders or directions, the subject is understood to be *you.*

On the left side of the following chart are three examples of sentences that give orders or directions. The verbs are underlined twice. On the right side, the same sentences appear with the understood subjects shown in parentheses.

Order or Direction	With Understood *You* Added
Drive carefully!	(You) Drive carefully!
After waiting a moment, dial the number again.	After waiting a moment, (you) dial the number again.
Lucy, leave the room.	Lucy, (you) leave the room.

EXERCISE A: Recognizing Subjects That Give Orders or Directions. On your paper write the subject of each of the following sentences. Seven of the sentences give orders or directions. The other three are ordinary sentences in normal word order.

EXAMPLE: David, remember to turn out the lights.

(you)

1. Wash your face with soap and water. *(You)*
2. Tell us what happened, Frank. *(You)*
3. Marie, open the window about an inch. *(you)*
4. Paul tried to remove the splinter from Sue's finger.
5. After raking the leaves, spread an even coat of lime on the lawn. *(you)*
6. Girls, help us carry these packages into the house.

4. Paul 6. (you)

7. Measure the amount of rain that falls each morning.
8. The bread jammed the toaster and burned. *bread*
9. Get the doctor at once! *(You)*
10. She bought a portable radio. *She*

7. (You)

Subjects in Questions

A sentence not in normal word order will generally be in *inverted word order*. The subject in such a sentence comes after its verb. This order is seen perhaps most often in questions.

In questions the subject often follows the verb.

Many questions begin with a verb or a helping verb. Others begin with such questioning words as *what, which, whose, who, when, why, where,* and *how*. In the following examples, notice that the subject sometimes comes between the parts of a verb phrase.

VERB FIRST: Are the apples very sour?

HELPING VERB FIRST: Have you opened your present?

QUESTIONING WORD FIRST: Where are the sour apples?

When will they begin the play?

If you have trouble finding the subject in a question, you can use a trick. Simply reword the question as a statement. The subject will then appear before the verb.

Question	Reworded as Statement
Are the apples very sour?	The apples are very sour.
Have you opened your present?	You have opened your present.
Where are the sour apples?	The sour apples are where.
When will they begin the play?	They will begin the play when.

Although many questions use inverted word order, some do not.

EXAMPLES: Whose poems were selected for the school literary magazine?

Who has taken my notebook?

EXERCISE B: Finding the Subject in Questions. Copy the following sentences onto your paper. Underline the subject in each.

EXAMPLE: Which Dickinson poem do you like best?

1. When did she call from her office?
2. Which book did Billy choose?
3. Has Roberto left for college yet?
4. Were the flowers delivered on time?
5. Which team has won the trophy?
6. How did they accept the news?
7. Where is the signature on this check?
8. Are you certain about the record?
9. Who took my pencil?
10. Why has he objected to the title of the play?

Subjects in Sentences Beginning with *There* or *Here*

Sentences beginning with *there* or *here* are usually in inverted word order.

There or *here* is never the subject of a sentence.

There can be used in two ways at the beginning of sentences. First, it can be used just to start the sentence.

SENTENCE STARTERS: There are (V) two astronauts (S) from NASA in the office.

There is (V) no good reason (S) for our failure.

There can also be used as an adverb at the beginning of sentences, as can the word *here.* As adverbs these two words point out where and modify the verbs.

ADVERBS: There goes (V) the principal (S).

Here are (V) the invitations (S) to the party.

Be alert to sentences beginning with *there* and *here.* Remember that they are probably in inverted word order. If you have a problem finding the subject, mentally reword the sentence. Put it in normal word order. If *there* is just a sentence starter, it can be dropped from the sentence.

Sentence Beginning with *There* or *Here*	Reworded with Subject Before Verb
There is a mistake on your paper.	A mistake is on your paper.
Here comes the captain of the team.	The captain of the team comes here.

EXERCISE C: Finding the Subject in Sentences Beginning with *There* and *Here.* Copy the following sentences onto your paper. Underline the subject in each.

EXAMPLE: Here is the missing piece.

1. Here are the notes on the trip.
2. There were three steps to follow in the recipe.
3. There is a new sporting goods store in town.
4. There are the magazines on boating.
5. Here are three good mystery novels to read.
6. There is a bad winter storm approaching us.
7. There on the hill are the ruins of the ancient temple.
8. There can be only one choice.
9. Here sat the ambassador from Zimbabwe.
10. Here are your assignments for the next week.

Subjects in Sentences Inverted for Emphasis

Sometimes a subject is intentionally put after its verb to draw attention to the subject.

In some sentences the subject follows the verb in order to receive greater emphasis.

In the following example, notice how the order of the words builds suspense by leading up to the subject.

EXAMPLE: In the midst of the crowd outside the theater stood (V) Muhammed Ali (S).

Sentences such as this one can be reworded in normal word order to make it easier to find the subject.

Inverted Word Order	Reworded with Subject Before Verb
In the midst of the crowd outside the theater stood Muhammed Ali.	Muhammed Ali stood in the midst of the crowd outside the theater.

EXERCISE D: Finding the Subject in Inverted Sentences. Copy the following sentences onto your paper. Underline the subject in each.

EXAMPLE: Far in the distance came the first roar of thunder.

1. High atop the tree on a dead branch perched a vulture.
2. All about the neighborhood lay the debris from the tornado.
3. Suddenly, into the clearing came three deer.
4. On that distant hill once stood an old one-room schoolhouse.
5. Not far from the cabin was a clear, cold stream.

APPLICATION: Writing Sentences with Subjects in Various Positions. Write original sentences according to the

following directions. Add any missing subjects, using parentheses. Then underline the subject in each sentence. *Answers will vary; samples given for first two.*
1. There are four apples in the bowl. 2. (You) Choose your courses carefully.

EXAMPLE: Begin a sentence with *Were they.*

Were they really lost on a desert island?

1. Begin a sentence with *There are.*
2. Begin a sentence with *Choose.*
3. Begin a question with *What have.*
4. Begin a sentence with *How.*
5. Begin a sentence with *Here.*
6. Begin a question with *Did she.*
7. Begin a sentence with *There will be.*
8. Begin an order with *Stop.*
9. Write a sentence ending with the subject.
10. Write a question in which the subject comes before the verb.

Direct Objects 7.5

Often a subject and verb alone can express a complete thought. For example, "Birds fly" can stand by itself as a sentence even though it contains just a subject and a verb. In other sentences, however, the thought begun by a subject and its verb needs to be completed with other words. For example, the sentences "Toni bought," "The eyewitness told," "Our librarian is," and "Richard feels" all contain a subject and verb, but none expresses a complete thought. All these ideas need *complements.*

A **complement** is a word or group of words that completes the meaning of a subject and verb.

Complements are usually nouns, pronouns, or adjectives. They are located right after or very close to the verb. In the following chart, the subjects are underlined once, the verbs twice, and the complements are boxed and labeled.

DIFFERENT KINDS OF COMPLEMENTS
Toni bought cookies. (Complement: cookies)
The eyewitness told us the story. (Complements: us, story)
Our librarian is a poet. (Complement: poet)
Richard feels sad. (Complement: sad)

The next three sections will describe three types of complements: *direct objects, indirect objects,* and *subject complements.*

The Direct Object

Direct objects are complements that are used after action verbs.

> A **direct object** is a noun or pronoun that receives the action of a transitive verb.

A direct object can be found by asking *Whom?* or *What?* after an action verb.

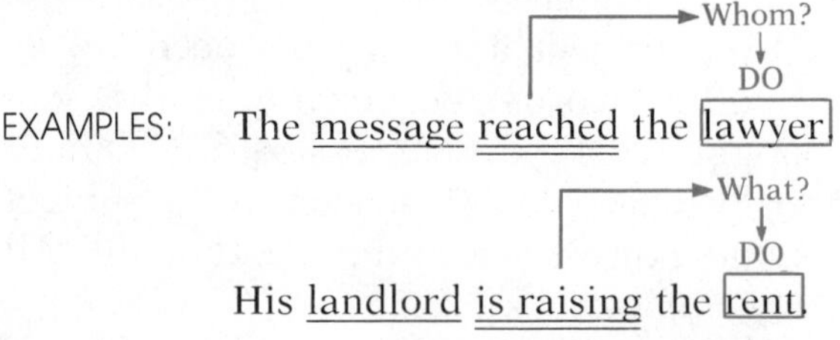

Whom?
DO
EXAMPLES: The message reached the lawyer.
What?
DO
His landlord is raising the rent.

In the examples *lawyer* and *rent* are the direct objects of the verbs. In the first sentence, the question is *Reached whom?* The answer is the *lawyer*. In the second example, the question is *Raised what?* The answer is the *rent.*

EXERCISE A: Recognizing Direct Objects. Each of the following sentences contains a direct object. Copy the sentences onto your paper and underline each direct object.

EXAMPLE: She quickly opened the letter.

1. My aunt approached the door cautiously.
2. Sally gave our puppy to the Wilsons.
3. The patients take their medicine three times a day.
4. My mother sent the clothing to the Red Cross.
5. At night she often eats frozen dinners.
6. We received oranges from Florida.
7. I want them here now.
8. He winds his gold watch each morning.
9. After lunch she gave an account of the accident.
10. They did not serve any dessert after dinner.

Compound Direct Objects

Direct objects, like subjects and verbs, can be compound.

> A **compound direct object** is two or more nouns or pronouns that receive the action of the same transitive verb.

If a sentence contains a compound direct object, asking *Whom?* or *What?* after the verb will give you more than one answer.

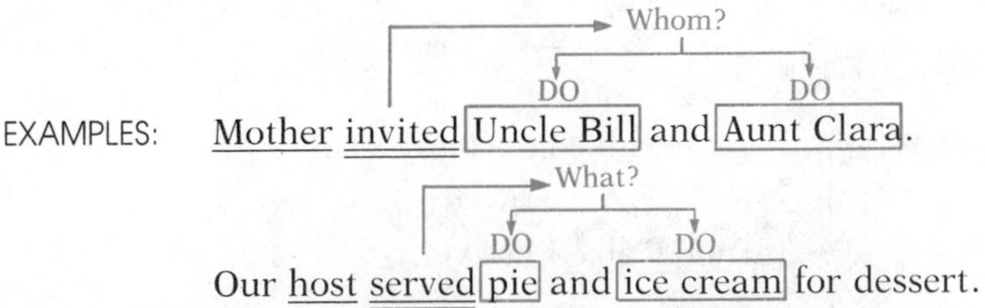

Whom?
DO
DO
EXAMPLES: Mother invited Uncle Bill and Aunt Clara.
What?
DO
DO
Our host served pie and ice cream for dessert.

EXERCISE B: Recognizing Compound Direct Objects. Each of the following sentences contains a compound direct object. On your paper write only the nouns or pronouns that make up each compound direct object.

EXAMPLE: Don't forget the carrots or the spinach.

carrots spinach

1. At the market buy some lettuce and tomatoes.
2. After class Mr. Simpson complimented Ned and him.
3. Did they buy a sedan or a convertible?
4. I shocked Mary and Bob with my story.
5. I saw him and her at the movies.
6. The train passed Providence and Boston while I slept.
7. Linda and Alan planted marigolds and petunias in their garden.
8. The poet Sylvia Plath wrote many poems and one novel.
9. She has always loved ships and the sea.
10. Sara bought a new blouse and a yellow skirt.

Direct Object, Adverb, or Object of a Preposition?

Not all action verbs have direct objects. Be careful not to confuse a direct object with an adverb or with the object of a preposition.

> A direct object is never an adverb or the noun or pronoun at the end of a prepositional phrase.

Compare the following examples. Notice that the action verb *walked* has a direct object only in the first sentence.

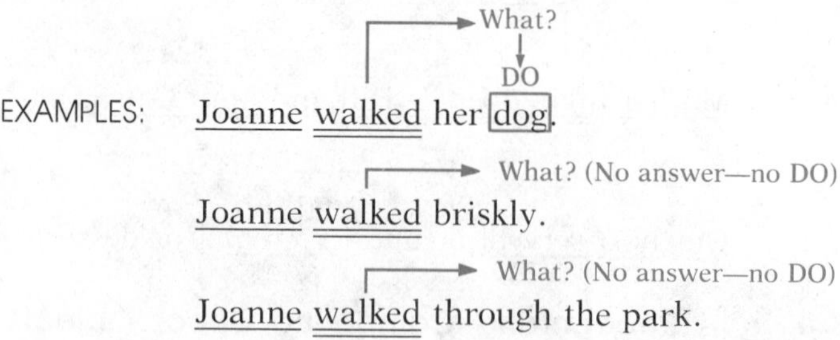

Each example shows a very common sentence type. The first consists of a subject, a verb, and a direct object. The noun *dog* is the direct object of the verb *walked.* The second example consists of a subject, a verb, and an adverb. Nothing answers the question *What?* so there is no direct object. *Briskly* modifies the verb. The third example consists of a subject, a verb, and a prepositional phrase. Again, no noun or pronoun answers the question *What?* The prepositional phrase tells where Joanne walked.

Notice also that a single sentence can contain more than one of these three.

EXAMPLE: Joanne walked her dog briskly through the park.
(DO: dog; Adv: briskly; Prep Phrase: through the park)

EXERCISE C: Distinguishing Between Direct Objects, Adverbs, and Objects of Prepositions. Copy each of the following sentences onto your paper. Underline each direct object. Circle any adverbs or prepositional phrases. Not every sentence has all three.

Adverbs and prepositional phrases are shaded.

EXAMPLE: The dragon roared (loudly) (in the night).

1. Fred drove the old truck into our driveway.
2. She opened the letter slowly and cautiously.
3. My mother attended the parade in the park.
4. The lion chased the frightened animals through the forest.
5. He practiced a new stunt for the competition.

Direct Objects in Questions

A direct object in a sentence in normal word order is found after the verb. In questions, which are often in inverted order, the position of a direct object in the sentence may change.

A direct object in a question is sometimes near the beginning of the sentence, before the verb.

Compare the position of the direct object in each of the sentences in the following chart. The sentences in the first column are questions. In the second column, the questions have been reworded as statements in normal word order.

Questions	Normal Word Order
DO Whom did you ask for help?	DO You did ask whom for help.
DO What does he want from us?	DO He does want what from us.
DO Which book does he want from the library?	DO He does want which book from the library.

If you have trouble finding the direct object in a question, change the sentence into normal word order, as shown in the examples.

EXERCISE D: Finding Direct Objects in Questions. Copy each of the following sentences onto your paper and underline each direct object. Note that in two of the sentences, the direct objects follow the verbs.

EXAMPLE: What were you thinking?

1. Which photograph did she take?
2. Whom does he expect this evening?
3. What did you do with the package?
4. Where will you spend your vacation?
5. Which books have they read?
6. How many records did you buy?
7. Which suggestions have they considered so far?
8. What have you heard about the astronauts?
9. When will the judges announce the awards?
10. Which color have they chosen for the new curtains?

APPLICATION: Writing Sentences with Direct Objects. Write an original sentence for each of the following patterns. You may add additional words or details as long as you keep the assigned pattern.

Answers will vary; samples given for first two.

EXAMPLE: Subject + Verb + Direct Object + Direct Object

Becky collected both records and marbles.

1. Subject + Verb + Direct Object
2. Subject + Verb + Direct Object + Prepositional Phrase
3. Direct Object + Helping Verb + Subject + Verb
4. Subject + Verb + Direct Object + Conjunction + Direct Object
5. Subject + Verb + Direct Object + Adverb + Prepositional Phrase

1. My cousin borrowed my blue sweater.
2. Dad is adding a toolshed to the garage.

Indirect Objects 7.6

Sentences that contain a direct object may also contain another kind of complement, called an *indirect object.*

The Indirect Object

A sentence can not have an indirect object unless it first has a direct object.

> An **indirect object** is a noun or pronoun that comes after an action verb and before a direct object. It names the person or thing that something is given to or done for.

An indirect object answers the question *To or for whom?* or *To or for what?* after an action verb. To find an indirect object, find the direct object first. Then ask the questions, as shown in the examples.

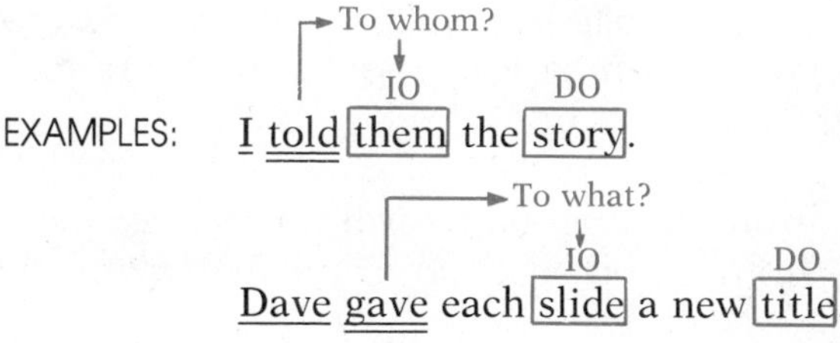

In the first of the sentences above, *them* answers the question *To whom did I tell the story?* In the second example, *slide* answers the question *To what did Dave give a title?*

Keep in mind the following pattern: Subject + Verb + Indirect Object + Direct Object. An indirect object will almost always come between the verb and the direct object in a sentence.

EXERCISE A: Recognizing Indirect Objects. Each of the following sentences contains a direct object and an indirect object. Copy the sentences onto your paper and underline each indirect object.

EXAMPLE: Finally, she told him the news.

1. The coach gave him a special award.
2. We sent her a bouquet of flowers.
3. After dinner they told us the good news.
4. Have you shown them the new puppy?
5. Lucille lent her brother her umbrella.
6. I later wrote my brother an explanation for my behavior.
7. Pass your sister the vegetables.
8. Vasco taught me several Portuguese words.
9. I will order you some breakfast now.
10. Did you really sell him your record collection?

Compound Indirect Objects

Like a subject, verb, or direct object, an indirect object can be compound.

> A **compound indirect object** is two or more nouns or pronouns that come after an action verb and before a direct object. It names the persons or things that something is given to or done for.

Compound indirect objects answer the same questions as single indirect objects: *To or for whom?* or *To or for what?*

To what?

IO IO DO

EXAMPLE: Dave gave each slide and photo a new title.

EXERCISE B: Recognizing Compound Indirect Objects. Each of the following sentences contains a compound indirect object. On your paper write only the nouns or pronouns that make up each compound indirect object.

EXAMPLE: Will he tell Jay and Cathy the truth?

Jay Cathy

1. Give him and her an equal amount.
2. Have you told Sally or Beth that story?
3. We gave the birds and the fish new homes.
4. Mother told the doctor and nurse our symptoms.
5. Did you get Marie and Steve their consent slips?
6. I gave the stairs and the porch a new coat of paint.
7. Have you told Mother and him the wonderful news?
8. Please read Bob and them the directions to the store.
9. In the morning I will give Joyce and her father our decision.
10. Take Uncle Bill and Aunt Lila a cold drink.

Indirect Object or Object of a Preposition?

Do not confuse an indirect object with the object of a preposition.

An indirect object never follows the preposition *to* or *for* in a sentence.

Compare the following examples.

EXAMPLES: Father bought him (IO) a present (DO).

Father bought a present (DO) for him.

In the first example, *him* is an indirect object. It comes after the verb and before the direct object. In the second example, *him* is the object of the preposition *for* and follows the direct object.

EXERCISE C: Distinguishing Between Indirect Objects and Objects of Prepositions. The following sentences contain either an indirect object or an object of a preposition. Copy each sentence onto your paper. Underline each indirect object. Circle each object of a preposition.
Objects of prepositions are shaded.

EXAMPLE: Strawberries gave him a rash.

1. Sheepishly, she told her father the story.
2. Raphael gave a bone to the collie.
3. Did you tell him the price?
4. Surprisingly enough, she gave her aunt the bracelet.
5. My mother brought her car to the repair shop.
6. I definitely will hold him to his promise.
7. In anger he gave him the money.
8. I did offer her a choice.
9. Please buy a new radio for them.
10. Have you shown your mother the test paper?

APPLICATION: Writing Sentences with Indirect Objects. Follow the directions to write five sentences.
Answers will vary; samples given for first two.

EXAMPLE: Write a sentence with three indirect objects.

Mary Beth told Cindy, Craig, and Joel her secret.

1. Mother Hubbard gave her dog a bone. 2. Mother Hubbard gave a bone to her dog.

1. Write a sentence that fits this pattern: Subject + Verb + Indirect Object + Direct Object.
2. Using the same subject, verb, and direct object as in the first item, change the sentence to Subject + Verb + Direct Object + Prepositional Phrase.
3. Write a sentence with a compound indirect object connected by *and*.
4. Write a sentence with a compound indirect object connected by *or*.
5. Rewrite the sentence in the example, changing the compound indirect object to a prepositional phrase.

7.7 Subject Complements

Both direct objects and indirect objects are complements used with action verbs. Linking verbs, however, have a different kind of complement, called a *subject complement.*

A **subject complement** is a noun, pronoun, or adjective that follows a linking verb and tells something about the subject.

Nouns and pronouns that act as subject complements are called *predicate nouns* and *predicate pronouns*. An adjective that acts as a subject complement is called a *predicate adjective.*

Predicate Nouns and Pronouns

Both nouns and pronouns are sometimes used as subject complements after linking verbs.

A **predicate noun** or **predicate pronoun** follows a linking verb and renames or identifies the subject of the sentence.

It is easy to recognize *predicate nouns* and *predicate pronouns.* The linking verb acts much like an equal sign between the subject and the noun or pronoun that follows the verb. Both the subject and the predicate noun or pronoun refer to the same person or thing.

PREDICATE NOUNS AND PRONOUNS	
Examples	**Relationship of Words**
Ronnie will be the captain (PN) of our team.	The predicate noun *captain* renames the subject *Ronnie.*
North America's longest river is the Mississippi (PN).	The predicate noun *Mississippi* identifies the subject *river.*
The two winners are they (Pred Pron).	The predicate pronoun *they* identifies the subject *winners.*

The verbs in these examples are all forms of the linking verb *be.* See Section 2.2 for a complete list of the forms of *be* and other linking verbs.

A predicate noun or pronoun will never be the object of a preposition. In the following example, the subject complement is *one,* not *stars.*

EXAMPLE: Diana Ross was one (Pred Pron) of the stars (Obj of Prep) in *The Wiz.*

EXERCISE A: Recognizing Predicate Nouns and Pronouns. Copy the following sentences onto your paper and underline each predicate noun or predicate pronoun.

EXAMPLE: That yellow shrub is a forsythia.

1. The capital of New Jersey is Trenton.
2. Peter Taylor has long been one of America's best short-story writers.
3. At this time Sheila appears the frontrunner.
4. According to legend Prometheus was a Titan.
5. That young woman may someday become a fine doctor.
6. Many years ago Simla was the capital of British India.
7. Carlos and Juan have remained buddies for years.
8. The last person in line is she.
9. My favorite sport has always been basketball.
10. That camera was an excellent choice.

Predicate Adjectives

A linking verb can also be followed by a *predicate adjective.*

A **predicate adjective** follows a linking verb and describes the subject of the sentence.

A predicate adjective is considered part of the complete predicate of a sentence because it comes after a linking verb. In spite of this, a predicate adjective does not modify the words in the predicate. Instead, it describes the noun or pronoun that serves as the subject in front of the linking verb.

PREDICATE ADJECTIVES	
Examples	**Relationship of Words**
The flight to Houston was PA swift.	The predicate adjective *swift* describes the subject *flight.*
Our congresswoman seems very PA sensitive to the needs of her constituents.	The predicate adjective *sensitive* describes the subject *congresswoman.*

EXERCISE B: Recognizing Predicate Adjectives. Copy the following sentences onto your paper and underline each predicate adjective.

EXAMPLE: The sky is murky.

1. The scent of the flowers is very sweet.
2. Many of the houses are quite old.
3. I felt sad about his misfortune.
4. At night this road becomes particularly dangerous.
5. The smoke from the fire remained heavy.
6. This chemical smells stronger than any other.
7. The view from the mountaintop was breathtaking.
8. The old windmill in Aruba is very attractive.
9. The carton seems too heavy to carry.
10. He has always been honest about his shortcomings.

Compound Subject Complements

Like other sentence parts, subject complements can be compound.

A **compound subject complement** consists of two or more predicate nouns, pronouns, or adjectives.

EXAMPLES: My two best friends are Phil and Mark. (PN: Phil, Mark)

The other speakers were he and she. (Pred Pron: he, she)

The highway seems slick and icy. (PA: slick, icy)

EXERCISE C: Recognizing Compound Subject Complements. Copy the following sentences onto your paper and underline each part of each compound subject complement. If a compound subject complement is made up of predicate adjectives, draw arrows pointing from each adjective to the subject.

EXAMPLE: The icing was rich and sweet.

Subjects modified by predicate adjectives are shaded.

1. Vacations in state parks can be interesting and inexpensive.
2. My favorite poets are Emily Dickinson and Langston Hughes.
3. The old bridge seems frail and dangerous.
4. The organizers of the crafts fair were Sonia and I.
5. That imported cheese tastes moldy and much too strong.
6. This fish is either flounder or sole.
7. Are the sails strong and seaworthy?
8. Their hands became raw and frostbitten in the icy wind.
9. The soup is neither too hot nor too cold.
10. The flame first turned orange, then blue, and finally brilliant white.

APPLICATION: Writing Sentences with Subject Complements. Use the following subjects and verbs to write sentences of your own. Include in each sentence the type of subject complement given in parentheses.

Answers will vary; samples given.

EXAMPLE: poem was (compound predicate adjectives)

The poem was short but moving.

1. ^feet feel ^ (predicate adjective) *My/cold.*
2. Bob and Stan will be ^ (predicate noun) *lifeguards.*
3. ^captains are ^ (compound predicate pronouns) *The/she and I.*
4. ^dog is ^ (compound predicate adjectives)
5. ^roast beef looks ^ (predicate adjective) *This/too rare.*
6. ^cities are ^ (compound predicate nouns)
7. ^cars appear ^ (compound predicate adjectives)
8. ^precious metals are ^ (compound predicate nouns)
9. ^music sounds ^ (predicate adjective) *His/old-fashioned.*
10. ^cousins are ^ (predicate noun and predicate pronoun) *My/Brenda and she.*

4. The/mangy and dirty. 6. My favorite/Montreal and Denver. 7. These/clean and new. 8. Two/gold and platinum.

The Four Functions of Sentences 7.8

Sentences are often classified according to what they do. A sentence may be *declarative, interrogative, imperative,* or *exclamatory*.

A **declarative sentence** states an idea and ends with a period.

DECLARATIVE: A strong wind whipped through the valley.

Royal Street in New Orleans is filled with expensive shops and horse-drawn carriages.

The cost is three hundred dollars.

An **interrogative sentence** asks a question and ends with a question mark.

INTERROGATIVE: Where is the old city hall?

Have you ever attempted to make lasagna?

Who is he?

An **imperative sentence** gives an order or a direction and ends with either a period or an exclamation mark.

Many imperative sentences begin with a verb. When the subject of such a sentence is left out, it is understood to be *you.*

IMPERATIVE: Wrap the package carefully.

Stop!

Imperative sentences, however, do sometimes have subjects. When they do, they sound very much like questions. But instead of ending with a question mark, they end with a period or exclamation mark. In the following examples, the subjects are italicized.

IMPERATIVE: Can *you* help us, please.

Will *somebody* answer the phone!

An **exclamatory sentence** conveys strong emotion and ends with an exclamation mark.

EXAMPLES: What a terrible accident that was!

He is a villain!

EXERCISE A: Identifying the Use of Sentences. Read each of the following sentences and identify its use as *declarative, interrogative, imperative,* or *exclamatory.* After each answer, write the appropriate punctuation mark for that sentence.

EXAMPLE: What a mistake that was

exclamatory !

1. Have you visited the dentist yet this year *inter* ?
2. Choose the hat with the best fit *imper* .
3. Between 1629 and 1640, almost 60,000 people emigrated from England *declar* .
4. She worked very hard as governor *declar* .
5. Would you stand absolutely still now, please *imper* .
6. What are the other ingredients needed for the cookies *inter* ?
7. I agree with the editorial in this newspaper *declar* .

8. What an excellent magazine this is *exclam* !
9. How much do they want for it now *inter* ?
10. Give two reasons supporting your opening statement *imper*

APPLICATION: Writing Sentences with Different Uses. Write a sentence according to the directions given for each of the following items.
Answers will vary; samples given for first two.

EXAMPLE: Write an imperative sentence that ends with an exclamation mark.

Do it now!

1. Close the door behind you.

1. Write an imperative sentence that begins with a verb.
2. Write a question beginning with *Which.*
3. Write a declarative sentence about your favorite hobby.
4. Write an exclamatory sentence showing your surprise at something.
5. Write a question beginning with a verb.

2. Which invitation should I accept?

Diagraming Basic Sentence Parts 7.9

Diagraming is a visual way to explain how the parts of a sentence are related. In a diagram the words from a sentence are positioned on horizontal, vertical, and slanted lines. Each line stands for something different. This section will explain how you can draw diagrams for each of the sentence parts that were discussed in this chapter.

Subjects and Verbs

The basic parts of any sentence are the subject and its verb. In a diagram both the subject and verb are placed on a horizontal line. They are separated by a vertical line, with the subject on the left and the verb on the right.

EXAMPLE: Cars race. (S: Cars; V: race)

Cars | race

Names and compound nouns are diagramed in the same way as *cars* in the preceding example. Verb phrases are diagramed as was the verb *race.*

EXAMPLE: Elizabeth Wilson has been called. (S: Elizabeth Wilson; V: has been called)

Elizabeth Wilson | has been called

EXERCISE A: Diagraming Subjects and Verbs. Each of the following sentences contains a subject and verb. Diagram each sentence, using the preceding examples as models. *Answers on page T-107.*

1. People grow.
2. Max spoke.
3. Mrs. Rodriguez has changed.
4. Oklahoma State Park has opened.
5. They have been notified.

Adjectives, Adverbs, and Conjunctions

Most sentences contain more than a subject and verb. Here are the ways to add adjectives, adverbs, and conjunctions to your basic diagrams.

Adding Adjectives. Adjectives are placed on slanted lines directly below the nouns or pronouns they modify.

EXAMPLE: *A strong, icy* wind appeared. (S: wind; V: appeared)

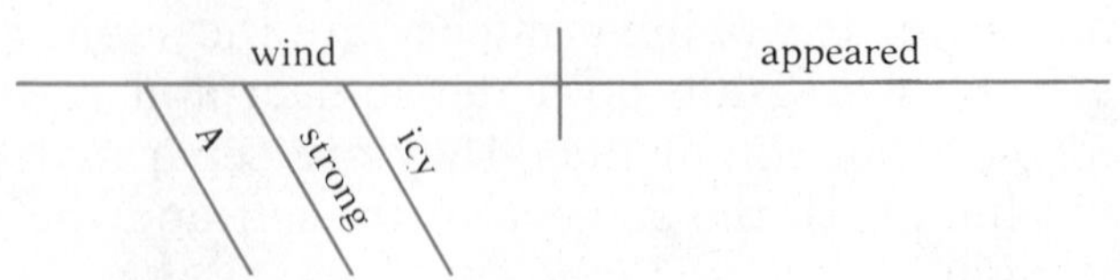

Adding Adverbs. Adverbs are also placed on slanted lines. They go directly under the verbs, adjectives, or adverbs they modify.

EXAMPLE: (Adj) *Quite* nervous, (S) Frank (V) spoke *very hesitantly.*

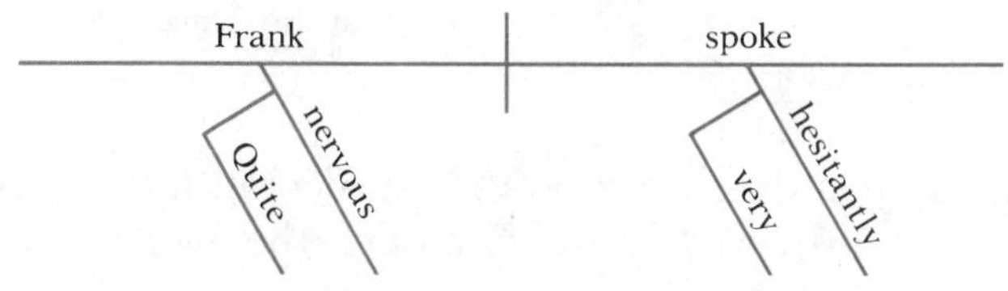

Adding Conjunctions. Conjunctions are diagramed on dotted lines drawn between the words they connect.

EXAMPLE: The (Adj) warm *and* (Adj) friendly (S) nurse (V) spoke (Adv) softly *but* (Adv) firmly.

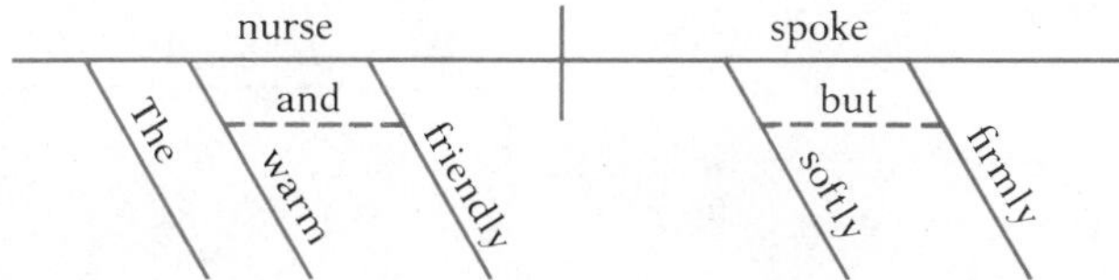

EXERCISE B: Diagraming Subjects and Verbs with Modifiers and Conjunctions. In addition to subjects and verbs, the following sentences contain adjectives, adverbs, and conjunctions. Diagram each sentence.

Answers on page T-108.

1. The old woman walked slowly.
2. The instructor spoke rapidly but quite distinctly.
3. The tiny but courageous dog yelped constantly.
4. The red and yellow tulips swayed very gently.
5. Extremely dense smoke was quickly drifting upward.

Compound Subjects and Verbs

It is necessary to split the horizontal line in order to diagram a sentence with either a compound subject or a compound verb.

Compound Subjects. A sentence with a compound subject has its subject diagramed on two levels.

EXAMPLE: Father and Mother are arriving.
(S: Father; S: Mother; V: are arriving)

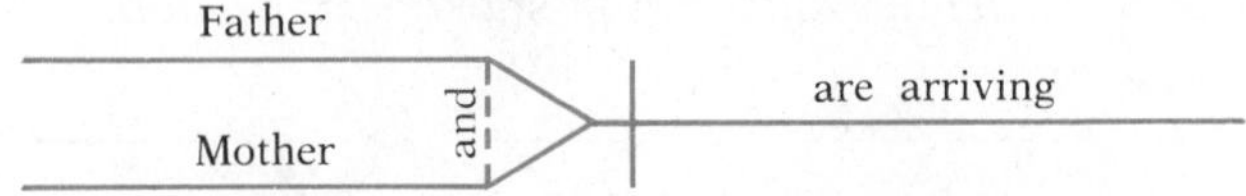

In diagraming compound subjects, take care to place any adjective directly under the word it modifies. If an adjective modifies the entire compound subject, place it under the main line of the diagram. In the following example, *several* modifies the entire compound subject. *Red* and *blue* modify separate subjects.

EXAMPLE: *Several red* balloons and *blue* kites floated overhead.
(S: balloons; S: kites; V: floated)

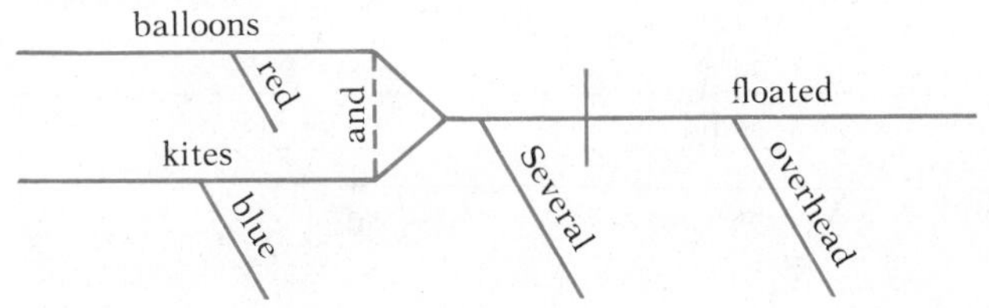

Compound Verbs. Sentences with compound verbs are diagramed much like sentences with compound subjects. In the following example, the adverb *magnificently* modifies both parts of the compound verb.

EXAMPLE: Jeffrey acts and sings *magnificently*.
(S: Jeffrey; V: acts; V: sings)

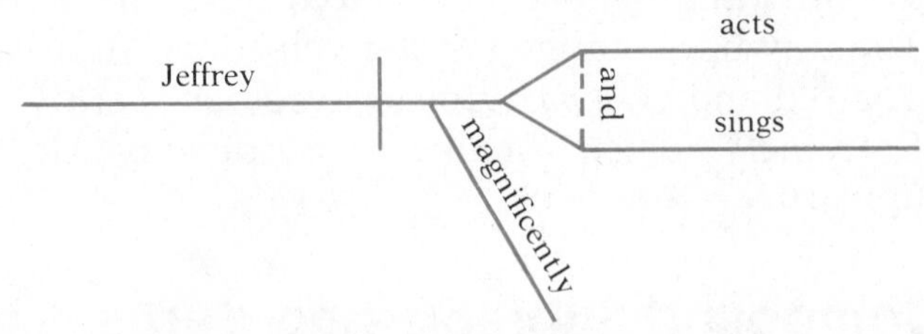

If the parts of a compound verb share a helping verb, the helping verb is placed on the main line of the diagram. If each part of the compound verb has its own helping verb, then each helping verb is placed on the line with its own verb.

EXAMPLE: Betty will (HV) win or lose.

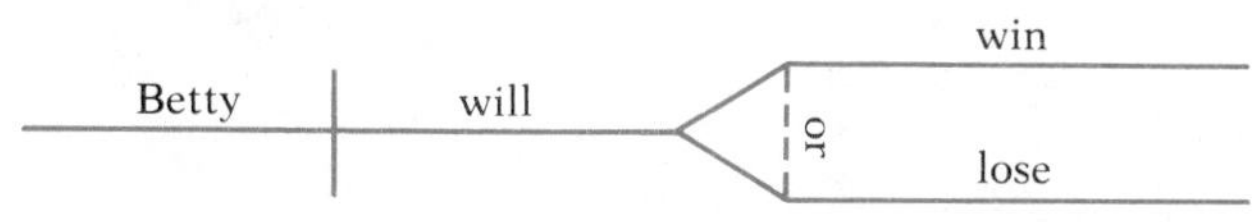

EXAMPLE; This project must (HV) grow or must (HV) shrink.

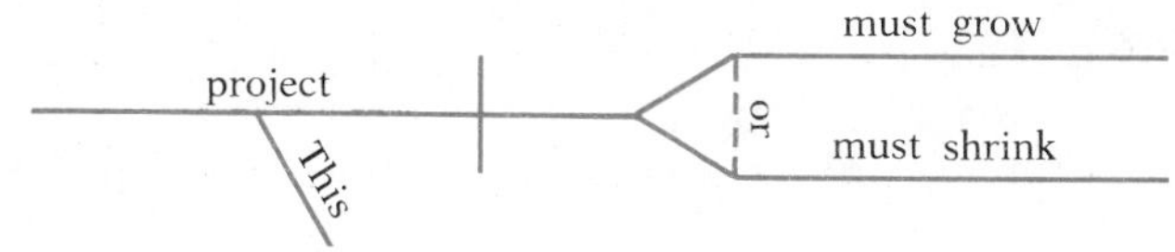

EXERCISE C: Diagraming Compound Subjects and Compound Verbs. Each of the following sentences has a compound subject, a compound verb, or both. Correctly diagram each sentence. *Answers on page T-109.*

1. Apples and grapes were served.
2. They can come or can stay.
3. The players, coaches, and parents cheered wildly.
4. The noisy crowd cheered, whistled, and applauded.
5. My brother and sister arrived early and left late.

■ Orders, Sentences Beginning with *There* and *Here*, and Interjections

Orders, sentences beginning with *there* or *here,* and interjections all follow special forms.

Orders. The subject of an order is usually understood to be *you.* The understood subject *you* is diagramed in the regular subject position, but in parentheses.

EXAMPLE: Stop (V) now.

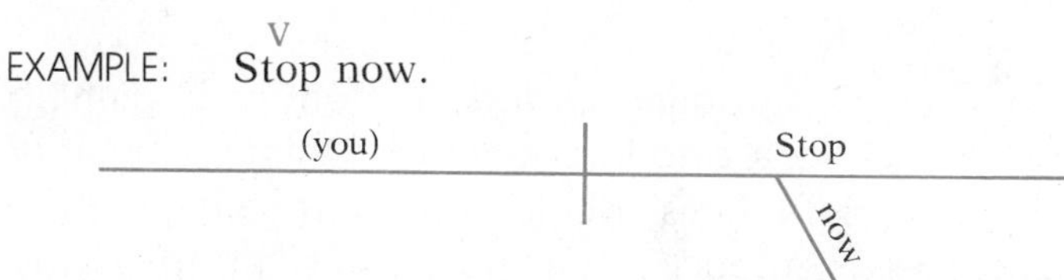

Sentences Beginning with *There* and *Here*. *There* and *here* sometimes appear at the beginning of sentences and are mistaken for subjects. They are usually adverbs that modify the verb.

V S
EXAMPLE: *Here* is your watch.

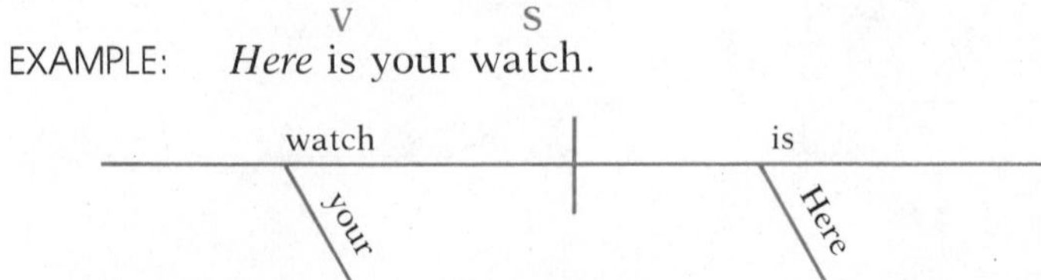

When *there* is used simply to start a sentence, it has no grammatical relation to the rest of the sentence. It is therefore placed on a short line above the subject.

V S
EXAMPLE: *There* is an important meeting now.

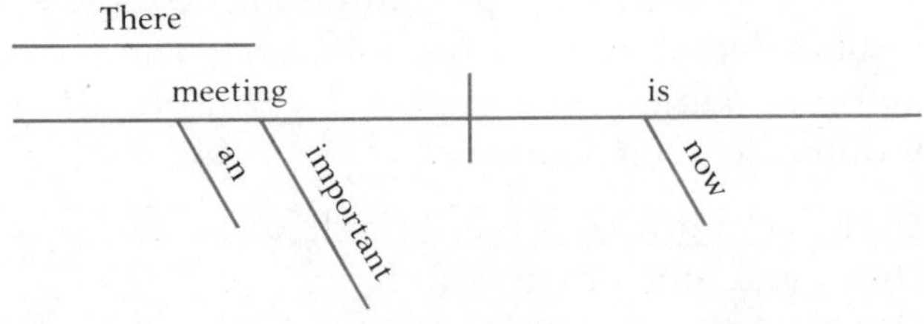

Interjections. Like the word *there* used simply to start a sentence, interjections have no grammatical relation to the other words in a sentence. For this reason interjections are also placed on a short line above the subject.

S V
EXAMPLE: *Wow!* I won.

Wow
I
won

EXERCISE D: Diagraming Orders, Sentences Beginning with *There* and *Here*, and Interjections. Diagram each of the following sentences. Make sure that you position the adverbs, sentence starters, interjections, and understood subjects correctly. *Answers on pages T-109–T-110.*

1. Begin now.
2. Here is my homework.
3. There once was a snake.
4. Whew! That hurt.
5. Gee! Watch out.

Complements

Direct objects, indirect objects, and subject complements are diagramed in three different ways.

Direct Objects. A direct object is placed on the same line as the subject and verb. The direct object follows the verb and is separated from it by a short vertical line.

DO

EXAMPLE: Children drink milk.

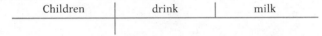

Children | drink | milk

A compound direct object is diagramed in a way similar to compound subjects and verbs. An adjective modifying both parts of the compound direct object is placed under the main line of the diagram. Otherwise, the adjective is placed directly under the word it modifies.

DO DO

EXAMPLE: I have read five books and magazines.

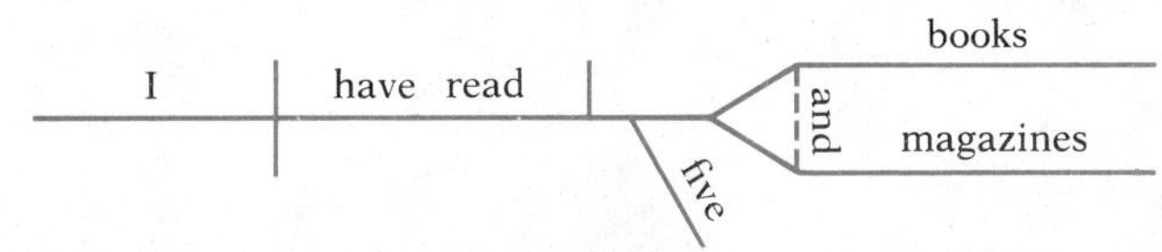

Indirect Objects. The indirect object is the only complement that is not placed on the main horizontal line. Instead, it is placed on a short horizontal line extending from a slanted line drawn directly below the verb.

IO

EXAMPLE: The teacher gave them the good news.

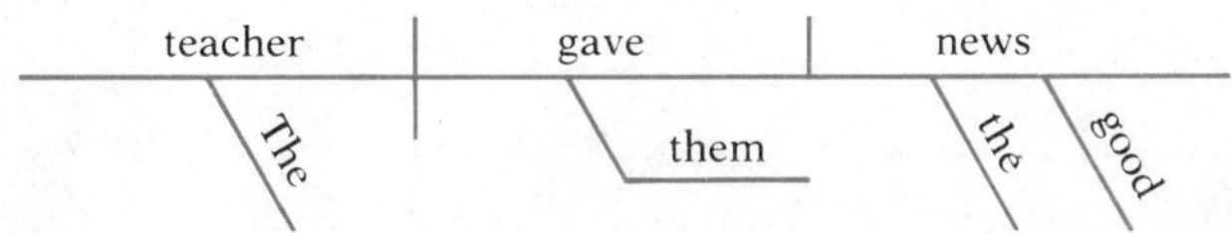

A sentence with a compound indirect object is diagramed in the following way.

EXAMPLE: Mother bought Billy [IO] and me [IO] new gloves.

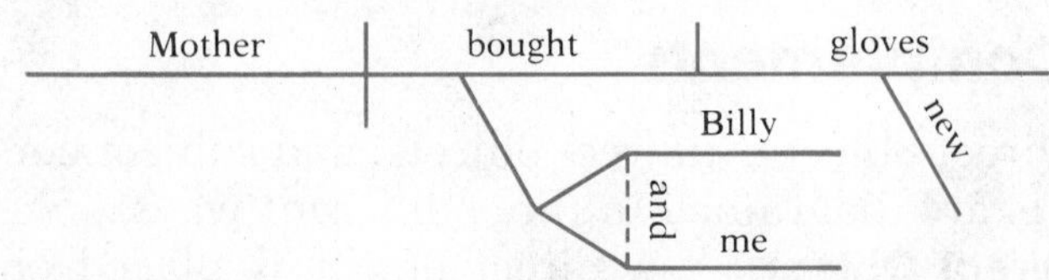

Subject Complements. The subject complements —predicate nouns, pronouns, and adjectives—follow linking verbs. All are diagramed in the same way. They are placed after the verb, separated from it by a short slanted line.

EXAMPLE: Julie will be our class president [PN].

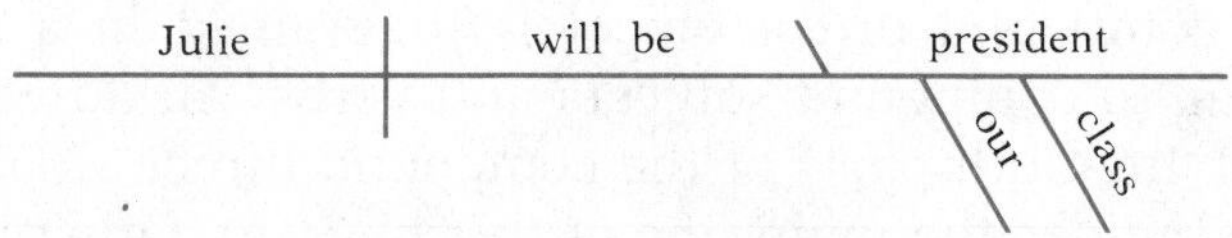

EXAMPLE: Julie seems very intelligent [PA].

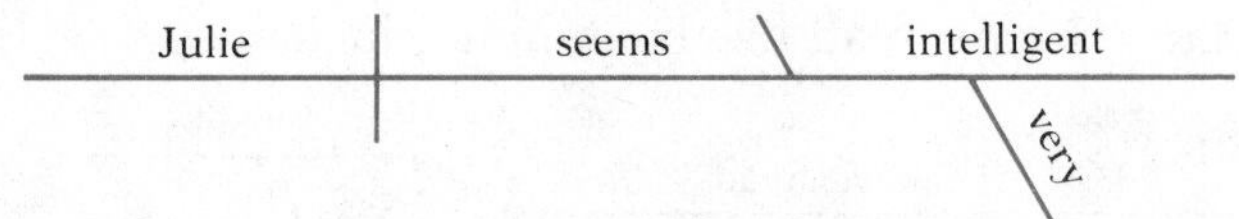

A compound subject complement is diagramed in the same way as a compound direct object, except that the separating line is slanted.

EXAMPLE: Those stamps are old [PA] and very valuable [PA].

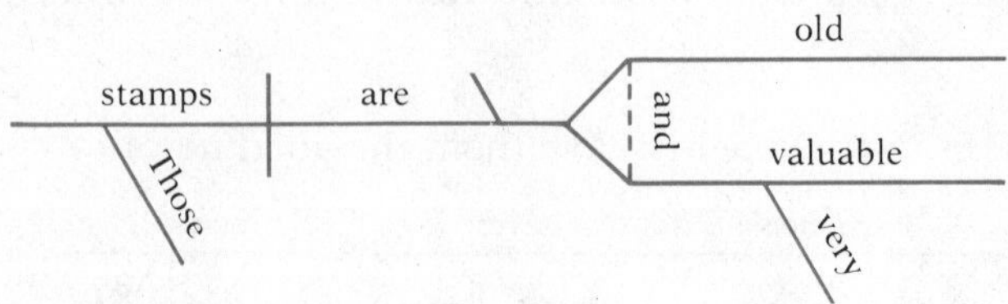

EXERCISE E: Diagraming Direct Objects and Indirect Objects. Diagram the following sentences. Some of the direct objects and indirect objects are compound.
Answers on pages T-110–T-111.

1. My sister owes me a dollar.
2. Our teacher gave Brad and me a new assignment.
3. Father later bought lettuce, radishes, and cucumbers.
4. I will tell my mother the story tomorrow.
5. The gymnast showed us her new routine.

EXERCISE F: Diagraming Subject Complements. Diagram the following sentences. Some of the complements are compound. *Answers on page T-111.*

1. The pool seems quite crowded.
2. The *Silver Streak* is a fine train.
3. Pat is the secretary and treasurer.
4. The river valley was unusually scenic.
5. Our new manager is honest and dependable.

APPLICATION: Diagraming Sentences with a Variety of Sentence Parts. The following sentences contain many of the sentence parts covered in this section: subjects, verbs, modifiers, conjunctions, and complements. Diagram each sentence. *Answers on pages T-112–T-113.*

1. My grandparents and uncle bought a small farm.
2. Our hotel rooms are clean, convenient, and airy.
3. There are three men and one woman outside.
4. The children wore mittens and boots.
5. Give them those books and the old magazines.
6. Amy and Joel wanted new bicycles.
7. They proudly carried the green and yellow banner.
8. The dentist smiled and put his drill away.
9. Those flowers are especially pretty.
10. Kerry will send us a letter soon.

Chapter 8

Expanding Sentences with Phrases

Chapter 7 explained the basic parts of a sentence: subjects, verbs, and complements. Sentences are built, however, with more than just these parts. For example, adjectives and adverbs can give color and clarify meaning. *Phrases* of all kinds also play an important role by adding information.

> A **phrase** is a group of words that functions in a sentence as a single part of speech. Phrases do not contain a subject and verb.

There are several kinds of phrases: *prepositional, appositive, participial, gerund,* and *infinitive.* They get their names from the word that begins the phrase or from the most important word in it. The first section in this chapter will discuss the kind of phrase with which you are probably most familiar, the prepositional phrase.

8.1 Prepositional Phrases

Section 5.1 explained that a *prepositional phrase* begins with a preposition and ends with a noun or pronoun called the object of the preposition.

	Prep	Obj	Prep	Obj	Prep	Obj
EXAMPLES:	under	the window	near	them	at	the store

Prepositional phrases may also have compound objects.

EXAMPLE: near the flowers and the trees (Prep: near; Obj: flowers; Obj: trees)

In a sentence, a prepositional phrase can act as an adjective and modify a noun or pronoun. It can also act as an adverb and modify a verb, adjective, or adverb.

Prepositional Phrases That Act as Adjectives

A prepositional phrase that acts as an adjective is called an *adjective phrase.*

An **adjective phrase** is a prepositional phrase that modifies a noun or pronoun by telling what kind or which one.

The following chart compares adjective phrases to one-word adjectives. Notice that an adjective phrase usually follows its noun or pronoun.

Adjectives	Adjective Phrases
A *double-decked* bus skidded.	A bus *with a double deck* skidded.
The *blue-eyed* acrobat slipped and fell.	The acrobat *with the blue eyes* slipped and fell.

The adjective phrases answer the same questions as the one-word adjectives. *What kind* of bus skidded? A bus *with a double deck* did. *Which one* of the acrobats slipped and fell? The acrobat *with the blue eyes* did.

An adjective phrase can modify nouns and pronouns used in many ways: as subjects, direct and indirect objects, predicate nouns and pronouns, and so on.

MODIFYING A SUBJECT: Everyone *on the committee* objected.

MODIFYING A DIRECT OBJECT: She has a television *with remote control.*

MODIFYING A PREDICATE NOUN: Ted is the captain *of the team.*

When two adjective phrases appear together, the second phrase often modifies the object of the preposition in the first.

MODIFYING THE OBJECT OF A PREPOSITION: The crack *at the top of the windshield* was caused by a pebble from the driveway.

At other times two or more adjective phrases may modify the same word.

MODIFYING THE SAME WORD: The bouquet *of roses on the table* arrived this morning.

EXERCISE A: Identifying Adjective Phrases. Each of the following sentences contains at least one prepositional phrase used as an adjective. Copy the sentences onto your paper. Underline each adjective phrase and draw an arrow pointing from it to the word it modifies. *Modified words are shaded.*

EXAMPLE: The room in the back is very damp.

1. Mr. Suarez bought a new car with a sun roof.
2. The book about Eleanor Roosevelt is inspiring.
3. Mary is the supervisor of all the nurses.
4. The house near the top of the hill has been sold.
5. The tree in the corner of the yard is a weeping cherry.
6. This is the way to the shopping mall.
7. The autographed picture of Reggie Jackson is one of my treasures.
8. The carton of eggs on the bottom of the pile has been crushed.

9. The captain of the precinct gave a talk about gun control.
10. The front steps of many houses in Baltimore are white marble.

Prepositional Phrases That Act as Adverbs

Prepositional phrases can also be used as adverbs.

An **adverb phrase** is a prepositional phrase that modifies a verb, adjective, or adverb. Adverb phrases point out where, when, in what manner, or to what extent.

The examples in the following chart show that *adverb phrases* serve basically the same function that one-word adverbs do.

Adverbs	Adverb Phrases
The bus left *late.*	The bus left *after a two-hour delay.*
Put the package *there.*	Put the package *in the closet.*

In the first pair of examples, both *late* and *after a two-hour delay* answer the question *Left when?* In the second pair, *there* and *in the closet* answer the question *Put where?*

Like one-word adverbs, adverb phrases can modify verbs, adjectives, or adverbs.

MODIFYING A VERB: The diplomat chose her words *with great care.* (Chose *in what manner?*)

MODIFYING AN ADJECTIVE: She was angry *at my refusal.* (Angry *in what manner?*)

MODIFYING AN ADVERB: We talked late *into the night.* (Late *to what extent?*)

Unlike adjective phrases adverb phrases do not always appear close to the words they modify. They can appear in almost any position in a sentence, very much like one-word adverbs.

EXAMPLES: The legions of Roman soldiers left *in a hurry.*

About two years later, Caesar's army mounted another campaign.

Very often two or more adverb phrases in different locations will modify the same word in a sentence.

EXAMPLE: *After dinner* we drove *to the lake.*

EXERCISE B: Identifying Adverb Phrases. Each of the following sentences contains at least one prepositional phrase used as an adverb. Copy the sentences onto your paper. Underline each adverb phrase and draw an arrow pointing from it to the word it modifies.
Modified words are shaded.

EXAMPLE: With increasing excitement she read the last chapter.

1. Our scout troop hiked through the forest.
2. At the traffic light, the road curves to the left.
3. They arrived early in the day.
4. Susan is upset about her science grades.
5. At the zoo many kinds of animals live in harmony.
6. The storm cleared by morning.
7. At noon the Museum of History and Science opens for visitors.
8. They placed the berries in straw baskets.
9. Larger type would be easier on the eye.
10. At the first signal, the fire trucks raced from their stations.

APPLICATION: Writing Sentences with Adjective and Adverb Phrases. Write an original sentence using each of the following prepositional phrases as an adjective or adverb according to the instructions in parentheses.

Underline each phrase and draw an arrow pointing from it to the word it modifies. *Answers will vary; samples given for first two.*

EXAMPLE: on the beach (as an adverb phrase)

On the beach the bonfire burned brightly.

1. in the dark raincoat (as an adjective phrase)
2. between dawn and dusk (as an adverb phrase)
3. at her constant excuses (as an adverb phrase)
4. near us (as an adjective phrase)
5. from Congress (as an adjective phrase)
6. with a great deal of hesitation (as an adverb phrase)
7. to the department store (as an adjective phrase)
8. under the bridge (as an adjective phrase)
9. by a little-used side road (as an adverb phrase)
10. of record albums (as an adjective phrase)

1. The man in the dark raincoat was eating peanuts.

2. They hiked for miles between dawn and dusk.

Appositives in Phrases 8.2

Appositives, like adjective phrases, give information about nouns or pronouns.

An **appositive** is a noun or pronoun placed after another noun or pronoun to identify, rename, or explain the preceding word.

Appositives are very useful in writing because they give additional information using a minimum of words.

APPOSITIVES
The poet *Robert Frost* is much admired.
This antique car, a *Studebaker,* is worth thousands of dollars.
The song *"I Am a Rock"* is a classic.

An appositive with its own modifiers creates an appositive phrase.

> An **appositive phrase** is a noun or pronoun with modifiers. It stands next to a noun or pronoun and adds information or details.

The modifiers in the phrase can be adjectives or adjective phrases.

APPOSITIVE PHRASES
Mr. Wilkie, *an old, experienced scoutmaster,* knows every trail.
The painting, *a mural in many bright colors,* highlights the entrance.
The medicine, *a dark liquid with a horrible smell,* seems to work.

Appositives and appositive phrases can also be compound.

EXAMPLES: Volunteers, *boys* or *girls,* are wanted.

These poems, *"The Sea Gypsy"* and *"Before the Squall,"* are about love of the sea.

EXERCISE A: Identifying Appositives and Appositive Phrases. Copy the following sentences onto your paper. Underline each appositive or appositive phrase and draw an arrow pointing from it to the noun or pronoun it renames. *Renamed words are shaded.*

EXAMPLE: Gwendolyn Brooks, an American poet, grew up on Chicago's South Side.

1. Our math teacher, Mrs. Cruz, helped us solve a puzzle.
2. Two O. Henry stories, "The Gift of the Magi" and "The Last Leaf," are my personal favorites.

3. Two low-calorie vegetables, kale and bean sprouts, are highly recommended.
4. George Patton, a general in World War II, was the subject of a prize-winning film.
5. The book *The Matarese Circle* pits an American spy against a Russian.
6. Beethoven wrote only one opera, *Fidelio*.
7. Senator Atkins, a wonderful speaker, made quite an impression.
8. Our destination, either Puerto Rico or Costa Del Sol, will be decided upon soon.
9. You must see Lincoln Center, the cultural mecca of New York.
10. The Beatles' movie *Yellow Submarine* won several awards.

APPLICATION: Writing Sentences with Appositives. Use the following words or phrases as appositives in your own sentences. *Answers will vary; samples given for first two.*

EXAMPLE: a real mistake

His choice, a real mistake, was greeted with laughter.

1. Dr. Dever, a fine teacher, will lead a tour of Spain this spring.

1. a fine teacher
2. the captain
3. a good driver
4. my oldest friend
5. a fascinating book
6. my favorite team
7. a restaurant in town
8. a beautiful song
9. a luscious dessert
10. a town landmark

2. Missy Sazonick, the captain, is the best swimmer on the team.

Participles in Phrases 8.3

The next three sections are about *verbals*. A *verbal* is a verb form that is used as another part of speech. There are three kinds of verbals: *participles, gerunds,* and *infinitives*. Each is used differently. Participles are used as adjectives, gerunds as nouns, and infinitives as nouns, adjectives, or adverbs.

Verbals keep two important characteristics of verbs: (1) They can be followed by a complement, such as a direct object, and (2) they can be modified by adverbs and adverb phrases. A verbal with a complement or a modifier is called a *verbal phrase.* This section will discuss the first kind of verbal, the participle, and explain how it can be used in phrases.

Participles

Many of the adjectives you commonly use are actually *participles.*

A **participle** is a form of a verb that acts as an adjective.

There are two kinds of participles: *present participles* and *past participles.* You can recognize these two different kinds of participles by their endings. Present participles end in *-ing.*

PRESENT PARTICIPLES: going, playing, growing, telling, reading, jumping

Past participles usually end in *-ed,* although those formed from irregular verbs will have different endings such as *-t* or *-en.* (See Section 11.1 for a list of irregular verb endings.)

PAST PARTICIPLES: marked, jumped, moved, hurt, chosen, eaten

The following chart shows how both types of participles can be used as adjectives in sentences. Like other adjectives participles answer such questions as *What kind?* or *Which one?*

Present Participles	Past Participles
A *growing* baby sleeps much of the day.	Our *chosen* representative resigned.
Crying, he threw himself on the bed.	*Troubled,* she asked for advice.

EXERCISE A: Identifying Present and Past Participles. Each of the following sentences contains a present or past participle used as an adjective. On your paper write the participle from each sentence. Then write whether the participle is *past* or *present.*

EXAMPLE: The cracked vase can not be repaired.

cracked past

1. A raging snowstorm struck the city. *pres*
2. Disturbed, she consulted her doctor about the symptoms. *past*
3. The police shined a glaring light on the robber. *pres*
4. Singing, she stepped from the shower. *pres*
5. The frozen pipe burst. *past*
6. Have you repaired the broken lamp? *past*
7. I have used reading glasses for some time now. *pres*
8. The story of the haunted house was very popular. *past*
9. Did you find the finished copies of the term paper? *past*
10. Laughing, she bowed several times to the audience. *pres*

Verb or Participle?

Sometimes verb phrases (verbs with helping verbs) are confused with participles. In the chart, however, note that a verb phrase always begins with a helping verb. A participle used as an adjective stands by itself and modifies a noun or pronoun.

Verb Phrases	Participles
The car *was racing* around the curve.	The *racing* car crashed into the wall.
I *was* greatly *disturbed* by the call.	The *disturbed* boy talked about his problem.

EXERCISE B: Distinguishing Between Verbs and Participles. On your paper identify each of the underlined words as either a *verb* or a *participle.* If the word is a participle, also write the word it modifies.
Modified words are shaded.

EXAMPLE: They found the written test easy to do.

participle test

1. The doctor is talking to a patient. *verb*
2. *part* She has a growing understanding of the problem.
3. A broken window was part of the evidence. *part*
4. Brian has finally chosen a topic for his report. *verb*
5. Do you have a thick marking pen? *part*
6. We drove past a deserted railroad terminal. *part*
7. In exchange she is asking for another radio. *verb*
8. I bought three pounds of ripened cheese. *part*
9. *verb* She is always playing Mozart on her phonograph.
10. The prisoner was brought before the judge. *verb*

Participial Phrases

A participle can be expanded into a phrase by adding one or more modifiers or complements to it.

A **participial phrase** is a present or past participle that is modified by an adverb or adverb phrase or that has a complement. The entire phrase acts as an adjective in a sentence.

The examples in the following chart show a few of the ways that participles can be expanded into phrases.

PARTICIPIAL PHRASES
The diner, *chewing rapidly,* started to choke.
The old woman, *assisted by her daughter,* moved to a new house.
The clerks, *eating their lunch,* refused to answer the phone.

The first participial phrase is formed by adding the adverb *rapidly.* The second is formed by adding the prepositional phrase *by her daughter.* The third is formed by adding the direct object *lunch.*

In these three examples, notice that each participial phrase appears right after the noun it modifies. All three sentences could be reworded to move the phrases before the modified words.

EXAMPLES: *Chewing rapidly,* the diner started to choke.

Assisted by her daughter, the old woman moved to a new house.

Eating their lunch, the clerks refused to answer the phone.

EXERCISE C: Recognizing Participial Phrases. Each of the following sentences contains a participial phrase. Copy the sentences onto your paper. Underline each participial phrase and draw an arrow pointing from it to the word it modifies. *Modified words are shaded.*

EXAMPLE: The frontier, spreading out endlessly to the west, excited the pioneers.

1. The plant, growing slowly, finally bloomed in June.
2. Chosen by the principal, Marie represented our school.
3. My father, walking the dog, met an old friend.
4. Laughing loudly, she ran from the room.
5. The coin, found in a cellar, proved to be valuable.
6. Telling her strange story, she began to giggle.
7. The detective, watching the suspect closely, discovered a clue.
8. Scolded by his father, he left the house and took a walk.
9. The students, listening carefully, followed the instructions perfectly.
10. The clipper, sailing majestically, reached the harbor in two hours.

APPLICATION: Writing Sentences with Participial Phrases. Write an original sentence using each of the following participial phrases.
Answers will vary; samples given for first two.

EXAMPLE: hitting a home run

Hitting a home run, Chris tied the score.

1. Speaking slowly, the teacher repeated the question.

1. speaking slowly
2. reminded twice
3. opening the door
4. speaking very slowly
5. followed by a puppy
6. reading a letter
7. frozen in the lake
8. meeting often
9. choosing another way
10. thinking clearly

2. Ellen, reminded twice, still missed the bus.

8.4 Gerunds in Phrases

Like present participles, *gerunds* end in *-ing*. Present participles, however, are used as adjectives. Gerunds are used as nouns.

A **gerund** is a form of verb that acts as a noun.

Gerunds

Like other nouns gerunds can be used as subjects, direct objects, predicate nouns, and objects of prepositions.

USE OF GERUNDS IN SENTENCES	
Subject	*Smoking* is not permitted in many public buildings.
Direct Object	Michael enjoys *painting*.
Predicate Noun	His favorite sport is *fishing*.
Object of a Preposition	Lucille never gets tired of *singing*.

EXERCISE A: Identifying Gerunds. Each of the following sentences contains one gerund. On your paper write the gerund from each sentence. Next to it write whether it is used as a *subject, direct object, predicate noun,* or *object of a preposition.*

EXAMPLE: Dancing is her favorite pastime.

Dancing subject

1. Walking is excellent exercise. *S*
2. My sister observes my birthday by phoning. *obj of prep*
3. This plant needs pruning. *DO*
4. Love is caring, and I always try to show I care. *PN*
5. Speeding led to the loss of her driver's license. *S*
6. Our goal has always been winning. *PN*
7. Don't you ever get tired of studying? *obj of prep*
8. Exercising is one way to burn up calories. *S*
9. After several months grandmother stopped writing. *DO*
10. The team finished practicing at five o'clock. *DO*

Gerund Phrases

A gerund, like a participle or an appositive, can be part of a phrase.

A **gerund phrase** is a gerund with modifiers or a complement, all acting together as a noun.

The following chart shows some of the many ways that gerunds can be expanded.

GERUND PHRASES	
Gerund with Adjectives	*The loud, shrill howling* continued all morning.
Gerund with Direct Object	*Practicing the violin* is part of his daily routine.
Gerund with Prepositional Phrase	He helped the police by *telling about his experience.*
Gerund with Adverb and Prepositional Phrase	My father tries to stay fit by *walking rapidly to the station.*

EXERCISE B: Identifying Gerund Phrases. Each of the following sentences contains one gerund phrase. On your paper write each gerund phrase. Next to it write whether the gerund phrase is used as a *subject, direct object, predicate noun,* or *object of a preposition.*

EXAMPLE: His favorite pastime was writing limericks.

writing limericks predicate noun

1. Drinking large amounts of water can help clear the kidneys. *S*
2. His favorite hobby is raising guppies. *PN*
3. A loud knocking interrupted their dinner. *S*
4. Nothing can be gained by choosing sides. *obj of prep*
5. He enjoys composing all sorts of music. *DO*
6. The secretary kept perfect records by writing the dates of each event. *obj of prep*
7. Insulating older homes helps conserve energy. *S*
8. Tourists at the Acropolis are warned against taking stones for souvenirs. *obj of prep*
9. Traveling by air is the fastest way to get there. *S*
10. My plans for summer vacation include redecorating my room. *DO*

APPLICATION: Writing Sentences with Gerund Phrases. Use each of the following gerund phrases in an original sentence according to the instructions in parentheses.
Answers will vary; samples given for first two.

EXAMPLE: singing in the shower (as a subject)

Singing in the shower was her only form of vocal exercise.

1. Andy frightened us by driving too fast.

1. driving too fast (as the object of a preposition)
2. exercising in the morning (as a subject)
3. collecting stamps and coins (as a direct object)
4. cleaning her room thoroughly (as the object of a preposition)
5. raising animals (as a subject)

2. Exercising in the morning helps her to wake up completely.

8.5 Infinitives in Phrases

Infinitives can be used as three different parts of speech.

An **infinitive** is the form of a verb that comes after the word *to* and acts as a noun, adjective, or adverb.

Three Uses of Infinitives

As a noun an infinitive can be used in several ways: as a subject, direct object, predicate noun, object of a preposition, or appositive.

INFINITIVES USED AS NOUNS	
Subject	*To succeed* is a popular goal.
Direct Object	As soon as she gets home, she hopes *to write.*
Predicate Noun	His dream has always been *to travel.*
Object of a Preposition	They had no choice except *to leave.*
Appositive	Her decision, *to listen,* was a wise one.

Infinitives can also be used as adjectives and adverbs. In the following chart, notice how the infinitives answer the usual questions for adjectives and adverbs.

INFINITIVES USED AS ADJECTIVES AND ADVERBS	
Adjective	The person *to contact* is the dean. (*Which person?*) She has the ambition *to succeed. (What kind of ambition?*)
Adverb	This is easy *to do.* (Easy *in what manner?*) Ready *to leave,* they locked the door. (Ready *in what manner?*)

EXERCISE A: Identifying Infinitives. Find the infinitive in each of the following sentences and write it on your paper.

EXAMPLE: They were always eager to answer.

to answer

1. She wants to go.
2. Impossible to miss, the monument is located right on the lake.
3. The recipe to try is on the package itself.
4. To listen is not easy with that uproar.
5. He wanted nothing except to sleep.
6. The librarian was happy to help.
7. His greatest wish, to fly, was never fulfilled.
8. This is the best reference book to consult.
9. Susan's dream is to dance.
10. To whistle is difficult for some people.

Infinitive Phrases

Infinitives, like gerunds and participles, can be combined with other words to form phrases.

An **infinitive phrase** is an infinitive with modifiers or a complement, all acting together as a single part of speech.

The following chart shows some of the ways infinitives can be expanded.

INFINITIVE PHRASES	
Infinitive with Adverb	It will be important *to listen carefully.*
Infinitive with Prepositional Phrases	They like *to jog through the park at dawn.*
Infinitive with Direct Object	She hopes *to write a novel.*
Infinitive with Indirect and Direct Objects	I need *to give you my new telephone number.*

EXERCISE B: Identifying Infinitive Phrases. Each of the following sentences contains one infinitive phrase. On your paper write each infinitive phrase.

EXAMPLE: To reach the peak was not possible in the blizzard.

To reach the peak

1. To graduate a year early is my goal.
2. The teacher to ask for a reference is Miss Stevens.
3. I find it difficult to talk with strangers.
4. Her ambition is to direct a musical at school.
5. This is an offer to take very seriously.
6. To get home during the storm was quite difficult.
7. Our plan was to reach southern Maine by noon.
8. She was told to reorganize her composition.
9. The person to ask about that is James.
10. They want to wait another week before acting.

APPLICATION: Writing Sentences with Infinitive Phrases. Write an original sentence using each of the following infinitive phrases according to the directions in parentheses. *Answers will vary; samples given for first two.*

EXAMPLE: to please Uncle Pete (as an adverb)

It was difficult to please Uncle Pete.

1. To succeed in English requires attention and practice.

1. to succeed in English (as a subject at the beginning of the sentence)
2. to go into business (as a direct object with the verb *want*)
3. to reach the station (as an adverb after the adjective *easy*)
4. to become a lawyer (as a predicate noun after the verb *is*)
5. to ask for advice (as an adjective after the noun *teacher*)
6. to study carefully (as a subject at the beginning of a sentence)
7. to leave for a vacation (as an adverb after the adjective *happy*)

2. Next year they want to go into business.

8. to travel to France and Italy (as a predicate noun after *was*)
9. to call home (as a direct object after the verb *forgot*)
10. to go to college (as an appositive after the noun *wish*)

8.6 Diagraming Prepositional Phrases and Appositives

Section 7.9 explained how to diagram subjects, verbs, complements, and modifiers. You may want to study or review the diagrams in that section before studying the diagrams presented here for two of the most essential phrases, prepositional and appositive phrases.

Prepositional Phrases

The diagram for a prepositional phrase is drawn under the word it modifies. The diagram has two parts: a slanted line for the preposition and a horizontal line for the object of the preposition. Any adjectives that modify the object are placed beneath the object.

Adjective Phrases. The diagram for an adjective phrase is placed directly under the noun or pronoun that the phrase modifies.

S — Obj of Prep — V

EXAMPLE: The person *in the first office* will help you.

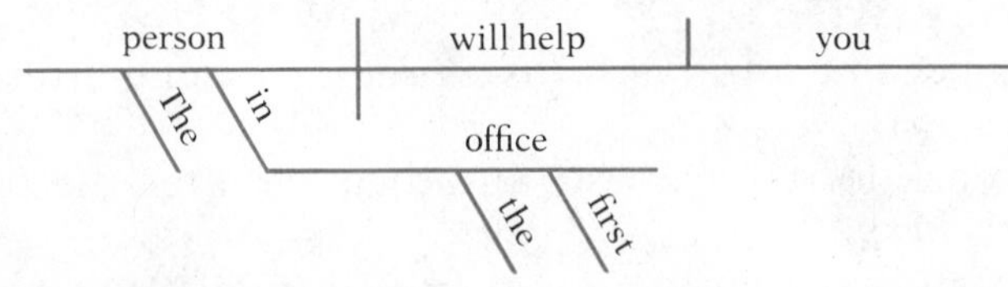

Adverb Phrases. The diagram for an adverb phrase is placed directly under the verb, adjective, or adverb that the phrase modifies.

S V Obj of Prep

EXAMPLE: I spoke later *with my best friend.*

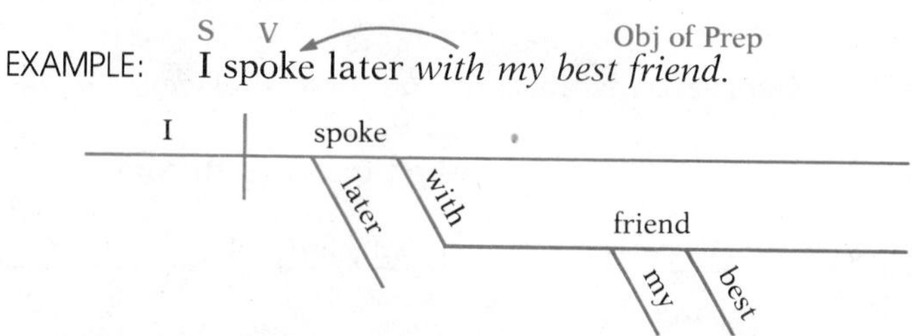

Compound Objects of a Preposition. A prepositional phrase with a compound object is diagramed in the following way.

S V DO Obj Obj Obj

EXAMPLE: We made a bouquet *of zinnias, asters, and marigolds.*

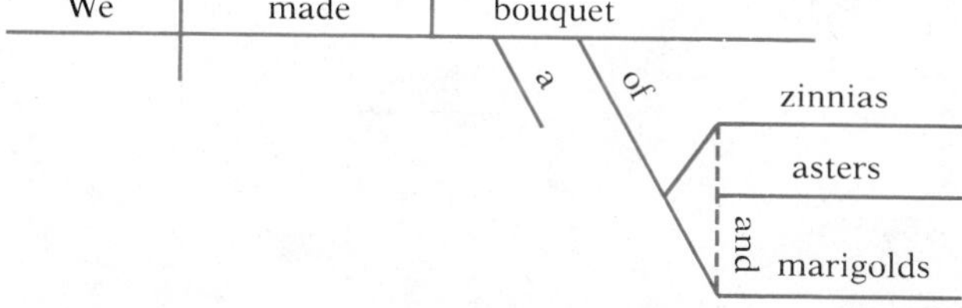

EXERCISE A: Diagraming Prepositional Phrases. Each of the following sentences contains one or two prepositional phrases. Diagram each sentence, using the preceding examples as models. *Answers on pages T-113–T-114.*

1. The man in the brown hat is my cousin.
2. I awoke suddenly at dawn.
3. A car with a faulty muffler roared up the street.
4. They moved to an apartment with two bedrooms, a large kitchen, and a balcony.
5. During the night he wrote a poem about loneliness.

■ Appositives

To diagram an appositive, place it in parentheses next to the noun or pronoun it renames. Any adjectives or adjective phrases that modify the appositive are positioned directly beneath it.

EXAMPLE: George Washington, *the first President of the United States,* established many traditions.

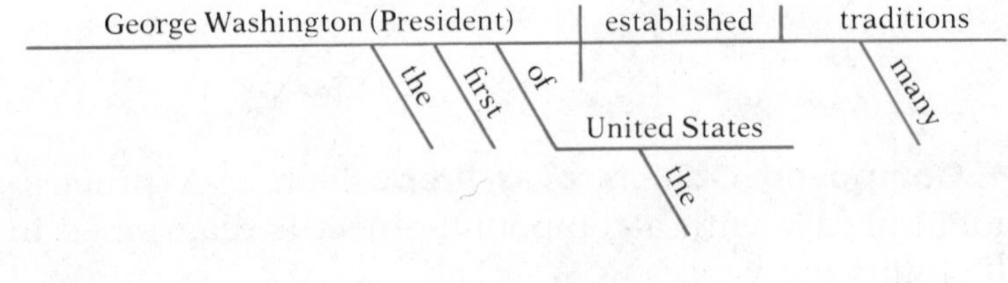

EXAMPLE: I wrote about George Washington, *our first President.*

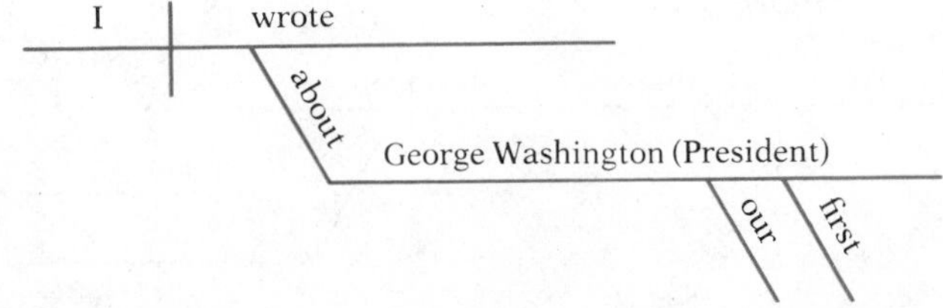

EXERCISE B: Diagraming Appositive Phrases. Each of the following sentences contains one appositive phrase. Diagram each sentence. *Answers on page T-115.*

1. We have a new pet, a furry, little kitten.
2. Joe Louis, the world heavyweight champion for twelve years, was an American hero.
3. The articles of Sylvia Porter, a financial columnist, appear in hundreds of daily newspapers.
4. We will be going to Zagreb, the capital of Yugoslavia.
5. This is a sonnet, a poem of fourteen lines.

APPLICATION: Diagraming Prepositional Phrases and Appositives. Diagram the following sentences according to the examples in this section. *Answers on pages T-116–T-118.*

1. A reporter from our local newspaper phoned.
2. The package was wrapped in yellow paper.

3. Beethoven, one of the greatest figures in music, composed nine symphonies.
4. Our art teacher talked about Picasso, the brilliant modern painter.
5. My parents are very happy about her great success.
6. Bob Andrews, a flight lieutenant, spoke at our last assembly.
7. Our puppy, a dachshund, always greets us at the door.
8. The ambassador from Peru attended the reception at the embassy.
9. She gave him his favorite present, a ticket to the concert.
10. They made their last trip to St. Louis in September.

Chapter 9

Expanding Sentences with Clauses

The last two chapters have dealt with various parts of a sentence: subjects, verbs, complements, and phrases. This chapter will explain the last important sentence element, the *clause.*

A **clause** is a group of words with its own subject and verb.

There are two basic types of clauses, and there is an important difference between them. The first type is called an *independent clause.*

An **independent clause** has a subject and a verb and can stand by itself as a complete sentence.

The length of a clause has little to do with whether it can stand alone as a sentence. Each of the following examples is an independent clause. Each can stand alone because it expresses a complete thought.

INDEPENDENT CLAUSES: The reporter (S) shouted (V).

Mother (S) wrote (V) a letter to my cousin in Florida.

At dawn the caravan (S) began (V) to cross the windy desert in an effort to reach the village before nightfall.

The second type of clause is called a *subordinate clause.* Like an independent clause, it contains both a subject and a verb. A subordinate clause, however, is not a sentence.

A **subordinate clause** has a subject and a verb but can not stand by itself as a sentence. It is only part of a sentence.

A subordinate clause does not express a complete thought even though it contains a subject and a verb.

SUBORDINATE CLAUSES:

when the phone (S) rang (V)

whom I (S) often admired (V)

since the constitution (S) was amended (V) at the last meeting

Each of these clauses has a subject and a verb, but each lacks something. Examine, for example, the first clause: *when the phone rang. When the phone rang,* what happened? More information is needed to make the thought complete.

Why does a subordinate clause not express a complete thought? The answer often can be found in the first word of the clause. Some subordinate clauses begin with subordinating conjunctions, words such as *if, since, when, although, because,* and *while.* Others begin with relative pronouns such as *who, which,* or *that.* These words are clues that the clause may not be able to stand alone. Compare, for example, the independent clauses and the subordinate clauses in the following chart. Notice how the addition of subordinating words changes the meaning of the independent clauses.

COMPARING TWO KINDS OF CLAUSES

Independent	Subordinate
He (S) arrived (V) this morning.	*since* he (S) arrived (V) this morning
The room (S) is (V) not clean.	*if* the room (S) is (V) not clean

In order to make sense, a subordinate clause usually needs to be combined with an independent clause. In the following examples, the subordinate clauses are italicized; the independent clauses are not.

EXAMPLES: *Since he arrived this morning,* he has been working at top speed.

(S over "he", V over "arrived"; S over "he", V over "has been")

I will call the manager *if the room is not clean.*

(S over "I", V over "will call"; S over "room", V over "is")

This chapter will explain how subordinate clauses work with independent clauses to make complete sentences. It will also explain how subordinate clauses can act within sentences either as adjectives or as adverbs.

9.1 Adjective Clauses

Some subordinate clauses act as adjectives.

An **adjective clause** is a subordinate clause that modifies a noun or pronoun.

Adjective clauses, like one-word adjectives or adjective phrases, answer the questions *What kind?* or *Which one?*

Recognizing Adjective Clauses

Most adjective clauses begin with one of the five relative pronouns: *that, which, who, whom,* and *whose.* Sometimes an adjective clause will begin with an adverb such as *when* or *where.*

Study the examples in the following chart. The adjective clauses are italicized. The arrow in each sentence points to the word in the independent clause that the adjective clause modifies. Note also that an adjective clause usually comes right after the word it modifies.

ADJECTIVE CLAUSES

She wrote the story *that won first prize.*

That British stamp, *which depicts Queen Victoria,* will be sold at auction.

The man *who opened the door* is my brother-in-law.

Marcia is the student *whom we chose to represent us in the debate.*

The boy *whose book I borrowed* is the class president.

In the period *since the war ended* much has happened.

This is the time *when I like to read.*

EXERCISE A: Identifying Adjective Clauses. Each of the following sentences contains an adjective clause. Copy the sentences onto your paper and underline each adjective clause. Be prepared to identify the word each clause modifies. *Modified words are shaded.*

EXAMPLE: I like science fiction books that are believable.

1. The tailor who shortened my skirt is very reasonable.
2. This museum, which is described in our travel guide, was built in 1876.
3. The man whose dictionary I borrowed is a retired teacher.
4. Have you found a show that you would like to see?
5. In the month since he had the accident, his condition has improved greatly.
6. Have you visited the plaza where the statue was dedicated?
7. The painter whom she most admires is Georgia O'Keeffe.
8. The book that you wanted is no longer in print.
9. A play that I particularly liked was *All My Sons.*
10. That package, which just arrived, is for you.

Combining Sentences with Adjective Clauses

Two sentences sometimes can be combined into one by changing one of them into an adjective clause. Such a combination is particularly useful when the information in both sentences is closely related. Notice how the two sentences in the following example are changed into one sentence. The new sentence consists of an independent clause and an adjective clause.

TWO SENTENCES: My history teacher has written books on John Adams and Benjamin Franklin. My teacher is considered by many scholars to be an expert on the American Revolution.

SENTENCE WITH ADJECTIVE CLAUSE: My history teacher, *who is considered by many scholars to be an expert on the American Revolution,* has written books on John Adams and Benjamin Franklin.

EXERCISE B: Using Adjective Clauses to Combine Sentences. Change the second sentence in each of the following groups into an adjective clause. Then make the adjective clause part of the first sentence. You will need to add a comma before and after each of these adjective clauses. *Answers will vary; samples given for first two.*

EXAMPLE: Phillis Wheatley was an early American poet. She was born in Africa.

Phillis Wheatley, who was born in Africa, was an early American poet.

1. John Steinbeck, who won the Nobel Prize in 1962, wrote. . . .

1. John Steinbeck wrote *The Grapes of Wrath* and *The Pearl.* He won the Nobel Prize in 1962.
2. Albany has changed greatly in the last twenty-five years. It now boasts the lavish Empire State Plaza.
3. This hotel room will be more expensive. It has a view of the mountains.

2. Albany, which now boasts the lavish Empire State Plaza, has. . . .

4. Katherine Hepburn won an Academy Award for her performance in *The Lion in Winter.* Her film career spans fifty years.
5. My mother recently bought a small economy car. She had always preferred large sedans.

APPLICATION: Using Adjective Clauses in Sentences. Copy the following sentences onto your paper, filling in each blank with an adjective clause.

Answers will vary; samples given.

EXAMPLE: Choose the book ______.

Choose the book that you like best.

1. Abraham Lincoln, *whom many once reviled*, has grown in stature over the years.
2. This is the old house *that used to scare us*.
3. Have you read the book *that Ms. Lyon assigned*?
4. I will never forget the day *when I learned to float*.
5. The students *who write this paper* will be exempted from the final exam.
6. Washington, D.C., *where I grew up*, is an exciting place to visit.
7. The guitarist played the song *that his wife composed*.
8. Our new car, *which we drove out West*, is extremely fuel efficient.
9. The school play, *which stars my brother*, will be performed next weekend.
10. The guest of honor, *who is a well-known poet*, received a gold medal.

Adverb Clauses 9.2

Some subordinate clauses act as adverbs.

An **adverb clause** is a subordinate clause that modifies a verb, an adjective, or an adverb.

Adverb clauses can answer any of the following questions about the words they modify: *Where? When?*

In what manner? To what extent? Under what condition? or *Why?*

Recognizing Adverb Clauses

Adverb clauses begin with subordinating conjunctions. The most common ones are listed here. Knowing them can help you recognize adverb clauses.

SUBORDINATING CONJUNCTIONS			
after	before	than	where
although	even though	though	wherever
as	if	unless	while
as if	in order that	until	
as long as	since	when	
because	so that	whenever	

In the following chart, the adverb clauses are italicized. The arrows point to the words that the clauses modify. Notice that each clause begins with a subordinating conjunction.

ADVERB CLAUSES	
Modifying Verbs	Sit *where I can see you.* The boys arrived *after the parade had begun.* He is acting *as if he had something to hide.* *If you care,* donate your time.
Modifying an Adjective	I was upset *because she forgot my birthday.*
Modifying an Adverb	The movie lasted longer *than I had expected.*

Each of these clauses answers one of the questions for adverb clauses. The first clause, for example, answers the question *Where?*

Most adverb clauses occur either at the beginning or at the end of a sentence. If an adverb clause follows the independent clause, no punctuation is required.

EXAMPLES: Marie phoned *when she reached the station.*

Grandmother keeps more active *than anyone else I know.*

When an adverb clause begins a sentence, however, a comma is used.

EXAMPLES: *When I reviewed his message,* I rushed to the telephone.

Since she accepted the new assignment, she has had second thoughts.

EXERCISE A: Identifying Adverb Clauses. Each of the following sentences contains an adverb clause. Copy the sentences onto your paper and underline each adverb clause. Be prepared to identify the verb, adjective, or adverb each clause modifies. *Modified words are shaded.*

EXAMPLE: Before she married, Pearl Buck's name was Pearl Sydenstricker.

1. Before we left on vacation, we took the dogs to the kennel.
2. Although you have explained your reasons, I must vote according to my own beliefs.
3. The plant will thrive as long as you do not overwater it.
4. The baby is sleepier than I have ever seen her.
5. If you can make the trip, you certainly will enjoy the scenery.
6. Barbara reads more rapidly than anyone in our class.
7. I finished my homework at seven so that I could watch the movie.

8. My best friend is much wiser than most of us ever realized.
9. She acted as if she didn't expect to win the scholarship.
10. While I generally respect your ideas, I can not agree with your present plan.

Elliptical Adverb Clauses

In certain adverb clauses, words are left out. These clauses are said to be *elliptical.*

In an **elliptical adverb clause,** the verb or the subject and verb are understood rather than actually stated.

Many elliptical adverb clauses are introduced by one of two subordinating conjunctions: *as* or *than.* In the following examples, the understood words have been added in parentheses. The first elliptical adverb clause is missing a verb; the second is missing a subject and a verb.

EXAMPLES: My brother can eat as much *as I (can).*

I liked this book more *than (I liked) that one.*

EXERCISE B: Recognizing Elliptical Adverb Clauses. Each of the following sentences contains an elliptical adverb clause. Draw two columns on your paper as shown in the example. In the first column, write the elliptical clause. In the second write out the full adverb clause, adding the understood words.

EXAMPLE: She is stronger than I.

Elliptical Clause	Full Clause
than I	than I am

1. Our sports car is faster than his. is.
2. This book is just as interesting as that one. is.
3. Mrs. Wilson is as pleasant as Miss Grogan. is.
4. Jennifer gave more to him than to her. she gave
5. We are more willing to serve than they. are.

APPLICATION: Writing Sentences with Adverb Clauses. Combine each of the following pairs of sentences into a single sentence by making one of them an adverb clause. Write the new sentences on your paper and underline the adverb clause in each. Refer to the chart of subordinating conjunctions on page 154, if necessary.

Answers will vary; samples given for first two.

EXAMPLE: Joe stayed at school. The others went home.

Joe stayed at school after the others went home.

1. She left the house early because she didn't want to disturb anyone.

1. She left the house early. She didn't want to disturb anyone.
2. You went into the kitchen. Did you notice anything new?
3. Margie was very tired. She did enjoy most of the game.
4. Yeats first studied art. He soon realized that his real talents lay in writing poetry.
5. We have finished all our homework. We want to go ice skating this afternoon.
6. Mr. Wilkens acted strangely all morning. He couldn't remember where he was.
7. They went to the shopping center. I returned home from school.
8. Your parents won't object. I will drive you to the bazaar.
9. I was in Spain last summer. I learned about the languages of the different regions.
10. The author Richard Wright was born in Natchez, Mississippi. He later moved to Memphis, Tennessee.

2. When you went into the kitchen, did you notice anything new?

Classifying Sentences by Structure 9.3

All sentences can be classified by the number and kinds of clauses that they contain. There are four basic sentence structures: *simple, compound, complex,* and *compound-complex.*

The Simple Sentence

Most writers use *simple sentences* more than any other type.

A **simple sentence** consists of a single independent clause.

A simple sentence can be short or long. It must contain a subject and a verb. It may also contain complements, modifiers, and phrases. Some simple sentences contain various compounds—a compound subject or a compound verb or both. Other parts of the sentence may also be compound. A simple sentence, however, does not contain any subordinate clauses.

The following examples show a few of the many possible variations of the simple sentence. The subjects have been underlined once and the verbs twice.

ONE SUBJECT AND VERB: The siren sounded.

COMPOUND SUBJECT: Ice cream and cookies are my two favorite desserts.

COMPOUND VERB: My sister acts and sings in the play.

COMPOUND SUBJECT AND VERB: Frank and Bill crossed the mountain but failed to reach the campsite by nightfall.

WITH PHRASES AND COMPLEMENTS: At breakfast we gave them the news about his victory.

EXERCISE A: Recognizing Simple Sentences. The following are simple sentences. Copy each one onto your paper and underline the subject once and the verb twice. Some of the subjects and verbs may be compound.

EXAMPLE: Many streets and schools are given the names of famous people.

1. He swam to the canoe and paddled the rest of the way to the shore.
2. Waiting near the bridge, we finally spotted the caravan of trucks.
3. Jennie passed French but failed algebra.
4. My mother, my father, and my grandparents all attended the graduation.
5. Both the bus and the taxi had engine trouble and arrived late.

EXERCISE B: More Work with Simple Sentences. In a book or magazine, find ten simple sentences. On your paper copy each sentence and mark it as in Exercise A.

You might suggest that students include at least two sentences with compound subjects or verbs.

The Compound Sentence

Independent clauses are the key elements in a *compound sentence.*

A **compound sentence** consists of two or more independent clauses.

The independent clauses in most compound sentences are joined by a comma and one of the coordinating conjunctions *(and, but, for, nor, or, so, yet).* Sometimes a semicolon (;) is used to join independent clauses in a compound sentence. Like simple sentences compound sentences contain no subordinate clauses.

EXAMPLES: The roads are relatively safe, but the bridges are icy.

She visited Cornell University this weekend; she also spent some time at Ithaca College nearby.

EXERCISE C: Recognizing Compound Sentences. The following are compound sentences. Copy each onto your paper. Underline the subject once and the verb twice in each independent clause.

EXAMPLE: Bolivia has no seacoast; Paraguay is also landlocked.

1. Our first stop was the port of Hamilton in Bermuda; our second stop was at Nassau in the Bahamas.
2. Several tiles fell off the space shuttle during lift-off, but the craft nonetheless landed safely.
3. Susan baked the bread, and Ron prepared the salad.
4. Your argument is weak, for you have no proof to support your ideas.
5. Many islands dot the coast of Yugoslavia, yet few of them have inhabitants.

EXERCISE D: More Work with Compound Sentences. In a book or magazine, find ten compound sentences. On your paper copy each sentence and mark it as in Exercise C. *Students might try to find at least two sentences in which semicolons are used to separate the clauses.*

The Complex Sentence

A sentence with an adjective or adverb clause is called a *complex sentence.*

A complex sentence consists of one independent clause and one or more subordinate clauses.

The independent clause in a complex sentence is often called the *main clause* to distinguish it from the subordinate clause or clauses. The main clause and each subordinate clause have their own subjects and verbs. Those in the independent clause are called the *subject of the sentence* and the *main verb.*

EXAMPLE:

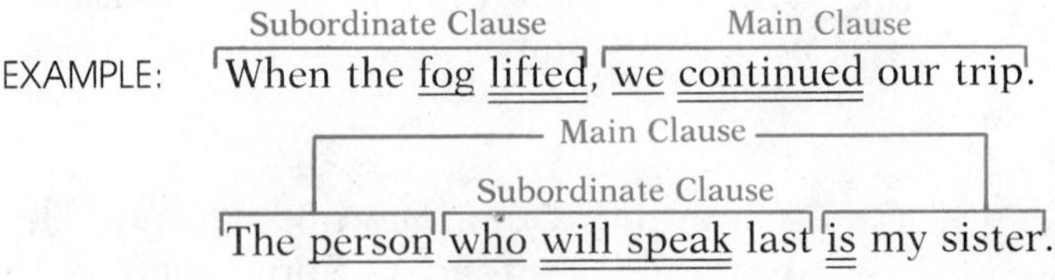

Subordinate Clause
Main Clause
When the fog lifted, we continued our trip.
Main Clause
Subordinate Clause
The person who will speak last is my sister.

In the first example, *we* is the subject of the sentence, and *continued* is the main verb. In the second example, *person* is the subject of the sentence, and *is* is the main verb.

EXERCISE E: Recognizing Complex Sentences. The following are complex sentences. Copy each onto your paper. In each clause underline the subject once and the verb twice. Then put parentheses around each subordinate clause.

EXAMPLE: The player (who scores the most points) wins.

1. I will leave (after you are safely indoors.)
2. (Although he is a marvelous science student,) he is weak in mathematics.
3. The noise (that shattered the window) was a sonic boom.
4. You may sit here (if you like.)
5. The museum (that we wanted to visit) is not open today.

EXERCISE F: More Work with Complex Sentences. In a book or magazine, find ten complex sentences. On your paper copy each sentence and mark it as in Exercise E.

Students might try to find at least one sentence with two subordinate clauses.

The Compound-Complex Sentence

A *compound-complex sentence,* as the name indicates, contains the elements of both a compound sentence and a complex sentence.

> A **compound-complex sentence** consists of two or more independent clauses and one or more subordinate clauses.

EXAMPLE: [As he was leaving for school,]Subordinate Clause [Larry remembered to take his lunch,]Independent Clause but [he forgot the report]Independent Clause [that he had finished the night before.]Subordinate Clause

EXERCISE G: Recognizing Compound-Complex Sentences. The following are compound-complex sentences. Copy each onto your paper. In each clause underline the subject once and the verb twice. Then put parentheses around each subordinate clause that you find.

EXAMPLE: The person (who knows it best) is not here, but we can try it anyway.

1. The mountain areas are barren, but the valleys are fertile (since they are irrigated daily.)
2. The musicians (who appeared for the audition) were generally excellent, but a few were real amateurs.
3. (Since the blizzard ended,) the schools have remained closed, but shops in town have reopened.
4. Our school band seems ready for the concert, and the chorus will again be in top shape (because its leading tenor has returned after a long illness.)
5. (Although the two-hundred-year-old house has been declared a landmark,) its plumbing is nearly in ruins, and few people have shown any interest in buying it.

EXERCISE H: More Work with Compound-Complex Sentences. In a book or magazine, find five compound-complex sentences. On your paper copy each sentence and mark it as in Exercise G.

Students might try to find at least one sentence that has two subordinate clauses as well as two independent clauses.

APPLICATION 1: Identifying the Structure of Sentences. On your paper identify the structure of each of the following sentences as either *simple, compound, complex,* or *compound-complex*.

EXAMPLE: Without thinking, we asked again.

simple

1. If this offense is reported, he will receive a severe fine. *cpx*
2. The apples, peaches, and pears are in the lower part of the refrigerator. *smp*

3. Father will fly home from Dallas tomorrow, or he will phone the family. *cpd*
4. She carefully described the people that she had seen. *cpx*
5. The room is dark in the morning, but sunlight floods it in the afternoon. *cpd*
6. He left suddenly in the middle of the committee meeting and did not reappear until more than two hours later. *smp*
7. She gave him a battered copy of *Bartlett's Familiar Quotations*, and he used it until his fiancée gave him a new dictionary of quotations. *cpd-cpx*
8. The book is very long; it does, nevertheless, have many interesting passages. *cpd*
9. Marco Polo was born on the walled island of Korcula in the Adriatic. *smp*
10. She described the method that she had used to save her brother's life. *cpx*

APPLICATION 2: Writing Sentences with Different Structures. Write original sentences according to the following instructions. *Answers will vary; samples given for first two.*

EXAMPLE: Write a complex sentence that ends with an adverb clause.

Louisa May Alcott kept a diary when she was young.

1. Chub caught his kite in the tree and began to cry.

1. Write a simple sentence with a compound verb.
2. Write a complex sentence that begins with an adverb clause.
3. Write a compound-complex sentence consisting of two independent clauses followed by a subordinate clause.
4. Write a complex sentence in which the adjective clause comes right after the subject in the independent clause.
5. Write a compound sentence in which the two independent clauses are joined by a comma and the conjunction *but*.

2. Until I saw it for myself, I didn't believe the size of the statue.

9.4 Diagraming Clauses

The previous sections on diagraming dealt with different forms of simple sentences. This section will introduce diagrams for clauses in compound and complex sentences.

Compound Sentences

A compound sentence is a combination of two or more independent clauses. To diagram a compound sentence, begin by diagraming each clause separately, one above the other. Then join the clauses at the verbs using a dotted line shaped like a step. Place the conjunction or semicolon on the horizontal part of the step.

EXAMPLE: Mary slowly opened the package, and then she smiled happily.

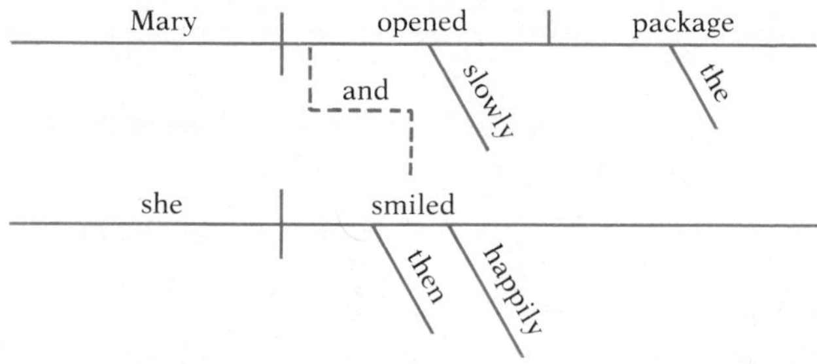

EXERCISE A: Diagraming Compound Sentences. Diagram each of the following compound sentences.
Answers on pages T-118–T-119.

1. The roads are safe, but the bridges are icy.
2. Bob left for Boston yesterday; we will go today.
3. She wrote herself a note, yet she still forgot her appointment.
4. We must paint the fence; otherwise, it may rot.
5. We will give him three guesses; she will then tell him the answer.

Subordinate Clauses

A complex sentence contains one independent clause and one or more subordinate clauses. In a diagram of a complex sentence, each clause is placed on a separate horizontal line.

Adjective Clauses. A subordinate adjective clause is placed on a horizontal line of its own beneath the independent clause. The two clauses are then connected by a dotted line. This dotted line connects the noun or pronoun being modified in the independent clause with the relative pronoun in the adjective clause.

S S V V

EXAMPLE: The person *whom you described* is the principal.

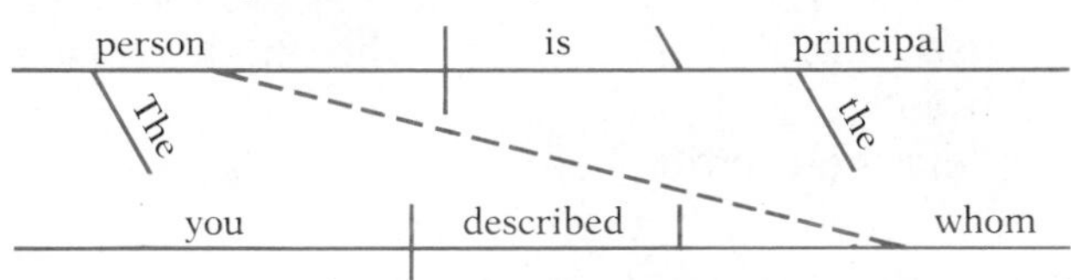

S V S V

EXAMPLE: This is the man *whose car was stolen.*

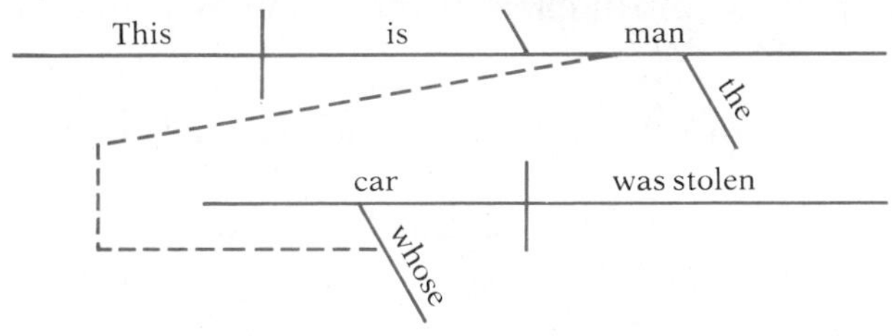

Adverb Clause. A subordinate adverb clause is diagramed in the same way a subordinate adjective clause is. The adverb clause is also written on a horizontal line of its own beneath the independent clause. In a diagram of an adverb clause, however, the subordinating conjunction is written along the dotted line. This line extends from the modified verb, adverb, or adjective in the independent clause to the verb in the adverb clause.

S V S V

EXAMPLE: They left *before the parade began.*

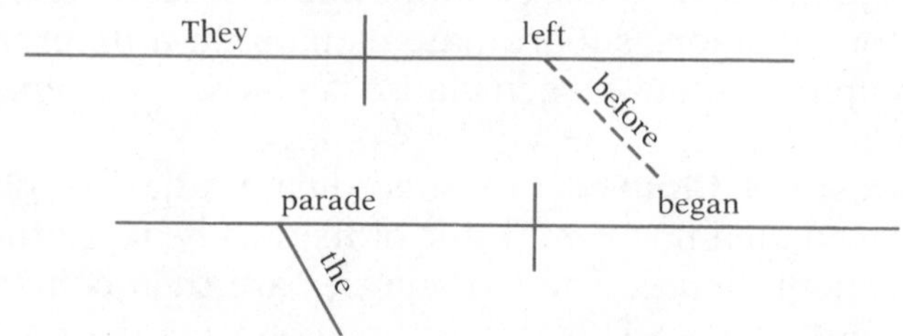

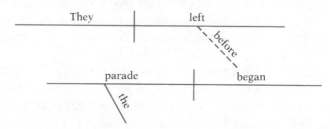

EXERCISE B: Diagraming Subordinate Clauses. Each of the following sentences contains an adjective or an adverb clause. Diagram each sentence. *Answers on pages T-119–T-1*

1. I discovered the culprit who had caused the problem.
2. We left the theater before the play began.
3. The milk that I bought is sour.
4. When the judge entered, everyone rose.
5. The plans that they discussed remain a mystery.

APPLICATION: Diagraming Compound and Complex Sentences. Diagram each of the following sentences.
Answers on pages T-120–T-122.

1. The lady who scolded us walked away slowly.
2. My grandfather opened his newspaper after he had his lunch.
3. I want his old bicycle, but I will not pay his price.
4. She likes their new house because it is near a public park.
5. They chose a house that has no attic.
6. He is happier than I am.
7. They will reach the coast today, or they will certainly get there in the morning.
8. I gave him his ticket since he will meet us at the theater.
9. This is the album that he recommended.
10. We have been expecting a letter, but none has arrived.

Chapter 10

Correcting Sentence Errors

A knowledge of sentence structure can help you avoid several common problems that often appear in writing. For example, knowing what elements are needed to make a complete sentence can help you avoid writing either incomplete or overcrowded thoughts. In addition, knowing how phrases and clauses act to modify words can help you be sure that your sentences actually express the ideas intended.

This chapter will discuss three common sentence errors and give you practice in correcting them.

Avoiding Fragments 10.1

There are many different kinds of *fragments,* but they all have one thing in common.

A **fragment** is a group of words that does not express a complete thought.

A fragment is only part of a sentence. Any group of words that can not stand alone is a fragment.

Recognizing Fragments

A sentence must contain a subject *and* a verb. If it does not, the result is a fragment. Often the fragment will be made up of one or more phrases. A fragment may also include a verb without a subject or a word that could be used as a subject without a verb. A fragment might even include a subject and a word that could be used as *part* of a verb. A subordinate clause is a fragment even though it includes a subject and a verb. Missing in this case are the *main* subject and verb.

FRAGMENTS
About five o'clock.
Should have left by now.
The man in the dark overcoat.
The car swerving around the corner.
If she expects me to finish the job.

One good way to spot a fragment is to read the words aloud. Read each fragment in the preceding chart and listen carefully. Your ear will tell you that something is missing. Now compare these fragments with the complete sentences in the following chart. The original fragments are printed in italics.

COMPLETE SENTENCES
My uncle arrived *about five o'clock.*
We *should have left by now.*
The man in the dark overcoat knocked on the door.
The car was *swerving around the corner.*
If she expects me to finish the job, she will have to give me more time.

Notice what was added in each case to make a complete sentence from the fragment. The first fragment became complete with the addition of a subject and verb. The second became complete with the addition of a subject, while the third became complete with the addition of a verb and a modifying phrase. The fourth became complete when a helping verb was added. The fifth, a subordinate clause, needed a full independent clause.

EXERCISE A: Recognizing Sentence Fragments. Each of the following groups of words is either a sentence or a fragment. For each group write *F* if it is a fragment and *S* if it is a complete sentence.

EXAMPLE: Near the end of the story. F

1. On top of the hill. F
2. A policeman standing on the corner. F
3. The money stolen from the largest bank in town. F
4. This road leads to the state assembly building. S
5. The person waiting for us at the bus stop. F
6. When Aunt Millie stepped from the plane. F
7. Near the ledge by the window in the living room. F
8. Backed into the billboard. F
9. Because she waited too long to call for help. F
10. The robber rattled by the noises in the attic. F
11. A beautiful baby smiling at us. F
12. Should report to the manager's office. F
13. Although I always try to be on time. F
14. Between you and me. F
15. A severe winter storm raged for more than a day. S
16. A man identifying himself as a CIA agent. F
17. Since my last visit to Chile and Peru. F
18. Only a part of the sentence. F
19. The two top brands are about equal in quality. S
20. Two or three miles down the highway at the traffic light. F

Phrase Fragments

You can easily learn to recognize many different types of fragments. One of the most common types is the *phrase fragment.* Since a phrase does not contain a subject and a verb, it can not stand alone as a sentence.

> A phrase should not be capitalized and punctuated as if it were a sentence.

Four kinds of phrases—prepositional, participial, gerund, and infinitive—are sometimes used alone by mistake as fragments. If you recognize that a phrase fragment has been treated as a sentence, you should correct it. Often the fragment can be added to a nearby sentence in the passage.

PREPOSITIONAL PHRASE FRAGMENT: My uncle arrived after a long trip. *On a specially chartered plane.*

ADDED TO NEARBY SENTENCE: My uncle arrived after a long trip *on a specially chartered plane.*

PARTICIPIAL PHRASE FRAGMENT: *Walking in the rain.* I developed a sore throat.

ADDED TO NEARBY SENTENCE: *Walking in the rain,* I developed a sore throat.

Sometimes it is not possible to add a phrase fragment to a nearby sentence. In such a case, you must make a complete sentence from the fragment itself. You will often have to add both a subject and a verb as well as any other words that are needed to make a sentence that expresses a complete thought.

GERUND PHRASE FRAGMENT: Growing flowers successfully.

COMPLETED SENTENCES: *Growing flowers successfully* requires great skill.

He enjoys *growing flowers successfully.*

In the first corrected sentence, a verb and an object have been added. In the second sentence, a subject and a verb have been added.

Look at another example, this one using an infinitive phrase.

INFINITIVE PHRASE FRAGMENT: To swim well.

COMPLETED SENTENCES: *To swim well* was her ambition.

Her ambition was *to swim well.*

In the first corrected sentence, a verb and a complement have been added. In the second sentence, a subject and a verb have been added.

The variety of phrase fragments possible is almost endless. If you think a sentence is actually a fragment, check for three things: a subject, a verb, and a complete thought.

EXERCISE B: Changing Phrase Fragments into Sentences. Use each of the following phrase fragments in a sentence. You may use the phrase at the beginning, at the end, or in any other position in the sentence.

Answers will vary; samples given for first two.

EXAMPLE: In Chicago and St. Louis.

Major fairs have been held in Chicago and St. Louis.

1. We saw a baseball bat near the broken window.

1. Near the broken window.
2. Chewing gum.
3. Lost for several hours.
4. In the kitchen.
5. Chosen by the committee.
6. To eat too fast.
7. Holding my grandmother's hand.
8. In the morning after breakfast.
9. Crossing the street carefully.
10. To read a newspaper.

2. Chewing gum is not permitted in many classes.

Clause Fragments

A clause, as you may remember, has a subject and a verb. But not every clause can stand alone as a sentence. Some are *clause fragments.*

A subordinate clause should not be capitalized and punctuated as if it were a sentence.

Subordinate clauses are among the most common types of fragments. Because they contain subjects and verbs, a writer may sometimes think that subordinate clauses express complete thoughts. But a subordinate adjective or adverb clause by itself is *not* a complete thought. It must be joined to, or made into, an independent clause.

An adjective clause usually begins with a relative pronoun such as *that, which, who, whom,* or *whose.* The best way to correct an adjective clause fragment used as a sentence is to add the entire adjective clause to an independent clause.

ADJECTIVE CLAUSE FRAGMENTS: That you explained to me.

Whom you decided to pick.

COMPLETED SENTENCES: This is the agreement *that you explained to me.*

The girl *whom you decided to pick* won't serve on the committee.

An adverb clause usually begins with a subordinating conjunction such as *since, although, if, while, because,* or *when.*

ADVERB CLAUSE FRAGMENTS: If I can reach him soon.

Since you offered him another chance.

This type of fragment can usually be corrected in either of two ways. One way is to drop the subordinating conjunction.

SENTENCES: I can reach him soon.

You offered him another chance.

If taking away the conjunction changes your intended meaning, then add the entire subordinate clause to an independent clause.

COMPLETED SENTENCES: *If I can reach him soon,* I will drive him to the game.

He agreed to try again *since you offered him another chance.*

EXERCISE C: Changing Clause Fragments into Sentences. Use each of the following clause fragments in a sentence. *Answers will vary; samples given for first two.*

EXAMPLE: If I ever see Paris.

If I ever see Paris, I will send you a post card.

1. When the delivery man rang the bell, the dogs began to bark.

1. When the delivery man rang the bell.
2. Who reserved rooms in the new motel.
3. That he wanted to use.
4. Which she had saved for over a year.
5. That he intends to carry out.
6. Whom he later married.
7. Although she has collected old silver coins for a long time.
8. Since the electricity has been off for the last two days.
9. If they decide to travel by railroad.
10. When the chimney in back of the school began to smoke.

2. These are the people who reserved rooms in the new motel.

APPLICATION: Changing Fragments into Sentences. Read the following fragments and decide what is missing from each one. Then use the fragment as part of a complete sentence. *Answers will vary; samples given for first two.*

EXAMPLE: Thinking about you everyday.

I have been thinking about you everyday.

1. Opening the door to the garage, he hurt his thumb.

1. Opening the door to the garage.
2. With soft rolls, white bread, and vanilla cookies.
3. Since I received his letter last week.
4. On the top shelf of the closet.
5. Taken from the top drawer in the desk.
6. Buying buttons, snaps, and zippers.
7. Which reached us the next morning.
8. Replacing a cylinder in the old engine.
9. Whose house he rented.
10. Because I won't accept his advice.
11. If we can't reach them by Monday.
12. To report to the principal.

2. The bakery cases were filled with soft rolls, white bread, and vanilla cookies.

13. In a map of the old part of town.
14. Waiting for more than an hour at the bus stop.
15. Whose book I borrowed yesterday.
16. When the delivery truck pulled up.
17. Smiling and showing their approval.
18. Under the pile of papers on the bookcase.
19. While I am willing to do my part.
20. With roses and marigolds.

10.2 Avoiding Run-ons

Fragments lack essential parts that would make them sentences. Another kind of sentence error is found in sentences that are crowded with too much information. An overcrowded sentence is called a *run-on.*

A **run-on** is two or more complete sentences that are not properly joined or separated.

Run-ons are usually the result of haste. The writer fails to take the time to see where one sentence ends and a new sentence begins.

Two Kinds of Run-ons

You should learn to recognize run-ons when you see them. One type of run-on consists of two sentences that are not joined or separated by any punctuation at all. An even more frequent kind of run-on consists of two sentences punctuated only with a comma.

RUN-ONS	
With No Punctuation	**With Only a Comma**
The hall was dark and dreary-looking a row of wooden chairs was placed against the far wall.	The coach welcomed the new players, he explained his rules for practice.

A good way to distinguish between a run-on sentence and a correct sentence is to read the words aloud. Hearing the words will help you decide whether they express one complete thought or more than one complete thought.

EXERCISE A: Recognizing Run-ons. Some of the following items are full sentences; others are run-ons. On your paper write *S* if the item is a complete sentence and *RO* if the item is a run-on.

EXAMPLE: Her horse fell, she ended in a ditch. RO

1. A comedy of manners usually deals with the behavior of people these witty plays are often about middle- and upper-class men and women. RO
2. The Johnstown Flood was brought about by the collapse of the Conemaugh Reservoir in Pennsylvania, it occurred during a period of very heavy rainfall. RO
3. In an attempt to correct the leak, he actually caused much more damage. S
4. Beethoven's Seventh Symphony has often been called the *Dance Symphony,* the composer himself conducted the first performance of it in Vienna in 1813. RO
5. A highlight of a trip through the coastal region of Norway usually is a cruise through the beautiful fjords. S
6. He had read all of Jack London's books the first one was *Call of the Wild.* RO
7. Cigar smoking is now prohibited on most airline flights, cigarette smoking, however, is still permitted in special sections. RO
8. Irrigation of arid land was first begun in the United States by the Mormons sometime before the Civil War. S
9. The storm flooded major highways, motorists were warned to stay at home. RO
10. In 1700 the Natchez Indians lived between the Yazoo and Pearl rivers on the east side of the Mississippi. S

Three Ways to Correct Run-ons

Once you have spotted a run-on, there are three relatively simple ways to correct it.

Using End Marks. End marks are periods, question marks, and exclamation marks.

Use an end mark to separate a run-on into two sentences.

An end mark breaks a run-on into two shorter but complete sentences. Use whichever end mark is needed at the end of the first sentence.

RUN-ON: Last Friday this traffic light was not working an emergency crew repaired it the same day.

CORRECTED SENTENCES: Last Friday this traffic light was not working. An emergency crew repaired it the same day.

RUN-ON: Stop complaining, it won't make things any better.

CORRECTED SENTENCES: Stop complaining! It won't make things any better.

Using a Comma and a Coordinating Conjunction. If the ideas in both parts of a run-on are related, you can usually change the run-on into a compound sentence.

Use a comma and a coordinating conjunction to combine two independent clauses into a compound sentence.

The five most frequently used coordinating conjunctions are *and, but, or, for,* and *nor.* In using this method, it is important to remember that both a *comma* and a *coordinating conjunction* are needed.

RUN-ON: My father eats a full breakfast each morning, my mother has only juice and coffee.

CORRECTED SENTENCE: My father eats a full breakfast each morning, *but* my mother has only juice and coffee.

RUN-ON: I enjoy belonging to different clubs I expect to join the community center soon.

CORRECTED SENTENCE: I enjoy belonging to different clubs, *and* I expect to join the community center soon.

Using Semicolons. A semicolon can also be used to punctuate the two parts of a run-on.

Use a semicolon to connect two closely related ideas.

Semicolons should not be used too often. In addition, they should be used only when some type of relationship exists between the ideas in both parts of the sentence.

RUN-ON: The first speaker outlined some general ideas, the second filled in the details.

CORRECTED SENTENCE: The first speaker outlined some general ideas; the second filled in the details.

A semicolon is often used when the second part of a run-on includes such words as *however, for example,* or *moreover.* When a semicolon comes before one of these words, a comma is used after the word to separate the word from the rest of the clause. Study the following corrected example carefully for the positions of both the semicolon and the comma.

RUN-ON: His suggestions are not always sound, for example he wanted to spend all that money without doing any research first.

CORRECTED SENTENCE: His suggestions are not always sound; for example, he wanted to spend all that money without doing any research first.

EXERCISE B: Correcting Run-ons. Rewrite each of the following run-ons using any of the three methods described in this section. Use each method at least four times. *Answers will vary; samples given for first two.*

EXAMPLE: They were in a hurry, the crowd was enormous.

They were in a hurry, but the crowd was enormous.

1. The first rocket launching was unsuccessful, but the second fulfilled all our expectations.

1. The first rocket launching was unsuccessful the second fulfilled all our expectations.
2. Tell the truth, it is easier than lying.
3. My father watches football, basketball, and baseball on TV my mother prefers to watch comedies, concerts, and documentaries.
4. The book itself was poor, the film version was a disaster.
5. The Marquis de Lafayette reached New York on August 16, 1824, he had been invited by President Monroe.
6. I hope to visit Denmark and Sweden this summer, however, I will have to see how expensive it will be.
7. Our plants are not doing well they seem dry and lifeless.
8. Lotteries go back to pre-Revolutionary times, even then they were used to raise money for schools, roads, and bridges.
9. My brothers and I always crave dessert all my parents ever have is black coffee.
10. The first English settlers brought a primitive loom to this country, a better Dutch loom with a fly shuttle soon replaced the English loom.
11. The American author Harriet Beecher Stowe wrote *Uncle Tom's Cabin* before the Civil War, she did not die until 1896.
12. I am saving for a new turntable, however, my old one still works well.
13. "The Playground of the World" is what Atlantic City likes to call itself it does have beautiful hotels, casinos, and a fine beach.

2. Tell the truth; it is easier than lying.

14. I am amused by the different beverage fads in this country now bottled water has become popular in many places.
15. Nathan Hale is undoubtedly the most famous spy from the Revolutionary War era, however, Lydia Darrah, another spy during that period, is credited with actually saving Washington's army on one occasion.
16. Franklin loves to make soup he told me that there are three basic soup stocks: chicken, meat, and fish.
17. Fables are stories that teach a moral sometimes they are about animals that speak and act like humans.
18. Edgar Allan Poe was an orphan at two, the rest of his life was also tragic.
19. Gershwin wrote the music for *Porgy and Bess,* many experts consider it America's first great folk opera.
20. The robin is the state bird of Michigan, the state flower is the apple blossom.

APPLICATION: Correcting Run-ons in a Composition. Three of the sentences in the following paragraph are run-ons. Rewrite the entire paragraph and correct each run-on. Do not use the same method to correct all the run-ons. *Corrections for 2, 3, and 5 may vary; sample given for 2.*

EXAMPLE: American pioneers ran into many different problems one of them was housing.

American pioneers ran into many different problems. One of them was housing.

(1) Early settlers on the prairie had problems finding timber to build homes. (2) Sod houses first appeared about 1830, in one period about 90 percent of the people west of the Missouri River lived in these mud huts. (3) The settlers learned to build sod houses from the Plains Indians they had long made their winter homes from earth. (4) Sod houses had walls three feet thick. (5) These huts were dark and poorly ventilated they were warm in winter and cool in summer.

2. Sod houses first appeared about 1830; in one period about 90 percent of the people west of the Missouri River lived in these mud huts.

10.3 Avoiding Misplaced Modifiers

When phrases and clauses that act as adjectives or adverbs are placed too far from the words they modify, confusion can result. A modifier that is placed incorrectly is called a *misplaced modifier.*

A modifier should be placed as close as possible to the word it modifies.

Recognizing Misplaced Modifiers

When a modifier is placed too far from the word it modifies, the sentence may be difficult to understand.

MISPLACED MODIFIER: I bought a stereo at the store *with pushbutton controls.*

The misplaced modifier is the phrase *with pushbutton controls.* In the sentence it sounds as though the store, and not the stereo, has pushbutton controls. The sentence can be improved by placing this modifier closer to *stereo* and placing the other phrase at the beginning of the sentence.

CORRECTED SENTENCE: At the store I bought a stereo *with pushbutton controls.*

Look now at a slightly different kind of misplaced modifier.

MISPLACED MODIFIER: *Suffering from a cold,* her test mark was poor.

Here the problem is more complicated. The sentence begins with the phrase *suffering from a cold.* That phrase should modify a person. Instead it incorrectly modifies the word *mark.* The sentence should be rewritten to include the name of the person who has a cold.

CORRECTED SENTENCE: *Suffering from a cold,* Diana did poorly on the test.

EXERCISE A: Recognizing Misplaced Modifiers. Some of the following sentences are correct, but most of them contain misplaced modifiers. If the sentence is correct, write *C* on your paper. If the sentence contains a misplaced modifier, write *MM*.

EXAMPLE: Writing a letter, his signature is almost always illegible. MM

1. Crossing the bridge, a tollbooth was hit by the car. *MM*
2. I always prefer a room in a motel with a window. *MM*
3. Choosing his words carefully, my father began to speak. *C*
4. Having had our dinner, the boat continued the journey. *MM*
5. Having received a medal, my dream was fulfilled. *MM*
6. She gave the letter to Mr. Gross with the envelope. *MM*
7. Driven to the station early, we decided to have lunch. *C*
8. I chose that hat for my mother with the flower. *MM*
9. Reaching the end of the road, the farm came into view. *MM*
10. Frightened by the noise, my screams were heard down the hall. *MM*

Correcting Misplaced Modifiers

Three kinds of modifiers that are commonly misplaced are prepositional phrases, participial phrases, and adjective clauses. For each of these modifiers, the rule is the same: Place the modifier as close as possible to the word it modifies.

A misplaced prepositional phrase usually occurs in a sentence with two or more phrases in a row. The misplaced prepositional phrase should be moved closer to the word it modifies. Any other phrases that might also be confused should be moved as well.

MISPLACED PHRASE: My older brother chose a car at the showroom *without optional equipment.*

CORRECTED SENTENCE: At the showroom my older brother chose a car *without optional equipment.*

Participial phrases are often used at the beginning of sentences. The word that the phrase modifies should appear right after the phrase. Sometimes it is necessary to rephrase the sentence to get the modified word next to the phrase.

MISPLACED PHRASE: *Driving into the park,* the statue of Eisenhower was seen.

Who did the driving? Who saw the statue? Someone performed both these actions. The sentence should be rephrased to show who did the driving.

CORRECTED SENTENCE: *Driving into the park,* we saw the statue of Eisenhower.

A misplaced adjective clause should also be brought closer to the word it modifies. In the following example, the clause is too far away from *man.*

MISPLACED CLAUSE: The police arrested a man after a long investigation *that was seen often in the vicinity.*

CORRECTED SENTENCE: After a long investigation, the police arrested a man *that was seen often in the vicinity.*

EXERCISE B: Correcting Misplaced Modifiers. Rewrite the following sentences to eliminate the misplaced modifiers. In your rewritten sentences, underline the modifier that was misplaced in the original and draw an arrow pointing from the modifier to the word it modifies. *Answers may vary; samples given for first two.*

EXAMPLE: Swimming leisurely, his worries were left behind.

Swimming leisurely, he left his worries behind.

1. The book that he wanted was not available.

1. The book was not available that he wanted.
2. Entering the movie, my best friend was seen in the last row.
3. We are sending you a package of seeds by parcel post with planting instructions.
4. The man was really very stingy that many people admired.
5. Eating lunch rapidly, my trip was soon continued.
6. Mother bought strawberries at the supermarket with delicious flavor.
7. Swimming as fast as possible, the drowning girl was reached.
8. The train was unusually late that I always take into the city.
9. Told to remain silent, the crying of the baby grew even louder.
10. I welcomed my old friend as soon as he arrived with great affection.

2. Entering the movie, I saw my best friend in the last row.

APPLICATION: Correcting Misplaced Modifiers in a Composition. Three of the sentences in the following composition contain misplaced modifiers. Rewrite the entire paragraph and correct these errors.

Corrections for 2, 3, and 4 may vary; sample given for 2.

EXAMPLE: Herodotus is best remembered for his works about history by many people.

By many people Herodotus is best remembered for his works about history.

(1) Except from his writings, almost nothing is known of Herodotus' life. (2) Born between 490 and 460 B.C. in Asia Minor, several years of his early adulthood were spent by him in travel. (3) As a person of Greek heritage, he must have been filled by the lands he visited—Egypt, Mesopotamia, Palestine, southern Russia—with awe. (4) At Thurii in southern Italy, he wrote his famous *History*, where he had retired in later

2. Born between 490 and 460 B.C. in Asia Minor, he spent several years of his early adulthood in travel.

life. (5) Reading Herodotus' accounts of strange lands and wondrous events, one almost envies the life of the man who is called the Father of History.

Review Exercises: Grammar

REVIEW EXERCISE 1: Recognizing Parts of Speech

Read the following paragraph and answer the questions that follow it.

EXAMPLE: Find the verb in the first sentence.

peered

(1) Donna peered into the bright and noisy auditorium from backstage. (2) She could hear many people in the audience chatting with friends as they waited for the show to start. (3) Who was present tonight? (4) Donna felt both hot and cold in her costume, and she tugged at the Indian sari that she had painstakingly wrapped around her. (5) The house lights flashed and went down very slowly. (6) Donna waited until the auditorium was completely dark. (7) Then she took her position in front of the curtain. (8) The spotlight lit her and she heard herself utter her first line in a strong, confident voice: "Aha!"

and 1. Find the coordinating conjunction in the first sentence.
2. Find the proper noun in the first sentence. *Donna*
3. Find the collective noun in the second sentence.
many 4. Find the indefinite adjective in the second sentence.
5. Find the helping verb in the second sentence. *could*
Who 6. Find the interrogative pronoun in the third sentence.
7. Find the adjective in the third sentence. *present*
8. Find the linking verb in the fourth sentence. *felt*
9. Find a correlative conjunction in the fourth sentence. *both . . . and*
10. Find the proper adjective in the fourth sentence.

3. audience 10. Indian

11. Find the relative pronoun in the fourth sentence. *that*
12. What part of speech is *down* in the fifth sentence?
13. What word does *very* modify in the fifth sentence?
14. Find an intransitive action verb in the sixth sentence. *waited*
15. Find the subordinating conjunction in the sixth sentence. *until*
16. Find the compound preposition in the seventh sentence. *in front of*
17. Find the possessive adjective in the seventh sentence. *her*
18. Find the compound noun in the eighth sentence.
19. Find the definite article in the eighth sentence. *The*
20. Find the interjection in the eighth sentence. *Aha*

12. adverb 13. slowly 18. spotlight

REVIEW EXERCISE 2: Writing Sentences Using Parts of Speech

Make the following short sentences longer by adding nouns, pronouns, adjectives, adverbs, prepositional phrases, and conjunctions. *Answers will vary; samples given for first two.*

EXAMPLE: Birds fly.

In the morning, birds of all kinds fly up to our bird feeder.

1. Home movies seldom entertain anyone outside of the immediate family.

1. Movies entertain.
2. The puppy plays.
3. Mother works.
4. The moon rose.
5. Winfield sang.
6. Friends will visit.
7. Katharine studies.
8. Earl eats.
9. The architect draws.
10. Zack travels.

2. The Dalmatian puppy plays with the rubber crocodile.

REVIEW EXERCISE 3: Recognizing Parts of a Sentence

Read the following paragraph and answer the questions that follow it.

EXAMPLE: Find the verb in the first sentence.

will begin

(1) Next September, Lunar Lines, America's first interplanetary travel agency, will begin a series of luxury cruises to the moon. (2) Our special tour package offers you and your family the vacation of a lifetime. (3) You will voyage out of this world on one of our beautiful mooncrafts. (4) Your flight attendants and tour guides on this journey will be former astronauts. (5) On the moon you will stay at our deluxe Casaluna Hotel and will experience low gravity and other moon marvels in the comfort of our own private park. (6) Does the idea of an extraterrestrial vacation thrill you? (7) Then act quickly. (8) There are only a few places left on our maiden flight. (9) Join us and become the very first moonwalker on your block!

1. Identify the subject in the first sentence. *Lunar Lines*
2. What is the function of the world *moon* in the first sentence? *obj of prep*
3. Find a direct object in the first sentence. *series*
4. What is the function of the word *voyage* in the third sentence? *V*
5. What is the function of the word *astronauts* in the fourth sentence? *PN*
6. What is the subject in the sixth sentence? *idea*
7. What is the direct object in the sixth sentence? *you*
8. What is the verb in the sixth sentence? *Does thrill*
9. What is the subject in the eighth sentence? *places*
10. What is the subject in the ninth sentence? *you*
11. What is the function of the word *moonwalker* in the ninth sentence? *PN*
12. *5* Which sentence contains a compound direct object?
13. Which sentence contains a compound indirect object? *2*
14. Which sentence contains a compound subject? *4*
15. Find the first sentence with a compound verb. *5*
16. Find the first sentence with a linking verb. *4*
17. How many imperative sentences are in the paragraph? *2*
18. How many declarative sentences are in the paragraph? *6*

19. How many interrogative sentences are in the paragraph? *1*
20. Find the last three prepositional phrases in the paragraph. *of . . . vacation/on . . . flight/on . . . block*

REVIEW EXERCISE 4: Writing Sentences According to Patterns

Write one sentence for each of the following patterns, adding modifiers and conjunctions where appropriate.
Answers will vary; samples given for first two.

EXAMPLE: Subject + Verb + Direct Object

Yesterday, I made a long-distance telephone call to my friend in Hawaii.

1. Jack and Jill were climbing all afternoon.

1. Subject + Subject + Verb
2. Subject + Verb + Indirect Object + Direct Object
3. Subject + Verb + Verb + Direct Object
4. Subject + Linking Verb + Predicate Adjective
5. Subject + Verb + Indirect Object + Indirect Object + Direct Object
6. Subject + Linking Verb + Predicate Noun + Predicate Noun
7. Subject + Subject + Verb + Verb
8. Subject + Verb + Direct Object + Direct Object
9. Subject + Linking Verb + Predicate Pronoun
10. Verb + Indirect Object + Direct Object

2. Gwen promised Eric a new ten-speed bike.

REVIEW EXERCISE 5: Recognizing Different Kinds of Phrases and Clauses

Read the following paragraph and answer the questions that follow it.
Sentence numbers are given for questions that require phrases and clauses.

EXAMPLE: Find an adjective phrase in the first sentence.

of a huge gray city

(1) The park, the green heart of a huge gray city, is always crowded on fine days with visitors hungering for nature. (2) It can be enjoyable simply to watch the

various people flocking into the park, for they include individuals of all ages, backgrounds, and temperaments gathered in one place for many different reasons. (3) Jogging, bicycling, and roller skating remain the most popular athletic activities among those who frequent the park for the purpose of improving themselves. (4) For others merely to be out of doors is sufficient reason to come to the park whenever they can. (5) Babies doze complacently, carried or pushed by proud parents; racing children loudly pursue objects that catch their fancy; and young and old couples wander tranquilly, holding hands as they walk. (6) On such days the park gives the people that enter it the feeling that the human race might be able to solve its problems, if only the sun could shine all the time.

1. Find an appositive phrase. *1*
2. Find a prepositional phrase with a compound object. *2*
3. Find a compound sentence. *2*
4. Find an infinitive phrase used as an adjective. *4*
5. Find the first infinitive phrase that is used as an adverb. *2*
6. Find the first adverb clause in the paragraph. *4*
7. How is the word *jogging* used in the third sentence? *subj*
8. Find the first adjective clause that modifies a word used as a direct object. *5*
9. Find an adjective clause that modifies a word used as an indirect object. *6*
10. Find a compound-complex sentence in the paragraph. *5*
11. How many complex sentences are there in the paragraph? *3*
12. Find an adjective clause that modifies the object of a preposition. *3*
13. Find the first present participle in the paragraph. *1*
14. How does the prepositional phrase *out of doors* function in the fourth sentence? *adv*
15. Find the past participle in the second sentence.
16. Find a simple sentence in the paragraph. *1*
17. What kind of clause is *as they walk* in the fifth sentence? *adv*

15. gathered

18. Find the last adverb clause in the paragraph. *6*
19. How does the word *that* function in the fifth sentence? *subj of adj clause*
20. Find the first five prepositional phrases in the paragraph. *1 and 2*

REVIEW EXERCISE 6: Writing Sentences with Different Phrases and Clauses

Expand each of the following phrases and clauses into sentences as called for in each item.
Answers will vary; samples given for first two.

EXAMPLE: Use the adjective phrase *in the dark* in a simple sentence.

A shot in the dark often misses.

1. The person who finds the hiding place can keep the chocolate eggs.

1. Use the adjective clause *who finds the hiding place* in a complex sentence.
2. Use the adjective clause *which we all forgot* in a complex sentence.
3. Use the adverb clause *when the rain stops pouring* in a compound-complex sentence.
4. Use the infinitive phrase *to eat tacos* as the direct object in a simple sentence.
5. Use the participial phrase *burning brightly* in a simple sentence.
6. Use the infinitive phrase *to write a paper* as a predicate noun.
7. Use the infinitive phrase *to be alone* as an adjective.
8. Use the gerund phrase *climbing a mountain* as the object of a preposition.
9. Use the gerund *swimming* as an appositive.
10. Use the past participle *defeated* as an adjective in a compound sentence.

2. The math test, which we all forgot, had been announced weeks ago.

REVIEW EXERCISE 7: Recognizing Sentence Errors

The following paragraph contains a number of faulty sentences. Read the paragraph carefully and then answer the question that follow it.

EXAMPLE: What sentence errors are found in the first sentence?

misplaced modifier and run-on

(1) Born in 1564, the work of William Shakespeare represents the largest body of masterpieces produced by a single writer, he is undoubtedly our greatest author. (2) Shakespeare's literary output includes a total of thirty-seven plays. (3) Among them, seventeen comedies, ten history plays, and ten tragedies, which include the powerful dramas of *Hamlet, Othello,* and *King Lear.* (4) Very little is known to scholars living in the twentieth century of Shakespeare's early life. (5) As the son of a leatherworker, Shakespeare was given an education that was adequate but not extensive. (6) Though he may have served as a schoolmaster in his youth. (7) At the age of nineteen, he married Anne Hathaway they had three children. (8) For a period of seven years, he disappeared during which he may have gone to London as an actor in a touring company. (9) However, Shakespeare emerged from these "lost years" as an actor of recognized ability and a playwright with a growing reputation around 1592.

1. How many correct sentences can you find in the paragraph? *2*
2. Identify the first sentence fragment. *3*
3. Identify the second run-on sentence. *7*
4. Identify the first two sentences that contain misplaced modifiers. *1 and 4*
5. What should the modifier in the first of these two sentences correctly modify? *William Shakespeare*

REVIEW EXERCISE 8: Correcting Sentence Errors

On your paper rewrite the paragraph in Review Exercise 7, correcting all the sentence errors.
Corrections for 1, 3, 4, 6, 7, 8, and 9 may vary; sample given for 1.

EXAMPLE: Shakespeare is said to have been born on April 23, he died on the same date many years later.

Shakespeare is said to have been born on April 23. He died on the same date many years later.

1. Born in 1564, William Shakespeare created the largest body of masterpieces produced by a single writer. He is undoubtedly our greatest author.

UNIT II

Usage

Chapter 11

Using Verbs

The term *usage* refers to the way a word or expression is used in a sentence. Over the years rules have been established that reflect the way most educated Americans use their language. What the majority of Americans now consider to be the correct use of language for most situations is known as *standard English.* What they consider to be incorrect usage is known as *nonstandard English.* The rules in this and the following chapters are those of standard English. They are the rules that you will probably be expected to apply in most of the writing and speaking you do in school.

One area of usage that causes people many problems is verbs. Since verbs have many forms and uses, you may find yourself occasionally making mistakes with them. This chapter will help you learn their various forms and will give you guidance in using them correctly in your speaking and writing.

11.1 The Principal Parts of Verbs

Verbs have different forms to express time. The form of the verb *talk* in the sentence "She *talks* about her plans" expresses action in the present. In "She *talked* about her plans," the form of the verb shows that the action happened in the past. These forms of verbs are known as *tenses.* To use the various tenses of verbs correctly, you should first know how to form the *principal parts* of a verb.

A verb has four **principal parts:** the *present,* the *present participle,* the *past,* and the *past participle.*

Here are the four principal parts of the verb *talk.*

PRINCIPAL PARTS OF *TALK*			
Present	**Present Participle**	**Past**	**Past Participle**
talk	(am) talking	talked	(have) talked

Notice in the chart the first principal part, the present. This is the form of the verb that you would find listed in a dictionary. Notice also the second and fourth principal parts and the words before them in parentheses. When these two principal parts are used as verbs in sentences, helping verbs are always used with them.

Here are four sentences, each using one of the principal parts of the verb *talk.*

EXAMPLES: I sometimes *talk* too much.

We *were talking* to the guidance counselor.

They *talked* together for hours.

He *has talked* about a trip to Greece.

By looking at the third and fourth principal parts of a verb, you can learn whether the verb is *regular* or *irregular.*

Regular Verbs

Most verbs in English are *regular.*

The past and past participle of a **regular verb** are formed by adding *-ed* or *-d* to the present form.

The past and past participle of such regular verbs as *lift* and *contain,* which do not end in *-e,* are formed by adding *-ed* to the present form. With regular verbs that end in *-e,* such as *save* and *change,* you simply add *-d* to the present form.

PRINCIPAL PARTS OF REGULAR VERBS			
Present	**Present Participle**	**Past**	**Past Participle**
lift	(am) lifting	lifted	(have) lifted
contain	(am) containing	contained	(have) contained
save	(am) saving	saved	(have) saved
change	(am) changing	changed	(have) changed

EXERCISE A: Recognizing the Principal Parts of Regular Verbs. On your paper write the verb or verb phrase from each of the following sentences. Then identify the principal part used to form the verb.

EXAMPLE: Frank was serving dinner when he heard the news.

was serving present participle

1. I practice my music every day. *pres*
2. Luis rubbed his hiking boots carefully with saddle soap. *past*
3. Celia has wanted to meet my twin cousins for a long time. *past part*
4. The twins are competing against each other in the debate next week. *pres part*
5. Henry mailed the letter without a stamp and without a ZIP code. *past*
6. Were you laughing at the actor's joke or at her costume? *pres part*
7. Because of the thunderstorm, we postponed our trip to the beach. *past*
8. Roy had already changed his mind twice before breakfast. *past part*
9. Those dogwood trees in the park always blossom in the spring. *pres*
10. What is she placing over the door? *pres part*

EXERCISE B: Using the Principal Parts of Regular Verbs. Copy each of the following sentences onto your paper, writing the correct form of the word given in parentheses.

EXAMPLE: The caterpillar has (change) into a moth.

The caterpillar has changed into a moth.

1. Meredith is (lift) weights to increase her strength. *lifting*
2. Edgar had already (straighten) his tie six times before the interview began. *straightened*
3. The baby tipped over the cup and (spill) the milk on his feet. *spilled*
4. I am happy that they still (visit) me every summer. *visit*
5. Alexis is (design) a special table for her work room. *designing*
6. Car chases in movies have always (frighten) me. *frightened*
7. Had you (finish) your newspaper before the bus arrived? *finished*
8. His grandmother has (create) her own exotic desserts for years. *created*
9. Who was (knock) at the back door? *knocking*
10. He has (base) the character in his story on his uncle. *based*

Irregular Verbs

Most verbs in the English language are regular. Many of the most commonly used English verbs, however, are *irregular*.

The past and past participle of an **irregular verb** are *not* formed by adding *-ed* or *-d* to the present form.

The third and fourth principal parts of irregular verbs are formed in different ways and must be memorized.

SOME IRREGULAR VERBS WITH THE SAME PAST AND PAST PARTICIPLE			
Present	**Present Participle**	**Past**	**Past Participle**
bring	(am) bringing	brought	(have) brought
build	(am) building	built	(have) built
buy	(am) buying	bought	(have) bought
catch	(am) catching	caught	(have) caught
fight	(am) fighting	fought	(have) fought
find	(am) finding	found	(have) found
get	(am) getting	got	(have) got *or* (have) gotten
hold	(am) holding	held	(have) held
lay	(am) laying	laid	(have) laid
lead	(am) leading	led	(have) led
lose	(am) losing	lost	(have) lost
pay	(am) paying	paid	(have) paid
say	(am) saying	said	(have) said
sit	(am) sitting	sat	(have) sat
spin	(am) spinning	spun	(have) spun
stick	(am) sticking	stuck	(have) stuck
swing	(am) swinging	swung	(have) swung
teach	(am) teaching	taught	(have) taught

SOME IRREGULAR VERBS WITH THE SAME PRESENT, PAST, AND PAST PARTICIPLE			
Present	**Present Participle**	**Past**	**Past Participle**
bid	(am) bidding	bid	(have) bid
burst	(am) bursting	burst	(have) burst
cost	(am) costing	cost	(have) cost
hurt	(am) hurting	hurt	(have) hurt
put	(am) putting	put	(have) put
set	(am) setting	set	(have) set

SOME IRREGULAR VERBS THAT CHANGE IN OTHER WAYS			
Present	**Present Participle**	**Past**	**Past Participle**
arise	(am) arising	arose	(have) arisen
be	(am) being	was	(have) been
begin	(am) beginning	began	(have) begun
blow	(am) blowing	blew	(have) blown
break	(am) breaking	broke	(have) broken
choose	(am) choosing	chose	(have) chosen
come	(am) coming	came	(have) come
do	(am) doing	did	(have) done
draw	(am) drawing	drew	(have) drawn
drink	(am) drinking	drank	(have) drunk
drive	(am) driving	drove	(have) driven
eat	(am) eating	ate	(have) eaten
fall	(am) falling	fell	(have) fallen
fly	(am) flying	flew	(have) flown
freeze	(am) freezing	froze	(have) frozen
give	(am) giving	gave	(have) given
go	(am) going	went	(have) gone
grow	(am) growing	grew	(have) grown
know	(am) knowing	knew	(have) known
lie	(am) lying	lay	(have) lain
ride	(am) riding	rode	(have) ridden
ring	(am) ringing	rang	(have) rung
rise	(am) rising	rose	(have) risen
run	(am) running	ran	(have) run
see	(am) seeing	saw	(have) seen
shake	(am) shaking	shook	(have) shaken
sing	(am) singing	sang	(have) sung
sink	(am) sinking	sank	(have) sunk
speak	(am) speaking	spoke	(have) spoken
spring	(am) springing	sprang	(have) sprung
swear	(am) swearing	swore	(have) sworn

swim	(am) swimming	swam	(have) swum
take	(am) taking	took	(have) taken
tear	(am) tearing	tore	(have) torn
throw	(am) throwing	threw	(have) thrown
wear	(am) wearing	wore	(have) worn
write	(am) writing	wrote	(have) written

Check a dictionary whenever you are in doubt about the correct form of an irregular verb.

EXERCISE C: Completing the Principal Parts of Irregular Verbs. Without looking back at the charts in this section, write the missing principal parts for the following irregular verbs on your paper.

EXAMPLE:

Present	Present Participle	Past	Past Participle
______	writing	______	______
write	writing	wrote	written

	Present	Present Participle	Past	Past Participle
1.	*freeze*	*freezing*	froze	*frozen*
2.	run	*running*	*ran*	*run*
3.	*lie*	*lying*	*lay*	lain
4.	swing	*swinging*	*swung*	*swung*
5.	*set*	*setting*	set	*set*
6.	*hold*	holding	*held*	*held*
7.	*teach*	*teaching*	*taught*	taught
8.	*pay*	paying	*paid*	*paid*
9.	bring	*bringing*	*brought*	*brought*
10.	*lay*	*laying*	laid	*laid*
11.	*go*	*going*	went	*gone*
12.	*drink*	*drinking*	*drank*	drunk
13.	*know*	knowing	*knew*	*known*
14.	ride	*riding*	*rode*	*ridden*
15.	*shake*	*shaking*	shook	*shaken*
16.	*do*	doing	*did*	*done*
17.	catch	*catching*	*caught*	*caught*

18.	rise	rising	rose	risen
19.	tear	tearing	tore	torn
20.	burst	bursting	burst	burst

EXERCISE D: Using the Past of Irregular Verbs. For each of the following sentences, choose the correct verb from the choices in parentheses and write it on your paper.

EXAMPLE: We (freezed, froze) the vegetables.

froze

1. The camping trip was fun, but my sister (catched, caught) a bad cold.
2. The pitcher (threw, throwed) the ball to third base.
3. This bicycle (costed, cost) much more than my last one.
4. After dinner Earl (lay, lied) down for a rest.
5. Maggie's father (built, builded) their house himself.
6. Ron (swore, sweared) that he would never go near that highway again.
7. Jessie (blowed, blew) the balloons up for Seth's party.
8. The bear quickly (put, putted) her paw into the beehive.
9. The baseball (broke, breaked) the new bay window of the shoe store.
10. Last winter we (flied, flew) down to Orlando to visit my grandmother.

EXERCISE E: Using the Past Participle of Irregular Verbs. For each of the following sentences, choose the correct verb from the choices in parentheses and write it on your paper.

EXAMPLE: Angel Clare should not have (spoke, spoken) to Tess that way.

spoken

1. Has the sun (rose, risen) yet?
2. Gary has (drawn, drew) these designs for our parade float.

3. I had (ran, run) home to meet you, but you never came.
4. Since moving to the city, Colleen and Marcie have (ate, eaten) many unfamiliar foods.
5. The bell had already (rung, rang) when the new teacher walked into the room.
6. I have (came, come) to study, not to waste time.
7. Don must have (grown, grew) at least four inches in the last year.
8. Joyce had (wore, worn) a bathing suit to the picnic.
9. The sandbar had already (sunk, sank) out of sight by the time we arrived.
10. I was surprised to see that you had (chose, chosen) that album.

EXERCISE F: Supplying the Correct Principal Part of Irregular Verbs. Copy each of the following sentences onto your paper, writing the correct past or past participle form of the verb given in parentheses.

EXAMPLE: Sandy had ___(draw)___ up a plan of attack.
Sandy had drawn up a plan of attack.

1. The spider had ___(spin)___ a lovely web in the corner of the empty room. *spun*
2. In the first place, you should never have ___(swing)___ the bat so hard. *swung*
3. For her birthday Karen's aunt ___(give)___ her a pair of skis. *gave*
4. Lenny ___(begin)___ to work on this puzzle three days ago. *began*
5. Who ___(be)___ that masked man? *was*
6. If you had not ___(fall)___ down, you wouldn't have noticed that flower. *fallen*
7. The two athletes have already ___(shake)___ hands.
8. The truth has always ___(lie)___ somewhere between the two positions. *lain*
9. Dressed in silver, the dancer ___(spring)___ out of the shadows. *sprang*
10. The two families have always ___(take)___ their vacations at the same beach. *taken*

7. shaken

11. He had told it so many times that his story, though true, had ___(wear)___ thin. worn
12. Through the telescope Juanita ___(see)___ the rings of Saturn very clearly. saw
13. We have ___(throw)___ enough seeds and crumbs to that sparrow to make several loaves of bread. thrown
14. Deborah had never ___(sing)___ that song before. sung
15. Sam thought that we had ___(go)___ for the day since the office was locked. gone
16. As soon as Susan ___(drink)___ the cup of soup, she felt drowsy. drank
17. Barking urgently, the terrier ___(lead)___ us deeper into the woods. led
18. The two artists have ___(fight)___ over the years, but they always make up. fought
19. Jean's accusation ___(hurt)___ me, but I didn't know how to reply. hurt
20. The politician had ___(speak)___ the same words many times before. spoken

APPLICATION: Using the Principal Parts of Verbs. Write a brief account of something exciting or frightening that has happened to you recently. Use at least five of the verbs in the following list. *Answers will vary. You may wish to check both for correct use of principal parts and for unnecessary shifts in tense.*

EXAMPLE: write

The letter that he had written was a real surprise.

1. rise	5. frighten	9. shake
2. say	6. choose	10. escape
3. find	7. do	
4. be	8. run	

The Six Tenses of Verbs 11.2

In English verbs have six *tenses*.

A **tense** is a form of a verb that shows time of action or state of being.

Each of the six tenses has two categories: six *basic* forms and six *progressive* forms. This section will explain how the basic forms are made. The next section will explain the progressive forms.

The Basic Forms of the Six Tenses

The following chart shows the *basic* forms of the six tenses, using as an example the verb *speak*. As you can see in the third column, the six basic forms make use of just three of the principal parts: the present, the past, and the past participle.

BASIC FORMS OF THE SIX TENSES OF *SPEAK*

Tense	Basic Form	Principal Part Used
Present	I speak	The Present
Past	I spoke	The Past
Future	I will speak	The Present
Present Perfect	I have spoken	The Past Participle
Past Perfect	I had spoken	The Past Participle
Future Perfect	I will have spoken	The Past Participle

Study the chart carefully. Learn what the tenses are called and which principal parts are needed to form them. Then learn to recognize the four tenses that need helping verbs.

EXERCISE A: Identifying the Basic Forms of Verbs. On your paper write the verb from each of the following sentences. Then identify the tense of the verb.

EXAMPLE: We have collected a ton of newspapers for recycling.

have collected present perfect

1. Gabriel will present his report first. *fut*
2. We lived in Idaho for ten years. *past*
3. They had notified us of their arrival. *past perf*

4. Elaine and June practice their figure skating every day. *pres*
5. Our dogs have bitten no one. *pres perf*
6. The family will have finished dinner by seven. *fut perf*
7. She arrived at school earlier than usual. *past*
8. We have seen that movie twice. *pres perf*
9. I will stay here no longer. *fut*
10. The Lochtefeld family owns an art gallery on Nantucket. *pres*

Conjugating the Basic Forms of Verbs

A helpful way to become familiar with all the forms of a verb is by *conjugating* it.

A **conjugation** is a list of the singular and plural forms of a verb in a particular tense.

Each tense in a conjugation has six forms that correspond to the first-, second-, and third-person forms of the personal pronouns. (See Section 1.2 for a review of personal pronouns.)

To conjugate any verb, begin by listing its principal parts.

PRINCIPAL PARTS OF *GO*			
Present	**Present Participle**	**Past**	**Past Participle**
go	going	went	gone

The conjugation in the chart below and on the next page shows all the basic forms of *go* in all six tenses.

CONJUGATION OF THE BASIC FORMS OF *GO*		
	Singular	**Plural**
Present	I go you go he, she, it goes	we go you go they go

Past	I went you went he, she, it went	we went you went they went
Future	I will go you will go he, she, it will go	we will go you will go they will go
Present Perfect	I have gone you have gone he, she, it has gone	we have gone you have gone they have gone
Past Perfect	I had gone you had gone he, she, it had gone	we had gone you had gone they had gone
Future Perfect	I will have gone you will have gone he, she, it will have gone	we will have gone you will have gone they will have gone

An important verb to learn to conjugate is the verb *be*. It is both the most common and the most irregular verb in English. The following charts list the principal parts and all the basic forms of *be* in the six tenses.

PRINCIPAL PARTS OF *BE*

Present	Present Participle	Past	Past Participle
be	being	was	been

CONJUGATION OF THE BASIC FORMS OF *BE*

	Singular	Plural
Present	I am you are he, she, it is	we are you are they are

Past	I was you were he, she, it was	we were you were they were
Future	I will be you will be he, she, it will be	we will be you will be they will be
Present Perfect	I have been you have been he, she, it has been	we have been you have been they have been
Past Perfect	I had been you had been he, she, it had been	we had been you had been they had been
Future Perfect	I will have been you will have been he, she, it will have been	we will have been you will have been they will have been

EXERCISE B: Conjugating the Basic Forms of Verbs. On your paper conjugate each of the following verbs. The first two verbs are regular; the second two are irregular. Use the conjugation of *go* on pages 203 and 204 as your model. Begin each of your conjugations by listing the principal parts of the verb.

Answers should follow the model given.

1. ask 2. move 3. speak 4. begin

APPLICATION 1: Supplying the Correct Tense. Copy each of the following sentences onto your paper, supplying the basic form of the verb as directed in parentheses.

EXAMPLE: Helen Keller (speak—past) her first word when she was an infant.

Helen Keller spoke her first word when she was an infant.

1. We (ask—past) the police officer for directions to the museum. *asked*
2. The Johnsons (move—present perfect) three times in the past year. *have moved*
3. They (see—past perfect) everything they wanted to by the end of their vacation. *had seen*
4. Steve always (begin—present) his homework right after dinner. *begins*
5. By the end of their tour, the group (perform—future perfect) in eleven cities. *will have performed*
6. We (visit—future) the Uffizi Gallery when we go to Florence this summer. *will visit*
7. Sharon (talk—past perfect) to her counselor earlier in the day. *had talked*
8. He never (do—present) what he is told to do. *does*
9. We (grow—present perfect) very fond of our new neighbors. *have grown*
10. She (give—past) you a chance yesterday to change your mind. *gave*

APPLICATION 2: Using the Basic Forms of the Six Tenses. Write six sentences of your own for each verb in the following list. Use a different tense in each of your sentences. *Answers will vary; samples given for first one.*

EXAMPLE: give

She gives us flowers every spring.

She gave us flowers last year.

(and so on)

1. need 2. walk 3. sing 4. draw 5. be

1. The door needs a new lock. The door needed a new lock, and we bought one. The door will need a new lock eventually. The door has needed a new lock for a long time. The door had needed a new lock for years before it was fixed. By tomorrow, the door will have needed a new lock for exactly one month.

11.3 The Progressive Forms of Verbs

Section 11.2 gave the six tenses in their basic forms. Each of these tenses also has a *progressive* form. All six of the progressive forms of a verb are made using just one principal part: the present participle. This is the principal part that ends in *-ing*.

Recognizing Progressive Forms

The following chart shows the progressive forms of the six tenses.

PROGRESSIVE FORMS OF THE SIX TENSES OF *SPEAK*

Tense	Progressive Form	Principal Part Used
Present	I am speaking	
Past	I was speaking	
Future	I will be speaking	
Present Perfect	I have been speaking	The Present Participle
Past Perfect	I had been speaking	
Future Perfect	I will have been speaking	

EXERCISE A: Identifying the Tense of Progressive Forms of Verbs. Study the preceding chart. Then identify the tense of each of the following verbs.

EXAMPLE: was thinking past

1. will be going *fut*
2. have been seeing *pres perf*
3. am helping *pres*
4. will have been hiking
5. was carrying *past*
6. had been visiting
7. am leaving *pres*
8. will be making *fut*
9. was playing *past*
10. had been practicing
11. have been buying *pres perf*
12. will have been trying
13. was teaching *past*
14. am writing *pres*
15. had been catching *past perf*
16. will be singing *fut*
17. have been putting *pres perf*
18. was sitting *past*
19. will have been waiting
20. am collecting *pres*

4. fut perf 6. past perf 10. past perf 12. fut perf 19. fut perf

Conjugating the Progressive Forms of Verbs

Conjugating the progressive forms of any verb is easy if you know how to conjugate the basic forms of the verb *be.*

To conjugate the progressive forms of a verb, add the present participle of the verb to a conjugation of the basic forms of *be.*

A complete conjugation of the basic forms of *be* is shown on pages 204 and 205. Compare that conjugation with the following conjugation of the progressive forms of *go.* To form the progressive forms of a verb, you must know the basic forms of *be.*

CONJUGATION OF THE PROGRESSIVE FORMS OF *GO*

	Singular	Plural
Present Progressive	I am going you are going he, she, it is going	we are going you are going they are going
Past Progressive	I was going you were going he, she, it was going	we were going you were going they were going
Future Progressive	I will be going you will be going he, she, it will be going	we will be going you will be going they will be going
Present Perfect Progressive	I have been going you have been going he, she, it has been going	we have been going you have been going they have been going

Past Perfect Progressive	I had been going you had been going he, she, it had been going	we had been going you had been going they had been going
Future Perfect Progressive	I will have been going you will have been going he, she, it will have been going	we will have been going you will have been going they will have been going

EXERCISE B: Conjugating the Progressive Forms of Verbs. On your paper conjugate the progressive forms of each of the following verbs. Use the chart on pages 208 and 209 showing the progressive forms of *go* as your model.

Answers should follow the model given; note that 2 is irregular.

1. move 2. freeze

APPLICATION 1: Supplying the Correct Tense. Copy each of the following sentences onto your paper, supplying the progressive form of the verb as directed in parentheses.

EXAMPLE: He (go—present progressive) to Alabama to visit his relatives.

He is going to Alabama to visit his relatives.

1. I (write—past progressive) to you when you telephoned me. *was writing*
2. Clarissa (study—future progressive) music at a special camp this summer. *will be studying*
3. Reggie (carry—present perfect progressive) a heavy course load this year. *has been carrying*
4. Despite her height, Kate (hope—present progressive) to make the basketball team. *is hoping*
5. I was very relieved because I (expect—past perfect progressive) a much lower grade. *had been expecting*

6. The rain (ruin—present progressive) all of our party decorations. *is ruining*
7. They (swim—future perfect progressive) for three hours by noon. *will have been swimming*
8. Nick (have—present perfect progressive) second thoughts about the concert. *has been having*
9. The last ferry (leave—future progressive) soon.
10. We (watch—past perfect progressive) the dancer carefully all evening. *had been watching*

9. will be leaving

APPLICATION 2: Using the Progressive Forms of the Six Tenses. Write six sentences of your own for each verb in the following list. Use a different tense in the progressive form in each of your sentences.
Answers will vary; samples given for first one.

EXAMPLE: ask

We are asking for three tickets.

We were asking about their dog.

(and so on)

1. move 2. have 3. say 4. give 5. think

1. We are moving our headquarters to a new building. We were moving when the car bumped us. We will be moving to San Antonio next week. We have been moving away from that policy for a while now. We had been moving in the wrong direction until we changed course. We will have been moving furniture for six hours by lunch time.

11.4 Active and Passive Voice

Just as verbs change tense to show time, they may also change form to show whether or not the subject of the verb is performing an action. In English most verbs have two *voices,* one to show that the subject is performing an action and one to show that the subject is having an action performed upon it.

A **voice** is a form of a verb that shows whether or not the subject is performing the action.

■ Two Voices

The two voices are called *active* and *passive.*

Active Voice. Any action verb can be used in the *active* voice.

A verb is **active** when its subject performs the action.

ACTIVE VOICE: Sharon (S) *reported* (V) the good news (DO).

Bob (S) *left* (V) early.

In each of these examples, the subject performs the action. Sharon did the reporting; Bob did the leaving. Notice also in the examples that an active verb may or may not have a direct object.

Passive Voice. Most action verbs can also be used in the *passive* voice.

A verb is **passive** when its subject does not perform the action.

PASSIVE VOICE: The good news (S) *was reported* (V) by Sharon.

Bob (S) *was left* (V) with the bill.

In each of these examples, the subject is the receiver rather than the performer of the action. In the first sentence, the performer is named: Sharon. *Sharon,* however, is the object of the preposition *by* and is no longer the subject. In the second sentence, the performer of the action is not named. The sentence does not tell *who* left Bob with the bill. Notice finally that neither of these sentences has a direct object. An active verb may or may not have a direct object, but a passive verb almost never does.

EXERCISE A: Distinguishing Between Active and Passive Voice. On your paper write the verb or verb phrase from each of the following sentences. Then identify its voice as either *active* or *passive*.

EXAMPLE: Those flowers were sent without a card.

were sent passive

1. Ted was hurt by Julie's reaction to his song. *pass*
2. The play was pronounced a great success by the producer. *pass*

3. Unfortunately, nobody believed him. *act*
4. That sapling was bent by last December's ice storm. *pass*
5. Hot, tired, and out of breath, Kim finally reached the top of the Statue of Liberty. *act*
6. The desk clerk directed us to the hotel dining room. *act*
7. The note was left in this bottle more than fifty years ago. *pass*
8. Simon jumped over the porch railing into the lilac bush. *act*
9. After a long wait, Georgina was admitted to the advanced drawing class. *pass*
10. Franklin befriended me on my first day in this town, five years ago. *act*

Forming the Tenses of Passive Verbs

A passive verb always has two parts.

A **passive verb** is always a verb phrase made from a form of *be* plus a past participle.

Here is a short conjugation of the passive forms of the verb *report* with the pronoun *it*.

CONJUGATION OF THE PASSIVE FORMS OF *REPORT*	
Tense	**Passive Form**
Present	it is reported
Past	it was reported
Future	it will be reported
Present Perfect	it has been reported
Past Perfect	it had been reported
Future Perfect	it will have been reported

EXERCISE B: Conjugating Verbs in the Passive Voice. Using the chart on this page as your model, conjugate the following two verbs in the passive voice. In each conjugation include the pronouns indicated in parentheses. *Answers should follow the model given; note that 1 is irregular.*

1. do (with *it*) 2. scold (with *he*)

Using Active and Passive Voices

Each of the two voices has its proper use in English.

Use the active voice whenever possible.

Sentences with active verbs are less wordy and more forceful than those with passive verbs. Compare, for example, the following sentences. Notice the different number of words each sentence needs to report the same information.

ACTIVE: The movers *lugged* the piano up the steps.

PASSIVE: The piano *was lugged* up the steps by the movers.

Though you should aim to use the active voice in most of your writing, at times you will need to use the passive voice.

Use the passive voice to emphasize the receiver of an action rather than the performer of the action.

In the following example, the receiver of the action is the subject *paintings.*

EMPHASIS ON RECEIVER: The three priceless paintings *were damaged* by vandals.

The passive voice should also be used when there is no performer of the action.

Use the passive voice to point out the receiver of an action when the performer is unknown or unimportant and is not named in the sentence.

PERFORMER UNKNOWN: The paintings *were stolen* sometime during the night.

PERFORMER UNIMPORTANT: The museum *was* quickly *ordered* closed while the police searched for clues.

EXERCISE C: Using the Active Voice. Rewrite each of the following sentences, changing the verb from the passive voice to the active voice and making whatever other changes are necessary.

Revisions may vary; samples given for first two.

EXAMPLE: This old watch was found by me in my grandmother's bureau.

I found this old watch in my grandmother's bureau.

1. We ate all the hamburgers in less than five minutes.

1. All the hamburgers were eaten by us in less than five minutes.
2. Television is hardly ever watched by Randy and Caroline.
3. The story was blurted out by the twins to everyone in the room.
4. A decision was suddenly reached by the President.
5. A home run was hit by Hank Aaron in his first time at bat.
6. Sequined tank suits were worn by the members of the precision swim team.
7. Many books have been read by me since I got a library card.
8. The javelin was forcefully hurled into the air by Don.
9. A remarkable opportunity was missed by you a few minutes ago.
10. Four languages are spoken by him fluently.

2. Randy and Caroline hardly ever watch television.

APPLICATION: Correcting Unnecessary Use of the Passive Voice. Most of the underlined verbs in the following paragraph are in the passive voice. Rewrite the paragraph changing as many of the passive verbs into active ones as you think necessary to improve the paragraph. It is not necessary to change every passive verb.

Answers will vary; sample given on page T-123.

EXAMPLE: Vehicles of many different sorts have been sent into space by the United States.

The United States has sent vehicles of many different sorts into space.

(1) After years of preparation and many delays, the first space shuttle was launched by the United States in 1981. (2) The shuttle had been designed by NASA engineers to make a number of voyages into outer space. (3) The very first voyage was made by the spacecraft *Columbia* on April 12, 1981. (4) The spaceship was manned by astronauts John Young and Robert Crippen. (5) These men had been carefully trained for many years by NASA to participate in the space shuttle program. (6) The *Columbia* was lifted into space from Cape Canaveral by several rockets that could be reused by the space program. (7) These rockets were later recovered by the Navy from the Atlantic Ocean. (8) The spacecraft with its human cargo orbited the earth for two days. (9) It was finally guided back to the earth and was landed on the ground at Bakersfield, California, by astronauts Young and Crippen. (10) The successful flight was heralded by millions of Americans as this country's return to outer space.

Glossary of Troublesome Verbs 11.5

The following verbs cause problems for many speakers and writers. Some of the problems involve using the principal parts of certain verbs. Other problems involve learning to distinguish between the meanings of certain confusing pairs of verbs. As you read through the following list, note those verbs that have caused you difficulty in the past and concentrate on them. Use the exercises to test your understanding. When you are writing and revising your compositions, refer to this section to check your work.

(1) *Ain't.* *Ain't* is not considered correct English. Avoid using it in speaking and in writing.

INCORRECT: He *ain't* coming to the movies with us.

CORRECT: He *isn't* coming to the movies with us.

(2) *Burst.* This irregular verb has the same form for three of its principal parts. The present, past, and past participle of *burst* all are *burst*. *Bust* and *busted* are not considered correct. If you find you are using these incorrect forms, try replacing them with the present, past, or past participle of the verb *break*. *Break, broke,* or *broken* may be easier for you to use correctly.

INCORRECT: If you drop the model airplane, it *will bust.*

She *busted* the blister on her hand.

This radio *has been busted.*

CORRECT: If you drop the model airplane, it *will break.*

She *burst* (or *broke*) the blister on her hand.

This radio *has been broken.*

(3) *Did* and *Done.* Remember that *done* is a past participle and can be used as a verb only with a helping verb such as *have* or *has*. Instead of using *done* without a helping verb, use *did*. Otherwise you can add the helping verb before *done*.

INCORRECT: I already *done* my homework.

CORRECT: I already *did* my homework.

I *have* already *done* my homework.

(4) *Dragged* and *Drug.* *Drag* is a regular verb. Its principal parts are *drag, dragging, dragged,* and *dragged*. *Drug* is never correct as the past or past participle of *drag*.

INCORRECT: I *drug* the heavy suitcases up the stairs.

You *should have drug* the sack of potatoes out of the rain.

CORRECT: I *dragged* the heavy suitcases up the stairs.

You *should have dragged* the sack of potatoes out of the rain.

(5) *Drowned* and *Drownded.* *Drown* is a regular verb. Its past and past participle are formed simply by adding *-ed* to the present form: *drown-+-ed. Drownded* is wrong. Do not add the extra *d* either in speaking or in writing.

INCORRECT: The lemmings raced into the sea and *drownded.*

CORRECT: The lemmings raced into the sea and *drowned.*

(6) *Gone* and *Went.* *Gone* is the past participle of *go* and can be used as a verb only with a helping verb such as *have* or *has. Went* is the past of *go* and is never used with a helping verb.

INCORRECT: Jean and Frank *gone* to the beach.

We *should have went* along with them.

CORRECT: Jean and Frank *have gone* to the beach.

Jean and Frank *went* to the beach.

We *should have gone* along with them.

(7) *Have* and *Of.* In conversation the words *have* and *of* often sound very similar. Be careful not to write *of* when you really mean the helping verb *have* or its contraction *'ve.*

INCORRECT: You should *of* stayed until the end of the show.

CORRECT: You should *have* stayed until the end of the show.

You *should've* stayed until the end of the show.

(8) *Lay* and *Lie.* These verbs are troublesome to many people because they look and sound almost alike and have similar meanings. The first step in learning to distinguish between *lay* and *lie* is to become thoroughly familiar with their principal parts. Memorize the principal parts of both verbs.

PRINCIPAL PARTS:	lay	laying	laid	laid
	lie	lying	lay	lain

The next step is to compare the meaning and use of the two verbs. *Lay* usually means "to put (something) down" or "to place (something)." This verb is almost always followed by a direct object.

EXAMPLES: Marie always *lays* her notes (DO) on her desk.

The workers *will be laying* new carpeting (DO) soon.

This morning I *laid* my lab materials (DO) on the floor.

The builders *have laid* the foundation (DO) for the new school.

Lie usually means "to rest in a reclining position." It also can mean "to be situated." This verb is used to show the position of a person, place, or thing. *Lie* is never followed by a direct object.

EXAMPLES: My mother usually *lies* down before dinner.

The dog *is lying* in front of the fire.

The ancient city of Palmyra *lay* in the Syrian desert.

The broken glass *has lain* in the alley for a week.

Pay special attention to one particular area of confusion between *lay* and *lie*. *Lay* is the present tense of *lay*. *Lay* is also the past tense of *lie*.

PRESENT TENSE OF LAY: I *lay* the mail on that table every morning.

PAST TENSE OF LIE: My cousin *lay* down with a headache.

(9) *Learn* and *Teach.* *Learn* means "to receive knowledge." *Teach* means "to give knowledge." Do not use *learn* in place of *teach.*

INCORRECT: Dan *learned* me how to ice-skate.

CORRECT: Dan *taught* me how to ice-skate.

(10) *Leave* and *Let.* *Leave* means "to allow to remain." *Let* means "to permit." Do not reverse the meanings.

INCORRECT: *Leave* me finish!

Let the dog alone!

CORRECT: *Let* me finish!

Leave the dog alone!

(11) *Raise* and *Rise.* *Raise* has several common meanings: "to lift (something) upward," "to build (something)," to grow (something)," or "to increase (something)." This verb is usually followed by a direct object.

DO

EXAMPLES: *Raise* the lamp just a bit.

DO DO

My uncle *has been raising* wheat and corn on his farm.

DO

The town *raised* a monument to the war hero.

DO

Our volunteers *have raised* 1,500 dollars in a month.

Rise, on the other hand, is not usually followed by a direct object. This verb means "to get up," "to go up," or "to be increased."

EXAMPLES: The sun *rises* in the east.

Our rooster *will be rising* soon.

She *rose* for a moment and then dropped back into her seat.

Has the rate of inflation *risen* as sharply this month as last?

(12) *Saw* and *Seen.* *Seen* is a past participle and can be used as a verb only with a helping verb such as *have* or *has*. Instead of using *seen* without a helping verb, use *saw*. Otherwise you can add the helping verb before *seen*.

INCORRECT: I *seen* that show already.

CORRECT: I *saw* that show already.

I *have seen* that show already.

(13) *Says* and *Said.* A common mistake in reporting what someone said is to use the present tense *says* rather than the past tense *said*.

INCORRECT: First he turned ghostly white, and then he *says*, "I need to sit down."

CORRECT: First he turned ghostly white, and then he *said*, "I need to sit down."

(14) *Set* and *Sit.* The first step in learning to distinguish between *set* and *sit* is to become thoroughly familiar with their principal parts.

PRINCIPAL PARTS:	set	setting	set	set
	sit	sitting	sat	sat

To avoid confusing these two verbs, compare their meanings. *Set* commonly means "to put (something) in a certain place." It is usually followed by a direct object.

EXAMPLES: *Set* (not *sit*) the vase (DO) down carefully.

They *are setting* decoys (DO) out on the lake.

Frank *set* the table (DO) for dinner.

We *have set* those plants (DO) in direct sunlight for the winter.

Sit usually means "to be seated" or "to rest." In its usual meanings, the verb *sit* is not followed by a direct object.

EXAMPLES: The house where Grandmother was born *sits* (not *sets*) atop that hill.

The delegates *have been sitting* in a hot room all day.

Mona *sat* in the first seat.

The owl *has sat* in the hemlock tree since sunset.

(15) *Sneaked* and *Snuck*. *Sneak* is a regular verb. Its principal parts are *sneak, sneaking, sneaked,* and *sneaked. Snuck* is sometimes heard in conversation in place of *sneaked.* You should avoid using *snuck,* however, in your writing.

INCORRECT: The cat *snuck* up, then sprang at the bird.

CORRECT: The cat *sneaked* up, then sprang at the bird.

EXERCISE A: Avoiding Problems with Troublesome Verbs 1–5. For each of the following sentences, choose the correct verb from the choices in parentheses and write it on your paper.

EXAMPLE: Amelia Earhart (did, done) what few other people dared to do.

did

1. The child (dragged, drug) his stuffed bear across the playground.
2. (Ain't, Aren't) you finished with your homework yet?
3. The happy guests (busted, burst) into the dining room.
4. The patriot said, "I (done, did) my best for my country."
5. Her answer was (drowned, drownded) in catcalls.
6. My bicycle is (busted, broken) and can't be fixed.
7. You look like something the cat (drug, dragged) in.
8. The workers (done, have done) everything on our list.
9. It (ain't, isn't) right to drop pennies from tall buildings.
10. The weak swimmer almost (drowned, drownded) in the brutal current.

EXERCISE B: Avoiding Problems with Troublesome Verbs 6–10. For each of the following sentences, choose the correct verb from the choices in parentheses and write it on your paper.

1. Ms. Barker should (of, have) given us more time to finish that job.
2. When we left, we (lay, laid) a blanket over the antique chair to protect it.
3. I wish you would (learn, teach) me how to water-ski.
4. (Let, Leave) your brother alone!
5. (Let, Leave) him go!
6. My mother would have (went, gone) to college if she had had the money.
7. Children, (lie, lay) still until I call you.
8. I am going to (teach, learn) myself how to cook in a Chinese wok.
9. You should (of, have) seen your face when they called out your name.
10. They (went, gone) away without saying goodbye.

EXERCISE C: Avoiding Problems with Troublesome Verbs 11–15. For each of the following sentences, choose the correct verb from the choices in parentheses and write it on your paper.

1. The beam isn't balanced; (rise, raise) your end a little bit.
2. We (set, sat) down to a delicious lobster dinner.
3. The space shot was the most spectacular thing I've ever (saw, seen).
4. He pointed to the carrot and (said, says), "Let's feed the rabbit."
5. Harriet and Shirley (snuck, sneaked) back to the wings of the theater.
6. He was proud that I (seen, saw) how well he did.
7. Then the witch smiled and (says, said), "Look, I'll take a bite of the apple myself."
8. "(Sit, Set) the bird cage in that corner, please."
9. Inflation occurs when prices (raise, rise).
10. Allen (snuck, sneaked) a look at his birthday presents.

APPLICATION: Using Troublesome Verbs Correctly. Write an original sentence for each of the following verbs. *Answers will vary; samples given for first two.*

EXAMPLE: seen

She has seen many changes in the past eighty years.

1. The balloon burst when it hit the branch. 2. What have you done with my keys?

1. burst	8. lie	15. let
2. done	9. went	16. set
3. dragged	10. leave	17. rise
4. drowned	11. raise	18. said
5. gone	12. sneaked	19. sit
6. did	13. lay	20. saw
7. have	14. teach	

Chapter 12

Using Pronouns

Some pronouns change form depending on how they are used in a sentence. For example, in "I hit the ball," the pronoun *I* is a subject. But in "The ball hit me," *I* changes to *me* to show that the pronoun is now a direct object. The relation between a pronoun's form and its use is known as *case.*

This chapter will explain the three cases that pronouns can have and will show you how to use the various forms of pronouns correctly in sentences.

12.1 Cases of Personal Pronouns

The many forms of personal pronouns that are listed in Section 1.2 are arranged in three groups. Pronouns in the first group refer to the person speaking; those in the second group refer to the person spoken to; and those in the third to the person, place, or thing spoken about. These same pronouns can be grouped in another way—that is, according to their *cases.*

English has three **cases:** *nominative, objective,* and *possessive.*

Three Cases

The following chart shows the personal pronouns grouped according to the three cases. On the right is a list of the uses that each of the cases can have.

THE THREE CASES OF PERSONAL PRONOUNS	
Nominative Case	**Use in Sentence**
I, we you he, she, it, they	Subject of a Verb Predicate Pronoun
Objective Case	**Use in Sentence**
me, us you him, her, it, them	Direct Object Indirect Object Object of a Preposition
Possessive Case	**Use in Sentence**
my, mine, our, ours your, yours his, her, hers, its, their, theirs	To Show Ownership

EXERCISE A: Identifying Case. On your paper identify the case of the personal pronouns that are underlined in the following sentences.

EXAMPLE: Melvin left the theater without us.
objective

1. His photograph was awarded second prize. *poss*
2. Frances wrote me about the party for Vickie. *obj*
3. The first actors onstage will be he and I. *nom*
4. The collie caught the frisbee and ran away with it. *obj*
5. Laurent and I haven't finished the kite yet. *nom*
6. As soon as the lights came on, Rennie saw them. *obj*
7. Uncle Norman forgave us for playing that band's music. *obj*
8. According to your count, how many people came to the second performance? *poss*
9. Unfortunately, he was the last person to leave the house. *nom*
10. Don't tell me any more bad news. *obj*

The Nominative Case

Personal pronouns in the *nominative case* have two uses.

Use the **nominative case** (1) for the subject of a verb and (2) for a predicate pronoun.

In the following examples, note that all of the predicate pronouns follow linking verbs.

SUBJECTS: *I* build model sailboats.

She hopes to become a surgeon.

With great glee *they* are planning a surprise party.

PREDICATE PRONOUNS: It was (LV) *I* who suggested a picnic.

The first caller could have been (LV) *he*.

The best dancers are (LV) *we* and *they*.

People seldom forget to use the nominative case for a pronoun that is used by itself as a subject. Problems sometimes arise, however, when the pronoun is part of a compound subject.

INCORRECT: John and *me* build model sailboats.

To make sure you are using the correct case of the pronoun in a compound subject, use just the pronoun with the verb in the sentence. Trying this test in the preceding example, you would see that "Me build" is obviously wrong. The nominative case *I* should be used instead.

CORRECT: John and *I* build model sailboats.

You should also note that in speaking and in casual writing people often use the objective case for any personal pronoun after a linking verb. In formal writing, however, you should still use the nominative case.

INFORMAL: "Who is it?" "It's *me.*"

FORMAL: The organizers of the dance were Maria, Juan, and *I.*

EXERCISE B: Using Pronouns in the Nominative Case. Complete each of the following sentences by writing a nominative pronoun on your paper. Then tell how each pronoun is used in the sentence.
Pronouns may vary; samples given.

EXAMPLE: Without question ________ had to care for the pony herself.

she subject

1. After losing the match, ___we___ boarded a bus and drove silently out of town. S
2. Georgina and ___he___ both wanted something more extravagant. S
3. The winner would obviously be ___she___. pred pron
4. Only ___he___ knows the spot where the best mushrooms grow. S
5. ___They___ are sanding an old oak desk for the study. S
6. Doris always answered the telephone very formally by saying, "It is ___I___." pred pron
7. When the airport came into view, ___we___ began to talk excitedly. S
8. The first person in line was ___he___. pred pron
9. In addition to that old letter, ___we___ found two high-buttoned shoes. S
10. Unfortunately, ___I___ can't possibly finish the job by tomorrow morning. S

■ The Objective Case

Personal pronouns in the *objective case* have three uses.

Use the **objective case** (1) for a direct object, (2) for an indirect object, and (3) for the object of a preposition.

DIRECT OBJECTS: Frank's comment upset *me.*

Luis saw *us* in the library.

INDIRECT OBJECTS: Tell *her* the good news.

I sent *them* a postcard from San Diego.

OBJECTS OF PREPOSITIONS: Take the packages from *them.*

The wasps swarmed around *me.*

Mistakes usually occur only when the object is compound.

INCORRECT: Frank's comment upset Kathy and *I.*

Tell Dorothy and *she* the good news.

The wasps swarmed around Lucy and *I.*

Again, to test whether the case of a pronoun is correct, use the pronoun by itself after the verb or preposition. In the preceding examples, "upset I," "Tell she," and "around I" all sound wrong. Objective pronouns are needed.

CORRECT: Frank's comment upset Kathy and *me.*

Tell Dorothy and *her* the good news.

The wasps swarmed around Lucy and *me.*

EXERCISE C: Using Pronouns in the Objective Case. Complete each of the following sentences by writing an objective pronoun on your paper. Then tell how each pronoun is used in the sentence.

Pronouns may vary; samples given.

EXAMPLE: His grandmother's stories gave ________ ideas that he later used in his writing.

him indirect object

1. Rain or shine, Ellen always brought happiness with ___*her*___. *obj of prep*
2. Henry visited ___*us*___ on his trip out West. *DO*
3. Please tell ___*me*___ your problems. *IO*

4. In the 1000-meter run, Jonathan timed ___them___ with a stopwatch. DO
5. Richard dedicated his book to ___her___. obj of prep
6. The weather gives ___us___ very little opportunity for swimming. IO
7. Caroline sent Max and ___me___ a message about the change in plans. IO
8. Beth ran behind ___him___ and hid the present. obj of prep
9. Jerry should show ___them___ his prize lamb. IO
10. We left ___him___ at home with the baby. DO

The Possessive Case

Personal pronouns in the *possessive case* all show ownership of one sort or another.

Use the **possessive case** of personal pronouns before nouns to show possession. In addition, recognize that certain personal pronouns may be used by themselves to indicate possession.

BEFORE NOUNS: The kitten licked *its* paws.

Chris held *my* hand.

BY THEMSELVES: Is this book *yours* or *mine?*

Hers was the best composition.

Personal pronouns in the possessive case are never written with an apostrophe. Keep this in mind especially with possessive pronouns that end in *-s.*

INCORRECT: Did you see *his'* new bicycle?

These seats are *our's,* not *their's.*

CORRECT: Did you see *his* new bicycle?

These seats are *ours,* not *theirs.*

When the pronoun *it* ends with an apostrophe and an *-s,* it is not a possessive pronoun but a contraction meaning *it is.*

CONTRACTION: *It's* going to rain.

POSSESSIVE PRONOUN: The parakeet feels safe in *its* cage.

EXERCISE D: Using Pronouns in the Possessive Case. For each of the following sentences, choose the correct word from the choices in parentheses and write it on your paper.

EXAMPLE: Fortunately, the sinking boat was not (our's, ours).

ours

1. (His, His') exceptional voice brought Len to the conductor's attention.
2. The chimpanzee and (it's, its) master go for a walk in the park each afternoon.
3. I will never understand (you, your) joy in working on a stamp collection.
4. The bicycles were (theirs, their's).
5. (My, Me) last letter to him was ten pages long.
6. You may use this room while (your's, yours) is being painted.
7. The album was clearly (hers, her's).
8. The bird was so friendly that (its, it's) chirps ceased to irritate us.
9. George grabbed the pie and yelled, "(Its, It's) mine!"
10. Fred now felt he could call the house of his host (his', his) own.

APPLICATION 1: Checking the Case of Personal Pronouns. Some of the underlined pronouns in the following sentences are incorrect. On your paper identify each error and supply the correct form of the pronoun. For sentences without any errors, write *correct.*

Incorrect pronouns are shaded.

EXAMPLE: I sent invitations to Jeremy and he.

he him

1. The lion in the center ring kept looking at her and me. C

2. Donald gave no real reason for leaving his' suitcase in the station. *his*
3. This room and it's furnishings were designed by my uncle's firm. *its*
4. He will probably decide to sit between you and I at the concert. *me*
5. The flowers wilting in the heat are theirs. *C*
6. The person on the other end of the line was him. *he*
7. Harry, Jessie, and me worked all afternoon. *I*
8. We will never forget the way that you told that joke. *C*
9. The students finally chosen were they and us. *we*
10. These books used to be Regina's, but now they are your's. *yours*

APPLICATION 2: Using Pronouns Correctly. Use each of the following pronouns in a sentence of your own according to the instructions in parentheses.
Answers will vary; samples given for first two.

EXAMPLE: her (as the object of a preposition)

They left for the fair grounds without her.

1. The debate between us and them lasted for hours.

1. us and them (with a preposition)
2. he and I (as predicate pronouns)
3. its (to show possession)
4. your (to show possession)
5. her (as an indirect object)
6. him (as a direct object)
7. hers (to show possession)
8. you and I (as a subject)
9. it's (to mean *it is*)
10. his (to show possession)

2. The people for the job are he and I.

Cases of *Who* and *Whom* 12.2

The pronouns *who* and *whom* have two common uses in sentences. They can be used in questions, and they can be used to begin subordinate clauses in complex sentences.

Questions	Complex Sentences
Who is knocking at the door?	I don't know the person *who* is knocking at the door.
Whom did you invite to your party?	One guest *whom* you invited will not be able to attend.

Separate Uses in Sentences

Many people have problems deciding when it is correct to use *whom* instead of *who*. Like personal pronouns *who* and *whom* indicate case. *Who* is nominative; *whom* is objective.

The Nominative Case: *Who*. Just like the nominative personal pronouns, such as *I* or *she*, *who* is used as a subject.

Use **who** for the subject of a verb.

You will often find the word *who* used as the subject of a question.

SUBJECT IN A QUESTION: *Who* hit the most home runs?

Who may also be used as the subject of a subordinate clause in a complex sentence.

SUBJECT IN A SUBORDINATE CLAUSE: I admire the player *who* hit the most home runs.

In the example *who* is part of an adjective clause: *who hit the most home runs*. Within the clause itself, *who* is the subject of the verb *hit*.

The Objective Case: *Whom*. The uses of *whom* are similar to those of the objective personal pronouns, such as *me* or *him*.

Use **whom** (1) for the direct object of a verb and (2) for the object of a preposition.

The following examples show *whom* used in questions.

DIRECT OBJECT: *Whom* did he meet at the movies?

OBJECT OF PREPOSITION: From *whom* did she receive the flowers?

Whom were you talking about?

Questions that include the word *whom* will generally be in inverted word order. If you reword the first example so that it follows normal word order, you will see that *whom* is the direct object of the verb *did meet: he did meet whom at the movies.* In the second example, it is easy to see that *whom* is the object of a preposition because it comes right after the preposition *from.* In the last sentence, *whom* is separated from its preposition *about.* Again, rewording may help: *you were talking about whom.*

Rewording is also useful when *whom* is part of a subordinate clause.

DIRECT OBJECT: I wonder about the person *whom* he met at the movies.

OBJECT OF PREPOSITION: Janet thanked her aunt, from *whom* she had received a bracelet.

A subordinate clause that should begin with *whom* will always be in inverted word order. To check whether you have used the correct case of the pronoun, isolate the clause and put it in normal word order. In the first of the preceding examples, the subordinate clause is *whom he met at the movies.* In normal word order, the clause would be *he met whom at the movies.* The objective pronoun *whom* is a direct object.

In the second example, the subordinate clause is *from whom she had received a bracelet.* You can probably guess that *whom* is the object of a preposition since it follows *from.* In normal word order, the clause would be *she had received a bracelet from whom. Whom* is the object of the preposition *from.*

EXERCISE A: Using *Who* and *Whom* in Questions. For each of the following sentences, choose the correct pronoun from the choices given in parentheses and write it on your paper.

EXAMPLE: (Who, Whom) did you ask to the party?

Whom

1. To (who, whom) were you just speaking?
2. (Who, Whom) among us has met a famous person?
3. This article was written by (who, whom)?
4. (Who, Whom) were you helping in the cafeteria the other day?
5. Of the two (who, whom) is more capable?
6. (Who, Whom) is your favorite singer?
7. (Who, Whom) wouldn't know you, even in that disguise?
8. (Who, Whom) did she leave with the children?
9. For (who, whom) should I ask at the Governor's office?
10. (Who, Whom) in this group could be at the theater by seven o'clock?

EXERCISE B: Using *Who* and *Whom* in Subordinate Clauses. On your paper, write the subordinate clause in each of the following sentences. Then indicate the way in which *who* or *whom* is being used in the subordinate clause. *Subordinate clauses are underlined.*

EXAMPLE: What is the name of the person who is calling?

who is calling subject

1. My sister Emily, for whom I wrote this poem, is hiding in the maple tree. *obj of prep*
2. I know the singer who performed at your party. *S*
3. I can introduce you to Walter, whom you have been admiring from afar. *DO*
4. We were eager to meet the woman who will be our candidate. *S*
5. You'll never guess the name of the person who told me that. *S*

6. Give it to the person whom you place the most trust in. obj of prep
7. Guess what happened to the man whom we met in the lobby at intermission. DO
8. Gil is one person whom I have absolute confidence in. obj of prep
9. Please don't invite the person who spilled the coffee last time. S
10. I asked Jim to tell me the name of the person who wrote the limerick. S

APPLICATION: Using *Who* and *Whom* in Sentences. Choose between *who* and *whom* in completing each of the following sentences and write the appropriate pronoun on your paper.

EXAMPLE: To ________ did you mail that letter of complaint?

whom

1. Morgan, for __whom__ the party is being given, doesn't know anything about it.
2. I don't know the person __whom__ you are talking about.
3. You asked __whom__ for information about the class trip?
4. Can't you see the character __who__ is playing the villain?
5. The hero is a character __whom__ I admire.
6. No one __whom__ I questioned could give me a satisfactory answer.
7. __Who__ should elect the President—the people or the Senate?
8. __Who__ has been plotting this prank?
9. Don't be alarmed when you hear the name of the person __whom__ the Mayor has promoted.
10. With __whom__ are you going to California this summer?

Chapter 13

Making Words Agree

Subjects and verbs work together in sentences. For example, you would never say, "*I are* the first in line," or "*Am you going* to the party?" You would immediately hear that something is wrong with these sentences. The problem is that the subjects and verbs do not *agree.*

In most of the sentences you speak and write, making subjects and verbs agree takes little thought; you do it automatically. In some sentences, however, the mind can be tricked into making the verb agree with a word that is not the subject of the sentence. In such a case, you must check the sentence carefully to find the real subject and to make sure it agrees with its verb.

Subjects and verbs are not the only parts of sentences that must agree. Pronouns too must agree with the words they stand for. This chapter will explain the importance of agreement between subject and verb and between pronoun and antecedent and will give you practice making the parts of sentences work together perfectly.

13.1 Agreement Between Subjects and Verbs

One main rule governs *agreement* between subjects and verbs.

A subject must agree with its verb in number.

In grammar the concept of *number* is simple. The number of a word can be either *singular* or *plural.* A singular word indicates *one.* A plural word indicates *more than one.* Only nouns, pronouns, and verbs have number.

The Number of Nouns and Pronouns

The difference between the singular and plural forms of most nouns and pronouns is usually easy to recognize. Compare, for example, the singular and plural forms of the nouns in the following chart.

NOUNS	
Singular	**Plural**
girl	girls
bus	buses
child	children
goose	geese

Most nouns are made plural by adding *-s* or *-es* to the singular form (girl*s,* bus*es*). Some nouns become plural in other ways (child*ren,* g*ee*se). (See Section 20.2 for more information about making nouns plural.)

Sections 1.2 and 1.3 listed the singular and plural forms of the various kinds of pronouns. For example, *I, he, she, it, this,* and *anyone* are singular; *we, they, these,* and *both* are plural; and *you, who,* and *some* can be either singular or plural.

Being able to recognize the number of nouns and pronouns will help you to determine whether a subject is singular or plural.

EXERCISE A: Recognizing the Number of Nouns and Pronouns. On your paper indicate whether each of the following words is *singular* or *plural.*

EXAMPLE: mice plural

1. houses *pl*
2. player *sing*
3. someone *sing*
4. I *sing*
5. boxes *pl*
6. others *pl*
7. bees *pl*
8. it *sing*
9. friendship *sing*
10. gas *sing*
11. bird *sing*
12. we *pl*
13. mess *sing*
14. those *pl*
15. women *pl*
16. they *pl*
17. mouse *sing*
18. both *pl*
19. roses *pl*
20. each *sing*

The Number of Verbs

As shown in the conjugations in Sections 11.2 and 11.3, verbs have many forms to indicate tense. Few of these forms cause problems in agreement because most of them can be used with either singular or plural subjects (I *go,* we *go;* he *ran,* they *ran*). Problems involving the number of verbs usually occur only with third-person forms in the present tense and with forms of *be.*

The following chart shows all of the basic forms of two different verbs—*send* and *go*—in the present tense.

SINGULAR AND PLURAL VERBS IN THE PRESENT TENSE

Singular		Plural
First and Second Person	**Third Person**	**First, Second, and Third Person**
(I, you) send	(he, she, it) send*s*	(we, you, they) send
(I, you) go	(he, she, it) go*es*	(we, you, they) go

Notice that the verb form changes only in the third-person singular column, where an *-s* or *-es* is added to the verb. Unlike nouns, which usually become *plural* when *-s* or *-es* is added, verbs with *-s* or *-es* added to them are singular.

The helping verb *be* may also indicate whether a verb is singular or plural. The chart on the following page shows only those forms of the verb *be* that are always singular.

FORMS OF THE HELPING VERB *BE* THAT ARE ALWAYS SINGULAR			
am	is	was	has been

EXERCISE B: Recognizing the Number of Verbs. For each of the following items, choose the verb from the choices in parentheses that agrees in number with the pronoun. After each answer write whether the verb is singular or plural.

EXAMPLE: he (begin, begins)

begins singular

1. we (knows, know) *pl*
2. they (was, were) *pl*
3. she (knows, know) *sing*
4. I (is, am) *sing*
5. he (were, was) *sing*
6. we (is, are) *pl*
7. they (have, has) *pl*
8. it (was, were) *sing*
9. she (have, has) *sing*
10. we (argues, argue) *pl*

Agreement with Singular and Plural Subjects

To check the agreement between a subject and a verb, begin by determining the number of the subject. Then make sure the verb has the same number.

A singular subject must have a singular verb.

A plural subject must have a plural verb.

In the following examples, the subjects are underlined once and the verbs twice.

SINGULAR SUBJECT AND VERB: Larry never arrives on time.

She is happy about her grade.

According to the announcement, the plane is preparing to land.

PLURAL SUBJECT AND VERB: Those boys never arrive on time.

We are happy about our grades.

According to the announcements, both planes are preparing to land.

In the preceding examples, the subjects stand next to or near their verbs. Often, however, a subject is separated from its verb by a prepositional phrase. In these cases it is important to remember that the object of a preposition is never the subject of a sentence.

A prepositional phrase that comes between a subject and its verb does *not* affect subject-verb agreement.

In the following examples, the correct subject is *poster;* the word *coins* is the object of the preposition *of*. Since *poster* is singular, it can not agree with the plural verb *show*.

INCORRECT: This poster of ancient coins show the portraits of all the Roman emperors.

CORRECT: This poster of ancient coins shows the portraits of all the Roman emperors.

EXERCISE C: Making Verbs Agree with Singular and Plural Subjects. For each of the following sentences, choose the correct verb and write it on your paper.

EXAMPLE: The books on the shelf (was, were) dogeared.

were

1. The wind always (makes, make) the screen door rattle during the summer.
2. The keys to our house (is, are) on a ring in the garage.
3. The geese (migrates, migrate) north every year at this time.
4. My friends never (knows, know) what I will do next.

5. A famous painting of those trees and windmills (hangs, hang) in the art museum.
6. The parents of my best friend (has, have) invited me to the ballet.
7. The silence (was, were) deafening after the prosecution rested its case.
8. The secret of her many successes (lies, lie) in her diligence.
9. Red roses on a white wooden trellis (blooms, bloom) in my aunt's lovely garden.
10. The child with two sets of grandparents (enjoys, enjoy) the attention of many doting adults.

Agreement with Compound Subjects

A compound subject is two or more subjects that are joined by a conjunction, usually *or* or *and.* (See Section 7.3 for information about finding compound subjects in sentences.) A number of different rules govern the way in which verbs must agree with compound subjects.

Two or more singular subjects joined by *or* or *nor* must have a singular verb.

In the following example, the conjunction *or* joins two singular subjects. Although two names make up the compound subject, it does not take a plural verb. Either Alice or Mike will help, not both.

EXAMPLE: Either Alice or Mike is going to help us.

Problems often occur when the parts of a compound subject joined by *or* or *nor* are mixed in number.

When singular and plural subjects are joined by *or* or *nor*, the verb must agree with the closest subject.

In the following examples, notice how the verb depends on the subject that is closer to it.

SINGULAR SUBJECT CLOSER: Neither the students nor their teacher is waiting for us in the auditorium.

PLURAL SUBJECT CLOSER: Neither the teacher nor the students are waiting for us in the auditorium.

Compound subjects joined by *and* create still another situation for you to consider when you decide whether to use a singular or a plural verb.

A compound subject joined by *and* is usually plural and must have a plural verb.

And usually acts as a plus sign. Whether the parts of the compound subject are all singular, all plural, or mixed in number, they usually add up to a subject that calls for a plural verb.

EXAMPLES: The cup and the glass are broken.

The cups and glasses are broken.

Three cups and one glass are broken.

This rule has two exceptions. If the parts of the compound subject are thought of as a single thing, then the compound subject is considered singular and must have a singular verb. The other exception involves the words *every* and *each.* Either of these words used in a sentence before a compound subject in a sentence indicates the need for a singular verb in that sentence. The following examples show these exceptions.

EXAMPLES: Cucumbers and yogurt is a popular Middle Eastern dish. (Cucumbers + yogurt = one dish)

Every cup and glass is broken.

Each cup and glass is broken.

EXERCISE D: Making Verbs Agree with Compound Subjects Joined by *Or* and *Nor*. For each of the following sentences, choose the correct verb from the choices in parentheses and write it on your paper.

EXAMPLE: Neither the soup nor the salad (was, were) ready.

was

1. Because I am ill, either Mary or John (is, are) going in my place.
2. Neither Kate nor her parents (has, have) ever met anyone as eccentric as Ace.
3. Bread or fruit always (goes, go) well with cheese.
4. Neither the nails nor the hammer (was, were) within my reach.
5. Either Joanna or Howard (takes, take) the children to school each day.
6. Neither the hat on that shelf nor the scarves on this one (belongs, belong) in a shop like yours.
7. Either the kittens or the dachshund (has, have) frightened the baby.
8. Fred or his brothers (watches, watch) the store at lunchtime.
9. Neither Emily nor Marian (knows, know) how to get to the library.
10. I suspect that either the maids or the butler (is, are) not telling the inspector the whole truth.

EXERCISE E: Making Verbs Agree with Compound Subjects Joined by *And*. For each of the following sentences, choose the correct verb from the choices in parentheses and write it on your paper.

EXAMPLE: Every knife and fork in the house (has, have) disappeared.

has

1. Clocks and sundials (measures, measure) time.
2. Chocolate cake and cherry pie (is, are) Murray's favorite desserts.

3. The gingham dog and the calico cat (does, do) not get along with each other.
4. The decorations and the centerpiece (was, were) beautiful.
5. Every book and record in this library (shows, show) signs of wear.
6. On this issue Congress and the President (finds, find) the present law to be inadequate.
7. Macaroni and cheese (was, were) served as the main course.
8. Each sheet and pillowcase in our hotel (is, are) freshly laundered every day.
9. Every student and teacher in this school (knows, know) what must be done to improve class attendance.
10. The horse and the mule (was, were) once the major means of transportation in this country.

APPLICATION 1: Recognizing Subjects and Verbs That Agree. For each of the following sentences, choose the correct verb from the choices in parentheses and write it on your paper.

EXAMPLE: Either Elizabeth Blackwell or Amelia Earhart (is, are) the subject of her report.

is

1. Marcy and Julio (is, are) composing the score for the class play.
2. Because of the wind, the doors in the deserted house next to the cemetery (creaks, creak) open and shut all night long.
3. Either Vanessa or Robert (has, have) enough votes to win the election.
4. To decorators a combination of red and green (represents, represent) Christmas.
5. Every cat and dog (was, were) adorned with a large ribbon.
6. Neither the walls nor the floor of your room (looks, look) very clean.
7. Spaghetti and meatballs (is, are) an inexpensive and popular dinner.

8. Each television and radio in the store (was, were) tuned to a different station.
9. Either my mother or my brothers (cleans, clean) the fish we catch.
10. The mice in our attic (scampers, scamper) overhead when we sleep.

APPLICATION 2: Correcting Errors in Subject and Verb Agreement. In some of the following sentences, the subjects and verbs do not agree in number. If a sentence is correct, write *correct* on your paper. If it is faulty, rewrite the sentence correctly.

EXAMPLE: Neither Don nor his brothers is coming.

Neither Don nor his brothers are coming.

1. Molly and her brother Tom skates faster than anyone else. skate
2. Ann and Reggie have been friends for years. C
3. Every chair and table in the restaurant were painted canary yellow. was
4. Neither the bushes nor the tree in the yard block our view of the ocean. blocks
5. Each dog and cat receives a prize at the end of the pet show. C
6. The rabbits were running through the forest. C
7. Either Rodney or Carl have to write your campaign speech. has
8. Ham and cheese is a popular sandwich combination. C
9. Both the chairman and the secretary of the department meets regularly with the faculty. meet
10. The three of them eats here every Monday. eat

Special Problems with Subject-Verb Agreement 13.2

Some sentences may cause you special problems when you check for agreement between subjects and verbs.

Agreement in Sentences with Unusual Word Order

In most sentences the subject comes before the verb. Sometimes, however, this normal word order is inverted, or turned around. (See Section 7.4 for more information about sentences with inverted word order.) In sentences that are inverted, look for the subject after the verb and apply the following rule.

When a subject comes after the verb, the subject and verb still must agree with each other in number.

Some sentences may be inverted for emphasis. Such a sentence usually begins with a prepositional phrase that is followed by the verb and then the subject. Always make sure the verb agrees with the subject, not with a word placed before the verb. In the following example, the plural verb *were growing* agrees with the plural subject *tulips*. The singular noun *sidewalk* is the object of a preposition.

EXAMPLE: Near the fence along the sidewalk were growing many bright-red tulips.

Sentences beginning with *there* or *here* are almost always in inverted word order. Again, look for the subject after the verb (or after the helping verb) and make sure that the subject and verb agree.

EXAMPLES: There were many tulips growing by the fence.

Here is the magazine I promised to lend you.

The contractions *there's* and *here's* contain the singular verb *is: there is, here is.* Do not use these contractions with plural subjects.

INCORRECT: Here's the magazines I promised you.

CORRECT: Here are the magazines I promised you.

Finally, many questions are in inverted word order. Check questions carefully to find the subject and make sure that it agrees with the verb.

INCORRECT: Where's the magazines you promised me?

CORRECT: Where are the magazines you promised me?

EXERCISE A: Checking Agreement in Sentences with Inverted Word Order. On your paper write the subject from each of the following sentences. Then choose the correct verb from the choices in parentheses.

Subjects are shaded.

EXAMPLE: There (is, are) the missing giraffes.

giraffes are

1. Where in your desk (is, are) your yellow pencil?
2. Beyond this town and across the river (looms, loom) the Empire State Building.
3. Here (is, are) the letter I mentioned to you.
4. Why (is, are) all three outfielders looking the wrong way?
5. There (is, are) many possible reasons for their behavior.
6. Crawling behind the sofa (was, were) two loudly giggling children.
7. Here in this box (is, are) several toys from my childhood.
8. How often (does, do) he manage to take a break from his responsibilities?
9. How silently and softly (falls, fall) the rain.
10. There (is, are) no excuse for such table manners.

Agreement with Indefinite Pronouns

When used as subjects, indefinite pronouns can also cause problems.

Depending on its form and meaning, an indefinite pronoun can agree with either a singular or a plural verb.

Look again at the list of indefinite pronouns in Section 1.3. Notice that some of the pronouns are always singular. Included here are those ending in *-one (anyone, everyone, someone),* those ending in *-body (anybody, everybody, somebody),* and those that imply one *(each, either).* Other indefinite pronouns are always plural: *both, few, many, others,* and *several.* A few can be either singular or plural: *all, any, more, most, none,* and *some.*

The following examples show pronouns from each of the three categories. Notice in the first group that the prepositional phrases between the subjects and verbs do not affect agreement.

ALWAYS SINGULAR: One of the lamps is broken.

Everybody at the movies was frightened by the film.

Neither of your ideas seems workable.

ALWAYS PLURAL: Many are bringing their own lunches.

Others are buying their lunches at school.

Several eat at home.

EITHER SINGULAR OR PLURAL: Most of the salad has been eaten.

Most of the apples have been eaten.

When an indefinite pronoun can be either singular or plural, the number of the pronoun's antecedent becomes the determining factor. In the first sentence of the last set of examples, the antecedent of *most* is *salad.* Since *salad* is singular, the verb is singular. In the second sentence, the antecedent of *most* is *apples.* Since *apples* is plural, the verb is plural.

EXERCISE B: Checking Agreement with Indefinite Pronouns. For each of the following sentences, choose the correct verb from the choices in parentheses, and write it on your paper.

EXAMPLE: All of the trees in the garden (was, were) swaying in the wind.

were

1. Both of you (writes, write) well enough to enter the essay contest.
2. Everyone (remembers, remember) the day the emergency sprinklers flooded our classroom with six inches of water.
3. Most of the movie (was, were) shown at the wrong speed.
4. Some of the students (drives, drive) to school.
5. Few of those television sets (works, work) properly.
6. Most of the books we read (expands, expand) our knowledge of the world.
7. (Does, Do) any of them play on the field hockey team?
8. Some of the bread (feels, feel) stale.
9. Each of you (deserves, deserve) to receive the award.
10. All of the subjects in the paper (has, have) been researched thoroughly.

APPLICATION 1: Checking Special Problems in Agreement. For each of the following sentences, choose the correct verb from the choices in parentheses and write it on your paper.

EXAMPLE: Here (is, are) the rings you asked to see.

are

1. Most of the students (comes, come) to every session.
2. Some of the tourists (doesn't, don't) speak English.
3. Over the roof and down the pillar (creeps, creep) the ivy.
4. Each of the boys (has, have) both oils and watercolors.
5. Here (is, are) the report and the book that were missing.
6. How often (has, have) that story been told?
7. One of the antiques (was, were) very valuable.

8. Everybody on the two teams (is, are) waiting.
9. There (is, are) at least three reasons why the dog must stay at home.
10. What (was, were) the total price of all of your purchases?

APPLICATION 2: Correcting Problems in Agreement. In some of the following sentences, the subjects and verbs do not agree in number. If a sentence is correct, write *correct*. If a sentence is faulty, rewrite it correctly.

EXAMPLE: All of the apples is ripe.

All of the apples are ripe.

1. Why don't he wear a coat in such cold weather?
2. In the orchard was three old cherry trees. *were*
3. Most of the film deals with the problem of water pollution. *C*
4. There's flies in my soup, waiter. *There are*
5. Why was the basket of flowers delivered to the patient in Room 1404? *C*
6. Over the river and through the woods ride the highwayman. *rides*
7. Many of the pages in the book were dogeared. *C*
8. Here is the same sweater again at a lower price. *C*
9. When is the relatives coming? *are*
10. All of the students is involved in the project. *are*

1. doesn't

13.3 Agreement Between Pronouns and Antecedents

An antecedent is the noun for which a pronoun stands. Sometimes a pronoun's antecedent is a group of words acting as a noun, or even another pronoun. This section will show you how pronouns agree with their antecedents. If you are not sure you can quickly recognize pronouns and antecedents, review Sections 1.2 and 1.3.

Making Personal Pronouns and Antecedents Agree

Personal pronouns should agree with their antecedents in two ways.

A personal pronoun must agree with its antecedent in both person and number.

Person indicates whether a pronoun refers to the person speaking (first person), the person spoken to (second person), or the person, place, or thing spoken about (third person). *Number* indicates whether a pronoun is singular (referring to one) or plural (referring to more than one). A personal pronoun must agree with its antecedent in both person and number.

EXAMPLE: *Lisa* presented *her* report on careers in medicine to the class yesterday.

In the example, the pronoun *her* is third person and singular. It agrees with its antecedent *Lisa,* which is also third person and singular.

Avoiding Shifts in Person. A common error in agreement occurs when a personal pronoun does not have the same person as its antecedent. This error usually involves the careless use of *you* with a noun in the third person.

INCORRECT: *Dino* is practicing the backstroke, a stroke *you* need to master if *you* want to compete in the swim meet.

CORRECT: *Dino* is practicing the backstroke, a stroke *he* needs to master if *he* wants to compete in the swim meet.

Whenever you use *you* in your writing, make sure it refers only to the person you are addressing (your reader). It should never be used to refer to the person you are writing about.

Avoiding Shifts in Number. Achieving agreement in number is sometimes a problem when the antecedent is a compound joined by *or* or *nor.*

Use a singular personal pronoun to refer to two or more singular antecedents joined by *or* or *nor.*

Two or more singular antecedents joined by *or* or *nor* must have a singular pronoun, just as they must have a singular verb.

INCORRECT: Either *Bob* or *Jim* is bringing *their* guitar to the picnic.

CORRECT: Either *Bob* or *Jim* is bringing *his* guitar to the picnic.

When a compound antecedent is joined by *and,* a plural personal pronoun is used.

EXAMPLE: *Andrea* and *Jane* brought *their* books.

EXERCISE A: Making Pronouns and Antecedents Agree. Rewrite each of the following sentences, filling in the blank with an appropriate pronoun.

EXAMPLE: The trees had dropped __________ leaves all over the brick path.

The trees had dropped their leaves all over the brick path.

1. Philip and Carla were proud of ___*their*___ new kitchen.
2. Each boy on the soccer team had ___*his*___ own special memories of the game.
3. The people in the park all seemed to have smiles on ___*their*___ faces.
4. Julie is going to Japan, a country ___*she*___ has always wanted to visit.
5. Paul would never forget ___*his*___ day at the fair.

6. The poodle, a new mother, was carefully guarding ___her or its___ litter.
7. Either Sarah or Susan will certainly remember to bring ___her___ book.
8. The three children were proudly wearing ___their___ new boots.
9. All travelers can benefit from planning ___their___ trips ahead of time.
10. Neither Ian nor Peter was sure about ___his___ answer on the test.

EXERCISE B: Avoiding Shifts in Person and Number. Each of the following sentences contains a single error in pronoun-antecedent agreement. On your paper rewrite each sentence correctly, underlining the pronoun that you have changed and its antecedent.

Incorrect pronouns are underlined; antecedents are shaded.

EXAMPLE: Bill wants to know where you can go to study art in this area.

Bill wants to know where he can go to study art in this area.

1. Alex has put together a racing bike you couldn't buy in a store. *he*
2. Neither Caroline nor Lee has decided whether they can come to the party. *she*
3. All Brownie leaders should gather with her troops at 3:15 sharp. *their*
4. Each bronco tried their luck at unseating the champion. *its*
5. Jill is going to a clinic where you can get a flu immunization shot. *she*
6. Terry and Gene forgot his lines in the play. *their*
7. Each sandwich was packed in their own vacuum-sealed wrapper. *its*
8. Either Loretta or Harriet will lend their textbook to the new student. *her*
9. Jeff lives in Chicago, where you can make many train and plane connections. *he*
10. All applicants must sign the register before you can take the examination. *they*

Agreement Between Personal Pronouns and Indefinite Pronouns

Indefinite pronouns (listed in Section 1.3) are words such as *each, everyone, neither,* and *one.* Pay special attention to the number of a personal pronoun when the antecedent is a singular indefinite pronoun.

Generally use a singular personal pronoun when its antecedent is a singular indefinite pronoun.

In making a personal pronoun agree with an indefinite pronoun, ignore the object of any prepositional phrase that might fall between them. In the first two of the following examples, *their* mistakenly agrees with *dogs* and *records.*

INCORRECT: *Neither* of the dogs has received *their* shots yet.

Put *each* of the records in *their* cover.

CORRECT: *Neither* of the dogs has received *its* shots yet.

Put *each* of the records in *its* cover.

EXERCISE C: Making Personal Pronouns and Indefinite Pronouns Agree. For each of the following sentences, choose the correct pronoun from the choices in parentheses and write it on your paper.

EXAMPLE: Each of the boys has (his, their) money in hand.

his

1. Neither of the parakeets has eaten (its, their) food.
2. Not one of the apples had fallen from (its, their) branch.
3. Give each of the girls a lab coat of (her, their) own.
4. Several of the players were eating (his, their) lunches.
5. Fortunately, each of the books was filed in (its, their) correct location.
6. Neither of the students has written (her, their) paper yet.

7. The director asked all of the actors to practice (his, their) lines.
8. Few of the musicians were playing (his, their) instruments correctly.
9. Some of the dogs actually resembled (its, their) masters.
10. Take all of these shoes and clean (it, them).

APPLICATION 1: Checking Agreement Between Pronouns and Antecedents. Some of the following sentences contain errors in pronoun-antecedent agreement. On your paper rewrite the incorrect sentences, and write *correct* for those without errors.

EXAMPLE: Neither of the girls brought their parents.

Neither of the girls brought her parents.

1. Each of the flowers had closed their petals for the night. *its*
2. Only one of the women had given their real name. *her*
3. Some of the speakers were confused and forgot his points in the debate. *their*
4. Lee Anne is boarding a plane that will take you to Hawaii by way of San Francisco. *her*
5. Not one of the directors felt good about her work in the festival. *C*
6. Neither Henry nor Edwin has started their homework. *his*
7. All of the dogs obeyed their trainer. *C*
8. Every term paper was given their grade by the same teacher. *its*
9. Each one of the five men on the crew started their lunch break at the stroke of noon. *his*
10. Several of the stories were criticized for its blandness. *their*

APPLICATION 2: Correcting Mistakes in Pronoun-Antecedent Agreement. Some of the sentences in the following paragraph contain errors in pronoun-antecedent agreement. Rewrite the paragraph to correct the errors. *Errors are underlined; corrections are given after the paragraph.*

EXAMPLE: Every young woman is likely to have a slightly different view of their own future.

Every young woman is likely to have a slightly different view of her own future.

(1) Neither Natalie nor Beth planned her future in ordinary terms. (2) Each of the two sisters had their own ambitious plans. (3) Natalie wanted to become a writer. (4) She knew that you would have to work very hard to write well and that not all good writers can earn a living from their work. (5) Nevertheless, she was willing to commit her life to her art. (6) Beth, on the other hand, wanted to become a champion speed skater. (7) She had chosen a difficult path, too, for you would have only a few years to excel in this physically demanding discipline. (8) Both girls expected to be frustrated sometimes in reaching her dreams, but both also felt that her hopes had some chance of being fulfilled.

2. her 4. she 7. she 8. their/their

Chapter 14

Using Adjectives and Adverbs

Adjectives and adverbs can be used to compare two or more people, places, or things that share the same basic qualities. These two parts of speech have different forms in sentences depending on the kind of comparison that is being made.

ADJECTIVE: Lena is *young*.

Lena is *younger* than Roy.

Fran is the *youngest* member of the class.

ADVERB: This engine runs *smoothly*.

This engine runs *more smoothly* than that one.

This engine runs *most smoothly* of all.

The different forms of adjectives and adverbs are known as *degrees of comparison.*

Most adjectives and adverbs have three **degrees of comparison:** the *positive*, the *comparative*, and the *superlative* degree.

The *positive* degree is the basic form of an adjective or adverb—the form that you will find listed in a dictionary. The positive degree is used when no comparison is being made. The *comparative* degree is the form used when two things are being compared. The *superlative* degree is the form used when three or more things are being compared.

The first four sections in this chapter will explain how the three degrees are formed and will show you how different degrees should be used in sentences. The fifth section will discuss certain troublesome adjectives and adverbs and will give you practice using them correctly.

14.1 Regular Adjectives and Adverbs

Like verbs, adjectives and adverbs can be either *regular* or *irregular.* Happily, most adjectives and adverbs in English are regular. That is, their comparative and superlative degrees are formed in predictable ways.

Two rules govern *regular* modifiers. The first covers adjectives and adverbs of one or two syllables. The second concerns adjectives and adverbs of three or more syllables.

Modifiers of One or Two Syllables

The comparative and superlative degrees of most adjectives and adverbs of one or two syllables can be formed in either of two ways.

Use *-er* or *more* to form the comparative degree and *-est* or *most* to form the superlative degree of most one- and two-syllable modifiers.

Adding *-er* and *-est* is the most common way.

COMPARATIVE AND SUPERLATIVE DEGREES FORMED WITH *-ER* AND *-EST*

Positive	Comparative	Superlative
tall	taller	tallest
strong	stronger	strongest
happy	happier	happiest
friendly	friendlier	friendliest

More and *most* can also be used to form the comparative and superlative degrees of most one- and two-syllable modifiers. They should not be used, however, when they sound awkward, as in "He is *more tall* than I am" or "This is the *most strong* rope we have." Notice in the following chart that two of the modifiers from the preceding chart, *happy* and *friendly*, can use *more* and *most* to form the comparative and superlative degrees. *More* and *most* are also used with most adverbs ending in *-ly* and with one- and two-syllable modifiers that would sound awkward with *-er* and *-est*.

COMPARATIVE AND SUPERLATIVE DEGREES FORMED WITH *MORE* AND *MOST*

Positive	Comparative	Superlative
happy	more happy	most happy
friendly	more friendly	most friendly
slowly	more slowly	most slowly
brisk	more brisk	most brisk

Try using *-er* and *-est* with the last two examples in this chart. Notice how awkward they sound. If you are in doubt about which form to use, say the words aloud. Then use the method that sounds better.

EXERCISE A: Forming the Comparative and Superlative Degrees of One- and Two-Syllable Modifiers. On your paper write the comparative and superlative degrees of the following modifiers. If the degrees can be formed in either way, write the *-er* and *-est* forms.

1. cloudier/cloudiest 2. sunnier/sunniest 3. more hopeful/most hopeful

EXAMPLE: sad

sadder saddest

4. more rapid/most rapid 5. more rudely/most rudely 6. more just/most just

1. cloudy
2. sunny
3. hopeful
4. rapid
5. rudely
6. just
7. narrow
8. strange
9. lucky
10. awkward

7. narrower/narrowest 8. stranger/strangest 9. luckier/luckiest 10. more awkward/most awkward

Modifiers of Three or More Syllables

When a modifier has three or more syllables, its comparative and superlative degrees are easy to form.

Use *more* and *most* to form the comparative and superlative degrees of all modifiers of three or more syllables.

Never use *-er* or *-est* with modifiers of more than two syllables.

DEGREES OF MODIFIERS WITH THREE OR MORE SYLLABLES

Positive	Comparative	Superlative
eagerly	more eagerly	most eagerly
favorable	more favorable	most favorable
difficult	more difficult	most difficult

Less and *least,* which mean the opposite of *more* and *most,* can be used to form the comparative and superlative degrees of any of the modifiers in the chart. *Less* and *least* can also be used with modifiers of one or two syllables.

EXAMPLES:	eagerly	less eagerly	least eagerly
	favorable	less favorable	least favorable
	difficult	less difficult	least difficult

EXERCISE B: Forming the Comparative and Superlative Degrees of Modifiers with More than Two Syllables. On your paper write the comparative and superlative degrees of the following modifiers. First use *more* and *most* and then *less* and *least* for each modifier.

All words should follow the model given in the example.

EXAMPLE: happily

more happily most happily

less happily least happily

1. intelligent
2. effective
3. affectionate
4. overburdened
5. glittery
6. industriously
7. infamous
8. popular
9. intricate
10. protected

APPLICATION: Forming the Comparative and Superlative Degrees of Regular Modifiers. On your paper write two sentences for each of the following modifiers. Write one sentence using the comparative degree of the modifier and one sentence using the superlative degree.

Answers will vary; samples given for first one.

EXAMPLE: ambitious

Bernadette was more ambitious than her sister Kitty.

Leslie, however, was the most ambitious one of all.

1. She is kinder than I. In fact, she is the kindest person I know.

1. kind
2. lonely
3. careful
4. exciting
5. handsome
6. hopeless
7. simple
8. adventurous
9. hard
10. windy

Irregular Adjectives and Adverbs

14.2

The comparative and superlative degrees of a few adjectives and adverbs are *irregular* in form and must be memorized.

Learn the irregular comparative and superlative forms of certain adjectives and adverbs.

The chart on the following page lists the most common irregular modifiers. Memorizing the degrees of these irregular adjectives and adverbs will help you use them correctly in your sentences.

DEGREES OF IRREGULAR ADJECTIVES AND ADVERBS		
Positive	**Comparative**	**Superlative**
bad	worse	worst
badly	worse	worst
far (distance)	farther	farthest
far (extent)	further	furthest
good	better	best
well	better	best
many	more	most
much	more	most

EXERCISE A: Recognizing the Degree of Irregular Modifiers. On your paper identify the degree of the underlined word in each of the following sentences.

EXAMPLE: After a short talk with the coach, Chris did not feel at all bad.

positive

1. Visitors to the Finger Lakes region in upstate New York can see many lovely lakes and waterfalls. *pos*
2. Farther out, white sails glinted in the sunlight.
3. Which is worse, being too hot or being too cold?
4. Actually, I dislike being wet most of all. *super*
5. The plowing was going well when the thunderstorm began. *pos*
6. Peter gave me the worst wrench in the toolbox and told me to remove the wheel. *super*
7. Mary Ellen likes field hockey more than any other sport. *compar*
8. Although the weather was bad, Shelly had a wonderful time. *pos*
9. José has never been in better form than he was in today's debate. *compar*
10. I thought that of all the speakers he handled the controversial issues best. *super*

2. compar 3. compar

EXERCISE B: Using the Comparative and Superlative Degrees of Irregular Modifiers. Copy each of the following sentences onto your paper, supplying the form of the modifier requested in parentheses.

EXAMPLE: Joanna feels (well—comparative) today.

better

1. Milt did (badly—comparative) on this test than on the previous one. *worse*
2. Jean can speak (many—comparative) languages than anyone else in our class. *more*
3. I always work (well—superlative) under the pressure of a deadline. *best*
4. Leonardo da Vinci is admired (much—superlative) for the versatility of his genius. *most*
5. Marilyn's (bad—superlative) fears were realized when she forgot to study for her history examination. *worst*
6. One thousand miles is the (far—superlative) I have ever been from home. *farthest*
7. Your antique car will look (good—comparative) after you polish it. *better*
8. Who found the (many—superlative) items in the scavenger hunt? *most*
9. Jan enjoys reading poetry (much—comparative) than any other kind of writing. *more*
10. Michael's (good—superlative) character trait is his honesty. *best*

APPLICATION: Forming the Comparative and Superlative Degrees of Irregular Modifiers. On your paper write two sentences for each of the following modifiers, one using the comparative degree and one using the superlative degree.

Answers will vary; samples given for first one.

EXAMPLE: much

I like cider more than apple juice.

However, the drink I like most is papaya juice.

1. far 2. bad 3. many 4. well 5. good

1. This car can go farther on a gallon of gas than our old one. The farthest we have taken it is to Texas and back.

14.3 Using Comparative and Superlative Degrees

Keep two rules in mind when you use the comparative and superlative degrees.

Use the **comparative degree** to compare *two* people, places, or things.

Use the **superlative degree** to compare *three or more* people, places, or things.

Usually you need not mention specific numbers when you are making a comparison. The other words in the sentence should help make it clear whether you are comparing two items or three or more items.

EXAMPLES: Joanna feels *better* today.

This is Gene's *best* drawing.

In the examples, the comparative degree *better* clearly compares Joanna's present condition to a single previous condition. The superlative degree *best* obviously compares one of Gene's drawings to all his others.

Pay particular attention to the modifiers you use when you are comparing just two items. Do not make the mistake of using the superlative degree.

INCORRECT: Of Gene's two drawings, that one is *best.*

This is the *most exciting* book of the two.

CORRECT: Of Gene's two drawings, that one is *better.*

This is the *more exciting* book of the two.

Pay attention also to the form of the modifiers you use in the comparative and superlative degrees. Do not make *double comparisons.* You should never use both *-er* and *more* to form the comparative degree or both

-est and *most* to form the superlative degree. Use one or the other method, but not both. Moreover, be sure you never use *-er* and *-est* or *more* and *most* with an irregular modifier.

INCORRECT: Debbie and Rick are the *most happiest* couple we know.

The situation in that country could not be *more worse.*

CORRECT: Debbie and Rick are the *happiest* couple we know.

The situation in that country could not be *worse.*

EXERCISE A: Correcting Errors in Degree. Some of the following sentences contain errors in degree. On your paper rewrite the incorrect sentences. Write *correct* if the sentence contains no errors.

EXAMPLE: He was the most intelligent of the two brothers.

He was the more intelligent of the two brothers.

1. Her watercolors were the most palest in the painting class. *palest*
2. Of those two jackets, I like the tweed one best. *better*
3. That Hitchcock movie was one of the most frightening films I have ever seen. *C*
4. It was hard to say which of the two children looked youngest. *younger*
5. Joyce's words became even more louder when Ted refused to explain his actions. *louder*
6. Which of these three letterheads looks more informal to you? *most*
7. Hank was the most diligent of the twins, but Holly was the smartest. *more/smarter*
8. Her voice carried better on high notes than low notes. *C*
9. That book would head my list of the ten most worst novels of all time. *worst*
10. Which of your parents do you resemble most? *more*

APPLICATION: Using the Comparative and Superlative Degrees. Write two sentences for each of the following modifiers, one using the comparative degree and one using the superlative degree.

Answers will vary; samples given for first one.

EXAMPLE: slowly

The molasses dripped more slowly than the maple syrup.

However, the honey dripped most slowly of the three.

1. Your pine tree is taller than ours. In fact, it's the tallest pine on the block.

1. tall
2. ancient
3. difficult
4. fearful
5. beautiful
6. strong
7. much
8. terrible
9. quickly
10. badly

14.4 Making Logical Comparisons

In most situations you will have no problems forming the degrees of modifiers and using them correctly in sentences. Sometimes, however, you may find that the way you have phrased a sentence makes your comparison unclear. You will then need to think about the words you have chosen and revise your sentence, making sure your comparison is logical.

Balanced Comparisons

Most comparisons make a statement or ask a question about the way in which basically similar things are either alike or different. For example, one sentence might compare the sound of two radios. Because the sentence compares sound to sound, the comparison is *balanced.* Problems can occur, however, when a sentence compares basically dissimilar things. For example, it would be illogical to compare the *sound* of one radio to the *size* of another radio. Sound and size are not basically similar things and can not be compared meaningfully.

Make sure that your sentences compare only items of a *similar* kind.

An unbalanced comparison is usually the result of carelessness. The writer generally has simply left out something. Read the following incorrect sentences carefully.

INCORRECT: This book's index is larger than that book.

Our classroom is larger than the sixth-graders.

In the first sentence, an *index* is mistakenly compared to an entire *book*. In the second sentence, a *classroom* is compared to *sixth-graders*. Both sentences can easily be corrected to make the comparisons balanced.

CORRECT: This book's index is longer than that book's index.

Our classroom is larger than the sixth-graders' classroom.

EXERCISE A: Making Balanced Comparisons. Rewrite each of the following sentences, making the illogical comparisons more balanced.

EXAMPLE: This dog's coat is shinier than that dog.

This dog's coat is shinier than that dog's coat.

1. Bernie's roller skates look newer than Jodie.
2. This year's fair was better attended than last year.
3. Our morning newspaper's circulation is much larger than our afternoon newspaper. *newspaper's circulation*
4. Pia's project covered more material than Eddie.
5. Because he is dead, this painter's work is more valuable than that painter. *painter's work*
6. Andrea's family is smaller than Jane. *Jane's family*
7. My record collection is not as large as my sister.
8. David's vegetable garden produced more tomatoes than Philip. *Philip's vegetable garden*
9. My mother's car looks better than my father. *father's car*
10. This pond's frogs are much noisier than that pond.

1. Jodie's roller skates 2. year's fair 4. Eddie's project 7. sister's record collection 10. pond's frogs

Other and *Else* in Comparisons

Another common error in writing comparisons is to compare something with itself.

When comparing one of a group with the rest of the group, make sure your sentence contains the word *other* or *else.*

Adding *other* or *else* in such situations helps make the comparison clear. For example, since Queen Victoria was herself a British monarch, she can not logically be compared to *all* British monarchs. She must be compared to all *other* British monarchs.

Problem Sentences	Corrected Sentences
Queen Victoria reigned longer than any British monarch.	Queen Victoria reigned longer than any *other* British monarch.
The captain scored more touchdowns than anyone on the team.	The captain scored more touchdowns than anyone *else* on the team.

EXERCISE B: Using *Other* and *Else* in Comparisons. Rewrite each of the following sentences, adding *other* or *else* to make the comparisons more logical.

EXAMPLE: George types faster than any student in his class.

George types faster than any other student in his class.

1. My mother sings more beautifully than any member of my family. *any other*
2. Theodore Roosevelt took office at a younger age than any American President. *any other*
3. Our English teacher is stricter than anyone on the faculty. *anyone else*
4. I like chocolate better than any food. *any other*
5. Julie was funnier than anyone in the stunt show.
6. In the semifinals Carrie served more aces than any player in the whole tournament. *any other*

5. anyone else

7. William Shakespeare is more admired than any English playwright. *any other*
8. *Roots* reached a wider audience than any television show. *any other*
9. In our house baseball is more popular than any sport. *any other*
10. In many ways, Greta Garbo was more famous than any actress of her time. *any other*

APPLICATION: Writing Logical Comparisons. On your paper write a sentence that makes the comparison specified in each of the following items. Make sure that your comparisons are balanced and logical.

Answers will vary; samples given for first two.

EXAMPLE: Compare the records of two basketball teams.

Our basketball team's record is much better than their basketball team's record.

1. This book's events are much more exciting than that book's events.

1. Compare the events in two different books.
2. Compare the humor on two television shows.
3. Compare one President with all the rest, using the word *better.*
4. Compare one popular singer with all the rest, using the word *worse.*
5. Compare one city with all the rest.

2. Taxi's *humor is much wittier than* Three's Company's *humor.*

Glossary of Troublesome Adjectives and Adverbs 14.5

Certain commonly used adjectives and adverbs often cause people problems both in speaking and writing. As you read through the following list, make a note of those words that have puzzled you in the past and use the exercises to test your understanding. When you are writing and revising a composition, refer to this section to check your work.

(1) *Bad* and *Badly*. *Bad* is an adjective; *badly* is an adverb. Use *bad* after linking verbs, such as *appear,* *feel, look,* and *sound.* Use *badly* after action verbs, such as *act, behave, do,* and *perform.*

INCORRECT: I felt (LV) *badly* after the long hike in the rain.

The small children behaved (AV) *bad* at the museum.

CORRECT: I felt (LV) *bad* after the long hike in the rain.

The small children behaved (AV) *badly* at the museum.

(2) *Fewer* and *Less.* The adjective *fewer* answers the question "How many?" Use it to modify things that can be counted. The adjective *less* answers the question "How much?" Use it to modify amounts that can not be counted.

HOW MANY: *fewer* calories, *fewer* doses, *fewer* worries

HOW MUCH: *less* starch, *less* medicine, *less* worry

(3) *Good* and *Well.* *Good* is an adjective. *Well* can be either an adjective or an adverb. Most mistakes in the use of these modifiers occur when *good* is placed after an action verb. Use the adverb *well* instead.

INCORRECT: I did (AV) *good* on the test.

CORRECT: I did (AV) *well* on the test.

As adjectives these words have slightly different meanings. *Well* usually is limited to a person's health.

EXAMPLES: I always feel *good* after jogging three miles.

The soup is especially *good* today.

He has not been *well* for several months.

(4) *Just.* As an adverb *just* often means "no more than." When *just* has this meaning, make sure it is placed right before the word it logically modifies.

INCORRECT: I *just* want one slice of turkey.

CORRECT: I want *just* one slice of turkey.

(5) *Only.* The position of *only* in a sentence sometimes affects the sentence's entire meaning. Consider the meaning of the following sentences.

EXAMPLES: *Only* he takes care of that dog. (Nobody else takes care of the dog.)

He *only* takes care of that dog. (He does nothing else for the dog.)

He takes care of *only* that dog. (He takes care of that dog and no other dog.)

Problems can occur when *only* is placed in a sentence in such a way that it makes the meaning imprecise.

IMPRECISE: *Only* mark your mistakes.

BETTER: Mark *only* your mistakes.

EXERCISE A: Correcting Errors Caused by Troublesome Adjectives and Adverbs. Some of the following sentences contain errors in the use of the modifiers discussed in this section. On your paper rewrite the faulty sentences, writing *correct* if a sentence contains no errors.

EXAMPLE: They sang good together.

They sang well together.

1. We found less seashells on the beach this year. *fewer*
2. Greg looked badly after running the marathon. *bad*
3. Our vacation begins in just two weeks. *C*
4. Ellen did good in the auditions, but Kathryn did better and won the role. *well*
5. I only want three things for my birthday this year.
6. The pineapple tasted especially well served with bananas and ice cream. *good*

5. want only

7. My uncle has been responding very well to treatment for his arthritis. C
8. Mort just needs three more points to beat the scoring record in our league. needs just
9. Unfortunately, Roger is taking the news very bad. badly
10. Less than a hundred people came to the annual bike auction. Fewer
11. Static made the rock group sound very badly. bad
12. They only called once. called only
13. Her recovery has taken a long time, but Maria is finally well again. C
14. Ed just had fifteen minutes to finish his test. had just
15. Water actually occupies fewer space than ice. less
16. I can't understand why Jim ran so bad today. badly
17. I gained fewer pounds than I expected over summer vacation. C
18. His control of his voice is especially well today. good
19. You only have one chance to guess the right answer, so take your time. have only
20. Be good and you will look good. C

APPLICATION: Using Troublesome Adjectives and Adverbs Correctly. On your paper write a sentence according to the directions given in each of the following items. *Answers will vary; samples given for first two.*

EXAMPLE: Use *badly* to describe some action.

Because of the sun in his eyes, he threw the ball badly.

1. Only Simon finished the test in an hour. 2. I felt bad about spoiling the surprise.

1. Use *Only* at the beginning of a sentence.
2. Use *bad* with a linking verb.
3. Use *fewer* to compare two sets of items.
4. Use *less* to compare two sets of items.
5. Use *well* as an adverb.
6. Use *only* after a verb.
7. Use *well* as an adjective.
8. Use *good* as an adjective.
9. Use *badly* with an action verb.
10. Use *just* to mean "no more than."

Chapter 15

Recognizing Special Problems in Usage

Many common errors in writing and speech do not fit into the major categories of usage that have been covered so far in this unit. Some of these problems involve the use of words or expressions that have traditionally been considered wrong in most kinds of writing. Other problems are caused by words that are spelled almost alike and so are easily confused. As you study the following sections, concentrate on those problems that occur in your own writing.

Double Negatives 15.1

Negative words, such as *never* and *not,* are used in sentences to deny something or to say *no.* Hundreds of years ago, it was often the custom to use two or more negative words in one clause for emphasis. Over the years custom has changed. Today only one negative word is needed to give a sentence a negative meaning.

The Mistaken Use of Double Negatives

Few people today could crowd a sentence with three negative words, but some people mistakenly use *double negatives,* two negative words, when one alone is called for.

Do not write sentences with **double negatives.**

In the following chart, the sentences on the left contain double negatives. Notice on the right how each sentence can be corrected in either of two ways.

Double Negatives	Corrected Sentences
We did*n't* see *no one.*	We did*n't* see anyone. We saw *no one.*
She has*n't* *no* money.	She has*n't* any money. She has *no* money.
You *never* gave me *nothing.*	You *never* gave me anything. You gave me *nothing.*

EXERCISE A: Correcting Double Negatives. The following sentences contain double negatives. On your paper rewrite each sentence in *two* ways.

EXAMPLE: We didn't tell Frank nothing about the surprise.

We didn't tell Frank anything about the surprise.

We told Frank nothing about the surprise.

1. Jennifer didn't see nobody she knew at the conference. *didn't see anybody/saw nobody*
2. Michael couldn't find nothing about his topic in the encyclopedia. *couldn't find anything/could find nothing*
3. Franklin never suggests nothing really original.
4. I haven't never eaten octopus. *haven't ever/have never*
5. Don't say nothing about the contest to Don.
6. Phyllis hasn't no extra time this term. *hasn't any/has no*
7. Chris will not show Paul none of her sketches until tomorrow. *will not show Paul any/will show Paul none*
8. Don't never ride your bicycle on that road.
9. I don't make no excuses for my behavior.
10. William can't remember nothing about the end of the movie. *can't remember anything/can remember nothing*

3. never suggests anything/suggests nothing 5. Don't say anything/Say nothing
8. Don't ever/Never 9. don't make any/make no

APPLICATION: Writing Negative Sentences. Use each of the following words in a negative sentence.

Answers will vary; samples given for first two.

EXAMPLE: nobody

When I called her house, nobody answered.

1. There wasn't any cereal left. 2. I have never seen a ring like yours.

1. wasn't
2. never
3. not
4. didn't
5. none
6. can't
7. nowhere
8. nothing
9. wouldn't
10. no

Twenty Common Usage Problems 15.2

This section presents twenty usage problems in alphabetical order. Some of the problems are expressions that you should avoid entirely. Others are words that are often confused because they have a similar spelling or meaning.

As you read through the list, note especially those words that have caused you difficulty in the past. Then use the exercises for practice.

You may also wish to refer to this section for guidance when you are writing and revising your compositions. If you do not find the explanation of a problem anywhere in this section, check for it in the index at the back of the book.

(1) *Accept* and *Except*. Do not confuse these words, which sound alike but differ in spelling and in meaning. *Accept,* a verb, means "to take what is offered" or "to agree to." *Except,* a preposition, means "leaving out" or "other than."

VERB: We *accept* your plan.

PREPOSITION: No one *except* her agreed to the idea.

(2) *Advice* and *Advise*. Do not confuse the spelling of these related words. *Advice* is a noun meaning "an opinion"; *advise* is a verb meaning "to give an opinion to."

NOUN: Ask your teacher for *advice* about the assignment.

VERB: Our teacher *advised* us about what to do.

(3) *Affect* and *Effect*. *Affect* is almost always a verb meaning "to influence" or "to bring about a change in." *Effect,* usually a noun, means "result." Occasionally, *effect* is a verb. Then it means "to cause."

VERB: The wrong kind of diet can *affect* a person's health.

NOUN: You should feel the *effect* of the medicine immediately.

VERB: The administration *effected* many changes in the budget.

(4) *All Ready* and *Already*. *All ready* is used as an adjective to mean "ready." *Already,* an adverb, means "by or before this time."

ADJECTIVE: We were *all ready* to leave.

ADVERB: The mail had *already* arrived.

(5) *Among* and *Between*. *Among* and *between* are both prepositions. *Among* always refers to three or more. *Between* usually refers to just two.

EXAMPLES: The kite became caught *among* the branches.

Let's keep this secret *between* you and me.

(6) *At*. Do not use *at* after *where.* Simply eliminate the word *at.*

INCORRECT: I don't know *where* we're *at.*

CORRECT: I don't know *where* we are.

(7) *Because*. Do not use *because* after *the reason.* Eliminate one or the other.

INCORRECT: *The reason* for his absence is *because* he is sick.

CORRECT: He is absent *because* he is sick.

The reason he is absent is that he is sick.

(8) *Beside* and *Besides*. As prepositions, these two words have different meanings and can not be interchanged. *Beside* means "at the side of" or "close to." *Besides* means "in addition to."

EXAMPLES: Sit here *beside* me.

No one *besides* me knew the answer.

(9) *Different From* and *Different Than*. *Different from* is generally preferred over *different than*.

EXAMPLES: The movie was *different from* what I had expected.

This movie is *different from* that one.

(10) *Due To The Fact That*. All these words are unnecessary. Use *since* or *because* instead.

INCORRECT: *Due to the fact that* you were late, we began without you.

CORRECT: *Since* you were late, we began without you.

(11) *Farther* and *Further*. *Farther* usually refers to distance. *Further* means "additional" or "to a greater degree or extent."

EXAMPLES: The school I will attend next year is much *farther* away.

Lisa wanted *further* information.

(12) *In* and *Into*. *In* refers to position. *Into* suggests motion.

POSITION: Three rabbits are *in* the vegetable garden.

MOTION: The dog chased the rabbits *into* the woods.

(13) *Kind Of* and *Sort Of*. Do not use *kind of* and *sort of* to mean "rather" or "somewhat."

INCORRECT: She felt *kind of* good about her grade.

CORRECT: She felt *rather* good about her grade.

(14) *Like*. *Like* is a preposition that usually means "similar to" or "in the same way as." It should be followed by an object. Do not use *like* before a subject and a verb. Use *as* or *that* instead.

Obj
PREPOSITION: The creature's hands looked *like* claws.

Obj
He was howling *like* a coyote.

S V
INCORRECT: Your plan worked just *like* you said it would.

S V
It seems *like* the movie has started.

CORRECT: Your plan worked just *as* you said it would.

It seems *that* the movie has started.

(15) *Than* and *Then*. *Than* is used in comparisons. Do not confuse it with the adverb *then,* which usually refers to time.

COMPARISON: Felicia is older *than* Alexander thought she was.

TIME: The party ended at six o'clock, and *then* we left for home.

(16) *That, Which,* and *Who*. *That* can refer to either things or people. *Which* should be used only with things and *who,* only with people.

THINGS: The book *that* (or *which*) you borrowed from the library is overdue.

PEOPLE: The person *that* (or *who*) delivered the speech is my teacher.

(17) *Their, There,* and *They're.* *Their,* a possessive adjective, always modifies a noun. *There* can be used either as a sentence starter or as an adverb. *They're* is a contraction of *they are.*

POSSESSIVE ADJECTIVE: Our guests forgot *their* coats.

SENTENCE STARTER: *There* are two ways to solve the puzzle.

ADVERB: Put the books *there.*

CONTRACTION: *They're* leaving for Canada tomorrow.

(18) *This Here* and *That There.* Avoid using these expressions by simply leaving out *here* and *there.*

INCORRECT: *This here* pair of jeans costs twenty-five dollars.

CORRECT: *This* pair of jeans costs twenty-five dollars.

(19) *To, Too,* and *Two.* *To* is a preposition used to begin a prepositional phrase or an infinitive. *Too* is an adverb that modifies adjectives and other adverbs. Do not forget its second *o. Two* is a number.

PREPOSITION: *to* the bank, *to* Chicago

INFINITIVE: *to* see, *to* receive

ADVERB: *too* short, *too* slowly

NUMBER: *two* friends, *two* canaries

(20) *When, Where,* and *Why.* Do not use *when, where,* or *why* directly after a linking verb. Reword the sentence.

INCORRECT: Parties *are when* I always have a good time.
The park *is where* we play baseball.
Because I need advice *is why* I am calling.

CORRECT: I always have a good time at parties.
We play baseball in the park.
I am calling because I need advice.

EXERCISE A: Avoiding Usage Problems 1–5. For each of the following sentences, choose the correct form from the choices in parentheses and write it on your paper.

EXAMPLE: (Among, Between) the six of them, we should be able to find someone with a sense of humor.

Among

1. Evelyn gave me some good (advice, advise).
2. The huge sandwich was divided (between, among) Kit, Mary, and Stan.
3. The team members were (all ready, already) for the game.
4. (Accept, Except) for Steven no one had any difficulty finding the restaurant.
5. Hot weather (affects, effects) people in different ways.
6. This place is (all ready, already) beginning to look more attractive.
7. The senator asked several experts to (advice, advise) her on the subject of energy.
8. Joan's words had a strange (affect, effect) on him: He fainted.
9. The conversation (among, between) the two sounded like a vaudeville routine.
10. It is always difficult to (accept, except) one's own limitations.

EXERCISE B: Avoiding Usage Problems 6–10. For each of the following sentences, choose the correct form from the choices in parentheses and write it on your paper.

1. The hayride was canceled (due to the fact that, because) rain was predicted.
2. I don't know where my algebra book could (be, be at).
3. The reason we came is (because, that) your letter alarmed us.
4. (Due to the fact that, Since) Janet has studied Italian, she will give the waiter our order.

5. (Beside, Besides) the four of us, who will help decorate the gym for the dance?
6. Chris didn't want his new room to be any different (from, than) his old one.
7. Do you know of a store where fish sauce can be (found, found at)?
8. His reason for resigning was (because, that) his family needed him.
9. The girls moved the picnic table so that they could eat (beside, besides) the lake.
10. This version of the song is very different (from, than) the one you like.

EXERCISE C: Avoiding Usage Problems 11–15. For each of the following sentences, choose the correct form from the choices in parentheses and write it on your paper.

1. Kathleen walked (in, into) the room and announced the name of the winner.
2. His progress in his studies was greater (than, then) his friends imagined.
3. It seems (like, that) you were expecting us all along.
4. Wynn looked (kind of, rather) green after eating all those peppers.
5. (In, Into) the closet Kelly found the missing keys.
6. Nathan has a good speaking voice, but he sings (as, like) a frog.
7. First I dropped the turkey, and (than, then) I spilled the gravy.
8. Andy wrote every day, just (like, as) she had promised.
9. It looks (sort of, rather) silly for you to leave after just arriving.
10. As you climb (farther, further) up the mountain, the trees become sparser.

EXERCISE D: Avoiding Usage Problems 16–20. For each of the following sentences, choose the correct form from the choices in parentheses and write it on your paper.

1. Put (this, this here) cover on the bicycle.
2. The woman (which, that) wrote our textbook gave a lecture to the science club.
3. There are two sisters in his family, but (their, they're) both engaged.
4. Twilight is (when, the hour when) everything seems most tranquil.
5. The dog (who, that) ran out to greet you is eleven years old.
6. Independence Hall is (where, the place where) the Liberty Bell is displayed.
7. Mattie and Teresa built (they're, their) model dinosaur out of toothpicks.
8. Two hundred dollars is (to, too) high a price for this stereo.
9. He told me that (his cold is why he skipped practice, he skipped practice because of his cold).
10. The carpenter (which, who) made these bookcases is very skillful.

APPLICATION: Correcting Usage Problems. Some of the following sentences contain one or more usage errors. On your paper rewrite the faulty sentences, writing *correct* for the sentences without errors.

Answers to some items may vary within reason.

EXAMPLE: Hillary's opinion is quite different than yours.

Hillary's opinion is quite different from yours.

1. One of the affects of the New Deal was an increase in the size of the government. *effects*
2. The library is where you can find information on that subject. *the place where*
3. The baseball player that I admire most is Frank Robinson. *C*
4. Her choice was quite different than his. *from*
5. Even though I often disagree with you, this time I except your advise. *accept/advice*
6. There are too very controversial issues on the agenda for this meeting. *two*
7. Weren't you already this time? *all ready*
8. This here dress was designed in Paris. *This*

9. Due to the fact that he forgot his textbook, he had little to do in class. *Because*
10. The students need to discuss their proposal further before submitting it. *C*
11. It seems like their to tired to accomplish much this afternoon. *as if/they're/too*
12. The tall stranger walked into the room and began mingling among our guests. *C*
13. The music piped in the dentist's office was bland but kind of soothing. *into/rather*
14. The boxer floated like a butterfly, but then he stung like a bee. *C*
15. She knows where the money is at, but she won't tell anyone beside the sheriff. *is/besides*
16. This astronaut has been further from the earth then any other human being. *farther/than*
17. The story was sort of difficult for my little brother to follow. *rather*
18. The reason you didn't see us was because we weren't there. *that*
19. To see Robert Redford was why she went to the rally. *the reason why*
20. I can give them advice, but their not obliged to follow it. *they're*

Review Exercises: Usage

REVIEW EXERCISE 1: Identifying the Principal Parts, Tense, and Voice of Verbs

Read the following paragraph and answer the questions that follow it.

EXAMPLE: What is the tense of the verb in the first sentence?

present perfect

(1) Today has been a strange day. (2) The weather has been changing wildly from one hour to the next. (3) It began with the solid gray sky that usually means hours of rain. (4) I was resigned to a long day of working indoors, but by midmorning the sun had begun to poke through the clouds, and by noon it was shining brightly above. (5) No sooner had I stepped outside, however, than I noticed the dense black clouds that had been piling up to the west. (6) They were being churned eastward by some powerful force. (7) A furious thunderstorm broke and raged for several hours. (8) Now the sun is shining once again, although electrical power has been cut off. (9) It will have been restored by midnight, according to the authorities. (10) I wonder what melodramas tomorrow's weather will bring.

1. What is the tense and form of the verb in the second sentence? *pres perf prog*
2. Find the first two verbs in the paragraph that are in the past perfect tense. *had begun/had stepped*
3. Find the last two verbs in the passive voice.
4. Which sentence contains a verb in the present progressive? *8*
5. What are the tenses of the second two verbs in the fifth sentence? *past/past perf*
6. Which sentence contains one verb in the past and one in the present? *3*
7. What is the tense of the verb in the ninth sentence?
8. Which sentence contains one verb in the future tense? *10*
9. What principal part is used to form the verbs in the seventh sentence? *past*
10. Rewrite the sixth sentence to change the voice of the verb. *Some powerful force was churning them eastward.*

3. has been cut/will have been restored 7. fut perf

REVIEW EXERCISE 2: Correcting Errors in Verb Usage

Rewrite each of the following sentences, correcting all errors in verb usage as well as any awkward uses of the passive voice.

EXAMPLE: He has chose to bring his lunch with him.

He has chosen to bring his lunch with him.

1. Rosina will have drank eight glasses of water before she lays down to sleep. drunk/lies
2. With a little luck, we could of broke the track record last week. have broken
3. Leave me rest; I must have ran ten miles in practice today. Let/run
4. The present the child had brought with him was busted within a few hours. broken
5. The story of Cinderella was told by me to my nephew. I told the story of Cinderella to my nephew.
6. I seen the sun when it raised this morning. saw/rose
7. He says to me, "You should have went with us."
8. Have you shook this package to see what is inside?
9. Set down and chat with me; we haven't spoke like this in years. Sit/spoken
10. They have lain down their swords, for they were defeated in battle. laid

7. said/gone 8. shaken

REVIEW EXERCISE 3: Identifying the Case of Personal Pronouns

On your paper identify the case of the personal pronouns that are numbered and underlined in the following paragraph.

EXAMPLE: Television constantly amazes me.

objective

(1) I find that watching (2) my television without (3) its sound can sometimes be more interesting than watching the usual way. For example, soundless news makes the events of (4) our world much easier to understand. Newscasters use only three basic expressions throughout the broadcasts. (5) They can look grave, humorous, or intelligent, depending on the story (6) they are reading. Soap operas, on the other hand, seem to increase in depth if (7) they are seen and not heard. In one scene an actor pulls (8) his hair and seems to

1. nom 2. poss 3. poss 4. poss 5. nom 6. nom 7. nom 8. poss

exercise every single muscle in (9) his face. And yet the actress in the scene with (10) him simply nods (11) her head pleasantly. What can (12) he be telling (13) her that upsets (14) him so much? Why is (15) she taking (16) it so calmly? (17) I know that what is actually going on must be much less interesting than what (18) my imagination invents for (19) me. On television (20) it is certainly true that one picture is worth a thousand words. *9. poss 10. obj 11. poss 12. nom 13. obj 14. obj 15. nom 16. obj 17. nom 18. poss 19. obj 20. nom*

REVIEW EXERCISE 4: Correcting Errors in Pronoun Case

Rewrite each of the following sentences, correcting all errors in pronoun case. If a sentence is correct, write *correct.*

EXAMPLE: She was certain that the final decision would be her's.

She was certain that the final decision would be hers.

1. This opinion is held by both he and I. *him/me*
2. The captain this year will be her. *she*
3. The man who Leslie telephoned from the airport is her uncle. *whom*
4. The woman in this photograph is not the person whom you identified. *C*
5. The fly seemed to be wringing it's hands. *its*
6. On our math test, Mrs. Warner gave Gail and I the top scores. *me*
7. Who was Leon walking with the other day? *Whom*
8. I don't understand him when he begins speaking quickly. *C*
9. This catcher's mitt is ours', not theirs'. *ours/theirs*
10. My younger sister doesn't like Jean and he. *him*

REVIEW EXERCISE 5: Identifying Subject-Verb and Pronoun-Antecedent Agreement

In each of the following sentences, words that should agree with each other are underlined. If they do agree, write *correct*. If they do not agree, rewrite the sentence to make it correct. *Incorrect forms are shaded.*

EXAMPLE: Neither my sister nor my brothers was at the party.

Neither my sister nor my brothers were at the party.

1. Both Kennedy and Johnson were candidates for the Democratic nomination in 1960. *C*
2. Has each of the girls found their own bowling shoes? *her*
3. No one in the family expect to go away this summer. *expects*
4. Lloyd and Ben took their mothers out to dinner. *C*
5. Neither Peg nor Franny will spend their time helping us plan for the party. *her*
6. Either the walls or the ceiling need to be painted this year. *needs*
7. One of the boys lost their mitt. *his*
8. Most of the leaks in the roof have been repaired. *C*
9. The father and mother of a newborn baby is often too delighted to speak. *are*
10. The members of the construction crew have all signed this get-well card for you. *C*

REVIEW EXERCISE 6: Correcting Errors in Agreement

The following paragraph contains a number of errors in subject-verb and pronoun-antecedent agreement. Find these errors and rewrite the paragraph to correct them. *Errors are underlined; corrections are given below.*

EXAMPLE: Everyone on a debating team are faced with certain pressures.

Everyone on a debating team is faced with certain pressures.

(1) The students of Redwood Junior High School was discussing its strategy for the finals of the annual debate competition. (2) They knew that you had to plan carefully before a debate. (3) Although most of the

1. were/their 2. they

competition were over, the scores of several competing schools was very close. (4) The students of Redwood School realized that neither they nor the students at Lincoln, their greatest rival, was able to afford a mistake in the finals. (5) Redwood's captain and co-captain was arguing about whether the captain should choose to go first or last if she won the toss. (6) Finally, the co-captain said, "Everyone know that we have a hard case to argue tomorrow. (7) However, there's several mistakes that we might make if we speak first. (8) If we speak after Lincoln, all of our debaters will have more time to strengthen his arguments, and it will allow Lincoln's debaters to make a few mistakes of their own. (9) Neither the captain nor the other students was able to disagree with this logic. (10) The next day, the students of Redwood Junior High School was successful in its debate and won the first place.

3. was/were 4. were 5. were 6. knows 7. there are 8. their 9. were 10. were/their

REVIEW EXERCISE 7: Identifying Degrees of Modifiers

On your paper identify the degree of the modifier that is underlined in each of the following sentences.

EXAMPLE: They felt good after they finally reached the end of the trail.

positive

1. She never does any more work than she has to. *compar*
2. Now that I understand the subject fairly well, I can begin to organize my paper. *pos*
3. We have not seen much of you this fall. *pos*
4. Heidi was most anxious to arrive before dark. *super*
5. My room is quieter now that I have a rug. *compar*
6. Of all composers of popular American music, I like Gershwin best. *super*
7. Elliott found fewer reasons than I did for this change of policy. *compar*
8. Many students are now electing to study Latin. *pos*
9. His condition has not improved, but it has not gotten worse. *compar*
10. Sometimes even our dearest friends can disappoint us. *super*

REVIEW EXERCISE 8: Correcting Errors in Adjective and Adverb Usage

The following sentences contain errors in adjective and adverb usage. Rewrite the sentences to correct these problems.

EXAMPLE: France has sent us less immigrants than most other countries in Europe.

France has sent us fewer immigrants than most other countries in Europe.

1. Bob likes Boston better than any American city. *any other*
2. I just found this letter two days ago. *found this letter just*
3. A person who speaks good has a better chance for success in public life. *well*
4. Her awkwardest moment came when she dropped her lecture notes in the soup. *most awkward*
5. Which is worst, a hurricane or a tornado? *worse*
6. Although they are the same age, my hamster is fatter than my older brother. *brother's hamster*
7. There were less people than expected at the rock concert. *fewer*
8. Carlo thought that the senator looked badly in the debate yesterday. *bad*
9. I need to see her more than anyone. *anyone else*
10. His expression grew more sterner as he listened to the report. *sterner or more stern*

REVIEW EXERCISE 9: Identifying Special Usage Problems

The following paragraph contains a number of special usage problems. On your paper write the faulty word or words from each sentence. If a sentence is correct, write *correct*. *Answers to some items may vary within reason.*

EXAMPLE: Their are a number of things that can be learned from sports.

Their

(1) The marathon race was when Claudia first learned that she could discipline herself farther than

she had ever thought possible. (2) She had always been sort of athletic, due to the fact that she had grown up besides three brothers. (3) They hadn't never treated her different than themselves, and their was considerable rivalry in sports and games between them all. (4) But Claudia was the only one of them which signed up for the marathon. (5) Her brothers thought that the race would be to much for her, but she did not except their advise. (6) As she settled in her training routine, Claudia noticed that her physical routine effected her schoolwork as well. (7) Her concentration improved greatly and her grades hadn't never been better. (8) By the day of the actual race, it seemed to Claudia like the marathon itself was less important then the lessons she had learned from training. (9) She was proud that her brothers saw her cross the finish line. (10) But she knew that the real reason the whole effort had been worthwhile was that she had finally learned to compete with no one accept herself.

REVIEW EXERCISE 10: Correcting Special Usage Problems

Rewrite the paragraph in Review Exercise 9, correcting the errors in usage. *Revisions will vary; examples given.*

EXAMPLE: Their are a number of things that can be learned from sports.

There are a number of things that can be learned from sports.

1. was the time when/further 2. rather/because/beside 3. had never/different from/there/among 4. who 5. too/accept/advice 6. into/affected 7. had never 8. that/than 9. C 10. except

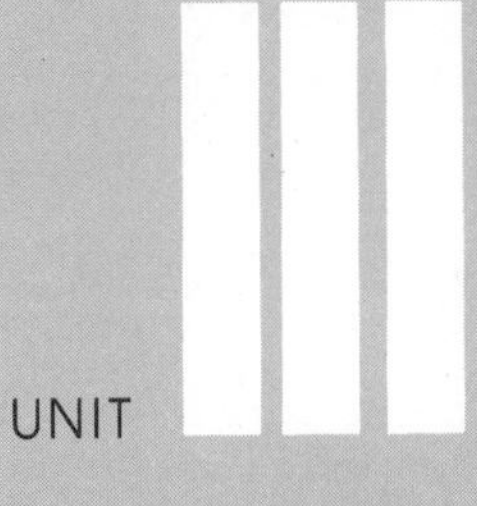

UNIT III

Mechanics

16

Using Capitals

17

Using Abbreviations

18

Using Punctuation Marks

Chapter 16

Using Capitals

In the English language, *capital letters* are used as signals. For example, capitals may signal the beginning of a sentence or an important word within a sentence. As you can see in the following example, a sentence written without capitals is confusing.

EXAMPLE: mr. bailey conducted the band from youngstown as they played a march by sousa.

With the addition of capitals, the same sentence is easier to read.

EXAMPLE: Mr. Bailey conducted the band from Youngstown as they played a march by Sousa.

The meaning of a sentence is clearer when it is capitalized correctly.

To **capitalize** means to begin a word with a capital letter.

The six sections in this chapter present a number of rules that will help you capitalize correctly.

16.1 Capitals for First Words

Capital letters are used for the first words in all sentences and in many quotations. They are also used for the word *I*, whatever its position in a sentence.

Sentences

One of the most common uses of a capital is to signal the beginning of a sentence.

Capitalize the first word in declarative, interrogative, imperative, and exclamatory sentences.

DECLARATIVE: Strong gusts of wind made it dangerous to drive on the bridge.

INTERROGATIVE: Who found the clue leading to the suspect's arrest?

IMPERATIVE: Think carefully before you decide.

EXCLAMATORY: What an amazing coincidence this is!

Sometimes only part of a sentence is written out. The rest of the sentence is understood. In these cases a capital is still needed for the first word.

EXAMPLES: When? Why not? Certainly!

EXERCISE A: Using Capitals to Begin Sentences. Copy the following items onto your paper, adding the missing capitals. *Underline letters are to be capitalized.*

EXAMPLE: great! when will we leave?

Great! When will we leave?

1. few students have shown more determination than she.
2. i left my book somewhere. but where?
3. what? would you repeat that?
4. please refer to an encyclopedia for a more detailed explanation.
5. next weekend? we thought the play opened tonight.
6. how talented you are!
7. stand at attention during the inspection.
8. when is the science project due?
9. wow! that was a surprise!
10. his bicycle is considerably older than he is.

Quotations

A capital letter also signals the first word in a quoted sentence.

Capitalize the first word in a quotation if the quotation is a complete sentence.

In each of the following examples, the first word of the quotation is capitalized because it begins a complete sentence.

EXAMPLES: Several people shouted, "Stop the bus!"

"She really wants to play first base," Arlene confided.

When a quotation consists of one complete sentence in two parts, only one capital is needed.

EXAMPLE: "How much longer," asked Brian, "are you going to need that book?"

If a quotation contains more than one sentence, capitalize the first word of each sentence.

EXAMPLE: "Please distribute these maps to everyone," explained the director. "They show the location of each exhibit."

EXERCISE B: Using Capitals for Quotations. Copy each of the following sentences onto your paper, adding the missing capitals. *Underlined letters are to be capitalized.*

EXAMPLE: "where did you find this one?" he asked.

"Where did you find this one?" he asked.

1. "begin tuning your instruments," the conductor told the musicians.
2. the telephone operator asked, "what number did you dial?"
3. "let me do the driving," said Earl. "sit back and relax."

4. "turnips are good for you," he stated as he served the steaming dish.
5. "cardinals devour the birdseed," she explained, "but woodpeckers prefer suet."
6. after an hour the audience began to shout, "we want Joe! we want Joe!"
7. "all the important documents are in the filing cabinet," the secretary explained. "notice, however, that they are not in alphabetical order."
8. Marty whispered, "let me borrow some paper."
9. "collecting rock samples," Jill told the class, "is a fascinating hobby."
10. "dependable equipment is a must," the skiing instructor noted.

■ The Word *I*

The pronoun *I* is always written as a capital.

Capitalize the word *I* wherever it appears in a sentence.

EXAMPLE: I worked two years as a clerk before I received the promotion.

EXERCISE C: Using the Pronoun *I*. Copy the following sentences onto your paper, adding the missing capitals.
Underlined letters are to be capitalized.

EXAMPLE: she and i were the last to arrive.

She and I were the last to arrive.

1. am i late?
2. i hope i answered the question correctly.
3. "sometimes," i told her, "i feel as discouraged as you do."
4. when they finally announced the winner, it was i.
5. the following pronouns are singular: i, she, and he.

APPLICATION: Using Capitals for First Words. Each of the following patterns represents a complete sentence. Write sentences that fit the punctuation of each pattern, using capitals where they are needed.
Answers will vary; samples given.

EXAMPLE: ________! ______________________!

Darn! He let the cat in again!

1. ___Is the dog outside___?
2. "___I think so___," ___he said___.
3. ___She asked___, "___Are you going___?"
4. ___What a day we had___!
5. ___The rains began___.
6. ___Wow___! ___Aren't you excited___?
7. ___The dog is hungry___. ___Why___?
8. "___Let's go___," ___I said___. "___We're late___."
9. "___Throw it___," ___he said___, "___now___."
10. ___Where is the party___? ___When___?

16.2 Capitals for Proper Nouns

Because a proper noun names a specific person, place, or thing, it is capitalized.

Capitalize all proper nouns.

Names of People

One kind of proper noun is the name of a specific person.

Capitalize each part of a person's full name.

EXAMPLES: Michelle T. Como P.A. Sullivan

When a two-part last name begins with *Mc, O',* or *St.,* the second part of the last name must also be capitalized.

EXAMPLES: McMurphy O'Connor St. John

For two-part last names that do not begin with *Mc, O',* or *St.,* the capitalization varies. Check with a reliable source for the correct spelling.

EXERCISE A: Using Capitals for Names of People. On your paper write each name that you find in the following sentences, adding the missing capitals.
Underlined letters are to be capitalized.

EXAMPLE: Her best friend was andrea mcmahon.

Andrea McMahon

1. We asked cindy to join us on our class trip.
2. This book by e.b. white is a children's classic.
3. My cousin, paul mcbride, is a talented trumpet player.
4. helen st. james invited us to her graduation party.
5. The firm is managed by t.l. johnson and her partner, b.r. whitaker.
6. She usually relaxes by listening to the music of brahms or beethoven.
7. Short stories by o. henry were among his favorites.
8. The convention was organized by elizabeth cady stanton and susan b. anthony.
9. With a friendly smile, maria lopez invited the unexpected visitors to enter.
10. The patriot paul revere was an expert silversmith.

Geographical Places

The names of specific geographical places are also proper nouns.

Capitalize geographical names.

According to this rule, any place listed on a map should be capitalized.

GEOGRAPHICAL NAMES	
Streets:	First Avenue, Spencer Road
Towns and Cities:	Plainfield, Los Angeles, Tokyo
Counties:	Orange County, Wayne County
States and Provinces:	Oklahoma, Manitoba
Nations:	France, Ecuador, Saudi Arabia
Continents:	South America, Africa, Asia

Valleys and Deserts:	Death Valley, the Mojave Desert
Mountains:	the Rocky Mountains, Mount Rushmore
Sections of a Country:	New England, the Southwest, the Northeast
Islands:	Iceland, Pitcairn Island
Scenic Spots:	the Everglades, Yosemite National Park
Rivers and Falls:	the Colorado River, Rainbow Falls
Lakes and Bays:	Lake Superior, Saginaw Bay
Seas and Oceans:	the Dead Sea, the Indian Ocean

Compass points, such as north, southwest, or east, are considered proper nouns only when they name specific geographical locations. In those cases, they are capitalized. When they simply refer to directions, they are not.

EXAMPLES: We spent our vacation in the East.

Bitterly cold winds swept southeast across the mountains.

EXERCISE B: Using Capitals for Geographical Places. On your paper write each geographical place name that you find in the following sentences, adding the missing capitals. *Underlined letters are to be capitalized.*

EXAMPLE: They had seen niagara falls in 1954.

Niagara Falls

1. A few miles south of buckhorn lake is the cumberland national park.
2. The Blakes bought a cottage on lake drive in schuyler county.
3. Our tour included a visit to india and china, neighboring countries in asia.
4. The trip was extended to include a week's stay in ceylon, an island in the indian ocean.

5. The st. johns river flows into the atlantic ocean near jacksonville, florida.
6. The sahara covers most of the land of north africa.
7. We lived in providence, rhode island, before moving to the west.
8. mount everest, the highest of the himalaya mountains, has claimed many lives.
9. During the summer we visited friends in toronto, canada.
10. The plane flew west over the atlantic ocean and landed in halifax, nova scotia, before continuing on to bangor, maine.

Other Proper Nouns

Other kinds of proper nouns also require capital letters.

Capitalize the names of specific events and periods of time.

The following chart gives examples of events and times that are capitalized.

SPECIFIC EVENTS AND TIMES	
Historical Periods:	the Golden Age, the Renaissance, the Industrial Revolution
Historical Events:	the Boxer Rebellion, World War I
Documents:	the Declaration of Independence, the Bill of Rights, the Homestead Act
Days:	Friday, Sunday
Months:	March, June
Holidays:	Memorial Day, St. Valentine's Day, New Year's Day
Religious Days:	Easter, Pentecost, Muharram
Special Events:	the Orange Bowl, the State Fair of Texas

The names of seasons are an exception to this rule. Even though they represent specific times of year, they are not capitalized.

EXAMPLE: Last winter was the coldest in a decade.

Like specific events the names of specific groups are considered to be proper nouns.

Capitalize the names of various organizations, government bodies, political parties, races, and nationalities, as well as the languages spoken by different groups.

The following chart shows examples of each of these kinds of groups.

SPECIFIC GROUPS	
Clubs:	the Lincoln School Camera Club, the Philadelphia Pioneer Track Club
Organizations:	the International Red Cross, the Girl Scouts
Institutions:	Georgia Institute of Technology, Tenakill School, Beth Israel Hospital
Businesses:	General Electric Company, L.L. Bean, Inc.
Government Bodies:	the Congress of the United States, the Supreme Court, the Los Angeles City Council
Political Parties:	the Republican Party, the Democratic Party
Races and Nationalities:	Caucasian, Algerian, Japanese, Mexican, American
Languages Spoken by Different Groups:	English, Portuguese, Arabic, Norwegian

The names of religions and many religious terms are also proper nouns.

Capitalize references to religions, deities, and religious scriptures.

The following chart shows the words that the major religions use to refer to important religious figures and holy writings. Note that the name of each religion is also capitalized.

RELIGIOUS REFERENCES	
Christianity:	God, the Lord, the Father, the Son, the Holy Ghost, the Bible, books of the Bible (such as Genesis, Exodus, Matthew, Mark)
Judaism:	God, the Lord, the Father, the Prophets, the Torah, the Talmud, the Midrash
Islam:	Allah, the Prophet, Mohammed, the Koran
Hinduism:	Brahma, the Bhagavad-Gita, the Vedas
Buddhism:	Buddha, Mahayana, Hinayana

An exception to this rule occurs when the word *god* or *goddess* is used in reference to ancient mythology. Do not use a capital for the word *god* or *goddess*.

EXAMPLE: the god Mars the goddess Athena

Many other proper nouns also require capitalization.

Capitalize the names of other special places and items.

The following chart shows specific examples of these other kinds of proper nouns.

OTHER SPECIAL PLACES AND ITEMS	
Monuments:	the Eiffel Tower, the Statue of Liberty
Memorials:	the Tomb of the Unknown Soldier
Buildings:	the Museum of Natural History
Celestial Bodies: (except the moon, the sun, and generally the earth)	the Spiral Galaxy, Jupiter, Orion
Awards:	the Pulitzer Prize, the Nobel Peace Prize
Air, Sea, Space, and Land Craft:	*Air Force One,* the *Lusitania, Apollo 12,* a Ford Model A
Trademarks:	Kellogg's Rice Krispies, Polaroid

EXERCISE C: Using Capitals for Other Proper Nouns. On your paper write each proper noun that you find in the following sentences, adding the missing capitals.

Underlined letters are to be capitalized.

EXAMPLE: The temple was dedicated to the goddess minerva.

Minerva

1. The english and americans have been allied for many years.
2. Janet bought a box of hershey's to make cocoa for the ice-skating party.
3. Many cards sent on valentine's day picture the god cupid.
4. For Jed the most impressive monument in washington was the lincoln memorial.
5. In our country thanksgiving is traditionally celebrated on the last thursday in november.
6. After graduating from westchester community college, she worked for gaylord ad agency.
7. John was a democrat when he was first elected to the house of representatives.
8. In the spring christians celebrate easter.

9. Colorful fireworks blazed across the sky on that fourth of july.
10. The founder of the religion now known as islam was mohammed.
11. Paul thoroughly enjoyed his visit to the museum of modern art.
12. Sheila sailed the *albatross* to victory in a race sponsored by the west shore yacht club.
13. The bill of rights guarantees freedom of religion, speech, and assembly.
14. During the winter our pantry shelves are stocked with boxes of cheerios.
15. A small statue of buddha was placed in a corner of the room.
16. In 1899 jane addams founded hull house, a settlement house that offered educational and health services to the poor.
17. During the renaissance a new interest in learning spread throughout europe.
18. The spacecraft *voyager 1* photographed saturn's many rings.
19. Jamie and her brother have each won a national merit award.
20. To protest great britain's policy of taxation without representation, americans staged the boston tea party.

APPLICATION: Using Capitals for Proper Nouns. Write a brief description of a real or fictional vacation area. Your description should include proper nouns from at least ten of the twelve categories in the following list. Try to make the area appeal to tourists by writing in the style of a travel brochure. Be sure to capitalize correctly.

Descriptions will vary; samples of proper nouns are given.

1. A town or city
2. A language *Spanish*
3. A special event
4. A historical event or period
5. A body of water
6. A mountain *Mount Whitney*
7. A building *the Sears Tower*
8. A celestial body *Venus*
9. A monument *Grant's Tomb*
10. A month *May*
11. A religious holiday
12. A section of a country

1. Brownsville, Texas 3. the Danbury Fair 4. World War II 5. the Gulf of Mexico 11. Christmas 12. the Southwest

16.3 Capitals for Proper Adjectives

Proper adjectives are proper nouns and proper noun forms that are used as adjectives to describe, or modify, another word.

■ Proper Adjectives

A single capitalization rule applies to most proper adjectives.

Capitalize most proper adjectives.

In the following examples, notice that both proper nouns and proper adjectives are capitalized. Common nouns modified by proper adjectives, however, are not capitalized.

PROPER NOUNS: World War I the Congress

PROPER ADJECTIVES: a World War I battle

a Congressional report

A trademark, the name of a company's product, is considered a proper noun. If you use only part of the trademark, the brand name, to describe a common noun, the brand name becomes a proper adjective. In this case capitalize only the proper adjective.

PROPER NOUN: Kellogg's Rice Krispies

PROPER ADJECTIVE· Kellogg's cereal

EXERCISE A: Using Capitals for Proper Adjectives. Complete each of the following sentences by supplying a proper adjective that is correctly capitalized.

Answers will vary; samples given.

EXAMPLE: Her most treasured possession was a ________ sofa.

Victorian

1. Philip's dog, an ___Irish___ setter, won a prize.
2. The ___London___ buses run twenty-four hours a day.
3. This Sunday we will have a ___Halloween___ party.
4. I asked you to buy ___Palmolive___ dish detergent.
5. The ___American___ car proved to be the best buy.
6. Saul's parrot nibbled on the ___Ritz___ cracker.
7. The librarian located a translation of the ___French___ novel.
8. It is easier to write with a ___Parker___ pen.
9. The ___Wallis___ family attended a reunion in Maryland.
10. ___Minnesota___ winters are usually long and cold.

APPLICATION: Using Capitals for Proper Adjectives. Use each of the following words as a proper adjective in an original sentence. Be sure to capitalize the proper adjectives correctly. *Answers will vary; samples given for first two.*

EXAMPLE: italian

He returned with many stories about the friendliness of the Italian people.

1. Sheila is fond of Mexican food. 2. That was a Biblical reference.

1. mexican
2. biblical
3. roman
4. kraft
5. californian
6. danish
7. canadian
8. new england
9. african
10. japanese

Capitals for Titles of People 16.4

Several rules govern the use of capitals for titles of people.

■ Social and Professional Titles

Social and professional titles may be written before a person's name or may be used when speaking directly to another person.

Capitalize the title of a person when it is followed by the person's name or when it is used in direct address.

The following chart gives examples of some of these titles.

TITLES OF PEOPLE	
Social:	Mister, Madam or Madame, Miss, Sir
Business:	Doctor, Professor, Superintendent
Religious:	Reverend, Father, Rabbi, Bishop, Sister
Military:	Private, Ensign, Captain, General, Admiral, Colonel
Government:	President, Secretary of State, Ambassador, Senator, Representative, Governor, Mayor

Notice how these titles can be used both before a person's name and in direct address with or without the person's name.

BEFORE A NAME: Private Jacobson and Captain Wilkins arrived together.

DIRECT ADDRESS: Doctor Bennett, your patient needs you.

Please, Miss, hurry.

The titles of high government officials, such as the President of the United States, the Chief Justice of the Supreme Court, and the Queen of England, are generally capitalized even if no name or direct address is involved.

Capitalize the titles of certain high government officials even when the titles are not followed by a person's name or used in direct address.

WITH A PERSON'S NAME: Queen Victoria ruled England for over sixty years.

WITHOUT A PERSON'S NAME: The President greeted the Queen as she entered the room.

The titles of lower government officials may also be capitalized when there is no name given, but only when they refer to the specific person who has that title.

SPECIFIC REFERENCE: Tell the members of the press the Mayor will speak with them now.

GENERAL REFERENCE: The mayor of a large city often has a difficult job.

See Section 17.1 for information about capitalizing abbreviated social and professional titles.

EXERCISE A: Using Capitals for Social and Professional Titles. If the title in each of the following sentences is correctly capitalized, write *correct* on your paper. If it is incorrectly capitalized, rewrite the title, correcting the error.

EXAMPLE: The president was seated in the Oval Office of the White House.

President

1. Pardon me, professor, but would you repeat that quotation? *Professor*
2. Several sermons given by reverend Donne have been published. *Reverend*
3. After serving the school district for ten years, superintendent Mills retired. *Superintendent*
4. There was limited television coverage of the President's last press conference. *C*
5. All of the army's Generals agreed that a military attack was not possible. *generals*
6. I heard that senator Carr is widely respected. *Senator*
7. Our teacher asked Sir Richard to speak to the class about British royalty. *C*
8. The queen of England will attend the celebration next month. *Queen*
9. Representative Wilkins voted against the revised plan. *C*
10. In 1898 admiral Dewey defeated the Spanish fleet.

10. Admiral

Family Titles

A different rule is needed for titles that show family relationships.

Capitalize titles showing family relationships when the title is used with the person's name or in direct address. The title may also be capitalized in other situations when it refers to a specific person, except when the title comes after a possessive noun or pronoun.

BEFORE A NAME: We invited Aunt Rebecca to the party.

IN DIRECT ADDRESS: Watch out, Uncle, or you'll slip.

REFERRING TO A SPECIFIC PERSON: Is Grandmother going?

AFTER A POSSESSIVE NOUN: I helped Linda's aunt.

AFTER A POSSESSIVE PRONOUN: Your uncle is wonderful.

EXERCISE B: Using Capitals for Family Titles. Complete each of the following sentences by filling the blank with a family title or a title with a name.

Answers will vary; samples given.

EXAMPLE: Please, ___________,send more pineapples.

Please, Grandfather, send more pineapples.

1. My ___aunt___ likes to spend her spare time working on our car.
2. While the rest of us danced, ___Grandpa___ played the fiddle.
3. His ___brother___ is now on the junior varsity soccer team.
4. "Come quickly, ___Mom___!" Cindy cried.
5. Their ___aunt___ knits sweaters for all the children.
6. Few people are as widely traveled as Randy's ___father___.
7. "Let me tell you, ___Grandma___, about that fish I almost caught," he said.
8. Before the race began, ___Uncle Jay___ tried to remain calm.
9. I told Jill's ___mother___ that we would be home later than usual.

10. Slowly ___Dad___ began to shovel a path through the deep snow.

APPLICATION: Using Capitals for Titles of People. Write ten sentences of your own, using in each sentence one title as described in the following items. Be sure to capitalize correctly.

Answers will vary; samples given for first two.

EXAMPLE: A family member's title and name

We will visit Aunt Roberta this summer.

1. The group will be addressed by Doctor Jonas Bower.

1. A business or professional title and a specific name
2. A government title and a specific name
3. An English monarch's title
4. A military title and a specific name
5. A family member's title used in direct address
6. A reference to the President of the United States
7. A family member's title used with a possessive pronoun
8. A social title and a specific name
9. A government title not followed by a specific name
10. A family member's title used with a possessive noun

2. Senator Smith voted for the bill.

Capitals for Titles of Things 16.5

Titles of certain things must also be capitalized.

Works of Art

Works of art cover a variety of items, including written, printed, sung, drawn, painted, or sculpted materials. The titles of works of art should be capitalized properly.

Capitalize the first word and all other important words in the titles of books, periodicals, poems, stories, plays, paintings, and other works of art.

All the words in a title should be capitalized except for articles *(a, an, the)* and conjunctions and prepositions of fewer than five letters. These words should be capitalized only when they are used as the first word of a title.

Notice the use of underlining and quotation marks in the following examples. See Section 18.7 for more information on the punctuation of these titles.

BOOK: The Red Pony

PERIODICAL: National Geographic

POEM: "Stopping by Woods on a Snowy Evening"

SHORT STORY: "The Gold Bug"

PAINTING: A Girl with a Watering Can

EXERCISE A: Using Capitals for Works of Art. Rewrite each of the following titles, adding the missing capitals. Use underlining and quotation marks as shown.
Underlined letters are to be capitalized.
EXAMPLE: rose in bloom

Rose in Bloom

1. as you like it
2. the call of the wild
3. "jabberwocky"
4. better homes and gardens
5. tales of a wayside inn
6. the mystery of the old clock
7. field and stream
8. the old man and the sea
9. "the ransom of red chief"
10. in the rain

School Courses

Sometimes titles of school courses are capitalized, and sometimes they are not. Titles of courses should be capitalized according to the following rule.

Capitalize titles of courses when the courses are language courses or when the courses are followed by a number.

EXAMPLE: My schedule includes Latin, English, and Science 101.

Although languages are always capitalized, other school subjects should not be capitalized when discussed in a general manner.

EXAMPLE: This semester I will study typing, algebra, and Spanish.

EXERCISE B: Using Capitals for Courses. For each of the following, choose the correctly written course title from the choices in parentheses and write it on your paper.

EXAMPLE: My most difficult course is (german, German).

German

1. I signed up for Miss Albee's (earth science 201, Earth Science 201).
2. Susan is glad that she took an extra course in (math, Math).
3. In (english, English) we are studying lyric poetry.
4. The most popular elective course in our school is (cooking, Cooking).
5. Dennis found that (algebra I, Algebra I) was easier than he had thought.

APPLICATION: Using Capitals for Titles of Things. Copy each of the following sentences onto your paper, supplying a title as directed in parentheses. Use underlining and quotation marks as shown and be sure to capitalize correctly. *Answers will vary; samples given.*

EXAMPLE: (Play title) is my favorite play.

The King and I is my favorite play.

1. Linda tried to read (book title) as the bus sped along the highway. *The Pearl*
2. Our local theater company presented (play title) last Saturday night. *Our Town*
3. Branden passed (course title) after getting a tutor's help. Geometry 1
4. To read the short story ("short story title") takes only a few minutes. "A Day's Wait"
5. I usually read every issue of (magazine title). *Newsweek*

16.6 Capitals in Letters

An additional rule applies specifically to the special parts of letters.

Capitalize the first word and all nouns in letter salutations and the first word in letter closings.

SALUTATIONS: Dear Mr. Perkins: Dear Aunt Maude,
My dear Friends,

CLOSINGS: Sincerely yours, Yours truly,
Affectionately,

EXERCISE A: Using Capitals for Letter Salutations and Closings. Rewrite each of the following letter parts, adding the missing capitals.
Underlined letters are to be capitalized.

EXAMPLE: dear cousin jo,
Dear Cousin Jo,

1. my dear anna and fred,
2. dear family,
3. dear sir or madam:
4. with deepest regret,
5. respectfully yours,

APPLICATION: Using Capitals in Letters. Write a brief letter inviting a friend to a party. Use a salutation and closing that are different from the ones in the previous exercise. Be sure to capitalize correctly throughout the letter. *Answers will vary; sample given on page T-124.*

Chapter 17

Using Abbreviations

Most *abbreviations* are formed by using the first letter of a word along with a few other important letters in the word.

To **abbreviate** means to shorten an existing word or phrase.

Abbreviations can be valuable tools in writing if you know when and how to use them. Most abbreviations should not be used in formal writing. However, they can be very helpful in informal writing situations—when you are taking notes or writing lists, for example. Moreover, a few abbreviations can help you save time in any writing situation.

Abbreviations of Titles of People 17.1

Perhaps the most common abbreviations are those used with names.

Social Titles

Mr. and *Mrs.* are the most familiar of the abbreviations used for social titles.

Abbreviations of social titles before a proper name begin with a capital letter and end with a period. They can be used in any type of writing.

SOCIAL TITLES: Mr.

Mrs. or Mme. (Madame)

Messrs. (plural of Mr.)

Mmes. (plural of Mrs. and Mme.)

EXAMPLES: Mr. Comstock sells furniture as a second job.

Mrs. Ridley made an appointment with the firm's auditors.

NOTE ABOUT MISS AND MS.: *Miss* and the plural form *Misses* are social titles used before the names of single women. They are not abbreviations and are not punctuated with a period. The title *Ms.* can be used before the name of a single or a married woman. Although *Ms.* is not the abbreviation of another word, it is followed by a period.

EXAMPLES: Miss Kelly requested a leave of absence.

His question was answered by Ms. Hartley.

EXERCISE A: Using Abbreviations of Social Titles. Copy the following sentences onto your paper, adding an abbreviation of an appropriate social title or the word *Miss, Misses,* or *Ms.* before each name or pair of names. Use at least five different abbreviations.

Answers will vary; samples given.

EXAMPLE: The law firm was owned by ________ Ryan and James.

The law firm was owned by Messrs. Ryan and James.

1. ___*Mme.*___ Zola modeled the designer's new line.
2. ___*Mr.*___ York claims that his parking ticket was not deserved.
3. No one had foreseen ___*Miss*___ Clark's reaction.
4. ___*Misses*___ Black and Haynes wore identical costumes to the masquerade party.
5. My teacher, ___*Mr.*___ Cole, assigns homework every night.

6. A solution to the problem was suggested by Messrs. O'Keefe and Martinez.
7. We asked Misses Dennison and D'Anastasio to lead the hike.
8. The jury waited for Ms. Thomas to present the evidence.
9. Messrs. Wheeler and Pine have both worked as foreign correspondents.
10. Even as an experienced secretary, Mrs. Hawkins was dismayed by the stack of papers on the desk.

Other Titles

Many other titles can be written before a name to identify a person's business or profession.

Abbreviations of other titles used before proper names also begin with a capital letter and end with a period. These abbreviations are used less often in formal writing.

The following chart shows some abbreviations of governmental, military, and professional titles commonly used before names.

ABBREVIATIONS OF COMMON TITLES BEFORE NAMES					
Governmental		**Military**		**Professional**	
Supt.	Superintendent	Pvt.	Private	Dr.	Doctor
Rep.	Representative	Sgt.	Sergeant	Atty.	Attorney
Sen.	Senator	Lt.	Lieutenant	Prof.	Professor
Gov.	Governor	Capt.	Captain	Hon.	Honorable
Treas.	Treasurer	Lt. Col.	Lieutenant Colonel	Rev.	Reverend
Sec.	Secretary	Maj. Gen.	Major General	Fr.	Father
Amb.	Ambassador	Ens.	Ensign	Sr.	Sister
Pres.	President	Adm.	Admiral	Br.	Brother

In most formal writing, these titles should be spelled out, especially when only the last name is written.

EXAMPLES: Governor Herrick was reelected twice.

Captain Bixby inspected the ship carefully.

The parish appreciated Father Perry's dedication.

In certain cases it is acceptable to use the abbreviated forms. *Dr.* may be used in formal writing if it comes before a proper name. Nonreligious titles may also be abbreviated if they are used along with a person's first name or initials.

EXAMPLES: Dr. Fenson was still on duty in the emergency room.

Prof. Mariana Peres requested several books at the library.

Sometimes the abbreviation of a title appears after a name.

Abbreviations of titles after a name start with a capital letter and end with a period. They can be used in any type of writing.

The following chart shows abbreviations of titles that come after names.

ABBREVIATIONS OF COMMON TITLES AFTER NAMES			
Social		**Professional**	
Jr.	Junior	D.D.S.	Doctor of Dental Surgery
Sr.	Senior	M.D.	Doctor of Medicine
		Ph.D.	Doctor of Philosophy
		R.N.	Registered Nurse

Notice that when an abbreviation is written after a name within a sentence, a comma is placed before and after the abbreviation. When an abbreviated title occurs at the end of a sentence, only the comma before the abbreviation is used.

EXAMPLES: Anthony Petri, Jr., attends Brighton Academy.

The psychology course will be taught by Eleanor Adams, Ph.D.

EXERCISE B: Using Abbreviations of Other Titles. Copy the following sentences onto your paper, using the abbreviated form of each of the titles.

EXAMPLE: The missing clue was found by Professor Ashley Crewes.

The missing clue was found by Prof. Ashley Crewes.

1. A sign on the door read, "Jacqueline Bartley, Doctor of Dental Surgery." *D.D.S.*
2. Jacob Schmidt, Doctor of Philosophy, teaches at the local college. *Ph.D.*
3. Lieutenant Daisy Murphy prepared her locker for inspection. *Lt.*
4. Arthur Schlesinger, Junior, is a well-known expert in U.S. history. *Jr.*
5. Ambassador Sidney Rochester joined the speakers at the convention. *Amb.*
6. Our town's pediatrician, Doctor Whitaker, actually makes house calls. *Dr.*
7. The jury listened carefully as Attorney Arlene Clemens questioned the witness. *Atty.*
8. Professor William Anderson polished his glasses as he spoke to the class. *Prof.*
9. Janice Summers, Registered Nurse, discussed career opportunities with the students. *R.N.*
10. The club members waited until Secretary Chris Morganthal read the minutes. *Sec.*

APPLICATION: Using Abbreviations of Titles Correctly. Write a sentence for each of the following, correctly using an abbreviation of each of the titles described. Follow the rules for formal writing.

Answers will vary; samples given for first two.

EXAMPLE: A man who has the same name as his father

Percy Bysshe McCoy, Jr., always used his initials when signing his name.

1. I saw Mrs. Bernstein in the supermarket today.

1. A married woman
2. A club treasurer
3. A registered nurse
4. A man
5. A colonel
6. An ambassador
7. A lawyer
8. Two men
9. A medical doctor
10. Three married women

2. We listened to Treas. Robert Clark discuss our deficit.

17.2 Abbreviations for Time and Historical Dates

Abbreviations for time and historical dates are found in all types of writing.

Time

Abbreviations are used to express time before noon and after noon.

For abbreviations of time before noon and after noon, either capital letters followed by periods or small letters followed by periods are acceptable. These abbreviations can be used in any type of writing.

ABBREVIATIONS: A.M. *or* a.m. *(ante meridiem,* before noon)

P.M. *or* p.m. *(post meridiem,* after noon)

These abbreviations should only be used with numerals.

WITH NUMERALS: The first earthquake tremor registered at 7:20 a.m.

By 1:00 P.M. the train had crossed the Canadian border.

WITHOUT NUMERALS: At six o'clock each day, my family sits down to dinner.

EXERCISE A: Using Abbreviations of Time. From the words given in parentheses, choose the abbreviation or phrase that correctly expresses time in each of the following sentences and write it on your paper.

EXAMPLE: When going fishing, he always gets up at 4:30 (in the morning, A.M.).

A.M.

1. If we leave now, we can see the 7:30 (in the afternoon, P.M.) show.
2. The police sergeant arrived at his desk at five o'clock (in the morning, A.M.).
3. Set your alarm clock for 7:30 (in the morning, A.M.) if you plan to be on time.
4. The cafeteria will be open until three o'clock (in the morning, a.m.).
5. June punched her time card at exactly three o'clock (in the afternoon, P.M.).

■ Dates

Abbreviations can also be used to express historical dates before and after the birth of Christ.

Abbreviations for historical dates before and after the birth of Christ require capital letters followed by periods. They can be used in any type of writing.

ABBREVIATIONS: B.C. (before Christ)

A.D. (*anno Domini,* in the year of the Lord)

Use B.C. and A.D. with numerals that express the year. B.C. always follows the number. A.D. may be written after or before the number.

EXAMPLES: Alexander conquered Babylon in 331 B.C.

The death of Ptolemy in 180 A.D. halted the progress of astronomy for a time.

The Empress Theodora died in A.D. 548.

EXERCISE B: Using Abbreviations of Historical Dates. Copy the following sentences onto your paper, writing the abbreviated form for each historical date given in parentheses. *Numbers and abbreviations given.*

EXAMPLE: According to one historian, Rome was founded in (753 before Christ).

According to one historian, Rome was founded in 753 B.C.

1. The Greek philosopher Socrates died in (399 before Christ). *399 B.C.*
2. Eleanor of Aquitaine, queen of both France and England, died in (1204 in the year of the Lord).
3. In (1000 in the year of the Lord), Leif Ericsson is said to have landed on the coast of America.
4. Hannibal crossed the Alps in (218 before Christ).
5. The ancient city of Pompeii was buried in (79 in the year of the Lord). *79 A.D. or A.D. 79*

2. 1204 A.D. or A.D. 1204 3. 1000 A.D. or A.D. 1000 4. 218 B.C.

APPLICATION: Using Abbreviations of Time and Dates. Write a sentence for each of the following items, including an abbreviation of the indicated time or date and using the information given in parentheses.
Numbers and abbreviations given.

EXAMPLE: eleven o'clock before noon (the British often have a coffee break)

At 11:00 A.M. the British often have a coffee break.

1. 1603 in the year of the Lord (Elizabeth I ended a reign of forty-five years) *1603 A.D. or A.D. 1603*
2. 214 before Christ (the Great Wall of China was begun) *214 B.C.*
3. two o'clock after noon (sirens summoned volunteer firefighters) *2:00 P.M. or p.m.*
4. 54 before Christ (Julius Caesar invaded Britain)
5. six o'clock after noon (newscasters described a local water shortage) *6:00 P.M. or p.m.*
6. fifteen minutes past eight o'clock after noon (the baseball game was cancelled) *8:15 P.M. or p.m.*

4. 54 B.C.

7. 1431 in the year of the Lord (Joan of Arc died)
8. seven o'clock before noon (an airplane made an emergency landing) *7:00 A.M. or a.m.*
9. 1215 in the year of the Lord (the Magna Charta was written) *1215 A.D. or A.D. 1215*
10. ten o'clock before noon (the crafts fair started)

7. 1431 A.D. or A.D. 1431 *10. 10:00 A.M. or a.m.*

Geographical Abbreviations 17.3

Geographical terms and locations are often used in informal writing, such as notes and lists, and in addressing envelopes.

Abbreviations for geographical terms before or after a proper noun begin with a capital letter and end with a period. They are seldom used in formal writing.

The following chart shows some of the most commonly used of these abbreviations.

ABBREVIATIONS OF GEOGRAPHICAL TERMS					
Ave.	Avenue	Ft.	Fort	Prov.	Province
Bldg.	Building	Hwy.	Highway	Pt.	Point
Blk.	Block	Is.	Island	Rd.	Road
Blvd.	Boulevard	Mt.	Mountain	Rte.	Route
Co.	County	Natl.	National	Sq.	Square
Dist.	District	Pen.	Peninsula	St.	Street
Dr.	Drive	Pk.	Park, Peak	Terr.	Territory

Each of the fifty states may also be abbreviated.

Traditional abbreviations for states begin with a capital letter and end with a period. They are seldom used in formal writing.

The following chart shows these abbreviations.

TRADITIONAL ABBREVIATIONS FOR STATES					
Ala.	Alabama	Me.	Maine	Okla.	Oklahoma
Alaska	Alaska	Md.	Maryland	Ore.	Oregon
Ariz.	Arizona	Mass.	Massachusetts	Pa.	Pennsylvania
Ark.	Arkansas	Mich.	Michigan	R.I.	Rhode Island
Calif.	California	Minn.	Minnesota	S.C.	South Carolina
Colo.	Colorado	Miss.	Mississippi	S. Dak.	South Dakota
Conn.	Connecticut	Mo.	Missouri	Tenn.	Tennessee
Del.	Delaware	Mont.	Montana	Tex.	Texas
Fla.	Florida	Nebr.	Nebraska	Utah	Utah
Ga.	Georgia	Nev.	Nevada	Vt.	Vermont
Hawaii	Hawaii	N.H.	New Hampshire	Va.	Virginia
Ida.	Idaho	N.J.	New Jersey	Wash.	Washington
Ill.	Illinois	N. Mex.	New Mexico	W. Va.	West Virginia
Ind.	Indiana	N.Y.	New York	Wis.	Wisconsin
Iowa	Iowa	N.C.	North Carolina	Wyo.	Wyoming
Kans.	Kansas	N. Dak.	North Dakota		
Ky.	Kentucky	O.	Ohio		
La.	Louisiana				

The traditional abbreviation for the District of Columbia is D.C. Use the traditional abbreviation in formal writing whenever the abbreviation follows the word *Washington*.

EXAMPLE: We visited Washington, D.C., on our class trip last spring.

In 1963 the Postal Service introduced a new set of abbreviations for state names.

The official Postal Service abbreviations for states require capital letters with no periods. They are generally not used in formal writing.

The Postal Service prefers that you use these abbreviations when you address envelopes or packages for mailing.

OFFICIAL POSTAL SERVICE ABBREVIATIONS

AL	Alabama	ME	Maine	OK	Oklahoma
AK	Alaska	MD	Maryland	OR	Oregon
AZ	Arizona	MA	Massachusetts	PA	Pennsylvania
AR	Arkansas	MI	Michigan	RI	Rhode Island
CA	California	MN	Minnesota	SC	South Carolina
CO	Colorado	MS	Mississippi	SD	South Dakota
CT	Connecticut	MO	Missouri	TN	Tennessee
DE	Delaware	MT	Montana	TX	Texas
FL	Florida	NB	Nebraska	UT	Utah
GA	Georgia	NV	Nevada	VT	Vermont
HI	Hawaii	NH	New Hampshire	VA	Virginia
ID	Idaho	NJ	New Jersey	WA	Washington
IL	Illinois	NM	New Mexico	WV	West Virginia
IN	Indiana	NY	New York	WI	Wisconsin
IA	Iowa	NC	North Carolina	WY	Wyoming
KS	Kansas	ND	North Dakota		
KY	Kentucky	OH	Ohio		
LA	Louisiana				

The Postal Service abbreviation for the District of Columbia is DC.

EXERCISE A: Recognizing Geographical Abbreviations. On your paper write the traditional abbreviations for the geographical terms given in parentheses in each of the following sentences.

EXAMPLE: In April they will move from Johnson (Street) to Hastings (Boulevard).

St. Blvd.

1. The correct address is this: 49 Wilmot (Avenue), Dorchester, (Nebraska). *Ave./Nebr.*
2. Few people have registered to vote in (District) 6 of Tompkins (County). *Dist./Co.*
3. Follow (Route) 75 northwest until it crosses the (Tennessee) border. *Rte./Tenn.*

4. Sandy's brother is stationed at (Fort) Wayne. Ft.
5. We visited Dinosaur (National) Monument, (Colorado). Natl./Colo.
6. (Mount) Fuji erupted with sudden force. Mt.
7. We passed through Sullivan (County) on our way to the cabin. Co.
8. Remember this address: 16 Chamblee (Drive), Decatur, (Alabama). Dr./Ala.
9. Chincoteague (Island) is off the coast of (Maryland).
10. Alberta (Province) in Canada is north of (Montana).

9. Is./Md. 10. Prov./Mont.

APPLICATION: Understanding Geographical Abbreviations. On your paper write ten sentences, each using the word that one of the following abbreviations stands for.

Sentences will vary; words abbreviations stand for are given.

EXAMPLE: Hwy.

The bank robbers sped along Highway 66.

1. UT	3. Me.	5. Natl.	7. Pk.	9. CA
2. Sq.	4. Blvd.	6. Okla.	8. Co.	10. Rd.

1. Utah 2. Square 3. Maine 4. Boulevard 5. National 6. Oklahoma 7. Park or Peak 8. County 9. California 10. Road

17.4 Abbreviations of Measurements

Using abbreviations for measurements makes technical writing easier.

Traditional Measurements

Periods are used with traditional measurements.

With traditional measurements use small letters and periods to form the abbreviations. These abbreviations are not used in formal writing except with numerals.

The following chart shows examples of these abbreviations. Notice that the *F.* for *Fahrenheit* is an exception to the rule about small letters.

TRADITIONAL MEASUREMENTS					
in.	inch(es)	tsp.	teaspoon(s)	pt.	pint(s)
ft.	foot; feet	tbsp.	tablespoon(s)	qt.	quart(s)
yd.	yard(s)	oz.	ounce(s)	gal.	gallon(s)
mi.	mile(s)	lb.	pound(s)	F.	Fahrenheit

WITHOUT ABBREVIATION: The ball missed by eleven inches.

WITH ABBREVIATION: The ball missed by 11 in.

EXERCISE A: Using Abbreviations of Traditional Measurements. On your paper write the abbreviations for the traditional measurements that are underlined in each of the following sentences.

EXAMPLE: The baby weighed six pounds, four ounces.

6 lb. 4 oz.

1. Bought separately, four quarts of ice cream cost more than one gallon. *4 qt./1 gal.*
2. Johanna is five feet, four inches tall. *5 ft./4 in.*
3. Beat one teaspoon of vanilla into one pint of cream. *1 tsp./1 pt.*
4. This week I lost two pounds, eight ounces. *2 lb./8 oz.*
5. Sam said that the hundred yards he ran seemed like five miles. *100 yd./5 mi.*

Metric Measurements

Abbreviations of metric measurements do not require periods.

With metric measurements use small letters and no periods to form the abbreviations. These abbreviations are not used in formal writing except with numerals.

Notice in the following chart that the abbreviations of *liter* and *Celsius* are exceptions to the small letter rule.

METRIC MEASUREMENTS					
g	gram(s)	mm	millimeter(s)	L	liter
kg	kilogram(s)	cm	centimeter(s)	C	Celsius
		m	meter(s)		
		km	kilometer(s)		

WITHOUT ABBREVIATION: Last night the temperature was zero degrees Celsius.

WITH ABBREVIATION: Last night the temperature was 0°C.

EXERCISE B: Using Abbreviations of Metric Measurements. On your paper write the abbreviation for the metric measurement that is underlined in each of the following sentences.

EXAMPLE: We traveled only forty-two kilometers that day.

42 km

1 mm 1. Bob joked that he grew only one millimeter a year.
2. As a fashion model, Esther keeps her weight at fifty kilograms. *50 kg*
3. The average body temperature is thirty-seven degrees Celsius. *37 °C*
3 cm 4. Most paper clips are about three centimeters long.
5. Did you know that a dollar bill weighs about one gram? *1g*

APPLICATION: Using Abbreviations of Traditional and Metric Measurements. On your paper write ten sentences, each using one of the following measurements and measurement abbreviations.
Answers will vary; samples given for first two.

EXAMPLE: F.

His favorite temperature is 78°F.

1. We bought several pints of milk. 2. Water boils at 100 °C.

1. pints
2. C
3. kilogram
4. oz.
5. gal.
6. meters
7. ft.
8. mm
9. lb.
10. grams

Chapter 18

Using Punctuation Marks

Punctuation marks in sentences act as signals to direct readers. Punctuation marks tell readers when they should pause or stop, when they should read with a questioning tone, and when they should read with excitement. Punctuation marks may also be used to show the relationship between ideas, by connecting the ideas or by setting them apart.

Punctuation is a commonly accepted set of symbols used in writing to convey specific directions to the reader.

The following chart shows the most commonly used punctuation marks.

COMMON PUNCTUATION MARKS			
period	.	colon	:
question mark	?	quotation marks	" "
exclamation mark	!	hyphen	-
comma	,	apostrophe	'
semicolon	;		

This chapter will help you become more familiar with these punctuation marks and the rules for using them. Using these marks effectively can improve the clarity and flow of your writing.

18.1 End Marks

End marks signal the end or conclusion of a sentence, word, or phrase.

There are three **end marks:** the **period** (.), the **question mark** (?), and the **exclamation mark** (!). They usually indicate the end of a sentence.

Uses of the Period

The *period* is the most frequently used of all the end marks. The following rules explain its use.

Use a period to end a declarative sentence, that is, to end a statement of fact or opinion.

STATEMENT OF FACT: Monticello was Thomas Jefferson's home.

STATEMENT OF OPINION: I believe that we can be optimistic.

A period is also used for imperative sentences.

Use a period to end an imperative sentence, that is, to end a direction or command.

DIRECTION: Turn left at the next intersection.

COMMAND: Come here.

Sometimes a declarative sentence contains an indirect question. An indirect question is one that needs no response.

Use a period to end an indirect question.

INDIRECT QUESTION: Jackie asked what time it was.

The period is also used with many abbreviations.

Use a period to end most abbreviations.

Although some abbreviations do not end in periods, most do.

INITIALS: L. J. Fergusson

TITLES: Mr. Mrs. Dr. Gen.

PLACE NAMES: St. Mt. Calif. Mass.

When a sentence ends with an abbreviation that makes use of a period, it is not necessary to put a second period at the end.

EXAMPLE: The person she called on was Arthur Jones, Jr.

EXERCISE A: Using the Period. The following sentences do not have periods. Copy each of the sentences onto your paper, adding periods as needed.

EXAMPLE: Jacob Jones, Sr, was not pleased when his son ran off to join the circus

Jacobs Jones, Sr., was not pleased when his son ran off to join the circus.

1. Straighten your tie and comb your hair
2. I think Mrs Berg gave the message to her son, Chris Berg, Jr
3. Sgt S P Casey wrote the ticket that Mr Gillespie received
4. Fill out the form and sign it at the bottom
5. Dr Birch asked me if Sally Ryan, R N , works at the hospital

Uses of the Question Mark

An interrogative sentence, which asks a question requiring an answer, ends with a *question mark.*

Use a question mark to end an interrogative sentence, that is, to end a direct question.

INTERROGATIVE SENTENCES: Where are you staying in Florida?

Was there a valid reason for her absence?

Do not confuse an interrogative sentence, which is a direct question, with an indirect question. An indirect question requires no answer and should end with a period.

Sometimes a single word or phrase is used to ask a question.

Use a question mark to end an incomplete question in which the rest of the question is understood.

EXAMPLE: Of course, I will meet you. When?

A question that shows surprise is sometimes phrased as a declarative sentence. Use a question mark to indicate that the sentence is a question.

Use a question mark to end a statement that is intended as a question.

EXAMPLES: There is no electricity?

You invited him for dinner?

EXERCISE B: Using the Question Mark. The following sentences do not have end marks. Some sentences are direct questions requiring question marks. Others are indirect questions requiring periods. Still others are statements intended as questions. Copy each of the sentences onto your paper, adding the correct punctuation mark.

EXAMPLE: She wondered if she would ever be famous

She wondered if she would ever be famous.

1. How many people attended the play the first night ? The second night ?
2. I wondered why my car would not start .

3. You lost the money I gave you for the tickets to the concert?
4. The students asked if any more assemblies were scheduled.
5. Who developed a successful vaccine for smallpox? When?
6. The children asked whether any refreshments would be served.
7. Which planet is the red one?
8. A stork built its nest on your chimney?
9. Would you repeat that?
10. The puppy scratched you?

■ Uses of the Exclamation Mark

The *exclamation mark* is used to indicate strong emotions such as anger or amazement.

Use an exclamation mark to end an exclamatory sentence, that is, to end a statement showing strong emotion.

EXAMPLES: I finally understand the problem!

That was a terrifying experience!

The exclamation mark may also be used to end an urgent imperative sentence.

Use an exclamation mark after an imperative sentence if the command is urgent and forceful.

EXAMPLE: Run for your life!

In addition, an exclamation mark often follows an interjection.

Use an exclamation mark after an interjection expressing strong emotion.

EXAMPLE: Oh! You've ruined the surprise.

NOTE ABOUT USING EXCLAMATION MARKS: Exclamation marks should not be used too often. Overusing them makes writing too emotional and less effective.

OVERUSED: I made brownies for dessert! They are made with semisweet chocolate, walnuts, and other rich ingredients! You will never taste better brownies!

CORRECT: I made brownies for dessert. They are made with semisweet chocolate, walnuts, and other rich ingredients. You will never taste better brownies!

EXERCISE C: Using the Exclamation Mark. Exclamation marks have been left out of each of the following items. Copy the items onto your paper, adding exclamation marks as needed. Then identify each item that required an exclamation mark as an *exclamatory sentence*, an *imperative sentence*, or an *interjection*.

EXAMPLE: Watch out

Watch out! imperative sentence

1. Surprise! We tricked you. *interject*
2. We broke the record for having the most people in a telephone booth! *exclam*
3. That's impossible! *exclam*
4. Don't touch! Those vases are priceless. *imper*
5. If only I could remember! *exclam*
6. Well! This is a deliberate insult. *interject*
7. He repaired the television in less than five minutes! *exclam*
8. I haven't eaten since yesterday! *exclam*
9. Foul! That was a double dribble. *interject*
10. Stop dragging your feet! *imper*

APPLICATION: Using End Marks Correctly in Sentences. On your paper write ten original sentences according to the following instructions. Be sure to use the correct end marks for the sentences, words, or phrases that require them.

Answers will vary; samples given for first two.

EXAMPLE: Write a sentence beginning with an interjection.

Wow! That's more what I had in mind.

1. We went to a movie last night. 2. I thought the movie was very funny.

1. Write a statement of fact.
2. Write a statement of opinion.
3. Write a declarative sentence followed by an interjection.
4. Write a direction.
5. Write a command.
6. Write an indirect question.
7. Write a declarative sentence containing the initials of a person's name.
8. Write a statement intended as a question.
9. Write an exclamatory sentence followed by an incomplete question.
10. Write an urgent command.

Commas That Separate Basic Elements 18.2

A *comma* (,) in a sentence signals the reader to pause briefly. Many writers tend either to neglect commas or to overuse them. If you use a comma only when you have a specific rule in mind, your writing will be smoother and clearer.

Generally, commas function in one of two ways: (1) to *separate* items, such as two independent clauses, from each other or (2) to *set off* items, such as introductory words, from the rest of the sentence. This section shows you how to use commas to *separate* items from each other.

Commas with Compound Sentences

A compound sentence consists of two or more independent clauses that are joined by a coordinating conjunction. Coordinating conjunctions include *and, but, for, nor, or, so,* and *yet.*

Use a comma before the conjunction to separate two independent clauses in a compound sentence.

COMPOUND SENTENCES: I filled my canteen with fresh spring water, and we began the long hike back to town.

Storm clouds were gathering overhead, so the children brought their kites inside.

Use a comma before a conjunction only when there are complete sentences on both sides of the conjunction. Do not use a comma before a conjunction when a word, phrase, or subordinate clause appears on either side of the conjunction.

WORDS: *Glue* or *tape* will hold the sign in place.

PHRASES: We could go *to the movies* or *for a walk.*

SUBORDINATE CLAUSES: Try to buy a car *that has low mileage* and *that is in good condition.*

Sometimes the independent clauses in a compound sentence are so short and their meaning so clear that the comma may be left out.

EXAMPLE: Adam tried to speak but he could not.

EXERCISE A: Using Commas with Compound Sentences. Commas have been left out of the following compound sentences. Read each sentence and decide where the comma goes. On your paper write the word before the comma, the comma, and the conjunction following the comma.

EXAMPLE: She was tired yet she was determined to finish the race.

tired, yet

1. The sheep bleated fearfully, but the shears never cut their skin.

2. The freshly painted walls and newly waxed floors made the apartment pleasant, yet major repairs were still needed.
3. Sarah is inclined to exaggerate, but her stories are usually entertaining.
4. Mr. Klein's kitchen has been remodeled, and it now contains many modern conveniences.
5. There were no trees growing on the desert island, nor was there any water.
6. We could hear music blaring inside the house, but no one answered when we knocked.
7. Tom had mixed peat moss with the soil, and Eliza had trimmed some of the branches.
8. Wind rattled the windows of the cabin, yet the campers slept soundly.
9. She was forced to dismount, for her horse could no longer carry her.
10. Many people have reptiles as pets, but few of them know how to care for reptiles properly.

Commas Between Items in a Series

A series consists of three or more similar items.

Use commas to separate three or more words, phrases, or clauses in a series.

Notice that the number of commas used is one fewer than the number of items in the series. For example, in the first of the following sentences, *four* items in a series are separated by *three* commas.

SERIES OF WORDS: The buffet included *turkey, ham, roast beef,* and *lamb.*

SERIES OF PHRASES: The treasure map directed them *through the woods, over the mountain,* and *past the bridge.*

SERIES OF CLAUSES: The house was rather quiet *before she arrived, before her luggage was piled up in the hall,* and *before her three poodles took over.*

One exception to the rule for commas with series occurs when each item is joined to the next by a conjunction. In this case no commas are necessary.

EXAMPLE: For this exam you will need two pencils *and* an eraser *and* a slide rule.

A second exception to the rule concerns words that are considered to be one item. Paired words such as *macaroni and cheese* should not be split by a comma.

EXAMPLE: Every table in the diner was set with *a knife and fork, a cup and saucer,* and *salt and pepper*.

EXERCISE B: Using Commas Between Items in a Series. Copy each of the following sentences onto your paper, adding commas as needed.

EXAMPLE: Alex threw back the covers stamped across the room and pounced on the alarm clock.

Alex threw back the covers, stamped across the room, and pounced on the alarm clock.

1. The pioneers crossed deserts, scaled mountains, and forded rivers before they reached the West.
2. Silk, cotton, and wool are natural fibers.
3. I must mow the lawn, trim the hedges, and weed the garden.
4. Studying your notes, listening to directions, and feeling confident can help you do well on the exam.
5. The performers ran off the stage, down the aisles, and through the exit doors.
6. For dinner Lauren wanted spaghetti and meatballs, bread and butter, and ice cream and cake.
7. Becky first requested, then insisted on, and finally pleaded for permission to visit her cousin for the weekend.
8. Bring a wrench, a pair of pliers, and a hammer and nails out to the garage.
9. Elizabeth polished the silverware, set the table, and lit the candles.

10. Ted walked to the end of the diving board, leaped into the air, and dived gracefully into the pool.

Commas Between Adjectives

Sometimes two or more adjectives are placed before the noun they describe. Use the following rule to determine whether to use a comma between them.

Use commas to separate adjectives of *equal rank*.

There are two ways to decide if adjectives are of equal rank. First, if the word *and* can be placed between the adjectives without changing the meaning of the sentence, then the adjectives are of equal rank. Second, if the order of the adjectives can be changed, then they are equal.

After reading the following examples, try both methods for determining whether the adjectives are of equal rank.

EXAMPLES: She left *detailed, precise* instructions for the substitute.

A *smooth, round* stone was cupped in her hand.

As you can see, the adjectives in the examples are equal, and commas are necessary to separate them. Sometimes, however, placing *and* between the adjectives or changing their order can destroy the meaning.

Do not use commas to separate adjectives that must stay in a specific order.

In the following examples, you can see that either adding *and* or changing the order of the adjectives results in sentences that make no sense.

EXAMPLES: *Three brief* paragraphs will be enough.

In a *few short* hours, we will be finished.

NOTE ABOUT COMMAS WITH ADJECTIVES: Never use a comma to separate the last adjective in a series from the noun it modifies.

INCORRECT: A *yellow, long-stemmed,* rose lay on the table.

CORRECT: A *yellow, long-stemmed* rose lay on the table.

EXERCISE C: Using Commas Between Adjectives. In each of the following sentences, two adjectives have been underlined. Copy the adjectives onto your paper, adding commas only where necessary.

EXAMPLE: The two little girls were playing jacks.

two little

1. We noticed an unfamiliar, musky odor inside the cave.
2. Many shallow pools formed on the beach after the light rain.
3. Several faint giggles brought the librarian to his feet.
4. On the door was a heavy, ornate knocker in the shape of a wreath.
5. Slow, steady rowing soon brought the boat to shore.

APPLICATION: Using Commas to Separate Basic Elements in Your Writing. Follow the directions to write five sentences of your own. Use commas only where necessary. *Answers will vary; samples given for first two.*

EXAMPLE: Write a sentence containing a series of clauses.

They finally relaxed when the meal was over, when the guests had left, and when they had cleared the table.

1. We tried repeatedly, yet we couldn't budge the rock.

1. Write a compound sentence using the conjunction *yet* to join two independent clauses.
2. Write a sentence containing a series of at least three nouns.

2. Leroy enjoys only music, art, and English.

3. Write a sentence containing three nouns, each joined to the next by *and*.
4. Write a sentence containing two adjectives of equal rank that modify the same noun.
5. Write a sentence containing two adjectives that belong in a specific order.

Commas That Set Off Added Elements

18.3

In addition to separating similar kinds of words and word groups, such as adjectives or independent clauses, commas are also used to *set off* or isolate certain groups of words that are added to sentences. Included in this category are introductory words and phrases, words and groups of words inserted in the middle or at the end of a sentence, and a few special elements such as dates.

■ Commas After Introductory Material

Commas are often used to set off information at the beginning of a sentence.

Use a comma after an introductory word, phrase, or clause.

As you study the following chart, notice how a comma sets off the introductory word or words in each of the sentences.

KINDS OF INTRODUCTORY MATERIAL	
Introductory Words:	*No,* we don't need any. *Fran,* give me your camera. *Smiling,* the flight attendant greeted the passengers.

Introductory Phrases:	*Inside the warm and comfortable stable,* the calf struggled to its feet. *Shattered into many sharp fragments,* the window was now a hazard. *To succeed in business,* you must have perseverance.
Introductory Adverb Clauses:	*When the huge elm tree became diseased,* we called a tree surgeon. *Although the police responded quickly,* they arrived too late.

An exception is made for short prepositional phrases. If an introductory prepositional phrase is only two or three words long, it generally will not need a comma to set it off.

EXAMPLE: *After the exam* Monica felt relieved.

EXERCISE A: Using Commas After Introductory Material. Each of the following sentences needs a comma to set off introductory material. On your paper write the introductory word or words, the comma, and the word following the comma.

EXAMPLE: To get a better view Fran climbed to the top of the hill.

To get a better view, Fran

1. For better or for worse, we were committed to the task.
2. If you are easily frightened, don't see that movie.
3. Gripping the man's cuff in his jaws, the bulldog braced his legs and pulled.
4. Yes, these plastic treads should make the stairs safer.
5. To calm the jittery horse, Irene stroked its neck and spoke quietly.
6. Please, isn't there any way you could make an exception?

7. Remember, no one is admitted beyond this point.
8. With dry clothing and warm food, the climbers soon recovered.
9. After the brief intermission, we returned to our seats.
10. Marsha and Bill, will you please stop arguing?

Commas with Parenthetical Expressions

A *parenthetical expression* is a word or phrase that is not essential to the meaning of the sentence.

Use commas to set off parenthetical expressions.

Parenthetical expressions usually appear in the middle or at the end of a sentence. A parenthetical expression in the middle of a sentence needs two commas. A parenthetical expression at the end of a sentence needs only one.

The following chart shows some common kinds of parenthetical expressions. Notice that each of the sentences makes sense with or without the parenthetical expression.

KINDS OF PARENTHETICAL EXPRESSIONS	
Names of People Being Addressed:	Listen carefully, *Bob and Lucinda,* while I explain. That's a logical conclusion, *Pete.*
Certain Adverbs:	The other team, *therefore,* won the game. She will not be able to go with us, *however.*
Common Expressions:	The math test, *I think,* will be very difficult. They believe in her ability, *of course.*
Contrasting Expressions:	These apples, *not those,* are ripe enough to use. The decision should be mine, *not yours.*

EXERCISE B: Using Commas with Parenthetical Expressions. Copy each of the following sentences onto your paper, adding commas as needed to set off the parenthetical expressions.

EXAMPLE: Her hope of course was that he would return.

Her hope, of course, was that he would return.

1. Check the yellow pages of the telephone directory, Melissa.
2. Charles, we believe, is the right man for the job.
3. Audrey's hair is black, not red.
4. We assumed, nevertheless, that you would still come to the party.
5. This kitten, however, believes your hen is its mother.
6. If you bring in the painting, Mr. Curtis, we can help you choose a frame.
7. Beth's grades, therefore, need improvement.
8. Hurry up, Armando, or we'll miss our bus.
9. Their younger son, not the older, showed an interest in the family business.
10. Everyone is eagerly anticipating the holiday, of course.

Commas with Nonessential Expressions

Some writers have trouble determining when a phrase or clause should be set off with commas. It helps to know whether the phrase or clause is *essential* or *nonessential* to the meaning of the sentence. Expressions that are essential can not be left out without changing the meaning of the sentence. Expressions that are nonessential are additional phrases or clauses that, in contrast, can be left out.

Use commas to set off nonessential expressions.

The following chart shows examples of essential and nonessential phrases and clauses. Notice that removing an essential expression alters the sentence's meaning; removing a nonessential expression does not.

ESSENTIAL AND NONESSENTIAL EXPRESSIONS	
Appositives and Appositive Phrases	
Essential:	The famous dramatist *Ben Jonson* wrote these comedies.
Nonessential:	Ben Jonson, *a famous dramatist,* wrote these comedies. These comedies were written by Ben Jonson, *a famous dramatist.*
Participial Phrases	
Essential:	The girl *waiting in the car* is my sister.
Nonessential:	My sister, *waiting in the car,* wished we would hurry. The time passed slowly for my sister, *waiting in the car.*
Adjective Clauses	
Essential:	We need someone *who can play a harmonica and a guitar.*
Nonessential:	Bob Dylan, *who can play a harmonica and a guitar,* was applauded enthusiastically. We applauded enthusiastically for Bob Dylan, *who can play a harmonica and a guitar.*

EXERCISE C: Using Commas with Nonessential Expressions. Read each of the following sentences carefully to determine whether the underlined expression is essential or nonessential. If the material is essential, write *E*. If the material is nonessential, copy the sentence onto your paper, adding any commas needed.

EXAMPLE: The New England poet <u>Emily Dickinson</u> lived a very quiet life.

E

1. Our new kittens, who could not find their mother, meowed loudly.
2. Grandmother's old quilt, filled with soft eiderdown, was a family heirloom.
3. My favorite book is a spell-binding story written by the famous author Robert Louis Stevenson. E
4. My favorite author, Robert Louis Stevenson, wrote *Treasure Island.*
5. Only a person who was a genius could have formulated this theory. E
6. Albert Einstein, who was a genius, formulated the theory of relativity.
7. Our school newspaper, published twice a month, won an award.
8. The person wearing a new red coat boarded the plane. E
9. Fred, my younger brother, has just learned to swim.
10. I would like you to meet Miss Jorgenson, my new neighbor.

Commas with Dates and Geographical Names

Dates usually have several parts, such as months, days, and years. Commas prevent such dates from being unclear.

When a date is made up of two or more parts, use a comma after each item except in the case of a month followed by a day.

In the following examples, notice that commas follow most of the words and numbers in the dates. An exception is found in all cases where a month is followed by a day.

EXAMPLES: Saturday, July 20, is their anniversary.

January 1, 1945, was the beginning of an exciting year for my grandfather.

On September 7, 1982, school began.

When dates contain only months and years, commas are optional.

EXAMPLES: Before February 1981 the house had no central heating system.

Before February, 1981, the house had no central heating system.

Geographical names may also consist of more than one part. Again, commas help prevent confusion.

When a geographical name is made up of two or more parts, use a comma after each item.

EXAMPLES: Our neighbors moved from Columbus, Ohio, to Temperance, Michigan.

This cheese was shipped from Montigny, Moselle, France, by my friend Robert.

EXERCISE D: Using Commas with Dates or Geographical Names. Copy each of the following sentences onto your paper, adding commas where they are needed.

EXAMPLE: The new student had come from San Juan Puerto Rico in March.

The new student had come from San Juan, Puerto Rico, in March.

1. On March 15, 1917, the Czar of Russia gave up his throne.
2. The exchange student explained that Nairobi, Kenya, is located almost directly on the Equator.
3. This recipe for clam sauce comes from a restaurant in Milan, Italy.
4. Thursday, March 15, is Lynn's birthday.
5. She will leave for Paris, France, on Monday, October 10.

Other Uses of the Comma

The following rules govern the use of commas in addresses, letter salutations and closings, numbers, and quotations. A final rule concerns using commas to avoid misunderstandings.

The first rule covers commas used in addresses.

Use a comma after each item in an address made up of two or more parts.

As you can see in the following example, commas are placed after the name, street, and city. No comma separates the state from the ZIP code.

EXAMPLE: Write to Maxwell Hunnicutt, 54 Monmouth Avenue, Dallas, Texas 75243.

Fewer commas are needed when an address is written on an envelope.

EXAMPLE: Maxwell Hunnicutt
54 Monmouth Avenue
Dallas, Texas 75243

Letter salutations and closings also make special use of commas.

Use a comma after the salutation in a personal letter and after the closing in all letters.

SALUTATIONS: Dear Bill, My dear Aunt,

CLOSINGS: Sincerely, With best wishes,

Another use of commas is to make it easier to read large numbers.

With numbers of more than three digits, use a comma after every third digit, counting from the right.

EXAMPLES: 1,750 feet 3,608,787 square miles

NOTE ABOUT COMMAS WITH NUMBERS: Do not use commas with ZIP codes, telephone numbers, page numbers, or serial numbers.

ZIP CODE: 14301

TELEPHONE NUMBER: (212) 555-2473

PAGE NUMBER: on page 1022

SERIAL NUMBER: 059 94 6106

Commas can also show where direct quotations begin and end.

Use commas to set off a direct quotation from the rest of a sentence.

As you read the following examples, notice that the correct location of the commas depends upon the "he said/she said" part of the sentence. (See Section 18.6 for more information about the punctuation used with quotations.)

EXAMPLES: Bret said, "Hold the door open."

"I can't," Lorna replied, "because my arms are full of books."

The final rule covers special situations when a comma is needed to avoid confusion.

Use a comma to prevent a sentence from being misunderstood.

Without any commas the following sentences are confusing. The addition of commas keeps the reader from having to puzzle over the meaning.

UNCLEAR: Beyond the mountains were clearly visible.

CLEAR: Beyond, the mountains were clearly visible.

UNCLEAR: After watching Zack asked to join the game.

CLEAR: After watching, Zack asked to join the game.

EXERCISE E: Using Commas in Other Situations. Commas have been left out of the following sentences and groups of words. Copy each item onto your paper, adding commas as needed.

EXAMPLE: There were 1407 people in the audience, all demanding an encore.

There were 1,407 people in the audience, all demanding an encore.

1. Send this postcard to Jimmy Murphy, 509 Cliff Street, Newfield, New York 14867.
2. The Zambian census taken in 1963 indicated a population of 3,405,788 Africans and 84,380 non-Africans.
3. In the spring Mandy planted 3,000 flowers.
4. Arlene advised, "Take the train instead of the bus."
5. While racing, John's dog developed a limp.
6. Maryann's permanent residence is 3 Hill Drive, Apartment 3E, New Milford, Connecticut 06776.
7. Inside, Mr. Martin took off his coat and warmed himself by the fire.
8. "Your request is unreasonable," Barry stated.
9. My dear Patricia, Sincerely,
   Nathaniel
10. "The serial number," said Sue, "is 101 27 304."

APPLICATION: Using Commas to Set Off Added Elements. Write ten original sentences, each containing the material described in the following directions. Use commas when necessary. *Answers will vary; samples given for first two.*

EXAMPLE: Use the word *however.*

Nothing, however, could have pleased them more.

1. The members of our team, listening to the weather report, feared the game would be canceled.

1. Use the phrase *listening to the weather report* as nonessential information.
2. Use the clause *who volunteered* as essential information.
3. Use the word *Oh* at the beginning of a sentence.
4. Indicate the full date, including the day of the week, of your next birthday.
5. Write a direct quotation consisting of one sentence interrupted by *Dennis said.*

2. Everyone who volunteered was given a job.

6. Use your area code and telephone number.
7. Use the expression *not the green one.*
8. Use the phrase *Under the surface of the crystal-clear water* to begin a sentence.
9. Directly address *Cindy,* asking her a question.
10. Use the name and complete address of a friend.

The Semicolon 18.4

The *semicolon* looks like a period above a comma (;). Like the two punctuation marks that make it up, the semicolon indicates a pause in a sentence. However, the semicolon is less final than a period and indicates more of a pause than a comma does.

Two basic functions of the semicolon are (1) to join related independent clauses and (2) to take the place of commas that would cause confusion for the reader.

■ Semicolons Used to Join Independent Clauses

Semicolons are used to join independent clauses only in specific situations.

Use a semicolon to join independent clauses that are *not* already joined by the conjunctions *and, or, nor, for, but, so,* or *yet.*

Two independent clauses joined by a conjunction usually require a comma before the conjunction.

CLAUSES WITH COMMA: Shelly's birthstone is an amethyst, *and* Faith's is an opal.

Sometimes no conjunction is used to join clauses. Then, the semicolon replaces both the comma and the conjunction.

CLAUSES WITH SEMICOLON: Shelly's birthstone is an amethyst; Faith's is an opal.

A semicolon should never be used simply as a shortcut. When two independent clauses are not closely related, a semicolon should not be used. Instead, the clauses should be written as separate sentences.

INCORRECT: The fire began with a casually tossed match; many years must pass before a forest can recover from a fire.

CORRECT: The fire began with a casually tossed match. Many years must pass before a forest can recover from a fire.

The fire began with a casually tossed match; a moment of carelessness resulted in terrible destruction.

When a sentence contains three or more related independent clauses, they may still be separated with semicolons.

EXAMPLE: The birds vanished; the sky grew dark; all was still.

Semicolons are also used when independent clauses are separated by certain special words.

Use a semicolon to join independent clauses separated by either a conjunctive adverb or a transitional expression.

Certain words or phrases—conjunctive adverbs and transitional expressions—establish the relationship between sentence parts.

CONJUNCTIVE ADVERBS: also, besides, furthermore, however, indeed, instead, moreover, nevertheless, otherwise, therefore, thus

TRANSITIONAL EXPRESSIONS: as a result, at this time, consequently, first, for instance, in fact, on the other hand, second, that is

When these words separate two independent clauses, a semicolon generally goes before the conjunctive adverb or transitional expression.

EXAMPLE: We were very impressed with the child's knowledge of science; *indeed,* she was remarkably well-informed.

Remember to place a comma after the conjunctive adverb or transitional expression. The comma sets off the conjunctive adverb or transitional expression, which acts as an introductory expression to the second clause.

EXERCISE A: Using Semicolons to Join Independent Clauses. Semicolons have been left out of the following sentences. Read each sentence and decide where one or more semicolons are required. On your paper write the word before each semicolon, the semicolon, and the word that follows it.

EXAMPLE: I like the color of the leaves in October however, I do not like raking them.

October; however

1. Jeb hurried to finish his project; as a result, his work was slipshod and unacceptable.
2. Some of the volunteers were assigned the task of painting; others were responsible for repairing the playground equipment.
3. Lester sent the hamburger back; it was too rare.
4. The soup was cold; the salad was limp; the chicken was burned.
5. The prairie dog barked a warning; immediately, all the rodents scampered for safety.

6. Marge had a cast on her leg; nevertheless, she was the first one on the dance floor.
7. I expect you to be on time; furthermore, be ready to work hard.
8. Ornamental fans were arranged on the walls; large, comfortable cushions were scattered on the rug.
9. Mrs. Walker forgot to mail the payment; consequently, the electricity was turned off.
10. The fans droned overhead; the temperature rose steadily; the students sat listlessly at their desks.

Semicolons Used to Avoid Confusion

Occasionally a semicolon may be used in place of a comma.

Consider the use of a semicolon to avoid confusion when independent clauses or items in a series already contain commas.

In the following example, there are several commas in the first clause. Adding another comma before the word *but* would create unnecessary confusion for the reader. Therefore, the use of a semicolon is appropriate in this particular sentence.

EXAMPLE: This side of the lake, which has never had any public beaches, has always been a secluded, private retreat for our family; but we will have to abandon it now because of the high taxes.

You may also use a semicolon to separate items in a series when the items already contain a number of commas. The semicolon shows where each *complete* item ends.

EXAMPLE: The waiter brought fresh shrimp, which was heaped on a bed of lettuce; herring, which had been marinated in a sour cream sauce; and soft shell crabs, which were sautéed in lemon and butter.

EXERCISE B: Using Semicolons to Avoid Confusion. Read the following sentences and decide where semicolons should be used instead of commas. Copy each sentence onto your paper, making the necessary corrections.

EXAMPLE: Heather, who was eight, had always loved living in Aspen Park, a suburb of Detroit, but she faced the move without fear.

Heather, who was eight, had always loved living in Aspen Park, a suburb of Detroit; but she faced the move without fear.

1. In a house with poor insulation, heat escapes through the walls and the roof, but adding more insulation can help keep the heat inside and can thus lower fuel bills. *roof; but*
2. This delicatessen, which is only a few blocks away from our house, has delicious roast beef, ham, and corned beef sandwiches, so Jerry and I always come here for lunch. *sandwiches; so*
3. The three puppies that we kept from our poodle's first litter were Coco, a light brown female, Snowflake, a white female, and Tippy, a gray male.
4. Before the town restored this area, the street was lined with neglected homes, but now the houses, each with many rooms, have been remodeled as professional buildings. *homes; but*
5. In our family Christine, who is seventeen, plays the guitar, Julie, who is fifteen, plays the trombone, and Maxine, who is only nine, plays the bassoon. *guitar; Julie/trombone; and*
6. On Fridays and Saturdays, I work as a cashier first, from three-thirty to five o'clock, as a filling station attendant second, from five-thirty to seven o'clock, and as a baby sitter last, from eight o'clock until late in the evening. *o'clock; as/o'clock; and*
7. Jenny, who rarely finds fault with anything, criticized the food, the company, and the entertainment, yet the rest of us were quite content.
8. Even with his help, we had still not addressed all of the envelopes, not even all of those on the first list, and time was running out. *list; and*

3. female; snowflake/female; and 7. entertainment; yet

9. This car needs a new hood, a new grill, and new headlights, but the engine, transmission, and interior are all in excellent condition. *headlights; but*
10. The wagon, sagging and missing a wheel, hardly seemed a bargain for the price, and Jack, disappointed but firm, refused to buy it. *price; and*

APPLICATION: Using Semicolons in Your Writing. Write five original sentences, each using semicolons as indicated in the following directions.

Answers will vary; samples given for first two.

EXAMPLE: Use a semicolon in a sentence with a conjunctive adverb.

The Johnsons were pet lovers; indeed, they had three cats, six dogs, and a dozen hamsters.

1. The wind blew hard; the shutters rattled; the house shook.

1. Use two semicolons to join three independent clauses in the same sentence.
2. Use a semicolon to join two independent clauses separated by *on the other hand.*
3. Use a semicolon with two independent clauses that already contain commas.
4. Use two semicolons in a sentence to separate a series of three items that are already punctuated with commas.
5. Use a semicolon to join two independent clauses not joined by a conjunction.

2. The cake looks good; on the other hand, fruit would be a lighter dessert.

18.5 The Colon

The *colon* looks like one period placed above another (:). This mark directs the reader's attention to the information that comes after it.

The Colon as an Introductory Device

As the following rule shows, one of the most important uses of the colon is to introduce a list of miscellaneous items.

Use a colon before a list of items following an independent clause.

EXAMPLE: His disguise included the following touches: large sunglasses, a black wig, a handlebar mustache, and platform shoes.

Notice that an independent clause comes before the colon. Although it may include words that hint there is more to come, such as *the following,* the clause must make sense by itself. Never use a colon to introduce a list that does not follow an independent clause. A colon should never, for example, separate a verb or a preposition from its object.

INCORRECT: As additions to her spring wardrobe, she purchased: white cotton gloves, a straw hat, and a lightweight coat.

Her new spring wardrobe consisted of: white cotton gloves, a straw hat, and a lightweight coat.

CORRECT: She added three new items to her spring wardrobe: white cotton gloves, a straw hat, and a lightweight coat.

EXERCISE A: Using Colons as Introductory Devices. Colons have been left out of some of the following sentences. Write the word before each missing colon, the colon, and the word following the colon. Write *correct* for any sentence that does not need a colon.

EXAMPLE: José wanted three things a horse, a saddle, and boots.

things: a

1. We finally located several constellations: Orion, Taurus, Pisces, and Virgo.
2. Merry carried the following items on her first day of class: a pencil sharpener, an eraser, a box of crayons, and a lunch box.

3. It was once believed that the universe was made up of four elements: earth, water, air, and fire.
4. My favorite movies include *Star Wars, 2001,* and *Superman.* C
5. The value of our property increased because of several improvements: landscaping the yard, blacktopping the driveway, and insulating the house.

■ Special Uses of the Colon

A colon is frequently used to indicate time with numerals, to end salutations in business letters, and to signal important ideas.

Use a colon in a number of special writing situations.

The following chart shows examples of these special uses of the colon.

SPECIAL USES OF THE COLON	
Numerals Giving the Time:	3:04 P.M. 5:00 a.m.
Salutations in Business Letters:	Gentlemen: Dear Ms. Langly:
Labels Used to Signal Important Ideas:	Warning: If taken internally, consult a physician immediately. Notice: Shop is closed for repairs.

EXERCISE B: Using Colons in Special Situations. Colons have been left out of the following expressions. Copy each item onto your paper, adding colons as needed.

EXAMPLE: Note The beach closes at dusk.

Note: The beach closes at dusk.

1. Dear Colonel Landstrom:
2. 400 A.M.

3. Caution: Proceed at your own risk.
4. Dear Voter:
5. Warning: The Surgeon General has determined that cigarette smoking is dangerous to your health.

APPLICATION: Using Colons in Your Writing. Write five original sentences or examples according to the following directions, using colons as needed.

Answers will vary; samples given for first two.

EXAMPLE: Write a salutation of a business letter.

Dear Senator Craig:

1. There are only three choices on the menu: steak, chicken, and fish.

1. Write a list of items following an independent clause.
2. Write a list of items following a verb.
3. Write a list of items following a preposition.
4. Write a sentence containing a numeral and an abbreviation giving the time.
5. Write a label and an important idea it signals.

2. We visited Seattle, Vancouver, and Calgary.

Quotation Marks with Direct Quotations

18.6

There are many reasons for using quotation marks. Sometimes you may want to show that you are repeating the exact words spoken by a person or printed in a book. At other times, in writing fiction, for example, you may want your characters to reveal themselves in their own words or to show action through dialogue.

Direct and Indirect Quotations

There are two types of quotations: *direct* and *indirect.* A direct quotation requires the use of special punctuation.

A **direct quotation** represents a person's exact speech or thoughts and is enclosed in quotation marks (" ").

EXAMPLES: Margo said, "Let me do it for you."

"Why didn't she call me?" Don wondered.

An indirect quotation, on the other hand, does not need special punctuation.

An **indirect quotation** reports the general meaning of what a person said or thought and does not require quotation marks.

EXAMPLES: Margo said that she would do it for me.

Don wondered why she hadn't called him.

EXERCISE A: Distinguishing Between Direct and Indirect Quotations. Read each of the following sentences carefully to determine whether it contains a direct quotation that requires quotation marks or an indirect quotation. If the sentence contains a direct quotation, write *D* next to the appropriate number on your paper. If it contains an indirect quotation, write *I*.

EXAMPLE: It was the same old story repeating itself, thought Bruce.

D

1. Carol complained that her sister was never on time. *I*
2. I have noticed that, commented Bruce. *D*
3. I wish she would hurry, continued Carol. *D*
4. Bruce thought that the delay might make them miss the movie. *I*
5. He said that they should probably leave without her. *I*
6. Maybe she has a reason, said Carol. *D*
7. I, however, object to the casual way she operates, she added. *D*
8. Beginning to worry, Bruce decided that he should try to remain calm. *I*
9. Let's give her five more minutes, he suggested. *D*
10. That's a good idea, Carol agreed. *D*

Direct Quotations with Introductory, Concluding, and Interrupting Expressions

A writer will generally identify a speaker by using words such as *he asked* or *she said* with a quotation. These expressions can introduce, conclude, or interrupt a quotation. The following rule shows how to punctuate sentences with introductory expressions.

When an introductory expression precedes a direct quotation, place a comma after the introductory expression and write the quotation as a full sentence.

EXAMPLES: The animal trainer explained, "All wild animals should be treated with caution."

Barney asked, "Is it difficult to train a lion to perform?"

When an explanatory expression comes at the end of a direct quotation, the punctuation changes.

When a concluding expression follows a direct quotation, write the quotation as a full sentence ending with a comma, question mark, or exclamation mark inside the quotation mark. Then write the concluding expression.

Notice that the comma in the first of the following examples is placed where a period would usually be appropriate. Since the sentence is not yet complete, the comma signals the reader to pause rather than stop.

EXAMPLES: "That depends on several factors," the trainer replied.

"Could you show us one of your lions?" interrupted Barney.

"Please!" everyone chorused.

Notice also that the concluding expressions do not begin with capitals.

An expression that interrupts a quotation requires twice as many quotation marks.

When the direct quotation of one sentence is interrupted, end the first part of the direct quotation with a comma and a quotation mark. Place a comma after the interrupting expression, and then use a new set of quotation marks to enclose the rest of the quotation.

Each of the following examples consists of *one* sentence. As you study the quotations, pay special attention to these items: (1) the comma inside the quotation mark at the end of the first part of the quotation; (2) the small letter at the beginning of the interrupting expression; (3) the comma inserted after the interrupting expression; (4) the small letter at the beginning of the second part of the quotation; and (5) the end mark inside the last quotation mark.

EXAMPLES: "This," the trainer said, "is Rufus, a lion I trained myself."

"What would he do," asked Corina, "if I tried to touch him?"

Often a quotation consists of two sentences, with a complete sentence on each side of the interrupting expression.

When two sentences in a direct quotation are separated by an interrupting expression, end the first quoted sentence with a comma, question mark, or exclamation mark and a quotation mark. Place a period after the interrupter, and then write the second quoted sentence as a full quotation.

Study the examples that follow and look closely at these items: (1) the varied punctuation at the end of the first quoted sentence; (2) the small letter used at the beginning of the interrupting expression; (3) the period following the interrupting expression; (4) the capital at the beginning of the second quoted sentence; and (5) the end mark inside the last quotation mark.

EXAMPLES: "That would be dangerous," the trainer quickly explained. "Rufus is usually very gentle, but he is not a house cat."

"Did you see those teeth?" asked Mark. "I wouldn't dream of touching him."

EXERCISE B: Using Direct Quotations with Introductory, Concluding, and Interrupting Expressions. The following direct quotations have not been correctly punctuated or capitalized. Copy each of the sentences onto your paper, making the necessary corrections.

Underlined letters are to be capitalized.

EXAMPLE: Elena said we will need at least twelve more

Elena said, "We will need at least twelve more."

1. there will be no exceptions to this rule the teacher announced
2. brian added after the wood is sanded, apply a thin coat of varnish
3. two heads are better than one said Sandra
4. have you ever considered a permanent the hairdresser politely inquired
5. do it now shouted Jake
6. please go ahead said Andy as he examined the broken chain on his bicycle I can't go anywhere until this is repaired
7. i think speculated Denise that his summer job will be a good one
8. repeatedly the young man insisted I must have your answer
9. can't you wait for me shouted Hector from the balcony I'll be ready in two minutes
10. as the fog became thicker, Mother said use your low beams

Quotation Marks with Other Punctuation Marks

Sometimes it may be hard to decide whether to place another punctuation mark inside or outside a quotation mark. You have seen that a comma or period used with a direct quotation goes inside the final quotation mark. In some cases, however, an end mark comes after the quotation mark. The following rules can help you choose the correct placement.

The first rule applies to a quoted declarative sentence.

Always place a comma or a period *inside* the final quotation mark.

EXAMPLES: "This lawn needs attention," Mrs. Finch told her children.

She added, "This looks more like a field than a yard."

Question marks or exclamation marks used with quotation marks can be more confusing. Both the sense of the quotation and the sense of the entire sentence must be considered.

Place a question mark or exclamation mark *inside* the final quotation mark if the end mark is part of the quotation.

The following examples are declarative sentences. The first example contains a quotation that asks a question; the second contains a quotation that shows strong emotion. The end mark in each case depends on the sense of the quotation.

EXAMPLES: Joseph asked, "Don't I mow the lawn every week?"

His brother protested loudly, "I mow more often than you do!"

In the preceding examples, each complete sentence seems to call for a period. However, two final punctuation marks are unnecessary, so the period is dropped.

INCORRECT: Rodney asked, "Will you stop arguing?".

CORRECT: Rodney asked, "Will you stop arguing?"

Sometimes the entire sentence, not the quotation, requires a question mark or an exclamation mark. Then the order of the punctuation changes.

> Place a question mark or exclamation mark *outside* the final quotation mark if the end mark is part of the entire sentence, not part of the quotation.

In the following examples, the quotations are declarative, but the sentences are not. The first sentence is a question, and the second is an exclamation.

EXAMPLES: Did anyone say, "You have been negligent"?

I'm shocked that you can say, "I'm not responsible"!

EXERCISE C: Using End Marks with Direct Quotations. End marks have been left out of the following sentences. Read each sentence and decide if the missing punctuation goes inside or outside the quotation marks. Copy the sentences onto your paper and include the necessary punctuation.

EXAMPLE: Has anyone said, "Please"

Has anyone said, "Please"?

1. Noel commented, "I can't think of a better reason."
2. Who said, "Waste not, want not"?
3. How could the owner have said, "My dog is friendly"?
4. How dare you say, "You weren't invited"!
5. My friend asked, "Why does firing a pistol start the race?"
6. The pilot continued, "Is this your first flight?"

7. Zelda excitedly announced, "I got the job!"
8. Ben said, "All he had ever asked for was a fair chance."
9. Will anyone say, "That is not what I meant"?
10. As the artist sketched, he muttered, "This still isn't right."

■ Quotation Marks for Dialogue

Dialogue is direct conversation between two or more people.

When writing dialogue, begin a new paragraph with each change of speaker.

EXAMPLE: "Will you be going with us on the family camping trip this year?" Noreen asked her cousin.

Gwen hesitated before answering, "I'm afraid so. My parents think I enjoy the experience."

"You fooled me, too," Noreen replied. "Maybe the trip will be better this year."

"Well, at least it can't be any worse," sighed Gwen. "On the last trip, I got a case of poison ivy that lasted for weeks!"

Notice that each sentence is punctuated according to the rules discussed earlier in this section. When writing dialogue, you also need to remember to indent whenever a new speaker talks.

EXERCISE D: Using Quotation Marks with Dialogue. The following selection is a dialogue. However, it is missing some punctuation marks and paragraph indentations. Decide where quotation marks, other punctuation marks, and indentations are needed. Then copy the paragraphs onto your paper, making the necessary changes. *Answer on page T-124.*

(1) This is quite a large crowd Andrea whispered to her friends. (2) You're right answered Paul. (3) I understand that this speaker is a famous expert on the Old

West. (4) Bill, who was sitting on Andrea's left, joined the conversation by asking Why do you think that topic is so popular? (5) It may have something to do with the programs on television Andrea suggested.

APPLICATION: Using Quotation Marks in Your Writing. Choose one of the following topics or make up a topic of your own. Then write a dialogue consisting of at least fifteen sentences. Use as many different quotation rules as possible, and remember to punctuate and indent correctly. *Answers will vary. Students could be motivated for this activity by watching pantomimes based on these topics acted out by volunteers.*

A day at the beach
A broken promise
A moment of anger
A situation to be avoided
A change of opinion

Underlining and Other Uses of Quotation Marks 18.7

Underlining and quotation marks help make titles and other special words and names stand out in your writing. *Underlining* is used only in handwritten and typed work. In printed materials *italics* take the place of underlining.

UNDERLINING: The Call of the Wild

ITALICS: *The Call of the Wild*

This section explains when it is correct to underline and when it is correct to use quotation marks.

When to Underline

One of the most common uses of underlining is for titles of long written works such as novels.

Underline the titles of long written works and the titles of publications that are published as a single work.

The following chart shows some of these kinds of titles.

WRITTEN WORKS THAT ARE UNDERLINED	
Title of a Book:	The Adventures of Tom Sawyer
Title of a Play:	A Raisin in the Sun
Title of a Long Poem:	Paradise Lost
Title of a Magazine:	Seventeen
Title of a Newspaper:	The New York Times

NOTE ABOUT NEWSPAPER TITLES: The portion of the title that should be underlined will vary from newspaper to newspaper. The New York Times should always be fully capitalized and underlined. Other papers, however, can usually be treated in one of two ways: for example, either the Los Angeles Times or the Los Angeles Times. Unless you know the exact name of a paper, choose one of these two forms and use it consistently.

Certain other titles also need underlining.

Underline the titles of movies, television and radio series, and works of music and art.

The following chart illustrates some of these titles.

ARTISTIC WORKS THAT ARE UNDERLINED	
Title of a Movie:	Rocky
Title of a Television Series:	Happy Days
Title of a Long Work of Music:	Surprise Symphony
Title of a Record Album:	Elton John's Greatest Hits
Title of a Painting:	Christina's World
Title of a Sculpture:	The Thinker

The names of individual planes, ships, space vehicles, trains, and cars are also underlined.

Underline the names of individual air, sea, space, and land craft.

AIR:	the Kitty Hawk	SPACE:	Gemini 5
SEA:	the Titanic	LAND:	the Tom Thumb

Other words, letters, and numbers are sometimes underlined also.

Underline words, letters, or numbers used as names for themselves.

EXAMPLES: The word maybe is not part of her vocabulary.

On this typewriter the o is blurry.

Six is my lucky number.

EXERCISE A: Underlining Titles, Names, and Words. Each of the following sentences contains a title, name, or word that needs underlining. Write the items that require underlining on your paper and underline them.

EXAMPLE: The Lusitania sank in 1915 off the coast of Ireland.

Lusitania

1. I've seen Doctor Zhivago twice at the movies and once on television.
2. One of the three ships that brought Columbus to the New World was the Santa Maria.
3. Njal's Saga is a long epic poem written in Icelandic.
4. Grant Wood's American Gothic can be seen in the Art Institute of Chicago.
5. Lydia wanted to play the part of Helen Keller in the production of The Miracle Worker done at our school.
6. In the novel The Yearling, Jody learns that he can not run away from his grief.
7. Many people think the number thirteen is unlucky.
8. Howdy Doody was one of the first television shows for children.

9. The librarian explained that back issues of the Herald Tribune were on microfilm in the periodical room.
10. Charles Lindbergh made the first solo flight across the Atlantic in the Spirit of St. Louis.

When to Use Quotation Marks

In general, quotation marks are used for short works and works that are a part of a longer work.

Use quotation marks around the titles of short written works.

The following chart contains examples of titles that you should enclose in quotation marks.

WRITTEN WORKS THAT TAKE QUOTATION MARKS	
Title of a Short Story:	"The Gift of the Magi"
Chapter from a Book:	"The Test Is in the Tasting" from No-Work Garden Book
Title of a Short Poem:	"Lucy"
Title of an Article:	"How to Build Your Own Greenhouse"

The titles of other short works of art are also placed in quotation marks.

Use quotation marks around the titles of episodes in a series, songs, and parts of a long musical composition.

Examples are given in the following chart.

ARTISTIC WORKS THAT TAKE QUOTATION MARKS	
Title of an Episode:	"The Homecoming" from The Waltons
Title of a Song:	"Beautiful Dreamer"
Title of a Part of a Long Work of Music:	"Waltz of the Flowers" from the Nutcracker Suite

Sometimes a long work is mentioned as part of an even longer work.

Use quotation marks around the title of a work that is mentioned as part of a collection.

The play *Uncle Vanya* would normally be underlined. In the following example, however, the title is placed in quotation marks because it is cited as part of a larger work.

EXAMPLE: "Uncle Vanya" in Eight Great Comedies

EXERCISE B: Using Quotation Marks with Titles. Each of the following sentences contains a title that needs quotation marks. Some of the sentences also contain titles that need underlining. Copy the titles onto your paper, either enclosing them in quotation marks or underlining them.

EXAMPLE: My favorite song is Getting to Know You from The King and I.

"Getting to Know You" The King and I

1. Song of High Cuisine is a brief poem by Phyllis McGinley that ridicules such delicacies as snails and nightingales' tongues.
2. My favorite song from the musical Brigadoon is There But for You Go I.
3. Did you see The Battle of the Clingons on Star Trek?
4. As do most of Ray Bradbury's short stories, The Whole Town's Sleeping has a startling conclusion.
5. While listening to Sunrise, the first movement of the Grand Canyon Suite, we could almost see the morning light.
6. National Geographic has a fascinating article this month called The Trouble with Dolphins.
7. Tonight's assignment is to read The Valley of Humiliation, a chapter in the novel The Mill on the Floss.
8. After reading I'll Give You Love, a short story by Molly Picon, the class began to discuss its theme.

9. In Friday's English class, we will be reading the play "Twelfth Night" from our textbook The World's a Stage.
10. Edgar Allan Poe's short story "The Tell-Tale Heart" sends chills up and down my spine.

APPLICATION: Using Underlining and Quotation Marks. Write ten original sentences, each including a specific example of one of the following items. Be sure to punctuate and capitalize correctly.

Answers will vary; samples given for first two.

EXAMPLE: The title of a short poem

Reading the poem "Little Boy Blue" always makes me cry.

1. Picasso's Guernica is now in Spain.

1. The title of a painting
2. A book title
3. The name of a specific ship or airplane.
4. A song title
5. A magazine title
6. A short-story title
7. A movie title
8. The title of one work within a collection
9. A newspaper title
10. A letter used as a name for itself

2. Her favorite book is Through the Looking Glass.

18.8 The Hyphen

The *hyphen* is used to combine numbers and word parts, to join certain compound words, and to show that a word has been broken between syllables at the end of a line.

When to Use the Hyphen

Many numbers require a hyphen so that they can be read more easily.

Use a hyphen when writing out the numbers *twenty-one* through *ninety-nine*.

EXAMPLES: There were *thirty-four* people at the meeting.

Your paper has *twenty-one* spelling errors.

Sometimes fractions also require hyphens.

Use a hyphen when writing fractions that are used as adjectives.

EXAMPLE: A *four-fifths* majority indicated overwhelming approval.

Notice, however, that a fraction used as a noun, rather than as an adjective, does not need a hyphen.

EXAMPLE: *Two thirds* of the pie has been eaten.

Hyphens are also used to combine certain prefixes and suffixes with other words.

Use a hyphen after a prefix that is followed by a proper noun or adjective.

The following prefixes are often used before proper nouns: *ante-*, *anti-*, *mid-*, *post-*, *pre-*, *pro-*, and *un-*.

EXAMPLE: The *pre-Columbian* artifacts were discovered by a team of archeologists.

Three prefixes and one suffix in particular always require a hyphen.

Use a hyphen in words with the prefixes *all-*, *ex-*, and *self-* and the suffix *-elect*.

EXAMPLES: all-powerful self-determined

ex-leader governor-elect

Hyphens are also used to join certain compound words.

Use a hyphen to connect two or more nouns that are used as one word, unless the dictionary gives a different spelling.

Some compound nouns are written as one word, and others are written as separate words. The following examples show some of the many compound nouns that are written with hyphens.

EXAMPLES: lady-in-waiting cave-in

great-grandfather secretary-treasurer

Modifiers may also consist of two or more words joined by hyphens.

Use a hyphen to connect a compound modifier that comes before a noun.

In each of the following examples, the first part of the modifier describes the second part of the modifier, not the noun. The hyphen shows the connection between the words in each modifier.

EXAMPLES: This *long-winded* essay is unacceptable.

Don't ignore a *once-in-a-lifetime* opportunity such as this one.

No hyphen is necessary when a compound modifier follows the noun it describes.

BEFORE: Nicole is a *well-disciplined* person.

AFTER: Nicole is *well disciplined.*

BEFORE: An *almost-perfect* term paper is expected.

AFTER: This term paper is *almost perfect.*

However, if a dictionary spells a word with a hyphen, the word must always be hyphenated, even when it follows a noun.

EXAMPLES: This *poor-spirited* horse will never win a race.

This horse is *poor-spirited.*

A few special compound modifiers never take hyphens.

Do not use a hyphen with a compound modifier that includes a word ending in *-ly* or in a compound proper adjective.

INCORRECT: clearly-written

CORRECT: clearly written

INCORRECT: West-Indian music

CORRECT: West Indian music

EXERCISE A: Using Hyphens in Numbers, Word Parts, and Compound Words. Examine the following items and decide where hyphens are needed. If an item does not require a hyphen, write *correct.* If an item does require hyphenation, rewrite the item to make it correct.

EXAMPLE: a newly minted coin

correct

1. nine tenths of the population c
2. anti-Soviet activities
3. self-explanatory letters
4. a never-to-be-forgotten day
5. a jack-in-the-box
6. newly appointed officials c
7. mid-Victorian ideas
8. an all-encompassing study
9. a pre-Babylonian civilization
10. star-shaped designs
11. well-deserved recognition
12. sixty-five employees
13. Jenkins, our president-elect
14. a pro-Mexico delegation
15. an answer quickly determined c

16. a two-thirds majority
17. appetizers before dinner *C*
18. Miss Humphrey, ex-consultant
19. horse-and-buggy days
20. the North American continent *C*

Rules for Dividing Words at the End of a Line

Avoid dividing words at the ends of lines whenever possible. Too many divided words can make your writing seem choppy. When it is necessary to divide a word, use the following rules to divide words correctly.

If a word must be divided, always divide it between syllables.

EXAMPLE: You must not feel that a contri-
bution of five dollars is insig-
nificant.

In carrying out this rule, make sure you place the hyphen at the end of the first line, not at the beginning of the second line.

INCORRECT: These chemicals cause lime particles to dis
-solve.

CORRECT: These chemicals cause lime particles to dissolve.

In addition, take care never to divide one-syllable words, even if they seem long or sound like words with two syllables.

INCORRECT: sch-ool bru-ised thro-ugh

CORRECT: school bruised through

Another rule points to a major exception to the first rule.

Do *not* divide a word so that a single letter stands alone.

The following words are correctly broken into two syllables. However, because the break leaves one letter standing alone, these words should not be divided at the end of a line.

INCORRECT: a-mid ver-y o-kay

CORRECT: amid very okay

Also, to avoid awkward pronunciations, you should not place *-ed* at the beginning of a new line.

INCORRECT: halt-ed

CORRECT: halted

Proper nouns and proper adjectives also require a special rule.

Do *not* divide proper nouns or proper adjectives.

INCORRECT: Mar-tin Lat-vi-a

CORRECT: Martin Latvia

A final rule applies to words that already have hyphenated spellings.

Divide a hyphenated word only after the hyphen.

INCORRECT: We lost the game in spite of our well-inten-
tioned efforts.

CORRECT: We lost the game in spite of our well-
intentioned efforts.

EXERCISE B: Using Hyphens to Divide Words. Imagine that you have to decide either to hyphenate each of the following words at the end of a line or to write the complete word on the next line. If you can divide a word, write the part of the word that would appear at the end of the first line on your paper. If you can not divide the word, write the complete word.

EXAMPLE: old-fashioned

old-

1. ready *ready*
2. laugh *laugh*
3. promised *prom-*
4. Thailand *4. Thailand*
5. self-serving *self-*
6. grocery *gro-*
7. Maryann *Maryann*
8. handed *handed*
9. forty
10. evasive *9. for-* *10. eva-*

APPLICATION: Using Hyphens in Your Writing. Write ten original sentences, each including a hyphenated word. Divide at least four words at the ends of lines. Try to apply as many of the different rules for hyphenation as you can. *Answers will vary. You may want to try to determine the most common types of hyphen errors first in a class discussion and then have students concentrate on these.*

EXAMPLE: The ex-governor had once been all-powerful.

18.9 The Apostrophe

The two main uses of the *apostrophe* (') are (1) to show possession in nouns and pronouns and (2) to indicate that letters are left out of contractions.

Apostrophes with Possessive Nouns

Apostrophes are used with nouns to show ownership or possession. The rule for singular nouns is quite simple.

Add an apostrophe and *-s* to show the possessive case of most singular nouns.

EXAMPLES: The role of the *parent* becomes the *parent's* role.

The sound of the *trumpet* becomes the *trumpet's* sound.

The fur of a *mole* becomes a *mole's* fur.

Even when a singular noun already ends in *-s,* you can usually still add an apostrophe and *-s* to show possession.

EXAMPLES: The color of an *iris* becomes an *iris's* color.

The blade of a *cutlass* becomes a *cutlass's* blade.

The cow of *Bess* becomes *Bess's* cow.

Sometimes the addition of an apostrophe and *-s* makes it difficult to pronounce a noun ending in *-s.* In this case only an apostrophe is added to show possession.

AWKWARD: Slim Pickens's role was that of a cowboy.

BETTER: Slim Pickens' role was that of a cowboy.

The possessive of a plural noun depends on the ending of the noun.

Add just an apostrophe to show the possessive case of plural nouns ending in *-s* or *-es.*

EXAMPLES: The mother of the *kittens* becomes the *kittens'* mother.

The belief of the *multitudes* becomes the *multitudes'* belief.

Add an apostrophe and *-s* to show the possessive case of plural nouns that do not end in *-s* or *-es.*

EXAMPLES: The squeaking of the *mice* becomes the *mice's* squeaking.

The father of the *children* becomes the *children's* father.

The advice of the *women* becomes the *women's* advice.

The possessives of compound nouns also follow a basic rule.

Add an apostrophe and *-s* (or just an apostrophe if the word is a plural ending in *-s*) to the last word of a compound noun to form the possessive.

NAME OF A BUSINESS: The Army and Navy Store's sale

NAME OF AN ORGANIZATION: the Girl Scouts' cookie sale

TITLE OF A RULER: the Queen of England's horse

HYPHENATED TITLES: my father-in-law's car

the treasurer-elect's position

In forming the possessive case, you may have trouble deciding where the apostrophe belongs or whether an *-s* is necessary. Your decision will be easier if you use the steps in the following chart.

STEPS FOR DECIDING WHERE AN APOSTROPHE BELONGS

1. Determine the owner of the idea, object, or personality trait. Ask yourself, "To whom or what does it belong?"
2. If the answer to the question is a singular noun, follow the rule for forming the possessive of a singular noun. If the answer is a plural noun, follow the rules for forming the possessive of a plural noun.

In the phrase *the flowers fragrance,* ask yourself, "To what does the fragrance belong?" If the answer is singular, "the flower," then the possessive is *the flower's fragrance*. If the answer is plural, "the flowers," then the possessive is *the flowers' fragrance*.

EXERCISE A: Using Apostrophes to Form the Possessives of Nouns. The following sentences contain underlined singular or plural nouns. Copy each underlined noun onto your paper, putting it into the possessive form by adding an apostrophe and *-s* as needed.

EXAMPLE: The children hour at the public library has been a great success.

children's

1. According to legend, a dragon breath was quite dangerous. dragon's
2. All of the pencils points were broken and the sharpener would not work. pencils'
3. The pond became the geese home for the summer.
4. Many have benefited from reading Do-It-Yourself advice in the newspaper. Do-It-Yourself's
5. Most designers believe that garments colors attract buyers. garments'
6. This yarn was purchased at the Jack and Jill Craft Store sale. Jack and Jill Craft Store's
7. Ross lizard must be kept on a leash at all times. Ross's
8. Elected officials represent the people choice. people's
9. Chancellor Helmut Schmidt reelection seemed likely. Schmidt's
10. Discard the lettuce outer leaves. lettuce's

3. geese's

Apostrophes with Pronouns

Both indefinite and personal pronouns can show possession. The possessive case of indefinite pronouns is formed in the same manner as the possessive case of singular nouns.

Use an apostrophe and *-s* with indefinite pronouns to show possession.

EXAMPLES:	another's preference	nobody else's business
	anybody's help	no one's ticket
	each other's privacy	one's choice
	everyone's advice	somebody's hat

The personal pronouns that show possession are treated differently.

Do *not* use an apostrophe with possessive personal pronouns.

None of the following personal pronouns needs an apostrophe to show possession: *my, mine, your, yours, his, her, hers, its, our, ours, their,* and *theirs.*

Some of these pronouns act as adjectives.

EXAMPLES: The spider caught a fly in *its* web.

Our house is for sale.

Others act as subjects, objects, and subject complements.

EXAMPLES: *Mine* is the yellow crayon.

Someone broke *yours*.

The red one is *his*.

The important thing to remember is not to use an apostrophe when these pronouns are used to show possession.

EXERCISE B: Using Apostrophes with Pronouns. The following sentences contain pronouns used as possessives. If all pronouns in a sentence are used correctly, write *correct*. If a pronoun is used incorrectly, rewrite it to make it correct.

EXAMPLE: When they divided up the property, the lake became his and the island became their's.

theirs

1. Everybody else's favorite dessert is not necessarily yours' or mine. *yours*
2. The tools in your garage are our's, not your's.
3. Someones' cat was howling in the alley while our's was sleeping peacefully. *Someone's/ours*
4. The veterinarian examined her' parakeet and said it's wing was broken. *her/its*
5. Ours is the preferred method, even though their's is almost as good. *theirs*
6. Listen to his' idea for a solution before you accept hers. *his*
7. Her's is the best solution to our problem. *Hers*
8. I will help you finish your math work if you will help Leon with his. *C*

2. ours/yours

9. It is still not too late to file your' tax return. *your*
10. Their's is always the first yard on the block to have its' leaves raked. *Theirs/its*

Apostrophes with Contractions

Contractions are shortened forms of words or phrases.

Use an apostrophe in a contraction to indicate the position of the missing letter or letters.

People often use contractions in informal speech and writing both for convenience and to save time. For example, instead of saying, "Let us go," a person is more likely to say, "Let's go." The following chart shows some other contractions formed with verbs.

COMMON CONTRACTIONS WITH VERBS		
Verb + *not*:	are not (aren't)	could not (couldn't)
	is not (isn't)	did not (didn't)
	was not (wasn't)	do not (don't)
	were not (weren't)	should not (shouldn't)
	can not (can't)	would not (wouldn't)
Pronoun + the Verb *will*:	I will (I'll)	we will (we'll)
	you will (you'll)	they will (they'll)
	he will (he'll)	who will (who'll)
	she will (she'll)	
Pronoun or Noun + the Verb *be*:	I am (I'm)	we are (we're)
	you are (you're)	they are (they're)
	he is (he's)	who is (who's)
	she is (she's)	where is (where's)
	it is (it's)	Lee is (Lee's)
Pronoun or Noun + the Verb *would*:	I would (I'd)	we would (we'd)
	you would (you'd)	they would (they'd)
	he would (he'd)	who would (who'd)
	she would (she'd)	Nancy would (Nancy'd)

An apostrophe is also used to form contractions of years.

EXAMPLE: the 1984 yearbook (the '84 yearbook)

Still another use of the apostrophe is with the letters *o, d,* and *l. O'* is a shortened version of the longer phrase *of the. D'* in Spanish means *of the,* and *l'* in French simply means *the.* These letters and an apostrophe have become part of certain words and proper names and are always used with them.

EXAMPLES: o'clock (of the clock)

O'Brien (of the Brien family)

d'Agostino (of the Agostino family)

L'Engle (the Engle family)

Although apostrophes are always used in the examples above, you should avoid using most contractions in formal writing.

INFORMAL WRITING: No one could've guessed the outcome.

FORMAL WRITING: No one could have guessed the outcome.

EXERCISE C: Using Contractions in Informal Writing. Each of the following sentences contains one or more word groups that can be written as contractions. On your paper write each of these word groups as a contraction.

EXAMPLE: Where is the new science-fiction book I ordered?

Where's

1. Who is the new student representative? *Who's*
2. I am not certain whether he is upstairs or downstairs. *I'm/he's*
3. This pen will write if you will just keep shaking it.
4. You are ignoring what I am saying. *You're/I'm*
5. Glenda is the one I would like to invite. *Glenda's/I'd*
6. There can not be any doubt about who will be invited. *can't/who'll*

3. you'll

7. You will enjoy looking at these old pictures of the class of 1956. *You'll/'56*
8. They were not sure who would be on the committee or when the meetings would be held.
9. I will look for the book in the public library since the school library does not have it. *I'll/doesn't*
10. Where is the one who said she would be here early? *Where's/she'd*

8. They're or weren't/who'd

Special Uses of the Apostrophe

Apostrophes are also used in forming certain plurals.

Use an apostrophe and *-s* to write the plurals of numbers, symbols, letters, and words used to name themselves.

EXAMPLES: two *5*'s and six *7*'s three *!*'s

a's first and *z*'s last

Don't begin sentences with *well*'s.

EXERCISE D: Recognizing Special Uses of the Apostrophe. Write five original sentences, each using the plural of one of the following numbers, symbols, letters, or words. Be sure to underline each plural form and use apostrophes where they are needed.

Sentences will vary; plural forms given.

EXAMPLE: t

Please take greater care in crossing your t's.

1. 9 2. m 3. huh 4. ? 5. please

1. 9's 2. m's 3. huh's 4. ?'s 5. please's

APPLICATION: Using Apostrophes in Your Writing. Write a brief dialogue between two friends. You can use one of the following topics or make up your own. Apply as many of the rules for apostrophes as you can. If necessary, see page 364 for rules governing the punctuation of dialogue. *Answers will vary. You may want to have students read their dialogues aloud, stopping the students at certain possessive words and having volunteers give the spellings.*

A discussion of math homework
A discussion of an abstract painting
A discussion of a movie's plot

Review Exercises: Mechanics

REVIEW EXERCISE 1: Identifying Errors in Capitalization

The following sentences have not been capitalized correctly. Copy each sentence onto your paper, adding the missing capitals. Use underlining as shown.

Underlined letters are to be capitalized.

EXAMPLE: "please send me three turkish stamps," she said, "so i can complete my collection."

"Please send me three Turkish stamps," she said, "so I can complete my collection."

1. "the orbits of uranus and neptune are over one billion miles apart," jill explained, "while the orbits of the moon and earth are much closer."
2. listen, uncle fred, while my dad tells the boy scout troop how to build a campfire.
3. in art history 193, professor tilden told the students to write an essay describing the painting entitled portrait of a boy.
4. the correct address is 1307 maple tree lane, cincinnati, ohio 45202.
5. while in gimbels miss henderson bought the revlon cosmetics that she had seen advertised in glamour.
6. "who wrote the bill of rights," asked peter jones, "and when was it written?"
7. the last monday in september was set aside for the first meeting of the german students at bridgeton school.
8. after driving all the way from oklahoma to spend the fourth of july in yellowstone national park, dave and i were exhausted.
9. rosh hashana, a major jewish holiday, is a time of repentance.
10. his family watched as lieutenant mike o'toole received a purple heart for injuries received while flying a martin b-26 marauder during a world war II bombing mission.

REVIEW EXERCISE 2: Writing Sentences Using Capitals

Use ten of the following twenty items in a letter that tells a story. Add capitals where necessary in each item and capitalize correctly throughout the rest of the letter. *Compositions will vary; underlined letters are to be capitalized.*

1. dear miss whekens:
2. delaware river
3. port jervis, new york
4. whekens' boat shop
5. the rock bottom
6. memorial day
7. kiwanis club
8. aunt grace
9. mayor sheldrick
10. 66 plainview avenue
11. sally r. cohen
12. michael o'reilly
13. saturday and sunday
14. polish ham
15. american flag
16. hiker magazine
17. "don't stand up!"
18. lake erie
19. girl scout troop
20. sincerely yours,

REVIEW EXERCISE 3: Identifying Abbreviation Errors in Formal Writing

Decide if the underlined words, phrases, and abbreviations in the following passage of formal writing are used correctly. If they are correct, write *correct* on your paper. If they are incorrect, write the correct form.

EXAMPLE: Many private detectives work almost around the clock, sometimes as late as three or four a.m.

in the morning

Last Saturday (1) Mr. Norman Goodman and Ms. Angela Bright, private detectives, met at the corner of Center (2) St. and Market Avenue at 9:30 (3) *ante meridiem*. Both wore tan raincoats, and Mr. Goodman also sported a ten- (4) gal. hat. Angela excitedly described their next case. An ancient golden statue, which was to be given to the (5) Pres. as a gift, was to arrive by plane at (6) one o'clock P.M. The statue had been made in (7) 79 B.C., but it had not been discovered by archeologists

1. C 2. Street 3. A.M. or a.m. 4. gallon 5. President 6. 1:00 7. C

until (8) A.D. 1937. The statue was now worth millions of dollars. The precious statue would be stored temporarily by Oldart Gallery in their warehouse in (9) PA. 8. C 9. Pennsylvania

Quickly, the two detectives made plans to protect the statue. They would guard the truck carrying the five- (10) ft., ten- (11) inch statue by following it along (12) Rte. 95 until it reached the warehouse on Green Avenue. 10. foot 11. C 12. Route 95

Unfortunately, two thieves from (13) N.H. had decided to steal the statue from the truck after it turned into Oldart Gallery's driveway. The thieves, (14) Dr. Jeremiah Crook and his sister (15) Mrs. Teresa Wrong, did manage to steal the statue, right after the detectives left. But Crook and Wrong had driven only three (16) km from the scene of the crime when their car broke down under the weight of the thousand- (17) kilogram statue. 13. New Hampshire 14. C 15. C 16. kilometers 17. C

"I want my (18) atty.!" shouted Crook as he and his sister were taken in by (19) Sgt. Reynolds at the police station. Reporter Diane Taknow and her photographer (20) Ira Shoot, Jr., covered the story for the local newspaper. 18. attorney 19. Sergeant 20. C

REVIEW EXERCISE 4: Using Abbreviations in Your Own Writing

Write the abbreviation for each of the following terms. Then choose ten abbreviations that would be appropriate in formal writing and use them in a short story of your own. *Compositions will vary; abbreviations are given.*

1. *ante meridiem* A.M. or a.m.
2. Celsius C
3. Avenue Ave.
4. Registered Nurse R.N.
5. Junior Jr.
6. Captain Capt.
7. centimeter cm
8. Doctor Dr.
9. Delaware Del. or DE
10. *post meridiem* P.M. or p.m.
11. Secretary Sec.
12. Mister Mr.
13. Oregon Ore. or OR
14. mile mi.
15. Road Rd.
16. before noon A.M. or a.m.
17. in the year of the Lord
18. kilometer km
19. before Christ B.C.
20. Professor Prof.

17. A.D.

REVIEW EXERCISE 5: Identifying Errors in Punctuation

Read the following passage, which contains errors in punctuation. Then answer the questions that follow.

EXAMPLE: Which sentence needs an exclamation mark?

(1)

(1) "Watch out for the shark" Ernie yelled. (2) Youre not going to get me into that water, he added.

(3) "Are you serious" Randy asked. (4) She knew that "the great white shark had an overrated reputation" (5) This was probably because of movies such as Jaws or Jaws II that horrified everyone with tales of sharks, that ate people.

(6) There are actually fewer than 1,00 shark attacks reported worldwide in a year yet white sharks are often the culprits when there are attacks. (7) The white shark which is a meat-eating fish usually stays in warm or tropical waters and seldom strays to northern beaches. (8) However, there have been some, documented cases of white shark attacks in cold waters. (9) The white shark can of course be very frightening; for the following reasons its sharp edged teeth its great size and its grim reputation.

(10) Experts advise swimmers to follow a few-practical rules when swimming in waters that are known to contain sharks. (11) In addition to swimming only when others are present, you should never try to touch a shark, even if it looks injured, and you should not swim if you have a wound, especially if the wound is open. (12) In spite of the odds against an attack by a great white shark it pays to know the rules that can save your' life.

1. Which sentence needs a period? *4*
2. Which sentence could best use a question mark? *3*
3. In which sentence is a comma used incorrectly between adjectives? *8*
4. In which sentence are commas missing between items in a series? *9*
5. Which compound sentence is missing a comma? *6*

6. Which sentence needs a comma after introductory material? *12*
7. Which sentence needs commas around a parenthetical expression? *9*
8. Which sentence needs commas with a nonessential expression? *7*
9. In which sentence is a comma used incorrectly with an essential expression? *5*
10. In which sentence is a comma used incorrectly with a number? *6*
11. In which sentence is a semicolon used incorrectly? *9*
12. Which sentence could use a semicolon instead of a comma to avoid confusion? *11*
13. Which sentence needs a colon? *9*
14. Which sentence needs quotation marks? *2*
15. In which sentence are quotation marks used incorrectly? *4*
16. Which sentence needs words underlined? *5*
17. Which sentence needs a hyphen with a compound word? *9*
18. In which sentence is a hyphen between two adjectives used incorrectly? *10*
19. Which sentence needs an apostrophe in a contraction? *2*
20. In which sentence is an apostrophe incorrectly used to show possession? *12*

REVIEW EXERCISE 6: Writing Sentences Using Punctuation Correctly

Use one of the two topics listed below to write a story at least eight sentences long. Include the following punctuation marks in your writing. *Stories will vary. You may want students to exchange papers to correct each other's punctuation.*

1. 4 periods
2. 1 question mark
3. 1 exclamation mark
4. 4 commas
5. 1 semicolon
6. 1 colon
7. 2 quotation marks
8. 1 underlining
9. 1 hyphen
10. 2 apostrophes

A room that fits all your needs
A mysterious package

UNIT IV

Vocabulary and Spelling

Chapter 19

Building Your Vocabulary

You may not realize it, but you already have hundreds of words in your vocabulary. Even if you know many hundreds of words, however, your vocabulary contains only a tiny fraction of the words in the English language. This chapter will suggest various methods for learning and remembering the meanings of new words so that the words become part of your vocabulary. As your vocabulary grows, your pleasure in reading and your ease in writing will grow also.

19.1 Ways to Enlarge Your Vocabulary

A small investment of time and effort can lead to a big increase in the size of your vocabulary. The most important tool in vocabulary building is a good dictionary. There you will find the meaning of a word, its pronunciation and part of speech, and often information about its history.

Setting Up a Vocabulary Notebook

You may find it useful to set up a vocabulary notebook with separate sections for each of your subjects. Whenever you are reading or studying, jot down on a piece of paper any words that are new to you. When you have finished reading, write the words in your notebook. Then use a dictionary to find out the meaning of each word.

Set up a vocabulary notebook and use a dictionary to add new words to your vocabulary.

A good plan is to divide each page of your vocabulary notebook into three columns. Label the first column "Words" and use it for new words and, if you wish, their pronunciations. Label the second column "Bridge Words" and use it for hints or helping words that will make it easier for you to remember the meanings of new words. Label the third column "Definitions" and use it to write the meanings of new words.

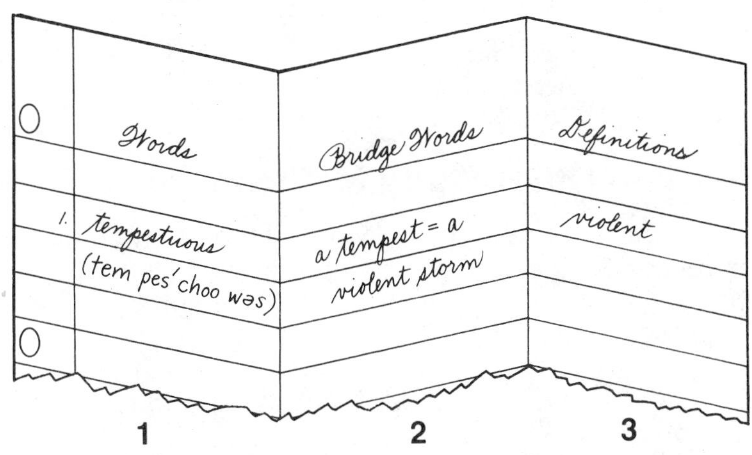

This three-column format will make it easier for you to learn the meanings of the new words you list. When you study, cover the third column with a piece of paper or fold the page back so you can test yourself on the definitions. The bridge words in the middle column will give you hints. When you think you have learned a word, you can cover the middle column as well as the third column and then try to give the word's definition. Study four or five words at a time using this method. You might want to write the definitions on a piece of paper and then compare these with the definition column. Each time you define a word correctly, place a check in your notebook next to the word. Three checks should mean that you are gaining familiarity with the word and that it has become part of your vocabulary.

EXERCISE A: Working with Your Vocabulary Notebook. Set up a vocabulary notebook with separate sections for each of your subjects. For each subject go over your corrected papers or look through the reading assignments in your textbooks and choose five words whose meanings you are not sure of. Using the three-column format, list the vocabulary words you have chosen in your notebook.
Students should follow the format in the example.

EXAMPLE:

Words	Bridge Words	Definitions
amendment (ə mend′ mənt)	to mend	a change for the better

■ Using Other Study Methods

Frequent review of the words in your vocabulary notebook is an excellent way of improving your vocabulary. Other study methods, however, might also work well for you.

Use a variety of methods for studying and reviewing new words.

Try each of the following methods to see which works best.

Reviewing New Words with Flash Cards. A good way to expand your vocabulary is to review words using a set of flash cards. Just as a vocabulary notebook can act as your personal dictionary, so can flash cards be tailored to meet your own needs. The following steps can help you prepare flash cards.

MAKING FLASH CARDS

1. Using index cards, make a flash card for each word in your vocabulary notebook.
2. Write or print the word on one side of the card. If the word is hard to pronounce, copy the phonetic spelling given for it in the dictionary.
3. In the lower right-hand corner of the card, pencil in one or more bridge words that will give you a hint about the meaning of the word. These words can later be erased when you find that you no longer need them.
4. On the back of the card, write the definition of the word. You may also want to note in the upper left-hand corner whether the word is from a particular subject area or from your general reading.

The following illustration shows the front and back of a card you might make.

Front	Back
solidify (sə lid'ə fī') *solid = firm or hard*	*Science* *to make or become solid, firm, hard*

You can carry your flash cards with you and flip through them whenever you have time. If you feel sure of the definition of a word, put that card aside in a "review set." Go through the review set from time to time to make sure you have not forgotten any words.

Reviewing New Words with a Tape Recorder. Some people learn new words more easily by hearing them than by reading them. If you have access to a tape recorder, you may find the following procedure helpful.

REVIEWING WITH A TAPE RECORDER

1. Read a vocabulary word into the tape recorder.
2. Leave approximately five seconds of blank space on the tape and then give the definition.
3. Follow the definition with a sentence using the word. The sentence is to help you remember the word and its meaning.
4. Leave another blank space of about five seconds.
5. Record the rest of the words in the same fashion.
6. Study the words by replaying the entire tape, filling in the first blank space with a definition spoken aloud and the second blank space with the vocabulary word spoken aloud.
7. Rerun the tape until you are able to give all of the definitions and words without hesitation.

If you listen to your tape several times a week, the new words will soon become a permanent part of your vocabulary.

Reviewing New Words with a Partner. All the methods described so far work well when done with a partner. You can alternate between using your vocabulary notebooks, your flash cards, or a tape recorder. One person can read the words listed in one of your notebooks while the other defines the words. If the person defining the words hesitates, the reader can offer bridge words. You might also drill each other on difficult words by using the flash cards. In either case, you might use the tape recorder as a final review.

EXERCISE B: Making Flash Cards or Tapes. Using the preceding instructions as a guide, make a set of flash cards or a tape. Use five of the following words, concentrating on those whose meanings you do not know.

Students might exchange cards or tapes, check each other's work, and become familiar

1. context	5. fanatic	9. plausible
2. disperse	6. intolerant	10. sardonic
3. elongate	7. koala	
4. evade	8. malice	

with words they did not choose.

APPLICATION: Using New Vocabulary Words in Sentences. Select five words from the notebook you made in Exercise A and five words from Exercise B. For each word write an original sentence that will give a reader a clear understanding of the meaning of the word.
Different sentences using the same word might be compared.

EXAMPLE: disperse

The pigeons gathered from all directions waiting for him to disperse the bread crumbs.

Using Context 19.2

If *context* was one of the words you looked up in Exercise B of Section 19.1, you now know that it refers to the sentence, the surrounding words, or the situation in which a word is used. The context of a word can be very useful in learning new words.

Use **context clues** to guess the meanings of unfamiliar words.

Often, without even realizing it, you will guess at the meaning of an unfamiliar word as you read. Context clues are what enable you to figure out the meaning of a word in this way. For example, look at the word *muffed* in the following sentence.

SENTENCE: Jon was on his way to becoming an instant hero when he *muffed* an easy fly ball.

CLUES: The reader knows that something happened to keep Jon from becoming a hero. The word *easy* is another clue.

GUESS: Jon must have missed the ball.

DEFINITION OF *MUFF*: to fail to catch, to fumble

The following chart give steps to follow when using context clues.

USING CONTEXT CLUES

1. Reread the sentence, leaving out the unfamiliar word.
2. Examine the surrounding words to see if they provide any clues.
3. Use the clues to guess the meaning of the word.
4. Read the sentence again, substituting your guess.
5. Check your guess by looking up the word in a dictionary.
6. Write the word and the dictionary definition in your notebook.

The rest of this section offers some opportunities for you to use context clues in your reading.

Using Context in Daily Reading

The following passage contains the kind of material you might read in a newspaper or a magazine. Although the paragraphs describe an experiment, the words used are not scientific or technical; they are general words such as those you are likely to meet when you read for pleasure.

Read the paragraphs and try to determine the meaning of each underlined word from its context. On a separate piece of paper, write down what you think each of the words means.

EXAMPLE: Michel Siffre entered a <u>subterranean</u> cave near Del Rio, Texas, on February 14, 1972. His goal was to learn how long he could live without human companionship. Michel brought supplies, including food, water, a radio, and a lamp, to the floor of the cave, where he set up a shelter about one hundred feet below the surface of the earth. The cave was completely silent and, except for the small circle of light cast by his lamp, totally dark. It seemed like a suitable <u>retreat</u> for the experiment.

In the beginning Michel spent much of his time reading, but after a few weeks this activity became tedious. Except for occasional radio contact with friends on the surface, he was completely alone. As time passed, his isolation began to affect him. After ninety-four days his behavior was quite changed. He spoke to his friends rarely, and then in a disjointed and expressionless way, as though they were no longer a part of his life. His condition continued to deteriorate.

After four months in the cave, Michel was reduced to a passive existence, sitting motionless for hours in the darkness that surrounded him. His friends urged him to terminate the experiment, but he refused.

After more than five months, Michel spotted a tiny mouse. He felt a sudden burst of joy—now he would have a companion to alleviate his loneliness! He managed to trap the mouse with a large dish, but his exaltation was short-lived. Soon after Michael had caught the mouse, it died. Once again, Michael was completely alone in the cave.

On August 10 Michel finally left the cave. He had proven to his own satisfaction that an important element in life is companionship.

EXERCISE A: Defining Words. Use your list of guessed meanings from the preceding passage to answer the following multiple choice questions. For each word choose the definition that most closely matches the meaning of the word as it was used in the passage. Then check your answers in a dictionary and record in your vocabulary notebook any words that you missed.

EXAMPLE: cave — (a) ditch; (b) capsule; (c) cavern; (d) hill

(c)

1. alleviate — (a) share; (b) lessen; (c) alter; (d) destroy
2. deteriorate — (a) improve; (b) be dejected; (c) get worse; (d) prevent
3. disjointed — (a) dissatisfied; (b) slow; (c) angry; (d) disconnected

4. exaltation	(a) feeling of joy; (b) great discovery; (c) anticipation; (d) honor
5. passive	(a) sad; (b) unreal; (c) inactive; (d) former
6. reduced	(a) made smaller; (b) brought to a poorer state; (c) took off weight; (d) divided
7. retreat	(a) quiet place; (b) signal; (c) enemy; (d) go back
8. subterranean	(a) train; (b) overground; (c) underground; (d) below
9. tedious	(a) long; (b) difficult; (c) boring; (d) technical
10. terminate	(a) end; (b) continue; (c) determine; (d) transfer

Using Context in Science

The material presented in science textbooks often includes technical words as well as ordinary words used with a special meaning. The following passage is similar to material you might read in a science textbook. At first glance it might seem difficult, but if you pay attention to context as you read, you will find hints about the meanings of the unfamiliar words.

After you read through the paragraphs, try to determine the meaning of each underlined word by its context. Write down what you think each word means.

EXAMPLE: Although water constitutes over 70 percent of the earth's surface, there are some areas of extreme aridity. For example, neither the Great Basin nor the Mojave Desert receives enough rainfall to support luxuriant plant growth. The plants and animals of those areas have all had to adapt to the harsh desert environment.

In contrast to the deserts of the Southwest, the Ozark Plateau has a temperate climate with warm summers, cold winters, and abundant rainfall spread over the entire year. As a result vast, dense forests flourish there. The leaves dropped every fall by deciduous trees create decaying matter, or humus, that becomes a rich, fertile soil on the forest floor. The several strata, or layers, of this material provide an excellent environment for a variety of wildlife. Herbivorous creatures such as deer, rabbits, and small birds find plentiful food in the forest, and these in turn support such carnivorous creatures as birds of prey, foxes, and weasels.

EXERCISE B: Defining Words. Use your list of guessed meanings to answer the following multiple choice questions. For each word choose the definition that most closely matches the meaning of the word as it was used in the passage. Then check your answers in a dictionary and record in your vocabulary notebook any words that you missed.

EXAMPLE: desert (a) swamp; (b) cake; (c) garden; (d) wasteland

(d)

1. adapt — (a) make one's own; (b) give in; (c) skillful; (d) adjust
2. aridity — (a) humidity; (b) dryness; (c) temperature; (d) area
3. carnivorous — (a) flesh-eating; (b) fiesta; (c) very large; (d) grass-eating
4. constitutes — (a) presses together; (b) settles (c) makes up; (d) contracts
5. deciduous — (a) poisonous; (b) dishonest; (c) leaf-shedding; (d) definite
6. herbivorous — (a) plant-eating; (b) cooked with herbs; (c) flesh-eating; (d) weasel
7. humus — (a) funny; (b) dry soil; (c) meek; (d) decaying matter
8. luxuriant — (a) expensive; (b) comfortable; (c) growing in abundance; (d) harsh
9. strata — (a) environment; (b) degrees; (c) fertile; (d) layers
10. temperate — (a) moderate; (b) timely; (c) dry; (d) tropical

Using Context in Social Studies

The following passage includes material that you might find in a social studies textbook. After you read the paragraphs, look back at the underlined words and try to determine their meanings from the context. Write down what you think each word means.

EXAMPLE: The first settlers faced unprecedented physical hardships after they stepped onto the rocky New England shores in the winter of 1620. Never in a quandary about their spiritual mission, the small band of men and women faced the problem of earthly survival in a harsh land. They erected temporary shelters, later replacing them with sturdy log cabins, filling in the crannies between the logs with a mud plaster made of dirt, water, grass, and leaves. At the same time, they cleared the land and prepared it for cultivation.

There was little deviation from the basic pattern of life in the settlement: work and worship, worship and work; every man, woman, and child had tasks to complete. They had little time for revelry since all their energy was directed toward living from day to day.

Steadfast of purpose, the settlers endured their first year. Each week and month that passed saw their lives become less and less vulnerable to the forces of nature. In the fall they affirmed their belief in the omnipotence of God by setting aside a day of praise and thanksgiving for a bountiful harvest.

EXERCISE C: Defining Words. Use your guessed meanings to answer the following multiple choice questions. For each word choose the definition that most clearly matches the meaning of the word as it was used in the passage. Then check your answers in a dictionary and record in your vocabulary notebook any words that you missed.

EXAMPLE: settler (a) old inhabitant; (b) new inhabitant; (c) dog; (d) nomad

(b)

1. affirmed (a) denied; (b) suggested; (c) declared firmly; (d) strengthened greatly
2. bountiful (a) reasonable; (b) plentiful; (c) prayerful; (d) bordering on
3. crannies (a) plasters; (b) windows; (c) narrow openings; (d) bark shelves
4. deviation (a) turning away; (b) acceptance; (c) good; (d) evil
5. omnipotence (a) lack of power; (b) great power; (c) knowledge; (d) angry feeling
6. quandary (a) mistake; (b) large amount; (c) uncertainty; (d) sailing vessel
7. revelry (a) competition; (b) merrymaking; (c) act of vengeance; (d) revelation
8. steadfast (a) firm; (b) unsure; (c) hopeful; (d) endurance
9. unprecedented (a) usual; (b) infrequent; (c) unpleasant; (d) unheard of
10. vulnerable (a) impolite; (b) strongly defended; (c) open to injury; (d) affectionate

APPLICATION: Using Words in Context. Choose any ten vocabulary words from the passages you have read. For each word write an original sentence that will give a reader a clear understanding of the meaning of the word. *Different sentences using the same word might be compared.*

EXAMPLE: affirmed

She affirmed her belief in his words by staking her life on them.

19.3 Using Structure

Another way to expand your vocabulary is to use the *structure* of words to get an idea of their meanings. For example, the word *intervention* has three parts whose individual meanings add up to the meaning of the word itself.

WORD PARTS: inter- + -ven- + -tion

MEANING OF PARTS: between + come + the act of

MEANING OF WORD: intervention = the act of coming between

The three word parts in English are *prefix, root,* and *suffix.* A prefix, such as *inter-*, is one or more syllables added at the beginning of a root. A root, such as *-ven-*, is the base of the word. A suffix, such as *-tion,* is one or more syllables added at the end of a root.

Use **prefixes, roots,** and **suffixes** as clues to the meanings of unfamiliar words.

Some words consist of a root alone *(pay),* some words have a prefix and a root *(repay),* some words have a root and a suffix *(payment),* and some have all three word parts *(repayment).* Not all roots, however, can stand by themselves. Such roots as *-dic-*, which means "to say," and *-spec-*, which means "to see," must be combined with a prefix or a suffix in order to make a complete word.

Using Prefixes

An easy way to enlarge your vocabulary is to learn the meanings of a few common *prefixes*. Once you have learned them, you can add these prefixes to words you already know to make new words.

TEN COMMON PREFIXES			
Prefix	**Meaning**	**Example**	
ad-	to, toward	ad- + -here	to stick to
com-	with, together	com- + -pile	to gather together
dis-	away, apart	dis- + -grace	to lose favor
ex-	from, out	ex- + -port	to send out
mis-	wrong	mis- + -lead	to lead in a wrong direction
post-	after	post- + -war	after the war
re-	back, again	re- + -occupy	to occupy again
sub-	beneath, under	sub- + -merge	to place under water
trans-	across	trans- + -oceanic	across the ocean
un-	not	un- + -beatable	unable to be defeated

As you combine these prefixes with words or roots, you will notice that some of them change their spelling when they are joined to certain roots.

EXAMPLES: *ad-* becomes *ac-* in accept
ap- in apply
as- in assume
com- becomes *co-* in cooperation
con- in confess
cor- in correct
sub- becomes *suc-* in succeed
suf- in suffix
sup- in support

EXERCISE A: Working with Prefixes. Divide your paper into two columns. Then use the preceding chart to find a prefix you can join to each of the following words. In the first column, labeled "Words," write the word you

form. In the second column, labeled "Definitions," write a brief definition, using your knowledge of the prefixes and the information in the chart. Check your definition in the dictionary. If you have chosen a valid word but the wrong definition, write the word in your vocabulary notebook, giving its correct definition.
Answers will vary; sample words are given.

EXAMPLE: take

Words	Definitions
mistake	something that is understood or done incorrectly

1. press *compress*
2. read *misread*
3. play *replay*
4. arm *disarm*
5. form *reform*
6. change *exchange*
7. marine *submarine*
8. venture *adventure*
9. reliable
10. place

9. unreliable
10. replace

Using Roots

Of the three word parts, the *root* is the most important because it carries the basic meaning of the word. The following chart lists ten common roots. These are only a few of the roots in the English language, but you can combine them with other word parts to make many words. Notice that each of these roots has more than one spelling. A variant spelling for each root is shown in parentheses.

TEN COMMON ROOTS

Root	Meaning	Example	
-cap- (-capt-)	to take or seize	capt- + -ivate	to take or hold
-dic- (-dict-)	to say or point out in words	pre- + -dict	to foretell
-mit- (-mis-)	to send	re- + -mit	to send back
-mov- (-mot-)	to move	mov- + -able	able to be moved

-pon- (-pos-)	to put or place	com- + -pose	to put together
-spec- (-spect-)	to see	spec- + -tator	one who sees or watches
-ten- (-tain-)	to hold	de- + -tain	to hold back
-ven- (-vent-)	to come	con- + -vene	to come together
-vert- (-vers-)	to turn	in- + -vert	to turn upside down
-vid- (-vis-)	to see	vis- + -ible	able to be seen

EXERCISE B: Using Roots to Define Words. Match the words in the first column with their meanings in the second column.

EXAMPLE: postpone

to put off until later

1. prospect *f*
2. inversion *d*
3. diction *a*
4. mobility *j*
5. intervention *b*
6. transpose *i*
7. submission *c*
8. supervise *e*
9. attain *h*
10. captive *g*

a. way of using words
b. the act of coming between
c. something sent for approval
d. a turning upside down
e. to oversee
f. future outlook
g. someone taken as a prisoner
h. to reach
i. to change places
j. ease of movement

Using Suffixes

A *suffix* is one or more syllables added at the end of a root to form a new word. The following chart shows seven suffixes, their meanings, and a word using each one. It also tells you the part of speech formed by each suffix. Using these suffixes together with the prefixes and roots you have been learning, you can form many words. In addition when you come upon a new word you can analyze its various parts and get clues as to its meaning and part of speech.

SEVEN COMMON SUFFIXES			
Suffix	**Meaning**	**Example**	**Part of Speech**
-able (-ible)	capable of being	comfort- + -able	adjective
-ance (-ence)	the act of	confid- + -ence	noun
-ful	full of	joy- + -ful	adjective
-ity	the state of being	senior- + -ity	noun
-ly	in a certain way	firm- + -ly love- + -ly	adverb or adjective
-ment	the result of being	amaze- + -ment	noun
-tion (-ion, -sion)	the act or state of being	ten- + -sion	noun

EXERCISE C: Using Suffixes to Change Words from One Part of Speech to Another. Using the suffixes in the preceding chart, change each of the following words to the part of speech indicated. Because the spelling of some of the words will change slightly, you will need to use a dictionary. Then write a brief definition of each new word. Check your definition, again using the dictionary. Enter in your vocabulary notebook any words whose definitions you missed.

Answers may vary; sample words are given.

EXAMPLE: Change *grace* to an adjective.

graceful full of grace

1. Change *perform* to a noun. *performance*
2. Change *regret* to an adjective. *regrettable*
3. Change *act* to a noun. *action*
4. Change *like* to an adjective. *likable*
5. Change *attend* to a noun. *attendance*
6. Change *timid* to a noun. *timidity*
7. Change *cheer* to an adjective. *cheerful*
8. Change *mobile* to a noun. *mobility*

9. Change *predictable* to an adverb. *predictably*
10. Change *correspond* to a noun. *correspondence*

APPLICATION: Using Structure to Form New Words. Try your hand at combining word parts to form words. Choose from among the prefixes, roots, and suffixes in the charts in this section. Combine the parts to make ten words. Then write ten sentences using the words.
Different sentences using the same word might be compared.

EXAMPLE: transmit

They will transmit the message at dawn.

Exploring Word Origins 19.4

You can use words to tell stories, but many words have interesting stories of their own. Some words have traveled here from other lands, including familiar words such as *chowder* (taken from a French word), *dollar* (from a Dutch word), and *algebra* (from an Arabic word). Some words acquire new meanings over the years; others team up to form new words with new meanings. *Magazine* is an example of the first type of word; *spacewalk* and *southpaw* are examples of the second. Other words have been made up, or *coined,* because scientists and inventors needed names for things that were unknown or that never existed before. Some examples of coined words are *laser, scuba,* and *quark.*

This section will examine the origin and development, or *etymology,* of a number of interesting words in all of these different categories.

Loanwords

Many English words are borrowed from other languages. Although some of these words are part of your everyday vocabulary, it probably never occurs to you that they came from another language.

Loanwords are words in the English language that have been borrowed from other languages.

Of all the *loanwords* in the English language, by far the greatest number can be traced back to Latin and French. The Latin words are usually words that refer to philosophy, religion, and other intellectual topics. Many of the French words describe literature, the arts, and government. By contrast, many of the simple words you use daily, such as *sky, house, mother, winter,* and *summer,* can be traced back a thousand years to the Scandinavian influence that began with the Viking conquests of England. Loanwords have also come into English from other European languages—Spanish, Italian, and German—and from the languages of the East and of Africa.

Along with all the words borrowed from various foreign languages, there are a number of loanwords that were borrowed from the languages of the Native Americans. Many of these words name foods, plants, and animals that were unknown to the early settlers and for which they thus had no words. Some examples of these loanwords are *squash, succotash, skunk,* and *moccasin*. Of the words borrowed from the Native American languages, perhaps the most important are those used as place names. For example, Kansas, itself a Siouan tribal and river name, has for its capital Topeka, another Siouan name that means "good place to dig potatoes." Among the counties of Kansas are Chautauqua, a Seneca word that means "one has taken out fish there"; Cheyenne, a Dakota word meaning "to speak unintelligibly"; and Shawnee, an Algonquian word for "southerners."

EXERCISE A: Discovering the Sources of Borrowed Words. In a dictionary that provides etymologies, look up each of the underlined words in the following paragraph. On your paper write the language of origin next to the number for each word. When more than one origin is given for a word, use the first. If your dictionary uses abbreviations for languages, use the guide to abbreviations in the front or back of the dictionary to find the full name of each language.

EXAMPLE: loyal

French

1. Fr 2. Hebrew 3. Irish 4. Fr 5. Algonquian 6. Narragansett 7. Fr 8. Fr

On their way to the (1) concert, (2) Sarah and (3) Kevin stopped at a (4) restaurant. (5) Squash and (6) succotash were on the (7) menu, but the couple decided to order an (8) omelet, (9) spaghetti, and a salad of (10) tomatoes, lettuce, and (11) mayonnaise. For (12) dessert, they had (13) tapioca, (14) chocolate cake, and (15) coffee. Sarah was wearing a (16) shawl and a new (17) denim skirt. Kevin was wearing a (18) parka and (19) dungarees. Fortunately, they had an (20) umbrella, because when they left to go to the concert, it was raining. 9. It 10. Sp 11. Fr 12. Mid Eng 13. Port 14. Fr 15. It 16. Urdu 17. Fr 18. Aleut 19. Hindi 20. It

EXERCISE B: Matching Words with Their Origins. On your paper match the words in the first column with their origins in the second column. Since many of the words have changed in meaning over the years, you may have to look some of them up in a dictionary that provides etymologies in order to match them correctly.

EXAMPLE: powwow

a conference (Algonquian)

1. escape *c*	a. great water (Algonquian)
2. radical *h*	b. brotherly love (Greek)
3. janitor *g*	c. out of one's cloak (Latin)
4. plaid *f*	d. an arm (Latin)
5. geometry *j*	e. to tremble (Latin)
6. pretzel *d*	f. blanket (Gaelic)
7. Lake Michigan *a*	g. doorkeeper (Latin)
8. prairie *i*	h. root (Latin)
9. Philadelphia *b*	i. meadowland (French)
10. tremendous *e*	j. to measure the earth (Greek)

EXERCISE C: Finding Loanwords in the Dictionary. In a dictionary that provides etymologies, find words from any five of the following languages. For each word that you find, give yourself points for the word according to the number in parentheses after each language. A total score of 25 would be considered excellent for this exercise.

Students might exchange papers and verify each other's etymologies. Words that students have found might also be listed on the board.

EXAMPLE: Hindi (7)

bungalow 7 points

1. French (1)
2. Italian (2)
3. German (3)
4. Spanish (3)
5. Yiddish (4)
6. Chinese (4)
7. Japanese (4)
8. Native American (5)
9. Sanskrit (7)
10. Arabic (7)
11. Persian (7)
12. Hindi (7)

Old Words with New Meanings

Another way speakers of English have expanded the language is by giving new meanings to existing words. Sometimes the original meaning falls into disuse and is forgotten. *Camera,* for example, originally meant "chamber" or "room." More often a word simply gains one or more additional meanings. *Rig,* for example, still means "the arrangement of sails and masts on a ship." Today, however, *rig* also means "oil drilling equipment" and "a tractor-trailer."

The English language grows by giving new meanings to existing words.

Think of all the different meanings for words that describe parts of the body. Look up the words *head, arm, elbow, hand,* and *heart,* for example. Each has many meanings, both old and new. In addition, all but one of the five words can easily be used as either a noun or a verb.

Existing words also take on new meanings by working together. From the time of its origin, the English language has combined words to create new words with new meanings. Common examples are *lion-hearted, breakfast,* and *freeway.*

EXERCISE D: Combining Words to Create New Words. Match each word in the first column with the appropriate word in the second column and write the words you have formed on your paper.

EXAMPLE: waste paper

wastepaper

1. hitch	a. book	*1. hitchhike*
2. copy	b. sick	*2. copycat*
3. text	c. way	*3. textbook*
4. home	d. pack	*4. homesick*
5. search	e. hike	*5. searchlight*
6. free	f. ball	*6. freeway*
7. back	g. tack	*7. backpack*
8. basket	h. weight	*8. basketball*
9. thumb	i. light	*9. thumbtack*
10. feather	j. cat	*10. featherweight*

Coinages

In addition to borrowing words and adding new meanings to existing words, the English language grows through the creation of new words called *coinages*.

The English language grows through the addition of newly coined words.

New words are needed to describe new inventions, new ideas, and new situations. There are several different methods of inventing new words.

Acronyms. An acronym is a word coined from the first letter or first few letters of a series of words. Many acronyms were invented to describe scientific advances. The words *radar* (*ra*dio *d*etecting *a*nd *r*anging) and *sonar* (*so*und *n*avigation *a*nd *r*anging) were formed this way. Others were invented as abbreviations for organizations or acts of government. The word *SAC* (*S*trategic *A*ir *C*ommand) falls into this category. Like other similar words, it is made up of capital letters.

"People" Words. A surprising number of words have their origin in the name of a person. When you speak of eating a sandwich, driving along a macadam road, or wearing sideburns, you are memorializing the Earl of Sandwich, a Scottish engineer named McAdam, and a Civil War general named Burnside.

Clipped Words. Some new words are simply shortened versions of old words. Examples are *ad* (advertisement), *hi-fi* (high fidelity), and *bike* (bicycle).

Blends. Some words are formed by combining parts of other words. For example, *motel* was formed when someone wanted to describe a hotel intended for people traveling by motor car. *Chortle* was invented by Lewis Carroll to describe the way a character could chuckle and snort at the same time.

Brand Names. The brand names created by companies to describe new products are another fertile source of new words. Often, one of these names eventually becomes the word used for the whole group of products, even though some of them may be manufactured by other companies. The word *Kleenex* is a good example. If you look up *Kleenex* in the dictionary, you will find that the word is used to refer to tissues in general.

EXERCISE E: Finding the Origins of Acronyms and "People" Words. In a dictionary that provides etymologies, look up each of the following words. On your paper write the definition and the origin of the word next to the appropriate number. *Answers on page T-125.*

EXAMPLE: mackintosh

raincoat, named after a Scottish inventor named Mackintosh

1. scuba
2. chauvinism
3. nicotine
4. quasar
5. ZIP code
6. NASA
7. pasteurize
8. diesel
9. OPEC
10. cardigan

EXERCISE F: Finding the Origins of Clipped Words, Blends, and Brand Names. In a dictionary that provides etymologies, look up each of the following words. On your paper write the word or words from which each of the clipped words or blends was derived. If the name was coined by a manufacturer, write *brand name* next to the appropriate number.

EXAMPLE: stereo

stereophonic record player

1. motor pedal 2. taxicab 3. brand name 4. breakfast lunch 5. omnibus 6. splash surge

1. moped
2. taxi
3. Band-Aid
4. brunch
5. bus
6. splurge
7. zoo
8. Xerox
9. Levi's
10. sci-fi

7. zoological garden 8. brand name 9. brand name 10. science fiction

APPLICATION: Determining Origins of Words. From the following list of words, find four that have come from Latin, three that are combinations of common words, two that have been derived from names of people, and one that is Native American in origin.

EXAMPLE: motorcycle

combination

1. combination 2. Latin 3. combination 4. Latin 5. person (C. C. Boycott) 6. combination

1. airmail
2. circus
3. motorboat
4. virus
5. boycott
6. baseball
7. auditorium
8. genius
9. valentine
10. Oklahoma

7. Latin 8. Latin 9. person (St. Valentine) 10. Native American (Choctaw)

Chapter 20

Improving Your Spelling

The ability to write effectively has always been recognized as a valuable skill. One of the first steps in improving your writing is to improve your spelling. Accurate spelling is important whether you are writing a letter to a friend or a report for a teacher.

This chapter will show you a number of ways to solve most spelling problems. The first section describes several techniques for learning the spelling of problem words. The second section focuses on specific types of spelling errors and provides rules to help you avoid them.

20.1 Solving Your Spelling Problems

Before you can begin a successful program of spelling improvement, you must identify the words that you yourself have problems with. This section will help you to identify the words that you most frequently misspell. It will also give you useful suggestions about how to correct the spelling problems that you have found.

■ Your Personal Spelling List

One of the best ways to improve your spelling is to keep a personal spelling list. Set aside a special section in your notebook to list words that you use often but have trouble spelling. To start your list, gather together a group of corrected papers from all of your courses. A quick review of your spelling errors on these papers should supply you with enough words for a small list.

Make a list of words that you misspell, write the list in your notebook, and review it regularly.

The following example shows one useful way of setting up a spelling list. Each page of the list is divided into four columns. Each entry includes a spelling word, its correct pronunciation, a simple definition, and a short sentence using the word. The fourth column can also be used for memory aids, which are described later in this section. Note that troublesome letters have been underlined in the first column and the fourth column of the spelling list to make the problem areas stand out.

Spelling List

Word	Pronunciation	Definition	Sentence / Memory Aid
accept	ək sept′	to take or receive willingly	Carla was asked to accept the trophy for the basketball team.
cafeteria	kaf′ə tir′ē ə	a self-service restaurant	Meet me in the cafeteria for lunch.
necessary	nes′ə ser′ē	required	Plenty of sun and rain are necessary for a good crop.
schedule	skej′ ool	a list of details or times when certain things will happen	Do you have a schedule for every school day?

To prepare your own list begin by looking up each word in a dictionary and entering it in the first column. If you have difficulty finding the word, you can refer to the Word Finder Chart on pages 502 and 503 of Section 23.3. In the same section, under the heading "Understanding Main Entries," there is an explanation of pronunciation. Since dictionaries differ slightly in the pronunciation symbols they use, the symbols used on page 415 may vary from those in your dictionary. It will be useful for you to become familiar with the pronunciation symbols used in your own dictionary since those are the ones you should use in the second column of your notebook. Finally, add a definition and a short sentence for each entry.

When you have completed your list, proofread each spelling entry to be sure that the information you have written is correct. Proofreading, incidentally, is a good way to check the spelling in all of your written work. When you proofread your papers, check a dictionary for the spelling of any words you are not sure of. Every student who is serious about spelling improvement should acquire the "dictionary habit."

To carry out a spelling improvement program, you must also keep your personal spelling list up to date. Once a week review your written work and spelling tests for new words to add to your list.

EXERCISE A: Starting Your Personal Spelling List. Select at least five words that you have trouble spelling and enter them into a special spelling list in your notebook. Follow the model given on page 415. You will need to consult a dictionary to find the correct spelling, pronunciation, and definition of each word.

Students might compile a class list of generally troublesome words, listing all words that show up on three or more of their individual lists.

EXAMPLE: secretary

Word	Pronunciation	Definition	Sentence/ Memory Aid
secretary	sek′ rə ter′ ē	a person who carries out clerical duties	Her secretary was excellent.

EXERCISE B: Adding More Words to Your Personal Spelling List. Each of the following sentences has one misspelled word. Find the word and rewrite the sentence, using the correct spelling of the word. Then exchange papers with a classmate and correct each other's papers. After checking a dictionary, add to your personal spelling list any words that you misspelled.

EXAMPLE: The lines were separate but paralel.

The lines were separate but parallel.

3. anonymous 4. library 8. restaurant 9. substitute 12. lightning

1. Sarah loves to do experiments in the science labratory. *laboratory*
2. Nate accidentaly spilled his glass of milk. *accidentally*
3. The detective just received an anonimous tip.
4. How many books did you borrow from the libary?
5. The camel is well adapted to dessert life. *desert*
6. The magician made the rabbit dissappear. *disappear*
7. Do you have an extra pair of scissers? *scissors*
8. The twins had spaghetti at the resturant.
9. Our teacher was absent, so we had a substatute.
10. Tomorow is Terry's birthday party. *Tomorrow*
11. Bart has a brother in the eigth grade. *eighth*
12. Some people are afraid of thunder and lightening.
13. Mathmatics is Rosa's favorite subject. *Mathematics*
14. Did you bring me back a souvenier from your trip?
15. I wonder wheather Jennifer will win the race.
16. The jury found the defendent not guilty. *defendant*
17. Mark was dissappointed with his test grade.
18. Who was the villan in the play? *villain*
19. Tina went to the beauty salon for a permanant.
20. Bill is my next-door neighber. *neighbor*

14. souvenir 15. whether 17. disappointed 19. permanent

A System for Improving Your Spelling

To improve your spelling, you should review the words on your spelling list frequently.

Use the following method to study the words on your personal spelling list.

The method given in the chart can be very helpful if you use it regularly.

A METHOD FOR LEARNING PROBLEM WORDS

1. *Look* at each word. Does it have a pattern of letters that you could memorize? For example, the word *committee* has two *m*'s, two *t*'s, and two *e*'s. Notice how the letters are arranged in the word. Then cover the word and try to get a mental picture of it.
2. *Pronounce* the word, syllable by syllable. If, for example, you pronounce *library* carefully, you will note that there is an *r* after the *b*.
3. *Write* the word on a sheet of paper. Say each syllable aloud as you are writing it down.
4. *Compare* the word that you wrote on the paper with the word in your notebook. If you spelled the word correctly, put a small check in front of the word in your notebook. If you misspelled the word, circle the letter or letters on your paper that are incorrect and start over again with the first step.

Once a week you might also have a member of your family or a friend read your spelling words to you. As each word is read, write it. In addition, try to use these words in any writing assignments that you have. Using the words will help you to master them more quickly. You may consider a word mastered when you have spelled it correctly at least three times in your own written work.

EXERCISE C: Spelling Difficult Words. Read the following sentences, looking carefully at each underlined word. If the word is spelled correctly, write *correct* next to the appropriate number on your paper. If the word is misspelled, write the correct spelling of the word. When you are finished, check each underlined word in a dictionary. Add to your personal spelling list the correct spellings of any words that you misspelled. Review these words using the Look, Pronounce, Write, and Compare method.

EXAMPLE: Missing our train was just the first event in an extrodinary day.

extraordinary

1. The captain of the ship wore a blue uniform. *C*
2. Grandma served warm apple pie for dessert. *C*
3. Molly Pitcher was a couragous figure during the Revolutionary War. *courageous*
4. Jason wrote the address on the envelope, using invisible ink. *C*
5. Check the calender to see when spring vacation begins. *calendar*
6. The school band marched to the rythm of the drums. *rhythm*
7. Dale, an expert gymnast, excells on the parallel bars. *C*
8. The principal gave awards for perfect attendence.
9. Do you know the capital of Alaska? *C*
10. Someone left a blue hankerchief on the desk.
11. The ambulance drove up to the emergency entrance. *C*
12. Debbie's cat, Penelope, was particularly fond of fish. *C*
13. What mystery book would you reccommend? *recommend*
14. The cashier forgot to put my receipt in the bag. *C*
15. Friday morning the superintendant spoke to us.
16. The glee club stayed after school to rehearse. *C*
17. Have you ever seen a prairie dog? *C*
18. Occassionally my grandfather drives me to school.
19. This car needs a thorough cleaning. *C*
20. What foriegn language can you speak? *foreign*

8. attendance 10. handkerchief 15. superintendent 18. Occasionally

Developing Memory Aids

If, after several practice sessions, there are some words that you are still misspelling, you can make up a short memory aid for each word.

Use memory aids to help you remember the spelling of words that are difficult for you.

You can often associate some of the letters in troublesome words with the same letters in related words.

EXAMPLES: The lib*rar*y has *rar*e books.

Station*er*y is another word for lett*er* pap*er*.

Sometimes you may find a shorter word within the problem word.

EXAMPLES: The *air* smells fresh on the pr*air*ie.

There is a *mile* in *mile*age.

A *law*yer studies the *law*.

A *rat* is in the labo*rat*ory.

Did you *hear* the band re*hear*se?

EXERCISE D: Writing Memory Aids. Write a memory aid for each of the following spelling words.

Answers will vary; samples given for first two.

EXAMPLE: There's iron in the environment.

1. An ally should not be chosen accidentally. 2. Her mate is an amateur actor.

1. accidentally
2. amateur
3. attendance
4. believe
5. clothes
6. criticize
7. foreign
8. handkerchief
9. mathematics
10. secretary

EXERCISE E: Making Your Own Memory Aids. Select five words from your personal spelling list. In your notebook write a short memory aid for each word.

Students might share their favorite memory aids with their classmates.

EXAMPLE: A principle is a rule.

Studying Common Spelling Demons

When you have mastered most of the words on your personal spelling list, it is time to expand your spelling program. Studying a list of words that people frequently misspell can help you further improve your spelling skills. Words that are often misspelled are commonly called *spelling demons*.

Study the words on a list of spelling demons to find out which ones you need to work on.

The following chart of spelling demons contains one hundred words that students often misspell. Divide this list into groups of ten words. Use the Look, Pronounce, Write, and Compare method described on page 418 to study each group of words. When you find a word that you have trouble spelling, add it to your personal spelling list and review it along with the other words on your list.

100 COMMON SPELLING DEMONS			
absence	courageous	knowledge	receipt
accidentally	criticize	laboratory	recommend
achieve	curious	lawyer	rehearse
acquaintance	deceive	library	restaurant
aisle	defendant	lightning	rhythm
amateur	desert	mathematics	scissors
analyze	desperate	mileage	secretary
anniversary	dessert	misspell	separate
anonymous	disappear	naturally	similar
appearance	disappoint	necessary	sincerely
argument	dissatisfied	neighbor	souvenir
athletic	eighth	nuisance	spaghetti
attendance	embarrass	occasion	straight
awkward	emergency	occasionally	substitute
barrel	envelope	opinion	succeed
behavior	environment	parallel	superintendent
believe	exercise	particularly	suspicious
calendar	explanation	permanent	technique
capital	extraordinary	physician	temporary
capitol	familiar	possession	thorough
captain	foreign	prairie	tomorrow
cemetery	guarantee	preparation	unnecessary
clothes	handkerchief	privilege	vacuum
committee	independence	probably	villain
condemn	interfere	pronunciation	whether

EXERCISE F: Adding the Missing Letters. Each of the following spelling demons has one or more letters missing. Write the complete words on your paper. Then check your answers against the chart of common spelling demons. Add to your personal spelling list any words that you misspelled.

EXAMPLE: mi _ _ pell

misspell

1. ach _i_ _e_ ve
2. bel _i_ _e_ ve
3. calend _a_ r
4. capt _a_ _i_ n
5. courag _e_ _o_ _u_ s
6. ei _g_ _h_ th
7. emergen _c_ y
8. lab _o_ _r_ atory
9. lib _r_ _a_ ry
10. light _n_ ing
11. perman _e_ nt
12. prep _a_ ration
13. privil _e_ ge
14. re _c_ ommend
15. r _h_ _y_ thm
16. s _c_ _i_ ssors
17. sep _a_ rate
18. spa _g_ _h_ etti
19. vac _u_ _u_ m
20. vill _a_ _i_ n

EXERCISE G: Using Spelling Demons. From the chart on page 421, choose ten spelling demons that you need to practice. On your paper write a sentence for each word. Then proofread your work carefully. *Students can correct each other's papers. Any words misspelled can be added to students' personal spelling lists.*

EXAMPLE: dissatisfied

We were dissatisfied with the results of the first experiment.

APPLICATION: Using Spelling Words in a Story. Write a short story using at least ten words from the chart of spelling demons on page 421 and ten additional words from your own personal spelling list. Underline each of the words that you have chosen from the chart and your list. Then proofread your story carefully for misspelled words.

EXAMPLE: Although we had rehearsed the play for weeks, the opening night held a number of surprises for us all.

Selected stories can be read to the class, students can be asked to guess which words might be underlined, and then students can give the correct spelling for each guess.

Following Spelling Rules 20.2

Certain kinds of spelling errors are very common. Some people have difficulty forming plurals. Others make mistakes when adding a prefix or a suffix. Still others have problems with certain combinations of letters such as *ie* and *ei* or *-cede* and *-ceed*. This section will help you find out which of these situations cause problems for you. It will also provide you with one or more rules for each situation in order to help you avoid misspelling the problem words.

Forming Plurals

When you change a noun from its singular form to its plural form, you may sometimes be unsure about what ending to add. This is because the plural ending is not always the same. Most nouns in English form their plurals according to a few simple rules. The plurals of these words are called *regular plurals*. The plurals of nouns that do not follow these rules are called *irregular plurals*. Recognizing the differences between these two types of plurals can help you find the right endings, as can a knowledge of two simple rules that cover compound nouns.

Regular Plurals. Most nouns in English form the plural by adding *-s* or *-es*.

A regular plural is one that is formed by adding either *-s* or *-es* to the singular form of the noun.

Most regular plurals are formed simply by adding *-s*.

EXAMPLES:	bell	bells
	opinion	opinions
	athlete	athletes

A number of other regular plurals, such as the plurals of *mix* and *wish*, are formed by adding *-es*. In other cases you may need to change the spelling of the singular before adding the plural ending. The following chart will help you to form regular plurals correctly.

FORMING REGULAR PLURALS

Word Ending	Rule	Examples
-s, -ss, -x, -z, -ch, -sh	Add *-es*.	gas, gases success, successes fox, foxes waltz, waltzes branch, branches ash, ashes
-o preceded by a consonant	Add *-es*.	hero, heroes potato, potatoes EXCEPTIONS: alto, altos soprano, sopranos (and other musical terms)
-o preceded by a vowel	Add *-s*.	rodeo, rodeos
-y preceded by a consonant	Change *y* to *i* and add *-es*.	berry, berries party, parties
-y preceded by a vowel	Add *-s*.	toy, toys monkey, monkeys
-f	Add *-s*. OR Change *f* to *v* and add *-es*.	roof, roofs half, halves loaf, loaves
-ff	Add *-s*.	staff, staffs sheriff, sheriffs
-fe	Change *f* to *v* and add *-s*.	knife, knives wife, wives

Irregular Plurals. Some words have irregular plurals. They do not follow the rules in the preceding chart.

Use your dictionary to check the correct spelling of words with irregular plurals.

The following chart gives examples of some common irregular plurals.

FORMING IRREGULAR PLURALS		
Singular Form	**Rule**	**Plural Form**
ox	Add *-en.*	oxen
child	Add *-ren.*	children
foot	Change vowels.	feet
mouse	Change vowels and one other letter.	mice
moose	Make the plural the same as the singular.	moose
radius	Change *-us* to *-i.*	radii
crisis	Change *-is* to *-es.*	crises
medium	Change *-um* to *-a.*	media

If you are unsure about spelling the plural form of a word that does not appear in the charts, look it up in a dictionary. If no plural form is listed, then the plural is regular: Simply add *-s* or *-es* to the word. If a spelling change is necessary, the plural form will be listed after the entry word.

You should also know that some words have two ways to spell the plural. The plural of *mosquito,* for example, can be spelled either *mosquitoes* or *mosquitos*. In such cases the preferred form is listed first in the dictionary.

Plurals of Compound Nouns. Some compound nouns are written as one word *(handbook),* some are hyphenated *(father-in-law),* and some are written as separate words *(left field).*

Most compound nouns written as single words form their plurals regularly.

EXAMPLES: driveway driveways

armchair armchairs

If a compound noun is written with hyphens or as separate words, use the following rule.

Compound nouns written with hyphens or as separate words generally form the plural by making the modified word plural.

EXAMPLES: mother-in-law mothers-in-law

field mouse field mice

EXERCISE A: Writing Plural Forms. On your paper write the plural for each of the following words. If you are not sure of the spelling, refer to your dictionary. Add to your personal spelling list the plural form of any words that you had to look up.

EXAMPLE: station wagon

station wagons

1. veto *es*
2. house *s*
3. ax *es*
4. tariff *s*
5. thief *thieves*
6. turkey *s*
7. crisis *crises*
8. wolf *wolves*
9. activity
10. crash *es*
11. piano *s*
12. tractor *s*
13. tomato *es*
14. raspberry
15. leaf *leaves*
16. loss *es*
17. woman *women*
18. handkerchief *s*
19. ferry *ferries*
20. boardwalk *s*
21. shelf *shelves*
22. beach *es*
23. magnet *s*
24. baseball *s*
25. emergency
26. rodeo *s*
27. deer *deer*
28. dollar sign *s*
29. tooth *teeth*
30. chimney *s*

9. activities 14. raspberries 25. emergencies

EXERCISE B: Using Plurals in Sentences. Write ten sentences of your own, each using the plural form of one of the following words. *Sentences will vary; plurals are given.*

EXAMPLE: child

The children were eager to see what was inside the package.

1. sheep *sheep*
2. loaf *loaves*
3. cherry *cherries*
4. sandwich *sandwiches*
5. igloo *igloos*
6. goose *geese*
7. axis *axes*
8. starfish *starfish or starfishes*
9. echo
10. cliff

9. echoes
10. cliffs

Adding Prefixes

A prefix is one or more syllables added at the beginning of a word to form a new word.

When a prefix is added to a root word, the spelling of the root word stays the same.

When a familiar prefix such as *un-* is added at the beginning of a root word that you already know, you should be able to spell the new word without any trouble. Misspellings sometimes occur, however, when the last letter of a prefix is the same as the first letter of the root word. Remember to keep both letters when you are forming the new word.

EXAMPLES: re- + -cover = recover

un- + -necessary = unnecessary

dis- + -satisfield = dissatisfied

mis- + -spell = misspell

EXERCISE C: Using Prefixes. Combine the prefixes and root words in the following twenty items to form new words.

EXAMPLE: mis- + -lead

mislead

1. in- + -complete
2. mis- + -read *misread*
3. dis- + -solve *dissolve*
4. un- + -usual *unusual*
5. re- + -fill *refill*
6. dis- + -appear
7. un- + -fortunate
8. in- + -visible *invisible*
9. dis- + -appoint
10. un- + -noticed
11. re- + -gain *regain*
12. mis- + -place *misplace*
13. dis- + -agree *disagree*
14. con- + -serve *conserve*
15. in- + -numerable
16. re- + -play *replay*
17. in- + -expensive
18. mis- + -manage
19. dis- + -cover *discover*
20. re- + -paint *repaint*

1. incomplete 6. disappear 7. unfortunate 9. disappoint 10. unnoticed 15. innumerable 17. inexpensive 18. mismanage

Adding Suffixes

A suffix is one or more syllables added at the end of a word to form a new word.

Be aware of spelling changes needed in some root words when a suffix is added.

When a suffix is added to a root word, the spelling of the root word often changes. In these situations misspellings can easily occur.

The following chart shows the kinds of spelling changes that can take place.

SPELLING CHANGES TO MAKE WHEN ADDING SUFFIXES

Word Ending	Rule	Examples
-*y* preceded by a consonant	Change *y* to *i*.	lazy, laziness EXCEPTIONS: When the suffix begins with *i*: deny, denying fry, frying
-*y* preceded by a vowel	Make no change.	play, playful EXCEPTIONS: day, daily gay, gaily

-e	Drop the final *e* if suffix begins with a vowel.	like, likable value, valuable EXCEPTIONS: courage, courageous foresee, foreseeable notice, noticeable
-e	Make no change if suffix begins with a consonant.	grace, graceful sincere, sincerely EXCEPTIONS: argue, argument true, truly
One-syllable word ending in a single consonant preceded by a single vowel	Double the final consonant if suffix begins with a vowel.	bat, batted plan, planning EXCEPTIONS: Words ending in *-x* or *-w*: fix, fixed tow, towing
Word accented on the final syllable and ending in a single consonant preceded by a single vowel	Double the final consonant if suffix begins with a vowel.	begin, beginner EXCEPTIONS: Words in which the accent changes when the suffix is added: confer', con'ference

EXERCISE D: Making New Words with Suffixes. Make a new word that completes each of the following sentences by combining the words and suffixes given in parentheses. Write each new word on your paper, making any needed spelling changes. Then check the spelling of the new words in your dictionary.

EXAMPLE: When the check finally arrived, he thought his __(happy- + -ness)__ was assured.

happiness

1. We spent a <u>(peace- + -ful)</u> Saturday afternoon in the country. *peaceful*
2. The <u>(shop- + -er)</u> had too many packages to carry. *shopper*
3. The manager of the local hardware store had a very <u>(response- + -ible)</u> job. *responsible*
4. Does this rocking chair seem <u>(comfort- + -able)</u> to you? *comfortable*
5. Lisa <u>(benefit- + -ed)</u> from the swimming lessons she took. *benefited*
6. Jack enjoys his new job at the lake, and he likes his <u>(employ- + -er)</u>, too. *employer*
7. Is the <u>(amplify- + -er)</u> working? *amplifier*
8. Do you think that the story Gerry told us Monday is <u>(believe- + -able)</u>? *believable*
9. <u>(Play- + -ing)</u> softball has always been Jody's favorite activity. *Playing*
10. Do you think a letter has been <u>(omit- + -ed)</u> from that word? *omitted*

EXERCISE E: Using Suffixes. Combine the following root words and suffixes to form twenty new words. Then write twenty sentences, using one of the new words in each sentence. Underline each new word in your sentences and check the spelling of each new word in your dictionary.
Sentences will vary; spellings for new words are given.

EXAMPLE: wax- + -ing

waxing <u>Waxing</u> the floor by hand took hours.

1. value- + -able *valuable*
2. grow- + -ing *growing*
3. imagine- + -ary
4. hope- + -ful *hopeful*
5. rely- + -able *reliable*
6. scarce- + -ly *scarcely*
7. refer- + -ence *reference*
8. busy- + -ness *business*
9. beauty- + -ful *beautiful*
10. pay- + -ment *payment*
11. slip- + -ery *slippery*
12. lucky- + -ly *luckily*
13. perform- + -ance
14. plenty- + -ful *plentiful*
15. final- + -ly *finally*
16. love- + -able *lovable*
17. amuse- + -ment
18. guide- + -ance *guidance*
19. break- + -able *breakable*
20. reside- + -ence *residence*

3. imaginary 13. performance 17. amusement

Deciding on *ie* or *ei*

A major source of difficulty for many spellers is deciding whether to use *ie* or *ei* in a number of common words. Following these few general rules can help you to make your choice.

When a word has a long *e* sound, use *ie*.

When a word has a long *a* sound, use *ei*.

When a word has a long *e* sound but is preceded by the letter *c*, use *ei*.

The following chart lists a few common words that follow the above rules.

COMMON *ie* AND *ei* WORDS		
Long *e* Sound Use *ie*	**Long *a* Sound Use *ei***	**Long *e* Sound Preceded by *c* Use *ei***
brief	eight	ceiling
chief	freight	deceive
niece	reign	perceive
piece	sleigh	receipt
relieve	vein	receive
shield	weight	
yield		

However, a few words are exceptions to these rules. The most important of these are shown in the next chart.

SOME EXCEPTIONS TO THE RULES		
either	neither	seize

When you are in doubt about how to spell a word that does not appear in the preceding charts, consult your dictionary.

EXERCISE F: Working with *ie* and *ei* Words. Write the incomplete word from each of the following sentences on your paper, filling in either *ie* or *ei* in the blanks. You may refer to the rules as you work. Then check each word in your dictionary and add to your personal spelling list any words that you misspelled.

EXAMPLE: He asked the clerk for a rec __ __ pt.

receipt

1. The c _e_ _i_ ling in the living room was powder blue.
2. We noticed that the farmer was in his f _i_ _e_ ld plowing the soil.
3. May I have a p _i_ _e_ ce of watermelon?
4. Tom is giving a report about nutrition today in hyg _i_ _e_ ne class.
5. We stopped at a Chinese restaurant for shrimp chow m _e_ _i_ n.
6. How many cars did you count on that fr _e_ _i_ ght train?
7. Sally's Irish setter likes to retr _i_ _e_ ve sticks when we throw them.
8. Queen Victoria had a long r _e_ _i_ gn.
9. Dennis forgot to bring a clean handkerch _i_ _e_ f with him.
10. How much does a full-grown Indian elephant w _e_ _i_ gh?

Using *-cede, -ceed,* and *-sede*

Many spellers find the words that end in *-cede, -ceed,* and *-sede* confusing. Fortunately, there are relatively few words that end this way.

Memorize the words that end in *-cede, -ceed,* and *-sede.*

The following chart lists those words ending in *-cede* that you are most likely to meet.

WORDS ENDING IN *-cede*		
concede	precede	secede
intercede	recede	

In contrast only three common words end in *-ceed*: *exceed, proceed,* and *succeed*. Only one word ends in *-sede*: *supersede*.

EXERCISE G: Spelling Words Ending in *-cede, -ceed,* and *-sede*. Some of the words in the following paragraph have missing letters. Write each word next to the appropriate number on your paper, with the letters correctly filled in. Then check the words in your dictionary and add to your personal spelling list any words that you misspelled.

EXAMPLE: Suc ___ ___ ___ ___ ing in an exploration of arctic regions can be difficult.

Succeeding

The tiny village (1) re _c_ _e_ _d_ _e_ d in the distance as explorer Colin Irwin set off across the ice. Irwin (2) super _s_ _e_ _d_ _e_ d the original leader, who had been removed from command even though Irwin had (3) inter _c_ _e_ _d_ _e_ d for him. (4) Pre _c_ _e_ _d_ _e_ d by his guide, the explorer and his team headed for Point Barrow, Alaska. Although Colin had not (5) suc _c_ _e_ _e_ _d_ ed in earlier attempts, he was not ready to (6) con _c_ _e_ _d_ _e_ defeat. Despite the fierce wind, the group (7) pro _c_ _e_ _e_ _d_ ed to make their way across the frozen bay. Their speed (8) ex _c_ _e_ _e_ _d_ ed that of any previous group.

APPLICATION 1: Using Spelling Rules in Writing a Story. Write a story using words that follow the spelling rules you have learned in this section. Use at least three words that represent rules for plurals, three words that represent rules for prefixes and suffixes,

and three words that represent rules for *ie* and *ei* words. Also include at least one word that ends in *-cede* or *-ceed*. Underline the words that you choose to represent the spelling rules you have learned. Proofread your story for misspelled words.
Students might check each other's stories to see that requirements have been met and underlined words spelled correctly.

EXAMPLE: Good stories often begin with good characters.

APPLICATION 2: Planning Regular Reviews. Review the spelling rules that you have learned in this section. Decide which ones you need more work on. Write these rules, together with examples of each, in your notebook for further study. *Students might be grouped according to the rules they have chosen and instructed to drill each other using the examples they have prepared.*

UNIT V

Study Skills

Chapter 21

Improving Your Study Habits

Good study habits can help you do well in school. The skills involved include planning, organizing, listening, note-taking, and speaking. This chapter discusses a variety of methods for improving your study habits. Applying the suggestions in this chapter will help you do your schoolwork in a faster, more efficient way. Improving your study habits can also give you more confidence in your work and lead to better grades.

21.1 Establishing Good Study Habits

Everyone has study habits. Some of your own study habits are probably good; some may be bad. Begin looking at your study habits by answering these important questions: Are you getting good results from the way you are studying? Could you get more studying done in less time? Could you study in a more interesting way? If your answers reveal that you have good study habits, this section will reinforce those habits. If your answers point to a need for improvement, this section will help you establish better study habits.

Setting Goals

If you set goals and work to achieve them, your study habits will improve. Goals give you something specific to work on, and they provide direction for your efforts. In setting study goals, continued progress should be your major concern. As soon as you reach certain goals, establish new ones to guide your further development.

Set realistic short-range and long-range study goals that you can achieve.

To improve your study habits, you should set two types of goals. The first type of goal is a *short-range goal.* Achieving short-range goals requires little prior training. Just by beginning to work on them you can find success.

SOME SHORT-RANGE GOALS
Keeping a daily assignment notebook
Reviewing your class notes each evening
Looking through each reading assignment before beginning to read
Having a pleasure-reading book always handy to read
Recording new vocabulary words in a special notebook

The second type of goal is a *long-range goal.* Reaching long-range goals requires the development of special skills and repeated practice. Thus, long-range goals may take weeks, months, or even years to accomplish.

SOME LONG-RANGE GOALS
Increasing reading speed by at least one hundred words per minute
Taking notes rapidly in clear outline form
Reading with greater comprehension
Preparing a report using a number of different sources
Giving oral reports with more confidence

Once you decide on some short-range and long-range goals that you would like to work on, you should write down these goals. You can record them in your notebook or on a card posted above your study area at home. Examine your goals often—at least every week. Then practice the skills you are trying to acquire.

EXERCISE A: Choosing Short-Range and Long-Range Goals. Divide the following goals into two groups: five short-range goals and five long-range goals.

1. Completing a homework assignment *short*
2. Increasing your vocabulary skills *long*
3. Reading more books purely for pleasure *long*
4. Finishing a book report *short*
5. Asking a teacher for help in outlining *short*
6. Keeping organized notes in all subject areas *long*
7. Reorganizing your notebook by subject *short*
8. Improving your grades in all major subjects *long*
9. Learning to speak up more during classroom discussions *long*
10. Recording tonight's homework assignments *short*

EXERCISE B: Setting Your Own Goals. Think about your study habits. Then write down three short-range goals and three long-range goals that you think you should work on. *Students might list goals on board and then discuss the length of time that might be needed to achieve each goal.*

■ Scheduling Study Time

Another way to improve study habits is to organize your time better. Your time is valuable and should not be wasted. Spending too much time studying is almost as bad as spending too little time.

Establish a regular study schedule and follow it each night.

You should plan a study schedule that includes time for homework, time for special projects, and time to review for tests. A study schedule will help you budget your time. It will also help you avoid putting off work that needs to be done.

When setting up a study schedule, take three important factors into consideration: your family routine, your household duties, and your interests and leisure activities. After time has been set aside for these regular matters, begin blocking in time for each subject. If you have no homework in a subject on certain days, use this block of time for review or for work on long-term projects. The following chart includes some additional hints about how to make the best use of the time you schedule for studying.

SUGGESTIONS FOR SCHEDULING STUDY TIME

1. Plan to study during the hours when you are most alert.
2. Plan to study in time blocks of about a half-hour each.
3. Plan to study your most difficult subjects first each night.
4. Plan to follow the same basic schedule from Monday through Thursday.
5. Plan to complete short-term projects before continuing with long-term projects.
6. Set aside a special time for pleasure reading each day.
7. Post your study schedule in a visible place as a daily reminder.

In addition to using free time to review for tests, you should review at least once a week in each subject. A review is most helpful right after new material has been covered in class. Three to four days later you should again concentrate on reviewing. If you review material four or five times over a period of several weeks, you should know the material well when it appears on a test.

EXERCISE C: Making a Study Schedule. The following steps for making a study schedule are out of order. Read them carefully. Then, on your paper, write them in a more logical order.

1. Block in time for less difficult subjects. *3*
2. Block in time for dinner and tennis practice. *1*
3. Block in at least a half-hour of study time for most difficult subject. *2*
4. Post study schedule in working area. *5*
5. Block in free reading time. *4*

EXERCISE D: Creating Your Own Study Schedule. Using the information you have just learned, make a study schedule for the coming week. Start with the time school ends and finish with the time you go to sleep.
Students might write short evaluations of each other's plans.

Keeping Track of Assignments

To complete class assignments, you should begin by recording them carefully. Writing an assignment down keeps you from forgetting to do the work and helps you to do a thorough job.

Keep track of daily assignments, test dates, and special projects.

Perhaps the easiest way to record assignments is simply to record them in your notebook, using a special assignment page for each subject. The assignment page should be placed directly after the divider for a particular subject. One simple way to set up this page is to make four vertical columns. Use one column for the date of the assignment, one for a description of the assignment, one for the due date, and one for a check when the assignment is completed.

Assignments			
Subject Area:			
Date Assigned	Description	Date Due	Completed

You may instead prefer to use a separate notebook for recording assignments. In this case a different format should be used. In the assignment book, you should record all the assignments given on a particular day on a single page. List the subject first, then give the assignment and date, and finally leave space so you can check off work that is completed. Long-term assignments should be carried over to succeeding pages or recorded on a special page.

	Assignments			
		Date:		
	Subject	Description	Date Due	Completed

With either method of recording assignments, it is important to have a column labeled "Completed" where you can place a check when you have finished each assignment. This column will show you at a glance which work is incomplete. Putting a check in the column can also give you a feeling of satisfaction when each piece of work is completed.

EXERCISE E: Recording Your Assignments. Choose a method for recording your assignments in each class every day. Use either one page under each subject in your notebook or a separate assignment notebook. Follow either the format on page 440 or the one on page 441.

Notebooks can be checked from time to time. Students might also make a class calendar showing test dates and due dates for long-term assignments.

Eliminating Distractions While Studying

There are distractions all around you, whether you are at school, at home, or at the library. Fortunately, you can learn to control most of these distractions.

Eliminate study distractions before they become bad habits.

You should first identify those things that can interfere with your concentration. It is easy to tell yourself that listening to the radio helps you study or that you can read when you are sitting and talking with your friends. However, these and similar distractions may actually be keeping you from reaching your full potential as a student. You may be spending more time studying than you really need to. Yet, because of distractions, you may not be learning as much as you could be. The suggestions in the following chart can help you eliminate and overcome distractions so that you can concentrate on your work.

SUGGESTIONS FOR ELIMINATING DISTRACTIONS

1. In class block out noises by reading or listening with a specific purpose in mind: for example, to learn what material will be on tomorrow's test.
2. Take notes when you are reading and when you are listening to lectures. Writing down information will keep you from daydreaming.
3. Do not get *too* comfortable while studying. Staying alert helps you concentrate and study well.
4. Turn off the radio, television, or stereo when you are studying.
5. Set aside a specific time when your friends can call on the telephone.
6. Change your study location if you are continually being distracted.

EXERCISE F: Cutting Down on Distractions. Copy the following chart onto notebook paper and check the column that best describes how often each item distracts you. If you checked "usually" for any item, use the suggestions in the chart on this page to try to change the habit. *Class discussion can be based on the filled-in charts, with students comparing answers and offering additional suggestions for avoiding distractions.*

Distractions at Home: While studying do you listen to	Usually	Sometimes	Rarely
radio			
television			
stereo			
Are you distracted by			
telephone calls			
family activities			
Distractions at School: During class and study periods, do you find yourself			
daydreaming			
doodling			
talking with other students			
listening to outside noises			

APPLICATION: Evaluating Your Study Habits. After two weeks of trying the preceding suggestions for improving study habits, answer the following questions about your study habits.

You may wish to use students' answers as the basis for individual conferences.

1. What short-range and long-range study goals have you decided to work on?
2. What have you done to achieve the goals you have set for yourself?
3. Have you established a study schedule and followed it each night?
4. How can you improve your study schedule to make it more useful?
5. Have you recorded in a notebook all your assignments for each class?
6. Have you checked the assignments off as you completed them?

7. What distractions have interfered with your studying lately?
8. What steps have you taken in the last week to eliminate distractions while studying?
9. What rating (poor, fair, good, excellent) would you give your study habits?
10. What particular study habits will you continue to work on?

21.2 Developing Your Listening Skills

In school you are likely to spend approximately 75 percent of your time listening. It is important that you train yourself to listen well so that you can understand and remember what you hear. Remembering what you hear will make you a better student and cut down the amount of studying you need to do out of class.

Selecting Information to Remember

Training yourself to listen means learning to listen for main ideas and major details. It also means finding ways to remember these ideas and details.

Learn to take mental notes of important ideas as you listen.

A person can truly remember only a portion of what he or she hears. Thus, you must be selective. When you are listening, decide what parts of the information you should try to remember by asking yourself the questions in the following chart.

QUESTIONS TO HELP YOU LISTEN
1. What is the general topic?
2. What important things are being said about the topic?
3. What needs to be remembered about this topic?

The answers to these questions will be main ideas and major details. You may hold these ideas in your mind, or you may write them down. By answering the questions in the chart, you can become an active and selective listener. You will be remembering only the most important information—information that you will probably need later.

Picture yourself hearing the following announcement one morning. Try to decide what you would need to remember if you were in Mr. Simmons' class.

A PUBLIC ANNOUNCEMENT:	"Mr. Simmons is out today. Because there is no substitute, all of Mr. Simmons' students are to report to Ms. Thomas in Room 212. Bring your social studies texts to Room 212, and be prepared to read and outline Chapter 6. For homework tonight Mr. Simmons' students should study for Friday's unit test. Basketball practice has also been cancelled due to Mr. Simmons' absence."

You could use the questions in the chart to help you remember the following information from the morning announcement.

GENERAL TOPIC AND MAIN IDEA:	Mr. Simmons is absent so certain changes will be made in today's schedule.	
WHAT TO REMEMBER:	Detail 1:	Go to Room 212 for social studies.
	Detail 2:	Read and take notes on Chapter 6.
	Detail 3:	Study for Friday's unit test tonight.

EXERCISE A: Listening for Main Ideas and Major Details. Work with one other student on this exercise. While one person reads aloud the first of the following two passages, the other should answer the three questions on page 444 mentally and then in writing. Reverse roles and repeat the steps with the second passage.

Answers will vary; samples given on page T-126.

(1) We are having a drought in our state. Reservoirs have less than 20 percent of the water they need, and weather forecasters say that the spring will be dry. Major companies in the state may have to shut down their plants unless they can follow rules to save water. Without the help of every person in the area, the problem will most likely get worse. All of us should begin saving water now. We can do this by cutting down on the following: taking showers, watering lawns, washing cars, and using dishwashers and washers. We can also fix leaking faucets, turn off the water when brushing our teeth and washing our hands, and use less water in cooking. If we don't conserve water now, we may have to ration water in the summer.

(2) Most folks tend to think of dehydration as a hot-weather problem, but in fact it can be a far more serious threat in the winter. You don't even have to be exercising and perspiring to become dehydrated in the winter, because the cold dry air continually robs your skin and breath of moisture. Experts recommend at least three to four quarts of water daily. Your food will provide part of that, and if there is no running water in the area, you must melt snow for drinking as well as for cooking. Don't count on handfuls of raw snow to supply much of your water intake. It takes about ten cups of snow to make one cup of water, and if you eat too much snow, it could lower your body temperature enough to induce shivering and lack of muscle control—the first symptoms of hypothermia, a cold-weather affliction in which the body's core temperature is dangerously lowered.—Constance Brown

Following Oral Directions

At least two or three times a day you are probably asked to follow spoken directions. You may be told how to complete a school assignment or take a test, how to locate a room or some other place, or how to make or repair something. In many cases the directions will be repeated several times. However, you should always be prepared for the times when directions are given only once.

Learn to listen to directions by performing certain mental steps.

Being able to follow a set of directions can save you effort and time. The suggestions in the following chart can help you to understand directions when you hear them and to remember them afterwards.

STEPS TO HELP YOU UNDERSTAND DIRECTIONS
1. When you are about to hear directions, prepare to concentrate.
2. Visualize each step as it is given.
3. Link each step in the directions using one or more key words from each direction.
4. Try to predict each step before it is given.
5. After hearing the directions, repeat them mentally, orally, or in writing.

Whenever possible, you may want to jot down notes about directions to help remember them. However, the preceding steps should also help you learn to keep directions in your mind.

One set of directions you might have to remember is how to proceed during a fire drill. Imagine that you are hearing the following directions. Try to decide what you should remember.

ORAL DIRECTIONS:

1. When the fire alarm sounds, get up quietly and leave the room in single file.
2. Walk quietly and calmly down the corridor.
3. Head directly for the nearest main exit.
4. Form two lines on the field or sidewalk.
5. Wait quietly while your teacher takes roll.
6. Wait for the principal to dismiss your class.

You could use the steps in the chart to help understand and remember these directions. You might visualize steps and link them together using the following words and mental pictures: (1–2) filing down corridor; (2–3) following corridor to exit; (3–4) exiting and lining up; (4–5) standing in line for roll; (5–6) waiting for roll and principal. You could reinforce your recall of these directions by repeating them to yourself silently or out loud.

EXERCISE B: Listening for Directions. For this exercise work with a student in your class whom you do not know well. On your paper write down clear, simple directions telling how to get from the school to where you live. Then, without letting the other person see your directions, slowly read the directions aloud *once*. While you read, your partner should take mental notes using the steps in the chart on page 447. Do not repeat any part of your directions. After you have given the directions, your partner should repeat the directions back to you. Then switch roles and do the exercise once more. *You might have students take notes on their partners' responses and then compare these with their written directions.*

APPLICATION: Evaluating Your Listening Skills. After one week of practicing the listening skills discussed in this section, answer these questions about your own listening skills.

A useful class discussion might be based on students' answers to the last question.

1. How often have you used the questions in the chart on page 444 to help remember important information?
2. In the last week, have you noticed an improvement in your ability to remember the information you have heard?
3. How often have you used the steps for understanding oral directions?
4. What rating (poor, fair, good, excellent) would you give your listening skills?
5. In the future what specifically do you plan to work on in order to improve your listening skills even more?

Developing Your Note-Taking Skills

21.3

Note-taking is one of the best ways to remember what you hear and what you read. It also helps you concentrate on what you are hearing or reading. When you take notes, you must constantly make decisions. You have to decide what information is important and how you can record the information clearly and quickly. This section will explain three ways to take notes and will suggest when to use them.

■ Using Modified Outlines

An *outline* is a precise ranking of main ideas, major details, and minor details. A *modified outline* is a loosely structured outline. It is one of the easiest forms of note-taking. In a modified outline, information is listed very briefly. Main ideas are turned into underlined headings. The important information related to each main idea is listed briefly under the heading, using numbers, letters, indentations, or dashes.

Use a **modified outline** for recording notes briefly and quickly.

You will probably use modified outlines more than any other form of note-taking. A modified outline is particularly helpful when you are taking notes on a lecture. As you listen, you can rapidly jot down the main ideas and important related information, using a modified outline. Later you may decide to fill in more complete details. You can also use a modified outline to sketch out ideas for a composition or to take quick notes from something you are reading. In addition, you will find that modified outlines are particularly easy to study from.

Read the following passage on snake charming and study the modified outline following the passage.

READING: Snake charming is an ancient art that began in Africa and the Orient. The art requires a thorough knowledge of snakes and much practice. Once a snake charmer becomes skilled, the charmer can perform at fairs, carnivals, and circuses.

The public is often unaware that snake charmers use various methods to avoid getting bitten. In some cases snakes are milked of their venom before they appear in an act. In other instances snakes have their fangs and venom glands removed or their lips sewn together. These last two methods can cause snakes to suffer and possibly to develop infections.

The public is also usually unaware that snakes do not dance to the charmer's flute music. Because snakes have no external ears, they can not hear. Instead, the snake is responding to the swaying movement of the snake charmer's body and flute, not to the sound of the flute itself.

MODIFIED OUTLINE: Snake Charming

1. Ancient art from Africa and Orient
2. Requires knowledge of snakes and practice
3. Is shown at fairs, carnivals, circuses

Methods of Preventing Snake Bites

1. Milking venom
2. Removing fangs and venom glands
3. Sewing lips together

Why Snakes Dance

1. Not caused by music
2. Respond to movement of charmer and flute

EXERCISE A: Making a Modified Outline. Group the following words into three categories using a modified outline. Choose three of the words as headings and underline them. Then, underneath the headings, list the words that are related details.

1. ball	6. sneakers	11. skates
2. horse	7. tennis	12. net
3. puck	8. beam	13. stick
4. rings	9. hockey	14. gymnastics
5. helmet	10. bar	15. racket

1, 6, 12, and 15 should be listed under Tennis; *3, 5, 11, and 13 should be listed under* Hockey; *2, 4, 8, and 10 should be listed under* Gymnastics.

Using Formal Outlines

Like modified outlines *formal outlines* group information under headings. Formal outlines, however, are more complete and exact than modified outlines. A formal outline breaks information into smaller and smaller groups and gives each group a precise ranking. Formal outlines can be used in many different ways: for outlining chapters in textbooks with many subsections and smaller parts, for taking or revising class notes, and for preparing compositions, especially detailed reports.

Use a **formal outline** to group detailed information precisely according to main ideas, major details, minor details, and subdetails.

A formal outline has a very specific structure. Roman numerals (I, II, III) are assigned to main categories or main ideas. Capital letters (A, B, C) are used for major details. Minor details are assigned regular numbers (1, 2, 3), and subdetails are given small letters (a, b, c).

FORMAL OUTLINE:

I. Main idea
- A. } Major details explaining I.
- B. }
  - 1. }
  - 2. } Minor details explaining B.
  - 3. }
    - a. } Subdetails explaining 3.
    - b. }

II. Main idea

When you make a formal outline, you should follow a few rules demonstrated in the preceding example and listed in the following chart.

RULES FOR MAKING FORMAL OUTLINES

1. Every level must have at least two items: An outline must have a I and a II; an A must have a B; a 1 must have a 2; and so on.
2. Every new level of detail should be indented.
3. All Roman numerals should be in line, all capital letters in line, all regular numbers in line, and all small letters in line.
4. The first word in each item should be capitalized.
5. A period should be placed after each number or letter.

There are two kinds of formal outlines: *sentence outlines* and *topic outlines.* Both have the same structure, but in a sentence outline, each piece of information is written as a complete sentence. In a topic outline, each item is written as a word or phrase. You will probably find that topic outlines are most useful for note-taking and organizing your compositions.

The following topic outline covers the information from the passage on snake charmers that was presented on page 450.

TOPIC OUTLINE:

I. Snake charming
    A. Ancient art
        1. Developed in Africa
        2. Developed in Orient
    B. Requirements
        1. Thorough knowledge of snakes
        2. Much practice
    C. Locations of performances
        1. At fairs
        2. At carnivals
        3. At circuses
II. Prevention of snake bites
    A. Venom removed by a milking process

- B. Venom removed by taking out fangs and venom glands
  1. Can cause suffering for snake
  2. Can cause infection
- C. Lips sewn together
  1. Can cause suffering for snake
  2. Can cause infection

III. Explanation of snake dancing
- A. Not a response to sound of flute
  1. No external ears
  2. Can not hear
- B. Response to swaying movement
  1. Of flute
  2. Of snake charmer

EXERCISE B: Making a Topic Outline. Read the following short article on the black plague and then take notes on it using a topic outline. Observe the rules in the chart on page 452, and use at least three levels: Roman numerals, capital letters, and regular numbers.
Sample outline on pages T-126–T-127.

During the Middle Ages gruesome epidemics swept across the Earth. The terrible poverty, poor sanitation, and continual migration of people from one place to another all contributed to the rapid spread of such sicknesses as typhus, cholera, influenza, and the black plague.

The last named was the most fearsome. Although other diseases killed thousands of people each year, the black plague killed in numbers so staggering as to be almost beyond comprehension. Between the years 1347 and 1351, one fourth of the population of Europe was eliminated by this scourge. There was almost no family that hadn't lost at least one member.

The onslaught threw all of humanity into a panic. People turned to their doctors, begging for an escape from death. But knowing nothing of the cause of the disease, doctors could do nothing but conjure up all sorts of ridiculous and worthless remedies.

These remedies included the following: sitting between two great fires; rubbing perfume all over the walls and furniture; letting spiders loose in the house to spin "vapor-catching" webs; drinking red wine in which new steel had been cooled; and placing a piece of warm bread on a dying person's mouth in hopes that the bread would absorb lethal vapors.

As you can imagine, none of these weird remedies worked. Not until 1894 was the cause of the disease identified (a bacillus carried by fleas), and not until 1940 did scientists, at long last, discover a cure for it.—Don Wulffson

Using Summaries

A third form of note-taking is summarizing. A *summary* is a shortened version of a longer body of information. For example, a summary of a chapter or a lecture might be a few sentences or a paragraph long. A summary includes only main ideas and a few major details, all presented in complete sentences. You can use summaries to help remember information or to gather the information you need for compositions, especially reports.

Use a **summary** to record information in a shortened form.

A summary should be brief, well-written, and informative. It should be considerably shorter than the original, generally just a few sentences. A summary should also be accurate, presenting only the information found in the original. You should not add your own opinions.

STEPS FOR WRITING SUMMARIES

1. Identify important words and main ideas as you hear or read them.
2. Hold the main ideas in your mind or jot them down.
3. Combine important information into general statements.
4. Express these statements in your own words, using complete sentences.

A summary of the article on snake charming follows.

SUMMARY: Performers of the ancient art of snake charming must have considerable experience with snakes. Many charmers also avoid injury by using snakes that have had their venom milked, their venom glands and fangs removed, or their lips sewn. The people watching may think that snakes dance to the flute music. Actually, snakes respond only to movement because they can not hear.

After you have practiced writing summaries, you may find them useful in a variety of settings, especially when you want to remember only main ideas or when you can not take notes while you are listening, for example, during a movie. You may also find that rewriting outlines as summaries can help you study.

EXERCISE C: Writing a Summary. Write a three to four sentence summary of the article on the black plague in Exercise B. Follow the steps in the chart on page 454.
Summaries can be checked for correspondence to important points in topic outlines.

APPLICATION: Evaluating Your Note-Taking Skills. After two weeks of practicing the different forms of note-taking, answer these questions.
Students can compare and discuss answers.

1. When have you taken notes in a modified outline?
2. When have you used a formal outline?
3. When have you taken notes in summary form?
4. Which form of note-taking do you use most? Why?
5. What are three specific ways that you can use each form of note-taking in the future?

Developing Your Speaking Skills 21.4

Speaking well in front of others is a study skill that makes many students anxious. To get over your uneasiness or fear about appearing in front of a group, you can follow some of the suggestions in this section. You will find that the more carefully prepared you are and the more you have practiced your speaking skills, the more comfortable you will feel about speaking.

Speaking in Classroom Discussions

Knowing how to take part in classroom discussions involves a number of skills. You must know how to listen and how to make judgments. You must also know when to speak and what to say. Finally, you must know how to use all four of these four skills together.

Develop confidence about participating in class through preparation and practice.

The following chart offers suggestions to help you become more actively involved in classroom discussions.

SUGGESTIONS FOR TAKING PART IN CLASSROOM DISCUSSIONS
1. Set goals for your participation; for example, you might decide to contribute at least once to each discussion.
2. Do extra reading on the topic you are studying so that you will have something of interest to say.
3. If possible, plan what you might say before the discussion begins.
4. Do not wait for the teacher to call on you. Raise your hand.
5. Follow the discussion carefully so that your response will be to the point.
6. Observe methods used by other students who make good contributions.

By using these suggestions, you can build your self-confidence. If you believe that what you have to say is valuable, you will probably say it well. In turn, if you believe you can express your ideas well, you will probably become a regular contributor to classroom discussions.

When you take part in classroom discussions, you become an active learner. You have an opportunity to test out your ideas on others and get a reaction from them. Furthermore, you become an important part of the group learning process.

EXERCISE A: Developing Your Participation in Classroom Discussions. For each of your major subjects, set up a page similar to the following in the appropriate section of your notebook. Include columns for the date, the topic of the discussion, a tally of your comments, and an evaluation of your comments. Then, over the next month, keep a record on your chart of your contributions to every class discussion. Try both to increase the number of times you participate and to improve the quality of your comments.

Notebooks can be checked periodically and encouragement given to efforts made.

CLASSROOM DISCUSSION CHART: ENGLISH			
Date	**Topic**	**Number of Contributions**	**Evaluation**
Oct. 21	The novel <u>Shane</u>: Western heroes	2	Made contributions but should have reviewed book first

Giving a Speech

Whenever you must speak at length in front of the class, you need to be prepared.

To hold the audience's attention, learn to speak naturally while using a brief outline written on note cards.

An outline allows you to keep your speech moving along in an organized way, while giving you freedom to add or reword ideas. Having an outline to spark your memory and to hold on to can make you feel secure. The short statements in an outline can be picked up quickly by the eye so that you can speak while facing the audience. In addition, the shortness of an outline will enable you to express your ideas naturally as you go along. The suggestions in the following chart can help you make an outline for a speech.

PREPARING AN OUTLINE FOR A SPEECH

1. Use only a few small index cards.
2. Print all information neatly.
3. Write quotations or facts that you want to remember exactly.
4. Write out beginning and ending statements if necessary.
5. Rely mainly on key words and phrases or clear abbreviations.
6. Letter and indent details under the ideas they support.
7. Use underlining, capital letters, and different colors to make important information stand out.
8. Number your cards to help keep them in order.

Once you have prepared your outline on note cards, you should practice giving the speech several times until you feel comfortable using the cards.

The following note cards have been developed for a demonstration speech on making a paper hat. The purpose of the speech is to teach someone else how to make a hat. Notice the step-by-step organization of the speech, the shortness of the outline, and the use of such things as underlining and capital letters.

① Making Newspaper Hats

Need a quick hat that anyone can make in a matter of seconds? Try a newspaper hat!

I. USES
- A. Costumes
- B. Boat - it floats
- C. Container for snacks

II. MATERIALS
- A. Newspaper (double sheet)
- B. Pencil & ruler

②
- C. Paint
- D. Seals (optional)

III. HOW TO FOLD
- A. Hold sheet with short length facing you
- B. Fold top ½ down to meet bottom
- C. On front, draw line 2" from bottom
- D. Fold left corner to line
- E. Fold right corner to line
- F. Separate 2" margin at bottom
- G. Fold front & back margins up

③ H. Open up △ part of hat & place on head
IV. DECORATE
A. Paint
B. Add seals or stickers
C. Add fringe
Newspaper hats may not be the most attractive of hats, but their price is right and materials are usually available.

EXERCISE B: Preparing and Giving a Demonstration Speech. Prepare a two- to four-minute demonstration speech using one of the following topics or one of your own. Outline your speech on note cards. Practice your speech at home and then give it for the class.

Note cards can be checked before students practice their speeches. You can also set up

Making a book jacket	Starting a campfire
Tying shoelaces	Asking someone to dance
Hitting a baseball	Braiding hair

guidelines for class discussion and evaluation of speeches.

APPLICATION: Evaluating Your Speaking Skills. After two weeks of practicing the speaking skills discussed in this section, evaluate your progress by answering the following questions.

In answering the last question, students might pool their ideas for improved preparation.

1. What goals have you set for your participation in class?
2. Have you scheduled time to prepare for class discussions?
3. Have you made a practice of raising your hand in class to contribute ideas?
4. If you have given a speech recently, did you use note cards? Did you make your note cards clear and easy to use?
5. How could you improve your preparation for a speech?

Chapter 22

Improving Your Reading Skills

Knowing how to read well is important to your success in school. You will be required to read much of the material that you must learn in your different subjects. Reading is also essential to many out-of-school activities and in many jobs.

One important reading skill is the ability to change your reading rate as you read different kinds of material. Another useful reading skill is knowing how to get the most from reading your textbooks. The sections in this chapter will help you improve your reading rate and your ability to read textbooks.

22.1 Developing Your Reading Rate

To be a good reader, you need to vary your reading rate for different kinds of material and different purposes. You also need to have a "usual" reading rate that is fairly rapid. This section will help you improve your reading skills by developing different reading rates and by learning to increase your usual reading rate.

■ Using Different Reading Styles

Your reading style and rate should vary according to the material you are reading and your purpose in reading it. For example, you should read one way when you are reading information in detail for the first time. You should read another way when you want just a general idea of what a chapter contains. And you should read yet a third way when you are searching for a specific fact or detail. Learning when and how to use each of these reading styles can expand your reading skills.

Phrase Reading. *Phrase reading* is the best method to use when you need to read and understand *all* of the material in an assignment. In phrase reading, a reader's eyes take in groups of words without eliminating any of the words. The smaller words simply become part of larger groups of words. To read words in groups, you must adjust your focus. Instead of focusing on individual words, focus on the center of a group of words and read the entire group.

Use **phrase reading** to read and understand an entire passage more efficiently.

Since words will have more meaning when you read them in groups, you can increase your comprehension as well as your rate by using phrase reading. Look at the following sentence. It has been divided into phrases for easier reading.

EXAMPLE: The French teacher // told the class // that the test // would begin soon. //

Reading this sentence in phrases takes only four eye stops, whereas reading each word separately would take twelve stops. The phrases also make the meaning of the sentence immediately clear.

Skimming. In *skimming,* a reader skips over many of the words, while concentrating on key words and phrases. In using this method, you must move along rapidly, looking for no more than a general idea of what the material is about. This style is especially useful in previewing new material. It is also helpful in reviewing material that has already been read thoroughly.

Use **skimming** to get a general idea of what material is about.

The use of skimming to preview material can save time. By skimming a textbook chapter before you read it closely, you can gain essential information that will help you understand what you read later. By skimming an article in a magazine, you can tell whether it contains the information you need. If it does, you can use phrase reading to take in the information more thoroughly.

Scanning. In *scanning,* a reader reads even less material than in skimming. To use this method, you must let your eyes move quickly down a page in search of a single piece of information. This style of reading is best suited to review and research work.

Use **scanning** to find a single piece of information.

Scanning is especially helpful for finding details you can not recall when you are studying for a test. It is the kind of reading you would use to look for the date of the Battle of Gettysburg in a history book or facts about the liver in a science book.

EXERCISE A: Identifying Reading Styles. Read each of the following descriptions and decide which reading style it describes: *phrase reading, skimming,* or *scanning.* On your paper identify each style.

1. Does not leave out words *phrase reading*
2. Is used to look for very specific pieces of information
3. Is used in careful reading and study *phrase reading*
4. Requires less actual reading than any other style
5. Is used for previewing and reviewing *skimming*

2. scanning 4. scanning

EXERCISE B: Deciding on a Reading Style. Indicate the style or styles of reading—*phrase reading, skimming,* or *scanning*—best suited to each of the following purposes. *Answers to some items may vary within reason.*

1. Looking up a word in the dictionary scanning
2. Deciding whether to read a particular novel skimming
3. Reading and taking notes for a report phrase reading
4. Finding the name of Andrew Jackson's Vice President scanning
5. Reading an editorial for a social studies discussion group phrase reading

Determining Your Phrase Reading Rate

When people ask you how fast you read, they probably want to know your phrase reading rate. There are many advantages to developing a fast phrase reading rate. The faster you read, the more you can read and learn in a given period of time. If you can read your school assignments more quickly, you will have more time for reading or other leisure activities.

Speed in reading, however, should never be your only goal. Speed should never replace comprehension. The suggestions beginning on page 464, if practiced regularly, should help you increase your reading rate without losing comprehension. First, however, you must know how to calculate your reading rate.

Calculate your phrase reading rate from time to time to note improvements.

There are several methods you can use to find your phrase reading rate. None of them is entirely accurate, but each one gives a reasonable estimate. Two of the methods are described in the following paragraphs.

Using Pages with Numbered Lines. The easiest way to find your reading rate is by using stories and books that list the number of words in each line. These materials are often available in reading labs and reading kits. Many books on reading improvement also have numbered lines. When you use this method, you should read for one minute and then check the number that appears at the end of the line where you stopped.

This number gives your approximate reading rate, plus or minus twenty words per minute.

Using Average Words Per Line. To use this method, first count the number of words in three consecutive full lines of type. Then divide the total by three to find the average number of words per line. You should next read for one minute and then count the number of lines you have read. By multiplying this number by the average words per line, you will find your reading rate. For example, if the three lines contain a total of twenty-two words, there is an average of seven words per line. If you read fifty-one lines in one minute, the total (51×7) will equal 357 words per minute.

If you are interested in determining your reading rate for technical material, choose readings from science, math, or social studies books. On the other hand, if you are looking for your reading rate for pleasure reading, use a short story or a novel.

EXERCISE C: Calculating Reading Rates. Compute the reading rate for each of the following.

1. If there are a total of forty-eight words in three lines and you read thirty lines in one minute, what is your reading rate? *480 words per minute*
2. If there is an average of twelve words per line and you read twenty-five lines in one minute, what is your reading rate? *300 words per minute*

EXERCISE D: Comparing Your Reading Rates for Different Kinds of Material. Use the average-words-per-line method and time yourself for one minute on the following materials: a section of a short story, part of a social studies chapter, and part of a science chapter. Record your rate for each type of material.
Students can also test themselves on other types of material, such as newspapers and magazines.

■ Improving Your Phrase Reading Rate

As you have seen, reading groups of words instead of individual words can help you cut down the number of times your eyes must stop while reading a line. To increase your phrase reading rate, you must simply learn how to take in larger groups of words more quickly. There are a number of activities that can help you do this.

Increase your phrase reading rate through nightly drills.

Any of the three methods described in the following paragraphs can be used as a drill. Once you have proven to yourself that you can read more rapidly, you should be able to transfer your increased reading rate from your practice sessions to other situations. Remember, though, not to give up comprehension for speed. Whenever you find that you are not understanding what you read, slow down. Always adjust your reading rate to the difficulty of the material.

While you are reading about the following methods, try to decide which method or which combination of methods might work best for you.

Charting. To use the charting method, you must first determine your reading rate, using one of the methods described on pages 463 and 464. Then you must chart it on a graph. Each night during your drill period, you should try to read a little faster than you did the night before. After four to five days, check your reading rate again and enter it on the graph. You should begin to see a noticeable increase after about three weeks of practice.

Pacing. To carry out the pacing method, place a ruler under the first line of print so that it covers the lines below. Then move the ruler down the page as you read each line. The time it takes you to uncover each line should be slightly faster than the rate at which you normally read. The rapid uncovering of lines should force you to speed up your reading rate.

Repeated Reading. In the repeated reading method, you must select a passage and read it over three or four times during the same session. Each time you read it, the passage will become more familiar and easier to read. This increased ease in reading should, in turn, increase your reading rate.

EXERCISE E: Charting Your Reading Rate. Use one of the methods on pages 463 and 464 to determine your reading rate and enter the results on a graph. Then use one of the methods for improving your rate regularly for three weeks. Record your reading rate once every four or five days. *Students might be reminded that their concern should be to improve their own reading rates rather than to compete with other students.*

APPLICATION: Evaluating Your Reading Skills. After working on the reading skills in this section for several weeks, evaluate your reading skills by answering each of the following questions. *Students might respond to these questions again later in the school year and discuss any changes in their answers.*

1. Do you use the kind of reading style best suited to your purpose and to the reading material?
2. Which reading style is easiest for you? Which style should you work on most?
3. What is the largest group of words that your eyes can take in at one stop?
4. Which method of increasing your phrase reading rate has helped you most?
5. By how much have you been able to increase your phrase reading rate?

22.2 Reading Textbooks

Textbooks are probably the basic sources of written information in most of your classes. They are likely to provide much of the information that you need in order to understand the subjects, do assignments, and prepare for tests. To help you acquire the information you need, most textbooks have special sections and a number of special features within each chapter that make reading and studying easier. Using a textbook's overall organization and the numerous reading aids found within each chapter should help you learn a subject more quickly.

Becoming Familiar with the Parts of Your Textbooks

Most textbooks include a number of helpful sections at the front and back. These sections can help you become familiar with the contents of the book. You can also use some of these sections as guides when you are studying.

Identify and make use of the special items at the front and the back of your textbooks.

Not all textbooks contain all of the special items mentioned here, nor will you need to use all of these special items regularly. But you should be aware of these features in the books you have and use them when necessary to further your understanding of the subject.

The *table of contents* is found in the front of the textbook. It will show you how the book is organized by giving a list of the units and chapters in the book and indicating the pages where topics may be found. The list of chapters and their contents also provides a good overview of the material covered in the text. The following chart shows you three of the ways you can use the table of contents.

USING THE TABLE OF CONTENTS
1. To locate general information
2. To get an overview of the book while previewing
3. To test your recall of information in each of the chapters while reviewing for a unit test or final exam

The *preface* or introduction to a textbook, generally located just after or just before the table of contents, states the author's purpose in writing the book. It may also explain some of the other special features of the book and how to use them. You should read this information once and then take advantage of it as you read the book.

The *index* is found in the back of the textbook. It lists alphabetically all of the topics covered in the textbook and the pages on which they can be found. You should use this section to locate specific information. By consulting the index, you can turn directly to the information that you want. You will also know the different places throughout the book where a topic is discussed.

The *glossary,* located near the index in the back of many textbooks, provides a list of terms with definitions. Generally, it will include only specialized words and related definitions taken directly from the textbook. The glossary will thus give you the meanings of the terms you must know in order to understand the textbook.

The *appendix,* if a book has one, is also found in the back of the textbook. It contains a variety of information that the author considers useful to a student studying the subject of the book. This information may include charts, lists, documents, essays, or almost any other kind of material. Using the appendix can often free you from having to go to other books to locate relevant information.

If you do want to consult outside sources on your subject, the *bibliography,* located near the end of many books, can be a valuable tool. The bibliography includes books that the author has referred to in writing the textbook as well as other books you might want to read in connection with a particular subject.

EXERCISE A: Examining Your Textbooks. Examine two of your textbooks to become acquainted with their special sections. Answer the following questions for each book. *This can be approached first as an oral exercise, using a common textbook. Each student can then examine another text independently.*

1. According to the table of contents, how many units and chapters does the text have? Are chapters divided into smaller sections in the table of contents? What additional facts can you learn about the text from the table of contents?
2. What specific information does the preface contain?

3. What are two specific pieces of information you can learn from the index?
4. Does the text have a glossary? If so, examine the glossary. What are two pieces of information you have learned?
5. If the text has an appendix or a bibliography, what information do these pages contain?

■ Using the Reading Aids in Textbooks

In addition to specialized sections in the front and back of the book, the chapters of a textbook will generally include a number of different reading aids designed to make your studying easier.

Use the reading aids in textbooks to improve your comprehension, note-taking, and preparation for tests.

Reading aids will vary from book to book. However, most of the texts you use will have many of the following helpful features.

Most texts use *titles, headings,* and *subheadings* to divide the textbook into sections and subsections in much the same way a formal outline divides up information. The words usually appear in big, bold print to signal a change in the main idea or the division of a section into more detailed subsections. The following chart explains how these features can help you.

USING TITLES, HEADINGS, AND SUBHEADINGS	
When to Use	**How to Use**
Previewing	Skim titles, headings, and subheadings for an overview.
Studying carefully	Turn titles, headings, and subheadings into questions. Then read for the answers.
Locating information	Scan titles, headings, and subheadings to find pieces of information.
Reviewing	Skim titles, headings, and subheadings to check your mastery of the topics.

You can also use a text's *chapter introductions* and *summaries* when you study. First skim them, then read them carefully using phrase reading, and finally read them at least once when you are reviewing. They will generally restate and explain the main ideas of the chapters in capsule form.

End-of-chapter questions and other *exercise material* can be used before and after reading a chapter. Skimming the questions during previewing can give you an idea of what information you should be looking for as you phrase read the chapter. These questions can direct your attention to the main ideas and supporting details. When you review a chapter, you should read these questions more carefully and answer them fully.

You can use *graphs, charts, tables,* and *diagrams* as you phrase read a chapter and as you scan for particular pieces of information. These aids provide visual explanations of important ideas in the text.

Illustrations and the *captions* that accompany them can also enhance your understanding of important ideas. As you preview, you should notice the illustrations. Then, as you phrase read, look at them more carefully and read the captions to gain additional information about the subject you are studying.

USING READING AIDS

Previewing (Skimming)	**Studying (Phrase Reading)**	**Locating Information (Scanning)**	**Reviewing (Phrase Reading, Skimming, Scanning)**
Titles and headings Introductions and summaries Questions and exercises Illustrations	All reading aids	Titles and headings Graphs and charts	Titles and headings Introductions and summaries Questions and exercises

EXERCISE B: Examining Reading Aids in Your Textbooks. Examine two of your textbooks to become acquainted with their reading aids. Answer the following questions for each book. *Students can be divided into two groups, with each group examining one classroom text. The groups can then compare texts.*

1. Within a typical chapter of your textbook, how many different kinds of titles and headings are used? How many main sections are there? How many subsections are there under a typical main section?
2. How long are the introductions and summaries in a typical chapter?
3. How many and what kind of questions come either at the end of the chapter or within the chapter?
4. What kind of graphs, charts, tables, and diagrams appear in the chapter?
5. If the book has illustrations, are they closely related to the content of the chapter or are they mostly decorative?

APPLICATION: Evaluating Your Skill in Reading Textbooks. After one week of applying your knowledge of textbooks, answer the following questions. *Class discussion of answers can help reinforce the value of the various textbook features.*

1. Which of the special items at the front and back of your textbooks have you used in the last week?
2. What information did you get from them?
3. Which reading aids in your textbooks have you found particularly helpful in the last week?
4. What information did you get from them?
5. What special sections and reading aids do you think you should use more often?

Chapter 23

Improving Your Library and Reference Skills

You have probably been using the books and other materials in libraries for years. You are also likely to be very familiar with dictionaries. You may not, however, be getting as much value out of these sources as you could.

The purpose of the first two sections in this chapter is to explain the resources of the library and show you how to find and use these resources. The third section explores the contents and special features of dictionaries.

23.1 Using the Library

Libraries exist to help you and everyone else in your school and community. Because many people use libraries, it is important for all users to follow a few useful rules. First, be considerate of the other people by trying to be as quiet as possible. Second, return books and materials that you check out on time, and take care of them while you are using them. This way other people will have a chance to use the materials, and you can avoid paying fines. Third, be careful with the copying machines, microfilm readers, and other equipment available in the library. If you do not know how to use these machines, ask someone to show you. Fourth, when you are puzzled about finding the information you need, ask a librarian to help you. The librarian is trained to guide people to the materials they want. Finally, learn about the contents and organization of libraries in general and your own library in particular so that you will know where to find things.

This section will explain the card catalog—the major key to the contents of the library—and then guide you to the shelves to find the books you want.

■ The Card Catalog

Often one of the first objects you see when you enter a library is the *card catalog.* It is very important for you to learn to use it properly. Using the card catalog, you can locate any book.

Use the **card catalog** as a key to finding books in the library.

The card catalog is made up of small file drawers that contain alphabetically arranged cards. Each drawer has a label on the outside that tells you what part of the alphabet is in that drawer. For example, a label that says BE—BRI means that the card headings in that drawer begin with words that start with BE and go through words that start with BRI. Inside the drawer are *guide cards.* Guide cards have tabs that stick up above the rest of the cards. These tabs can help you find the words you want. Between these guide cards, the catalog cards are filed alphabetically.

FILE DRAWER:

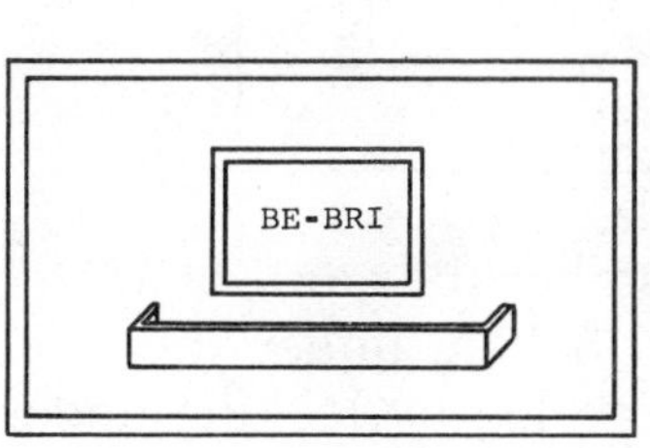

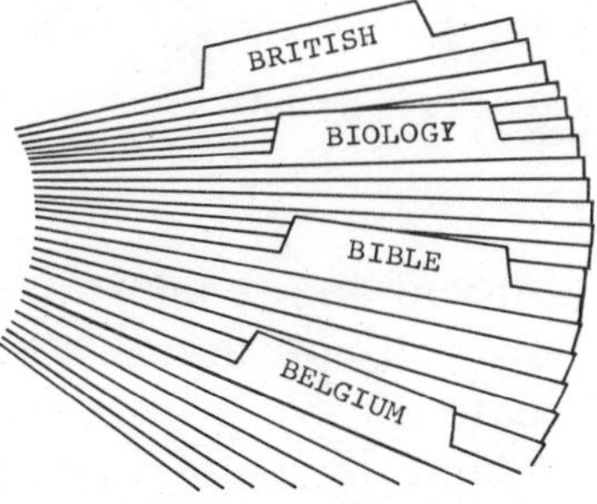

Usually the drawers are arranged alphabetically from top to bottom. If the drawer marked AAD–ALG is at the top, the drawer directly beneath it will continue listing the entries beginning with ALH. The same order will continue to the bottom of the row and then move to the top of the next row. Sometimes a library has separate sections of the card catalog for records or foreign language books. These sections may have labels of a different color on the front to identify them.

Kinds of Catalog Cards. Each nonfiction book in the library will have at least three cards in the catalog: an *author card,* a *title card,* and a *subject card.* Each fiction book will have an author card and a title card. For any single book, all the cards are identical except for the top line of each card.

Use the card catalog to find a book by author, title, or subject.

You can find any book by looking under the author's last name. For instance, if you had read a book by Cipriano and wanted to read other books written by him, you could look in the card catalog under C and find a card that looks like this one.

AUTHOR CARD:

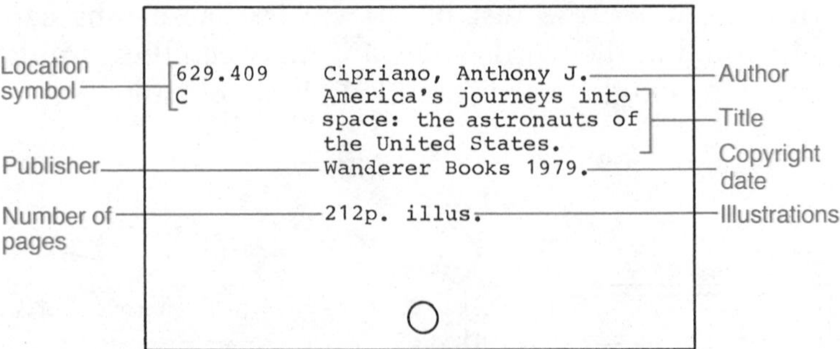

If you do not know or remember the name of an author, you can find a book by looking under the title. Locate the book in the card catalog by looking under the first letter of the first word of the title. If you wanted the book *America's Journeys into Space,* you would look under A.

TITLE CARD:

```
629.409   America's Journeys into Space
C         Cipriano, Anthony J.

          America's journeys into
          space: the astronauts of
          the United States.
          Wanderer Books  1979.

          212p. illus.
```

You can also find books by looking under the subject. If you have to write a report, you will probably be interested in finding as much information as you can about one specific subject. In such a case, you might begin by looking up the subject. If your paper were on astronauts, you might look under that word.

SUBJECT CARD:

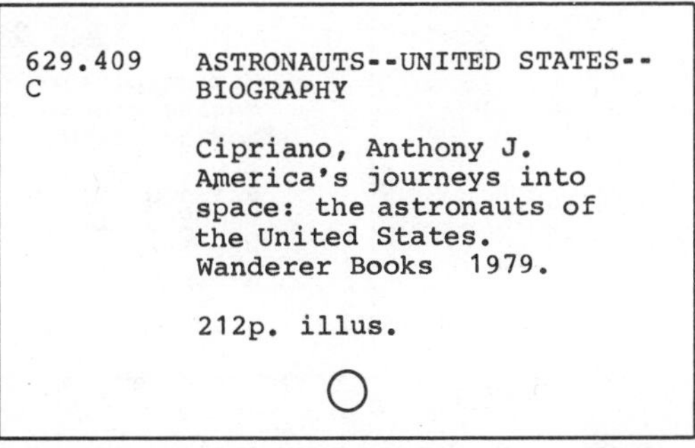

```
629.409   ASTRONAUTS--UNITED STATES--
C         BIOGRAPHY

          Cipriano, Anthony J.
          America's journeys into
          space: the astronauts of
          the United States.
          Wanderer Books  1979.

          212p. illus.
```

If you can not find a subject card in the card catalog, you may find *cross-reference cards* helpful. There are two kinds of cross-reference cards. The first is called a *see* card. A *see* card tells you that the library does not file cards under the subject you have looked up. The card directs you instead to a subject that the library does use. If you were looking for books about the American Army and found the following card, you would then have to look under the subject heading *United States, Army.*

CROSS-REFERENCE CARD:

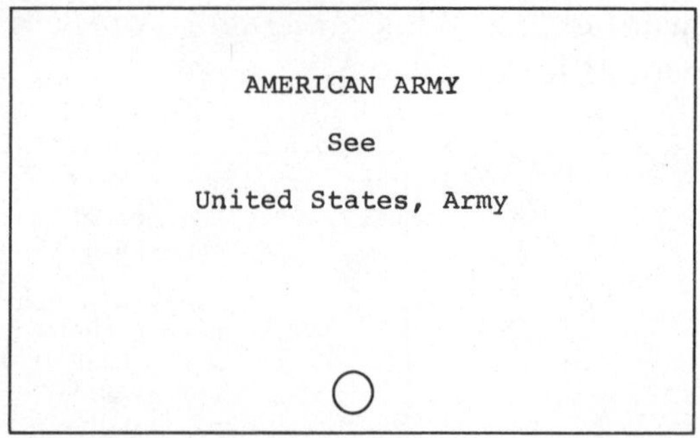

AMERICAN ARMY

See

United States, Army

The second kind of cross-reference card is a *see also* card. If you want additional books on a subject, a *see also* card can be useful. This card lists subjects related to the subject you have looked up. The following example of a *see also* card would be found under the subject heading *Moving pictures.* The card lists related topics, such as *Moving picture projection,* and more specialized parts of the subject, such as *Puppet films.*

CROSS-REFERENCE CARD:

MOVING PICTURES

See also

Moving picture projection
Moving picture theaters
Moving pictures in education
Puppet films
Science fiction films
Vampire films
War films
Western films

If you are having trouble finding a subject in the card catalog, cross-reference cards are just one source of help. You can also try to think of another word for your subject or a broader subject under which your subject might be included.

What Catalog Cards Tell You. In addition to giving you the author, title, and subject, catalog cards include other helpful information.

Consult catalog cards to find publishing information, a description of features, related subject headings, and the location symbol for each book.

You should be aware of how the information on catalog cards can be useful to you. Most cards will give you the book's publisher and the copyright date right after the title. For some subjects it is important to know how up-to-date the information in a book is. A card will also tell the number of pages and will indicate if the book has illustrations, a bibliography, or an index. If you are pressed for time, the length of the book may be a consideration. Furthermore, it may be important for you to have pictures on your topic, and a bibliography can help you find additional information. Some cards also include a summary of the contents of the book, sometimes called an *annotation.* At the bottom of the card, subject headings may be listed. There will be a card for the book filed under each of these headings. Finally, in the upper left-hand corner, you will find a *location symbol.* This code of numbers or letters will help you find the book on the shelf.

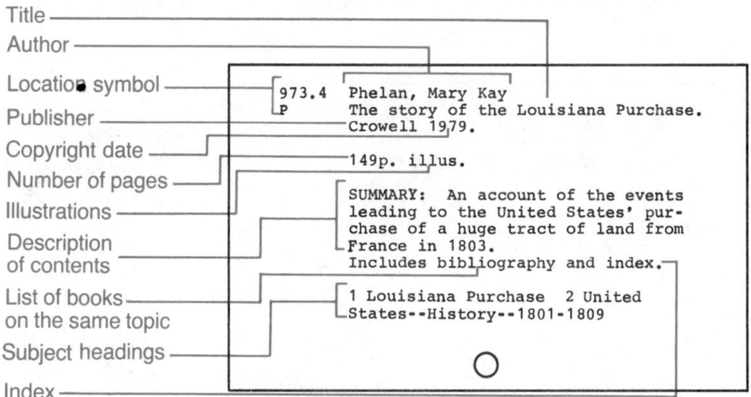

Arrangement of Cards. To use the card catalog effectively, you also need to know how the library alphabetizes cards.

Use word-by-word alphabetizing and a few additional rules to find cards in the catalog.

A library usually arranges cards in one of two ways. It may alphabetize author, title, and subject cards together or it may alphabetize the author and title cards together and the subject cards separately. Most smaller libraries alphabetize author, title, and subject cards together. In either case the library will indicate which system it is using.

There are two basic ways of alphabetizing: *word by word* and *letter by letter.* Letter-by-letter alphabetizing means that you look only at the order of the letters, regardless of the number of words. Letter-by-letter alphabetizing is used in dictionaries and in most encyclopedias. Word-by-word alphabetizing, on the other hand, is used in the card catalog. This method requires that you look first at the order of the letters in the first word of a group of words and then at the letters in the succeeding words. Thus, in letter-by-letter alphabetizing, which looks at all the letters together, *newspaper* would come before *New York.* However, in word-by-word alphabetizing, *New York* would come first because all groups of words beginning with the word *new* are listed before words that simply begin with the letters *new.* Look at some other examples.

TWO WAYS OF ALPHABETIZING

Library's Method: By Word	Other Method: By Letter
New Deal	New Deal
New Jersey	newer
New York	New Jersey
newer	newsletter
newsletter	New York

In addition to this general rule for alphabetizing, you should keep in mind the points in the following chart.

SPECIAL METHODS OF ALPHABETIZING IN THE CARD CATALOG

1. *A, an,* and *the* at the beginning of an entry are not used in alphabetizing; *The Enemy* would be alphabetized under *E.*

2. Abbreviations and numbers are alphabetized as if they were spelled out; *Dr.* is treated as *Doctor* and *100* as *one hundred.*
3. All *Mc's* and *Mac's* are alphabetized as if they were *Mac;* the following are in the correct order: *McBrien, MacDonald, machine, McInerney.*

EXERCISE A: Examining a Catalog Card. Use the following catalog card to provide each of the ten pieces of information requested after the card.

```
909.0492  Banks, Lynne Reid
B         Letters to my Israeli sons: the
          story of Jewish survival.
          F. Watts 1980.

          276p. maps

          Includes bibliography and index.

          1 Jews--History  2 Zionism--
          History  3 Palestine--History--
          1917-1948
                    O
```

1. The location symbol 909.0492 B
2. The author Lynne Reid Banks
3. The title Letters to My Israeli Sons: The Story of Jewish Survival
4. The copyright date 1980
5. The publisher F. Watts
6. The number of pages in the book 276
7. Any information about illustration includes maps
8. Any information about bibliography or index has both
9. Subject headings under which the book is listed
10. The kind of card this is author card

9. Jews—History/Zionism—History/Palestine—History—1917–1948

EXERCISE B: Alphabetizing Using the Library's Word-by-Word Method. Arrange the following items in card catalog order.

1. Santa Anna 7
2. Sanskrit 6
3. Sandwich Islands 3
4. San Juan 2
5. Sapphire 10
6. San Andreas Fault 1
7. Santiago 9
8. Sanitation 5
9. Sanhedrin 4
10. Santa Fe Trail 8

EXERCISE C: Following Special Rules for Alphabetizing. Arrange the following items in card catalog order.

1. Mt. Rainier 5
2. *100 Story Poems* 7
3. *An African Treasury* 1
4. McCullers, Carson 3
5. St. Catherine 9
6. *The Outsiders* 8
7. Mt. St. Helens 6
8. *A Wrinkle in Time* 10
9. MacLeish, Archibald 4
10. MacArthur, Douglas 2

Finding Books on the Shelves

Using the card catalog is the first step to finding books. The second step is letting the card catalog actually guide you to the books on the shelves. Usually a library divides and shelves books according to whether they are *fiction* or *nonfiction.* Works of fiction are made-up stories that may be based on facts but are created mainly from the authors' imaginations. Works of nonfiction are factual. A library may also categorize and shelve separately two subgroups of nonfiction—biographies and reference books—and various other materials as well.

Finding Fiction. The simplest shelving system in the library is the one used for *fiction.*

Fiction is arranged on the shelves alphabetically by the last name of the author and then by the title of the book.

The card catalog tells you that a book is fiction by the marking in the upper left-hand corner of the card. The location symbol for fiction usually consists of the letter F or the letters Fic along with the first few letters of the author's last name. Sometimes the fact that there is no location symbol will tell you that a book is fiction. No matter what marking the library uses, you will know that you must go to the shelves that hold fiction and look under the first few letters of the author's last name, which will often be printed at the bottom of the spine of the book. For example, a book by Marjorie Kellogg would be shelved before a book by John

Knowles. If there are several books by the same author, the books will be in alphabetical order by title.

Fiction Arranged Alphabetically

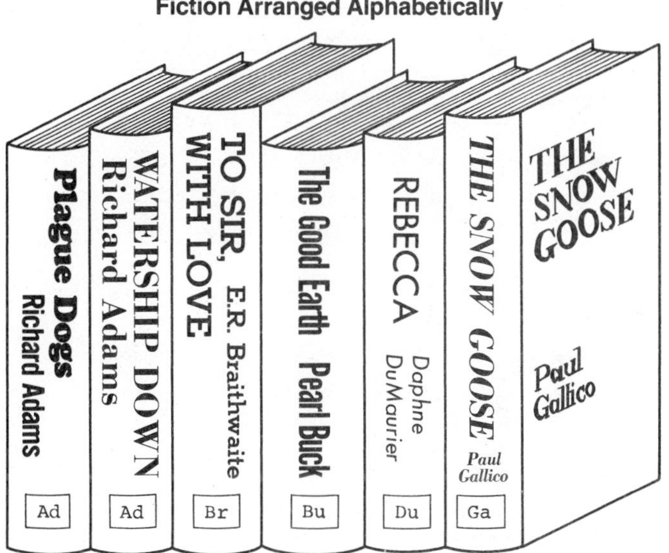

Finding Nonfiction Using Call Numbers. *Nonfiction* books are arranged differently. On many catalog cards, you will find a location symbol that is a number and the first letter or letters of the author's last name. This number and letter make up the book's *call number.*

Nonfiction is arranged on the shelf in call-number order.

The call number comes from a system used to classify nonfiction books. The call number on the card also appears on the spine of the book on the shelf. If you stop to think, you will realize that libraries must have agreed on some way to arrange all their books so that people can find books the same way in every library. There are two systems in general use: the Dewey Decimal System and the Library of Congress System. This section will focus on the Dewey Decimal System because the Library of Congress System is primarily used in college libraries and very large public libraries.

The Dewey Decimal System attempts to classify all knowledge. It does this by first breaking all knowledge down into ten main classes.

MAIN CLASSES OF THE DEWEY DECIMAL SYSTEM

Numbers	Subjects
000–099	Generalities
100–199	Philosophy and related disciplines
200–299	Religion
300–399	Social sciences
400–499	Language
500–599	Pure sciences
600–699	Technology (applied sciences)
700–799	The arts
800–899	Literature
900–999	General geography and history

Each main class is then subdivided into a number of smaller divisions. The second digit in a call number gives the division breakdown. For example, the following chart shows you part of the breakdown of the main class social sciences into smaller divisions. From this chart you can see that the 2 in 320 means political science.

FIVE DIVISIONS OF THE MAIN CLASS SOCIAL SCIENCES

Number	Division
300	Social sciences
310	Statistics
320	Political science
330	Economics
340	Law
350	Public administration

Each of the divisions is then further broken down into sections. The third number from the left gives you the section breakdown. In the following chart, you can see that the 4 in 324 means the political process.

FIVE SECTIONS OF THE DIVISION POLITICAL SCIENCE	
320	Political science
321	Kinds of governments and states
322	Relation of state to social groups
323	Relation of state to its residents
324	The political process
325	International migration

In call numbers there are often numbers beyond the decimal point as well. These divide the categories of knowledge into still more specific groups or subdivisions. For example, 324.2 is the number for political parties.

Although you do not have to memorize the Dewey Decimal System, understanding it will give you two advantages: (1) You will know that you can find more books about a subject by looking at books with the same call number; (2) you will know that a subject not covered in books with one number, say 324, might be talked about in chapters of a more general book having, for example, the number 320.

The call number of a book guides you to the book on the shelf. Call numbers appear on the spines of all nonfiction books, and books are arranged on the shelves in call-number order. Often a label on a row of shelves will indicate the range of numbers in that row. Knowing that the books are grouped numerically will help you find them. A book with the call number 300 will come before a book with the call number 310. A book numbered 312.1 will come before one numbered 312.12, and both of these will come before one numbered 312.2. When books have the same number, they are arranged alphabetically by the letters of the authors' last names: for instance, 312.3 will come before 312.3.
A B

Nonfiction in Call-Number Order

Finding Biographies and Special Materials. Besides grouping books on the shelves by fiction and nonfiction, libraries often use special location symbols and special organizations for biographies, reference books, and young-adult books.

Biographies, reference books, young-adult books, and other materials may be given special symbols and grouped separately.

Many libraries have a separate section for biography. This section includes biographies, which are factual books written about a person by another person, and autobiographies, which are factual books written by a person about himself or herself. The location symbol for biographies will generally be B or 92 followed by the first letter, the first few letters, or the entire last name of the person who is the subject of the biography. Biographies are arranged alphabetically by subject, not by author. For example, the book *First Woman Doctor: The Story of Elizabeth Blackwell, M.D.* by Rachel Baker would be labeled B (for biography) and B (for Blackwell). It would be placed on the shelf before *Kit Carson: Trail Blazer and Scout* by Shannon Garst, labeled B (for biography) and C (for Carson). Books containing biographies of several people, called *collective biographies,* are usually shelved with the main collection under the 920 division of the Dewey Decimal System.

Another special collection in most libraries is the reference collection. A reference book is usually indicated by the letter R before the call number. (See Section 23.2 for a discussion of reference books.)

Some libraries also have a separate section for young-adult books, which are books used primarily by junior high school students. The location symbol is usually YA followed by the proper call number or location symbol for fiction. For example, YA 324 means that the book is shelved in the young-adult collection.

In addition to knowing about these common markings, you should find out what special markings your library uses.

EXERCISE D: Locating Fiction. Arrange the following books in library shelf order.

1. *Mystery at Crane's Landing* by Marcella Thum *9*
2. *The Martian Chronicles* by Ray Bradbury *2*
3. *High Wind in Jamaica* by Richard Hughes *7*
4. *Little Women* by Louisa May Alcott *1*
5. *Summer of the Swans* by Betsy Byers *3*
6. *Old Yeller* by Fred Gipson *6*
7. *Lisa, Bright and Dark* by John Neufeld *8*
8. *Sea Glass* by Laurence Yep *10*
9. *The Pistachio Prescription* by Paula Danziger *4*
10. *Johnny Tremain* by Esther Forbes *5*

EXERCISE E: Locating Nonfiction. Arrange the following call numbers in library shelf order.

1. 150.1 G	3. 746.4 A	5. 150.2 A	7. 629 A	9. 629 M
2. 301.42 A	4. 600 G	6. 301.415 F	8. 300 F	10. 745 M

1. 1 2. 5 3. 10 4. 6 5. 2 6. 4 7. 7 8. 3 9. 8 10. 9

EXERCISE F: Locating Biographies. Arrange the following biographies in library shelf order.

1. *The Story of Eleanor Roosevelt* by Jeanette Eaton *5*
2. *Loretta Lynn* by Robert K. Krishef *4*
3. *Jack London: The Pursuit of a Dream* by Ruth Franchere *3*
4. *Trumpeter's Tale: The Story of the Young Louis Armstrong* by Jeanette Eaton *1*
5. *Arthur Ashe: Tennis Champion* by Louie Robinson *2*

APPLICATION: Using Your Knowledge of the Library. Use your knowledge of the library to carry out the following instructions. *After topics have been chosen, students might go to the school library in groups to complete the next three steps. The last item can be handled orally.*

1. Pick a topic.
2. Use the card catalog to choose three or four books about your topic. Remember to use cross-reference cards and to look for related subjects if necessary.
3. Go to the shelves and find the books. Examine the books to see how well they cover your topic.
4. List the books you have found.
5. In a few brief sentences, explain how you found them and describe how well they cover your topic.

23.2 Finding Reference Books in the Library

From your study of the card catalog, you probably know that the cards for reference books are marked with an R before the call number. These books are generally kept in a separate room or area and usually may not be borrowed.

A good way to describe a reference book is to say that it is a book to be consulted for information. It is not meant to be read from cover to cover. A reference book may be an index that leads you to information in other books or in magazines, or it may be a fact book that contains a large collection of information. Both indexes and fact books can be either general or specialized. A general reference book covers many subjects in broad outline. A specialized reference book covers one subject in greater detail. In this section you will learn how to use general and specialized reference books as well as some of the other kinds of materials in the library such as magazines and journals.

General Reference Books

General reference books are some of the most useful books in the library. Among them are encyclopedias, almanacs, atlases, and dictionaries. (See Section 23.3 for a detailed discussion of dictionaries.)

Encyclopedias. *Encyclopedias* contain basic facts on a great many subjects.

Use **encyclopedias** for basic facts, background information, and bibliographies.

Encyclopedias can be useful in several ways. If you need a piece of information quickly—for example, the date the Constitution was adopted—you can find the answer in an encyclopedia. Or perhaps you have to write a report on a subject you know little about. A general encyclopedia can serve as a good starting point. Besides giving you an overview of the subject, the bibliography at the end of the article may point you to additional sources you can consult.

Most encyclopedias consist of a number of volumes arranged alphabetically. Each volume contains a part of the alphabet. The volume number and the portion of the alphabet covered are marked on the spine. The pages of each volume also have guide words at the top to show you the first and last subjects included on those pages. Using the guide words, you can quickly determine if your subject is found on a particular page.

To aid you further, most encyclopedias have an index volume. An index is especially helpful if your subject does not have a complete article devoted to it. Notice the articles listed under the following subject in *The World Book* index.

Volume
Page number

INDEX ENTRY:

Space travel So:560 *with pictures and maps*
See also the Reading and Study Guide on this topic
Air Force, United States (The Air Force in Space) **A:185**
Altitude **A:372b**
Astronomy (Space Exploration) **A:813**
Computer (In Engineering) **Ci:742** *with picture*
Cosmic Rays (Effects of Cosmic Rays) **Ci:857**
Guided Missile (Postwar Developments) **G:413-414**
Life (The Search for Life on Other Planets) **L:245**
Mercury (Flights to Mercury) **M:340**
Moon (Man's Future on the Moon) **M:651**
Radar (In Space Travel) **R:66**
Research (Mathematics and Physical Sciences) **R:236** *with picture*
Rocket (Space Travel) **R:358** *with pictures;* (The Space Age) **R:360c**
Television *picture on* **T:85**
Thermocouple **T:192**
United States, History of the (Space Exploration) **U:123** *with picture*
World, History of (Modern Times) **W:360d-360e**
See also the list of Related Articles in the Space Travel *article*

As you can see, the first heading directs you to a main entry, giving the letters of the volume and the page of the article. In addition, volume letters and page numbers are given for a number of related articles on a variety of topics.

To be a valuable source of information, an encyclopedia must be kept up-to-date. The people who publish encyclopedias update their books in different ways. One way is continuous revision. Articles on subjects that change rapidly—subjects such as medicine and politics—are constantly revised to keep the facts current. Most encyclopedias also publish yearbooks. Yearbooks contain information about the events of the year and about new developments in many fields.

Your library is likely to have many encyclopedias. As you use the different encyclopedias, you will discover the strengths and special features of each set. For example, *The World Book* has good pictures and is useful for short, clear explanations. The *Encyclopedia Americana* is excellent for information about places in America.

POPULAR ENCYCLOPEDIAS	
Collier's Encyclopedia	*Encyclopedia Americana*
Compton's Pictured Encyclopedia	*Random House Encyclopedia*
The Encyclopaedia Britannica	*The World Book Encyclopedia*

Almanacs. *Almanacs* should be the first place you look for minor facts or certain types of specific information.

Use **almanacs** to find a number of different kinds of miscellaneous information.

Almanacs contain a wealth of specific information on a wide range of subjects—science, government, world history, religion, literary and motion picture awards, and sports, among others. Like encyclopedia yearbooks, almanacs include a summary of the events of the year. Unlike encyclopedias, however, they are not good for thorough background information. The information they include is generally sketchy, covering only a few key facts.

Almanacs are not arranged alphabetically. Instead, you must use the index at the front or back of each volume. The following entry from the index of the 1981 *World Almanac and Book of Facts* refers you to information about ice hockey.

INDEX ENTRY:

Hockey, ice—
Addresses, teams 848-849
All-Star teams . . . . 826 — Page number
Arenas 813
Canadian Intercollegiate 819
Hall of Fame 825
NCAA champions 826
Olympic records 810
Stanley Cup 824
World Hockey Association 826

If you wanted to find information about the National Hockey League's all-star hockey teams, you would turn to page 826 of the 1981 *World Almanac and Book of Facts.* There you would find lists of the players on the first and second teams for 1980.

TEXT ENTRY:

NHL All Star Team, 1980

First team	Position	Second team
Tony Esposito, Chicago	Goalie	Don Edwards, Buffalo
Larry Robinson, Montreal	Defense	Borje Salming, Toronto
Ray Bourque, Boston	Defense	Jim Schoenfeld, Buffalo
Marcel Dionne, Los Angeles	Center	Wayne Gretzky, Edmonton
Guy Lafleur, Montreal	Right Wing	Danny Gare, Buffalo
Charlie Simmer, Los Angeles	Left Wing	Steve Shutt, Montreal

The two best known almanacs are *The World Almanac and Book of Facts* and the *Information Please Almanac*. Each is published annually.

Atlases. From the pages and pages of maps that make up most *atlases,* you can gather many different kinds of facts.

Use **atlases** to find information from maps.

Most general atlases focus primarily on *political maps,* which show the boundaries of countries and the locations of cities, towns, rivers, and oceans. General atlases may also include *topographical maps,* which show the surface features of a region, and *economic maps,* which present information about the types of industry and the population.

The best way of using an atlas is generally by turning to the index at the back. The following entry from the index to Hammond's *World Atlas* shows you where to turn to look for maps of Hawaii.

INDEX ENTRY:

Havertown, Pa., 294
Havířov, Czech., 41
Havre, Mont., 262
Havre de Grace, Md., 245
Havre-Saint-Pierre, Que., 174
Hawaii (isl.), Hawaii, 218 ——— Page number
Hawaii (state), U.S., 218
Hawaiian (isls.), 218
Hawaii Volcanoes Nat'l Park, Hawaii, 218
Hawarden, Iowa, 229

If you turn to page 218, you will find various maps of Hawaii, some showing all of the islands and others showing parts of the state in greater detail. Each map also gives a scale of miles and kilometers so that you can figure out the distance between the different places shown on the map.

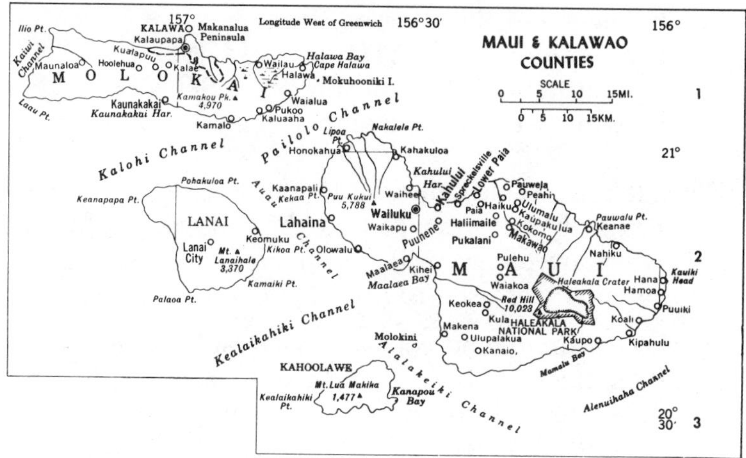

Other atlases that you may find useful are *The World Book Atlas,* the *National Geographic Atlas of the World,* and *Goode's World Atlas.*

In preparing reports you may also want to make use of atlases that provide historical information. A historical atlas is arranged to show the changes over time in the boundaries of territories, countries, and empires. Some examples are *Shepherd's Historical Atlas,* the *Atlas of American History,* and the *American Heritage Atlas of American History.*

EXERCISE A: Using Encyclopedias and Almanacs. Use the encyclopedias and almanacs in your school or public library to find the following information. On your paper write each piece of information and the book you used to find it. *Specific sources will vary; information given.*

2. chills and fever, spleen and liver enlargement, anemia, jaundice

1. The average temperature in Phoenix, Arizona, in March *60° F.*
2. The symptoms of malaria
3. The fourth fastest animal in the world and its speed *lion—50 mph*
4. Three accomplishments of Harriet Tubman
5. The name of the mayor of Honolulu, Hawaii, in 1982 *Eileen R. Anderson*
6. The cartoonist who created the character Dennis the Menace *Hank Ketchum*

4. "conductor" on Underground Railroad; led over 300 slaves to freedom; worked with Union forces in South; etc.

7. The legend of the Blarney Stone
8. Three countries in NATO *Belg, Can, Den, etc.*
9. Two painters of the Hudson River School
10. The winner of the Heisman Trophy in 1950 *Vic Janowicz*

7. Those who kiss it acquire skill in flattery. 9. Durand, Kensett, etc.

EXERCISE B: Using Atlases. Use the atlases in your school or public library to find the following information. On your paper write each piece of information and the book you used to find it. *Specific sources will vary; information given. 1. USSR and US 4. Chile, Peru, Braz, Para, Arg*

1. The two mainland countries nearest Wrangel Island
2. The states that border on Lake Erie *NY, Pa, O, Mich*
3. The states admitted to the Union between 1791 and 1803 *Vt, Ky, Tenn, O*
4. The countries that border on Bolivia
5. The countries that border the Mediterranean Sea

5. Sp, Fr, It, Yugo, Alban, Gr. Turk, Syr, Leb, Isr, Eg, Libya, Tun, Alg, Mor

■ Specialized Reference Books

A specialized reference book covers one topic in great depth. Many specialized reference books are available on a wide range of topics. This section will introduce you to some of the most useful ones.

Specialized Dictionaries. *Specialized dictionaries* cover many different aspects of words.

Use **specialized dictionaries** to find detailed information about words.

One kind of specialized dictionary you are likely to use focuses on synonyms—words with similar meanings. When you write, you should try to use language precisely, choosing words that best fit what you are trying to say. You should also try to avoid using the same words over and over again. A dictionary of synonyms can help you find other words that have approximately the same meaning as a particular word. Some dictionaries of synonyms are *Funk and Wagnall's Modern Guide to Synonyms, Roget's International Thesaurus, Roget's Pocket Thesaurus,* and *Webster's New Dictionary of Synonyms.*

Some dictionaries of synonyms are arranged alphabetically. Others are arranged by categories and approached through an alphabetical index. If you wanted to find a synonym for *nourish* in one of these, you would look under that word in the index and find references to various meanings of the word, each with a category number and a paragraph number.

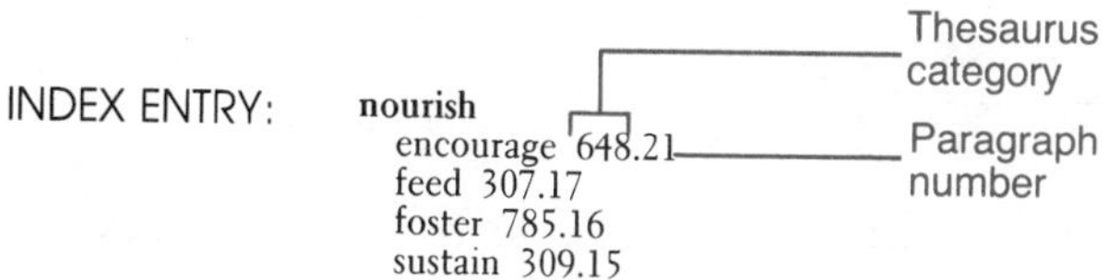

If you were interested in words that mean "to encourage," you would then look for category 648, paragraph 21, in the body of the book. The guide number at the top of the page would tell you that you were on the right page. There you would find the following list of words from which you could choose.

GUIDE NUMBER: 648.1–648.22

TEXT ENTRY: .21 **encourage,** give encouragement, pat *or* clap on the back; **invite,** ask for; **abet,** aid and abet, countenance, keep in countenance; **foster, nurture,** nourish, feed.

Other specialized dictionaries are devoted to foreign languages. Still others cover particular fields or topics, such as rhyming words or dialects.

OTHER SPECIALIZED DICTIONARIES

The Dictionary of American Slang

A Dictionary of Contemporary American Usage

The Harvard Dictionary of Music

James' Mathematical Dictionary

The Pocket Dictionary of American Slang

Steen's Dictionary of Biology

Specialized Encyclopedias. Some *specialized encyclopedias* are multivolume with extensive information; others are single volumes. All deal with particular fields and treat topics more thoroughly than general encyclopedias do. Usually, however, they are organized alphabetically, just as general encyclopedias are.

Use **specialized encyclopedias** to find detailed information on a topic.

Some multivolume sets specialize in subjects related to your school courses. For example, *The Book of Popular Science* gives good basic information on all areas of science and can thus be useful in preparing science reports. *Peoples of the Earth* provides information about people all over the world and can be used for many social studies assignments. Other single and multivolume works focus on subjects such as sports, art, music, and medicine.

Biographical Reference Books. When you need information about famous people, living or dead, you can consult reference books that specialize in people.

Use **biographical reference books** to find information about people.

One of the best *biographical reference books* is *Current Biography,* a multivolume set started in 1940. Each bound volume covers one year. *Current Biography* includes articles on athletes, politicians, scientists, and other famous people living at the time of publication. It is published eleven times a year, and at the end of the year all the monthly issues are combined into one volume. The long illustrated articles end with bibliographies that can suggest other sources of information.

To find articles in *Current Biography,* you should use one of the indexes. *Current Biography* has an index at the end of each volume. The indexes in the latest volumes can help you find articles on people who have been in the news recently. You can look in the 1980 ten-year index for people who have been important over a longer period of time. For someone whose fame stretches back over a number of decades, you can check the cumulated index volume, covering the years 1940–1970.

In the index of the 1980 volume of *Current Biography*, you would find the following entry for Meryl Streep, giving the month and year in which the article was published.

INDEX ENTRY:

Stravinsky, Igor (Fëdorovich) obit May 71
Subject — Streep, Meryl Aug 80 — Volume year
Strong, Maurice F(rederick) Dec 73
Strout, Richard L(ee) Apr 80
Struthers, Sally (Ann) Jan 74
Stump, Felix B(udwell) obit Sep 72
Suárez González, Adolfo May 77
Sullivan, A(loysius) M(ichael) obit Aug 80
Sullivan, Ed(ward Vincent) obit Nov 74

Then, looking in the volume listed, under Streep, you would find the article. Here is an excerpt from the article.

TEXT ENTRY: **Streep, Meryl**

June 22, 1949- Actress. Address: c/o International Creative Management, 40 W. 57th St., New York City, N.Y. 10019

One of the most intelligent, perceptive, and sensitive of the younger generation of contemporary American actresses, Meryl Streep has achieved stardom in the theatre, television, and motion pictures in an astonishingly brief span of time. She first came to the attention of critics in 1975, when, working under the aegis of the New York Shakespeare Festival and the Phoenix Theatre, she appeared in choice roles in half a dozen plays in the course of a single year. Since then she has gone on to win many honors, including an Emmy award for her performance in the NBC-TV miniseries *Holocaust* (1978) and an Oscar for her performance in the motion picture *Kramer vs. Kramer*.

The many *Who's Who* publications cover a number of different fields. These books are primarily helpful because they include so many people. For example, *Who's Who in America* is a book of basic facts about prominent living Americans. *Who Was Who in America* covers prominent people who have died. The articles in these books are very short. In addition, because the information is obtained directly from the people covered, it may not be totally objective. Even so, the *Who's Who* volumes can give you some useful information.

A good source for information on people no longer living is the *McGraw-Hill Encyclopedia of World Biography*. It is international in scope and gives short illustrated articles on a number of different people.

The following chart lists a few other biographical works that might be useful.

OTHER BIOGRAPHICAL REFERENCE BOOKS
Contemporary Authors
Dictionary of Scientific Biography
Modern Men of Science
Notable American Women

EXERCISE C: Using Specialized Dictionaries and Encyclopedias. Use specialized reference books in your school or public library to find the following information. On your paper write each piece of information and the book you used to find it. *Sources will vary; information given.*

1. absurdity, foolishness, senselessness, outrageousness, etc. 2. self-important person

1. Four synonyms for the word *nonsense*
2. The meaning of the slang term *big cheese*
3. The diameter of Mars *4,200 mi (6800 km)*
4. The titles of two paintings by Mary Cassatt
5. Three kinds of nonpoisonous snakes

4. Mother and Child, Lady at the Tea Table, *etc. 5. garter, black, king, etc.*

EXERCISE D: Using Biographical Reference Books. Use the biographical reference books in your school or public library to find answers to the following questions.

On your paper write each piece of information and the book you used to find it.
Specific sources will vary; information given.

1. When did Black Hawk live? *1767–1838*
2. Who is Toni Morrison? *black writer, author of* Song of Solomon
3. What awards did Marie Curie receive? *Nobel Prize, etc.*
4. Who is Katharine Meyer Graham?
5. When and where was Scott Joplin born?

4. former publisher of the Washington Post *5. 1868 in Texarkana, Tex*

Periodicals

Periodicals are publications that are issued at regular intervals during the year. They may be published daily, weekly, monthly, every two months, or every three months.

A *magazine* is a periodical with articles of general interest written for the general public. A *journal* is a more scholarly periodical with information on a special field. While a book will give you clear and often detailed information, a magazine or journal can provide information that is both concise and very recent. In these periodicals you can find information on new discoveries, recent happenings, and people in the news.

Use **magazines** and **journals** to find concise, current information.

The next question is, "How do you find specific information in periodicals?" Just as you used the card catalog to find books, so you can use indexes to find magazine articles. The most important index is *The Readers' Guide to Periodical Literature,* which indexes more than 180 popular magazines. In the front of every volume of *The Readers' Guide,* you will find an alphabetical list of the magazines indexed and a list of the abbreviations used in the index. Throughout most of the year, *The Readers' Guide* is published twice a month. At the end of each year, all the monthly volumes are collected into one volume for that year.

The Readers' Guide is an author and subject index. You can find articles if you know either the author or the subject. Usually you will be looking for articles on a particular subject. To find the most recent information, you can begin with the most recent volumes of *The Readers' Guide* and work backwards. By first looking under general subjects and then looking under the more specific subheadings, you will be able to find articles on almost any subject.

The following entry shows the information you can expect to find in *The Readers' Guide.* Note that the entries give you the names of the articles, the authors, the titles of the magazines, the volume and page numbers, and the dates. They also tell you whether there are illustrations. Like the card catalog, there are *see* and *see also* references.

ENTRY FROM *THE READERS' GUIDE:*

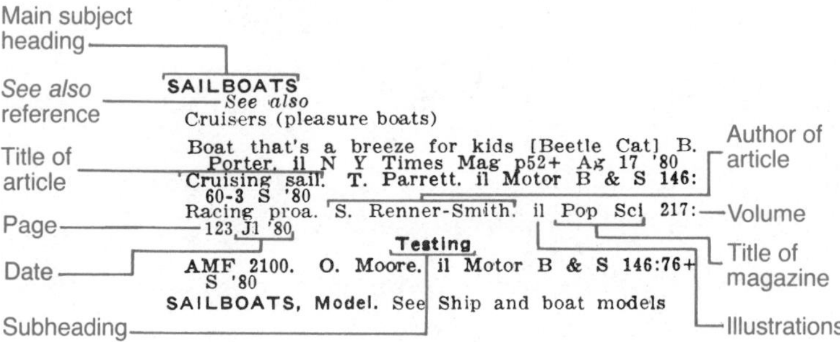

Once you have found an article covering your subject, there are several possible procedures for finding the magazine. Some libraries keep separate issues of the magazines. Others bind them together in volumes, and still others keep them on microfilm or microfiche. If your library stores magazines as single issues, you should write out the title of the magazine, the volume, and the date on a slip of paper and give it to the librarian. Then the librarian will go into the room where the periodicals are stored and find the one you have requested. Occasionally, periodicals will be bound and shelved, and you can locate them on the shelves yourself. At other times you may have to use a machine called a *reader* to read the articles that are on microfilm (rolls) or microfiche (sheets).

EXERCISE E: Interpreting *The Readers' Guide*. Examine the following excerpt from *The Readers' Guide*. Then, using complete words for all abbreviations, write out each of the five entries in the excerpt. Include the titles of the articles, the names of the authors when they are given, the titles of the magazines, the volume numbers when they are given, the page numbers, and the dates. Then explain the procedure you would follow to find one of these articles.
The first entry can be done orally to give students practice in translating abbreviations.

SMOKING
Hormones and tobacco smoke—when mixed, it's an ill wind [excerpt from The scientific case against smoking] R. Winter. Sci Digest 88:58-61 O '80
Kenya govt. bans smoking in public. il World Health p30-1 O '80
Mirkin on: nicotine addiction. G. Mirkin. il por Fam Health 13:20-1 Ja '81
Old argument. K. Cook. il Forbes 126:188 N 10 '80
Secondhand smoke and lung cancer [Japanese study] M. Clark and D. Shapiro. il Newsweek 97:63 Ja 26 '81
SMOKING and diet. See Diet

EXERCISE F: Using *The Readers' Guide*. Use a recent volume of *The Readers' Guide* in your school or public library to find two other articles on smoking. On your paper write the information you would need to obtain the magazines. *If the school library uses forms for obtaining magazines, students might fill out forms to answer this exercise.*

APPLICATION: Using the Research Tools in Your Library. Choose the best reference book to find information on each of the following items. Then use the reference book to find the information requested. Try to use as many different kinds of reference books as you can. On your paper write each piece of information and the book you used to find it.
Specific sources will vary; information given.

1. Who won the 1977 World Series? *NY Yankees*
2. Find a synonym for the word *mess* when it means "eat." *dine*
3. What are the physical effects of too little vitamin A in a person's diet? *night blindness, susceptibility to infection*
4. When was Nikki Giovanni born? For what is she known? *1943/writing poetry*
5. Who was Kublai Khan?
6. How many square miles are covered by the Pacific Ocean? *64,186,300*

5. Emperor of China at the time of Marco Polo's visits

7. What is the capital of Paraguay? *Asuncion*
8. What was Jacques Cousteau's first major achievement? *with Emil Gagnon, invented scuba equipment in 1943*
9. What is the best treatment for lead poisoning?
10. What was the population of Texas in 1980?

9. injections of metal-attracting compounds 10. 14,228,383

23.3 Using the Dictionary

Professional writers and people who read widely usually make it a practice to keep a dictionary handy. For them it is the first place to look for quick answers to questions they may have about the spelling and meaning of words.

As a student you may find it very useful to develop a similar habit. If you want to use words correctly when you write and wish to understand what you read, you should never be reluctant to consult a dictionary. The trick is to be able to find what you are looking for quickly and easily. As with any other skill, quickness and ease come with practice.

This section will explain how you can use a dictionary to find a great variety of information. As you read, apply what is said here to the particular dictionary that you use most often at school or at home.

A Dictionary for Everyday Use

Not all dictionaries are the same. Different writers and publishers offer a variety of dictionaries, each with a particular audience in mind. Some dictionaries are made for scholars. Others are designed for the special needs of college students. Still others are made for students in high school or elementary school. There are even dictionaries for children who are just learning to read. Since there are many kinds of dictionaries, the dictionary you use every day should be one that is right for you.

Use a dictionary that best suits your present needs.

Such a dictionary should be neither too easy nor too difficult for you. It should contain all the words you are likely to come upon in your schoolwork and should explain these words in language you can understand.

DICTIONARIES RECOMMENDED FOR STUDENTS
The Macmillan Dictionary
The Scott, Foresman Advanced Dictionary
Webster's New World Dictionary, Students Edition

Once you have found a dictionary that you think will suit your needs, use it often—even browse through it occasionally to see what new things you can discover. The more you use your dictionary, the easier it will be to use.

EXERCISE A: Examining Your Dictionary. Examine the dictionary that you use most often at home, in school, or in the library. Answer the following questions about it. *Answers will vary; if students have access to dictionaries at home, their responses can be compared in class. If school dictionaries are used, this can be an oral exercise.*

1. What is the complete title of your dictionary?
2. What company published it and when?
3. For what kind of audience was it made? (You should find the answer to this question in the preface or foreword at the beginning of the dictionary.)
4. Does the dictionary have an introduction that explains how to use the book? If so, how many pages are in this section?
5. List three technical terms that you have had to learn in science, history, English, or some other subject. Does your dictionary define them?

Using Your Dictionary to Check Spelling

A common complaint of students is, "How can I find the word if I can't spell it to begin with?" Checking the spelling of a word *can* sometimes be difficult because English often has many different spellings for the same sound.

Become familiar with the different spelling patterns of the sounds in English words.

Always begin with your best guess. The odds are that you will find the word you are looking for after a few tries. The more spelling patterns you know, the better your chances are of finding the word quickly.

The following Word Finder Chart should help you become familiar with the various spelling patterns for different sounds.

WORD FINDER CHART		
If the sound is like the . . .	try also the spelling . . .	as in the words . . .
a in fat	ai, au	pl*ai*d, dr*au*ght
a in lane	ai, ao, au, ay, ea, ei, eigh, et, ey	r*ai*n, g*oa*l, g*au*ge, r*ay*, br*ea*k, r*ei*n, w*eigh*, sach*et*, th*ey*
a in care	ai, ay, e, ea, ei	*ai*r, pr*ay*er, th*e*re, w*ea*r, th*ei*r
a in father	au, e, ea	g*au*nt, s*e*rgeant, h*ea*rth
a in ago	e, i, o, u	ag*e*nt, san*i*ty, c*o*mply, foc*u*s
ch in chin	tch, ti, tu	ca*tch*, ques*ti*on, na*tu*re
e in get	a, ae, ai, ay, ea, ei, eo, ie, u	*a*ny, *ae*sthete, s*ai*d, s*ay*s, br*ea*d, h*ei*fer, l*eo*pard, fr*ie*nd, b*u*ry
e in equal	ae, ay, ea, ee, ei, eo, ey, i, ie, oe	alumn*ae*, qu*ay*, l*ea*n, fr*ee*, dec*ei*t, p*eo*ple, k*ey*, mach*i*ne, ch*ie*f, ph*oe*be
e in here	ea, ee, ei, ie	*ea*r, ch*ee*r, w*ei*rd, b*ie*r
er in over	ar, ir, or, our, re, ur, ure, yr	li*ar*, elix*ir*, auth*or*, glam*our*, ac*re*, aug*ur*, meas*ure*, zeph*yr*
f in fine	ff, gh, lf, ph	cli*ff*, lau*gh*, ca*lf*, *ph*rase
g in go	gg, gh, gu, gue	e*gg*, *gh*oul, *gu*ard, prolo*gue*
i in it	a, e, ee, ia, ie, o, u, ui, y	us*a*ge, *E*nglish, b*ee*n, carr*ia*ge, s*ie*ve, w*o*men, b*u*sy, b*ui*lt, h*y*mn
i in kite	ai, ay, ei, ey, ie, igh, uy, y, ye	*ai*sle, *ay*e, sl*ei*ght, *ey*e, t*ie*, n*igh*, b*uy*, fl*y*, r*ye*
j in jam	d, dg, di, dj, g, gg	gra*d*uate, ju*dg*e, sol*di*er, a*dj*ective, ma*g*ic, exa*gg*erate

k in keep	c, cc, ch, ck, cqu, cu, lk, q, qu, que	*c*an, a*cc*ount, *ch*orus, ta*ck*, la*cqu*er, bis*cu*it, wa*lk*, *q*uick, li*qu*or, baro*que*
m in me	chm, gm, lm, mb, mm, mn	dra*chm*, paradi*gm*, ca*lm*, li*mb*, dru*mm*er, hy*mn*
n in no	gn, kn, mn, nn, pn	*gn*u, *kn*eel, *mn*emonic, di*nn*er, *pn*eumatic
o in go	au, eau, eo, ew, oa, oe, oh, oo, ou, ough, ow	m*au*ve, b*eau*, y*eo*man, s*ew*, b*oa*t, t*oe*, *oh*, br*oo*ch, s*ou*l, d*ough*, r*ow*
o in long	a, ah, au, aw, oa, ou	*a*ll, Ut*ah*, fr*au*d, th*aw*, br*oa*d, *ou*ght
oo in tool	eu, ew, o, oe, ou, ough, u, ue, ui	man*eu*ver, dr*ew*, m*o*ve, sh*oe*, gr*ou*p, thr*ough*, r*u*le, bl*ue*, fr*ui*t
oo in look	o, ou, u	w*o*lf, w*ou*ld, p*u*ll
ou in out	ough, ow	b*ough*, cr*ow*d
r in red	rh, rr, wr	*rh*yme, be*rr*y, *wr*ong
s in sew	c, ce, ps, sc, sch, ss	*c*ent, ri*ce*, *ps*ychology, *sc*ene, *sch*ism, mi*ss*
sh in ship	ce, ch, ci, s, sch, sci, se, si, ss, ssi, ti	o*ce*an, ma*ch*ine, fa*ci*al, *s*ure, *sch*wa, con*sci*ence, nau*se*ous, ten*si*on, i*ss*ue, fi*ssi*on, na*ti*on
t in top	ed, ght, pt, th, tt	walk*ed*, bou*ght*, *pt*omaine, *th*yme, be*tt*er
u in cuff	o, oe, oo, ou	s*o*n, d*oe*s, fl*oo*d, d*ou*ble
u in use	eau, eu, eue, ew, ieu, iew, ue, ui, you, yu	b*eau*ty, f*eu*d, qu*eue*, f*ew*, ad*ieu*, v*iew*, c*ue*, s*ui*t, *you*th, *yu*le
ur in fur	ear, er, eur, ir, or, our, yr	l*ear*n, g*er*m, haut*eur*, b*ir*d, w*or*d, sc*our*ge, m*yr*tle
v in vat	f, lv, ph	o*f*, sa*lv*e, Ste*ph*en
w in will	o, u, wh	ch*o*ir, q*u*aint, *wh*eat
y in you	i, j	on*i*on, hallelu*j*ah
z in zero	s, sc, ss, x	bu*s*y, di*sc*ern, sci*ss*ors, *x*ylophone
z in azure	ge, s, si, zi	gara*ge*, lei*s*ure, fu*si*on, gla*zi*er

Suppose, for example, that you had written the sentence "My sister will grajuate from college this June" and your teacher has noted that "grajuate" is misspelled. If you tried looking up this spelling in the dictionary, you would not find it. An educated guess, however, would tell you that you are right at least as far as *gra*. The problem, then, is with the fourth letter: *j* is wrong. After checking the letters given for the *j*-sound, the next logical step is to try the word with a *d:* gra*d*-uate. Looking up this spelling in the dictionary tells you that it is correct.

EXERCISE B: Correcting Spelling with Your Dictionary. Each of the following words is misspelled. Using the Word Finder Chart and your dictionary, write the correct spelling for each word.

1. agravated
2. rythm *rhythm*
3. recroot *recruit*
4. hymm *hymn*
5. vanaty *vanity*
6. lisense *license*
7. emfasize *emphasize*
8. hygene *hygiene*
9. tishue
10. ajency

1. aggravated 9. tissue 10. agency

Finding Words Quickly

Most of the time you will know how a new word is spelled because you will have just come across it in your reading. At these times you will want to find the word's meaning quickly and get back to your reading.

Learn to use alphabetical order quickly to find words in the dictionary.

Thumbing aimlessly through a dictionary to find a word wastes time. Here are three steps to help you find any word in the dictionary quickly.

STEPS FOR FINDING WORDS QUICKLY
1. Use the Four-Section Approach.
2. Next use the guide words.
3. Then follow strict, letter-by-letter alphabetical order.

The Four-Section Approach. Most dictionaries can be mentally divided into four roughly equal sections.

FOUR SECTIONS: ABCD
EFGHIJKL
MNOPQR
STUVWXYZ

Knowing the section of the dictionary in which a word will be found can help you open to that general area right away. The word *kinkajou,* for example, will be near the middle of the book, whereas *springbok* will be toward the end, near the beginning of the fourth section.

Guide Words. Once you have narrowed your search down to a general area, you should begin using the *guide words.* These are the two words printed in large type at the top of each page in a dictionary. The guide word at the left tells you the first word on that page. The one on the right tells you the last word on that page. If, for example, the guide words are *glower* and *go,* a glance at them will tell that a word such as *glucose* will be on that page.

Letter-by-Letter Alphabetical Order. All the items in a dictionary are listed in *strict alphabetical order*—that is, letter by letter right to the end of the entry. This rule holds even if the item is made up of more than one word.

EXAMPLES: okra *before* Olaf
Olaf *before* olden
olden *before* old hand

EXERCISE C: Alphabetizing. Put the following items into the order you would find them in in a dictionary.

1. riprap *4*
2. rise *7*
3. ripen *2*
4. rival *10*
5. riptide *5*
6. ritual *9*
7. ripe *1*
8. risk *8*
9. Rip van Winkle *6*
10. ripple *3*

EXERCISE D: Finding Words Quickly. Using the three steps for finding words quickly, look up the following items in your dictionary. Write the guide words on the page where each item is found. *Answers will vary. If classroom dictionaries are used, this exercise, with other words added, could be used as a game.*

1. tomahawk
2. impassive
3. paradox
4. biopsy
5. shilling

Understanding Main Entries

In a dictionary the words you look up combined with all the information given about them are known as *main entries.* The words themselves are called *entry words.* The following chart shows examples of different kinds of entry words.

KINDS OF ENTRY WORDS	
Single Word	**la·goon** (lə go͞on′) ***n.*** [< Fr. *lagune* & It. *laguna* < L. *lacuna,* lake] **1.** a shallow lake or pond, esp. one connected with a larger body of water **2.** the water enclosed by a circular coral reef **3.** shallow salt water separated from the sea by dunes
Compound Word	**national bank** **1.** a bank or system of banks owned and operated by a government ☆**2.** in the U.S., a member bank of the Federal Reserve System, chartered by the Federal government
Abbreviation	**nat.** **1.** national **2.** native **3.** natural
Prefix	**an·ti-** (an′ti; *also variously* -tē, -tī, -tə) [< Gr. < *anti,* against] *a prefix meaning:* **1.** against; hostile to *[antilabor]* **2.** that operates against *[antiaircraft]* **3.** that prevents, cures, or neutralizes *[antitoxin]* **4.** opposite; reverse *[antimatter]* **5.** rivaling *[antipope]*
Suffix	**-ant** (ənt, 'nt) [Fr. < L. *-antem* or *-entem,* acc. prp. ending] *a suffix meaning:* **1.** that has, shows, or does *[defiant, radiant]* **2.** a person or thing that *[occupant, accountant]*
Person (Family Name Usually First)	**An·tho·ny** (an′thə nē; *also, for 1 & 2,* -tə-) [< L. *Antonius,* name of a Roman gens] **1.** a masculine name: dim. *Tony;* var. *Antony* **2. Mark,** *see* ANTONY **3. Susan B(rownell),** 1820–1906; U.S. leader in the women's suffrage movement
Place	**La·gos** (lā′gäs, -gəs) capital of Nigeria; seaport on the Atlantic: pop. 665,000

As you can see in the chart, the information following an entry word varies depending upon the kind of word it is.

Learn to recognize and use the different kinds of information contained in a main entry.

Explanations of the different kinds of information that you can expect to find in a dictionary follow.

Spelling. Most words have only one correct spelling, as shown by the entry word. Some words, however, can be spelled in more than one way. The one most commonly used, called the *preferred spelling,* is listed first. Less commonly used spellings are called *variant spellings.* If the form of a word you are looking up is a variant spelling, the entry will refer you to the main entry that begins with the preferred spelling.

VARIANT SPELLINGS:

lah-di-dah, lah-de-dah (lä′dē dä′) ***adj.*** *same as* LA-DI-DA

PREFERRED SPELLING FIRST:

la-di-da, la-de-da (lä′dē dä′) ***adj.*** [Colloq.] affected in speech, manners, etc.; refined in a showy way

Syllabification. Centered dots, spaces, or slashes in an entry word indicate where the word may be divided if it is to be broken at the end of a line. In the following example, the centered dots indicate that the word *parliament* has three syllables.

EXAMPLE:

Syllabification

par·lia·ment (pär′lə mənt) ***n.*** **[**< OFr. *parlement* < *parler:* see prec.**]** **1.** an official conference or council concerned with public affairs **2.** [**P-**] the national legislative body of Great Britain, composed of the House of Commons and the House of Lords **3.** [**P-**] a similar body in other countries

Pronunciation. Pronunciations are given after most entry words. Exceptions are sometimes made for entries—such as abbreviations, prefixes, and suffixes—that are not complete words. Pronunciations are also avoided with compound words when pronunciations have already been given for the individual words that make up the compounds.

The dictionary tells you how a word is pronounced by respelling it in a *phonetic alphabet.* This is a set of special symbols. Each symbol is assigned one sound. Since phonetic alphabets vary from one dictionary to another, it is important for you to become familiar with the one in the dictionary you use. A *pronunciation key* at the front or back of your dictionary lists and explains all the symbols used throughout the book. Study this carefully. Most dictionaries for students also print short pronunciation keys on every other page to help you pronounce the words.

Besides helping you to pronounce the sounds correctly, the dictionary shows you which syllables are stressed. The syllable that gets the most emphasis has a *primary stress,* usually shown by a heavy mark after the syllable (′). Words of more than one syllable may have a *secondary stress,* shown by a shorter, lighter mark (') after the syllable. Unstressed syllables have no stress marks. Again, symbols may vary from one dictionary to another, so check the introduction of the book you use.

PRIMARY STRESS ONLY:

> **par·ley** (pär′lē) ***vi.*** **[**< Fr. *parler,* to speak < LL. < *parabola,* PARABLE**]** to hold a talk or conference, esp. with an enemy —***n.,*** *pl.* **-leys** a conference; specif., a military conference with an enemy to discuss terms

PRIMARY AND SECONDARY STRESSES:

> **an·ti·dote** (an′tə dōt') ***n.*** **[**ME. & OFr. < L. < Gr. < *anti-,* against + *dotos,* given < *didonai,* to give**]** **1.** a remedy to counteract a poison *[*milk and olive oil are common *antidotes]* **2.** anything that works against an evil or unwanted condition *[*education is a good *antidote* for prejudice*]* —**an′ti·dot'al** ***adj.***

When two or more pronunciations of a word are given, the pronunciation shown first is the one most frequently used. Any others are usually shown in abbreviated form.

MORE THAN ONE PRONUNCIATION:

> **par·tic·u·lar·ly** (pər tik′yə lər lē, pär-) ***adv.*** **1.** in detail **2.** especially; unusually **3.** specifically

Part-of-Speech Labels. The *part-of-speech labels* in a dictionary tell you whether a word can be used as a noun, verb, or some other part of speech. This information is given in abbreviated form, usually after the pronunciation, but sometimes at the end of the entry. When a word can be used as more than one part of speech, the word's meanings are grouped accordingly under each part-of-speech label.

After the appropriate part-of-speech label, the dictionary may also show the plural forms of certain nouns, the various forms of irregular adjectives or adverbs, or the principal parts of certain verbs. As the following example illustrates, such information is often shown in bold type.

EXAMPLE:

Noun

fo·cus (fō′kəs) ***n.***, *pl.* **fo′cus·es, fo′ci** (-sī) [ModL. < L., hearth] **1.** the point where rays of light, heat, etc. or waves of sound come together, or from which they spread or seem to spread; specif., the point where rays of light reflected by a mirror or refracted by a lens meet **2.** *same as* FOCAL LENGTH **3.** an adjustment of the focal length to make a clear image [to bring a camera into *focus*] **4.** any center of activity, attention, etc. **5.** a part of the body where an infection is most active **6.** *Math.* *a*) either of the two fixed points used in determining an ellipse: see illustration at ELLIPSE *b*) any similar point for a parabola or hyperbola —***vt.*** **-cused** or **-cussed, -cus·ing** or **-cus·sing** **1.** to bring into focus [to *focus* light rays] **2.** to adjust the focal length of (the eye, a lens, etc.) so as to make a clear image **3.** to concentrate [to *focus* one's attention] —***vi.*** to come to a focus —**in focus** clear; distinct —**out of focus** indistinct; blurred —**fo′cus·er** ***n.***

Plural forms of noun

Principal parts of verb

Intransitive verb

Transitive verb

Etymologies. The origin and history of a word is called its *etymology.* This information usually appears in brackets near the beginning of the entry.

Etymologies are printed in a code of symbols, abbreviations, and different kinds of type. The meaning of the code is explained in detail at the front of the dictionary.

EXAMPLE:

aq·ua·ma·rine (ak′wə mə rēn′, äk′-) ***n.*** [L. *aqua marina*, sea water] **1.** a transparent, pale bluish-green mineral: a variety of beryl, used in jewelry **2.** its color —***adj.*** bluish-green

Etymology

The etymology for *aquamarine* tells you that the word comes from the Latin (L.) words *aqua marina,* which mean "sea water."

Definitions. Many words have more than one meaning. Each meaning of a word is called a *definition.* When a word has two or more definitions, they will be numbered and grouped according to their part of speech. Related definitions may be divided even further and indicated by a series of small letters, as in the following example.

EXAMPLE:

Definition with two lettered parts

Numbered definitions

Example of word in use

lag (lag) ***vi.*** **lagged, lag'ging** [? akin to MDan. *lakke,* to go slowly] **1.** *a)* to fall, move, or stay behind; loiter [the tired hikers *lagged* behind] *b)* to move or develop more slowly than expected, hoped for, etc. [the assembly line was *lagging* in production] **2.** to become gradually less strong, energetic, etc.; wane; flag [her interest in sports was *lagging*] —***n.*** **1.** a falling behind or being slowed or delayed in motion, development, etc. **2.** the amount of such falling behind [a great *lag* between social behavior and scientific knowledge] —**lag'ger *n.***

As you can see in this example, many definitions are followed by a helpful phrase or sentence showing the word in use.

Special Labels. A definition may sometimes begin with a label that restricts that meaning of the word to a particular area of language. *Usage labels,* such as *Slang, Dialect,* and *Informal* (or *Colloquial*), tell you that a certain meaning is not generally used in formal, standard English. *Field labels,* such as *Biology, Mathematics,* and *Photography,* tell you that the word has a meaning that is limited to the particular occupation, activity, or branch of knowledge that is mentioned in the label.

EXAMPLE:

Field label

Usage label

wid·ow (wid'ō) ***n.*** [OE. *widewe*] **1.** a woman whose husband has died and who has not remarried ☆**2.** *Cards* a group of cards dealt into a separate pile, typically for the use of the highest bidder ☆**3.** [Colloq.] a woman whose husband is often away taking part in a certain sport, hobby, etc. [a golf *widow*] —***vt.*** to cause to become a widow [*widowed* by the war] **wid'ow-hood' *n.***

Idioms. *Idioms* are expressions such as *down at the heels* and *in the pink* that have meanings different from what the words would literally suggest. Most dictionaries for students list idioms near the end of the main entry. The following example shows the idioms that one dictionary lists for the word *peg.*

EXAMPLE:

peg (peg) ***n.*** [prob. < LowG. source] **1.** a short pin or bolt used to hold parts together, close an opening, hang things on, fasten ropes to, mark the score in a game, etc. **2.** a step or degree [the promotion moved me up a few *pegs*] **3.** any of the pins that hold the strings of a violin, etc. and are used to tighten or loosen them: see illustration at VIOLIN **4.** [Colloq.] the foot or leg [it knocked his *pegs* out from under him] **5.** [Colloq.] a throw [a good *peg* from the outfield] —***vt.* pegged, peg′ging** **1.** to put a peg or pegs into so as to fasten, mark, etc. **2.** to maintain (prices, etc.) at a fixed level **3.** [Colloq.] to identify or put in a category [she quickly *pegged* him as a fool] **4.** [Colloq.] to throw [to *peg* the ball to first base] —***vi.*** to move quickly (with *along*, etc.) —**peg away (at)** to work hard and steadily (at) —**round peg in a square hole** one in a position, etc. for which he is unfitted: also **square peg in a round hole** —**take down a peg** to make less proud or vain; humble

Idioms

Derived Words. Words formed by adding a common suffix, such as *-ly* or *-ness,* to an entry word are called *derived words.* Such suffixes change the word from one part of speech to another. Most dictionaries list derived words at the end of a main entry and do not give definitions for them. A derived word simply appears with its part-of-speech label and, sometimes, with its pronunciation.

EXAMPLE:

☆**pep·py** (pep′ē) ***adj.*** **-pi·er, -pi·est** [Colloq.] full of pep, or energy; brisk; vigorous —**pep′pi·ly *adv.*** —**pep′pi·ness *n.***

Derived words

Synonyms. A word that is closely related but not identical in meaning to another word is called a *synonym.* After certain main entries you may find a block of words labeled *SYN*. Here the differences in meaning among synonyms are explained. Some dictionaries list *antonyms*—words that are opposite in meaning—right after the synonyms.

EXAMPLE:

pen·i·tence (pen′ə təns) ***n.*** the state of being penitent
SYN.—**penitence** implies sorrow over having done wrong and a willingness to make up for one's wrongful act; **repentance** implies a full understanding of one's wrongs and a will to change one's ways; **contrition** implies a deep sorrow for one's wrongs, with a firm determination to change for the better; **compunction** suggests a sharp but passing feeling of uneasiness about one's wrongdoing; **remorse** implies a deep and torturing sense of guilt; **regret** may refer to sorrow over any unfortunate happening as well as over a fault or act of one's own

Synonyms

EXERCISE E: Understanding the Parts of Main Entries.

Read the following main entries carefully and then, on your paper, write the answers to the ten questions that follow.

char·a·banc, char-à-banc (shar′ə baŋk′, -baŋ′) ***n.*** **[**Fr., lit., car with bench**]** [Brit.] a sightseeing bus

char·ac·ter (kar′ik tər) ***n.*** **[**< OFr. < L. < Gr. *charaktēr,* an engraving instrument < *charattein,* to engrave**]** **1.** any figure, letter, or symbol used in writing and printing **2.** the basic quality or qualities that make up something **3.** the pattern of behavior or personality found in an individual or group **4.** moral strength; self-discipline, courage, etc. **5.** *a*) reputation *b*) good reputation *[left without a shred of character]* **6.** position or role *[in his character as a son]* **7.** a person in a play, novel, etc. **8.** [Colloq.] an odd or peculiar person **9.** a special trait or characteristic **10.** *Genetics* the color, shape, etc. caused in an individual by the action of one or more genes —see ***SYN.*** at DISPOSITION and QUALITY —**in** (or **out of**) **character** in keeping with (or not in keeping with) the role or general character

char·ac·ter·is·tic (kar′ik tə ris′tik) ***adj.*** that gives the basic quality or character to someone or something *[the characteristic sound made by an owl]* —***n.*** **1.** a trait, feature, etc. that makes a person or thing different from others **2.** the whole number, or integral part, of a logarithm, as 4 in the logarithm 4.7193: see also MANTISSA —**char′ac·ter·is′ti·cal·ly *adv.***
SYN. —**characteristic** suggests a quality that is typical of, and helps identify, a certain person or thing *[her characteristic honesty; the characteristic taste of honey]*; **individual** and **distinctive** refer to a quality that makes something different from others of its kind, **distinctive** often implying excellence *[an individual, or distinctive, style]*

char·ac·ter·ize (kar′ik tə rīz′) ***vt.*** **-ized′, -iz′ing** **1.** to describe or show as having particular qualities or traits *[Tennyson characterized King Arthur as wise and brave]* **2.** to be the distinctive character of; distinguish *[bribery characterized her term in office]* —**char′ac·ter·i·za′tion *n.***

cha·rade (shə rād′) ***n.*** **[**Fr. < Pr. *charrada* < *charrar,* to gossip**]** [*often pl.*] **1.** a game in which the players try to guess a word or phrase that another player is acting out without speaking, often syllable by syllable

chard (chärd) ***n.*** **[**Fr. *carde* < L. *carduus,* thistle**]** a kind of beet whose large leaves and thick stalks are used as food

charge (chärj) ***vt.*** **charged, charg′ing** **[**< OFr. *chargier* < VL. *carricare,* to load < L. *carrus,* CAR, wagon**]** **1.** to load or fill with the required material *[a firearm charged with gunpowder]* **2.** to saturate with another substance *[air charged with steam]* **3.** to add carbon dioxide to (water, etc.) ☆**4.** to add an electrical charge to (a battery, etc.) **5.** to give as a task, duty, etc. to *[the nurse is charged with giving medicine to the patients]* **6.** to give instructions to or command authoritatively *[the judge charged the jury]* **7.** to accuse of wrongdoing; censure *[the state charged her with murder]* **8.** to set as a price or fee *[barbers used to charge a dollar for a haircut]* **9.** to have recorded as a debt one is to pay later *[he charged his* purchases*]* **10.** to attack vigorously *[*our troops *charged* the enemy*]* —***vi.*** **1.** to ask payment (*for*) *[*to *charge* for a service*]* **2.** to attack vigorously or move forward as if attacking —***n.*** **1.** the amount, as of fuel, gunpowder, etc., used to load or fill something **2.** *a*) the amount of chemical energy stored in a battery to be a source of electrical energy *b*) a change from the condition of electrical neutrality by the gaining of electrons (*negative charge*) or by the loss of electrons (*positive charge*) ☆**3.** [Slang] a thrill **4.** responsibility or duty (*of*) *[*she took *charge* of the finances*]* **5.** care or custody (*of*) **6.** a person or thing entrusted to someone's care *[*the children were the nurses' *charges]* **7.** instruction or command, esp. instructions given by a judge to a jury **8.** accusation; indictment *[charges* of cruelty*]* **9.** the cost or price of an article, service, etc. **10.** a debt or expense ☆**11.** *same as* CHARGE ACCOUNT **12.** *a*) an attack, as by troops *b*) the signal for this **13.** *Heraldry* a bearing —see ***SYN.*** at COMMAND —**charge off** **1.** to regard as a loss **2.** to think of as due to a certain cause; ascribe *[charge off* her mistake to inexperience*]* —**in charge (of)** having the responsibility or control (of) —**in the charge of** in the care of or under the control of —**charge·a·ble** (chär′jə b'l) ***adj.***

1. Which entry shows both a preferred and a variant spelling? *charabanc*
2. Of the main entries given, which entry word has the most syllables? *characteristic*
3. Look at the entry word *charade* and tell which syllable is stressed. *second*
4. According to its etymology, what does *charabanc* literally mean? *car with bench*
5. Write the definition that explains the meaning of *charge* as it is used in each of the following sentences:
   a. The carpenter *charged* us $100 for the new kitchen cabinet. *to set as a price or fee*
   b. On that fateful day, the British cavalry *charged* at dawn. *to attack vigorously*
   c. The *charges* brought against him were proved false. *accusation; indictment*
6. As how many different parts of speech can *charge* be used? *two–verb and noun*
7. Which definition of *charge* is not considered formal English? *a thrill*
8. List three idioms found in the excerpt. Use them in sentences.
9. List the three derived words that can be found in the excerpt. *characteristically, characterization, chargeable*
10. List the synonyms that are explained in the entry for *characteristic*. *individual, distinctive*

8. Idioms are in (or out of) character, charge off, *and* in the charge of.

APPLICATION: Using Your Dictionary. Using your own dictionary, write the answers to the questions that follow.

Answers to 1, 4, and 5 may vary; samples given for all.

1. What is the first meaning of the word *key?*
2. According to its etymology, what does *gospel* mean? *good news*
3. In what country would you find *curb* spelled *kerb?*
4. What idioms are listed under the word *fall?*
5. What are some synonyms of the word *fatal?*

1. an instrument, usually of metal, for moving the bolt of a lock

3. Gr Brit

4. -(all) over oneself, -among, -away, -back, -back on, etc.

5. deadly, mortal, lethal, etc.

UNIT VI

Composition

Chapter 24

Improving Your Choice of Words

Accurate, interesting writing depends on careful word choices. If you choose words carelessly, you can confuse or bore a reader. On the other hand, if you choose words with care, you can make your ideas seem both clear and fresh to your audience. This chapter will show you a number of ways to improve your word choices in all of your writing.

24.1 Choosing Precise Words

Whenever you write, one of your basic goals is naturally to present your ideas in a clear and interesting way. If you concentrate on what you want to say, you will discover that many possible word choices are open to you. This section will show you how to avoid weak or dull word choices. It will also provide you with some new ways to find the most suitable words to express your ideas.

■ Using Action Words

Verbs are essential parts of your sentences. As you know from your study of grammar, some verbs are action verbs; other verbs are linking verbs. In addition verbs can be either in the active voice or in the passive voice. In general the more you use *action verbs* in the *active voice,* the more energetic and direct your sentences will be.

Use action verbs in the active voice to express your ideas forcefully.

Action Verbs. Although you will often need to use linking verbs, try to replace linking verbs with *action verbs* in many of your sentences. Note how action verbs make the sentences in the following chart more direct.

With Linking Verbs	With Action Verbs
He *is* a leader in many class projects.	He *leads* many class projects.
We *became* investors in the stock market.	We *invested* in the stock market.

You can rewrite many sentences that have linking verbs by looking for a word in the sentence that suggests an action verb and changing it into a verb. Notice how the use of the word *tutor* changes in the following examples.

LINKING VERB: Sheila *is* a tutor at the elementary school.

ACTION VERB: Sheila *tutors* at the elementary school.

Active Voice. You should also avoid using too many verbs in the passive voice. In the following chart, note how verbs in the *active voice* make the sentences more direct.

With Verbs in the Passive Voice	With Verbs in the Active Voice
We *were confused* by the question.	The question *confused* us.
The herd's survival *was threatened* by the plague.	The plague *threatened* the herd's survival.

Occasionally you will need to use verbs in the passive voice. However, a series of sentences with verbs in the passive voice is likely to sound roundabout. In addition the passive voice often adds words to sentences. Whenever you can, use the active voice to make your sentences more direct.

You can rewrite most sentences that have verbs in the passive voice by looking for the performer of the action at the end of the sentence and moving the performer to the beginning. In the following examples, *groom* and *ushers* are the performers of the action.

PASSIVE VOICE: Silver tuxedos *were worn* by the groom and his ushers.

ACTIVE VOICE: The groom and his ushers *wore* silver tuxedos.

EXERCISE A: Replacing Linking Verbs with Action Verbs. Rewrite each of the following sentences to make it more direct by replacing a linking verb with an action verb. *Answers will vary; samples given.*

EXAMPLE: Jed was a student of Greek civilization.

Jed studied Greek civilization.

1. Janet's good manners ~~are a pleasure to~~ my grandmother. *please*
2. Your order must be ~~in the mail~~ by midnight. *mailed*
3. The map in the bottle ~~was a guide for~~ us to Hammett's Cave. *guided*
4. Apparently my tutoring had really ~~been of help to~~ Marilyn. *helped*
5. Nobody ~~was of the belief~~ that I had actually flown an aircraft. *believed*
6. The handout sheet ~~was a list of~~ our assignments for the next four weeks. *listed*
7. Nobody expected that this television show would ~~be successful~~ in the competition for ratings. *succeed*
8. She ~~was a participant~~ in a number of different club activities. *participated*

9. Ants ~~are the creators of~~ tiny, endless underground tunnels. *create*
10. The hovering hawk ~~was an observer of~~ our every movement. *observed*

EXERCISE B: Replacing Verbs in the Passive Voice with Verbs in the Active Voice. Rewrite each of the following sentences to make it more direct by replacing a verb in the passive voice with a verb in the active voice. *Answers will vary; samples given.*

EXAMPLE: The shutters were rattled by the wind.

The wind rattled the shutters.

3. The/hinder store owners who wish to expand their businesses.

1. ~~The barbells were lifted by a~~ man of enormous strength. *A/lifted the barbells.*
2. ~~Mrs. Simpson, our teacher, was annoyed by the~~ builders pounding on the roof. *The/annoyed Mrs. Simpson, our teacher.*
3. ~~Store owners who wish to expand their businesses are hindered by the~~ new zoning laws.
4. ~~Many species of fish are endangered by industrial~~ wastes. *Industrial/endanger many species of fish.*
5. ~~Science students can be helped by the~~ physics review lectures offered on Saturdays. *The/can help science students.*
6. ~~Many of Leon Uris's novels were inspired by the~~ heroic deeds of World War II. *The/inspired many of Leon Uris's novels.*
7. ~~The tent was pitched and the fire was built by my~~ father and brothers. *My/pitched the tent and built the fire.*
8. ~~An article about whales was written by the~~ newest member of our news team, Marion Pratt.
9. The trouble began when the ~~bull was mistakenly released by a~~ gatekeeper. *mistakenly released the bull.*
10. Finally, ~~her stage fright was relieved by~~ the audience's enthusiasm. *relieved her stage fright.*

8. The/, wrote an article about whales.

Using Vivid Language

In addition to using action verbs in the active voice, you should try to use words that will paint pictures for your readers. Specific, vivid words can help the reader see what you have visualized in your own mind.

Choose language that is specific and precise rather than general and dull.

In the sentences in the following chart, note the difference between general language and specific language.

Examples of General Language	Examples of Specific Language
A *forest* surrounded the *building.*	*Dense pines* surrounded the *old barn.*
That *motion picture* was *silly.*	That *science fiction movie* was *ridiculously unbelievable.*
The *player moved* across the court.	The *young tennis champion sped* across the court.

The English language offers a great variety of words. You should not always be satisfied with the first words that come to mind. For example, do not write *look* when *glance* or *stare* would be more exact. If you search for the best words, using your memory, a dictionary, or a book of synonyms, you will find words that are both accurate and vivid.

You might begin by giving your verbs a "fitness" test. Ask yourself, "Would another verb help the reader see more clearly the action I am describing?" If the first verb that comes to mind is a common or general one, think about the action you are describing. For example, the verb *run* can be useful and appropriate, but it is general. A more specific verb can make the reader visualize the action exactly as you visualized it.

DULL, GENERAL VERB: Hillary *ran* across the finish line to the wild cheers of spectators.

VIVID, SPECIFIC VERB: Hillary *dashed* across the finish line to the wild cheers of spectators.

You should also examine your nouns and modifiers. Replace dull, general nouns and modifiers with words that will make your writing clearer. In the following example, the word *man* is vague, and the adjective *loud* is general. *Loud* could describe anything from a sigh to an explosion.

DULL, GENERAL WORDS: The *man* addressed the crowd in a *loud* voice.

VIVID, SPECIFIC WORDS: The *mayor* addressed the crowd in a *booming* voice.

While you are writing and especially when you are examining what you have written, question your words. Make sure that you have chosen specific and interesting words wherever they can be of help to your reader.

EXERCISE C: Using Specific, Vivid Words to Enliven Sentences. In the following sentences, the words in parentheses are dull, general verbs, nouns, or modifiers. Replace each item with one or more words that give a more vivid picture. *Answers will vary; samples given.*

EXAMPLE: Lisa (held) her little sister's hand as they crossed the street.

tightly gripped

1. After a (bad) experience in the dentist's chair, Chuck (said) that he would take better care of his teeth. *dreadful/vowed*
2. Officer Christie watched the (suspect) dart through the crowd and race around the corner. *thief*
3. The substitute player (stood) up when the coach called his name. *leaped*
4. Tyrone was (happy) when he won the basketball scholarship. *ecstatic*
5. Dancers (moved) to the beat of the drums.
6. The wrecking ball (hit) the side of the building.
7. With a (loud noise) the entire (structure) crumbled to the ground. *thundering crash/tenement*
8. The fire spread (fast). *quite rapidly*
9. The hungry trucker (ate) his food. *gobbled*
10. After spending three weeks in orbit, the astronaut reported that he was (glad) to be home. *delighted*

5. swayed gracefully 6. smashed

Choosing Words for Their Connotations

The *denotation* of a word is its literal meaning. The word *shivering,* for example, means "shaking." The words *trembling* and *quaking* also mean "shaking." These three words are synonyms because they share the same denotation.

The three synonyms, however, have different *connotations.* The connotation of a word is the set of ideas it brings to mind. *Shivering* generally suggests a physical reaction to cold. *Trembling,* on the other hand, might suggest a number of different emotions—for example, fear, love, anger, or excitement. Of the three words, *quaking* suggests the most violent action. Most people would also associate the act of *quaking* directly with the emotion of fear.

When you are considering synonyms, you should think about their different connotations.

Choose the words with the most appropriate connotations for your sentences.

Whenever you can think of several possible word choices, you are probably considering synonyms with different connotations. Remember that these different connotations can alter the meaning of your sentence. Notice how *shivering, trembling,* and *quaking* all change the idea presented in the following example.

EXAMPLE: *Shivering,* Orin approached the gray cottage.

Trembling, Orin approached the gray cottage.

Quaking, Orin approached the gray cottage.

In the first sentence, Orin could be going to the cottage to seek shelter from the cold. In the second the cottage might be Orin's former home or long-sought goal. In the third the cottage clearly holds something that frightens Orin.

Because their connotations are different, you will generally want to use these words to express different ideas. Note in each of the following sentences that one of the three words is more logical than the other two would be.

EXAMPLE: *Shivering,* Orin approached the icy river.

Trembling, Orin approached his long-lost brother.

Quaking, Orin approached the fiery dragon.

EXERCISE D: Understanding Connotations. List two synonyms for each of the following words. Next to each synonym, write a sentence that suits the connotation of that synonym. *Answers will vary; sample synonyms are given.*

1. wide *broad/large*
2. angry *irate/mad*
3. hurt *injure/damage*
4. pleasant *pleasing/agreeable*
5. strong *sturdy/tough*

EXERCISE E: Choosing Connotations. Each of the following sentences contains two or more synonyms in parentheses. Consider the different connotation of each synonym in a group. Then choose the word that you think best completes each sentence.

Answers may vary. Students can be asked to defend their choices.

EXAMPLE: The baby (chortled, guffawed) at the puppy.

chortled

1. Booster rockets (elevated, <u>lifted</u>) the missile from the launching pad.
2. The radio on the windowsill (<u>blared</u>, bellowed, howled) endlessly.
3. Robert had trouble making friends at first because he was (<u>shy</u>, wary, fearful).
4. After lifting weights for a year, Alfred had (<u>in-creased</u>, expanded, raised) the size of his arm muscles.
5. Pleasantly (<u>stuffed</u>, bloated) after Thanksgiving dinner, we retired to the living room to watch football on television.

6. The air was still too (icy, frozen, cold) for a light jacket.
7. She (made, shaped, created) more problems by never acknowledging her mistakes.
8. Holding the racket properly, Joni learned to (dominate, control) her serves.
9. State engineers have (invented, designed) a new type of roadway.
10. He made a (clumsy, gawky) attempt to apologize.

APPLICATION: Choosing the Best Words. Read the following passage carefully, looking for unnecessary linking verbs, verbs in the passive voice, and words that are dull, general, or inappropriate. Then rewrite the passage, using words that are direct, vivid, and suitable.

Revisions will vary; samples given.

(1) Charles Dickens' *The Christmas Carol* is an ~~interesting~~ story. (2) The story ~~is focused~~ on a man named Ebenezer Scrooge. (3) ~~Scrooge is interested only in money~~. (4) One Christmas Eve, however, ~~Scrooge is taught by a scary experience~~ to change his ways.

(5) ~~Scrooge is taken by three~~ phantoms—the spirits of Christmas past, present, and future—on a trip through his own past, present, and future. (6) He sees ~~things~~ from the future that ~~are frightening to~~ him. (7) Scrooge finally ~~sees~~ that his love of money can ~~be harmful to~~ him and others. (8) Then Christmas bells ~~are heard~~, and ~~Scrooge~~ wakes from his ~~reverie~~. (9) Scrooge is ~~happy~~ when he ~~comprehends~~ that he is still alive and that the future ~~can still be changed by him~~. (10) His life is completely ~~revolutionized~~, and he becomes a ~~nice~~ man.

1. entertaining 2. focuses 3. Only money interests Scrooge. 4. a terrifying adventure teaches Scrooge 5. Three/take Scrooge 6. scenes/frighten 7. understands/harm 8. Scrooge hears/he/dreams 9. thrilled/realizes/he can still change 10. changed/kind and generous

24.2 Avoiding Worn-out and Inappropriate Words

Using precise, clear language means choosing words that will be both interesting and clear. For this reason you should guard against two special problems: *clichés* and *slang*. This section will help you replace these words with original words and expressions.

■ Avoiding Clichés

A *cliché* is an overused expression such as *snug as a bug in a rug*. Your readers will be familiar with clichés—too familiar!

Use precise language in place of clichés.

Watch carefully for clichés. Tired-sounding, ready-made expressions such as *cute as a button* or *fit as a fiddle* will weaken your writing. Language that is more precise and original will convey much more meaning.

Examine the following examples. In each case a cliché makes an idea less precise than it could be. The revised version of each sentence provides a precise expression that makes the idea sharper.

CLICHÉ: The new administrator was afraid *to rock the boat*.

PRECISE EXPRESSION: The new administrator was afraid *to make any major changes in the organization*.

CLICHÉ: After painting his bedroom, Mike *ate like a horse*.

PRECISE EXPRESSION: After painting his bedroom, Mike *devoured two hamburgers and a pecan pie*.

EXERCISE A: Recognizing Clichés. Find five clichés by looking in books that discuss clichés, by listening to conversations around you, or simply by using your memory. On your paper list the five clichés, define each one, and write a sentence using the cliché in a way that shows its meaning. *Answers will vary. Clichés can be listed on the chalkboard and their definitions discussed by the class.*

EXERCISE B: Revising Clichés. Use the sentences you wrote in Exercise A. Underline the cliché in each. Beneath each sentence write a new version by substituting precise, original language for the cliché. *Answers will vary. Students can exchange papers, check the revisions, and suggest any improvements.*

Avoiding Slang

Slang is made up of words that are popular among certain groups of people at a particular time. Because slang words change over time and vary according to place, however, many people find slang confusing. Only a small percentage of slang words become well-known and permanent parts of the language. Except in very informal writing or in dialogue, slang should be avoided.

Use precise language in place of slang words and expressions.

The following examples are weakened by slang. Notice how more precise word choices clarify the ideas and sound less jarring.

SLANG: *It really blew Scott's mind* to find straight A's on his report card.

PRECISE EXPRESSION: Scott was *astonished* to find straight A's on his report card.

SLANG: The minister's sermon *was really far out.*

PRECISE EXPRESSION: The minister's sermon *included a gripping example from daily life.*

EXERCISE C: Replacing Slang. Find the slang word or expression in each of the following sentences. Consult a dictionary of slang if you do not understand some of the expressions. Then write a new sentence, replacing the slang with precise, original words.

Answers will vary; samples given.

EXAMPLE: His actions showed that he was made of the right stuff.

His actions showed that he was courageous and heroic.

1. Our team ~~blew them away~~. *defeated them soundly*
2. Proving once again that she was ~~an airhead~~, Gina left the apartment without her keys and allowed the door to lock behind her. *absent-minded*

3. Our neighbor, Mr. Sampson, ~~chewed my ear off~~ while I was trying to rake our lawn.
4. With his ~~wicked~~ curve ball, Jeremy struck out every batter. *exceptional*
5. When I told Jan to pick up her toys, she ~~got really ticked off~~. *became infuriated*
6. The pounding headache ~~bummed me out~~ all day.
7. Yesterday I was ~~nailed~~ by Mrs. DeStefano for not carrying a pass in the halls. *reprimanded*
8. With a grin on his face, Horace showed that he ~~was wise to~~ their plans. *knew of*
9. By grabbing the bridge's handrail, David saved himself from a ~~hairy~~ situation. *dangerous*
10. After rounding the last turn, the horse ~~burned up~~ the final stretch. *raced down*

3. chattered at me constantly 6. made me miserable

APPLICATION: Avoiding Worn-out and Inappropriate Words. List ten overused or currently popular expressions that are inappropriate in formal writing. Include both clichés and slang. Then complete the following steps.

1. Write a passage using any five of the expressions on your list.
2. Exchange papers with a partner. Then find and underline the five inappropriate expressions on your partner's paper and write a revised version of the passage.

Answers will vary. You may want to allow students to choose clichés from those listed in Exercise A and look for slang expressions in a dictionary of slang.

Chapter 25

Writing Better Sentences

Writing style is a term used to describe the way in which a person generally writes both individual sentences and groups of sentences. A poor style is usually one in which all the sentences are similar. The writing may be filled with short, choppy sentences that follow one after another. It may instead contain an endless series of long, confusing sentences. Or it might contain sentences that repeat the same patterns and structures over and over. In this chapter you will learn to recognize and avoid each of these problems.

25.1 Expanding Short Sentences

A short *simple sentence* sometimes contains too few details to make its idea clear and interesting. Moreover, too many short sentences in a series can sound awkward and choppy. However, by adding details to short sentences and by combining short sentences, you can produce a flowing style that readers are likely to find appealing.

■ Adding Details

Short sentences often deprive the reader of important information by leaving out the modifying words and phrases that would make the ideas come to life.

Improve short sentences by adding details to the subjects, verbs, or complements.

Short sentences are not errors in themselves. Using too many of them, however, can make your writing sound cold and empty, as well as choppy and awkward. As you write, you should concentrate first on the main parts that are needed in most sentences: the subject, the verb, and the complement. Then you should add to the main parts any details that will make the idea clearer for the reader.

The following chart provides examples of short sentences that have been expanded by adding details. In each case the additional information makes the idea more vivid.

ADDING DETAILS TO SHORT SENTENCES	
Details Added to the Subject	
A teddy bear sat in the rocking chair.	A *fuzzy* teddy bear *with only one ear* sat in the rocking chair.
Details Added to the Verb	
She hurled the javelin.	*In one arching motion,* she *gracefully* hurled the javelin.
Details Added to the Complement	
He found a silver dollar.	He found a *rare* silver dollar *hidden behind a jug on the shelf.*

EXERCISE A: Adding Details to Short Sentences. Each of the following items contains a short sentence. Beneath each item are details that you can add to the subject, verb, or complement of the sentence. Rewrite each item as a single longer sentence by adding all the details provided. *Answers may vary; samples given.*

EXAMPLE: The dog chewed a slipper.
a. blissfully b. lying on the living room floor
c. belonging to Mother

Lying on the living room floor, the dog blissfully chewed a slipper belonging to Mother.

1. ^Joey went to^camp^ *b/a/c*
   a. basketball b. full of excitement
   c. with his best friend Emil
2. ^The^sea was calm^ *c/a/b*
   a. bright blue b. in the still summer air
   c. except for the pencil-thin wake of a passing speedboat
3. The bishop's^silver collection was returned.^ ^ *b/a/c*
   a. by the police b. missing
   c. early in the morning
4. ^Mrs. Simmons strolled through the corridors.^ ^ *c/b/a*
   a. filled with the treasures of foreign lands
   b. of the museum c. excited and happy
5. The^sun set^over the^horizon. *a/b/c*
   a. golden b. rapidly c. distant
6. ^Sam watched^television^ *b/c/a*
   a. absent-mindedly b. while washing the dishes
   c. the new color
7. ^The^skaters^whirled across the ice. *a/b/c*
   a. with the grace of champions b. Olympic
   c. from Norway
8. ^The tiger lunged toward the^zebra^ *a/b/c*
   a. with lightning speed b. solitary
   c. grazing on the tundra
9. ^We watched the^game^ *c/a/b*
   a. football b. on television
   c. while eating dinner in silence
10. The^moonlight shone on the^snow^ *c/b/a*
    a. piled on the tree limbs b. glistening
    c. pale ivory

EXERCISE B: Adding Your Own Details. Rewrite each of the following sentences to make it more informative and descriptive. Add at least two different details to each. *Answers will vary; samples given for first two.*

EXAMPLE: I drank the water.

Hot and thirsty, I drank the cold water shooting out of the drinking fountain.

1. After dinner Mary quickly walked the dog around the block.

1. Mary walked the dog.
2. A herd of cattle grazed.
3. The waves broke violently.
4. A rainbow appeared.
5. His uncle spoke on television.
6. Flowers sprouted.
7. Our school won every game.
8. A submarine surfaced.
9. The scientist made a discovery.
10. I cut the grass.

2. A small herd of dairy cattle grazed in the open meadow.

Combining Sentences

A series of short sentences can sound choppy and awkward. One way to correct the problem is to use the ideas in some of the short sentences to make a few longer sentences.

Combine two or more short simple sentences to make a longer simple sentence, a compound sentence, a complex sentence, or a compound-complex sentence.

Two short sentences in a series often develop the same idea. You can easily join such ideas into one longer sentence. The chart below and on the next page shows different ways of combining ideas from two or more short sentences into one more interesting sentence.

COMBINING SENTENCES FOR VARIETY
Two Simple Sentences
We spent yesterday at the beach. We all got burned by the hot sun.
One Sentence Changed to a Modifying Phrase
At the beach yesterday, we all got burned by the hot sun.

One Sentence Changed to Make a Compound Verb
We spent yesterday at the beach and got burned by the hot sun.
Two Sentences Joined in a Compound Sentence
We spent yesterday at the beach, and we all got burned by the hot sun.
Two Sentences Joined in a Complex Sentence
Because we spent the whole day at the beach yesterday, we all got burned by the hot sun.
Two Sentences Joined with a Third Sentence in a Compound-Complex Sentence
Because the sun felt so good, we spent the whole day at the beach yesterday, and unfortunately we all got burned.

As you can see from the chart, the ideas in two short simple sentences can be combined to form a variety of new sentences. You might change the independent clause in one sentence to a modifying phrase or to a verb with an object or modifiers and then add the result to the other sentence, as in the second and third examples in the chart. Or you could use a coordinating conjunction to join the clauses in your simple sentences and produce a compound sentence, as in the fourth example. In many cases you can also use a subordinating conjunction to join the two clauses and produce a complex sentence, as in the fifth example. If you choose to expand on or change your ideas slightly, you could write a compound-complex sentence, as in the sixth example.

EXERCISE C: Combining Short, Choppy Sentences. Read each of the following groups of short, choppy sentences and then combine two or more of the sentences in each group. In any group that contains three sentences, you may decide to leave one sentence unchanged. Use your own judgment to make each passage clear and smooth. *Answers will vary; samples given.*

EXAMPLE: Jupiter was once thought to have only ten moons. Scientists have recently discovered new moons around the planet.

Although Jupiter was once thought to have only ten moons, scientists have recently discovered new moons around the planet.

1. ~~The~~ show ~~closed. Many~~ of the cast members auditioned for daytime soap operas. *After the/closed, many*
2. The city began to enforce the law against double-parking more ~~strictly. Too~~ many drivers had been ignoring the law. *strictly because too*
3. ~~The~~ sun rose beyond the ~~water. It~~ cast a pink glow on the lighthouse. *As the/water, it*
4. I enjoy seeing all the animals at the ~~zoo. The~~ gorillas are my favorites. *zoo, but the*
5. ~~Our~~ school's choral group is one of the finest in the ~~country. It~~ requires special auditions for admission.
6. The supermarket was ~~crowded. People~~ stood in checkout lines stretching back into the aisles.
7. The streets of that city can be quiet and ~~calm~~. ~~They can be~~ noisy and full of ~~life. It depends~~ on the time of day. *calm or/life, depending*
8. A burglar entered the house through the ~~window~~. ~~He~~ escaped with ~~the jewelry. The~~ jewelry ~~was~~ worth thousands of dollars. *window and*
9. Hockey is a fast-moving game. Players skate by with great ~~speed. Hockey~~ pucks can travel at more than eighty miles per hour. *speed, and hockey*
10. Alexander was a remarkable animal. ~~He could~~ understand words and sign ~~language. He~~ could also invent his own games and tricks.

5. Because our/country, it 6. so crowded that people 10. Not only could he/language, but he

APPLICATION: Expanding Short Sentences. Rewrite the following passage to make the style smoother. You will have to combine several sentences to eliminate choppiness and you should also consider adding some details. Note, however, that you do not need to change every sentence. *Answers will vary; samples given.*

(1) ~~Different~~ breeds of horses have ~~different strengths~~. ~~(2) People~~ through the years have relied on several different kinds of "horse power." (3) Draft ~~horses~~ are the strongest breed of ~~horse. (4) Draft horses pulled~~ heavy burdens on the American frontier. (5) A team of ~~four could~~ pull a twenty-ton ~~load. (6) They would be harnessed together. (7) They could do~~ the work of twenty human beings. (8) Arabians are a very fast breed of horse. ~~(9) Arabian horses are also very spirited~~. (10) ~~They~~ can cover long ~~distances. (11) They~~ were used most effectively in the past for trips over hundreds of miles. (12) Tennessee Walkers, another popular breed, have a smooth but fast gait. (13) They can maintain a steady running walk for hours. (14) Owners of big farms, particularly in the South, once used many of these ~~horses. (15) They rode them~~ around their property. (16) What if these and other kinds of horses had not existed? (17) The country's growth might have been slower. *1–2. Because different/varied strengths, people 3–4. horses, which/horse, pulled 5–7. four, harnessed together, could/load, which was 8–9. horses/and very spirited 10–11. Because they/distances, they 14–15. horses for riding/extensive 17. economic/much*

25.2 Simplifying Long, Confusing Sentences

The overuse of long sentences can weaken your style just as much as the overuse of short sentences can. Too many ideas strung together can produce an awkward, rambling style. It can also make your ideas sound more complicated than they really are. This section shows several basic ways to shorten sentences while maintaining a lively, interesting style.

Shortening Long Compound Sentences

A *compound sentence* contains at least two independent clauses. Too many independent clauses in a compound sentence can sound long-winded.

Recognize compound sentences that ramble, and separate them into two or more shorter sentences.

When you find a sentence that contains too many independent clauses strung together one after another, look for places where you can end one sentence and begin a new one. In the following example of a rambling compound sentence, notice that so many ideas are contained in its three independent clauses that the sentence is difficult to understand. The revised version groups the ideas into two sentences that a reader can absorb comfortably.

RAMBLING COMPOUND SENTENCE: We receive presents from Aunt Amy every year, and this year my gift, a sweater, was a perfect fit, but Leo's gift, a brown leather belt, was too large.

REVISED: We receive presents from Aunt Amy every year. This year my gift, a sweater, was a perfect fit, but Leo's gift, a brown leather belt, was too large.

EXERCISE A: Shortening Compound Sentences. Each of the following compound sentences rambles because it contains too many independent clauses. Rewrite each sentence by breaking it up into shorter sentences.
Answers will vary; samples given.

EXAMPLE: The batter slugged a line drive to left field and easily made it to first base, and then the ball was thrown to the infield, and he slid into second head first, and the shortstop missed the tag, so the runner was safe with a double.

The batter slugged a line drive to left field and easily made it to first base. Then the ball was thrown to the infield, and he slid into second, head first. The shortstop missed the tag, so the runner was safe with a double.

1. The myths of ancient Greece have inspired writers for ~~centuries, and~~ writers have studied the personalities of many Greek characters, and they have followed many of the plots of classical Greek stories. *centuries. These*
2. A dog can be both an ally and a burden to its ~~master, and it~~ can often be a source of protection and

love, but it can also be both an expense and a continuous responsibility. *master. It*

3. To wire the driftwood as a lamp, you must drill a hole through ~~it, and then~~ you must mount it on a ~~stand, and next~~ you must pull electrical wire through the wood and attach a light socket to the top. *it. Then/stand. Next*
4. We had been driving only four hours in Alaska, and already the Cassier Mountains had stopped looking like bumps on the ~~horizon, but instead~~ they began to look like a giant tidal wave of snow, and they seemed to grow steadily in height.
5. Break up six or seven slices of bread into small pieces, and place the pieces in a mixing ~~bowl, and then~~ add two eggs and a quarter cup of milk, and beat the ~~mixture, and finally~~ add a cup of raisins, and salt the entire ~~concoction, and you~~ will then have stuffing for your chicken.

4. horizon. Instead 5. bowl. Then/mixture. Finally/concoction. You

Shortening Long Complex Sentences

A *complex sentence* contains one independent clause and two or more dependent clauses. A sentence with too many dependent clauses can become overly complicated.

Recognize complex sentences that are too complicated, and separate them into shorter sentences.

In the following example of a long complex sentence, there are three dependent clauses. Notice in the revised version that the ideas are presented in two separate sentences. Notice also that some of the words have been changed and that the ideas are in a slightly different order. The new sentences express the ideas in a clearer, more logical way.

COMPLICATED COMPLEX SENTENCE: Because our washing machine was broken, we took our clothes to the laundromat, which was so crowded, however, that we decided to return home and wash our things by hand.

REVISED: We took our clothes to the laundromat because our washing machine was broken. The laundromat was so crowded, however, that we decided to return home and wash our things by hand.

When you see that too many dependent clauses cause confusion in a sentence, look for different ways to group the ideas into shorter sentences. As the preceding example shows, you should try to group together the ideas that are most closely related to each other. You may also want to change the order of ideas and add or eliminate some of the words. Your goal should be to clarify the logical relationships among your ideas and to create a pleasant, flowing style.

EXERCISE B: Shortening Complicated Complex Sentences. The following complex sentences are overly complicated. Rewrite each item by breaking it up into shorter sentences. Change the order of ideas and add or eliminate words as you see fit. *Answers will vary; samples given.*

EXAMPLE: New York is a fast-paced city that can never bore the people who visit it because it contains fascinating museums and historical sights, which tourists can explore, as well as many restaurants, concerts, and plays, which they can enjoy.

New York is a fast-paced city that can never bore the people who visit it. It contains fascinating museums and historical sights, which tourists can explore, as well as many restaurants, concerts, and plays, which they can enjoy.

1. Although Joe had not been fishing in a number of years, he surprised himself by catching a very large ~~swordfish, which, when~~ it was measured, set a local record, which was mentioned in the newspapers. *swordfish. When/the fish's size*
2. Some of today's television stars seem to worry more about contracts than they do about providing ~~entertainment, which, as~~ a result, ~~leaves~~ the audience wondering which star will disappear next from their favorite shows. *entertainment. As/is left*

3. My last trip to Africa included my first safari, which was very ~~exciting and which~~ began at sunrise and lasted until the late afternoon when we all sat together and recounted the adventures that we had enjoyed in the bush country. *exciting. It*
4. ~~When we~~ heard that school would end early because the storm that was headed our way was closing in sooner than forecasters had ~~thought~~, we were not very worried until the principal spoke over the public address system to warn us about flooding and electrical power lines that had fallen.
5. Although Shirley was a newcomer to Gainesville, she soon felt at ~~home because~~ neighbors in her apartment building showed her the town, which she found charming, and introduced her to several people, whom she immediately liked. *home. The*

4. We/thought. However,

APPLICATION: Simplifying Long, Confusing Sentences. Study the following passage. Then improve the sentence style by breaking up each of the five sentences. You may add or eliminate words as you see fit.

Answers will vary; samples given.

(1) Because accidents are rare, traveling by air is very ~~safe, and, in~~ fact, it is statistically safer than driving a car or taking a shower. (2) In particular, modern equipment enables planes virtually to fly themselves with very little assistance from the ~~pilots, who~~ are nevertheless vital to ~~navigation, and who~~ are particularly needed during turbulent weather and for take-offs and landings, when they must guide the aircraft. (3) Pilots and airplanes also benefit from the work done by navigation control personnel on the ~~ground, and they depend greatly on these~~ people ~~who~~ monitor airplanes in flight and plan safe routes for planes in the air.

(4) In contrast, the highways are peopled by drivers who act entirely as ~~individuals, and no~~ central control offers them ~~guidance, and instead~~ drivers must guess the next movements of others on the road, a factor that pilots do not usually have to consider. (5) In short, then, it is not surprising that airlines enjoy such an excellent safety ~~record, and people~~ should not be nervous about flying once they realize how much sophisticated equipment and attention guide the flight of every single craft in the sky. *1. safe. In 2. pilots. However, pilots/navigation. They 3. ground. These 4. individuals. No/guidance. Instead, 5. record. People*

Using a Variety of Sentences 25.3

Too many sentences that begin in the same way can add up to a dull style. A long series of sentences with similar structures can also be monotonous. To achieve a smooth style, you should try to vary both the beginnings and the structures of your sentences.

Using Different Sentence Openers

One of the best ways to avoid monotony in your writing is to avoid using the same kind of sentence opener over and over. If too many of your sentences begin with the most popular sentence opener, a subject, they will soon have a repetitious sound.

Begin your sentences with different openers: subjects, single-word modifiers, phrases, and clauses.

Many of your sentences should begin with subjects because the subject is often the most logical sentence opener. You should, however, avoid the monotony caused by beginning too many sentences with subjects. The following chart shows many different openers.

SENTENCE OPENERS
Subjects
The *movie* held our interest for only the first hour. *It* had been given too much publicity.
One-Word Modifiers
Happy, the child blew bubbles in his milk. *Gently,* his mother wiped his face.
Phrases
With great reverence the crowd knelt for the blessing. *Raising his arm,* the holy man addressed the crowd. *To record the event,* photographers took many pictures.

Clauses
Because she was pleased with her reception, the violinist played several encores. *When she finished,* the crowd clapped for ten minutes.

As you can see, many different kinds of words can replace a subject at the beginning of a sentence. You can use an adjective such as *happy* or an adverb such as *gently*. You can use a prepositional phrase such as *with great reverence,* a participial phrase such as *raising his arm,* or an infinitive phrase such as *to record the event*. Or you can use an adverb clause.

Varying your sentence openers can enliven the style of a whole passage. Look at the two passages in the following chart. The passage on the left sounds monotonous because every sentence begins with a subject. In the passage on the right, the sentence openers are varied, producing a smoother, more interesting style.

Same Sentence Openers	Varied Sentence Openers
Jan and Ed made a valuable discovery during their visit to the attic. They saw an old, rusted chest behind some boxes and old furniture. They had no idea what they would find when they first opened the old chest. They looked excitedly through the crumbling documents and yellowed photographs it contained. They then found beneath the tattered debris an old family Bible showing the birth and death dates of their ancestors.	Jan and Ed made a valuable discovery during their visit to the attic. Behind some boxes and old furniture, they saw an old, rusted chest. When they first opened the chest, they had no idea what they would find. Excitedly, they looked through the crumbling documents and yellowed photographs it contained. Then, beneath the tattered debris, they found an old family Bible showing the birth and death dates of their ancestors.

Compare the revised sentences to the originals. Note that the second sentence on the right moves a phrase from the end of the sentence to the beginning. The third sentence shifts a dependent clause from the end to the beginning, and the fourth and fifth sentences open with modifiers, making the paragraph as a whole flow more smoothly.

EXERCISE A: Using Different Sentence Openers. Each of the following sentences can be rewritten with a different opener. Look for a modifier, phrase, or clause that can be placed at the beginning of the sentence.

Answers will vary; samples given.

EXAMPLE: The robins used twigs, string, and newspaper to build their nest.

To build their nest, the robins used twigs, string, and newspaper.

4. To become proficient on a musical instrument, one

1. ~~We~~ ventured out in the new sailboat ~~when the bay became calm~~. *When the bay became calm, we*
2. ~~We can usually~~ count on Maxwell's help in the evenings. *Usually, we can*
3. ~~The~~ fighter planes soared in perfect formation ~~high above the clouds~~. *High above the clouds, the*
4. ~~One~~ must practice diligently ~~to become proficient on a musical instrument~~.
5. ~~The~~ board of trustees made painful cuts in services and personnel~~, although they saved the company from bankruptcy~~. *Although they saved the company from bankruptcy, the*
6. ~~The~~ entire audience stood ~~from the band's first note to its last~~. *From the band's first note to its last, the*
7. ~~The~~ sound of the collision ~~naturally~~ brought people running from their homes. *Naturally, the*
8. I met with Dr. Chung ~~at exactly 2:30 p.m.~~ *At exactly 2:30 p.m.,*
9. Mr. McCauley played basketball ~~while holding one hand behind his back~~. *While holding one hand behind his back,*
10. ~~The~~ convoy lost twenty minutes ~~waiting for a slow-moving freight train to pass~~.

10. Waiting for a slow-moving freight train to pass, the

EXERCISE B: Revising Sentence Openers. The following passage contains a series of sentences that all begin the same way. Find different openers for *most* of the

sentences. Then rewrite the passage to produce a smoother, more interesting style. *Answers will vary; samples given.*
2. Instantly, all 3. Then they 4. As the knock sounded again and again, no 5. At last

(1) A sharp knock at the door startled everyone in the room. (2) ~~All~~ heads ~~instantly~~ turned toward the door. (3) ~~They then~~ looked upward to the room where General Washington slept. (4) ~~No~~ one spoke ~~as the knock sounded again and again~~. (5) Margaret rose ~~at last~~ and walked unsteadily toward the door to face the enemy. (6) ~~A~~ captain of the British Army stood motionless, his face hidden in the darkness of the night~~, when the door swung open~~. (7) A small cluster of redcoats stood behind him. (8) ~~The~~ captain strode past Margaret ~~without a word~~ and swept into the room. (9) Four other soldiers followed him. (10) ~~They~~ began to search the house ~~at their officer's command~~.

6. When the door swung open, a 8. Without a word the 10. At their officer's command, th

EXERCISE C: Varying Sentence Openers as You Write. Write five to seven original sentences to complete the story begun in Exercise B. As you write, vary the types of sentence openers you use.
Answers will vary. Students might exchange papers and label the various openers used.

■ Using Different Sentence Structures

A group of sentences that all have the same structure can sound just as monotonous as a group of sentences that all have the same beginning.

> Use a variety of sentence structures—simple, compound, complex, and possibly compound-complex—in your writing.

If your writing relies too heavily on *one* kind of sentence, a passage will sound awkward. Too many simple sentences in a series will sound choppy even if some of them are relatively long simple sentences. Too many compound sentences in a series will produce a rambling pattern, and too many complex sentences will sound awkward and difficult. You should try to mix all three kinds of sentences in a passage and, when appropriate, use compound-complex sentences as well.

Look at the following passage. It sounds choppy because all of the sentences are simple.

Monotonous passage with all simple sentences

(1) The stage crew for this winter's annual variety show must be commended for a perfect job. (2) Jenny O'Reilly worked the sound effects equipment. (3) Lester Barrio operated the stage lights. (4) Phil Bernstein handled the props and curtains. (5) Supervising this efficient crew of hard workers was Cindy Adamson, the stage manager. (6) At the end of the evening, the entire show received overwhelming approval from the audience. (7) Unquestionably, the stage crew deserves much of the credit for this success.

Now look at the revision. It combines and alters some of these sentences to create several different kinds of sentences. As a result the passage reads more smoothly.

(1) Simple; (2) Compound-Complex; (3) Simple; (4) Compound

(1) The stage crew for this winter's annual variety show must be commended for a perfect job. (2) Jenny O'Reilly worked the sound effects equipment, and Phil Bernstein handled props and curtains, while Lester Barrio operated the stage lights. (3) Supervising this efficient crew of hard workers was Cindy Adamson, the stage manager. (4) At the end of the evening, the entire show received overwhelming approval from the audience, and the stage crew unquestionably deserves much of the credit for this success.

EXERCISE D: Using a Variety of Sentences. The following passage repeatedly uses the same kind of sentence. Rewrite the passage to create a variety of sentences. You may shorten, separate, and combine sentences as you see fit. *Answers will vary; samples given.*

(1) I was glad to arrive home after the long trip was over. (2) However, when I got there, I found the house unlocked. (3) ~~When~~ I walked in~~, I became frightened~~. (4) ~~As I became~~ more and more nervous, I searched the

3. Frightened, 4. Becoming

house for signs of a burglary. (5) ~~After I searched and found~~ nothing unusual, I decided to call the police. (6) ~~Although~~ they discovered nothing suspicious, I remained perplexed. (7) After a few days ~~had passed~~, I finally figured out the mystery. (8) I had simply left the door unlocked when I had left for my trip originally. (9) ~~Because I was relieved~~, I sank into a chair and sat there numbly for several minutes. (10) After ~~I had thoroughly analyzed~~ the situation, I vowed never to be so careless again. *5. After searching and finding 6. However,/and 9. Relieved, 10. thoroughly analyzing*

APPLICATION: Varying Your Sentences. Practice writing sentences with different beginnings and a variety of structures by using *one* of the following sets of directions. *Answers will vary. Students choosing the first set of directions might also be asked to label openers and structures.*

1. Write a passage of at least seven sentences on any topic that you wish. Make sure it contains different sentence beginnings and varied sentence structures.
2. Take a short composition that you have recently written. Identify the sentence openers and kinds of sentences that you have used. Then make any changes needed to achieve a variety of beginnings and structures.

Chapter 26

Looking at Paragraphs

Paragraphs are easy to recognize because the first line of a paragraph will generally be indented to show the beginning of a new idea. You will also find that one sentence usually states the main idea of the whole paragraph. Other sentences relate to the main idea and develop it by adding information about it. In addition, all of the sentences will generally follow some logical order. This chapter will give you more information about these key features of paragraphs.

Recognizing Topic Sentences 26.1

All of the sentences in a paragraph work together to present one main idea. However, one sentence usually clarifies the main idea by telling what the whole paragraph is about.

■ The Topic Sentence in a Paragraph

To find the *topic sentence* in a paragraph, look for the sentence that captures the idea behind the whole paragraph.

The **topic sentence** of a paragraph presents the main idea, which all the other ideas in the paragraph support or explain.

You will usually find the topic sentence at the beginning of a paragraph. In this position the topic sentence provides the reader with an immediate understanding of the paragraph's main idea. The rest of the paragraph will then support or develop this main idea. The following paragraph by a student begins with the main idea, followed by supporting information.

TOPIC SENTENCE

Supporting information

The Nile River served as a basis for ancient Egyptian society. It provided the Egyptians with many important resources. One was papyrus, a reed that grew around the banks of the river. It was used to make many things including shoes, mats, ropes, boxes, small boats, and the first form of paper. The Nile also supplied food for the Egyptians. They caught fish in the river. The birds and animals attracted by the water were also a source of food for Egypt's people. Another important purpose the Nile served was transportation. The Egyptians traveled up and down the river for pleasure and for trade. Most important, the Nile provided silt, the fertile mud that overflowed the banks, and water, both of which were crucial for survival. The river gave the Egyptians good farming land and the only water source in the middle of the surrounding desert. Without these resources, ancient Egyptian civilization might never have existed.—Laura Harris

Sometimes a paragraph may offer a few introductory ideas before presenting the main idea. In this case the topic sentence will be found near the middle of the paragraph. The first two sentences in the following paragraph lead up to the topic sentence. Note how the information after the topic sentence answers the question raised by the topic sentence.

The bird next to me was immature. He still had brown and tawny plumage instead of the predominantly black color of the adult.

TOPIC SENTENCE — *But why was he so unafraid?* For one thing, he may never have seen another human being.

Supporting information — But there is a better explanation: In the remote Galapagos Islands, 600 miles west of Ecuador, there are hardly any land mammals, and the hawk is very nearly the sole predator. With no enemies and almost no competitors, it has nothing to fear and plenty to eat.—Tui de Roy Moore

There is also a third possible position for a topic sentence—at the end of a paragraph. When the topic sentence comes at the end of a paragraph, it will generally draw a conclusion or act as a summary. In the following paragraph, the topic sentence follows a series of descriptive details and summarizes them.

Supporting information — Dark clouds blocked the sun as it peeked over the farthest mountain. The clouds moved forward and played hide-and-seek with beams of sunlight and slowly overtook them. The clouds began to release large drops of rain. With the clouds a wind made its entrance, and it swirled across the hillsides.

TOPIC SENTENCE — *A storm was brewing.*

EXERCISE A: Identifying Topic Sentences. Read each of the following paragraphs carefully. Then write the topic sentence of each paragraph on your paper. Note that one of the paragraphs has a topic sentence at the beginning, one has a topic sentence in the middle, and one has a topic sentence at the end.

(1) Rynek Glowny is almost as lively at night as during the day. From a window seat in a restaurant on the corner of the square, we could see street musicians strolling about as young boys kicked a soccer ball and couples strolled arm in arm. Every few minutes, a horse-drawn cab would roll by, often with a pretty girl and her date inside. After dinner, we strolled around ourselves, delighting in the contrast of old ladies sweeping out dark doorways as the sounds of modern jazz poured into the street from the Klub Pod Jaszczurami.—David Alpern

(2) The Virginia Preparatory School lies just off the Shirley Highway between Washington, D.C., and Richmond. It is a small Southern school with dull-red brick dormitories and classroom buildings, quiet old school buildings with quiet old Southern names—Page House, Stuart Hall, Randolph Hall, Breckinridge, Pinckney, and Coulter. The high brick wall that surrounds the school is known as the Breastworks, and the shallow pond behind the football field is the Crater. V.P.S. is an old school, with an old school's tradition.—C.D.B. Bryan

(3) A gleaming silver swan perches majestically on the hood of the old car. Unscarred by the years, the car's body still has its original shiny red coat of paint. Even the trim on the thick, black tires shines a glossy white. Considered by many car fans as a work of art, this 1952 Packard remains in good condition because it is rarely driven. Most of the time the car remains sheltered from heavy snows and winter ice, stored in a garage. Only during the summer months does its owner bring the car into the driveway where sunshine gleams from the finlike fenders and polished chrome. And then the 1950's live again.—Lynn Green

APPLICATION: Finding Topic Sentences. Pick a topic that interests you—for example, space travel, a vacation spot, or some particular craft or hobby. Find a book on your topic. Choose five paragraphs from the book, and write the topic sentence of each on your paper. If you can not find the main idea stated in a single sentence, write a topic sentence for the paragraph. Your topic sentence should express the main idea that all the other information in the paragraph explains.

Students might exchange papers and evaluate each other's answers. Any disagreements could be discussed in class.

26.2 Recognizing Supporting Information

A topic sentence may be supported by many different kinds of information. A paragraph about the items for sale in a certain store might offer four or five examples of these items or it might instead give details describing just a few of the most notable items. Some paragraphs will focus mainly on one kind of supporting information; others will offer several different kinds. Every good paragraph, however, must include specific information that thoroughly develops the main idea.

Learning more about the different kinds of supporting information that can be used to develop a main idea will help you write your own paragraphs.

Examples, Details, and Facts

Examples, details, and *facts* are all useful in helping a reader understand the main idea of a paragraph.

> Paragraphs may be developed with examples, details, and facts.

Examples show specific instances of some general idea. A paragraph about the dangers of lightning might give three or four examples of the destruction lightning can cause: knocking out the electricity in a town, starting a fire in a building, or causing a forest fire.

Details are pieces of descriptive information. A paragraph that describes a dazzling sunset might give details about color, the shapes of the clouds, and the changes that take place in the sky.

Facts are specific pieces of information that can be shown to be true. A paragraph about the results of an election might include such facts as the number of votes for each candidate and the percentage of people who voted.

The following paragraph about Nepal uses all three kinds of support. It contains examples of Nepal's varied geography, details about its animal and plant life, and facts about its location, size, and animals.

TOPIC SENTENCE — *Nepal has one of the world's most remarkable environments.* Just half the size of Italy, the country is tucked between the vast plains

Supporting information: Examples, details, and facts

of northern India and rugged, isolated Tibet. But Nepal consists of far more than mountains. In addition to alpine slopes that nourish Norway pines and "edelweiss," it has tropical forests with banyan trees, banana palms, and lush ferns. Within its boundaries are more than 800 species of birds, including the jungle fowl and the Impeyan pheasant, the national bird, which makes its home 12,000 feet above sea level. There are mugger and gharial crocodiles in the low-lying rivers, while the mysterious snow leopard prowls the remote mountain heights and is rarely seen by humans.—Adapted from Denis D. Gray

EXERCISE A: Recognizing Examples, Details, and Facts. Read the following paragraphs. On your paper make a list of the supporting information in each paragraph. Then indicate whether the supporting information is made up mainly of (a) different examples that all contribute to the main idea, (b) descriptive details that help the reader "see" the point made in the main idea, or (c) specific facts that back up the main idea. Note that the topic sentence in each paragraph is underlined.

Lists of support may vary within reason; basic types of support are given.

(1) Along Greenland's west coast about 100 glaciers reach the sea. Of those, about twenty are the main iceberg makers. Some of the bergs are mammoth. They may be several city blocks long and occasionally a mile or more long. Once a berg several miles long was sighted, but it was exceptionally large. Many tower 200 to 300 feet above the water. Some over 500 feet! Greenland sends out 10,000 to 15,000 good-sized bergs each year and uncountable numbers of smaller ones. The largest are calved from the glaciers along Melville Bay and from Humboldt Glacier farther north in the northwestern part of the island.—Gwen Schultz *facts*

(2) The little Pachang River in southeastern Connecticut is typical of the placid streams near the seacoast that provide a glimpse of marsh life. Near sea

level, the Pachang meanders through a fairly high-and-dry marsh that can be explored on foot. The marshland is interrupted and bordered by a forest of red oak, pine, and graceful hemlock. Shuttle transportation is unnecessary since the current is so slow that you can paddle effortlessly in either direction. It's a short river, but the miles add up along its twisted path. Near Voluntown, a good day can be spent between Beach Pond and downstream Beachdale and Pachang Ponds. Lazy bass nibble among the acres of water lilies and ripple away at your approach, while the air is filled with songbird calls. —Jack Waller *details*

(3) An airport flight departure announcement meant diverse things to those who heard it. To some, it was a routine summons, a prefix to another tedious, work-oriented journey which—had free choice been theirs—they would not have made. For others, a flight announcement spelled a beginning of adventure; for others still, the nearing of an end—the journey home. For some it entailed sadness and parting; for others, in counterpoint, the prospect of reunion and joy. Some who heard flight announcements heard them always for other people. Their friends or relatives were travelers; as to themselves, the names of destinations were wistful not-quite-glimpses of faraway places they would never see. —Arthur Hailey *examples*

Reasons and Incidents

Other kinds of supporting information can also be used to make a main idea clear.

Paragraphs may be developed with reasons and incidents.

Reasons can be used to answer any questions raised by the main idea. If the topic sentence presents an opinion, reasons can help to defend that opinion. Note how the following paragraph presents and supports an opinion about guitars.

TOPIC SENTENCE

Supporting information: Reasons

The guitar leads all fretted instruments in popularity. It is amazingly versatile. You can play single bass notes, chords, and single melody notes. It's traditional for singing cowboy, hillbilly, and folk songs. It's intimate. "You hold it close and feel its heart beat," says Burl Ives. Its harmony sounds good with a number of instruments, notably the recorder. Its incisive rhythm fits into a dance band. —Adapted from Doron K. Antrim

An *incident* is a brief story or set of events offered to illustrate a main idea. By telling a story, an incident helps to explain the idea in the topic sentence. The following paragraph is developed by an incident.

TOPIC SENTENCE

Supporting information: Incident

I remember Arthur Rubinstein's return to Poland after World War II. . . . People stood in line for tickets all night long, and those who did not succeed used bribes and every means ingenuity could devise to get in. As a result, the hall was so closely packed that several people fainted and had to be carried out. When the announced program came to an end, the audience simply refused to let Rubinstein go; they shouted titles of pieces they wanted him to play, and the pianist, obviously moved, obliged. Then, when it finally became clear that he wouldn't go on any longer, the audience spontaneously broke into song. "Sto lat, sto lat . . ." they shouted, which means "May he live a hundred years" and is sung on celebratory or joyful occasions. —Eva Hoffman

EXERCISE B: Recognizing Reasons and Incidents. Read the following paragraphs. On your paper either list the reasons used in the paragraph or briefly describe the incident used to develop the paragraph. Note that the topic sentence in each paragraph is underlined. *Lists of support and descriptions may vary within reason; basic types of support are given.*

(1) The main reason why attacks have been increasing has less to do with bears than with people. In re-

cent years, public use of national parks in Canada and the U.S. has exploded. As a result, people-bear confrontations have mushroomed, and the bears have suffered many more provocations. What is surprising, in fact, is not that bear attacks have increased, but that there have not been more of them. Given the amount of people pressure these days, actual bear attacks have been relatively rare. —Paul Grescoe *reasons*

(2) The first inkling of the earthquake came from a ham radio operator near Seattle, Washington, who happened to be talking to another ham in Anchorage. It was Good Friday. The stores had just closed, and people were homeward bound for the Easter weekend. The man in Anchorage mentioned that it appeared they were having a small earthquake. Then as it worsened, he shouted that the "ground was waving like an ocean." Communications broke off, and the Seattle man phoned the news to a radio station. He and many other amateurs then stayed at their shortwave sets, taking and relaying messages to anxious relatives and friends. There was no doubt that a catastrophe had occurred, but it was impossible to determine the extent till some time afterward. —Norma Spring *incident*

APPLICATION: Recognizing Support in Paragraphs. Reexamine the second paragraph in Exercise A of Section 26.1. On your paper list the supporting information used in the paragraph and identify it as mainly examples, details, facts, reasons, or incidents. Then, using that paragraph as a model, list *five* pieces of specific information that you could use in a paragraph that describes your school.

The supporting information in the original paragraph consists mainly of details. Students might list details about their school together as a class exercise.

Recognizing Unity 26.3

A paragraph has *unity* when *all* of the supporting ideas in the paragraph work together to develop the topic sentence.

The Unified Paragraph

To tell whether a paragraph is unified, you should first look for the main idea in the paragraph. Then you should look at the relationship between the pieces of supporting information and the main idea.

> A paragraph is unified if all of the ideas work together to support or develop the main idea.

If you examine a unified paragraph, you will notice that all of the ideas seem to belong together. For example, if the main idea of a paragraph focuses on the three finalists in a dog show, the supporting material will also focus on the three finalists. The supporting information might offer details describing each winning dog, or it might give the reasons why the judges chose each of these dogs. The paragraph would be unified because all of the supporting ideas would help to develop the main idea.

In order to write good paragraphs, you should also learn to recognize when a paragraph is *not* unified. Unrelated pieces of information or unnecessary details can destroy the unity of a paragraph. The following paragraph about home safety contains two pieces of information that do not support the main idea. The paragraph therefore lacks unity.

TOPIC SENTENCE	The National Safety Council warns against letting your home become a dangerous place. Instead, follow some sensible procedures to make your home a safer place. First of all, keep electrical equipment at a safe distance from sinks and bathtubs since contact with water can cause electrical shocks. To reduce the chance of burns—or fires that can result from cooking accidents—keep a dry chemical fire extinguisher in the kitchen.
Unrelated idea	*Many school buildings have fire extinguishers in the hallways, in the cafeteria, and in other key locations.* Check entrance ways and walkways for loose steps, slippery rugs, stray electrical extension cords—anything that someone might

Unrelated idea — trip over. *People fall more in the winter.* Inspect every room for potential hazards: Does the fireplace have a safety screen? Do staircases have sturdy handrails? Are medicines and harmful chemicals out of the reach of small children?

The paragraph focuses on ways to make your *home* safer. The ideas about fire extinguishers in school buildings and about people falling in the winter, however, do not develop the main idea.

Unrelated ideas can confuse a reader. To preserve the unity of a paragraph, remove any information that will not help the reader understand the main idea.

EXERCISE A: Recognizing Unity in Paragraphs. Each of the following items includes a topic sentence and several supporting ideas. Some of these supporting ideas do not belong with the topic sentence. On your paper identify the unrelated idea or ideas in each item.

Unrelated ideas are underlined.

1. A visitor to Philadelphia can see many famous historical sights.
   a. Independence Hall
   b. The Liberty Bell
   c. Baseball games in the summer
   d. Betsy Ross's House
   e. Great variety of scenery in Pennsylvania
2. A horse requires much care.
   a. Regular brushing and occasional baths
   b. Riding exercise at least once a week
   c. Good idea to walk a dog regularly
   d. Cleaning hooves
   e. Mustangs descended from the horses ridden by Spanish explorers
3. The United States space program has made a great deal of progress.
   a. Television programs about space include *Cosmos* and *Nova*
   b. Moon landings began in 1969
   c. America's first manned space flight in 1961
   d. Space shuttle in 1981
   e. Popular movies such as *Star Wars* and *Close Encounters*

APPLICATION: Creating Unity in Paragraphs. Find the three unrelated ideas in each of the following paragraphs. Leaving out these ideas, rewrite each paragraph.
Unrelated sentences are underlined.

(1) I do not enjoy swimming in public pools. Often, and especially on weekends, the pools are crammed with people. Trying to swim any distance generally results in a collision with someone, and a person can forget about trying to swim in a straight line. In fact, swimming through a crowded pool is much like trying to run an obstacle course that has moving obstacles. Running the hurdles must be an equally frustrating sport. It is probably even more frustrating than trying to ski down a slalom course. Worst of all, I feel, are the people who jump into the pool, ignoring those who are trying to swim. These people should have splashing pools of their own so that they will not interfere with serious swimmers. Tennis courts are also overcrowded.

(2) Backgammon is an easy game to learn but a difficult one to master. It has an element of chance since the players' moves are determined by throwing dice. Dice are often made of ivory. But backgammon also offers many opportunities for using strategy. Checkers, on the other hand, is a boring game. Good backgammon strategy usually involves taking risks and playing aggressively. In backgammon the goal is both to advance oneself and to block one's opponent. Football also involves advancing and blocking and is probably the most aggressive of all games. Learning to do both of these things at the same time takes practice.

26.4 Recognizing Coherence

In addition to unity, a paragraph should have *coherence*. In a coherent paragraph, the ideas will be logically organized. They will also be presented in a way that makes it easy for the reader to see the connection between them. To make a paragraph coherent, you can use one of a number of different logical orders as well as certain connecting words, called *transitions*.

Logical Orders

In order to write coherent paragraphs, you should first become familiar with the different logical orders that can be used to organize information when you write paragraphs.

A coherent paragraph will follow some logical order: chronological order, spatial order, order of importance, comparison and contrast order, or some other logical order suggested by the topic sentence.

Chronological Order. In *chronological order* events or actions are arranged according to their sequence in time. For example, you can write about historical events simply by following the order in which the events took place. Or you can explain a laboratory process in terms of the steps that someone must follow to perform the process.

The following paragraph, written by a student, uses chronological order. Notice that the steps in a process are explained in their proper sequence. The words *first, next, then, after,* and *now* help to point out the sequence.

TOPIC SENTENCE

Chronological order of steps

If you like exotic foods, then you might enjoy making one of my banana splits. The only ingredients you need are bananas, ice cream (any flavor), all kinds of syrups, and toppings such as chopped nuts, M and M's, jimmies, and shredded coconut. To make this tasty snack, you *first* slice the banana and put it in a bowl. *Next* you scoop out three scoops of ice cream and put the ice cream on the banana. *Then* (this is the fun part) you pour lots of syrup on top. *After* the syrup, you sprinkle jimmies, chopped nuts, and M and M's on your dessert. *Now* that you have made your banana split, you have the thrill of eating your creation. "A sweet for the sweet" is an old saying; making your own banana split gives this phrase new meaning.—Ethan Kleinberg

Spatial Order. In *spatial order* physical details are presented according to their location in a scene. This order is particularly useful in descriptions of people, places, and things. It presents details in a way that a reader might actually see them: from top to bottom, from nearest to farthest, from the inside to the outside, and so forth.

Notice the spatial order of details in the following paragraph, which describes a room. The phrases *from the ceiling, along the walls, in the center,* and *to the floor* help you, the reader, follow the spatial order.

TOPIC SENTENCE Spatial order of details	After the explosion the room was a shambles. Pieces of plaster curled *from the ceiling. Along the walls* cracks had appeared; pictures hung crookedly; one window had shattered. A cloud of dust floated *in the center* of the room, and some of the furniture had been moved by the blast. A lamp and some dishes had fallen *to the floor* and were now smashed.

Order of Importance. In *order of importance,* supporting information is arranged from least important to most important. Going from the least powerful or least important idea to the most important is effective because it leaves the reader with the strongest idea. You can use order of importance when you are presenting reasons to support an opinion or when you are simply explaining an idea.

The following paragraph gives reasons that support the writer's feeling about a certain day. The first reason presents a minor problem. The second reason shows a more important problem. And the third reason presents the greatest problem. The words *first of all, even more,* and *but worst of all* show this ranking of ideas.

TOPIC SENTENCE Order of importance for ideas	It was not going to be a good day to play golf. *First of all,* I had awakened late and could not practice my swing in the back yard. *Even more* upsetting was the sore throat that I felt coming on. *But worst of all,* the weather promised to be miserable. Rain

had fallen all night, and drizzle greeted me in the morning. The low-hanging fog would reduce visibility, and the soggy, muddy course would have some new water hazards.

Comparison and Contrast Order. The ideas in a paragraph can be arranged in still other ways. Ideas or details can be *compared* because of their similarities, or they can be *contrasted* because of their differences. For example, the following paragraph focuses on the differences between two kinds of watches. The words *on the other hand, whereas,* and *in contrast* highlight the differences.

TOPIC SENTENCE

Comparison and contrast order of ideas

Conventional watches and digital watches both tell time, but they make us see time in very different ways. Conventional watches map time on a round face, with numbers and moving hands. Digital watches, *on the other hand,* simply display the hour, minute, and second in lighted numerals. In other words conventional watches give a picture of time, *whereas* digital watches present time as a series of changing numbers. Time on a conventional watch seems to have a past and a future as well as a present. *In contrast,* time on a digital watch at any moment is an isolated number that is quickly replaced by another isolated number.

Other Logical Orders. Other logical orders can be used to develop a particular topic sentence. For example, a topic sentence might mention three new cars. The paragraph would then discuss the cars in the order in which they are listed in the topic sentence. Another kind of logical order might arrange supporting information like a series of building blocks: Each new thought might be based on the idea before it.

The next paragraph follows a single logical arrangement, building idea upon idea to describe the main idea presented in the topic sentence. The word *additionally* helps to link the information at the beginning of the paragraph with the information at the end.

TOPIC SENTENCE

Logical order suited to topic sentence

The most unusual gait, perhaps, is the stott, also called the pronk or the spronk. All four legs take off and land nearly together, and during the period of suspension, the legs hang down vertically from the body. Used by many deer and antelope, ranging from wildebeest to small gazelles, it is slower than a gallop but effective in changing direction or climbing hills. *Additionally,* it probably serves as a warning system. A pronking animal jumps so high that it can be seen by others in its group. Some species make a noise while pronking, and others deposit a scent on the ground from glands in the foot. —Anne Innis Dagg

EXERCISE A: Recognizing Logical Orders. Read each of the following paragraphs carefully, examining the order of support. On your paper identify the order used in each paragraph as *chronological, spatial, order of importance,* or *comparison and contrast.* If the ideas follow none of these orders, write *other logical order.*

Orders are given; transitions are underlined for Exercise B.

(1) The Egyptian civilization of antiquity visualized the universe as a great box, with Egypt in the center of its long, narrow floor. The top of the box was the sky, from which lamps were suspended by means of ropes. These lamps were the stars. Other lamps, carried in heavenly boats, traveled about the sky and appeared as planets. The Milky Way was supposed to be the celestial equivalent of the Nile, and the regions through which it flowed were populated with dead Egyptians dwelling under the benign supervision of Osiris. At the corners of the universe box were four huge mountains supporting the sky, and joining them around the sides of the box were mountain ranges. Along these mountains a river circumscribed the universe. In this river each morning, in the east, the sun-god Ra was reborn in a boat, appearing as a ball of fire. —Arthur Beiser and Konrad B. Krauskopf *spatial*

(2) Today, America's hawks, kites, falcons, eagles, ospreys, vultures, and owls are faring much better.

Most experts caution that the situation is far from ideal, but they agree real progress is being made. Insecticides such as DDT, which breaks down into another compound that thins the eggshells of bald eagles, peregrine falcons, and other fish- and meat-eaters, have been banned for years and, in some areas, are finally beginning to fade from the environment. But, most important of all, the general public today seems to have a genuine appreciation for the birds, coupled with an understanding of how they fit into the overall scheme of things. —John Neary *order of importance*

(3) What is most important is an inspection tour of your garden in spring. Check first for any winter damage to tree limbs and branches of shrubs. Prune off anything that is damaged; if a branch is torn, cut it off neatly. Check next to see if the soil mulch is still at an even depth and whether or not it needs a bit of replenishing. Then look for cracks in the masonry of walls, planters, and flooring. Is there damage to the awning or other overhead protection? Snip off dead ends of vines and ground covers. Finally, give the shrubs a "bath" to clean off soot that has accumulated during the winter months. —Adapted from Carla Wallach *chronological*

Transitions

In the paragraphs presented earlier in this section, certain connecting words, such as *first, next, even more, on the other hand,* and *in contrast,* are printed in italics. These words are *transitions.* Transitions link ideas and guide the reader from one idea to the next.

A coherent paragraph will often use transitions to help connect ideas smoothly and logically.

The following chart lists some of the most frequently used transitions. Notice that certain ones help to show chronological order. Others are most useful to point out spatial order or order of importance. Still other transitions help to clarify other logical orders of ideas.

COMMON TRANSITIONS		
For Chronological Order		
after	finally	next
afterward	first	now
at last	formerly	previously
before	last	soon
earlier	later	then
eventually	meanwhile	until
For Spatial Order		
above	beneath	in the distance
ahead	beyond	near
away	in front of	next to
behind	inside	outside
below	in the center	to the right
For Order of Importance		
also	furthermore	one
even greater	more	perhaps the greatest reason
finally	moreover	second
first	most	third
first of all	most important	
for one reason	next	
For Comparison and Contrast Order		
also	instead	on the other hand
although	just as	similarly
both	like	similar to
but	likewise	so also
however	nevertheless	whereas
in contrast	on the contrary	yet
For Other Logical Orders		
accordingly	for example	in fact
additionally	for instance	namely
along with	furthermore	therefore
and	in addition	thus
as a result	in conclusion	
consequently	indeed	

Look again at the paragraphs on pages 557 through 560. As you read each paragraph, see how the transitions printed in italics help to connect the ideas.

Not all paragraphs require transitions. Nor do you need to introduce each new idea with a transition. However, you should always check your writing for places where transitions could make your ideas clearer for the reader.

EXERCISE B: Recognizing Transitions. Reread the three paragraphs in Exercise A. On your paper list the transitions used in each paragraph. Some paragraphs may have only one or two transitions; others may have several. *Transitions are underlined in Exercise A. Choices may vary within reason.*

APPLICATION 1: Choosing Orders and Transitions. In each of the following items, you will find a topic and three or four supporting ideas. Tell which kind of order you would use to organize the supporting information in each item. Then list at least two transitions that you could use to help a reader follow the order that you have chosen.
Answers will vary; probable orders are given along with possible transitions.

1. The beginning of a storm *chronological/first, then*
    a. Clouds rolling in
    b. Lightning flashing
    c. Sunlight disappearing
    d. Rain beginning to fall
2. A scene in the woods *spatial/above, beneath*
    a. Birds in the trees
    b. Vines hanging from branches
    c. Animals on the ground
3. Reasons behind someone's popularity
    a. Appearance
    b. Friendliness and personality
    c. Helpfulness towards others
4. The design of a certain building *spatial/in the distance, inside*
    a. Its appearance from a distance
    b. Its details close up
    c. Its halls and rooms
5. Steps in preparing for a vacation *chronological/earlier, finally*
    a. Deciding where and when to go
    b. Packing and closing the house
    c. Loading the car and leaving

3. order of importance/also, furthermore

APPLICATION 2: Creating Coherence in a Paragraph. Choose one of the items in Application 1, and develop a paragraph from it. Write a topic sentence that expresses a main idea. (For example, for the first item you might write, "The beginning of a storm always fascinates me.") Then develop the idea using the list of information for that item and any other related ideas. Your paragraph should follow the logical order you chose in Application 1 and use the transitions you chose to link the supporting ideas. When you finish your paragraph, complete the following steps.

1. Identify the logical order you used.
2. Circle all transitions.
3. Read your paragraph again and take another look at the chart on page 562. Decide if you have chosen transitions that make your paragraph flow smoothly and logically. Improve your choices wherever you can.

Students might read finished paragraphs aloud, while the other students identify the logical orders and transitions used.

Chapter 27

Writing Paragraphs

This chapter presents a number of useful steps you can follow in planning, writing, and revising paragraphs of your own. At every point in this three-part process, you will need to make important choices. Making wise choices can help you write stronger, clearer, and more interesting paragraphs.

Thinking Out Your Ideas and Writing a Topic Sentence 27.1

At the beginning of the planning stage, three steps can help you create a firm basis upon which to write a paragraph. First you should find a topic that you want to write about. Then you should identify the audience to whom you will write, the main idea you will write about, and the purpose behind your writing—to explain, to persuade, or to describe. Finally you should express your main idea in a topic sentence. This section will take you through each of these steps.

Finding and Narrowing a Topic

What should you write about? Sometimes this question will be answered for you by a particular assignment. But at other times you will need to choose your own topic. If you are enthusiastic about a topic and if you think you can cover it within the length of a paragraph, you are likely to have found a good paragraph topic.

Brainstorm for interesting topics. Then find a good paragraph topic by choosing a topic that is small enough to be covered well in a paragraph.

To discover some of the topics that you could write about, you can tap your memories, the things you have learned, and your current interests. You might, for example, think about experiences that have made a big impression on you—meeting a famous person, visiting a famous place, or winning a game. You might also think about what you have learned from books or through your work in school. In addition you might think about situations that concern you in your community, your city, the country, or the world. Observations that you have made while riding to school, walking a dog, or visiting a friend can also become topics for writing.

Brainstorming can help you find these ideas. When you brainstorm, you should write down all your thoughts without judging whether or not they are brilliant ones. By letting your mind come up with ideas while you quickly jot them down, you can produce a rough list of possible topics. If one topic particularly interests you, write down other more specific topics under it. The more topics you have jotted down, the more choices you will have.

When you have a list with some interesting possibilities, you should examine the topics to find one you want to write about. Some of your topics will probably be too general—that is, too big for you to cover well in one paragraph. It might be difficult, for example, to write a single paragraph that covers the topic *Parks* or even the more limited topic *Amusement parks*. On the other hand, you could probably write a very good paragraph on *Ferris wheels* or *The fastest roller coasters* or *The most exciting ride*. After considering each topic on your list, you should choose a topic that you know something about and find particularly interesting. If the topic is too general, like the topic *Parks* or *Baseball*, break it down into smaller topics. Then choose a smaller related topic that you think you can develop with specific supporting information.

In your brainstorming for a topic, you might make a list like the one in the following chart. Note that many of the topics that are too large for paragraphs have smaller related topics listed under them. A few of the other topics—*Best fishing spots* and *Making bread*—are probably already small enough to be paragraph topics. With such a list in hand, you should find it relatively easy to choose a topic.

BRAINSTORMING FOR A PARAGRAPH TOPIC	
Subways	Thunderstorms
Best fishing spots	Bears
Radios	—Grizzlies—a threatened species?
—Latest models	—Bears' habits
—Sound pollution	News coverage
Making bread	—Famous reporters
Taking a bicycle trip	—Evening news on television

EXERCISE A: Narrowing General Topics. Write *two* of the following general topics on your paper. Then, under each, list three to five smaller related topics that you or someone else could cover well in a paragraph.

You may want to use one of the items as a class exercise before students begin work on their own.

Food
Hobbies
Movie or television stars
Dangerous jobs
School sports

EXERCISE B: Discovering a Paragraph Topic of Your Own. Write the following topics on your paper. Then brainstorm for at least *five* more topics of your own. Choose one topic and then examine it to make sure it is small enough for one paragraph. If it is too big, list two or three smaller related topics under it and choose one of those as a paragraph topic.

Students might work in small groups or with partners in brainstorming for topics.

Music of the 1980's
New sports
Fads
Famous animals
Books

Deciding on Audience, Main Idea, and Purpose

Early in the planning stage, generally right after you have chosen a topic, you should make three important decisions that will give a certain direction to your writing. You should decide upon your *audience*—the people with whom you want to communicate in your paragraph. You should determine your *main idea*—what you want to say about your paragraph topic. And you should decide upon your *purpose*—whether you are writing your paragraph to explain, to persuade, or to describe.

Determine your audience, main idea, and purpose in order to focus your paragraph topic.

The order in which you make these decisions will vary depending on the particular writing situation. For instance, sometimes you may know your *audience* from the beginning. If you were asked to write a paragraph on a camp application, you would begin with the knowledge that you were writing to the director or administrator of the camp. Sometimes your *main idea* will come first, either as an assignment or as an obvious point you want to make about your topic.

Sometimes your *purpose* will be clear from the beginning. Your assignment may, for example, tell you to write a paragraph explaining something or a paragraph convincing someone of something.

If none of the three are given, you will have to make your own decisions. One way is to decide on your audience first. You can then use this knowledge to help zero in on a main idea and a purpose. Once you know your audience, you can ask yourself questions about your paragraph topic while thinking about the audience. These questions can help you determine the point of your paragraph. Begin by asking yourself general questions such as these: "What might my audience want to know about the topic?" "What do I think the audience should know about the topic?" "What interests me most about the topic?" From these general questions, you can develop questions that are more directly related to your topic and then answer them. Your answers will give you a number of possible main ideas for a paragraph.

For instance, if you had chosen to write about *Evening news on television,* you might decide to write to a general audience of people who watch the evening news fairly often. You might then ask yourself questions like those in the following chart.

ASKING QUESTIONS TO FIND A MAIN IDEA	
Paragraph Topic: Evening news on television	
Questions	**Possible Main Ideas**
Why are the evening news programs on television so popular?	To attract viewers, television news programs have come up with many new ideas.
What specific things do the different news programs provide?	While some of the news programs focus mainly on news, others provide news as well as many different kinds of special features.
What are the problems, if any, of evening news programs?	Most of the news stories on evening news programs are treated in such a light or rapid way that they lose their impact.

When you examine the possible answers you have written down in response to your questions, you will generally find that they are leading you toward main ideas suitable for different purposes. For example, the first main idea in the chart is a factual statement that you could explain in a paragraph. The second main idea is also a factual statement. The third main idea, however, is an opinion that you would have to defend. Your purpose in the third case would be to persuade those members of your audience who have not thought about the issue or who disagree with you that your opinion is right.

After thinking about the possible main ideas and the purposes that they suit, you should decide which one you will choose for your paragraph. For example, if you were writing about television news programs, you might choose the third idea in the preceding chart because you thought it was the most interesting.

EXERCISE C: Deciding on a Main Idea. Using the paragraph topic you selected in Exercise B, follow these instructions. *Assigned partners might evaluate each other's work as each step is completed, checking relevance to the chosen topic.*

1. Decide on an audience and briefly describe it.
2. Write down at least two questions about your paragraph topic. Make these questions that your audience might ask about your topic.
3. Answer each question briefly with a statement that could be used as a main idea for your paragraph.
4. Examine each of the possible main ideas you have listed. Decide which purpose each suits.
5. Finally, choose the main idea that you would most like to write about, keeping your audience and the purpose related to the main idea in mind.

■ Writing a Topic Sentence

Once you have decided upon your audience, main idea, and purpose, you can draft a topic sentence for your paragraph.

Keep your audience and purpose in mind as you express your main idea in a topic sentence.

To make your main idea as clear as possible to the reader, you should choose the best possible wording for your topic sentence. Think about your audience and purpose as you express your main idea in a well-developed, complete sentence. Choose each word carefully. Even though you can revise your topic sentence at any time throughout the writing process, you will be able to work more confidently and save time if you write a strong topic sentence at this stage. In fact, it is a good idea to write several possible topic sentences. Each might express your main idea in a slightly different way. You can then choose the one that you like best and that best suits your audience and purpose.

POSSIBLE TOPIC SENTENCES

Main Idea: Most of the news stories on evening news programs are treated in such a light or rapid way that they lose their impact.

1. Most of the news stories on evening news programs are treated in such a light or rapid way that they lose their impact.
2. Evening news programs on television skim over the events of the day so quickly that the events lose most of their impact on viewers.
3. Although they try to cover the major events of the day, evening news programs on television often end up by weakening the impact of the information they report.
4. Evening news broadcasts on television weaken the impact of the information they report for a number of reasons—some of which are caused by television itself.

Any of the topic sentences in the preceding chart would be appropriate for a paragraph about television news programs. Note that all of the topic sentences suit a persuasive purpose. The four versions differ mainly in their wording. The first and second are both strong and direct. The third and fourth are slightly more detailed. You might decide to use the third because it sounds the calmest and most reasonable.

EXERCISE D: Writing a Topic Sentence. Using the main idea that you chose in Exercise C, write two or more possible topic sentences that clearly express the main idea. Think about your audience and purpose as you write. Then decide which version of your topic sentence you like best. *Selected groups of topic sentences might be written on the chalkboard, with students choosing the one they like best in each group.*

APPLICATION: Shaping Ideas for a Paragraph. Practice all of the steps discussed in this section on your own by following these instructions.
Students might exchange papers with partners for comments and suggestions.

1. Brainstorm for topics, and jot down a rough list of at least five.
2. Choose a topic that especially interests you. If necessary, break it down into smaller related topics and choose one of those as your paragraph topic.
3. Decide on your audience.
4. With your audience in mind, ask and answer questions about your paragraph topic to find possible main ideas.
5. Decide what purpose suits each main idea.
6. Choose the main idea that you would most like to write about.
7. Write at least two possible topic sentences, and choose the clearest, most suitable one.

27.2 Developing Support for a Topic Sentence

The planning you have done so far for your paragraph will help you as you gather specific information to develop your main idea. Your earlier work will also help you to organize the supporting information. This section discusses some effective ways to carry out these gathering and organizing steps.

Brainstorming for Support

When you first chose your paragraph topic and then zeroed in on a main idea, you probably had in mind at least a few examples or facts that would help support what you wanted to say about the topic. At this point in the writing process, you should get down on paper as much specific information relating to your main idea as you can.

Brainstorm for examples, details, facts, reasons, and incidents related to your main idea.

Brainstorming for support involves remembering, discovering, and gathering specific information on your paragraph topic. Your goal should be to have a long list of interesting information from which you can select examples, details, facts, and so forth to develop your main idea. You should not throw out or organize information at this point. Instead, gather more information than you can use in one paragraph and plan to sort it later. From your long list, you can then choose the best information.

You can brainstorm in a number of ways. You can brainstorm with another person or by yourself. You can sit quietly and try to come up with things related to your topic, or you can guide your thinking by writing down some questions about your main idea. If you decide to use questions, you should begin by writing your topic sentence at the top of a blank sheet of paper. Then think about your audience and purpose, and jot down some questions that might occur to someone in your audience after reading your topic sentence. What information does your topic sentence indicate that your paragraph will cover? What specific questions should your paragraph answer in order to fulfill the audience's expectations? After you have written down at least two questions, brainstorm for examples, details, facts, reasons, or incidents that will help answer these questions. Your answers should include a fairly long list of specific pieces of information. If you were brainstorming on the topic sentence about television news programs, you might come up with questions and answers like those in the following chart.

QUESTIONING TO FIND SUPPORT FOR A TOPIC SENTENCE

Topic Sentence: Although they try to cover the major events of the day, evening news programs on television often end up by weakening the impact of the information they report.

How do news programs weaken the impact of most stories?

—time is limited

—major stories assigned no more than five minutes

  —often less than a minute

  —average one to two minutes

—need to keep show moving

—appeal to viewers, ratings, with variety, liveliness

—items introduced and developed, finished off neatly

—reporters must use short cuts, avoid heavy analysis

—stories wrapped up with catchy "tag lines"

—stories repeated throughout day, from night to night

—personalities of reporters have become important

Would longer stories improve the situation?

—even these lose impact because mixed in with so many different kinds of lighter material

  —shorter items, human interest stories, humorous notes

  —commercials, announcements, other interruptions, small talk

—constant flow of programs on television—talk shows, news, sitcoms—blend together

—television is often seen mainly as entertainment

  —people tune in for amusement, break from own problems

  —even news is a form of entertainment because it is on television

  —therefore, less important, less real than it should be

Note that this list, like the lists you will probably make, contains more information than you would want to include in a single paragraph. Furthermore, some of the information is not directly related to the main idea. Even so, a list like this can help you see all of the ideas that you could include in your paragraph.

EXERCISE A: Gathering Support for a Topic Sentence. Use the topic sentence you wrote in Exercise D of Section 27.1 to brainstorm for support. Write the topic sentence at the top of your paper and then do one of the following: Jot down every piece of information that comes to mind about your main idea, or write down a few questions that your audience might ask and then answer them as rapidly as you can with as much specific information as you can. However you go about brainstorming, try to list at least a dozen examples, details, facts, reasons, or incidents.

Students might work with partners or in small groups as they begin brainstorming for support.

■ Organizing Supporting Information

The organizing step includes two parts. First, you must evaluate the supporting information to make sure that what you select is clearly related to the topic sentence. Then, you need to find a logical order in which to present that information in your paragraph.

> Eliminate unrelated and extra information from your list of support, adding other information, if necessary. Then organize the supporting information so that it follows a logical order.

To start organizing your paragraph, you should examine your list of supporting information for unity and completeness. Think about each piece of information that you have written down. Ask yourself, "Does this information help the reader understand my main idea? Do I need every one of these examples and details? Would some other example be better than this one?" Questions such as these can help you weed out weak and unneeded support. For instance, if you have five similar examples, you may want to choose the best three or four. In addition, you may find that you have to revise your topic sentence to fit the supporting information you have gathered.

Look again at the chart of supporting information on page 574. Some of the items listed are not that clearly related to the topic sentence—for example, the point about the way the stories are reported throughout the day. Other items would simply overload the paragraph. You might, for example, choose to skip the point about ratings. From a long list such as the one shown in the chart, you might eliminate about one third of the items, leaving just the best support for the topic sentence.

After evaluating your list of support, you should look at it again to decide on the order you want to use to present your ideas. Your topic sentence may give you some clues. If your topic sentence mentions three or more things in a certain order, your paragraph should develop those things in the same order. For example, if a topic sentence about horses mentions walking, trotting, and galloping, you should discuss those three items in that order in the paragraph. If you are defending an opinion, you may want to rank your information from least convincing to most convincing. Or you may want to use chronological order to show events over time, spatial order to help the reader visualize your topic, or comparison and contrast order to make comparisons.

Once you have chosen an order for your paragraph, you should arrange your information according to that order. You can do this simply by numbering your pieces of support in the appropriate order, or you can make a modified outline of your paragraph. The following modified outline of the paragraph on television news programs lists the problems associated with evening news programs in the order of their importance, ending with the most important.

Topic Sentence: Although they try to cover the major events of the day, evening news programs on television often end up by weakening the impact of the information they report.

Time Limitations of News Programs Weaken Impact

1. Only a few minutes for each item
2. Stories developed without analysis
3. Stories finished off neatly, next item picked up

Mixture of Content on News Programs Weakens Impact

1. Longer, serious items mixed in with lighter material
   —humorous stories, brief announcements
   —commercials
2. Everything blends together

Nature of Television Itself Weakens Impact

1. Television is often seen as entertainment
2. People use it for recreation, as a break from their own problems
3. News less important, less real as a result

Your numbered list of support or modified outline will guide you in the writing of your paragraph. Even though you may think of more ideas as you write or may find an even better order for your information, this early thinking and organizing will help you to write a good paragraph. This early work can also make the actual writing of your paragraph easier and more enjoyable.

EXERCISE B: Evaluating Your Support. Read through the list of supporting information that you made in Exercise A, and examine it for unity and completeness. Cross out information that does not belong with your topic sentence as well as information that would overload your paragraph. If necessary, add new examples, details, and so on. Finally, make sure that your topic sentence fits the supporting information that you have gathered. If it does not, revise it. *Students might exchange papers and make further suggestions for adding or deleting supporting information.*

EXERCISE C: Arranging Supporting Information in a Logical Order. Look again at your revised list of supporting information. Choose a logical order that fits your topic sentence and your list of support. Then organize your support in that order either by numbering the information or by preparing a modified outline. *Students might read their results aloud while others identify the orders used.*

APPLICATION: Developing Support for a Paragraph. For this exercise use either the paragraph topic you worked with in the Application at the end of Section 27.1 or a new paragraph topic, main idea, and topic sentence of your own. Then follow these steps to develop a paragraph outline.
Students might again exchange papers to evaluate each other's finished plans.

1. Brainstorm for supporting information for your topic sentence, creating a list of examples, details, facts, reasons, or incidents.
2. Check the unity of your support, and cross out any information that might weaken or overload your paragraph. Add to your list or make changes in your topic sentence, if necessary.
3. Decide what order you will use to present your pieces of information. Then make a modified outline of your paragraph.

27.3 Writing the Paragraph

If you have carefully thought out your paragraph, writing it will probably be a satisfying experience. Because of your earlier planning, you will have no reason to worry about what you want to say. Instead, you can concentrate on presenting your ideas in a way that will make them clear and appealing.

Putting Your Paragraph Together

Your *first draft* should be a complete version of your paragraph, but it will seldom be your final version. In many ways you can think of it as a practice version. Preparing a first draft will give you a chance to try out your ideas and to see the paragraph as a whole, as one unit of thought.

Think about your audience and purpose as you write your first draft, using your outline as a guide and adding transitions where they are needed.

In addition to your outline, you can use the suggestions in the following chart as you prepare your first draft.

SUGGESTIONS FOR DRAFTING A PARAGRAPH

1. Let your awareness of your audience and purpose guide you as you choose your words.
2. Check any new ideas you decide to add against your topic sentence.
3. Feel free to change the order of your ideas if that will make things clearer.
4. Make sure you have used enough transitions to link your ideas clearly.
5. Consider ending your paragraph with a *concluding sentence*—a sentence that wraps up all the ideas in the paragraph.

Keeping your audience and purpose in mind will help you find the right words. It can also help you decide whether you need to add any ideas to make your point clearer, whether you need to make any changes in order, and whether you have used enough transitions. Your audience and purpose can even help you decide whether or not to add a concluding sentence. Simply ask yourself if such a sentence would help your audience understand the point you are trying to make.

The following is a final copy of the paragraph about television news programs. Note that the supporting information follows the order of ideas in the modified outline on page 577. Note also that the transitions (printed in italics) guide the reader from one idea to the next, while showing that the information is organized in order of importance.

TOPIC SENTENCE

Completed paragraph with unity and coherence

Concluding sentence

Although they try to cover the major events of the day, evening news programs on television often end up by weakening the impact of the information they report. *First,* because time is limited, only a few minutes can be given to each news item. Therefore, each story is presented without much detail and then finished off neatly so that the next item can be picked up. *Even* when a story is reported at greater length, it often loses importance because the broadcast mixes it in with a number of other, lighter stories, as well as with commercials and brief announcements. As a result, everything seems to blend together. *Perhaps the major problem* with broadcast news coverage lies in the fact that television is often seen mainly as entertainment. People turn on their televisions for relaxation. They are looking for a break from their daily routines and problems. Everything they view—even news—becomes somewhat less important and less real under these circumstances. With the problem of time, the blend of many different kinds of stories, and the view of television as entertainment, evening news programs can not help chopping up and watering down the news of the world into easily digested tidbits that people can enjoy each night with their evening meals.

EXERCISE A: Writing a First Draft. Pretend that you have prepared the following modified outline for a paragraph to be written for the audience and purpose listed. Following the suggestions in the chart on page 579, prepare a first draft of the paragraph.
Students might compare finished paragraphs, noting such things as transitions used.

Audience: Friends   Purpose: To explain

Topic Sentence: A bottle of mustard in the wrong hands can easily cause a disaster.

The Situation
1. My family busy packing for camping trip
2. My friend Jack making sandwiches for picnic lunch

What Jack Did
1. Got out plastic mustard bottle, which had not been used in months
2. Lined up slices of bread
3. Squeezed bottle lightly—nothing came out
4. Turned bottle upside down and tapped it
5. Squeezed bottle hard—caused a big pop like a balloon exploding

Results of Jack's Actions
1. Made me laugh and slip in the mustard
2. Splattered mustard everywhere—on the counter, on the refrigerator, on Jack's shirt and jeans, on the floor
3. Took us an hour to clean up the kitchen

APPLICATION: Drafting Your Own Paragraph. Use the outline you prepared for the Application at the end of Section 27.2 to draft a paragraph of your own. Follow the suggestions in the chart on page 579 as you write.
Students might exchange finished paragraphs and make suggestions for improvements.

Revising and Rewriting a Paragraph 27.4

Because communicating well in writing is a challenge, it often requires extra time and effort. Even after you have planned and drafted a paragraph, you may not have written exactly what you want to say. Or you may have overlooked problems in your main idea and supporting information that will mislead a reader. For these reasons *revising* is an important step. Revising means taking a fresh look at your writing. It means rethinking ideas, seeing your writing as another person would, and often rewriting sentences or even the whole paragraph to make improvements. This section discusses some of the weaknesses you should look for in your paragraphs and some of the ways you can revise your paragraphs to make them stronger.

Recognizing Problems in Topic Sentences

A topic sentence should always give the reader a clear idea of what the paragraph covers. When you revise, you may sometimes discover that your topic sentence does not do this. For one reason or another, it may simply not fit the supporting information you have chosen to use in your paragraph. A topic sentence might be too narrow; that is, it might cover only some of the supporting information. Or it might be too general and suggest that the paragraph will cover much more information than it does. In either case the topic sentence should be revised.

Rewrite a topic sentence that is too narrow or too general by expanding or narrowing its focus to express the main idea of the entire paragraph.

The statements that follow are three possible topic sentences for a paragraph about the different animals and plants on beaches. Read each topic sentence and notice why only one of the topic sentences is suitable for the paragraph.

TOO NARROW: Every type of beach has its own special plant life.

TOO GENERAL: The beaches around the world surprise us with their variety.

CLEARLY FOCUSED: Every type of beach—whether rock or pebble, sand or mud—has its own characteristic group of animals and plants.

Now read the paragraph with the clearly focused topic sentence at the beginning.

Paragraph with a focused topic sentence

Every type of beach—whether rock or pebble, sand or mud—has its own characteristic group of animals and plants. The beach is a world of transition, washed by the ebb and flow of the tides and subject to constant change. The upper reaches are covered by sea water only briefly at high tide, while the lower parts of the beach are rarely exposed. Consequently, the resident animal and plant species vary from top to bottom of the beach, those at the top having little tolerance of salt water, while those lower down are unable to survive for long without it. —Adapted from *Rand McNally Atlas of the Oceans*

If you were to place either of the other two topic sentences at the beginning of the paragraph, the reader would probably be confused. The topic sentence that is too narrow mentions plant life but not animal life. The topic sentence that is too general prepares the reader for a general discussion of the many different kinds of beaches around the world, not for a paragraph on the animal and plant life on beaches.

To find and correct problems in topic sentences, read the paragraph you have written and then check the supporting information against the topic sentence. If the paragraph holds together but the topic sentence does not fit, revise the topic sentence.

EXERCISE A: Improving Topic Sentences. Each of the following underlined topic sentences is either too narrow or too general. Read each paragraph, and briefly describe why the topic sentence needs to be revised. Then rewrite each topic sentence to fit its paragraph.

Revisions will vary; problems are identified and sample changes are given.

(1) <u>You should always practice certain safety measures</u>. Try to figure out exactly where you are going in the city before you set off. Carry street maps, addresses, and important phone numbers with you. Even if you do get lost, try to look as though you know where you are

Too general: When visiting an unfamiliar city, you should practice certain safety measures.

going. It is also a good idea not to wear expensive jewelry, especially gold chains and bracelets. Furthermore, for your own protection, do not act overly friendly or casually start conversations with strangers. Acting purposeful and occupied with your own thoughts will help you blend in safely with the other people in a big city.

(2) Katherine Sutton, the main character in the fantasy *The Perilous Gard,* has a sharp mind. When Queen Mary of England banishes her to a remote castle for something she did not do, Katherine does not feel sorry for herself. She rides for miles through cold, rainy forests without complaining to her guards. Once settled in the mysterious castle, she explores the nearby countryside alone. Her curiosity is aroused when the townspeople shut their doors in her face and the children run from her. Katherine determines to find the answers to these puzzles and to her questions about the castle. When the People of the Hill imprison the man she loves, she follows him into captivity. Every day she risks her life by going to his cell to talk to him so that he will not go insane. Finally, by speaking the truth in her blunt way, she breaks through the hypnotic trance that threatens to destroy him and saves his life. *Too narrow: Katherine Sutton, the main character in the fantasy* The Perilous Gard, *displays remarkable intelligence, strength, and courage.*

Recognizing Problems with Supporting Information

You should also examine the supporting information in your paragraphs. There are a number of ways you may be able to strengthen this information.

Revising Paragraphs That Do Not Have Enough Support. Sometimes a paragraph may simply not have enough supporting information to explain its topic sentence or to make the paragraph convincing to a reader.

Revise a paragraph that does not have enough support by adding more information.

When you reread your paragraph, you may discover either that it leaves the reader with unanswered questions or that it simply seems sketchy. If so, gather a few more examples, facts, or other kinds of supporting information that will help the reader understand or appreciate the main idea. You might also look for words or ideas that readers could find confusing. If you find any of these, add definitions and details that will help clarify your ideas.

The following paragraph is underdeveloped. It barely begins to support its main idea.

Paragraph with not enough supporting information

Law students face a terrifying world during their first year of law school. Their professors and their textbooks use legal language full of difficult words that the students do not understand. To make matters worse, they must read and remember hundreds of pages of legal material a week.

The preceding paragraph gives only two examples to explain why law students face a "terrifying world." To be clear, the paragraph should have at least two or three more examples.

Paragraph developed with complete supporting information

Law students face a terrifying world during their first year of law school. Their professors and their textbooks use legal language full of difficult words that the students do not understand. To make matters worse, they must read and remember hundreds of pages of legal material a week. Often, a professor will call on students in class and expect them to discuss in detail the cases they have read. Perhaps the worst part of first-year law school is learning to take the exams. Most college classes require several papers and exams during the semester; in contrast, law school puts more pressure on students by having their grades depend entirely on one exam given at the end of each course. On a single four- or eight-hour exam, students must show how well they have mastered the material covered in an entire course.

Revising Paragraphs with Weak Support. The supporting information in a paragraph can also be a problem if it consists mainly of generalizations and weak opinions. Such a paragraph will not inform or persuade a reader.

Revise a paragraph made up of generalizations and weak opinions by replacing them with specific examples, details, facts, and reasons.

On rereading your paragraph, you may find that some of your supporting information takes up space without expanding a reader's knowledge. Generalizations will not help the reader grasp your ideas. Similarly, opinions that are not supported with specific information will have little meaning for the reader. You should cross out these pieces of weak support and substitute examples, details, facts, or reasons that will help the reader visualize or understand your main idea. Note how the following paragraph is unclear because it consists mainly of generalizations and weak opinions.

Paragraph with generalizations and weak opinions

My brother's college graduation was a ceremony full of tradition and high spirits. As the audience arrived, a small band played music. Then groups of people in robes and other people carrying flags marched down the center aisle. Everyone acted proud and important. Next the students filed down to the front of the audience. Then members of the audience cheered as students they knew received their diplomas. The students displayed their enthusiasm when the president awarded their degrees. At the end the procession walked back down the aisle. The ceremony was really meaningful. It was fantastic.

Most likely, the preceding paragraph has failed to convince you that the graduation "was a ceremony full of tradition and high spirits." Simply saying that something is "meaningful" and "fantastic" will not impress most readers. The paragraph could also be made more effective if generalizations such as "groups of people" and "other people" were replaced by specific details and examples.

Paragraph with strong, specific supporting information

My brother's college graduation was a ceremony full of tradition and high spirits. While the audience poured into the rows of chairs on the huge lawn, a small band could be heard playing music from the top of the bell tower right above. Then five graduates of the class of 1923 walked proudly down the center aisle as the audience clapped. Soon robed marshals carried in the multicolored flags that stand for engineering, medicine, humanities, and the other schools of the college. Marching in two by two, the faculty followed in robes, caps, and hoods in the colors of their schools: light blue, copper, purple, lemon, orange, green, salmon, and scarlet. Next the graduate students and the undergraduates streamed in proudly, their black robes and tassels fluttering in the breeze. After several brief speeches, members of the audience applauded as students they knew received their diplomas. When the president of the college declared that the undergraduates had officially graduated, all eight hundred of them tossed their caps into the air and cheered. At the end, while people smiled and waved and cameras clicked, the whole procession swept down the aisle again.

EXERCISE B: Improving Supporting Information. Each of the following paragraphs has problems with its supporting information. Identify the problem in each paragraph as either *not enough supporting information* or *generalizations and weak opinions*. Then revise each paragraph by rewriting it. Either add more specific information or remove the weak support and then add specific information. *Revisions will vary; problems are identified.*

(1) Every student who needs economical transportation should consider a bicycle. A bicycle is a great way to get around. It is inexpensive to run. I really enjoy mine. A bicycle is better than a moped or a motorcycle. Most people who ride bicycles regularly recommend them highly. *generalizations and weak opinions*

(2) The arguments for giving away our kitten finally outweighed our reasons for keeping her. At first she was frisky, but eventually she became foul tempered. She scratched us when we picked her up, and she developed the habit of shooting across the room, leaping on us, and clinging with her claws. She started to bite with her little needle teeth. *not enough supporting information*

Recognizing Problems with Unity and Coherence

During the revising stage, you should also think about the way in which the ideas throughout your paragraphs relate to each other. Do any ideas begin to take off on another topic? Does the paragraph seem disjointed in any way? If so, changes are needed.

Revising Paragraphs That Lack Unity. Occasionally, information that does not add anything or that is definitely unrelated may creep into your paragraphs.

Revise a paragraph that lacks unity by removing unrelated information and unnecessary details.

The following paragraph lacks unity because the writer has gotten sidetracked in a few places and has included some details (printed in italics) that are not needed.

Paragraph with unrelated information and unnecessary details

During our vacation in the White Mountains in New Hampshire, I barely survived the insects. Whenever I stepped outside the cabin, the mosquitoes found me. In just a few hours, I had red itchy mounds on my legs, arms, neck, and even my forehead. *The mosquitoes bother me at home too.* Even when I

> used mosquito spray, I could hear them whining in my ears when we walked along the lake in the evening. I was not safe from bugs on the water, either. When I tried to slap a horsefly that had circled me for ten minutes, I nearly capsized the canoe. *Horsefly bites can be especially painful, and sometimes these insects carry diseases.* I was particularly disturbed by the assortment of insects that rested on the wall under our cabin's porch light. To enter the cabin, I had to whip open the door and dash inside, slamming the door in the same motion. Even so, a few beetles, mosquitoes, and little moths usually slipped in to buzz and flutter around the lamps. *The lamps are all beautiful, old kerosene lamps, but they are a little unstable.* The giant moths as big as my hand unnerved me most. Like bats they flapped against the screens each night, giving us all nightmares.

If you reread the paragraph, mentally leaving out the sentences in italics, you will see how much more direct the unified paragraph is. With some paragraphs, such as the preceding one, you can simply cross out unrelated sentences to make the paragraphs unified. With other paragraphs you may need to take out parts of sentences and then rewrite the parts of the sentences that are left.

Revising Paragraphs That Lack Coherence. A paragraph may be unified and complete but still not read logically or smoothly. A paragraph that lacks coherence can confuse a reader because its ideas are not clearly organized or well connected. When you revise, you should make sure that your ideas are presented as clearly as possible.

Revise a paragraph that lacks coherence by reorganizing the support in a more logical order, by adding any necessary transitions, and by adding a concluding sentence if you think it will help.

When you reexamine your paragraph during the revising stage, you may find that some of your ideas do not follow logically from one to the next. If a reader is likely to have trouble following the order of your ideas, you should reorganize all or some of them for coherence. Maybe a different logical order would be more suitable for your topic sentence and support. If the basic order of your ideas is clear but the reader needs more guidance in following them, you should add transitions. Sometimes just one or two transitions can make the order of ideas in your paragraph clearer. With some paragraphs a concluding sentence can also help tie your ideas together. Reading a paragraph aloud and listening for the sense and sound of the sentences will help you decide how you can improve its coherence.

The following paragraph lacks coherence because the writer jumps around too much. Notice how difficult it is to understand the ideas.

Paragraph with poorly organized supporting information

If new skiers follow some simple instructions, they will have few problems using the rope tows on ski slopes. The rope will yank the skiers forward. To get off skiers must head their skis away from the track, release the rope, and push with their bodies away from the tow. By keeping their weight evenly distributed on both skis and by holding both skis parallel in the track, the skiers will find that the rope will pull them steadily to the top of the slope. They should make sure that they have on their gloves or mittens because the moving rope can burn bare hands. When they are ready to get on, they should grab the rope with both hands. One hand should be in front of them and one hand behind. While the skiers get in line, they should loop the straps of their poles around the arm that will be closest to the rope tow. As their turn to get on approaches, they should slide their skis into the smooth track under the moving rope, which is about three feet off the ground.

In order to make the "simple instructions" listed in the paragraph clear, the paragraph needs to be reorganized. When the steps involved in using a rope tow are presented in the order in which a reader would follow them, the paragraph makes more sense. Adding a few transitions and a concluding sentence also helps.

Paragraph with logically organized supporting information and necessary transitions

If new skiers follow some simple instructions, they will have few problems using the rope tows on ski slopes. When the skiers get in line, they should loop the straps of their poles around the arm that will be closest to the tow. They should *also* make sure that they have on their gloves or mittens because the moving rope can burn bare hands. As their turn to get on approaches, they should slide their skis into the smooth track under the moving rope, which is about three feet off the ground. When they are ready to get on, they should grab the rope with both hands. One hand should be in front of them and one hand behind. *At first,* the rope will yank the skiers forward. *But* by keeping their weight evenly distributed on both skis and by holding both skis parallel in the track, the skiers will find that the rope will pull them steadily to the top of the slope. To get off, the skiers must head their skis away from the track, release the rope, and push their bodies away from the tow. The rest is all downhill!

EXERCISE C: Revising a Paragraph for Unity. Find the three sentences that do not belong in the following paragraph. Then write the new paragraph on your paper.

Revisions may vary; unrelated sentences are underlined.

(1) The city council has approved a number of new measures to beautify the waterfront area. (2) One measure, which will cost the city almost a quarter of a million dollars, involves sandblasting a row of townhouses. (3) The sandblasting will make these dingy brick buildings look fresh and elegant. (4) In cities all over the East, old buildings have been sandblasted and fixed up inside. (5) Then these buildings have been

rented as modern apartments. (6) Another measure calls for the installation of electrified gas lamps. (7) Although these lamps look antique, they will provide enough light to brighten the waterfront. (8) Some street lights can be glaring and ugly. (9) The council also voted money for borders of flowers along the walkways. (10) When these changes are complete, the waterfront will be one of the most charming sections of the city.

EXERCISE D: Revising a Paragraph for Coherence. The following paragraph is illogically organized. It should describe a scene as taken in by viewers turning in a circle clockwise from north to west. Rewrite the paragraph so the details are logically organized. Consider adding more transitions and a concluding sentence.

Revisions will vary; probable new order of sentences: 1, 6, 3, 2, 7, 5, 4.

(1) The 360° view of the San Francisco Bay area from Mount Tamalpais entranced us. (2) Directly east, the purple cone of Mount Diablo stood out above the folds of the Coastal Range, and nearer to us Berkeley, Oakland, and the other cities spread from the top of the nearest range to the edge of the bay. (3) Nearer still to the east, the Richmond-San Rafael Bridge formed a slender band over the bay. (4) The Pacific Ocean to the west fringed the rocky coast and curled over the horizon. (5) The buildings of San Francisco flashed and twinkled to our south, soon to be engulfed by the creeping layer of fog that had already hidden the coastline in that direction. (6) Looking north, we could see a puddle of blue—a reservoir—surrounded by gold hills and forests, and San Pablo Bay spread out to the northeast. (7) The San Francisco-Oakland Bay Bridge in the southeast looked like a chain strung from Oakland to Yerba Buena Island and from that island to San Francisco.

Using a Checklist to Examine a Paragraph

You should now be familiar with some of the most common weaknesses that a paragraph can have. Recognizing these weaknesses can help you revise your writing. So can the following practical methods.

Look at your writing after some time has passed, and use a checklist to help rethink your ideas and pinpoint problems.

In order to improve your writing, try to approach it from a new perspective. Leaving some time between writing and revising can help you see things you may have overlooked while writing. Sometimes hearing another person read your writing aloud can also help you be objective.

Once you are ready to take a fresh look at your writing, a checklist can help you find ways to make your writing stronger by pointing out some of the weaknesses discussed in this section. When you use a checklist, you should read each question and then reread your paragraph and think about that specific checklist item.

CHECKLIST FOR REVISING A PARAGRAPH

1. Does the topic sentence clearly express the main idea of the paragraph? If not, should you expand or narrow the focus of the topic sentence?
2. Have you included enough support to develop your topic sentence?
3. Can you find any generalizations and weak opinions that should be replaced with specific supporting information?
4. Are there any unnecessary pieces of information that your paragraph would be stronger without?
5. Would another order be better for your ideas? Would any of the ideas be clearer if they were introduced by transitions? Would a concluding sentence tie your paragraph's ideas together?
6. Could you make your paragraph more suited to your audience and purpose?
7. Could any of the sentences be lengthened, shortened, or combined for smoothness?
8. Are there any mistakes in grammar, usage, mechanics, or spelling?

Once you have revised your paragraph, you should write a neat, final copy of it. You should then proofread the final copy to correct any errors that were made in recopying.

The following first draft of a paragraph shows the kinds of changes you should be prepared to make in your own paragraphs. Note that space has been left between all of the lines in the original paragraph. This makes it possible for new words, ideas, and even sentences to be added in the right places throughout.

Both water-skiing and cross-country skiing are good ways
~~Waterskiing is a good way~~ to exercise. A summer sport, water-skiing depends on the arms and leg muscles to keep the skier riding along the water. *To begin, the* ~~The~~ skier grabs onto a tow line and is pulled up by a motorboat into standing position. Leg muscles and arm muscles help the skier pull up into position and *then* keep balanced as the boat races through the waves. *Like the water-skier, the* ~~The~~ cross-country skier depends on strong arm and leg muscles, too. In the winter, a person can get similar exercise by cross-country skiing. *However, the* ~~The~~ cross-country skier has no outside power pulling him or her along and must rely *even more* on arm and leg strength. ~~The sport is not as much fun because of this extra work. Some people prefer downhill skiing.~~ In cross-country skiing, the *skier* ~~skiier~~ works hard, using the legs to guide and push the skis and using the arms to jab the ski poles into and push off from the snow.
In summer or winter, the person who skis can get plenty of exercise.

As you can see from the revision, the first draft of the preceding paragraph had a number of problems. Revising has expanded the topic sentence to cover the entire paragraph. A weak opinion and a piece of unrelated information have been eliminated. One piece of supporting information has been moved, and several transitions have been added. Finally, a concluding sentence has been written to tie together the paragraph's ideas.

EXERCISE E: Revising Someone Else's Writing. With another student, exchange first drafts of the paragraphs you wrote for the Application in Section 27.3. Use the checklist on page 593 and the ideas in this section to improve the other student's paragraph. Make your revisions right on your partner's paper. *Students' work might be monitored to ensure that revision suggestions focus on all needed areas.*

APPLICATION: Revising Your Own Paragraphs. Use the paragraph that your partner revised in Exercise E and another paragraph that you have written recently to produce *two* revised paragraphs. First, examine your partner's revisions. If you agree with the changes, keep them. If you think other revisions would be better, make them. Then copy your paragraph in its final form and proofread it for errors. Next, take the other paragraph and use the checklist on page 593 to identify weaknesses. Make your changes right on your paper. Finally, recopy this revised paragraph, and proofread it for errors. *Students might discuss revisions with partners before making final changes. Partners could also help proofread each other's work.*

Chapter 28

Writing Different Kinds of Paragraphs

In this chapter you will study and write three different kinds of paragraphs: *expository, persuasive,* and *descriptive.* Each kind of paragraph serves a different purpose, and each creates a different kind of relationship between writer and audience. Paying special attention to your purpose in writing can help you write clearer, more effective paragraphs.

28.1 Writing Paragraphs That Explain

You have probably written many *expository paragraphs* in your life, and you will probably write many more. In school you may be asked to write expository paragraphs for science, social studies, and English. Outside of school you may write expository paragraphs in carrying out club activities and in writing letters. Anything written to explain something to a reader is expository writing. This section will focus on the basic features of expository paragraphs: an explanatory purpose and informative language. It will also give you practice in writing expository paragraphs.

Focusing on an Explanatory Purpose

Whenever you write a paragraph in order to explain something or to instruct your reader about something, your purpose will be explanatory. Your goal will be to share information with an audience. To carry out this purpose, you must make sure that your topic sentence is a factual statement. You should also make sure that the supporting information develops this statement with factual, specific information, arranged so that the reader can grasp it easily.

An **expository paragraph** explains a factual main idea with factual, specific support that is clearly arranged for the reader.

The topic sentence of an expository paragraph must be a factual statement. It must *not* offer an opinion. It should simply tell the reader what information the paragraph will develop. The first of the following topic sentences would make sense at the beginning of an expository paragraph. The second, which states an opinion, would not.

FACTUAL TOPIC SENTENCE: Many different methods can be used to learn a foreign language.

OPINIONATED TOPIC SENTENCE: The only way to learn a new language is to visit a country where the language is spoken.

The supporting information in an expository paragraph should also be factual, as well as easily understood. You should gather examples, details, and facts about your topic from your own life, from books, and from other sources. Then you should organize your support so that a reader can follow it easily. Consider the logical orders that you studied in Section 26.4, and choose one that suits your topic. As you gather and organize your information, keep in mind your audience's understanding of the topic. A less knowledgeable reader will need more background information than one who is familiar with your topic.

The following expository paragraph explains the history of a musical instrument: the recorder. The explanatory purpose of the paragraph is evident from the topic sentence. The paragraph develops the topic with historical facts, presenting the information chronologically so that readers who know little about music can still understand.

TOPIC SENTENCE (Factual statement) Support in chronological order	The recorder dates back to Shakespeare, who speaks of it in some of his plays. In Elizabethan England, sets of recorders were found in nearly every home. Henry VIII's collection numbered seventy-five of them and Samuel Pepys kept eulogizing this pipe in his writings. The instrument stood foremost among woodwinds until the development of the modern orchestra which supplanted it with the transverse or side-blown flute. A twentieth century revival of the recorder took place in England, the continent, and the United States following the last war. Now more than 250,000 people are playing it over the country and adult evening classes are to be found in some schools. —Doron K. Antrim

EXERCISE A: Examining a Paragraph That Explains. Read the following expository paragraph and answer the questions after it.

> Refinishing old wooden furniture takes time, patience, diligence, and a large supply of sandpaper. You should begin by thoroughly cleaning the piece you want to refinish. Once the surface is clean, you can remove old layers of paint or shellac with a commercial solvent, although most experts recommend shaving these layers off carefully with a sharp chisel. Then you can begin refining and smoothing the wood with sandpaper. You should use very coarsely grained paper at first, switching several times to increasingly finer grains. When the surface is perfectly smooth, you can apply a quick-drying stain to protect the wood and bring out its grain. Your old hand-me-down is now something you can show off proudly!

1. What is the topic sentence?
2. List the items of support.
3. How is the support organized?

1. first sentence 2. Answers may vary within reason. 3. chronological order

EXERCISE B: Planning an Expository Paragraph. Each of the following topics could be used as the basis for an expository paragraph. Identify a specific audience for each topic. Then write a topic sentence that states a main idea about the topic. Be prepared to explain what kind of information you would use to support each topic sentence.

You may want to use the first item as a class exercise before students begin work on their own.

Ways of conserving energy in the home
What causes a rainbow
Directions from school to your home
A comparison between two towns
How to find a book in a bookstore

■ Focusing on Informative Language

In expository writing you should use language that teaches and informs. Your words should be clear, so they will help the reader grasp your explanation.

The language in an expository paragraph should be informative. It should be made up of words that will help the reader understand each of the ideas you are presenting.

Your purpose will help you find the most appropriate language for your expository paragraph. Because you are explaining something, you should choose words that offer facts, not opinions, as clearly as possible. Try to keep your audience in mind as you write, explaining those terms that a reader may not understand. You should also try to choose very specific, precise language throughout your paragraph.

To help the reader follow the information that you are presenting, you should use transitions as well.

Look at how the expository paragraph about recorders on page 598 uses language to inform the reader. The paragraph is fairly simple but factual: It includes several numbers and refers to familiar historical figures such as Shakespeare and Henry VIII. It also explains that the term *transverse* means "side-blown."

Finally, it explains the history of the recorder in clear, precise words that are easy to follow, and it uses language that makes the historical progression clear: *dates back to, Elizabethan England, modern orchestra, twentieth century, last war,* and *now.*

EXERCISE C: Using Informative Language. Using one of the topic sentences that you wrote in Exercise B, write an expository paragraph using informative language. Keep your specific purpose and audience in mind as you write.
Paragraphs that cover the same topics could be compared in class.

APPLICATION: Writing a Paragraph to Explain. Choose a topic of your own for an expository paragraph. Decide who your audience is. Then write a topic sentence. Finally, write and revise your paragraph, making sure that it clearly explains your topic.
Students might exchange papers and suggest revisions in each other's work.

28.2 Writing Paragraphs That Persuade

There are many situations in which you may need to write persuasively. You might want to express your opinion about a problem in your school or community. You might be asked to argue for or against a political issue in your social studies class. Or you might someday want to convince an employer to use an idea of yours. Many different writing situations require an ability to persuade. This section will discuss the basic features of *persuasive paragraphs*: a persuasive purpose and reasonable language. It will also give you several chances to use your own persuasive skills.

■ Focusing on a Persuasive Purpose

Whenever you write a paragraph to convince someone to accept your opinion, take an action of some kind, or simply look at something in a new way, you will need to write persuasively. To do this, you must let your persuasive purpose shape your entire paragraph. Your topic sentence should state your opinion. Your support should offer specific and convincing evidence, and the entire paragraph should be presented in an effective order.

A **persuasive paragraph** attempts to convince a reader to accept the writer's opinion by using specific evidence that is arranged logically.

Your topic sentence should make your persuasive purpose clear by expressing your opinion in strong but reasonable terms. You should state your opinion firmly, but at the same time, you should try not to offend those who disagree with you. The following topic sentences manage to sound reasonable, even while expressing very definite opinions.

TOPIC SENTENCES FOR PERSUASIVE PARAGRAPHS

The proposal to eliminate art and music classes in our school should be vigorously opposed by students and parents because it would deprive students of many valuable experiences.

The major weakness in local news broadcasts is their emphasis on a few sensational stories at the expense of thorough coverage of issues that affect most of the people watching.

Like the topic sentence, the support in a persuasive paragraph should present your case forcefully while taking into account the opposing view. To convince an audience of your main idea, you should provide strong reasons, facts, examples, and other information to support your opinion. You might even try to answer possible objections to your arguments in order to win over readers who oppose your ideas. In addition, you should try to make the most of your evidence by organizing it effectively. One very useful method is to lead your reader up to your strongest argument by organizing your ideas according to the order of their importance.

The following persuasive paragraph offers arguments in support of an opinion about traffic restrictions. Note the firm but reasonable opinion in the topic sentence. Note also that the arguments are arranged in order of importance.

TOPIC SENTENCE (Opinion)	This city could solve a number of problems if it began restricting automobile traffic in downtown areas this fall.
Support in order of importance	Our public transportation system is excellent, and yet our streets are usually choked with private cars in addition to buses and taxicabs. This amount of traffic increases the pollution, dirt, and noise in our streets. Furthermore, heavily traveled streets need more frequent repairs, which the city can not afford. And, most important, the need to regulate automobile traffic spreads our police force too thin to perform its other duties. The protection of lives and property could be improved if fewer police officers were tied up in traffic duty. Limiting people's use of private automobiles would cause some inconvenience, it is true. But this inconvenience would be offset by the benefits of such a move. If automobile traffic were reduced, the city could then direct its human and financial resources toward making our streets cleaner, safer, and more pleasant for all of us.

EXERCISE A: Examining a Paragraph That Persuades. Read the following persuasive paragraph and answer the questions after it.

Despite their aches and pains, old houses have more appeal than modern homes. For one thing old buildings, designed before architects began to place a high value on light and space, have many odd corners and surprising little nooks. New houses may be airier and easier to clean, but one seldom finds surprises in their vast open spaces. Because materials and labor cost less in the past, old houses were usually built more solidly than their modern counterparts. There seems to be more to an old house—more material, more detail, more rooms, more *house.* Finally, the feeling of time is built into old houses. Newer homes often seem barren and nearly identical. In an old house, the plumbing may be rusting and the wallpaper may be curling away, but its character and atmosphere keep growing over the years.

1. What is the topic sentence? *first sentence*
2. Identify the major pieces of support in the paragraph. *Answers may vary within reason.*
3. How are these pieces of support arranged in the paragraph? *comparison and contrast order (or order of importance)*

EXERCISE B: Planning a Persuasive Paragraph. Each of the following topics could be used as the basis for a persuasive paragraph. Write each topic on your paper and decide what opinion or stand each paragraph might express. Decide on your audience as well. Then write a topic sentence for each topic. Be prepared to explain what kind of supporting information you would provide in the rest of each paragraph.

As in Section 28.1, the first item might be used as a class exercise before students begin work on their own.

A pass/fail grading system
A particular commercial on television
Having one's own room or apartment
Eliminating physical education
Using safety belts in cars

Focusing on Reasonable Language

Just as the topic sentence in a persuasive paragraph should be stated firmly without offending those who disagree, the language throughout the paragraph should be both forceful and reasonable.

Persuasive paragraphs should use convincing but reasonable language to win readers over to the writer's viewpoint.

With practice it is not difficult to state opinions strongly but unemotionally. Imagine that you are speaking directly to someone who disagrees with you but who is willing to listen to reason. To win over such a listener, you should find specific language that establishes your point clearly and directly without overstating it. If your arguments are good, they do not need to be pumped up with emotion-charged words. Above all you should avoid name-calling and other offensive references to opposing opinions. It only does your argument harm to make a remark such as "Any idiot could see that I am right."

Take another look at the persuasive paragraph on page 602 arguing in favor of limiting automobile traffic. Note that although the issue is important, the writer has used simple, specific words, letting the arguments speak for themselves. The writer does not ridicule or blame drivers of automobiles and even admits that the proposal would cause them some inconvenience. Note also how smoothly the transitions lead the reader to the writer's final and strongest argument.

EXERCISE C: Using Reasonable Language. Using one of the topic sentences that you developed for Exercise B, write a persuasive paragraph using reasonable language.

Students might exchange papers and underline any examples of unreasonable language.

APPLICATION: Writing a Paragraph to Persuade. Choose a topic of your own for a persuasive paragraph. Decide on both your opinion and your audience. Then write a topic sentence. Finally, write and revise your paragraph, making it as persuasive as possible while using reasonable language.

Before the revision stage, students might exchange papers and note which arguments they find most and least persuasive.

28.3 Writing Paragraphs That Describe

You probably write *descriptive paragraphs* often—in letters, on postcards, in notes to friends—in short, whenever you want your readers to appreciate how something appears to you. This section will discuss the basic features of descriptive paragraphs: a descriptive purpose and descriptive language. It will also give you a chance to exercise your creativity in writing descriptive paragraphs of your own.

Focusing on a Descriptive Purpose

The purpose of any descriptive paragraph is to provide a sharp, vivid picture for the reader. The descriptive paragraphs you write will naturally be based on your own powers of observation: your ability to note the exact details of your topic and to share them with your reader. Your choice of details and your organization of details are also important. Your goal should be to make it possible for your reader to form a specific *dominant impression* of your topic, to "see it with your eyes."

A **descriptive paragraph** creates a dominant impression of a person, place, or thing through the use of vivid details arranged so that the reader can also see or experience the thing described.

A descriptive paragraph should give the reader a single dominant impression of your topic. This dominant impression will be the main idea of your paragraph, the idea that holds your description together. The dominant impression in a descriptive paragraph can be a particular quality of what you are describing. For example, in describing your brother, you might emphasize his weird sense of humor. The dominant impression you create can also be a *mood*, an emotion that runs throughout your description. For example, you might describe a quiet room in a way that makes the reader feel tranquil and secure.

The dominant impression will generally be the topic sentence of a descriptive paragraph. In some cases, however, the dominant impression may not be expressed easily in a topic sentence. Instead, the various details of the paragraph may add up to a dominant impression that is implied rather than stated. Each of the following sentences expresses a dominant impression in a topic sentence.

TOPIC SENTENCES FOR DESCRIPTIVE PARAGRAPHS
In his black trenchcoat and dark glasses, Father became an altogether different—almost glamorous—personality.
After a few days, the normally comforting sound of rain drumming steadily on our roof grew more and more maddening.

Support in a descriptive paragraph should be made up of details based on careful observation. You should always try to select the most vivid details you can find. Include specific details of shape, color, size, and texture to make the picture clear. Use sensory impressions—sights, sounds, smells, tastes, and sensations—to bring your topic to life. If you are describing a thing, you will probably concentrate on physical appearance. If your topic is a person, you can describe behavior and movement as well as physical appearance. And if you are recreating a scene, you can write about the people involved as well as the surroundings. You should arrange your details in the order that best conveys your dominant impression. For physical descriptions spatial order will often give your reader the best idea of what you are describing.

The following paragraph gives a vivid picture of Simon Rodia's Watts Towers, a landmark in Los Angeles. The dominant impression of the structure is expressed in the first sentence. Note the numerous visual details that the writers use to recreate the towers for the reader. Note also the use of spatial order to tie all these details together.

TOPIC SENTENCE (Dominant impression)

It was not until the late 1960's that people began to realize that Simon Rodia's towers were not only unique, but possibly Southern California's most distinctive architectural landmark. The Watts Towers are

Support in spatial order

certainly the tallest thing around. They spiral upward like tall mosaic cages, or primitive twin Eiffel Towers. Below the two major spires are several smaller ones, two or three fountains, a thronelike entrance pavilion, a bejewelled concrete ship, and a scalloped wall that runs along the street. Everything seems connected to everything else, making the whole environment into a great enclosing web, sparkling with shells, glass, pottery, and tile. Etched into the wall by the main gate are the words "Nuestro Pueblo," which can mean "Our Town" or "Our People." It is Rodia's name for his very personal work, which has now been adopted by his neighbors as a symbol of community spirit.—Adapted from Jane and Michael Stern

EXERCISE A: Examining a Paragraph That Describes. Read the following paragraph and answer the questions after it.

The car is jet black, swooping low to the ground. Its wheels are fully covered and its tiny windows are darkened so that none may gaze inside. It is rounded and streamlined, a front sweep of chrome bumper the only flash in the glossy blackness. It appears to have an expression, like a fierce and silent warrior rearing back on its haunches, coiled, ready to spring. It looks as though it hardly needs a human driver to come to life. The doors are flush and invisible. The tiny windshield is like two lidded eyes.—Adapted from Jane and Michael Stern

1. Answers may vary but should include a general impression of mystery or danger.

1. This paragraph's dominant impression is implied through its details rather than stated directly in a single sentence. What dominant impression does the paragraph build up for you?
2. Identify three especially vivid details.
3. In what order are the details in the paragraph arranged?

2. Answers may vary within reason. 3. spatial order

EXERCISE B: Planning a Descriptive Paragraph. Each of the following topics could be used as the basis for a descriptive paragraph. Write each topic on your paper, and decide on the dominant impression that you would like to create for it. Then, for each topic, write a topic sentence that expresses this impression. Be prepared to identify supporting details that you would provide to develop each impression. *As in previous sections, you may want to use one of the items as a class exercise before students begin work on their own.*

A stranger that you once observed

A memorable Halloween costume

Inside your refrigerator

The ugliest animal you have ever seen

The atmosphere of a certain street

Focusing on Descriptive Language

The language in your descriptive paragraph should bring your dominant impression to life for your reader. It should be full of sharply drawn images and strong sensory impressions. You might also appeal to your reader's imagination by comparing your topic to another item. If you show how your topic resembles something else familiar to the reader, you will help the reader imagine your topic more vividly.

A descriptive paragraph should bring its topic to life with colorful and precise language, sensory impressions, and striking comparisons.

The language of description consists of strong verbs, precise nouns, and vivid modifiers. You should avoid general and colorless modifiers such as *large* and *nice* and instead find more exact and vivid words that will tell your reader more about your topic. For example, *brawny, bloated,* and *mountainous* are all more precise and vivid ways of saying *large.* Which modifier you chose will depend on the actual characteristics of your topic.

Your choice of language can also increase the descriptive power of your paragraph by involving your reader's senses. Find words that create vivid sensory impressions as in the following examples.

EXAMPLES: the silky feel of a petal

the screech of chalk on the blackboard

the sweet, penetrating smell of honeysuckle

Occasionally you will be able to help your reader see (and possibly hear, feel, taste, and smell) your topic much more sharply by comparing it to something else that your topic in some way resembles. Such comparisons are called *similes* and *metaphors.* Similes are comparisons that include the word *like* or *as.*

SIMILES: His painting was like a crazy quilt.

She moved as swiftly as an arrow.

Metaphors create comparisons without *like* or *as* and suggest a closer identification between the items they compare.

METAPHORS: The electric clock was a buzzing insect.

The clown darted into the studio, a rainbow streaking through the gray corridor.

The paragraph about the Watts Towers on pages 606 and 607 includes a simile and a metaphor: *like tall mosaic cages* and *making the environment into a great enclosing web.*

EXERCISE C: Using Descriptive Language. Using one of the dominant impressions that you developed for Exercise B, write a descriptive paragraph. Use vivid modifiers, sensory impressions, and at least one simile or metaphor in your description.

You may want to remind students to avoid using clichés in their paragraphs.

APPLICATION: Writing a Paragraph to Describe. Choose a topic of your own for a descriptive paragraph. Decide on the dominant impression you want to create for your audience. Then write a topic sentence expressing that impression. Finally, write and revise your paragraph, using precise and vivid language.

Students might exchange paragraphs and identify dominant impressions, as well as any similes or metaphors.

Chapter 29

Writing Essays

An *essay* is a composition made up of several paragraphs that focus on the same topic. These paragraphs work together to present and develop one main point for a particular audience and purpose. Because of its greater length, an essay covers its topic in greater depth and detail than would be possible in a paragraph.

In this chapter you will learn more about the features of essays. You will then follow some helpful steps for planning and writing essays of your own.

29.1 Looking at Essays

First of all, you should learn to recognize the parts of an essay. Every essay should have a title, an introduction with a thesis statement, a body, and a conclusion. Then you should learn to recognize how these different parts work together. Once you know how an essay works, you will find it easier to write your own essays.

Recognizing the Parts of an Essay

An essay begins with a *title,* which attracts the reader's attention and suggests the topic of the essay. After the title the structure of an essay parallels that of a paragraph. In a paragraph the topic sentence presents the writer's main idea. In an essay the *introduction* leads up to and includes the writer's main point.

The main point is presented in a *thesis statement,* which usually comes at the end of the introduction. A paragraph has supporting information; in the same way, an essay has information that develops the thesis statement. This supporting information is presented in paragraphs called *body paragraphs.* Just as a paragraph often has a concluding sentence that presents a closing idea, an essay ends with a *conclusion* that brings the essay to a satisfying close.

The following diagram can help you see the similarities between an essay and a paragraph.

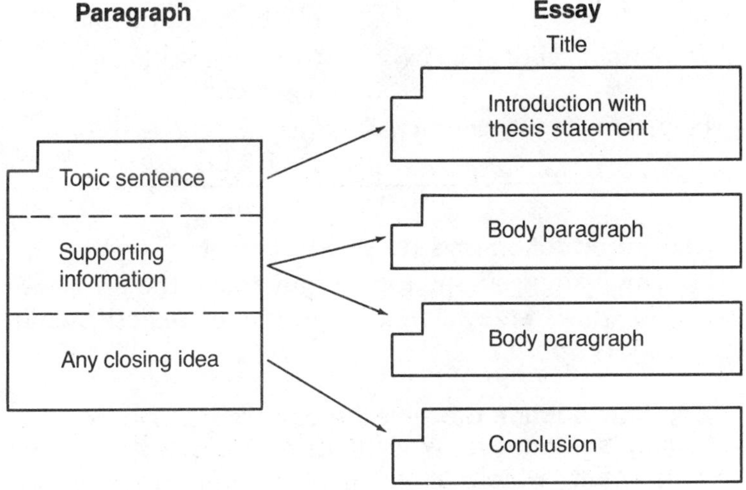

In the following pages, you will take a closer look at each of the parts of an essay.

The Title. The first thing that you see when you read an essay is the *title.* The title indicates the topic of the essay and often suggests the writer's main point. A good title should also capture the reader's interest.

The **title** of an essay suggests what the essay will be about while attracting the reader's attention.

A good essay title will be both accurate and interesting. It should provide a brief preview of what the writer has said in the essay and encourage the reader to read further. Titles can be straightforward or clever. But they should not simply state the topic flatly, nor should they be so creative that the reader is misled about the essay's content.

The following chart lists several sample topics and titles. All the titles give information about the essay's content as well as make the reader curious.

SAMPLE ESSAY TOPICS WITH TITLES

Topics	Titles
Basic ice hockey shots	What Every Hockey Player Needs to Know
Behind the scenes at a circus	Greasepaint, Spangles, and Sawdust
The making of ancient maps	Charting the Ends of the Earth

The Introduction and Thesis Statement. Unlike the title, which suggests the topic of an essay, the *introduction* and *thesis statement* tell the reader exactly what the essay is about.

> The **introduction** presents the essay's topic in an interesting, informative way. It also presents the **thesis statement,** which expresses the main point of the essay.

The introduction can offer incidents or examples to draw the reader into the essay. It may also provide any background information necessary for the reader to understand the writer's main point. In addition, the introduction should suit the writer's audience and purpose. It should let the reader know whether the essay is going to be serious or funny, formal or informal, explanatory or persuasive. Most important of all, the introduction gradually zeroes in on the writer's main point, which is presented in the thesis statement.

The thesis statement generally comes at the end of the introduction so that it will stand out. Because it focuses the essay's topic into one main point that the essay will develop or prove, the thesis statement is the single most important part of the essay. The rest of the essay works to support this main point.

Like the other sentences in the introduction, the thesis statement should suit the writer's audience and should be written with a particular purpose in mind.

SAMPLE THESIS STATEMENTS	
Thesis Statements	**Audience/Purpose**
To achieve precision as well as power in offensive action, hockey players must master three basic shots: the wrist shot, the slap shot, and the backhand shot.	To explain to an audience unfamiliar with ice hockey the three basic shots
One effect of television has been to break down some of the variety in American life.	To persuade a general audience to consider the writer's opinion about television

The Body. The *body* of the essay, which follows the introduction, will generally contain two or more paragraphs. These paragraphs present the supporting information.

The **body paragraphs** develop the thesis statement with specific and logically organized information—examples, details, facts, reasons, and incidents.

The body paragraphs should develop two or more *subtopics* of the main point. If a thesis statement makes a point about three different problems, then these problems would become the subtopics. The body paragraphs should also be clearly related to each other. A writer can show the relationship among subtopics by ordering them logically (for example, in chronological order, order of importance, or spatial order) and by using transitions. The simplest way to write the body of an essay is to devote one paragraph to each subtopic.

Each body paragraph should also have its own main idea, generally one of the subtopics of the thesis statement. In addition, each body paragraph should be unified, and each should be organized logically.

The Conclusion. The *conclusion* is the essay's ending. It can be a few sentences within the last paragraph of the body. But it is usually the entire final paragraph.

The **conclusion** ends the essay by recalling the thesis statement and completing the writer's thoughts.

The conclusion should tie the essay together. It should remind the reader of the thesis statement in some way without repeating the thesis statement word for word. It should also complete the essay with fitting and possibly memorable examples, statements, quotations, or incidents. Sometimes a writer will use a particularly interesting observation or incident that is related to the topic or a forceful or witty statement to end the essay. Such endings are called *clinchers* because they clinch the essay in the reader's memory.

EXERCISE A: Understanding Thesis Statements. Each of the following sentences is a thesis statement for an essay. For each statement identify the most likely audience and purpose. Then suggest two or three subtopics that the body paragraphs might develop. *Answers will vary; possible audiences and purposes are given; stated subtopics are underlined.*

1. Learning to make your own clothes is easy, fun, and, best of all, inexpensive.
2. Television game shows, variety shows, and crime dramas all appeal to different needs of viewers.
3. Although no summer would be complete without a vacation, winter vacations offer special pleasures.
4. There are a number of precautions that people can take to avoid being robbed.
5. Basketball is an exciting sport to watch.

1. people unfamiliar with sewing/to persuade 2. gen aud/to explain 3. gen aud/to persuade 4. people who have not been robbed/to persuade 5. people who are not yet fans/to persuade

Recognizing How the Parts of an Essay Work Together

Because an essay is made up of a number of parts and a number of paragraphs, care must be taken to make sure the parts work together and flow smoothly.

The title, introduction with thesis statement, body, and conclusion of an essay must all work together to present and develop the main point for the reader's understanding and enjoyment.

The best way to see how the parts of an essay work together is to read an essay. The following essay about hockey contains five paragraphs: an introduction, three body paragraphs, and a conclusion. As you read the essay, you will see how the paragraphs fit together logically and smoothly.

Title	What Every Hockey Player Needs to Know
Introduction Thesis statement with three subtopics	When an ice hockey player sends a speeding puck past a heavily padded goaltender, the player creates one of the most exciting moments in sports by scoring a goal. Certainly, hockey means both entertainment and tension for the spectators. For the players it is a game of skillful motion. Defensive and offensive movements in hockey are fast paced and sometimes dangerous. Hockey players often act like speeding machines on the ice, delivering shots that can reach 100 m.p.h. To achieve precision as well as power in offensive action, players must master three basic hockey shots: the wrist shot, the slap shot, and the backhand shot.
Body Paragraph 1 (Develops the first subtopic)	The easiest shot for players to learn is the wrist shot. Since this shot is often used when the puck—a small, hard disk—is traveling slowly, a player can aim quite accurately. The shot is taken by sweeping the puck with the stick while turning the wrists quickly.

This movement lets the player guide the puck in any direction. A wrist shot is especially practical when a player is close to the other team's net. It is a shot of accuracy and power, one that can make a goal.

Body Paragraph 2 (Develops the second subtopic)

A more difficult shot, the slap shot, is perhaps the most explosive move a player can make. In one motion the player pulls the hockey stick back off the ice to about waist level and then swings it forward and through, "slapping" the puck with the end of the stick. The shot sends the puck across the ice at a tremendous speed but is not always accurate, certainly not as accurate as the wrist shot. Players can not easily direct the puck with a slap shot; therefore, this shot is often used by those who are far away from the goal. A player who does not have a chance of scoring will often use this shot to forward the puck to teammates closer to the opponent's net.

Body Paragraph 3 (Develops the third subtopic)

By far the most difficult of the three shots is the backhand shot. Players can not plan to take such a shot. Instead they must decide upon it instantaneously at the moment that the puck is about to travel past them. To reach the puck, they must sweep the hockey stick across and behind their bodies, in much the same movement that tennis players make for a backhand shot. Then they must pull the puck across in front of them to propel it across the ice. Mastering the backhand shot can be a great asset to a foward, who plays near the opponent's net. Often forwards will have a chance to pick up a puck that rebounds off the goalies. The forward can then backhand the puck for a quick second attack against the goal.

Conclusion with reminder of thesis statement

These three shots are the most important moves of good offensive action in ice hockey. Players will generally use one of these shots to catch and deliver the puck. Because forwards are positioned close to the goal in the offensive zone, they will generally find wrist shots and backhands most useful. Defensive players, on the other hand, should concentrate on the slap shot because they are positioned farthest away from their goal. Of course, all players will use each of these shots at one time or another. This variety adds to the thrill and suspense of the game of hockey.

EXERCISE B: Understanding an Essay. Take another look at the preceding essay on ice hockey, and answer the following questions.

1. attention-getting remarks and thesis statement 2. wrist shot, slap shot, backhand shot

1. What information does the introduction provide?
2. What are the three subtopics?
3. How are the subtopics ordered in the body of the essay? *order of importance (or order of difficulty)*
4. Which sentence reminds the reader of the thesis statement? *first sentence in last paragraph*
5. What other information does the conclusion provide? *which players use each shot*

APPLICATION: Evaluating an Essay. Use the preceding essay on ice hockey to answer the following questions.

3. gives background information and thesis statement

1. In what ways does the title fulfill the purpose of a title? *suggests topic and gets reader's attention*
2. What other title might have been used? *Answers will vary.*
3. In what ways does the introduction fulfill the purpose of an introduction?
4. What other information might have been used in the introduction? *Answers will vary.*
5. What is the main point made in the thesis statement? *Three basic shots are necessary for power and precision.*
6. What audience and purpose is the writer likely to have had in mind? *audience unfamiliar with ice hockey/to explain*
7. In what way does the thesis statement in this particular essay prepare the reader for the order of the three body paragraphs?
8. What transitions help show the overall organization of the body paragraphs?

7. lists shots in the order they appear in the body 8. easiest/more difficult/By far the most difficult

9. In what ways does the conclusion fulfill the purpose of a conclusion?
10. What other information could have been included in the conclusion? *Answers will vary.*

9. recalls thesis statement and completes writer's thoughts

29.2 Thinking Out Your Ideas and Writing a Thesis Statement

Now that you are familiar with essays, you can practice writing your own. Following a few special steps can help you get started and can make writing easier. This section discusses the first steps in planning an essay: discovering something to write about, narrowing your topic to a suitable essay topic, deciding on your audience, main point, and purpose, and writing your thesis statement.

Finding and Narrowing a Topic

To get off to a good start, you must think carefully about topics for an essay.

Brainstorm for appealing topics and then find a suitable essay topic by narrowing down a general topic into smaller topics.

You should begin looking for an essay topic by jotting down a number of general topics that interest you. Jot down on a blank paper anything that occurs to you. You might think about your skills, hobbies, recent experiences, and daily activities. Any of these can provide you with an essay topic. Your classes and the books you have read might also offer ideas for topics. Movies, television shows, records, and news stories might give you topics. You might also try looking in a new way at familiar things or at things you have taken for granted. For example, you might think about why leaves fall in autumn, why dogs howl at sirens, why people become nervous before performing in front of an audience, or why escalators were invented.

Once you have jotted down a number of topics, you should examine your rough list to find one or more that particularly catch your interest. Then you should figure out if these topics are too general for one essay. For instance, it would be difficult to write a good essay on a topic as general as *Airplanes,* but you could probably write a very good essay about *The first passenger plane*. If a general topic interests you, you should think about it more and list smaller related topics under it.

The following chart shows a list similar to the one you should make for yourself. Note that some of the topics are narrow enough already while other more general topics have been broken down into smaller, more suitable topics.

BRAINSTORMING FOR AN ESSAY TOPIC

Yardwork as good exercise

Dinosaurs
—Why they became extinct
—Dinosaurs in North America
—How to make a dinosaur model
—A day in the life of Tyrannosaurus Rex

Plants
—Plants with unusual needs
—Terrariums
—Flower arranging

Twenty years from now
—My career
—Telephones of the future

Shopping
—Food budgets in 1960 and today
—Shopping malls

Cats
—Persian cats
—Caring for cats
—Cat shows

The curfew in our community

Learning to handle a sailboat

Your list of topics should give you a number of possibilities. Choose a topic that interests you greatly as well as one about which you have something to say. If terrariums were one of your hobbies, you might choose that topic.

EXERCISE A: Thinking of Suitable Essay Topics. Add to the following list of general topics by thinking of *five* topics of your own. Then, from the total list of fifteen topics, choose five topics and write them on your paper. Beneath each general topic, list at least three smaller essay topics. Finally, choose three topics suitable for an essay that you could write.

Students might work in small groups or with partners.

A musical instrument	Electronic games/gadgets
Automobiles	Friends
Status symbols	Cultural differences
Humor	Faces
Political campaigns	Oceans

Deciding on Audience, Main Point, and Purpose

Once you have a topic, you should make three important decisions. You should decide for whom you are writing—who will make up your audience. You should also decide what main point you want to make about your topic. And you need to decide why you are writing: to explain, to persuade, or to describe. The order in which you make these decisions may vary, but you should give some thought to each.

Focus an essay topic by deciding on your audience, main point, and purpose.

One good way to find a main point on which to base your essay is to think about your audience first. Will you be writing for other students in your class or school, for the adults in your community, for the staff of a local newspaper, for students who graduated from your school, or for a general audience made up of people of all ages and backgrounds? Will your audience be familiar with your topic beforehand? Will your audience agree with you?

Suppose, for example, that you were planning to write about terrariums, and you had chosen other students in your class as your audience. You would then be ready to explore possible main points for your essay. Thinking about your topic and your audience, you might ask some questions about your topic. Questions can help you discover what your audience might be interested in. They can also help you focus your topic to find a main point.

ASKING QUESTIONS TO FIND A MAIN POINT	
Essay Topic: Terrariums	
Questions	**Possible Main Points**
Why are terrariums interesting?	Terrariums are miniature plant worlds that show scientific principles in action.
Are terrariums better than other house plants?	Terrariums are better than house plants because they are easier to care for and more fun to observe.
How do you make a terrarium from scratch?	Making a terrarium is a three-step process.

When you ask yourself a series of questions with your audience in mind, the questions will lead you to possible main points. When you look at the points you have listed, you will see that they most likely suit different purposes. In the preceding chart, the first and third main points are factual and would be suitable if you wanted to explain an idea to your audience. The second main point is an opinion that you would have to persuade your audience to agree with.

At this stage you can decide on both your purpose and your main point. If you decided to teach other students how to make a terrarium, you would choose the last main point.

EXERCISE B: Coming Up with a Main Point for Your Essay. Choose *one* of the three topics that you selected in Exercise A. Then follow these instructions.
Students might exchange papers with partners for comments and suggestions.

1. Write a sentence telling who your audience is.
2. Think about your topic and audience. Then write down at least three questions that your audience might ask about your topic.
3. Answer your questions briefly. These answers will be your possible main points.
4. Decide which purpose each of the main points would suit.
5. Finally, choose the main point that you would like to use in your essay.

■ Writing a Thesis Statement

Your main point is actually a rough version of your thesis statement. To prepare a thesis statement, you should simply rewrite your main point to make it as clear and complete as possible.

> Keeping your audience and purpose in mind, write a thesis statement by expressing your main point in a clear and complete sentence.

Your thesis statement should present your main point clearly and accurately. It should suit your audience and purpose. Although you can revise your thesis statement once or many times throughout the writing of your essay, finding a thesis statement that you like now can speed up your writing. You may want to write several thesis statements expressing your main point. Try using different words in each.

The following chart presents several possible thesis statements for an essay on making a terrarium. It begins with the main point itself.

POSSIBLE THESIS STATEMENTS
Main Point: Making a terrarium is a three-step process.
1. Making a terrarium is a three-step process.
2. There are three steps involved in making a terrarium.
3. To make a terrarium, all you need to do is select the ingredients, prepare the soil, and root the plants you have chosen.
4. Making a terrarium is a three-step process: selecting the ingredients, preparing the soil, and rooting the plants.

After comparing the different versions, you might decide that the third version of the thesis statement is the clearest. By listing the three subtopics—the three steps in making a terrarium—you can help the reader see that the process is not difficult. This short but clear thesis statement might appeal particularly to students who have never made a terrarium.

EXERCISE C: Preparing a Thesis Statement. Use the main point that you chose in Exercise B, and write three practice versions of a thesis statement. Then decide which version appeals to you most. *Selected thesis statements might be listed, with students choosing the one they like best in each group.*

APPLICATION: Shaping Ideas for an Essay. Apply the thinking steps in this section by practicing them on your own, following these instructions.
Students might exchange final thesis statements, evaluate them, and suggest changes.

1. Brainstorm for topics and jot down a rough list of at least five.
2. Choose one or two topics that especially interest you. If a topic is too large for an essay, break it into smaller topics. Then choose one topic for your essay.
3. Decide on your audience.
4. To find two or more possible main points, ask and answer at least two questions that your audience might have about your topic.

5. Decide which purpose suits each of your main points.
6. Choose the main point that you want to use in your essay.
7. Write at least two versions of your thesis statement, and choose the one you like best.

29.3 Developing Support for a Thesis Statement

Your thesis statement sets the boundaries of your essay. It also makes it possible for you to begin planning the body of your essay. To plan the body, you will need to carry out two steps: finding supporting information and then organizing it so that it will clearly develop your thesis statement.

Brainstorming for Support

The first step after you have written your thesis statement is to find the best information you can to support and develop that statement.

Brainstorm for examples, details, facts, reasons, and incidents that will develop your thesis statement.

Brainstorming is not difficult, but it does require concentration. You might begin by simply writing down thoughts on your thesis statement as they occur to you. List as much specific information as possible. Do not weed out any information. Instead, try to come up with more support than you will actually use in your essay. The more you have on paper, the better your chances will be of finding the best information.

Another way to begin brainstorming is to write your thesis statement at the top of your paper. Then write down a few questions that your audience might ask after reading your thesis statement. The questions will help you come up with the information your audience needs to know in order to understand the thesis statement. Then brainstorm by listing examples, facts, and other specific information that answer the questions.

The following chart shows how you might use the second method to brainstorm for information to support the thesis statement about making a terrarium.

QUESTIONING TO FIND SUPPORT FOR A THESIS STATEMENT	
Thesis Statement:	**To make a terrarium, all you need to do is select the ingredients, prepare the soil, and root the plants you have chosen.**
What is a terrarium?	
—enclosed collection of plants —small world —self-sufficient—doesn't need to be watered or fertilized —miniature—from a few inches to several feet	—plants create own environment —can be attractive, decorative—different plants, shapes, colors —educational value—chance to observe plant life
What are the ingredients for a terrarium?	
—a clear container —fish tank or bowl —large jar —soil —charcoal (optional)	—sand —pebbles —small plants —ferns —mosses —tree seedlings
How do you prepare the soil?	
—line container with gravel 2 inches deep —put in a layer of charcoal (optional)—holds water, nutrients	—put in a layer of sand —put in a layer of soil—1 inch deep —make soil deeper in center (easier to add plants)

How do you root the plants?

—dig holes 1 inch deep—far enough apart to allow plants to grow

—press plant roots into holes

—pack dirt

—moisten soil

—place terrarium near window—should get some but not too much light

EXERCISE A: Gathering Supporting Information. Use the thesis statement you wrote in Exercise C of Section 29.2 to brainstorm for support. Write down three questions your audience might ask about the main point in the thesis statement. Then brainstorm for information to answer the questions.

Students might work with partners or in small groups as they begin brainstorming for support.

Organizing Your Ideas

The next step is to use your brainstorming list to organize the body of your essay.

> Choose the best pieces of support from your brainstorming list and organize them logically, first making a rough plan of subtopics and then making a modified outline.

Your list of support should give you more than enough information. You should now select the information that you will use in your essay. Look at your list. Cross out any ideas that are not closely related to your main point and add any new ideas. You might want to put aside a few pieces of support to use in your introduction and conclusion. At this time, however, you should concentrate mainly on the information you will present in the body of your essay.

After you have crossed out and possibly added some information, look again at your brainstorming list. Try to find logical groupings for the pieces of support that you plan to use. These groupings will be your subtopics. In some cases your thesis statement and the questions you asked while brainstorming will help you divide up your supporting information into subtopics. In other cases you will have to choose your subtopics now. For the essay on making a terrarium, the most logical subtopics would be the three steps of the process.

Next, decide on a logical organization for your subtopics. In the terrarium essay, the three most logical subtopics—the three steps—would naturally follow a chronological order. The subtopics in another essay might naturally follow some other logical order.

You should now see the body of your essay taking shape. Making a rough plan at this point can help. The following chart shows a possible plan for the essay on making a terrarium. The introduction and thesis statement makeup the first paragraph. Each subtopic can be developed in one body paragraph although sometimes you may want to use more than one paragraph for a subtopic. The conclusion can be a paragraph at the end.

POSSIBLE PLAN FOR AN ESSAY

First paragraph	= Introduction with thesis statement
Second paragraph	= Subtopic 1: Finding ingredients
Third paragraph	= Subtopic 2: Preparing the soil
Fourth paragraph	= Subtopic 3: Rooting the plants
Fifth paragraph	= Conclusion

With your subtopics in order, you can now begin to organize the information under each subtopic. To show your final plan, you may find it helpful to make an outline. The following is a modified outline for the body of the essay on making a terrarium.

Thesis Statement: To make a terrarium, all you need to do is select the ingredients, prepare the soil, and root the plants you have chosen.

Subtopic 1: Selection of Basic Ingredients

1. Finding a suitable container
   —glass-covered fish tank or bowl
   —wide-mouth gallon jar
2. Finding soil
   —rich, dark forest soil
   —gravel and sand, possibly charcoal and pebbles
3. Choosing plants
   —ferns
   —mosses
   —tree seedlings

Subtopic 2: Preparation of Soil

1. Lining bottom with two-inch layer of gravel or pebbles
2. Adding equal amounts of sand and soil on top of stones
3. Making sand and soil slope down on all sides

Subtopic 3: Rooting of Plants

1. Digging holes
2. Pressing roots into holes
3. Adding stones and bark for realism
4. Moistening soil, placing near a window (not too much light)

EXERCISE B: Organizing an Essay. Look again at the brainstorming list you made in Exercise A and follow these instructions. *Students' progress with these steps might be monitored closely to ensure effective supporting information.*

1. Cross out any ideas that now seem to be unrelated to the main point.
2. Add any new information you think of.
3. Examine your list of support and decide on subtopics.
4. Decide on a logical order for your subtopics, and make a plan for the essay like the one in the chart on page 627.
5. Organize the supporting information under each subtopic by making a modified outline of the body of the essay.

APPLICATION: Developing Support for an Essay. Using the thesis statement you wrote for the Application at the end of Section 29.2, follow the planning steps that you have learned in this section. First brainstorm for support, then select and group your supporting information, and finally prepare a modified outline for the body of your essay. *Students might exchange outlines to identify and then evaluate the orders used and to suggest any changes.*

Writing and Revising an Essay 29.4

All of your planning up to this point will make it possible for you to write your essay with confidence. Because you know what you plan to say, you can concentrate on presenting the information in the clearest and most interesting way. You may find it useful to begin by jotting down ideas for the beginning and end. Then you can use your brainstorming list, rough plan, and modified outline as guides for producing a first draft. Finally, you should go over your essay carefully to make any improvements you can in the ideas, organization, and writing.

Thinking About Your Introduction, Conclusion, and Title

The writing of your essay may go more quickly if you begin by jotting down ideas for your introduction, conclusion, and title.

Think of different possible ideas to introduce and end your essay. Give some thought to a title as well.

Your introduction should accomplish several very important tasks: grabbing the reader's interest, presenting the topic, and leading up to the thesis statement. As you plan your introduction, think about getting the reader interested. You might begin with a vivid example. You might start off by presenting a short incident. You might use a memorable quotation or ask an intriguing question about your topic. Use your imagination and check your brainstorming list to find ideas. Once you have found a "hook" to catch the reader's attention and have given any background information the reader will need to understand your topic, you will be ready to present your thesis statement.

Just as the introduction draws the reader into the essay, the conclusion leads the reader out. Its basic purpose is to tie together the thoughts that you have explored in the essay. A conclusion generally begins by referring to the thesis statement without repeating it word for word and then wraps up the essay in some interesting or memorable way. You may not want to write your conclusion before writing the body of the essay. However, it helps to have ideas in mind for the ending. You might think of a way to mention your main point using different words. You might also jot down examples, unusual facts, or incidents that expand upon your main point. Try to find something that will help make your essay stick in the reader's mind.

Finally, think about a few possible titles. Finding a good title can help spark your imagination.

EXERCISE A: Finding Ideas for an Introduction, Conclusion, and Title. Use the brainstorming list and outline that you developed in Exercises A and B of Section 29.3, and follow these instructions.

You may want to stress the need to find ideas that will catch the reader's interest.

1. Jot down ideas for an introduction to the essay.
2. Jot down ideas that you could use in a conclusion.
3. Write down three possible titles for the essay.

Writing the Essay

You now have everything you need to write your essay.

Write a first draft of your essay following your rough plan and outline. Include transitions to make your thoughts flow smoothly.

Your rough plan and outline should guide you in developing your main point logically. Try to make the main point and supporting information in your essay clear and connected. As you express your ideas in complete sentences, use transitions to move from one idea to another.

You should feel free to make both little changes and big changes as you write. If an idea no longer seems to fit, leave it out. Similarly, add any new examples or facts that you wish. If you decide to change the order of your ideas, you should check the outline to make sure the new order works as well as the old.

EXERCISE B: Writing a First Draft. Write a first draft of the essay with which you worked in Exercise A. Use your rough plan and your outline as a guide and connect your ideas with transitions. *You may find it useful to ask students to think of a few possible transitions before they begin writing.*

Revising the Essay

After you have written your first draft, there is still one major step to be completed.

Revise your first draft by looking for areas that could be improved.

Revising is an important part of the writing process. Few writers produce their best work the first time they try. Once you have your ideas down on paper in a first draft, you can usually find many ways to improve your essay. You might change words, rewrite sentences, or even add and take out ideas to make your essay clearer and more interesting.

In order to get a fresh perspective on your first draft, put it aside for a little while before you revise it. Pretend that someone else wrote it and has asked you for your suggestions. Make any changes right on the first draft. As a final check, answer the questions in the following checklist and make any additional changes that seem necessary.

CHECKLIST FOR REVISING AN ESSAY

1. Do you have a good title for your essay?
2. Is there any way you could make your introduction more interesting or informative?
3. Does the thesis statement fit the essay? Is it clear?
4. Are there any pieces of supporting information in the body of the essay that are not really needed?
5. Are there any examples, details, facts, reasons, or incidents that should be added to the body paragraphs to make the essay clearer or more interesting?
6. Would another order for the subtopics make the essay clearer?
7. Are there any transitions that you could add to make the essay read more smoothly?
8. Does the conclusion tie the essay together by referring to the main point? Are there ways in which you could make the conclusion more interesting for the reader?
9. Are there any mistakes in grammar, usage, mechanics, or spelling?

When you have expressed your ideas as clearly as you can, you should recopy your revised essay. Before you hand it in, you should also proofread it for mistakes that may have been added in recopying.

The following is the revised version of the essay about making a terrarium. Notice the transitions (printed in italics) that guide the reader through the steps in the process.

Title	Making a Small World
Introduction	A terrarium is a self-sufficient, miniature world for a group of plants. If you would like to have a terrarium to decorate a room or to observe for scientific purposes, you can learn
Thesis statement with three subtopics	to make one. It is not difficult. To make a terrarium, all you have to do is select the ingredients, prepare the soil, and root the plants that you have chosen.

Subtopic 1 *To begin,* you must find a suitable container, good soil, and plants. You can use a glass-covered fish tank or bowl or a wide-mouth gallon jar, which usually comes with a tightly fitting lid. You should thoroughly clean any container you choose. *In addition* to a container, you will need soil. You can use rich, dark forest soil as well as gravel and sand. You may want to collect charcoal and pebbles as well. You can use nearly any small plant, but assorted ferns, mosses, and even tree seedlings are especially good choices. However, you should avoid soil and plants that show any signs of having insects or parasites.

Subtopic 2 *After* you have chosen the outside of your terrarium and what will go into it, you are ready to prepare the soil. *First* line the bottom of the container with a two-inch layer of gravel or pebbles, which helps prevent root rot by allowing water to drain. You may want to place charcoal bits the size of peas in a one-inch layer on top of the pebbles. Charcoal is not necessary, but it will absorb moisture and supply nutrients. *Next* top the stones or charcoal with equal amounts of sand and soil. Try to make the sand and soil slope down on all sides so that the plants will be easy to see.

Subtopic 3 *When* you have finished placing the layers of soil in the terrarium, you can add the plants. You should root your plants with care. *First* dig holes that are an inch or so deep and far enough apart so that the plants will not be crowded. *Then* gently press the roots of the plants into the holes. Cover the roots with dirt and pack the dirt firmly with a fork or with your fingers. No part of the roots should be exposed. *When* the plants are in place, you can add stones and pieces of bark to make the scene realistic. *Finally,* you should moisten the soil thoroughly but gently by spraying or sprinkling water to avoid making holes in the soil. *After* you have completed this step, place the top firmly on your terrarium. *Then* place your terrarium near a window that has filtered light—that is, light that comes through a shade, blinds, or opaque glass. Too much light will encourage algae to grow on the glass.

Conclusion with reminder of thesis statement

When you have performed the three main steps, you can leave your terrarium on its own with little care. The water is prevented from escaping and will be used and reused by the plants in an endless process known as the water cycle. Filtered sunlight will provide the energy that the plants need for nourishment. With your work done, you can sit back and enjoy watching nature in action.

EXERCISE C: Revising an Essay. Reread the essay you prepared in Exercise B silently and aloud and note any changes that should be made. Then use the questions in the checklist on page 632 to examine the essay for further changes. Make all changes that are needed. Finally, recopy the revised essay and proofread it to catch any mistakes that have been added in recopying.

Before they begin revising, students might exchange papers for general suggestions.

APPLICATION: Drafting and Revising an Essay. Using the essay you prepared and organized in the Application at the end of Section 29.3, follow the steps you have learned in this section for completing an essay. Think up ideas for your introduction, conclusion, and title. Then draft the essay. Finally, exchange first drafts with another student in your class. Read the other student's essay carefully. Go over the essay using the checklist for revision on page 632. Circle any problems and make suggestions for improvements on the student's first draft. Then reread your own essay and the student's comments. Revise your essay according to the helpful comments you have received. Finally, recopy your revised essay and proofread it.

Students might discuss revisions with partners before making final changes. Partners could also help proofread each other's work.

Chapter 30

Writing Reports

In many of your classes, you will be asked to find information about a topic and present the information in a *report.* You will also be asked to read books and write *book reports.* Learning how to prepare effective reports will help you be a more successful student.

As you write both kinds of reports, you can use the skills you have already developed for writing paragraphs and essays. However, you should also recognize that both kinds of reports have special features of their own. This chapter will look first at the special features of a general report and then at the special features of a book report. It will also guide you through the steps you should follow to plan, write, and revise both kinds of reports.

Understanding and Preparing Reports 30.1

In many ways preparing a general *report* is similar to planning and writing an essay. Like an essay a report should develop a main point with facts and ideas. However, a report, unlike an essay, must be based on information that has been gathered by doing research. Much of the information in the report must be made up of facts and ideas that you find in other sources such as books and magazine articles. Your job is to put these facts and ideas together in a clear and interesting report.

The Special Features of a Report

Because a report is based on other sources, it contains two special features that an essay does not. *Footnotes* must be added throughout the paper to show where different pieces of information came from. In addition, a *bibliography* must be added at the end to give the reader a general list of all the outside sources used. In writing a report, you will need to add these two features. You will also need to combine the ideas from your sources with your own ideas to produce a clearly organized and unified paper.

Footnotes. Because so much of the information in a report is taken from outside sources, a special system has been developed for giving credit to these sources.

A report should contain **footnotes** giving credit to all outside sources.

You will need to use *footnotes* both when you quote someone else's words exactly and when you put someone else's ideas or words into your own words. You should also use footnotes for unusual facts.

Whenever you repeat, word for word, what someone else has said, you should enclose the statement in quotation marks and use a footnote to give credit to the speaker. You should also use a footnote when you state someone else's ideas in your own words; this will make it clear to the reader that the ideas are not your own but those of some authority. Well-known facts that are generally accepted do not need footnotes. For example, you would not need to cite the source for a famous baseball record such as Hank Aaron's home-run total. But you *would* need to mention a source for a lesser-known record—such as the longest game ever played in the major leagues.

To write a footnote, you should place a small number right after and just above the quotation, idea, or fact you are borrowing. This number will refer the reader to the footnote itself, which you can place either at the bottom of that page of your report or in a list at the end of the report. The footnote will tell the reader where you found the information used in your report.

When you write your report, you may have to use footnotes for a number of different kinds of sources: books by one or two authors, magazine articles with and without authors, and so forth. The following chart will help you decide what information to include in each of these footnotes.

FOOTNOTES FOR DIFFERENT SOURCES	
Kind of Source	**Footnote**
Book with one author	[1]Veronica Ions, Indian Mythology, p. 47.
Book with two authors	[2]Jane Stern and Michael Stern, Amazing America, p. 186.
Magazine article (signed)	[3]Marguerite Johnson, "Delay with Diplomacy," Time, May 18, 1981, p. 30.
Magazine article (unsigned)	[4]"Toys for Tots," Time, December 14, 1981, p. 68.
Encyclopedia article (signed)	[5]The World Book Encyclopedia, 1981 ed., "Berlin, Irving," by Ethan Mordden.
Encyclopedia article (unsigned)	[6]The Random House Encyclopedia, 1977 ed., "Hollywood."

A Bibliography. In addition to using footnotes throughout the report, you must also include a *bibliography* at the end listing all the sources you have used.

At the end of a report, a **bibliography** should list all the sources that were used in the preparation and writing of the report.

Your bibliography will give a general view of your research. If readers want to explore your topic further, your bibliography can help them find your sources in the library. For this reason you should list complete information about each source that you have used, whether or not you actually used information from that source in your report.

A bibliography entry differs from a footnote in a number of ways. In a bibliography entry for a book, you must list each author's last name first. You must also list your sources alphabetically, according to the first letter of each entry. Finally, you must use a reverse indent as shown in the following chart. As you write bibliography entries, use the samples in the chart as guides.

BIBLIOGRAPHY ENTRIES FOR DIFFERENT SOURCES

Kind of Source	Bibliography Entry
Book with one author	Ions, Veronica. Indian Mythology. London: Paul Hamlyn Limited, 1967.
Book with two authors	Stern, Jane and Stern, Michael. Amazing America. New York: Random House, 1977.
Magazine article (signed)	Johnson, Marguerite. "Delay with Diplomacy." Time, May 18, 1981, p. 30.
Magazine article (unsigned)	"Toys for Tots." Time, December 14, 1981, p. 68.
Encyclopedia article (signed)	The World Book Encyclopedia, 1981 ed., "Berlin, Irving," by Ethan Mordden.
Encyclopedia article (unsigned)	The Random House Encyclopedia, 1977 ed., "Hollywood."

A Unified Report. The overall structure of a report will generally be very similar to that of an essay. A complete report should include a title, an introduction that ends with the main point of the report (the thesis statement), two or more body paragraphs, and a conclusion. In addition a report should contain footnotes giving credit to information from sources as well as a bibliography. All of these parts should work together to present the information that you have gathered in a clear and unified report on your topic.

> A report is a unified paper on a single topic, based on information gathered from research. It has a title, an introduction with a thesis statement, a body, a conclusion, footnotes, and a bibliography.

Your report should not be simply a collection of all the information you have found in your research. Rather, it should be a unified paper that clearly presents your understanding of or opinions about the topic. Every piece of information that you present in the report should support and develop the main point stated in your thesis statement. The title and the introduction should help to lead up to the main point. The body of the report should present subtopics in a logical way in order to develop the main point clearly. The conclusion should tie the whole discussion together by referring to the main point. The footnotes and bibliography should tell the reader how much research has gone into developing your main point.

The following report on Brazil illustrates the features and structure that you should keep in mind as you prepare a report.

Title	Brazil: The Growing Republic
Introduction	Brazil, the fifth largest country in the world, covers nearly half of South America and contains nearly half the population of the continent along with an untold wealth of natural resources.[1] In a sense Brazil is two different countries. Most of its population is concentrated in the east along a narrow coastal strip, while the vast jungles and plains of the interior remain, for the most part, unexplored and unpopulated. During

the twentieth century, however, Brazil has made significant technological and economic progress and has begun to develop the resources of its vast interior. Both the country's rate of industrial growth and its agricultural potential are soon likely to thrust Brazil into the role of a major world power.

Thesis statement with two subtopics

Subtopic 1: industrial rate of growth

Brazil possesses enormous industrial potential. A wealth of minerals lies untouched under the Guiana highlands in the northern part of the country.[2] The country also has tremendous potential for hydroelectric power, largely because of the Amazon River, which could make Brazil a major producer of electricity. In addition the mining state of Minas Gerais contains nearly ten percent of the world's iron supply, and the huge Amazon forest contains a giant supply of wood that could be cut and exported.[3]

Brazil is beginning to take advantage of its industrial potential. Sao Paulo, the largest city in Brazil, hosts a wide range of industries and at present accounts for one third of the nation's income.[4] Yet other cities are catching up with Sao Paulo. According to Herbert Wendt, "in the past decade a number of major steel plants have been built in Minas Gerais in the vicinity of Santos."[5] And as the people of Brazil become better educated and trained, industrial growth will continue. Volkswagen, Incorporated, already manufactures cars in Brazil because the country has a healthy market for cars and because Brazilians are improving their skills in manufacturing.[6]

Subtopic 2: agricultural potential

Agriculture in Brazil has also grown rapidly. Brazil's great range of climates allows a variety of crops such as beans, cacao, cassava, and corn to be grown. And Brazil is so large that although only about two percent of the land is cultivated, the country produces more than a third of the world's coffee and half of South America's bananas, as well as large quantities of cotton, sugar cane, and rice.[7]

Conclusion Brazil, therefore, has the potential to become a major industrial and agricultural power. To do this the nation must continue to develop its vast undeveloped interior. So far the Brazilian government and people have worked with great determination and have achieved remarkable results in a very short time.

---

[1]National Geographic Atlas, 1975 ed., "Brazil."

[2]The Random House Encyclopedia, 1977 ed., "Brazil."

[3]National Geographic Atlas, "Brazil."

[4]Rose Brown, The Land and People of Brazil, p. 64.

[5]Herbert Wendt, The Red, White, and Black Continent, p. 421.

[6]The Random House Encyclopedia, "Brazil."

[7]The Random House Encyclopedia, "Brazil."

BIBLIOGRAPHY

Brown, Rose. The Land and People of Brazil. Philadelphia: J.B. Lippincott Company, 1972.

National Geographic Atlas, 1975 ed., "Brazil."

The Random House Encyclopedia, 1977 ed., "Brazil."

Wendt, Herbert. The Red, White, and Black Continent. Garden City, N.Y.: Doubleday and Company, Inc., 1966.

The World Book Encyclopedia, 1981 ed., "Brazil," by Manoel Cardozo.

EXERCISE A: Examining a Report. Read the report on Brazil again and then answer the following questions.

1. How many footnotes does the report contain? *7*
2. Which footnotes refer to facts and ideas? Which footnote is used for a quotation? *1–4, 6–7/5*

3. How many entries are listed in the bibliography? In what order are they listed? *5/alphabetical order*
4. What kinds of sources has the author used?
5. What are two additional sources on Brazil that your school library or local public library contains? List them as bibliography entries.

4. books, encyclopedias, atlas 5. Answers will vary but should follow bibliography form.

Preparing a Report

Now that you are familiar with the special features and the general structure of a report, you can begin to plan and write one of your own. Following a few special steps can help you carry out your planning and your research.

Finding a Good Topic. A good topic for a report is one that appeals to you and one for which you can find solid information. Thus, in looking for a topic, you should think about your own interests and check to see what sources are available in the library.

> For a report, choose a topic that interests you and one for which you can find at least three good sources of information.

Since preparing a report means searching for information, you will probably work best if you choose a topic that arouses your curiosity. Look for a topic that you already know something about but that you would like to know even more about. If your topic is too general, you can use the sources in the library to see how your topic might be narrowed down to more specific topics that you could cover in a report. Then, you can check further to see how much information you can find on one of these smaller topics.

In the library you can look up your topic in encyclopedias, the card catalog, and *The Readers' Guide to Periodical Literature.* The encyclopedias will give you general information and suggest ideas for more specific topics if you need them. The card catalog will tell you what books the library has on a number of subjects. It will also list subcategories of larger subjects. *The Read-*

ers' Guide will list magazine articles on a number of topics. Using these sources and your own imagination, find a topic that you want to write about and that you can cover in your report. Then you can use the same general sources to see if there is enough information about your topic. You should be able to locate at least three different sources for your topic. Try to find five or six. If possible, you should also gather information from different kinds of sources. In addition to encyclopedias and other books, try to use magazines as well.

Making Bibliography Cards. To help keep track of the books and articles that you find, you should make a bibliography card for each of your sources.

> For every book or article that you plan to use, make a bibliography card that lists the information you will need to know about each source.

Even before you begin to read through your sources, you should make a bibliography card for each of them. You can prepare many of your cards directly from the card catalog or *The Readers' Guide.* Your bibliography cards should list the call number and complete publishing information for each book and article that you plan to use. Making these cards will help you keep your research in order as you gather more and more information. The cards will also give you the information that you will need when you write your footnotes and bibliography. The following chart offers guidelines for preparing bibliography cards.

GUIDELINES FOR PREPARING BIBLIOGRAPHY CARDS

1. Use one note card for each source.
2. On each card write all of the information that you will need when you write the bibliography entry.
3. In addition, write down the call number, if the source has one, so you can find the source in the library.
4. Finally, note whether or not the source includes any illustrations or charts that you might want to use.

Taking Notes from Your Sources. Now that you have a good idea of the sources available to you, you can begin to gather your information.

Begin your research by jotting down several questions about your topic and writing a rough thesis statement. Then use these to decide what to focus on when you take notes from your sources.

Your research will go more smoothly if you do some planning before you actually start reading and taking notes. Jot down four or five questions about your topic that you think your report should answer. In addition, think about a main point you might want to develop in your report. Write down a rough thesis statement expressing this main point. Your research will now have a focus that can help you to take meaningful notes as you read your sources.

The following chart suggests how you can set up a good system for note-taking.

SUGGESTIONS FOR TAKING NOTES

1. Take notes on note cards, using one card for each aspect of your topic in each book or article.
2. In the upper left-hand corner of each card, write the author and title of the source as well as any other information that may be useful.
3. In the upper right-hand corner, write a subject heading that describes the information on that card.
4. Be sure to note the page number for each quotation, idea, or fact that you write down on your card. Record quotations exactly using quotation marks.
5. Keep the note cards from each source together, organized by subject headings.

Begin your note-taking with the source that seems to cover your topic most fully. Skim the material first, and then read it carefully and take notes on it. Each source might talk about several aspects of your topic, so plan to make several different note cards for each book or article you read. From some sources you might want to take exact quotations and other detailed notes. From others all you may need are short summaries. Use your own judgment, but try to limit your notes mainly to items that are related to the questions you have written about your topic and the rough thesis statement you have prepared.

The following sample note cards for a report on Halley's Comet show notes taken from two different sources.

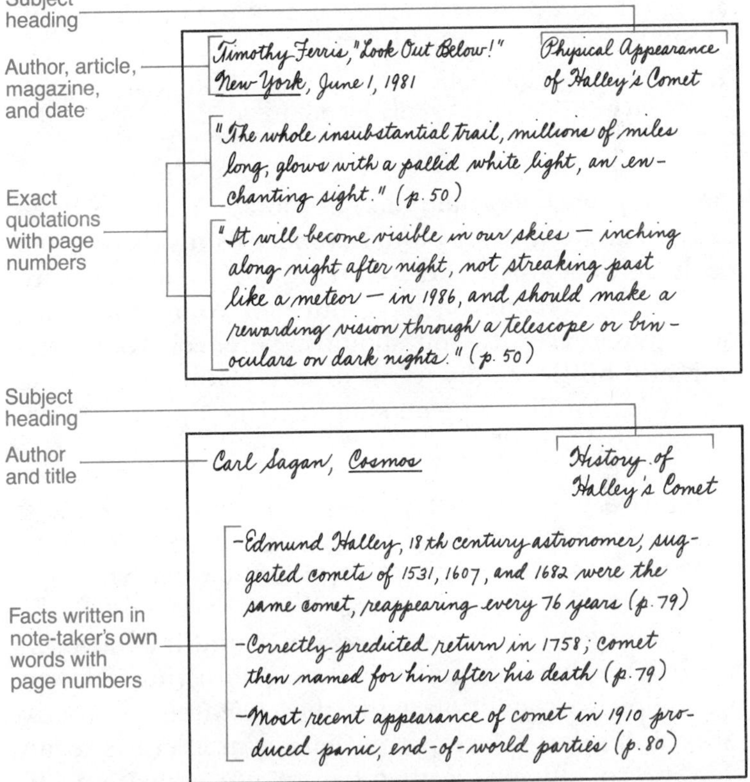

Organizing the Report. After you have found the information you need, you must arrange it to develop your main point logically.

Find a logical order for your information and write a modified outline for the body of your report.

The following chart will help you to put your information together. You may also want to study or review the information on organizing an essay in Chapter 29 since the steps are very much the same.

STEPS FOR ORGANIZING A REPORT

1. Looking at your note cards, decide on the major aspects of your main point that you want to develop in your report. These will be your subtopics.
2. Group your note cards according to your subtopics.
3. Decide on a logical order for presenting the subtopics and the information under each.
4. Write a modified outline that shows the organization of the body of your report by subtopic.

Writing and Revising the Report. You are now ready to write a draft of your report using the outline you have developed and following the basic structure of an essay. When you have finished your first draft, check and revise it. You should also check your footnotes and bibliography to make sure you have used the correct forms. Finally, you should write a polished version of your report.

Using your outline, write a first draft of your report with footnotes and a bibliography. Check and revise what you have written, and write a clean, final copy.

As you write your report, keep in mind the basic essay structure you are following: an interesting title, an interesting introduction with thesis statement, body paragraphs that develop the thesis statement, and an effective conclusion. Remember to use transitions to link your ideas throughout the report. When you have finished a first draft complete with footnotes and bibliography, take a look at the checklist for revising an essay on page 632. The following questions will also help you to revise your report.

CHECKLIST FOR REVISING A REPORT

1. Does your report include footnotes from at least three different sources?
2. Are all quotations, borrowed ideas, and little-known facts clearly credited?
3. Do your footnotes follow the appropriate form?
4. Are all sources listed correctly in the bibliography?
5. Is your bibliography in alphabetical order?

EXERCISE B: Finding a Topic and Preparing Bibliography Cards. Choose one of the following general topics or make up a general topic of your own. Then narrow it down to a topic suitable for a report. Finally, find at least three possible sources of information in the library, and make a bibliography card for each source. *At this point you might also want to establish a schedule for completing the various steps in writing the report.*

Aviation
Cartoons
Language
The Olympics
Musicians/Composers
American customs
Local history
Predatory animals
Astronomy
Women in sports

EXERCISE C: Taking Notes and Organizing the Report. After preparing a few questions and a rough thesis statement, take notes on each source that you have found in Exercise B. Make different cards for the different parts of your topic. Group your cards according to subtopics, and find a logical organization for your information. Then write a modified outline for the body of your report. *Before students begin outlining, you might check that each card has notes on only one subject, which is identified in a subheading.*

EXERCISE D: Drafting and Revising Your Report. Using your note cards and outline, write a first draft of your report including footnotes and a bibliography. Revise your report following the checklists on page 632 and on this page. Then write a final copy of your report and proofread it to catch any errors added in recopying. *Students might exchange first drafts, suggest revisions, and then later exchange final copies for a second proofreading.*

APPLICATION: Evaluating a Report. Exchange reports from Exercise D with another student. Read the other paper carefully, and answer the following questions.

1. How many footnotes does the paper contain?
2. What kinds of sources (books, magazines, and so on) have been used?
3. Are all the footnotes complete and correct?
4. How many sources has the writer used in all?
5. Are all the bibliography entries complete and correct?
6. What is the thesis statement? What are its subtopics?
7. How many body paragraphs are used to develop each of the subtopics in the report?
8. What logical order is used to arrange the subtopics in the report?
9. What are the strong points of the report?
10. What improvements could be made?

Answers will vary. The class might evaluate one or two reports as a group before students evaluate individual reports.

30.2 Writing Book Reports

When you are asked to write a *book report,* what should you include? Book reports come in many different forms, but most contain a few basic features designed to give the reader a good understanding of the book. This section will discuss the basic features of book reports and give you some specific things to think about when you write them.

■ The Basic Features of a Book Report

The book reports you write will probably vary depending on the kind of book you are writing about and the requirements of your teacher. Every book report you write, however, needs to have several basic features. It should identify the book by title and author, and it should give the reader some idea of the contents of the book. It should also show your understanding of the book by focusing on some elements of the book that particularly interest you. Finally, it should give some idea of how you feel about the book. Although these features can be arranged in many different ways, a simple three-part format covers all of the basic features.

> One particularly useful format for a **book report** has the following three parts: an introduction that identifies the book and gives a short summary of it, body paragraphs that focus on specific elements of the book, and a conclusion that makes a recommendation.

When you write a book report, you should generally assume that your reader has not read the book you are discussing. Therefore, it makes sense to begin by clearly identifying the book by title and author. You should also give your reader some idea of what the book is about. If you are writing about a work of nonfiction, you can simply mention the subject of the book. If you are discussing a novel, you should mention that the book is a work of fiction and give a capsule version of the story in a sentence or two.

Once you have given your reader some background information, you can present a few thoughtful ideas or opinions about the book and support them with evidence from the book itself. You can usually explore any of a number of topics, especially if you are writing about fiction. Every work of literature has certain basic elements, such as characters and setting. Since you will probably use one or more of these elements in the book reports you write, you can benefit from taking a few moments to become more familiar with them now. The following chart lists and briefly explains some of the most important elements you will find in books, particularly in fiction. There are other topics—for instance, a book's language—that you can also write about.

IMPORTANT ELEMENTS IN BOOKS	
Element	**Explanation**
Theme	A general truth or observation about life—the author's main point. It might not be stated directly in the book, but it is the idea that holds the work together.
Character	A person in a story. Characters are presented to the reader through their actions, dialogue, other characters' reactions to them, and sometimes through the author's comments on them.
Plot	The planned ordering of events in a story. The plot usually involves some *conflict,* a problem or struggle faced by the characters in the story. The conflict builds toward a *climax,* or turning point, when the conflict is resolved.
Setting	The time and place of the story. A story might take place in the past, present, or future. It might be set in a particular area of this country or in another country of even in another galaxy.

After you have discussed different elements of the book, it makes sense to give your own opinion of the book as a whole. This can be done in a concluding paragraph.

The following is a book report on the novel *Watership Down* by Richard Adams. After a short introductory paragraph, the book report focuses on two different elements of the novel. The book report then concludes with a paragraph that gives an evaluation of the book as a whole.

Report on *Watership Down*

Introduction

Watership Down, a fantasy novel by Richard Adams, follows the heroic struggles of a group of rabbits who journey through unknown territory in search of a new home. Along the way the rabbit characters must fight against overwhelming difficulties and danger.

First element

One of the most interesting things in the story is the way in which all of the rabbits work together to achieve their goal. The value of cooperation is stressed throughout. All of the rabbits seem to understand how they can best serve the group. The hero Hazel uses his courage and resourcefulness to lead the other rabbits to their new home. Even though he is not the largest rabbit, the others recognize that he is their leader. Bigwig, the largest rabbit, is clearly the best fighter, but he soon accepts his position as Hazel's lieutenant. Blackberry, the smartest rabbit, is given the job of figuring out strategy at various points in the journey. Fiver, Hazel's brother, is a small, weak rabbit, but he has the gift of second sight and so is regarded as the group's prophet. All of these individual rabbits and their companions are united by a deep sense of community, an instinct that goes beyond self-preservation.

Second element

The author also gives the reader a feeling for the special society of the rabbits by creating a special language for them. For example, *frith* means "sun," "day," and "God" to the rabbits while its opposite, *inle,* means "moon," "night," and "death." To *silflay* means to feed above ground, one of the rabbits' favorite activities. This language makes the book come alive. The reader soon begins to think in a kind of rabbit language. The special language also makes the adventures more believable.

Conclusion

It is difficult to put this book down after living through a few of these gripping rabbit adventures. By sympathizing with the struggles of the rabbit characters in *Watership Down,* the reader may even develop a feeling of kinship with real-life rabbits.

EXERCISE A: Examining a Book Report. Read the book report on *Watership Down* on pages 650 and 651 again carefully, and then write the answers to the following questions on your paper.

1. Where does the writer of the book report identify the title, the author, and the basic content of the novel? *first paragraph*
2. What elements of the novel do the two body paragraphs focus on? *theme/language*
3. What specific pieces of support are used in each body paragraph?
4. What is the writer's opinion of the book as a whole? *positive*
5. Would you like to read this novel? Why or why not? *Answers will vary. Students might present opinions in a class discussion.*

3. the roles of four specific rabbits in the society/the use of three words of the rabbit language

Preparing a Book Report

Writing a book report involves many of the same steps that writing an essay does. You will need to plan your report and organize it. After drafting your report, you will need to revise it. When you write a book report, however, you must begin by choosing the elements of the book you wish to examine, deciding what you want to say about each of the elements, and then finding appropriate support in the book itself to develop your ideas.

> In writing a book report, find something to say about the elements in the book, develop your ideas with specific information from the book, and then follow the basic steps for organizing, writing, and revising an essay.

The following chart shows some of the questions you can use to examine the various elements in a book as you plan your report. The answers to your questions should give you ideas for the body paragraphs of your report.

QUESTIONS FOR EXAMINING THE ELEMENTS OF BOOKS
Theme
1. In what way has the book changed your mind about something or made you see something in a new light? 2. What do you think the author's purpose was in writing the book? 3. What general idea seemed to hold the book together?
Character
1. Which character is your favorite? Why? 2. Which character did you like least? Why? 3. In what special ways did any of the characters change?
Plot
1. What was the most amusing, exciting, or moving incident in the book? 2. What was the major problem faced by the characters? 3. How did the writer create suspense?
Setting
1. What influence did the time or place of the story have on the plot and characters? 2. Would you like to live in the world created in the book? Why or why not? 3. Was the setting believable?

Once you have decided which elements you want to write about and what you want to say about them, you should gather supporting information. In order to develop your ideas, you should look through the book you have read for specific information: examples, details, incidents, and statements made by the author or the characters. If you are discussing theme, for instance, you might mention specific ideas about characters, plot, setting, or language since all of these elements can help to present the book's central idea. If your topic involves a character, you should look for examples of the character's thoughts, words, and actions. If you are focusing on plot, you could look at how events are related to each other in the story.

You should be able to find plenty of support for your ideas. Try to select the most interesting and significant information. If you decide to quote a description or something that a character says, write the words from the book exactly, enclose the statement in quotation marks, and indicate in parentheses the page on which it appears.

Once you have chosen your support and organized it, you can write your first draft. The first paragraph should identify the book for your reader and say enough about it so that your report will make sense to someone who has not read the book. The next few paragraphs should discuss the elements you have chosen. The last paragraph should end the report by giving an evaluation.

When you have completed your first draft, revise your book report carefully. The following chart suggests a few questions that you might use to improve your first draft.

CHECKLIST FOR REVISING A BOOK REPORT

1. Is there additional information that you could include to make your ideas clearer?
2. Is there any unnecessary information that you could take out?
3. Are there any examples that would be better than the ones you have used?
4. If you have used quotations, are they accurate?
5. Are there any transitions that you could add to make the book report read more smoothly?
6. Are there any ways in which you could make the introduction and the conclusion to your book report clearer or more interesting?
7. Does the report contain any mistakes in grammar, usage, mechanics, or spelling?

EXERCISE B: Planning a Book Report. From the books that you have read recently, choose one that you would like to write about. Use the list of questions on page 653 to find something to say about at least two of the elements in the book. Find as much specific support in the book as you can, and then choose the best support. Finally, organize the information for your body paragraphs using a modified outline. *Students might work with partners, evaluating the work done for each of the steps listed in the exercise.*

EXERCISE C: Writing and Revising a Book Report. Write a first draft of your book report. Be sure that it includes all of the basic features discussed in this section. Then revise your book report using the checklist on page 654. Finally, make a clean copy, proofread it, and correct any mistakes that were added in recopying. *Students might exchange first drafts, suggest revisions, and later help each other proofread.*

APPLICATION: Evaluating a Book Report. Exchange book reports with another student. Read your partner's book report carefully, and answer the following questions. *Answers will vary. As suggested in Section 30.1, the class might evaluate one or two reports as a group before students evaluate individual reports.*

1. What elements in the book does the writer focus on?
2. Has the writer given you a good understanding of what the book is about? Does he or she tell you too much or too little about the book?
3. What does the writer think of the book?
4. Does the report make you want to read the book? Why or why not?
5. How could the report be improved?

Chapter 31

Writing Stories

You probably enjoy reading fiction—novels and short stories—more than any other type of literature. Since fiction is generally based on things that have happened or might happen in real life, you can often develop an almost personal relationship with the characters and events you read about. You will probably enjoy writing fiction as well, since fiction, more than almost any other form of writing, gives you a chance to make full use of your experiences, your knowledge of people, and your imagination.

Fiction usually grows out of characters. In fiction the personalities and actions of the characters are often used to present the writer's views about life to the readers. For this reason the first section in this chapter focuses on character sketches. You will have a chance to use your imagination to bring a character to life for your reader. In the second section, you will have a chance to expand your creative writing skills by writing *short* short stories with dialogue between different characters.

31.1 Writing a Character Sketch

A *character sketch* is very much like an artist's sketch. Instead of using paint, however, you must use words. The goal is to present a single dominant impression of a person through the use of a few well-chosen details.

Recognizing the Basic Features of a Character Sketch

To create an interesting picture of another person, you must give the reader a strong, single impression of your character.

> A **character sketch** should focus on a dominant impression of a person. It should use lively details and exact language to support this impression, and it should end with a strong concluding idea.

The subject of your sketch can be a person you know, a character you have read about, or someone you have created in your imagination. The only real requirement is that it be someone whom you can write about in a vivid way.

The sketch should center on your *dominant impression* of this person. The person might have some outstanding quality, or you might have a special feeling or idea about the character, which could become your dominant impression. Your sketch can develop this impression in several ways. Physical descriptions that go beyond simple height, weight, and hair color can help you reveal your character. The person's actions and words can also help develop the impression.

A character sketch does not need to have a specific introduction, body, and conclusion. But it *should* have a strong, definite direction. It should build up more and more revealing details that create a sharper and sharper picture. A "telling" final detail can help you make your character memorable to the reader.

The following character sketch develops an impression of a young woman with several examples, details, and one striking incident.

Dominant impression	Lucy Graham has had more hair-raising adventures than anyone else I have ever met.
Examples	With a quick smile and a toss of her curly, red hair, she will launch into the story of her latest escapade the minute anyone asks. Her

blue eyes flashing with memories, she will describe, without taking a breath, anything from her latest rock-climbing adventure to a white-water kayak race. Every weekend finds Lucy enjoying the excitement of the world she loves best—the outdoors.

Examples and details

Lucy's room is a monument to her life style. In the corner a gray backpack that smells of campfire smoke leans against worn hiking boots and a battered tent. The rest of her gear—cooking equipment, bicycle helmet, rain poncho, and more—is stashed in a closet too small to hold it. Each time the door is opened, a stray pan or flashlight escapes with a loud crash. On the walls colorful posters and carefully cut out magazine photographs of forests, mountains, and rushing rivers cover almost all of the paint, along with bumper stickers that proclaim the joys of rock climbing and hiking. Several well-marked books on wilderness survival line the bookshelf above the desk, which is covered with travel and adventure magazines.

Incident

To Lucy every chance to explore the outdoors is a learning experience. Each trip she takes, she learns something new about herself and what she can do. Once, because she had misjudged a river's length, a white-water canoe trip stretched for over ten long hours. Hungry and exhausted, Lucy missed seeing a rock hidden beneath the river's surface and was suddenly catapulted into the swiftly moving current. As she was swept downstream, she kept calm, remembering that she would be safest from rocks if she kept her feet aimed downstream. Bruised and battered, Lucy called on her last reserves of strength as the current carried her near a large boulder, which she grasped to pull herself to safety. It was a terrifying experience and one Lucy did not forget. She made sure not to make the same mistakes the next time she went canoeing on that river—the following weekend!

EXERCISE A: Recognizing a Good Character Sketch. Look through novels, short stories, and magazines for character sketches, and choose two examples. For each one write a few sentences about (1) the author's dominant impression of the character and (2) the kind of descriptive material used to develop this impression.
Students' findings might be shared in class discussion.

Choosing a Subject and Focusing Your Ideas

The first step in planning your own character sketch is choosing a subject.

Choose a character who really interests you and decide on the particular impression of that person that you want to express.

Before selecting a character to write about, think over a number of possibilities. Think about characters from literature as well as people you know in real life. Search your imagination for other characters who may not be real but who appeal to you for some reason. Try to find a character about whom you feel strongly. Strong feelings—either positive or negative—will help you find things to say about your character.

Once you have chosen your character, you should focus on *one* major idea about that person. Your dominant impression can be a special feeling that you have about the character. It can be an unusual trait of your character. It can even be a combination of the physical appearance and the personality of your subject. Whatever your impression, it should be something *specific*. Never simply say that your character is "interesting" or "exciting" or "admirable." Instead, give your reader a clear idea of what makes your subject special.

WEAK IMPRESSION: My aunt is the most interesting person I know.

STRONGER IMPRESSION: Aunt Thelma was never willing to accept an obvious explanation.

EXERCISE B: Choosing a Character. Choose a real or imaginary character, using the following items as suggestions. Identify an outstanding characteristic of the person and write one or two sentences introducing the character and expressing a dominant impression.

Selected students might read their sentences aloud while the other students try to identify the dominant impressions.

1. A distant friend
2. A mysterious stranger
3. A memorable character from a book or play
4. A well-known person in your city or home town
5. Yourself (from another person's point of view)

Developing and Organizing Your Sketch

You can now begin to develop your sketch.

List physical details, incidents, and other information that will help develop the dominant impression you have chosen for your character. Then arrange your ideas in an order that will help your reader see the character vividly.

In much the same way that you prepare paragraphs and essays, you can brainstorm for information to support your character sketch. The following chart lists a few additional ideas that can help you develop support.

IDEAS FOR DEVELOPING A CHARACTER SKETCH
1. Describe the person's physical characteristics, including clothing, movements, and facial expressions, if these are particularly interesting.
2. Mention important facts about your character's past.
3. Use the character's own words if these help you focus on an aspect of the character's personality.
4. Describe the character's opinions and typical activities.
5. Show the character in action.
6. Describe your own and other people's feelings toward the character.

After you have listed a number of ideas, sort and arrange them. Look over your list and weed out the less effective or less important details. You should now be ready to arrange your best supporting items into a character sketch that will clearly present your dominant impression to the reader. If you want to show the character's development over time, chronological order will probably work best. On the other hand, if your sketch includes examples and details about your subject's appearance, habits, or ideas, the best way of organizing the support might be by order of importance. For example, if you were describing different habits of your character, you might plan three paragraphs, each describing a different habit of your subject, with the most unusual habit of all in the final paragraph.

EXERCISE C: Developing a Character Sketch. Beneath the dominant impression you wrote in Exercise B, list as many supporting details as you can think of, including physical details, incidents, and other information that supports your dominant impression. Eliminate weaker items, and arrange your information in the order most likely to produce a vivid picture for your reader.

Students might exchange papers, try to identify the orders used, and offer general suggestions.

Writing and Revising Your Sketch

You are now ready to begin your first draft of the sketch. While you write, you should concentrate on making your subject come alive on paper. Assume that the reader does not know your character. Your task is to make your character into a recognizable and familiar individual.

Use vivid language as you draft your character sketch. Then make any changes that will strengthen your sketch.

Because your purpose is to create a sharp picture of your subject, you must choose words that will let your reader see your character as you see him or her. Use strong action verbs, specific nouns, and lively modifiers as you write. You might also want to review the sections on word choice on pages 516–527.

When you have completed your first draft, reread it. Then make improvements wherever you can. The following checklist should help.

CHECKLIST FOR REVISING A CHARACTER SKETCH

1. Could your opening sentence establish a sharper impression of the person?
2. What additional details might strengthen your impression?
3. Would another arrangement of details make your sketch clearer or more interesting for your reader?
4. Are there places where more vivid word choices could be used to help make your subject come to life?
5. Is there any better way of closing your sketch?
6. Are there any mistakes in grammar, usage, mechanics, or spelling?

When you have made all the improvements you can, write a final copy. Then proofread your sketch to catch any errors added in recopying.

EXERCISE D: Writing a Character Sketch. Using the list you developed in Exercise C, write a first draft of your character sketch. Then revise your draft, using the checklist on this page. Finally, write a clean copy and proofread it to catch any errors added in recopying.

Before students begin writing, you might have them give examples of strong and weak descriptions.

APPLICATION: Evaluating a Character Sketch. Write another character sketch, following the steps you learned in this section. Then exchange sketches with another student, and answer the following questions. Finally, revise your own sketch, taking into consideration your partner's comments.

After the evaluations have been completed, students might discuss which kinds of improvements were suggested most often.

1. What is the dominant impression of the sketch? Could it be established more sharply?
2. Should the sketch have included more details? What kinds?
3. Are the writer's feelings about the person clear? What are they?
4. What, if anything, would have made the sketch more interesting to you?
5. Could the language be more vivid? Where?

Writing a Short Short Story 31.2

Just as a character sketch is like a picture, a *short short story* is like a short but complete scene in a movie. A short short story introduces a character or characters involved in an interesting or difficult situation. Then it shows what happens as a result of the characters' words or actions.

Recognizing the Basic Features of a Short Short Story

A short short story must include a number of different features in order to be convincing.

A **short short story** should describe characters and setting clearly, present and resolve a conflict, be told from a consistent point of view, follow a chronological order, and include dialogue where appropriate.

Characters and setting are the basic elements of any short short story. As you did in your character sketch, you will need to see these people and places in your mind and find ways of making them come alive for the reader.

The action in a short short story is usually based on some central *conflict,* or problem, that must be resolved. The conflict is usually between two or more characters, but it can also be within one character. The characters should think and act in order to work out the conflict.

In writing a short short story, you will also have to make a choice about who is telling the story. The teller of the story is called the *narrator*. The way in which the narrator tells the story is called the *point of view*. You can choose to tell the story through a first-person or "I" narrator, as if you were a character and the story were happening to you. Or you might use a third-person narrator, who does not take part in the story but is able to tell about one or several characters' thoughts as well as their actions. Whichever point of view you use, it must remain consistent throughout the story.

The following two passages tell the same story, first from a first-person point of view and then from a third-person point of view. Note the differences between the two points of view.

Passage with a first-person narrator	I walked into the cottage and saw that no one was home. Well, this didn't look too promising. Then I noticed that everything was covered with millions of coarse brown hairs. I definitely was not looking forward to meeting these people. Worst of all, there were three of everything—beds, chairs, bowls of porridge, you name it. I hate the number three. It always means that something weird is going to happen to me.
Passage with a third-person narrator	Goldilocks entered the cottage and soon realized that no one was home. This made her very uncomfortable. Then she noticed the coarse brown hairs that covered every inch of the room and wondered what sort of people lived there. But she was most upset by the fact that everything was in sets of three—three beds, three chairs, three bowls of porridge. Goldilocks had always hated the number three. She believed that it brought her bad luck.

Whatever the point of view, most short short stories will follow a chronological order, showing the action as it unfolds. Transitions such as *next, then, later,* and *soon* can help you show the order of events as well as the passing of time.

Finally, a short short story often includes dialogue between the characters. Dialogue helps to make both the events and the people involved in them more vivid.

The following short short story with a first-person narrator shows how these different elements work together.

First-person narrator

Character's actions and thoughts

Explanation of conflict

When a note was brought into my algebra class requesting my immediate appearance in the principal's office, my mouth became paste, my palms got wet, and my heart fluttered. As I walked the long, long corridors to the main office, my mind jumped back a week to April Fool's Day. Surely no one knew that I was the one who had rearranged the lane markers in the swimming pool so that they looked like a huge duck. I had done it after swim practice—who had seen me?

Dialogue

Finally, I reached the office. Mrs. Coveney, the secretary, looked at me over her glasses and said, "Have a seat, please. Mrs. Howard will be with you shortly." She was missing her normal friendly smile.

Description

Minutes ticked by on the large oak regulator clock as my world hung suspended. At last the door to the principal's office opened, and Mrs. Howard signaled for me to come into her office. She sat. I sat. Another moment passed. Then she broke the silence.

Dialogue

"Gerald," she began. Her voice locked my attention. "Gerald, the faculty is planning a little surprise party in honor of Mr. Burdett, who, as you probably know, is retiring after twenty years of coaching the swimming team."

Did she know? I searched her face for a hint of sarcasm. Nothing. She went on.

"So. We've decided to ask you, as a member of the team, to organize a committee to decorate the pool for the party. Can you manage that without his knowledge, do you think?"

Character's thoughts

What was going on here? Was she trying to trick me into a confession? I decided to stay innocent until proven guilty. I would go down fighting.

Dialogue

"Uh, sure. I'd be happy to." And I waited for the blow to fall.

It didn't. She just handed me a folded paper and said, smiling, "Fine. Now, I've jotted down a few of the things we have in mind for the party. Take a look when you get a chance." She nodded for me to go.

Character's actions and thoughts

Resolution

Relieved, I walked out of the office. This had certainly been a close one. But I had made it. In the safety of the hall, I smiled. Decorations? They probably want a bunch of crepe-paper streamers and other junk. Then I took a look at the sheet. This is what it said:

Dear Gerald,

Be good to your school.
Don't mess with the pool.
(Next time *won't* be cool.)

April Fool.

Sincerely,
Mrs. Howard

EXERCISE A: Examining a Short Short Story. Find a short short story in a book or magazine. Then answer the following questions.

This might be done as a class exercise first, using a story from a literature text.

1. Who are the characters?
2. What is the central conflict and how is it resolved?
3. From what point of view is the story told?
4. What transitions are used to guide the reader through the events of the story?
5. What role does dialogue play in the story?

Planning and Organizing Your Short Short Story

Writing a short short story calls for a good deal of creativity. Whether you make up the entire story or tell about something that really happened, you must think through the whole story in advance. The rest of this section suggests some steps you can follow to plan and write a story.

Deciding on Characters, Setting, Conflict, and Point of View. You can begin by letting your imagination take over. Has something happened to you that you can develop into a story? Is there a setting that seems ripe with possibilities? Can you imagine two or more characters—a customer and a clerk, two drivers, or two neighbors—involved in an interesting conflict?

Brainstorm for ideas about interesting characters, settings, and conflicts. When you know what story you will tell, choose the point of view you will use.

If you have a clear idea of either the characters, setting, or conflict, you can begin to fill in the other elements. Use your own experiences and those of people you know as ideas. Maybe you remember two customers arguing over a piece of merchandise. Or maybe a favorite family story can give you ideas for your own story. Your point of view is likely to grow naturally out of your choices of characters, setting, and conflict. Do you see yourself as a character in the story, or will you tell the story as a narrator removed from the story?

Developing and Shaping Your Story. Once you have a specific story in mind, you should list the key events of the story and begin thinking of specific details to enliven the story.

Make a chronological list of events and then brainstorm for specific details that will make the characters and happenings in your story come alive for the reader.

At this point you should give your story flesh and bones. Jot down the main things that happen, especially the actions of your characters. Then try to list as many details about the characters and the setting as you can. Just as you listed details for a character sketch, you should think of physical characteristics, gestures, expressions, or thoughts that will help the reader visualize and get to know your characters. Try to make the setting of your story clear by using revealing details, sights, sounds, and smells to capture the exact place.

Once you have a number of details to enliven your story, you will need to find a place for them in your outline of events. Although you will want to set the scene and sketch the characters at the beginning, be sure to save some details for later to give your reader a feeling of greater and greater understanding.

EXERCISE B: Choosing the Story You Will Tell. Think of ten different characters, five specific settings, and five conflicts or problems that need to be resolved. Then choose two or three characters, one specific setting, and one appropriate conflict. Decide what point of view you will use. Then develop an outline of events. Finally, brainstorm for specific details and add them to your outline in appropriate places. *In developing the items required in the first sentence, students might work with partners or in small groups.*

Using Dialogue to Show Character and Develop the Plot

Dialogue is not necessary in all short short stories. It can, however, add interest if you use it well.

> If you write dialogue for your characters, choose words and phrases that suit each personality and make sure that the dialogue helps move the action forward.

Dialogue breathes life into your characters when the words that you place in their mouths sound like things these people would actually say. An older person's words will be different from those of a ten year old. A police officer's phrasing is likely to differ greatly from that of a disc jockey. The situation can also have an effect on a character's words. If your character is nervous about something, for example, you should write dialogue that sounds anxious. Even slang and jargon may be appropriate if they are truly connected to the characters who use them.

Notice the difference between the following examples of dialogue, both written as the words of a young child who has just been scolded.

UNNATURAL: "It was truly an accident. The trash bag is enormous and I have difficulty handling it."

MORE NATURAL: "Okay, I'm sorry. But it wasn't my fault. The dumb bag is too big."

Dialogue should also contribute to the ongoing action of a story. You can use it to show the characters trying to resolve their problems. Or you can use it to help draw the reader from one event to the next. In the story about the April Fool's prank, the dialogue between the principal and the main character is an important part of the action. It shows the conflict between Gerald and the principal. It builds suspense, gives Gerald a false feeling of relief, and prepares the reader for Mrs. Howard's own April Fool's joke.

As you write dialogue, make sure the words of different characters are separated into different short paragraphs. You might also review the material on quotations in Section 18.6.

EXERCISE C: Developing a Short Short Story with Dialogue. Using the outline you prepared in Exercise B, decide on at least one place where dialogue might help to develop the characters or carry the action. Write three to five short paragraphs of dialogue, trying to make your characters sound as natural as possible.

To test for realistic dialogue, students might read samples aloud, with different students taking different characters' lines.

Writing and Revising Your Short Short Story

With an outline of events that shows where you will include description and dialogue, you can begin to write your short short story. When you have finished the first draft of your story, revise it thoroughly, and make a final copy.

Following your basic plan, write your first draft. Use a consistent point of view, and make your characters act, talk, and think to resolve the conflict. Then revise your draft using a checklist.

Writing the first draft gives you a chance to put all the parts together. Drafting your story should be fun. Play with your descriptions and dialogue. Try different ways to sharpen them and make them interesting. Do not be afraid to experiment with language, but remember to keep your story's point of view consistent. Add and take out events in your story line if such changes will help hold the reader's interest. Try not to leave out any necessary information, and make sure that the ending grows naturally out of the story.

When you read over your story, you may find many things to improve. Reading it aloud is a particularly good way to find awkward phrases, unnatural dialogue, and other weak spots. The following checklist can also help.

CHECKLIST FOR REVISING A SHORT SHORT STORY

1. Are the characters and setting clearly described? Will the reader see them as you do?
2. Have you presented and resolved some interesting conflict or problem?
3. Have you kept a consistent point of view throughout?
4. Does any dialogue you have included help make the story interesting and realistic?
5. Will the ending of your story leave the reader satisfied?

EXERCISE D: Writing a Short Short Story. Using the outline and dialogue you have developed, write the first draft of your short short story. Then use the preceding checklist to revise your work. Finally, write a clean copy and proofread it. *Students might exchange first drafts, identify characters, setting, conflict, and point of view, and suggest any revisions needed.*

APPLICATION: Writing and Evaluating a Short Short Story. Choose one of the following ideas or make up one of your own. Then write a short short story, following the steps you have learned in this section. When you have finished and revised your draft, write a final copy and exchange stories with another student. Finally, write a brief evaluation of your partner's story, identifying the conflict and point of view and commenting on the strongest and weakest parts of the story. *To evaluate the stories, students might also refer to the checklist on page 670 and check that correct paragraph indentations and punctuation are used for dialogue.*

1. A baby sitter encounters unusual children
2. A young person tries to gather enough courage to ask someone to dance
3. A family of very strong individuals has a hard time finding a vacation plan that will suit everyone
4. Two friends argue over reporting a possible UFO sighting
5. Confusion reigns in a school during a power blackout

Chapter 32

Writing Letters

In your school life and your personal life, you may often have to write letters. To be a good letter writer, you should know what special parts you must include in different kinds of letters, and you should practice writing letters that serve a number of different purposes.

This chapter will first show you the main parts of *friendly letters, social notes,* and *business letters*. It will then give you a chance to practice writing all three kinds of letters.

32.1 Looking at Friendly Letters, Social Notes, and Business Letters

A clear form is important to any letter. Both personal letters and business letters should have certain expected parts. In addition, each should follow a consistent style.

Setting Up Friendly Letters and Social Notes

There are many different reasons for writing a friendly letter or a social note: to correspond with a friend, to offer an invitation, to accept or decline an invitation, to offer congratulations, or to offer sympathy. Whatever your purpose in writing, you should include certain basic parts and follow a consistent style to make the letter look neat and orderly. In addition, the letter should be folded and the envelope prepared in a proper fashion.

The Basic Parts of a Friendly Letter or Social Note. To write a personal letter, you must be familiar with its five basic parts.

> A **friendly letter** or **social note** should include a heading, a salutation, a body, a closing, and a signature.

The *heading* should include your own address and the date on which you write the letter. The first line should contain your street address. The second line should contain your city or town, state, and ZIP code. The date on which you write the letter should appear in the third line.

HEADINGS:

141 Dogwood Drive
Clearwater, New York 11794
December 14, 1981

120 North 14th Street, Apt. 4A
Phoenix, Arizona 85005
May 20, 1982

The *salutation* is the part that greets your reader. You should generally use a formal salutation if you are not very familiar with the person to whom you are writing or if he or she is older than you. For a friend or close relative, you may want to use an informal salutation. Note in the following examples that a comma comes after each salutation.

FORMAL SALUTATIONS:	Dear Thomas,	Dear Mrs. Henry,
	Dear Uncle Ed,	Dear Ms. Ryan,
LESS FORMAL SALUTATIONS:	My good friend,	Hi, Brian,
	Hello, pal,	Greetings,

The *body* is the main part of your letter. In it you should write your basic message. You might share personal information with a friend, you might invite people to a party, or you might give any of a number of other kinds of information. Depending on the kind of information you wish to send, the body of your letter can vary in length. In a letter to a friend, the body may be several pages long. In an invitation the body will generally contain only a few sentences giving such things as the date and the location.

The *closing* of your letter should tell the reader that the message is finished. It may be only one word, or it may be a brief phrase. Note in the following examples that the first word of a closing is capitalized and that the closing is followed by a comma.

CLOSINGS:	My best wishes,	Love,
	Sincerely,	Very truly yours,

The *signature* signals the end of the letter. In writing your signature, you should use the name that the reader normally uses to address you. Always write your signature in ink, even if you have typed the rest of the letter.

You may also include a sixth part—an *R.S.V.P.*—in a letter of invitation. This abbreviation tells the reader to respond soon so that you will know if he or she plans to attend.

Two Styles for Friendly Letters and Social Notes. To set up your friendly letters and social notes, you must also know where each of the basic parts goes on the paper. The heading goes in the upper right-hand corner of the letter, and the salutation follows several lines beneath it along the left margin. The body is the middle of the letter. The closing follows in the lower right-hand section of the letter two or three lines beneath the body, and the signature follows beneath the closing. If you include an *R.S.V.P.,* write it in the lower left-hand corner of the letter. Although the basic positions are always the same, you can choose from two styles to present these parts of your letter.

To write the basic parts of a friendly letter or social note, use either the **indented style** or the **semiblock style.**

If you use the *indented style,* you must indent the lines of the heading and the signature as shown in the following example. If you use the *semiblock style,* the heading, the closing, and the signature should all be lined up one beneath the other.

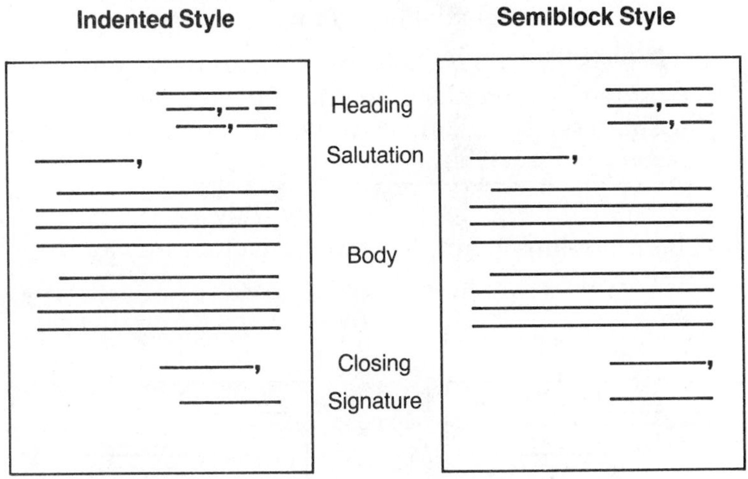

Indented Style | **Semiblock Style**

Heading

Salutation

Body

Closing

Signature

Envelopes for Friendly Letters and Social Notes. If you have used special stationery for your letter, you should use a matching envelope. In addition, if you have typed the letter, you should plan to type the envelope as well. Finally, you should write the mailing information on the front of the envelope using the same style that you used in the letter itself.

On the envelope include your full return address and a complete mailing address, using the same style as you used in the letter, either indented or semiblock.

On the envelope the first line of your return address should contain your full name. The second line should give your street address. The third line should give your city or town, state, and ZIP code. The mailing address should provide exactly the same information about the person to whom you are sending the letter. When preparing an envelope, you should also keep in mind a few additional guidelines.

GUIDELINES FOR ENVELOPES FOR PERSONAL LETTERS

1. Do not use titles—Mr., Miss, and Ms.—in writing your own name in the return address.
2. Avoid unclear abbreviations in both addresses.
3. Include ZIP codes in both addresses.
4. Be sure to use envelopes that are large enough to meet postal service regulations. Write the return address on the back of small envelopes.

The following examples show envelopes using each of the two styles.

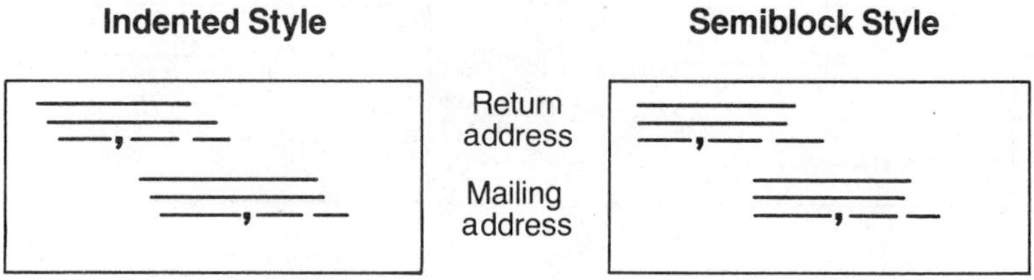

Indented Style **Semiblock Style**

Return address

Mailing address

Mailing the Letter. To mail your letter, follow a simple but important procedure.

Fold your letter properly and place it inside its envelope.

If you are writing on relatively small-size stationery, you will probably be able to fold the paper in half and slip it into the envelope. With some stationery you may even be able to fit it into an envelope without folding. With large paper you will generally need to fold your letter into thirds, creating a double-fold as shown in the following diagram.

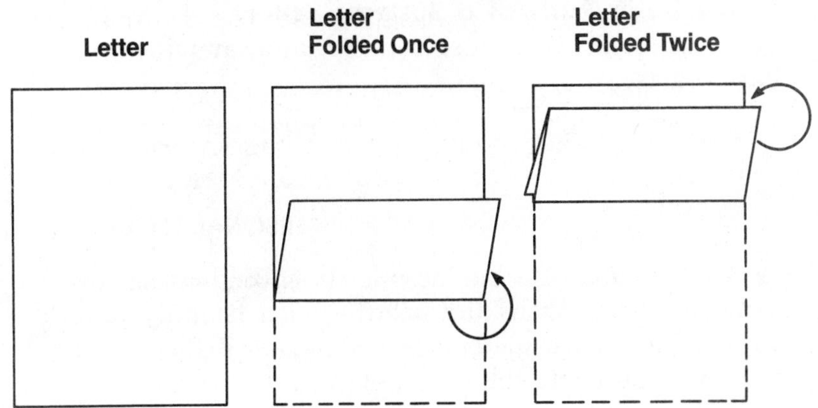

EXERCISE A: Setting Up the Parts of Friendly Letters and Social Notes. Use two separate sheets of paper to set up one letter in indented style and one letter in semi-block style. On each letter use your own address and today's date for the heading. Choose a different salutation for each letter, and draw lines to stand for the body. Then add the proper closing and signature.
Answers will vary. Students should follow the text examples of both letter styles.

EXERCISE B: Preparing Friendly Letters and Social Notes for Mailing. Following the style of each letter that you prepared in Exercise A, write an envelope for each letter. Use the information in each letter's heading to write a return address. Make up a mailing address to suit each salutation. Then fold each letter properly, and place it inside its envelope. *Answers will vary. Students should follow the text examples and match envelope style with letter style.*

■ Setting Up Business Letters

You may need to write business letters to order merchandise, to register a complaint or opinion, to answer an advertisement, or for any of a number of other purposes. As you will see, business letters contain many of the same parts that friendly letters and social notes contain, with a few additional features. The styles used for business letters are also similar to those used for personal letters, with a few minor changes.

The Basic Parts of a Business Letter. To write a business letter, you must become familiar with its six basic parts.

> A **business letter** should include a heading, an inside address, a salutation, a body, a closing, and a signature.

The *heading* of a business letter should contain the same information as the heading of a friendly letter: your street address, town or city, state, ZIP code, and the date you write the letter, arranged in three lines.

The *inside address,* placed two to four lines beneath the heading, should begin with the name of the person or business that you are writing to, sometimes including a title such as *President* or *Director.* The address of the person or business goes beneath the name.

INSIDE ADDRESSES:

Mrs. Joanne Burns, Editor
The Appleton Sun-Times
Appleton, Illinois 60771

Meyer's Discount Drugs, Inc.
1200 Turnpike Access
Hamilton, New York 10615

The *salutation* of a business letter, which should go two lines beneath the inside address, is your greeting to the reader of the letter. It should be formal and should be followed by a colon.

SALUTATIONS:

Dear Mrs. Ryan: Dear Sir or Madam:

Dear Sir: Gentlemen:

The *body* of the letter should give whatever information you need to include to achieve your purpose in writing. If you have written a business letter to order merchandise, for example, the body should contain your specific requests and provide all required information. The body can be any length—a few sentences or several paragraphs—but it should always be precise.

The *closing* of a business letter is a formal sign-off. It begins with a capital letter and ends with a comma.

The *signature* must be written in ink, even if the letter has been typed. If you have typed the letter, you should type your full name beneath your signature. In typed business letters, women sometimes write in parentheses before their name the title by which they wish to be addressed. The following are examples of closings and signatures from typed business letters.

CLOSING:	Yours truly,	Sincerely,
SIGNATURE:	*Harrison Martin*	*Betty Randolph*
NAME:	Harrison Martin	(Mrs.) Betty Randolph

Two Styles for Business Letters. The parts of a business letter are arranged in much the same fashion as a friendly letter. However, the exact position of a few of the parts depends on the style. For a business letter, you have a choice of two different styles.

> To write the basic parts of a business letter, use either the **block style** or the **semiblock style.**

The following examples show both styles.

Block Style | **Semiblock Style**

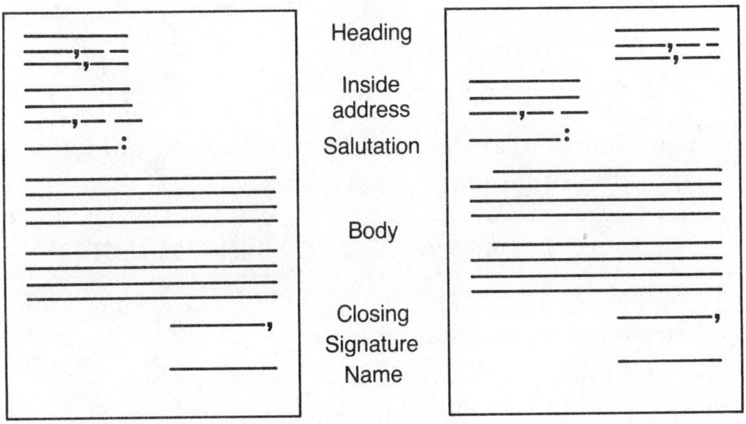

Heading

Inside address

Salutation

Body

Closing

Signature

Name

If you use the *block style,* you must line up all parts of the letter along the left margin of your paper. You should not indent any lines—not even the first lines of paragraphs. If you use the *semiblock style,* you should place the heading, the closing, and the signature on the right just as in the semiblock style for the friendly letter. As in the friendly letter, paragraphs are indented.

If your business letter is long enough to have a second page, you should write the name of the person receiving the letter, the page number *(Page 2),* and the date at the top of the second page.

Envelopes for Business Letters. Most business letters are written on white, business-size stationery. To match the standard letter paper, your envelope should also be white and of a standard business size.

On a business envelope, you should include your full return address and a mailing address that matches the inside address of the letter exactly.

All business envelopes should follow the style of the following example, regardless of the style you chose for the letter.

You should also follow a few additional guidelines when addressing business envelopes.

GUIDELINES FOR ENVELOPES FOR BUSINESS LETTERS
1. Do not use titles—Mr., Miss, and Ms.—in writing your own name in the return address.
2. Avoid unclear abbreviations in both addresses.
3. Include ZIP codes in both addresses.

Mailing the Letter. You should fold most business letters into thirds by making a double-fold, as shown on page 677, before placing them inside their envelopes.

Fold your letter properly and place it inside its envelope.

EXERCISE C: Setting Up the Parts of Business Letters. Use two separate sheets of paper to set up one letter in block style and one letter in semiblock style. On each letter use your own address and today's date for the heading. Use the following information to write an inside address. Choose a salutation, and draw lines to stand for the body. Then add a closing and signature.

Answers will vary. Students should follow text examples of both letter styles.

Mr. Harris Fontaine, the President of Comptons Department Stores, located at 500 North Main Street, Ocala, Florida, ZIP code 32668

EXERCISE D: Preparing Business Letters for Mailing. Obtain one business-size envelope and write an envelope for one of the letters in Exercise C. Then fold the letter and place it inside the envelope.

Answers will vary. Students should follow the text example for envelope style.

APPLICATION: Understanding Personal and Business Letters. Identify the types of letters (*friendly letters, social notes,* or *business letters*) described in each of the following questions. Note that some questions have more than one answer.

1. Which letters would most likely be typed?
2. Which letters might include an *R.S.V.P.*?
3. Which letters always use a comma in the salutation?
4. Which letters always use a colon in the salutation?
5. Which letters are written to accept or decline an invitation?
6. Which letters use a comma in the closing?
7. Which letters can be written using indented style?
8. Which letters can be written using block style?
9. Which letters will always show at least two different ZIP codes?
10. Which letters have only one style for envelopes?

1. business 2. social 3. friendly and social 4. business 5. social 6. all 7. friendly and social 8. business 9. business 10. business

32.2 Writing Different Kinds of Letters

Once you know the basic parts of letters, where they should be placed, and what styles can be used to present them, you can begin concentrating on the writing itself. This section will give you suggestions for writing a number of different kinds of personal and business letters.

Writing Friendly Letters and Social Notes

Many different kinds of personal letters are possible. Different social occasions often require special responses. No matter what kind of friendly letter or social note you are writing, however, it should be well organized and clearly written.

Learn the characteristics of friendly letters, invitations, letters of acceptance and regret, and other kinds of social notes.

Understanding the different kinds of letters you may need to write will help you respond appropriately in different situations. Keep in mind that you should make all letters clear and accurate, possibly by revising them, and always by proofreading them.

The Friendly Letter. Of all correspondence a friendly letter is usually the least formal. The purpose of such a letter is to share current personal news with friends and family members, to continue the communication of an earlier letter, or simply to maintain relationships with people. Your letter should show an interest in the reader by asking questions about his or her activities. You should also answer questions that the reader has asked you.

When you write a friendly letter, you can use either of the two styles for the parts of a friendly letter. The only requirement is that you be consistent within each letter. In the body you should also follow the rules of grammar, usage, mechanics, and spelling. Try to make the content of the letter specific, interesting, and enjoyable to read. You might include vivid descriptions and relate incidents of interest to the reader. Finally, you should always try to make your letter neat, and you should always proofread it for mistakes before you send it.

The following sample shows the basic characteristics of a friendly letter.

18 Sunrise Avenue
Miami, Florida 32986
June 1, 1982

Dear Sam,

How have you been? How do you like your new home? I hope the weather in Anchorage hasn't been too cold for you. This week the air here was so humid that it felt like a hot, wet towel. I'm beginning to wish that I could switch places with you.

Our baseball team is doing well. We beat Oscala's B-team the other day with a run-scoring single in the bottom of the seventh inning. Although we lost the next game to Granite Springs, I believe we have a chance for a spot in the sectionals.

I hope you've found some new friends in Alaska. Have you gone fishing on a salmon boat yet? Do you think that your family will stay there for more than a year? Frankly, I hope you return soon because the team needs you. Keep me informed.

Your friend,
D.J.

Invitations and Letters of Acceptance and Regret. An *invitation,* like any other social note, should be relatively short and precise. Within a few sentences, however, it should present a number of specific details: the date and time of the event, the location and nature of the event, and possibly what the person invited should bring or wear. When writing an invitation, try to put yourself in the reader's place and anticipate any questions that the reader might ask about the event. If you need a speedy reply to your invitation in order to complete your plans, you should also include an *R.S.V.P.*

10 Sanbar Place
Fresno, California 94182
June 16, 1982

Dear Liam,

My family is hosting a party to celebrate our graduation. The party will begin at 5:00 p.m. on June 30, and dinner will be served at approximately 7:00 p.m. Please dress casually and bring a Frisbee and baseball equipment.

I hope that you can attend.

Yours truly,
Sue Kiley

R.S.V.P.

A *letter of acceptance or regret* is a social note used to reply to an invitation. In a letter of acceptance, you should repeat the date, time, place, and any other information needed to prevent confusion. In a letter of regret, be sure to offer a reason why you can not attend. Whether you accept or decline, you should remember to express your appreciation for the invitation.

Other Social Notes. There are also a number of other occasions for writing social notes. You might want to write a thank-you note for a present. You might decide to write to a friend to offer your congratulations on a special award or honor. You might wish to send your sympathy to someone who has suffered a loss or an injury. Whatever your purpose in writing, follow the guidelines that you have learned in this chapter, and write clearly and precisely.

EXERCISE A: Writing Friendly Letters and Social Notes. Choose any one of the following ideas to write a friendly letter or social note. Be sure to include all five parts of the letter, and use your own name and address for the heading and envelope. Focus on the purpose of the letter and the person to whom you are writing. Then prepare an envelope for the letter, and place the letter inside the envelope. *Answers will vary. The grammar, mechanics, and content of letters could be checked, as well as their style.*

1. Write a friendly letter to a friend who is vacationing somewhere far away. Include personal news as well as the details of some interesting events. Use any of the following ideas:
   a. You struck out with bases loaded in the championship game.
   b. At a local restaurant you saw someone walk out without paying.
   c. You had a surprise visitor.
   d. You attended a party.
   e. A camera crew has just arrived to shoot a movie in your neighborhood.
2. You have decided to gather a group of friends to attend a concert in a nearby city. Write a letter of invitation to one of these friends, supplying all of

the information that your friend will need to know in order to reply.

3. You have received the invitation that was written following the idea in the second item. Write a letter of acceptance or a letter of regret in response to the invitation you have received.
4. Your cousin is away at school. You hear that she was named to the school's honor society. Write to congratulate her.
5. A friend is sick in the hospital. Write a letter wishing your friend a speedy recovery.

Writing Business Letters

Business letters can be used to achieve many different goals.

Learn the characteristics and purposes of a number of different kinds of business letters.

Because they serve specific business needs, business letters are usually more formal than personal letters. Focusing on the specific purpose of such a letter will help you make it a good letter. You should also develop the habit of revising and proofreading your business letters for clarity and accuracy.

Order Letters. Perhaps the most common kind of business letter is the *order letter.* It can be used to order almost any kind of merchandise through the mail. When you prepare an order letter, you should include all six parts of a business letter and take special care to make sure that the company address is accurate. The body of the letter should begin by stating your specific request. If the items are from a catalog and have order numbers, include these as well as sizes, prices, amounts, and so on. Think about any questions that the person filling your order may have, and provide all the information needed for billing and mailing. If you send a check or money order with your letter, be sure to state the amount in the letter.

The following order letter fills all the basic requirements.

3 Bagshot Row
Cleveland, Ohio 45201
October 30, 1982

Lesley Herman, Inc.
140 Main Street
Port Chester, New York 10850

Dear Sir or Madam:

I would like to order three items from your 1982 Christmas catalog. I have enclosed a money order for $25.25, which includes postage and handling costs.

Amount	Item	Price
1	Silver anniversary dish No. 5492	$19.25
2	German/English dictionaries No. 9910	6.00
TOTAL		$25.25

Thank you for filling my order.

Sincerely,

Ann Hoag

(Miss) Ann Hoag

Other Business Letters. At times you may have to write other kinds of business letters. If you need information for writing reports or planning trips, you may need to write to a business or agency, asking for specific information. At other times you may have to write a letter of complaint about faulty merchandise or services. You might also want to write a letter of opinion to a newspaper or a television station.

In writing any of these letters, you should try to keep the reader in mind at all times. In letters requesting information, you should state your purpose clearly and directly. In letters of complaint or opinion, you should be persuasive, including information that will help support the point you are making. Try to convince your reader to agree with you and to take action.

EXERCISE B: Writing Business Letters. Use any of the following ideas to write a business letter. Include all six parts of a business letter. Use your own address for the heading, and for the inside address, invent a person, business, or organization. Then write the letter, focusing on the reader and your purpose. When you have written, revised, recopied, and proofread your letter, prepare an envelope for it. *Answers will vary. Students might exchange letters, check that letter style is correct, and identify the purpose of each letter.*

1. Obtain a mail-order catalog and identify two or three items that you would like to purchase. Write an order letter, paying attention to necessary ordering and billing information.
2. Write to a local travel agency or a tourist office, requesting information about a place you would like to visit.
3. Write to the manager of a radio station, requesting changes in or additions to the kinds of music played.

APPLICATION: Writing a Friendly Letter, Social Note, or Business Letter. Identify a real purpose that you have for writing a friendly letter, social note, or business letter at this time. Review the characteristics of that kind of letter as presented in this section. Then write the letter, revise it, proofread it, and prepare an envelope for it. *Answers will vary. Students might exchange letters and then evaluate and answer their partners' letters.*

Preparing Papers

The composition unit of this book suggests many ways to develop, organize, and express ideas in your writing. It also has several checklists that can be used to polish your ideas. This short section on preparing papers covers a few additional points. It will give you a style to use in setting up your papers. It will also suggest certain questions you can answer if you are having problems with grammar, usage, mechanics, or spelling. Finally, it will give you a few useful symbols that you can use when you revise.

Setting Up Your Papers

Neatness counts. It may sometimes be a part of your grade, and it will almost always have a favorable effect on your reader. If you use the suggestions in the following charts, your reader will be able to concentrate on your ideas, not on the physical appearance of your paper.

Setting Up a Handwritten Paper. Use the following guidelines for a handwritten paper.

HANDWRITTEN PAPERS
1. Use white, lined, notebook-sized paper. Do not, however, use pages ripped from a spiral binder.
2. Use either blue or black ink.
3. Leave a margin of space on the right side.
4. Indent each paragraph.

Setting Up a Typed Paper. Use these guidelines for a typed paper.

TYPED PAPERS
1. Use white, unlined, notebook-sized paper.
2. Use a clear black ribbon.
3. Leave a margin of space on all sides.
4. Double-space all lines and indent each paragraph.

Identifying Your Papers. Your teacher may have a special form for you to follow in identifying your papers. If not, you can use one of the two forms below. The example on the left shows a full title page. You might use this form for long papers such as reports. The example on the right generally works best for short papers.

With Title Page

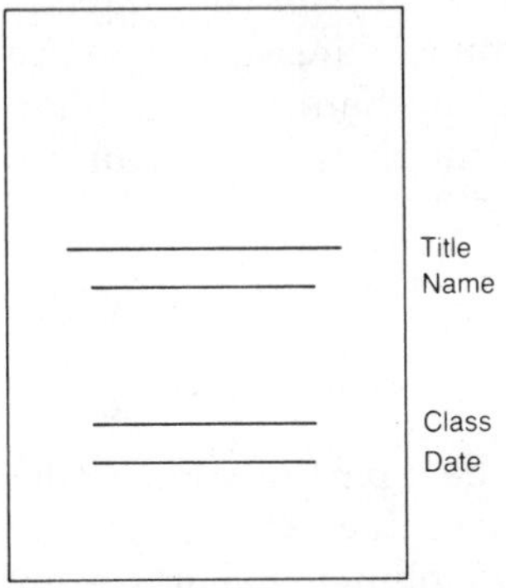

Title
Name

Class
Date

Without Title Page

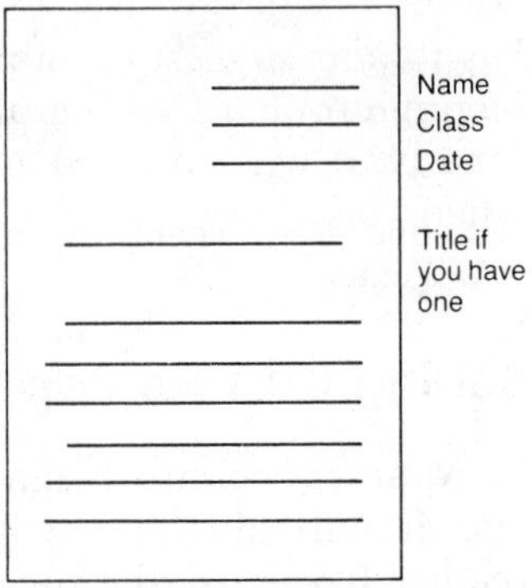

Name
Class
Date

Title if you have one

The second page and all additional pages should carry your name and the page number in the upper right-hand corner.

Checking for Errors

In revising and proofreading your papers, you should always look for errors in grammar, usage, mechanics, and spelling. If you are having problems in any of these areas, you may find that the following charts will help.

Errors in Grammar. Perhaps the most common errors in grammar are fragments and run-on sentences. Modifiers can also cause problems. The following chart gives questions to ask and sections to turn to in order to correct these problems.

Problems	Questions to Ask	Sections in Text
Fragments	Does each sentence have all of the necessary sentence parts?	10.1
Run-ons	Are any of your sentences really two sentences?	10.2

Misplaced Modifiers	Are all modifiers as close as possible to the words they modify?	10.3

Errors in Usage. Agreement causes many problems in usage. Certain verbs, modifiers, and other words can also be problems.

Problems	Questions to Ask	Sections in Text
Subject-Verb Agreement	Do all the subjects agree in number with their verbs?	13.1 and 13.2
Pronoun-Antecedent Agreement	Do all the pronouns agree in person and number with their antecedents?	13.3
Special Problems with Verbs, Modifiers, and Other Words	Have you chosen the wrong verb from certain troublesome pairs? Have you chosen the wrong adjective or adverb? Have you used the wrong word?	11.5 for Verbs 14.5 for Modifiers 15.2 for Words in General

Errors in Mechanics. Capitals and a few widely used punctuation marks generally cause the most problems in mechanics.

Problems	Questions to Ask	Sections in Text
Capitals	Are all proper nouns and proper adjectives capitalized correctly?	16.2 for Nouns 16.3 for Adjectives
End Marks	Does every sentence have the correct mark at the end?	18.1
Commas	Do you have a good reason for every comma you have used?	18.2 and 18.3
Apostrophes	Are apostrophes used incorrectly in personal pronouns such as *its* and *theirs*?	18.9

Errors in Spelling. Perhaps the most common errors in any paper are spelling errors.

Problem	Question to Ask	Sections in Text
Misspelled Words	Have you used a dictionary to check every word you are not sure of?	20.1 and 20.2

Using Correction Symbols

Correction symbols are special marks that make it easier to show where changes are needed in a paper. The following chart shows some of the most common.

Symbol and Meaning		Corrected Example	Final Version
—	take out	Randy admired the ~~the~~ lake.	Randy admired the lake.
^	add	It was a ^deep blue color.	It was a deep blue color.
¶	paragraph	¶Along the lake four hikers were walking.	Along the lake four hikers were walking.
frag	fragment	Very hungry and tired. (frag)	They looked very hungry and tired.
RO	run-on	The group had left camp at dawn, (RO) they had hiked for six hours.	The group had left camp at dawn, and they had hiked for six hours.
mod	misplaced modifier	(mod) Distant, Randy pointed to the campsite.	Randy pointed to the distant campsite.
sp	spelling	They picked up their packs and headed down the trale. (sp)	They picked up their packs and headed down the trail.

Index

Bold numbers show pages on which basic definitions and rules can be found.

Acknowledgments

The authors and editors have made every effort to trace the ownership of all copyrighted selections found in this book and to make full acknowledgment of their use.

The dictionary of record for this book is *Webster's New World Dictionary,* Students Edition, copyright © 1981 by Simon & Schuster, Inc. The basis for the selection of vocabulary words appropriate for this grade level is *The Living Word Vocabulary: The Words We Know* by Edgar Dale and Joseph O'Rourke, copyright © 1976.

Citations follow, arranged by unit and page for easy reference.

Study Skills. Pages 446 Constance Brown, "Camping in the Snow," copyright 1979 by the National Wildlife Federation. Reprinted from the December-January issue of NATIONAL WILDLIFE Magazine. **453–454** Don Wulffson, "The Black Plague," *Read* magazine. Special permission granted by *Read* magazine, published by Xerox Educational Publications © 1981, Xerox Corp. **488** Excerpted from *Research Guide/Index,* Volume 22 of *The World Book Encyclopedia.* © 1981 World Book-Childcraft International, Inc. **489, 490** (first item) *The World Almanac and Book of Facts,* 1981 edition, copyright © Newspaper Enterprise Association, Inc., 1980, New York, NY 10166. **490** (second item), **491** (map) *Hammond Citation World Atlas,* Hammond, Inc., Maplewood, NJ, 1980. **493** (index entry, text entry) From ROGET'S INTERNATIONAL THESAURUS, Fourth Edition (Thomas Y. Crowell Company). Copyright © 1977 by Harper & Row, Publishers, Inc. Reprinted by permission of the publisher. **495** (both items) From *Current Biography 1980.* Copyright © 1980 by the H.W. Wilson Company. Material reproduced by permission of the publisher. **498** *Readers' Guide to Periodical Literature* Copyright © 1980 by the H.W. Wilson Company. Material reproduced by permission of the publisher. **499** *Readers' Guide to Periodical Literature* Copyright ©1981 by the H.W. Wilson Company. Material reproduced by permission of the publisher. **502–503** (chart), **506–513** With permission. From *Webster's New World Dictionary,* Students Edition. Copyright © 1981 by Simon & Schuster, Inc.

Composition. Pages 546–457 Tui de Roy Moore, "Ruler of the Island Sky," copyright 1979 by the National Wildlife Federation. Reprinted from the July-August issue of INTERNATIONAL WILDLIFE Magazine. **547** David Alpern, "City at the Edge of Time," in TRAVEL/HOLIDAY MAGAZINE, March 1981. **548** C.D.B. Bryan, "So Much Unfairness of Things," *Ten Top Stories,* edited by David A. Sohn (New York: Bantam Books, Inc., 1977). **549–550** Denis D. Gray, "Crossroads in Katmandu," copyright 1980 by the National Wildlife Federation. Reprinted from the July-August issue of INTERNATIONAL WILDLIFE Magazine. **550** Gwen Schultz, *Icebergs and Their Voyages* (New York: William Morrow and Company, 1975). **551** (first item) Jack Waller in *Travel and Leisure Magazine* (June 1981). **551** (second item) Arthur Hailey, *Airport* (New York: Doubleday and Company, 1968). **552** (first item), **598** Doron K. Antrim, *Having Fun With Music* (New York: Thomas Y. Crowell Company, 1958). **552** (second item) Adapted from Eva Hoffman, "Poland," GEO Magazine (April, 1981). **552–553** Paul Grescoe, "Learning to Live With Old Grizz," copyright 1980 by the National Wildlife Federation. Reprinted from the July-August issue of INTERNATIONAL WILDLIFE Magazine. **553** Norma Spring, *Alaska: Pioneer State* (New Jersey: Thomas Nelson & Sons, 1966). **560** (first item) Anne Innis Dagg, "Legs, Legs, Legs," copyright 1978 by the National Wildlife Federation. Reprinted from the November-December issue of INTERNATIONAL WILDLIFE Magazine. **560** (second item) Arthur Beiser and Konrad B. Krauskopf, *Introduction to Earth Science* (New York: McGraw-Hill Book Company, 1975). **560–561** John Neary, "Hawks and Eagles," copyright 1980 by the National Wildlife Federation. Reprinted from the August-September issue of NATIONAL

WILDLIFE Magazine. **561** Adapted from Carla Wallach, *Gardening in the City* (New York: Harcourt, Brace, Jovanovich, 1976). **583** Adapted from ATLAS OF THE OCEANS © Mitchell Beazley 1977. Published in the U.S. by Rand McNally & Company. **606–607** Adapted from Jane and Michael Stern, *Amazing America* (New York: David Obst Books/Random House, 1977).

Key of Major Concepts

Grammar

Usage

Mechanics